This is a volume in

THE UNIVERSITY OF MICHIGAN HISTORY OF THE MODERN WORLD

Upon completion, the series will consist of the following volumes:

The United States to 1865 *by Michael Kraus*

The United States since 1865 *by Foster Rhea Dulles*

Canada: A Modern History *by John Bartlet Brebner*

Latin America: A Modern History *by J. Fred Rippy*

Great Britain to 1688: A Modern History *by Maurice Ashley*

Great Britain since 1688: A Modern History *by K. B. Smellie*

France: A Modern History *by Albert Guérard*

Germany: A Modern History *by Marshall Dill, Jr.*

Italy: A Modern History *by Denis Mack Smith*

Russia and the Soviet Union: A Modern History *by Warren B. Walsh*

The Near East: A Modern History *by William Yale*

The Far East: A Modern History *by Nathaniel Peffer*

India: A Modern History *by Percival Spear*

The Southwest Pacific to 1900: A Modern History *by C. Hartley Grattan*

The Southwest Pacific since 1900: A Modern History *by C. Hartley Grattan*

Spain: A Modern History *by Rhea Marsh Smith*

Africa: A Modern History *by Ronald Robinson*

SPAIN

A Modern History

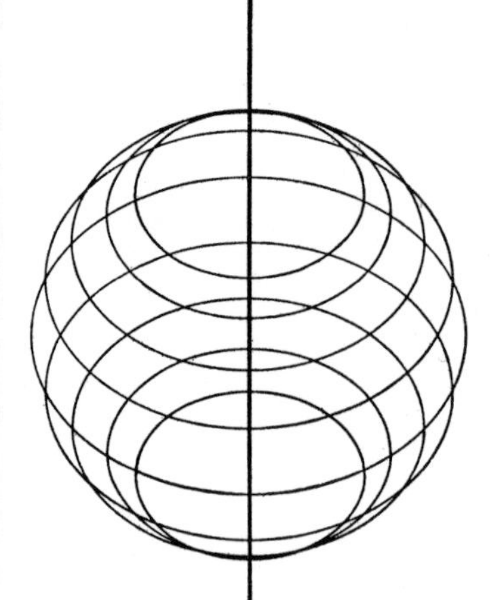

The University of Michigan History of the Modern World
Edited by Allan Nevins and Howard M. Ehrmann

SPAIN

A Modern History

BY RHEA MARSH SMITH

Ann Arbor: The University of Michigan Press

Library of Congress Catalog Card No. 65-15241
Published in the United States of America by
The University of Michigan Press and simultaneously
in Toronto, Canada, by Ambassador Books Limited
Manufactured in the United States of America by
Vail-Ballou Press, Inc.

TO THE MEMORY OF
GARRETT MATTINGLY

Contents

MAPS

SPAIN

A Modern History

CHAPTER I

Ancient Spain

The Iberian Peninsula, which from the Pyrenees to its southern coast bears on the map a false appearance of unity, was for centuries without any political cohesion whatever. The Greek name Iberia apparently referred at the outset only to a vague coastal strip. Not until Rome established an all-embracing authority did the prefiguring of a nation emerge, and this was centuries after the Phoenicians and Carthaginians had begun to mingle their blood with that of the people of the land.

The tardiness with which the outlines of a separate and identifiable country appeared may be attributed in part to the character of the tribes which in prehistoric times had entered Spain from North Africa, coming across the Strait of Gibraltar between the two great rocks which Greek mariners were to call the Pillars of Hercules. These hardy, independent-spirited migrants—perhaps seeking refuge from the aridity that was turning so much African soil into a desert—planted well-fortified settlements on mountain tops, whence they regarded each other with the suspicion and instant readiness for war which stamp most primitive peoples. Although the thrusts of invaders—first the Carthaginians, then the Romans—drove them to form loose confederacies, they never united in a truly national war against their enemies.

Spain, most of which is occupied by a massive tableland or meseta covering the central part of the peninsula, is intersected by numerous ranges of mountains. The tableland itself is isolated on the north by the Cantabrian Range and on the south by the Sierra Morena, and it is cut into parts by other highlands. The rugged chains give the land a wildly beautiful scenery of gorges, ridges, and peaks, with strong defensive centers. But they provide formidable barriers to the fusion of the inhabitants. The history of the land is written in separate valleys such as the Ebro, the Jalon, and the Guadalquivir, in separate minor plateaus like La Mancha, and in separate lines of heights rising to peaks like the

Pena Prieta—8300 feet high. From the beginning localism easily defeated nationalism, and localism remained the dominant tradition until modern times. Local customs and traditions, local autonomy and pride, local dialects nurtured by isolation, have always flourished; and they have reinforced the individualism of the men and women—who are as sternly independent as Swiss mountaineers or Scottish Highlanders.

In the dim twilight of the past, twelve or thirteen centuries before the Christian era, Celts from Western Europe found their way through the passes of the Pyrenees and scattered across the northwestern and western parts of the peninsula. They also occupied the Ebro Valley alongside the Iberians and penetrated the central meseta, but they never spread into the eastern and southeastern parts, where the Iberians retained all their cultural and political independence. The Celts were not strong enough to give any real measure of unity in language, customs, and outlook to the whole peninsula, or any great part of it. The task had been made more difficult, when they arrived, by the fact that competing migrants from the Mediterranean basin were placing their own strong imprint on the eastern reaches.

The first Near Eastern people to reach the peninsula by the sea lanes were the Phoenicians. Modern Spaniards proudly point to the foundations of the ancient Phoenician lighthouse at La Coruña as an historic monument established early in the twelfth century B.C. or thereabouts by hardy navigators from Sidon. This beacon served mariners cautiously following the coast northward to the British Isles in their quest for tin to be alloyed with copper in making bronze.

The sailors of another Phoenician city, Tyre, followed their compatriots to the west later in the twelfth century B.C. They not only found precious metals in Spain, but developed a flourishing commerce with the Iberians, planting trading posts in the Guadalquivir Valley and along the southern coast. The most important trade center was Gades, now Cádiz, founded about 1100 B.C., from which Phoenician products were widely distributed among the people of the region. The Phoenicians never tried to colonize the peninsula, but their trading posts were kept prosperous by their merchants and seamen.

The Greeks did not penetrate the western Mediterranean until much later than the Phoenicians. Reports of the wealth of the so-called Tartessians—apparently the Iberians in the Guadalquivir Valley—and of the profitable commerce which the Phoenicians had developed finally attracted seamen and merchants from the Greek islands. The earliest Greek to reach Tartessos was Kolaeus of Samos, about 630 B.C., and the profits of his trade with the country stimulated Greeks from Phocaea to follow. Their enterprise and sagacity so impressed the Tartessian king, Arganthonius, that he urged them to settle in his realm. They called the peninsula either Hesperia or Iberia.

After founding their principal establishment at Massilia (Marseilles), the Phocaeans opened the southern shores of France and the Catalan coast to Greek trade in competition with the Carthaginians. Emporion (Ampurias) was typical of these trading centers, consisting of two parts, one occupied by the Greeks and the other by the Iberians. The Greeks introduced the olive and grape into Spain, used the first coined money at Emporion, and exercised a great influence on the improvement of Iberian ceramics.

After the Persians conquered Tyre in the sixth century, the place of leadership in the western Mediterranean was inherited from the Phoenicians by the kindred city of Carthage, whose strategic position on the North African coast enabled her rulers to dominate the other Phoenician colonies and to extend her control over nearly the entire Iberian Peninsula. According to the historian Polybius, Carthage by the fourth century B.C. had established a protectorate over all the Iberian tribes as far north as the Pyrenees and had incorporated Iberian volunteers in her armies. The Carthaginians adopted a militant policy, alternating between brutality and conciliation, which aimed at the conquest of the peninsula and the exploitation of its mineral resources and manpower. The ambition of Carthage to dominate the land was stimulated by the First Punic War (264–241 B.C.) with Rome.

Hamilcar Barca, the father of Hannibal, who had won fame in the stubborn but unsuccessful attempt of the Carthaginians to gain control of Sicily, led an army across the Strait of Gibraltar into Spain with the far-sighted intention of bringing all the rich resources of the country under Carthaginian control (237 B.C.). He saw that this land could more than compensate Carthage for the loss of Sicily. The agricultural and mineral wealth, warlike tribesmen, and ports and fortresses would be invaluable if properly organized. And Hamilcar was sufficiently statesmanlike to use his army in a peaceable rather than a violent conquest of the land; he treated the people as allies, not subjects, encouraged the intermarriage of his soldiers with Spanish women—his own son Hannibal taking one as wife—and assisted the Spaniards in improving their economic position. Tradition credits him with the founding of Barcelona, which bears the family name, and it was he who developed New Carthage (Cartagena) as a splendid seaport.

By the time Hamilcar Barca died in 228 B.C., to be succeeded by his nephew, the equally statesmanlike Hasdrubal, the Carthaginians had established an ascendancy over the entire southern half of the peninsula. Their success aroused the jealous apprehension of the Romans, who were meanwhile fighting to extend their own sway over southern Gaul. In their alarm the Romans demanded from Hasdrubal an assurance that the Carthaginian advance would not be pushed northeast of the Ebro River, which flows to the Mediterranean south of the present city of Barcelona; they did not wish to be pushed entirely out of Spain.

When Hannibal succeeded Hasdrubal in 221 B.C., though not yet thirty, he recognized with the insight of genius that war with Rome was inevitable. He proceeded to reorganize the Carthaginian army—incorporating into it many Iberians as mercenaries—and to consolidate his power in Spain. The Romans had assumed the role of protector of the Greek colonies along the east coast, and one of these, Saguntum, a strong citadel, was the only obstacle to Carthaginian domination south of the Ebro River. Hannibal besieged and captured Saguntum while the Romans vainly protested and finally sent an ultimatum to Carthage. Thereupon the Carthaginians declared war on Rome (218 B.C.).

The Second Punic War (218–201 B.C.) was savagely contested in three theaters—Italy, Spain, and North Africa. The Romans prepared to dispute Carthaginian control of the Iberian Peninsula, but in one of the greatest offensive movements of history Hannibal, with his Carthaginians, Iberian mercenaries, Balearic slingers, and elephants, crossed the Alps and invaded Italy, annihilating a Roman army at Cannae. No match for Hannibal in pitched battle, the Romans adopted the Fabian policy of wearing down the Carthaginian army by attrition. Meanwhile, in Spain, the recklessly dashing Scipio Africanus revived the spirit of the Roman soldiers and gained the adherence of many Iberians. He carried the war into Carthaginian Spain, captured New Carthage by a sudden brilliant blow (210 B.C.), and forced the Carthaginians out of Gades into North Africa.

After the final defeat of the Carthaginians at the battle of Zama, the Romans under the able leadership of Scipio Africanus began to occupy the whole peninsula. By the end of the year 205 B.C. they had partly succeeded. An impressive new era in the history of the country began; indeed, one of the most impressive of all its eras, lasting more than six hundred years. The civilization of the Carthaginians, rich in commercial and military achievements though it was—its harsh power is graphically reflected in Flaubert's novel *Salammbô*—had been largely identical with the culture of the earlier comers, the Phoenicians. Now a much ampler and stronger authority had taken control, with one of the grandest civilizations of all history. Spain became the first great area assimilated by the Romans, and one of the most important overseas provinces of the empire. The country was soon divided into two great provinces, Farther Hispania west of the Ebro, and Hither Hispania east of that river, both governed by praetors. There was little homogeneity in either province, and neither of them was fully pacified for many decades. The Romans were forced to become conquerors of Spain by their eagerness to exploit all the values of its minerals and manpower, but at first they sadly underestimated the tenacity of native resistance. The conquest required nearly continuous warfare for two hundred years and exacted a heavy toll of Roman lives and treasure.

Although the Romans hoped—by developing the mineral resources and using the natives as mercenaries—to make the conquest of Spain pay for itself, they found this impossible. Profitable use of the mines required peace, which could be obtained only by the maintenance of standing armies. The disunity of the Iberians meant constant warfare, for their successive tribal defeats brought neither submission nor peace. While the Romans fought in massed array with heavy arms and elaborate equipment, the Iberians fought in small groups, surprising the invaders in sudden attacks, falling upon them from ambush, and taking full advantage of their familiarity with the terrain. As this guerrilla warfare was marked by savage desperation, service in the peninsula was dreaded by the Roman legionnaires.

A succession of violent and rapacious praetors excited a spirit of bitter resistance among the "Celtiberians." After 181 B.C., Rome belatedly adopted a more conciliatory policy and, through diplomacy and honest administration, induced numerous cities to submit, pay an annual tribute, and provide auxiliaries for the imperial forces. During the ensuing interlude of peace the Iberians accepted Roman authority and sought justice at the hands of Roman officials. But this happy period ended when Roman officials again abused their authority—pillaging villages, imposing excessive fines, and, in general, acting in the most arbitrary manner. The Celtiberians were goaded to rebellion in 153 B.C. by Roman treachery and withdrew to the settlement called Numantia, their principal stronghold near the river Douro, where they repeatedly repelled superior Roman armies until Scipio Aemilianus starved them into submission (132 B.C.).

Although the destruction of Numantia ended the Celtiberian revolt, another area had meanwhile become disaffected. Galba's perfidious attack on 30,000 Lusitanians—people of what is now western Spain and central Portugal—who had assembled under the protection of Roman arms, stimulated a rising under the leadership of Viriathus. Vigorous and eloquent, he defeated every Roman army sent against him for eight years until he was treacherously assassinated.

After these outbreaks a precarious peace was established with the Iberians, but their desire for independence was rekindled by the class struggles in Rome. Marius, the Roman general, had served in the peninsula during the siege of Numantia, and, later, as governor of Hither Spain. When his partisans were proscribed by Sulla, the leader of the aristocratic party in Rome, Quintus Sertorius took refuge in Spain and began to organize resistance to the dictator. He adopted the guerrilla tactics of the natives, found powerful allies among them, and refugees from Rome increased his forces. He wished to create an independent position for himself and to create a base for the reconquest of Italy, but he established a government with a senate, praetors, and tribunes and encouraged the natives to believe that he would restore their independence. At one time he seemed on the point of freeing the country from the Roman yoke, and for this—long afterward—he was mistakenly glorified by the Portuguese as a great patriotic leader.

But when dissension appeared in the faction of Marius, Pompey the Great was sent to Spain to subdue Sertorius. After some initial defeats Pompey successfully played upon the discontent among his enemies until in 72 B.C. Sertorius, abandoned by the Iberians and betrayed by his associates, was assassinated by a discontented officer. Pompey then returned to Rome to celebrate a magnificent triumph and to boast that he had conquered 876 cities!

Within a short time a far greater figure appeared on the Spanish stage. Julius Caesar, who became praetor in Rome in 59 B.C., went to Spain the following year to suppress the remnants of guerrilla warfare. He was doubly successful, for he not only gained the sympathy of the Iberians by reducing the tribute, but he also restored his personal fortunes and relieved himself of his enormous debts. When Caesar, Pompey, and Crassus as members of the First Triumvirate (60 B.C.) divided the territories under Roman jurisdiction, Pompey obtained control of Spain, which had become a more important source of wealth and manpower than ever, while Caesar held command in Gaul. In the ensuing struggle between Caesar and Pompey, Caesar first marched to Rome and then transferred his forces to Spain, where he quickly restored order. His decisive victories over the sons of Pompey, culminating in a great battle at Munda near present-day Córdoba in 45 B.C., made Caesar the master of the Roman world.

When the Roman Empire came into existence after the assassination of Caesar in 43 B.C., Octavian, as his heir, soon became its head, assuming the name of Augustus Caesar. He at once began to restore order in Spain, which was one of the most important parts of the empire, and completed its conquest; he crushed the last resistance to Roman arms in Cantabria and Asturias. The Iberian Peninsula then entered the longest period of calm and order ever enjoyed by its inhabitants. The process of romanization was already well advanced. Relations with the Roman legionnaires, both as friends and enemies, the use of Roman methods in developing mines, agriculture, and trade, and the tolerance of Roman colonies led the native tribes to accept Roman institutions and customs until they became as Latin as the Latins themselves. Abandoning the old intertribal wars, they devoted themselves to a great and healthy variety of pursuits. The population increased from some six millions under Augustus to nine millions by the year 400 A.D. The Iberians also adopted the conquerors' language, and Spain became a center of Latin culture.

As the romanization proceeded, new provinces were added in Betica and Gallecia. The Emperor Diocletian made Spain a part of the Prefecture of Gaul, and its five provinces—with Balearica and Mauretania—were placed under the direct control of the emperor. The extension of Roman political and civil rights was an important factor in the process of unification. Julius Caesar and Augustus Caesar labored to incorporate the mass of the natives into Roman life, to create new colonies, and to transform them and existing cities into Roman *municipia.* Several classes of cities evolved as the Romans erected distinctions between those which submitted and those which resisted. Thus, the Iberian centers were gradually transformed during six centuries of Roman rule into communities of Latin or Roman citizenship. The *municipia,* as free cities, enjoyed a large measure of autonomy and attained a skill in self-government that persisted into the Middle Ages.

In the Roman armies native components were organized as auxiliaries, largely independent and highly respected. After the peninsula was fully pacified, the Roman garrison in Spain was reduced to a single legion. While the armed forces were composed only of Roman citizens, the Spaniards could be recruited after the Emperor Caracalla admitted all provincials to citizenship. Special legions of Spaniards served as garrisons, and the cities where they were stationed became fertile markets for trade.

The southern part of the peninsula was more prosperous than other areas. In the fertile lands of the Guadalquivir Valley wheat, grapes, and olives flourished, and Spanish wheat and olive oil were highly esteemed in Rome. Although at first the Romans tried to restrict Spanish competition, later they encouraged the introduction of special varieties of grapes, and Spanish wines became celebrated.

The Iberians had little interest in commerce, but it flourished with Italy and Africa through the enterprise of Roman and oriental merchants. Internal commerce was facilitated by the construction of an excellent network of roads—undertaken for military purposes but utilized also for trade—which greatly accelerated the unification of the peninsula. A majority of the Spanish rivers were dry for part of the year, but some of them were navigable for considerable distances—the Guadalquivir as far as Seville. The Hispano-Romans also developed an excellent merchant marine and ports, which were improved with lighthouses and docks.

Two principal classes composed the society of Roman Spain, the freemen and the slaves. Among the freemen the aristocracy consisted of a small group of wealthy and privileged officials, who obtained title to extensive lands. As the conquest proceeded a middle class gradually appeared, including romanized freemen of mercantile and professional status and bureaucrats. The remaining freemen were manual workers in the cities and on farms, or served as soldiers and sailors. Some urban workers were organized into primitive cooperative societies (*collegia*). The burden of taxation fell most heavily on the lower and middle classes, and a majority of the rural workers were transformed into the *coloni* of the landed estates, the latifundia. Some slavery existed in Spain under Roman domination, but slaves were fewer than in Rome and less numerous than free workers.

Education was important as a means of diffusing Roman culture. While the Spaniards at first used Latin literary models, by the Augustan Age they began to exert an influence of their own on Roman literature. The list of Spaniards who attained prominent positions in the literary world in Rome is impressive. Julius Higinius became palace librarian of Augustus, and Marcus Porcius Latrus was a teacher of Ovid. The most influential family of Spanish origin in Rome was that of Seneca. Annaeus Seneca, the rhetorician, migrated from Córdoba. His son Lucius Annaeus Seneca, a versatile writer of verse and prose and a Stoic philosopher, was a principal adviser to Nero. Marcus Annaeus Lucanus, a nephew, was a poet celebrated for felicity of expression and original philosophical and political ideas. Also natives of Spain who made contributions to Latin literature were Quintilian, the rhetorician; Martial, composer of poetic epigrams; Columella, who retired to his native Cádiz to write twelve books on agriculture; and Pomponius Mela, author of the most ancient geographical work in Latin.

The most important event in ancient Iberian and Roman history, both for its immediate impact on the empire and for the future, was the conversion of the natives to Christianity. The Roman gods and the imperial cults had been introduced into the Iberian Peninsula largely as an exercise of patriotic duty. Then Christianity gained strength as the empire declined. The Spanish Church has always claimed the dignity of an apostolic origin, although no historic facts support the tradition of the missionary activity of St. James (Santiago) in the peninsula. Nevertheless, a belief in his residence, his martyrdom, and the translation of his body to Campus Stellae (Santiago de Compostela) is deeply woven into the national tradition. It is more probable that St. Paul was in Spain, perhaps between 63 and 67 A.D., although no evidence of his missionary labors has survived. The principal obstacle to the expansion of Christianity was the persistence of the imperial cult. The Christian converts, zealous in their pacifism and their denial of the pagan gods, were angrily opposed by officials and even by more tolerant citizens. The Emperors Decius, Valerian, and Diocletian were especially active in the persecution of the subversive sect.

Heresy soon began to appear among the less stalwart Christians under the Decian persecution, for they held that it was better to retract their faith than to become martyrs. But many were heroic even to death, and under later persecutions, martyrdom became a common avenue of escape to eternal life. The Catholic Church was recognized as a legal institution on an equal footing with other religions in 312, but then Hispanic individualism found expression in heretical divergence from orthodox opinion. The ideas of the Priscillians, who had absorbed some of the Iberian religious ideas and emphasized ascetic chastity, appealed especially to the natives and spread rapidly. Despite ecclesiastical condemnation the Priscillians dominated the peninsular church for a time, especially in Galicia; after the martyrdom of the founder, Bishop Priscillian of Ávila (d.385), they persisted until the sixth century. Meanwhile, an order of the Council of Iliberis (306) required clerical celibacy in the Spanish Church, this being probably the first prohibition of the marriage of priests.

In many ways the Romans united Spain. They unified the Iberians politically and culturally and gave them economic prosperity. As the Iberians became romanized they were the more easily converted to Christianity, which provided still another bond of unity. The Hispano-Romans finally became one of the most stable of all the peoples controlled by Rome and contributed their full share to the prosperity and strength of the Empire.

Six hundred years of Roman rule (205 B.C.–410 A.D.) made an indelible imprint on the population of Iberia. After reducing the inhabitants to submission, the conquerors proceeded to "romanize" them by giving them political and civil rights, recruiting them into the army, integrating their agricultural products into the imperial economy, and educating them in classical culture. The most obvious indication that the people had truly become Hispano-Romans was their adoption of Latin as the common language.

Christianity was introduced to the peninsula through Roman culture. It proved to be one of the most cohesive forces in Spanish civilization. The organized Church outlived the empire under which it had grown and played a vital part in the subsequent history of Spain.

CHAPTER II

The Visigothic Revolution

When the barbarians who had been sweeping over Europe poured through the passes of the Pyrenees in 409 A.D., a new ethnic element, the Germanic, entered the Iberian Peninsula, to be assimilated by the Hispano-Roman and the Christian. The invaders effected a revolution, for the ruling classes were overthrown and supplanted. The next quarter of a millennium witnessed the fusion in Europe of three elements of Western Christian civilization—the classical, the Christian, and the Germanic. In Spain this process was rudely interrupted by the Moslem invasion, which swept up out of Africa in 711. The rest of Western Europe was spared the intrusion of an alien civilization, but Iberian culture was deflected along a different route.

First, however, we must consider the three centuries during which the Visigoths—that is, the Goths of the West—dominated Spain. Many explanations have been offered for the decline of the Roman Empire. In Spain there was a gradual collapse. The Hispano-Romans, diverted from warfare to pacific pursuits and corrupted by Roman luxuries, fell easy prey to the barbarian tribes which entered the peninsula. The Roman Empire was subverted internally before the Germans assumed control.

Germanic peoples had periodically threatened the Rhenish and Danubian frontiers from the time of Julius Caesar. Migratory tribes from southern Scandinavia and the Baltic coast, they became more numerous, until, under pressure from the Huns and attracted by the prosperity and stability of the Roman Empire, they gradually infiltrated its frontiers. Tall, robust, and blonde, wearing their hair long to symbolize their freedom, they were accustomed to live without private property in a communal organization of tribes. Gradually, they adopted the principle of assigning land to individuals. Their government was a primitive democracy in which the warriors elected the king and the elders advised him. Military service was obligatory.

The Suevi, Alans, and Vandals, who must be differentiated from the Visigoths, were the first Germans to enter Spain. They fought their way through Gaul and invaded the peninsula at almost the same time that Alaric, the great leader of the Visigoths, sacked the city of Rome (410). While they sought to establish themselves, they also wished to retain their national identity. After wandering through the peninsula, ravaging the countryside and accumulating booty, they began to settle down. The Suevi and Asding Vandals occupied Galicia, the Alans settled in Lusitania and Cartaginense, and the Siling Vandals moved into Betica. The Hispano-Romans fled to strong cities and castles, especially in Tarraconense, which remained nearly free of the invaders and semi-independent under the local aristocracy.

The Visigoths meanwhile had entered Dacia (modern Romania) as Roman allies and in 376 crossed the Danube into Moesia (now parts of Yugoslavia and Bulgaria), where they were assigned lands for the defense of the frontier. They had been converted to Arian Christianity by Ulfilas (311–83), who modified their runic writing and translated the Bible into Gothic.

Wallia, ruler of the Visigoths after Alaric and his successor Ataulf, was the real founder of the Visigothic state. In a treaty with the Emperor Honorius he agreed to surrender Galla Placidia and conquer the Iberian Peninsula as an ally of the Romans. He established his capital at Toulouse in France, defeated the Siling Vandals, and nearly annihilated the Alans. The Asding Vandals migrated to Africa under Gaiseric, leaving only the Suevi to contest the supremacy of Spain with the Visigoths. Under Theodoric II (453–66) the Visigoths completely defeated the Suevi at Oporto, overran most of the Iberian Peninsula, and broke with the Roman Empire.

Euric (466–84), who succeeded his brother Theodoric, established his independence of the Roman alliance and completed the conquest of Spain and Lusitania, but under the attacks by the Franks lost the Visigothic centers in Gaul. Thus, Alaric II (485–507) was attacked by Clovis, king of the Franks, on religious pretexts and was defeated and killed at Vogladium. Amalric (511–31) married Clovis' daughter Clotilda, but his efforts to convert her to the Arian faith led to renewed conflicts with the Franks. Teudis (531–48) transferred his court to Spain and by adopting a more tolerant policy toward the orthodox Catholics, was able to resist Frankish attacks.

At this point a commander of high talent appeared. The Emperor

Justinian sent Count Belisarius with a Byzantine army to recover Spain for the empire. After conquering the Vandals in North Africa Belisarius was ready to cross the Strait of Gibraltar and invade the peninsula. The Byzantine forces soon gained control of southern and eastern Spain —the Greek fleet taking possession of the coastal towns, and the army occupying the region between the mouths of the Guadalquivir and Júcar rivers and the interior mountain ranges. Although the imperial forces occupied more territory than was stipulated in the treaty, they were encouraged to stay by the Catholic and Hispano-Roman population. Then came a confused series of kings, waging confused wars. The greatest of these rulers was Leovigild (573–86), who tried to curb the power of his unruly nobles and to subdue his enemies in Spain.

Sisebut (612–21), the most cultivated of the Visigothic monarchs, "brilliant in word, learned in thought, and well provided with literary knowledge," was forced to use his military talents upon his accession. He reconquered the area between the Júcar River and Gibraltar, and the Eastern emperor confirmed a peace by which he retained only a portion of the Algarve. The Visigothic domination of the peninsula was made complete when Swintilla (621–31) used force and astute diplomacy to push the imperial forces out of the Algarve (624).

The principal task of the Visigothic kings, from their first contact with the Hispano-Romans, was to assimilate the culture of the residents of the peninsula and fuse the various populations under their leadership. The people fell into four principal groups: the indigenous stock, the Germans (including the Visigoths), the western Romans, and the eastern (Byzantine) Romans. Euric had established a brilliant court at Toulouse, but he wanted to be more than a tribal chieftain and, in imitation of the Roman emperors, began to issue laws. He also wished to collect and perpetuate Visigothic customs and promulgated the code bearing his name. It was the work of Count León and constituted the first written Germanic law. While it was applied only to the Visigoths—the Hispano-Romans continued to live under their old Roman laws—it was the first step of the Visigoths toward political sophistication, there being a great deal of Roman influence in the formulation of the code.

Two legal systems, therefore, existed in the peninsula, with the Hispano-Romans observing a general, territorial law, and the Visigoths following their customary, personal law. A good deal of confusion soon appeared in judicial practices. Alaric II tried to codify the Hispano-Roman law to eliminate the obsolete in the *Lex Romana Visigothorum*. This code preserved imperial law and attempted to apply classical jurisprudence. The Code of Justinian was applied in the southeastern part of the peninsula after the Byzantine conquest, but its influence was not evident until the time of Leovigild.

Alaric II, Leovigild, and Recared revised the Code of Euric, and in the changes the emphasis was gradually shifted from personal to territorial law. Thus, the Visigothic code was revised to form the *Fuero Juzgo,* representative of the legislative unity which the Visigoths achieved. Another step toward the unity of the various peoples was the abolition of the prohibition of matrimony between the Visigoths and the Romans. Legal unification was finally accomplished through the *Liber judiciorum* of Recceswinth (649–72), which was made obligatory on both Visigoths and Hispano-Romans. Roman law ceased to prevail as such, but Roman influence persisted. The Visigoths were romanized, but in a sense primitive law was reborn under Visigothic influence and the Spaniards were deromanized.

Perhaps the greatest single advance toward unification lay in the fact that Latin took a commanding place as the language of the country, Gothic speech falling into disuse.

There was an insuperable obstacle in the fusion of the two populations in the religious differences. The Hispano-Romans had been converted to the orthodox creed of the Catholics, while the Visigoths were Arians. Euric, like his predecessors, was an Arian and believed that religious unity was essential to a united nation. The orthodox prelates in Gaul opposed him as a heretic, and he retaliated by persecuting the Catholics. He was determined to force them to submit to his rule, even if it were impossible to change their faith. The problem also had its political aspect because the orthodox clergy represented the Roman opposition to the Visigothic conquest. The Franks had used the heresy of the Visigoths as a pretext to attack their Gallic possessions, and their Arianism had persisted as an irritant in the relations of the two peoples. The orthodox Catholics in Spain constantly intrigued on behalf of the Franks against Alaric II and looked to Clovis for aid in their redemption from heretical rule.

While the Ostrogothic king of Italy, Theodoric, governed the Visigoths in the name of his grandson, Amalric (511–31), the persecution of the Catholics was abandoned and a more tolerant policy was formulated. Teudis and Athanagild followed a similar policy, but it was reversed by Leovigild, who brought the religious schism to a crisis. Since the Catholics were consistently intolerant of their Arian monarch and sought assistance from the Suevi and Franks against the king, he persecuted them and exiled their bishops.

Recared was immediately confronted with a serious division among his people. The urbanized Hispano-Romans were wealthy, cultivated, and powerful, whereas the Visigoths cherished rural and military traditions. As the Hispano-Romans were orthodox Catholics they not only represented a serious threat to internal tranquillity, but they were also an obstacle to national unity. Leovigild had already terminated the persecution, and in 589 at the Third Council of Toledo, Recared, with his family and many nobles, was publicly converted to Catholicism. Arianism ceased to be the official religion of the kingdom, but the Arian clergy, led by Goisuintha, began to conspire against Recared with the Franks. The religious division persisted throughout the Visigothic period and offered a ready excuse for intrigue among the disaffected nobility.

Another cause of disunity and discord was the presence of a large number of Jews in Spain. They had multiplied rapidly under Roman rule and had gained social distinction after Hadrian had transplanted 50,000 Jewish families to the peninsula. Additional thousands entered Spain after the Visigothic invasion. The Jewish academies attained an especially high level in education. But prejudice arose. Emperor Heraclius demanded that Sisebut expel the Jews, and they were given a year in which to accept Christianity or leave. Some 90,000 became Christians, and the remainder were severely persecuted. The objective was to attain religious unity in Spain, but although the Jews protected their lives and property by accepting the Christian faith, many of them were only superficially Christians. Chintila (636–40) renewed the persecution, and it was confirmed by the Sixth Council of Toledo (638).

Still another defect of Spanish civilization in the Visigothic era was that it produced no important cultural achievements. Architecture was imitative and weak, following Roman models at a distance. Libraries were small, common schools nonexistent. After Orosius in the fifth century, author of a long-famous work of church history, no important writer appeared until St. Isidore of Seville early in the seventh century furnished a long shelf of books. Of nonecclesiastical literature Spain had virtually none.

Visigothic tradition provided for the election of the king from among the nobles, the king being more chieftain than king. While Euric held the idea of kingship, Leovigild was the first to establish his own power in the kingdom. The electoral principle had produced a good deal of instability as well as successive assassinations of kings by ambitious rivals and disaffected nobles. Leovigild assumed the attributes of royalty to increase his prestige, surrounding himself with pomp, adopting Byzantine ceremonial customs, and issuing gold coins to commemorate his accession. He also associated his sons with the throne to assure the possibility of their succession. He was cruel and energetic in reprisals against the great nobles, some of whom were condemned to death, while others were exiled and their property confiscated.

Swintilla also tried to strengthen the right of hereditary succession to the throne of the kingdom by associating his son Ricimer with him in the government. Accused of cruelty and tyranny because of his severity toward those who conspired against him, he was finally overthrown by Sisenand, duke of Septimania, with the aid of Dagobert, king of Burgundy and Neustria. To secure his elevation to the throne Sisenand convoked the Fourth Council of Toledo and ordered it to approve his assumption of the crown. Chintila followed this precedent and had the Fifth Council of Toledo confirm his election. This council declared that the person of the king was sacred and inviolable and established certain conditions for aspirants to the throne, thereby reaffirming clerical intervention in the succession. The influence of important ecclesiastical personages, such as St. Leander, St. Isidore of Seville, and St. Fructuosus of Braga, in political affairs was increased in successive reigns. They supported the ideal of increased royal authority in return for religious unity and internal order under royal authority.

Recceswinth had been associated with his father, the severe Chindaswinth, and was not elected to the throne in the usual Visigothic tradition. A rebellion against him and an attempt to make the throne hereditary was suppressed. The reign of Wamba, the last great Visigothic king, came to an abrupt end as a result of a palace intrigue. He had a favorite, Ervigius, who was a Greek descendant of Hermenegild. Ervigius took advantage of his position to give the king a narcotic, and while he was drugged, his head was shaved, he was dressed as a monk, and it was pretended that he was dead. When Wamba recovered consciousness he believed himself so degraded that he did not dispute the succession of his favorite.

The anxiety of the Visigothic kings to establish the principle of hereditary succession produced continuous revolts and weakened the monarchy. A real threat to the stability of the throne had already appeared during the reign of Wamba. The Moslems had invaded North Africa, converted the Berbers, and taken Tangier from the imperial forces. Wamba repelled their attack on Algeciras with a numerous fleet. But the Visigoths were not well prepared to defend themselves against a Moslem invasion, for the Arians had not yet been reconciled with the orthodox Catholics, and many of the persecuted Jews who sought refuge in Mauretania maintained a close intelligence with the Jews remaining in Spain.

Egica (687–701) had associated his son Wittiza (701–10) in the government with him in an effort to insure his succession, but when Wittiza ascended the throne he was confronted with intrigue and revolt. The Visigoths had been able to restore the territorial unity of Spain and had tried to unite the inhabitants in a religious unity, but they were now confronted with an enemy in the expanding Moslem hordes in North Africa who was able to take advantage of their failure to complete the fusion of the basic elements of their heritage.

CHAPTER III

Visigothic Civilization

During the eras of prosperity among the Visigoths, the population of the Iberian Peninsula may have risen to ten million. The increase was not due to any large number of invaders because not more than 100,000 Visigoths and 80,000 Vandals moved through the peninsula. The very heterogeneous population was also redistributed: some cities being abandoned to the invaders, others losing most of their inhabitants, and the rural population greatly increasing at the expense of the urban.

The culture of the Visigothic invaders was gradually modified by their residence in the peninsula. They accepted Roman customs in dress and in luxuries and also adopted royal rites and practices from the Eastern Roman Empire. Although they became dominant, it was inevitable that the great numerical superiority of the Hispano-Romans should have a marked influence on cultural developments.

There were four principal influences on Visigothic civilization. The ruling classes provided the Germanic influence. Although the Suevi and Visigoths left a permanent impress on peninsular culture through the fresh energies which they gave the population, they were gradually romanized, despite the obstacles their Arian creed offered to full assimilation. The second important influence was the Latin. The Iberians had long since been thoroughly romanized, and in their absorption of the less numerous barbarians they gained the spiritual dominance. They provided the basis for cultural development and scattered nuclei of Iberians persisted and preserved their ancient traditions, especially the Asturians, Cantabrians, and Basques in their mountain retreats. This Latin influence had already become corrupt when the Visigoths arrived, and the self-centered, luxury-loving upper classes exploited the lower classes. The Byzantine or Greek influence strengthened the Latin through its influence on clerical and legal institutions.

A fourth influence, destined to become increasingly important, was that of the Franks, who although Germanic, were Catholic as opposed to

Arian. The Franks drove the Visigoths from Gaul, except for Septimania north of the Pyrenees, which became a constant stimulus to warfare and the spread of Frankish influence in northeastern Spain. The conversion of the Visigothic kings to Catholicism was the result of intermarriage with the ruling family of their Frankish neighbors. In the end, Germanic ideas were modified, while the Roman elements—both Latin and Byzantine—strengthened by Catholic dogma and intolerance, were persistent. The primary results of these interacting influences were instability, disorder, personal insecurity, vice, and immorality.

Two sports were quickly popularized by the Visigoths as a result of their admiration for valor and skill in military arts. While public spectacles diminished as the urban life decayed, the Romans had created a remarkably strong appetite for them by their gladiatorial combats and the circus. The Roman exhibitions were replaced by tourneys—public festivals at which warriors fought individually or in groups. Theodoric entertained his people with such festivals as early as the sixth century. Tourneys appealed to all classes—even in judicial matters there was recourse to trial by combat.

Bullfighting was an Iberian sport of ancient origin; it was probably introduced into Rome from Spain. There is a tradition that Julius Caesar brought the spectacle to Rome to amuse the mob after his sojourn in the peninsula. It also appealed to the Visigoths—a people for whom valor and stock-handling had long been held in high esteem.

In such a heterogeneous society, social distinctions were not based on race alone, for people from different racial groups might be found in any social class. Men held high position because of ownership of land, high office in the palace, military, administration, or church, and, especially, by right of blood. The most important and select class consisted of the privileged. The Visigothic nobility were nearly always the possessors of high military office, and many of the Hispano-Romans retained their land. The most numerous class consisted of the freemen, a mixed group of merchants and artisans in the cities and freedmen or manumitted serfs in the rural areas. Personal and economic liberty had already been restricted among the *coloni* and in the *collegia*. With the spread of insecurity there were many who became vassals, holding land or owing personal allegiance, and many small peasants exchanged their independence for protection. At the bottom of the social scale were the serfs, who owed their status to accidents of birth, sale, or capture in war. In general, the free cultivators were absorbed into the class of hereditary serfs bound to the land.

The higher clergy were members of the privileged class, with the rights of the nobility, but their positions were offices of the state and depended on nomination by the king. Both dioceses and parishes had their own property, so that the clergy were both officials and proprietors. In addition to their other privileges, the clergy could extend the right of asylum—exemption within the walls of a church or monastery from the penal law of the state. The political importance of the clergy increased when, after the Third Council of Toledo, they acquired the right of approving canons which could be converted into law with royal sanction. Above all, the strength of the clergy lay in their virtual monopoly of education and learning.

The inequality of classes became accentuated during the decay of the empire. There was a gradual but progressive loss of liberty for all classes but the privileged. The state steadily became more agricultural, ecclesiastical, and military, as the free activities of industry and commerce grew less important. Fixed capital, represented by land, became the primary form of wealth. Despite a certain amount of racial and social assimilation between Goths and Hispano-Romans, inequality increased as the privileged class became richer and the rest of the population more impoverished.

The upper classes maintained their position also by extralegal measures of terror, violence, and the coercion or subornation of the lower classes. They were exempt from corporal penalties and torture and had the right of participating in the election of the king, the most prized and zealously defended privilege of the Visigothic aristocracy.

In 418 Wallia signed a treaty of alliance with the Romans by which, in exchange for military service, two-thirds of the land was distributed among the Visigoths. Small and great properties were thus distributed among the nobles, but a large proportion of land remained under the exclusive control of the king. The latifundias which had existed in Roman times did not disappear. Also, extensive properties were formed through royal grants or concentration in the hands of the strong, while the total number of proprietors was reduced.

In the family life—after family unity had been dissipated under the influence of Roman law—there was a reaction toward primitive solidarity among relatives. Among the Germans the principle of blood revenge dominated the family. An offense against one member of the family was an offense against all of the surviving members, who thus inherited the duty of avenging the murder of a blood relative, either in blood or wergeld—compensation in gold. This practice contributed to greater disorder in an age already violent.

Visigothic law also upheld the authority of the husband over the wife.

He bought his bride with a dowry and recovered it on her death if there were neither heirs nor a will. Conjugal fidelity was highly prized and adultery by the wife was severely punished. Family inheritances were divided among the members of the family. The heirs received four-fifths of the property, but the widow enjoyed the income as long as she did not remarry.

As the trend toward the hereditary succession to the throne developed, royal authority in the Visigothic monarchy steadily increased, stimulated by the ambition of the monarch, the increase in the number of his subjects, the extent of his territory, his personal wealth, and royal control of the distribution of grants of land and public offices. The Visigothic king was never absolute in authority, his legislative power being restricted by the palace bureaucracy, while the high clergy and the nobility dominated the courts, despite their theoretical subjection to the king as chief judge.

After the Eighth Council of Toledo good habits became a prerequisite for a candidate for the throne. The new monarch was popularly acclaimed in Toledo, took the oath to fulfill the laws and protect the customs of the kingdom, and received the religious benediction. When they entered Spain the Goths did not have distinctive insignia, but after Leovigild they imitated the Byzantine practice of using a crown and a throne. By the time of Chindaswinth, they were using vestments of purple, a silver throne, a scepter, and a crown of gold and precious stones. The nobles constituted the court and an ill-defined advisory council, those who held positions at the royal palace being given the title of count. The court was at Narbonne or Toulouse until the reign of Amalric, later being moved to Seville, until Athanagild established it at Toledo in 584.

When the Visigoths abandoned tribal life for more sedentary ways, it was no longer possible to assemble the nation because of the dispersion of the tribes. The assembly of nobles replaced the assembly of all freemen, and Alaric modified the convocation by adding episcopal representatives. After the conversion of Recared the Councils of Toledo became political as well as religious. Composed of both clergy and nobility, they assumed a truly legislative character, while the sovereign acquired a certain religious sanctity. The clergy also began to exercise political influence. Although the royal will remained dominant in the imposition of laws, the council usually gained recognition and approval of its proposals. The king not only delegated power to the members of the council, but he used them for his own ends, especially to counteract the lawlessness of members of the aristocracy.

In general the Visigoths preserved the Roman administrative organization. The old system of provinces, directed by dukes as military officers, was continued with some modification. The principal innovation was the addition of the territories north of the Pyrenees to Narbonne. The cities were governed by counts, who bore civil duties and were assisted by vicars with judicial powers. Although many cities disappeared, the Visigoths actually favored the *municipia.* Until the elective counts became hereditary and councils were organized, the citizens of the towns assembled to deal with matters of common interest. The *curiales,* the members of the city councils, were released from their responsibility for the collection of taxes, and it became easier to get worthy citizens to accept membership on the council. In an age of anarchy when the central authority was striving to exert control, they enjoyed more independence than they had under the Roman Empire.

Judicial authority was usually delegated to justices in fixed districts, who were not permitted to act beyond their jurisdiction. The extraordinary judges for special occasions were remunerated with a percentage of the amount in litigation. The procedure in trials was simple and brief. Torture was applied, but only within certain well-defined limits, and to plebeians; tests of hot water and fire were not fully admitted as evidence. The most usual penalty consisted of cutting the hair, a symbol of degradation among the Visigoths. Criminals were also whipped and fined. Although sentences could be appealed to the count, duke, or king, justice remained uncertain and arbitrary. There were too many class distinctions to permit impartial justice.

When the Visigoths conquered the peninsula, they continued to collect the capitation tax on persons and lands, rents, and indirect taxes. They also required a special tax in kind on the lands of the conquered, while military service and support of the king and his court on their travels became additional public contributions. At first, only Hispano-Romans were forced to labor on public works, but later this obligation was imposed on the Visigoths. Fines for crimes, property confiscation, and special taxes on Jews were other sources of public revenue. The fiscal system of the Visigoths became very onerous, and insurrections occurred and delinquent taxes had to be written off. The Goth paid less than the Roman, the noble less than the plebeian, the freeman or freedman less than the serf, and the clergy were exempt from all taxes.

The Eighth Council of Toledo distinguished between the public and the private patrimonies of the king. It ordered that all wealth derived by virtue of his power and authority should belong to the kingdom and could not be bequeathed by testament; otherwise the king could dispose of the resources of the realm without any limitation. The administration of royal finances was entrusted to a count, and special officials were appointed to collect taxes.

When the Visigoths entered the peninsula they were organized on a military basis and had only to adapt their system to new conditions. The king was head of the army, the organization of which was based on the nobility. Custom and law made military service obligatory on all residents. While at first only Visigoths were called to military service, eventually Hispano-Romans were also included. Each lord led his own contingent, and the forces of the province were commanded by the duke, who was directly responsible to the king.

The royal guard, composed of the royal serfs, clients, and freedmen, was the only permanent military force. The feudal army was called only for military necessity in wartime. Each noble took a tenth of his servants to war and, until the time of Wamba, only the clergy were excepted. The vassal not only fought for his lord but shared the booty with him. Cavalry was the principal military arm, and the tactical objective was to surround —after scattered attacks—the enemy foot soldiers. Usually, in defensive tactics, the cavalry was held in reserve on the wings to charge at the propitious moment. The Visigoths, like the Romans, found that the traditional guerrilla warfare of the Iberians—especially the constantly defeated but never conquered Basques—was difficult to combat.

After the conversion of Recared the one supreme ecclesiastical authority beyond the control of the king was the bishop of Rome. He was consulted on important decisions, and disputed ecclesiastical cases were appealed to him. In turn, the bishop of Rome sent apostolic vicars to the peninsula. While there was no actual head of the Spanish Church, there were metropolitan sees at Toledo, Tarragona, Mérida, Seville, and Braga among the Visigoths and at Lugo among the Suevi, and the archbishop of Toledo exercised the primacy except during the Byzantine occupation of Cartagena, when it was contested.

By the seventh century there were seventy-seven dioceses in the Visigothic kingdom, sixty-nine of which were in the peninsula. The bishops had acquired great political influence as a result of their participation in the councils of Toledo. The king did not usually intervene in matters of worship and dogma, but left these matters to the bishops. The wealth of the Church was steadily increased by the construction of new churches —to compensate for the destruction during the invasion—and by donations and bequests from the pious, until it held extensive lands and many serfs. Matrimony and divorce were considered civil affairs, but the Church intervened in them. The monks in the increasing number of monasteries were independent under their abbots, but could appeal to civil tribunals.

Culture decayed with the collapse of Roman authority and the subsequent anarchy. Official schools disappeared, and the clergy—the most cultivated class and the only one not primarily preoccupied with war—gained control of education. New schools were established in connection with the churches and monasteries to provide instruction in both religious and general subjects. The sexes were separated, and the education of women was reduced to what could be learned at home.

Three languages were spoken in the peninsula during the Visigothic interlude. Gothic was introduced by the invaders, but it fell into disuse after the seventh century. Latin was the language of the Romans, the romanized natives, and the Church. When the conversion of Recared made Catholicism the official faith, Arian books in Gothic were destroyed and Latin, as has been noted, came into general and official use. In the southeast there was also a strong Greek influence. Many priests went to Constantinople to study, and Greek survived as a literary language among the cultivated. Hebrew and Chaldean were also taught in some cultural centers, especially among the Jews.

Intellectual life was centered primarily in the churches, cathedrals, and monasteries, and in some reigns at the court. The majority of the literary figures were churchmen, and their subjects were religious and moral. Many writers appeared, including Hidacius, a classical chronicler, and Oriencius and Merobaudes, poets of clerical distinction. During the sixth century a renaissance in letters was initiated as a result of foreign influences. It culminated in two great figures.

St. Leander (550?–?601), bishop of Seville, was the true father of the Hispano-Gothic Church. Born in Cartagena, he fled to Seville when the eastern area was ceded to the Byzantine Empire. By 578 he was archbishop of Seville. He assisted in the conversion of Hermenegild and was persecuted for a time by Leovigild. His school in Seville was an important center of the Visigothic renaissance. St. Isidore (560–636) succeeded as archbishop of Seville and became the leading figure of his century in the peninsula and one of the conspicuous figures of the Middle Ages. He not only exerted a great influence on the Spanish Church but collected a summary of ancient knowledge with encyclopedic care. He became a master of Greek, Latin, and Hebrew in his brother's school. His primary objective was the assimilation of the Gothic elements in the peninsula to form a homogeneous population through religion and education. He was the author of the *Etymologies, Chronicon,* and the

History of the Kings of the Goths, Vandals, and Suevi, one of the best sources for a knowledge of the Germanic peoples in the peninsula.

The leadership of St. Isidore gave Spain cultural dominance in the West during the seventh century. He was surrounded by disciples, who founded schools in Toledo, Mérida, Saragossa, and Palencia. The monasteries became the centers of the literary movement as foci of culture in the midst of general ignorance. They collected libraries and made Visigothic culture primarily a monastic culture. The idea of learning spread from the monasteries to the nobility. Many nobles collected libraries, studied Latin letters, and took Latin names.

A Visigothic style in art, based on a Latin foundation and influenced by oriental and Byzantine styles, evolved during the period. The Visigoths usually imitated classic styles, and their buildings were simple and solid rather than magnificent. Plans, materials, and decoration were inferior and there was a decline in taste, with a tendency toward barbaric ornamentation and ostentation. Painting did not develop, and such sculpture as appeared was rough and heavy. The richest remains of Visigothic art are the jewelry and the work in precious metals and stones.

The century and a half after Athanagild was the most brilliant period of the Visigothic civilization. Churches, palaces, and public buildings were erected, especially in Toledo, which became the real center of culture in the kingdom. The Visigoths took up their extensive estates in rural areas, and Roman life, which continued to flourish in such centers as Seville, Mérida, and Córdoba, in the end had a cultural influence on the Visigoths. They relinquished their primitive simplicity for luxuries, without really assimilating the refinement of the Latin spirit.

The entire Roman Empire had already declined internally when, in the fifth century, the Visigoths invaded and took control of Spain. These Germanic tribesmen brought with them the principle of kingship, whereby an assembly of warriors elected a chief and placed limits upon his authority. The Visigothic monarchs modified this original concept, however, making the kingship hereditary. Furthermore, when the Visigoths dispersed throughout the country, it was no longer possible to maintain the assembly of warriors. An assembly of nobles emerged instead, composed of the military and landowning elite and of the Catholic prelates.

Roman traditions generally prevailed over the more primitive Germanic customs, as evidenced by the fact that Latin replaced Gothic as the language of the new rulers. Nevertheless, Roman government and justice inevitably deteriorated. The weak central administration gave way to regional government under dukes or counts. Germanic personal law, in the form of the family vendetta or of local custom, came to exist alongside Roman territorial law. The old three-class system of privileged, free, and slave developed into a two-class system of privileged and serf.

The Christian element in Spanish society fared better than the Roman during the Visigothic age. The Catholic Church gained political power by associating itself with the monarchy. It also took over the educational process and preserved the remnants of classical learning in the monasteries.

Although the Visigoths ruled Spain for three hundred years, their kings failed to assert their authority, and so could not complete the fusion between the Roman-Christian and the Germanic elements of society. The result was a feeble and divided state, which the Moslems from North Africa overran in the eighth century.

CHAPTER IV

The Moslem Conquest

The Moslem invaders of the Iberian Peninsula were confronted with a Visigothic kingdom subverted by internal enemies, corrupted by romanization, and torn by strife for the succession to the throne. Wittiza's action in making his son a partner on the throne without the usual election by the nobles provoked intrigue and rebellion. In addition, the king had a personal feud to settle. While still a prince, he had become enamored of the wife of Duke Favila, and, in the quarrel which arose, he mortally wounded the duke. On his accession Wittiza exiled the duke's son, Pelayo, from Toledo.

Wittiza left three minor sons. His widowed queen, his brother the bishop of Seville, and a second brother supported the pretensions of Achila, his eldest son, but the nobles elected Rodrigo, duke of Betica, as sovereign. After a brief struggle the partisans of Achila fled to Africa and sought Moslem aid. Rodrigo was the last Visigothic king.

The Moslems—known as Moors because they were Moroccans—were still engaged in the conquest of Mauretania, although they had attacked Spain in 709 and 710 and raided the Spanish coast. Count Julian, a Visigothic or Byzantine governor of Ceuta but a Christian, had been sustained by aid from Spain in his resistance to the Moors. When the outbreak of civil war cost him that support, his vigilance over the strait was relaxed. Wittiza's sons fled to Ceuta and, in cooperation with Julian, sought an alliance with the Moorish leaders, Muza and Tarik.

Consequently, in 711 Tarik led 12,000 warriors and the Spanish allies in a landing at Gebel Tarik (rock of Tarik, or Gibraltar). Rodrigo hastened to Betica from the Basque country to meet the invaders. Tarik was reinforced, but had only 25,000 men to meet the 40,000 Visigoths at Guadalete. Rodrigo entrusted the command of his flanks to the two brothers of Wittiza, who gave way after the Visigothic cavalry had gained an advantage. Rodrigo was defeated and disappeared.

The triumphant Tarik divided his army into three contingents. One took Ecija, turned it over to the Jews, and advanced eastward along the coast to Málaga. The second army took Córdoba after fierce resistance, while Tarik led a third force on Toledo, which capitulated without resistance. Throughout the campaign Tarik was supported by the Jews and the adherents of Wittiza, who believed they were defending legitimacy and that the Moors came only to restore their rightful king. They soon realized that they had underestimated Muza, who landed at Algeciras in 712, captured Seville and Mérida, and advanced northward. Tarik besieged Saragossa, where Muza joined him after taking Salamanca and Astorga. By 714 the conquest of the major portion of the peninsula was complete. Only Theodomir, who resisted in the southeast and whose fragment of the Visigothic monarchy survived until 779, and scattered nuclei of resistance in the Pyrenees and Cantabrian mountains survived.

The Iberian Peninsula was now governed as a dependency of the Omayyad caliphate of Damascus, while the immediate ruler was an emir under the wali of North Africa at Kairwan. The choice of the caliph, who was both spiritual head of Islam and chief of the Moslem state, had created sharp rivalries among a variety of sects in the Mohammedan world. These were reflected in the society of Moslem Spain. The Sunnites, who were of Yemenite stock, believed that the caliphate should be an elective office, occupied by a member of Mohammed's tribe. The Shiites held that only Mohammed's son-in-law Ali and his descendants were qualified to be the caliph. Finally, the Kharijites, who dominated North Africa, regarded the caliphate as a freely elective office. The sects engaged in constant intrigue, and these dissensions among the conquerors, as well as the tribal feuds and the racial antagonism, kept the Moslem world disunited. The aristocratic Arabs had conquered and converted the democratic Berbers in North Africa, and their rivalry soon became evident in the dynastic struggles in Spain. As migration increased the numerical superiority of the Berbers, their influence became more evident.

Faith in Mohammed was the only common factor in the Moslem world, and the Moors lacked the unity to solve in permanent fashion the problems posed by their own differences and the resistance of the Christians in the north. Nevertheless, their first conquest of Spain was a brilliant accomplishment. In seven years of hard fighting (711–18) the combined forces of the African Berbers, the Yemenites, and the Mudarite Arabs drove with fanatical zeal past all obstacles—conquering the whole peninsula except narrow mountainous strips in the north.

Muza and Tarik were recalled to Damascus after their victories in Spain, but the conquest was consolidated by Abd-el-Aziz, the son of Muza. The Moors also crossed the Pyrenees and advanced as far as Poitiers in southern France before they were defeated and turned back by Charles Martel (732).

In 750 a new dynasty was established at Baghdad. The Abbasid family persecuted the remnants of the Omayyad family diligently. Among the few who escaped was Abd-er-Rahman, grandson of the Caliph Hisha, who fled through Egypt and North Africa to Spain. After preliminary investigation, and taking advantage of the factional strife, this prince defeated the ruling emir at Córdoba and founded an independent emirate in the peninsula.

Abd-er-Rahman I (756–88) proposed to reconcile the contending factions, terminate family, tribal, and sectarian rivalries, and establish a strong central government. He did not succeed in his design, and Charlemagne entered one of the combinations formed against him. When Charlemagne was unable to take Saragossa, he withdrew across the Pyrenees and the Basques ambushed and defeated his rearguard at the Pass of Roncesvalles. The heroic death of the French champion, Roland, in the battle has been celebrated in the *Chanson de Roland.*

While the emir assumed the title of "descendant of the caliphs," he continued to recognize their supremacy in religious matters. He adopted a policy of tolerance toward Christians and permitted Jews to return to the peninsula. His son and successor, Hisha I (788–96), was more fervently religious and attacked and defeated the Christians in Castile and Álava. He was constructively active in rebuilding Córdoba, in stimulating cultural progress and in strengthening the Moslem organization. A religious and intellectual aristocracy appeared, became a privileged caste, and began to intervene in political affairs. But his successor, Hakam I (796–822), suppressed this rising class with ferocious cruelty and added Mameluke slaves to the royal guard to intimidate the people. His energy strengthened and centralized the emirate, and he converted his military forces—paid from the royal treasury—into a permanent army.

Abd-er-Rahman II (822–52) was of a more peaceful temperament. He loved magnificence and so improved Córdoba that it attained its greatest splendor. While he devoted himself to poetry and learning, his wife and the perfidious Spanish renegade and eunuch, Nasar, ruled the emirate. At times he was roused to act against rebellion, and his armies engaged in continuous warfare against the Christians. In 844 the Northmen attacked Gijón and La Coruña; when repelled, they turned southward, occupied Cádiz, and advanced on Seville. The emir mobilized his forces and defeated them near that city. Some of the Northmen were captured and converted to the Moslem faith, settling down as dairymen, famous for their cheeses. After the raid Seville was fortified, the protection of the coast was improved, and the Moslems began to build a fleet.

The last years of Abd-er-Rahman were marked by the severe persecution of the Christians, the Mozarabs. The Christian communities, formerly tolerated, grew dissatisfied with the increasing Moslem influence among them and formed a group to combat their arabization. When Perfecto, a priest, bitterly blasphemed the Prophet and was executed, his martyrdom stimulated similar demonstrations, and the contagion increased with persecution, until in 852 a council of Mozarabs condemned such activity.

Rebellions took place in Toledo and Mérida under Mohammed I (852–86), and the Beni-Casi lords of Saragossa, Huesca, and Tudela became nearly independent on the northern frontier. Muza II even assumed the title of "Third King of Spain" and maintained close relations with the Christian kings. In the south a renegade son of a Visigoth, Omar ben-Hafsun, emerged as the leader of the mountaineers around Málaga and fortified the mountain of Bobastro, from whence he raided the surrounding countryside and attacked fortified cities. By the time of Abdallah (888–912) the authority of the emir had been reduced to its lowest ebb.

Abd-er-Rahman III (912–61), who was much the greatest of all the Moslem rulers of Spain, found the country when he came to power torn by civil dissension and threatened by foreign enemies. This emir was a handsome man of regular features, whose dark blue eyes and reddish hair betrayed his European blood, for he was the son of a Frankish concubine and the grandson of a Basque princess. He suppressed the defiant Omar ben-Hafsun—who had become a Catholic—and centers of rebellion at Seville, Badajoz, and Toledo. Then he turned on the Christians in the north, who had advanced to the Douro River, defeated them at Mentona (918) and Valdejunquera (920), and advanced northward to Pamplona. He forced Navarre to pay tribute and all of the states in the peninsula—except León and Catalonia—recognized his sovereignty.

While Abd-er-Rahman's predecessors had been content with *de facto* independence when the caliphs at Baghdad were still powerful, he was confronted with a weak caliph and a divided Moslem world. He abandoned the title of emir and ordered that he be called "Defender of the Faith" and "Prince of the Believers" in public prayers, thereby establishing the caliphate of Córdoba on a basis of equality with the caliphs of Baghdad and Egypt (929).

The caliph of Córdoba was an absolute monarch. He assumed all of the attributes of government and ruled without a vizier, surrounded by a bureaucracy of foreign slaves—brought to Córdoba by Jewish merchants—and freedmen, who enjoyed his full confidence. An expert administrator and an intelligent general, he was firm in the resolution of the problems which arose during his reign. He had the most powerful fleet in the Mediterranean. The power of the caliph was so increased that his fame spread beyond his frontiers and foreign embassies came to Córdoba to pay their respects. The treasury was filled with 20,000,000 gold coins. Córdoba became a magnificent city of 500,000 people, with innumerable mosques, baths, and palaces, rivaling Baghdad in splendor. Agriculture and industry flourished, the arts and sciences were stimulated, and the caliphate became one of the most civilized centers in the Western world.

Hakam II (961–76) was of a more pacific character, devoted to his books, until forced to defend the caliphate against León and the count of Castile. He launched an attack on the Christians in 963 and forced them to sue for peace; though they later besieged Gormaz, the caliph's favorite general, Galib, won a decisive victory. No caliph before Hakam II had demonstrated such interest in the arts and sciences as he did. He collected manuscripts and kept copyists, binders, and artists constantly occupied in his palace. His library contained more than 400,000 volumes, and he was prodigal in his generosity to learned men. Córdoba became a center of learning which attracted thousands of students.

Hisha II (976–1016) became his father's successor, despite a palace intrigue, at the age of twelve years. Dominated by his mother Sobh (Aurora), a Basque by birth, and the new vizier, Mohammed ibn-Abi-Amir, her lover—who had dreamed of becoming vizier since his youth—the caliph was too young to exercise authority and too weak to recover it when he came of age. Mohammed had been genial and unscrupulous as majordomo of the palace, but he had an iron will, great political cunning, singular military ability, and a mastery of intrigue which carried him to the height of his ambition. He was descended from an Arab who had entered the peninsula with Tarik, but his ancestors had been students rather than military men. He was educated to succeed his distinguished father in Córdoba in the transmission of Moslem traditions.

At the age of twenty-six Mohammed had been entrusted with the management of the property of Prince Abd-er-Rahman. He soon won the favor of the sultana by his courtesy and courtly manners and became administrator of her property. In time he became cadi, or judge, of Seville and Niebla, manager of various properties, and chief of police of Córdoba. He exercised such tact that, when sent to Mauretania, he not only satisfied the caliph, but also won the friendship of the generals he was sent to restrain.

Moshafi, the first minister, was an honest but mediocre bureaucrat, and, with the aid of Sobh, Mohammed exploited his weaknesses. He assumed the defense of the capital against Christian raids and in 977 increased his popularity by a victorious campaign in which he captured many prisoners and much booty. He had acquired a military reputation and won the gratitude of his fellow officials by careful gifts. A Berber of obscure origin, Moshafi had enjoyed a brilliant career, but his appointment as first minister had aroused jealousy. He had immediately challenged criticism by his policy of nepotism, and he incurred the disdain of Galib, the general commanding the frontier army, whose confidence Mohammed had already cultivated.

After a second raid against the Christians, Mohammed was made prefect of Córdoba through the influence of the general. He reestablished order in the capital and married Galib's daughter. It was inevitable that he should succeed Moshafi as first minister and share the supreme authority in the caliphate with his father-in-law, yet, as his ambition became more apparent, the opposition to him increased and his popularity began to wane. Sustained for a while by the sultana, Mohammed foiled a conspiracy to overthrow Hisha II and ingratiated himself with the influential, learned men of the capital by burning the philosophical books in the library collected by Hakam II. He was prepared to take the final, audacious step of transferring the administration from the alcazar to a new residence near Córdoba, where he would be absolute master, relieved of the necessity of rendering daily homage to his nominal sovereign.

Only his father-in-law remained as an obstacle to his ambition. Galib suspected his designs and their relations became strained. To counter Galib's military supremacy, Mohammed organized his own army—enrolling the Berbers who had been besieged at Ceuta as a permanent force and abolishing the old military organization by tribes. The crisis reached a breaking point when the old general reproached and attacked his son-in-law at a dinner party. Mohammed seized Galib's treasure and killed him in the battle which ensued.

As the final step in his ascent as dictator the first minister chose an honorific title, "al-Mansur bi-Allah," or "The Victorious by Allah." Sobh, who had become his implacable enemy, stimulated her son to make a feeble attempt to recover his authority, but the secret police discovered the plot and at a public festival in honor of the caliph al-Mansur issued an edict which delegated complete authority to him.

Al-Mansur justified his usurpation of power by his victorious campaigns against the Christians. In 981 he sacked Zamora, defeated the Christians at Rueda and Simancas, and pursued the fugitives to the gates of León. In the ensuing years he sacked and burned Barcelona, carried Moslem arms victoriously into the heart of Galicia, sacked and burned Santiago de Compostela—returning to Córdoba with the bells of the church—and ravaged Castile. In 1002 he became ill as he returned from his last campaign and died.

After al-Mansur the caliphate fell into anarchy and civil war. A succession of weak and ineffective caliphs, the intervention of the Berbers and slaves in political affairs, and the restlessness of the populace of Córdoba, ever ripe for revolt, brought the kingdom finally to disintegration. The relatively independent governors of the principal cities assumed the titles and powers of emirs. The city splinter states, known as *taifa,* were in constant warfare among themselves. In some states the old Arab aristocracy, formerly persecuted and humiliated, recovered power, in many of the eastern areas the emirs were slave generals, and in the central and western cities the Berbers gained the ascendancy. Each of the emirs sought to dominate the others and restore the position of caliph—they all tried piously to exterminate one another.

The conquest of Toledo by Alfonso VI placed the *taifa* in a critical position. Mutamid of Seville, the first emir to recognize the threat, proposed an appeal to the new Berber sect of the Almoravids in North Africa. As recent and fanatical converts to Islam, these Berbers from the Sahara, who complained of the lack of religious enthusiasm among the Moslems, represented a new political power. They called themselves Almoravids, religious men, and soon controlled a vast empire which extended from Senegal to Algiers.

At the time of Mutamid, the leader of the sect was Yusuf-ibn-Tashfin. Some of the petty kinglets, unsympathetic with his fanaticism, vacillated in their desire to request aid, but the Christian threat was the more immediate danger. Yusuf was invited to Spain on the condition that he respect the integrity of the existing states. After defeating and inflicting enormous losses on the Christians at Zalaca (1086), he failed to follow up his advantage and returned to Africa, but the campaign continued to be successful. The Christians were driven from Saragossa and Valencia and the states paying tribute to León and Castile were relieved of their burden.

Yusuf had become popular for his victory at Zalaca and was urged to return in 1090. The peninsular Moslems recognized that peace and tranquillity were possible only under his rule. Even the petty princes looked on him as an arbiter in their quarrels. The emirs underestimated Yusuf, for he soon dethroned several of the *taifa* kings and proclaimed himself lord of Spain. His successor, Ali (1106–43), defeated the Christians at Uclés (1108) and captured Saragossa. But the power of the Almoravids began to decline under the constant pressure of the Portuguese and Castilians. Intrigue and corruption produced discontent in Spain, and a new revolt broke out in North Africa.

The revolt in the Atlas Mountains was stimulated by ibn-Tumart, the Mahdi, whose followers were known as Almohads, or unitarians. The peninsula was left practically defenseless as Almoravid troops were recalled to defend the African territories. The Mahdi was killed (1130), but his successor, Abd-al-Mumin, soon gained control of Morocco. When rebellion broke out in Spain an appeal was made to the Almohads for aid. Abd-al-Mumin captured Seville, rapidly overran the southern half of the peninsula, and gained control of all Moslem Spain. The Berbers from Morocco were dominant in the peninsula.

Under the successors of Abd-al-Mumin there was constant warfare with the Christians. After defeating Alfonso VIII at Alarcos (1195) the Almohad ruler preached a new holy war against the Christians, but in 1212 Alfonso won the great battle of Navas de Tolosa, which marked the end of the Moslem effort to dominate Spain. Torn by revolt and discord over the succession, the Almohad empire began to disintegrate.

Just as the Moslems had overrun Spain because the Visigoths had not successfully united it, they declined because of division within their own ranks. In the end, only the state of Granada was left to sustain the Moslem tradition in the peninsula. Nevertheless, the Moors had placed a powerful stamp on the destiny of Spain. They kept the Christians occupied with the war on their southern frontier for nearly eight hundred years. The Arabs and Berbers contributed new blood to the heterogeneous inhabitants already there and gave them a new, fatalistic psychology. Under their sway the Jews returned to the peninsula. These factors not only gave a fresh eastern orientation to Spanish culture, but were a challenge to those who remained faithful to their Christian ideals.

When the caliphate of Córdoba reached the zenith of its prosperity, it was the most civilized state in Western Europe, and its wealth, industry, and culture had great influence on the continent. The Moslems turned the eyes of their Spanish and Portuguese successors toward Africa. They not only gave Spain a renovated culture but altered its foreign policy in a way which continuously influenced its future evolution.

Spain is an anomaly among the societies of the West in that it was affected not only by the Roman, Christian, and Germanic traditions, but also by the Moslem. In 711, a North African army entered Spain as an ally of the pretender to the Visigothic throne, but within seven years the Moslems had taken nearly the entire peninsula for themselves. Their state, the caliphate of Córdoba, reached its height of power during the reign of Abd-er-Rahman III in the tenth century.

The caliphate collapsed when the Moslem aristocracy broke away from several ineffective caliphs to establish themselves as independent lords. The Almoravids from North Africa reunited Spain briefly in the eleventh century, and the Almohads succeeded them. In the meantime, the small Christian kingdoms of the north had taken advantage of Moslem disunity to begin the reconquest of Spain for the Cross. They eventually succeeded, but Moslem influence persisted in every aspect of Spanish life: in language, government, law, science, and the arts.

CHAPTER V

The Civilization of Moslem Spain

The unification of Spain by the Moslems was even more difficult than it had been for the Visigoths. The constant warfare between the Christians and the Moslems for nearly eight hundred years and the diversity of the races that had accepted Mohammedanism were an obstacle to unity from the beginning. The rivalries of the different tribes and peoples persisted even after Abd-er-Rahman III tried to fuse them. Within the ranks of the conquerors there were Arabs, Persians, and Berbers, and among the Arabs were Yemenites and Syrians, separated by fierce hatred. These divergent factions struggled for their own particular objectives, tried to seize control of the state, and contributed to the anarchy which characterized a great part of the Moslem era in the peninsula.

The faith of Mohammed had civilized the Arabs, conquered the Berbers, and provided a broad basis for cultural unity despite racial antagonisms. Acceptance of this religion, founded on the Koran, signified belief in a single god, Allah, in his Prophet Mohammed, and in a glorious immortality for all believers. Mohammed adapted his religious system to the habits of the peoples to whom he gave religious and some political unity. Mecca was the ancient religious center of the Arab world; Mohammed sanctified pilgrimages to Mecca. The Arabs were accustomed to raiding and looting their neighbors; Mohammed made war a religious duty and reserved a fifth of the booty for Allah. He gave the Arabs a simple but effective ritual of prayer, and enjoined abstinence, charity, and pilgrimages to Mecca. His law was contained in the Koran and the Hadith—the word of Allah as understood through the revelations of the Prophet and the method of observing the traditions narrated by Mohammed and his companions.

While three religions coexisted in Spain—the Moslem, the Christian, and the Jewish—the official religion of the South was the Moslem, the religious leader of which was the caliph. While the aristocracy was somewhat skeptical and sophisticated in its attitude toward religion, the extremely pious middle and lower classes heeded the calls to prayer from the mosques and observed Friday as a holy day. The interpreters of the doctrine—the muftis—were usually important persons. Except in times of persecution the Christians could worship freely. The Catholic organization of the Visigothic period was left unchanged, although the caliph intervened in the appointment of the bishops and in convocations of councils. There were three Christian churches and eleven monasteries in Córdoba, where the Jews also had an important synagogue.

Mohammedanism also transformed customs and social organization, introducing a new civilization into the Iberian Peninsula. The family, the basis of Moslem society, was under the supreme authority of the father, to whom the wife and children owed absolute obedience as long as his orders did not conflict with religious duty. This limitation prevented him from exercising the power of life or death, but did not keep him from arranging the marriages of his children. He was obligated to support his family and to provide his sons with an education after they had passed from their mother's tutelage at the age of seven. Daughters remained under the care of their mother.

Polygamy was permitted in accordance with existing customs. A Moslem could have four legitimate wives and any number of concubines, but he had to endow each wife, which made polygamy a luxury restricted to wealthy Moslems. Abd-er-Rahman I had eighty-seven children and Mohammed I had fifty-four. Since the Moslems held matrimony to be a civil and not a religious contract, a man might repudiate his wife without legal formality, while a woman could appeal to judicial authority for a divorce. In either repudiation or divorce the husband had to return half of the dowry provided for in the matrimonial contract. No restriction was placed on marriage between a Moslem and a Christian, and the caliphs frequently married Christians from the north. In Spain the condition of a woman was, on the whole, not so subordinate as it was in the Orient. Although not usually permitted to appear in public without being veiled, and restricted to the harem, women at times wielded great influence.

Social lines were, in general, similar to those in other countries. In theory Moslem society was very democratic—no social differences existed in Moslem communities except those established by nature or age. But in fact, in the conquered countries, an aristocracy soon developed, for the conquered people were considered inferior. The aristocracy varied in composition. A special nobility consisting of the descendants of the Prophet wore a green turban and received marked consideration. Immediately after the Moslem conquest, the elite of the peninsula consisted of Arabs from Yemen or, as the migrations proceeded, from Syria, Palestine, or Egypt. The sects also differed violently in their concepts of theology and the caliphate. In the end the more democratic elements prevailed—partly from the radical revolution accomplished in the establishment of the caliphate of Córdoba and the strong policy of Abd-er-Rahman III and from the numerical superiority of the more democratic Berbers.

The dominant aristocracy in the Moslem part of the peninsula came to be that of the Berbers. Even though the Arabs retained a great deal of influence in the cities, the Berbers, constantly reinforced by migrations from Africa, formed on the one hand an aristocracy of the sword and on the other a middle class of merchants, professional men, and artisans who concentrated in the important cities and amassed considerable wealth. The Arab and Berber aristocracies were also the most important rural class. Land was wealth, and the emirs distributed great areas to tribal chiefs as rewards for services in war or to quiet discontent. Those who formerly cultivated the land were the serfs, and they gave their lords the portion of the harvest previously reserved for the state. In this fashion great landed properties controlled by independent lords were created.

The greater part of the Spanish population did not flee before the Moslem advance, partly because of the expected tolerance of the Moslems, partly because they concluded that the invasion was temporary, and partly because of relief from the harsh rule of the Visigoths. The majority converted to Mohammedanism and continued to enjoy the status of free men or freedom from serfdom. The new converts to Islam occupied an intermediate position and, with those who remained firm in their Christian faith, the Mozarabs, resided in the principal cities. There were several classes of apostates. The *maulas* were Christian captives who accepted Islam and became part of an Arab tribe as clients, thereby recovering their liberty. The *muladies,* another class of converts, were the children of a Moslem father and a Christian mother or of any mixed marriage and were obliged by law to be Moslems. A third class, the renegades—Spaniards subjugated at the time of the conquest who had abjured their religion—were usually known as *muladies* but were considered inferior to Moslems even when they accumulated great wealth and power. Many Christians gave up their faith to gain freedom from slavery or serfdom. The number of apostates increased after the period of Abd-er-Rahman II.

At first, the Moslems were very intolerant toward those who remained staunch in their Christian faith. Those conquered by the Moslems in the Holy War were obliged to choose between Islam and the payment of tribute. If they submitted voluntarily they were placed under the protection of the state, but if they were conquered by force of arms, the men were killed and the women enslaved. The Mozarabs also suffered certain restrictions, such as exclusion from public office and inability to hold Moslem serfs or slaves. The persecution was intensified after each new invasion, and the fanatical Almoravids and Almohads sought to unify Moslem Spain religiously by force.

Although arabized, the Mozarabs remained a distinct community within the Moslem state, subject to their own law—the *Fuero Juzgo*—and their own governors. In Córdoba a special official was designated to represent their interests and defend them in the court of the caliph. Despite the general toleration of the Mozarabs, the Moslems would not permit any offenses against the Mohammedan religion, such as apostasy and blasphemy. The Mozarabs usually lived in special sections of the cities in an effort to retain their identity, although they were in daily contact with the Moslems. In their loyalty to their faith they provided a threat to the Moslems, and they maintained intelligence with the Christians in the north. This threat, their fanatical devotion to Christianity, and the increasing intolerance of the Berbers as they were reinforced by successive invasions explain in large measure the periodic persecutions of the Mozarabs.

Of the men of two classes, serfs and slaves, the serfs were in a somewhat easier situation than they had been under the Visigoths, who did not possess as many slaves as did the Moslems. Also, freedom was always within their reach if they accepted Islam. Some of the slaves attained enviable and highly privileged positions—especially the eunuchs, who held places of great importance in the palace and served as special guards. The slaves finally constituted an aristocracy and gained great influence in political affairs. Abd-er-Rahman III increased the number of slaves in the army to provide its permanent basis, giving them lands and slaves of their own and important civil and military functions.

After the Moslem conquest the condition of the Jews was strikingly improved. Instead of adopting the restrictive policy of the Visigoths, the Moslems at first tolerated the Jews and conceded them generous privileges. They had aided in the conquest and had often been placed in charge of conquered cities. Commerce and industry flourished in the Jewish communities with ample liberty, especially in Córdoba. The

Jews engaged in diplomacy, business, and literary activities, and their number increased with their prosperity. Some cities, such as Lucena, had only Jewish inhabitants. Later, under the reforming Almoravids, persecution was renewed, and they were ordered to accept Islam or go into exile. Many Jews emigrated to Castile, where they were hospitably received.

The most famous Jew under Abd-er-Rahman III was the physician and politician Hasdai ibn Shaprut. Born in Jaén in 915, he dedicated himself to the study of medicine from his youth. His fame as a healer attracted the attention of Abd-er-Rahman III, who made him his first secretary and entrusted him with delicate diplomatic missions. He became a kind of minister of foreign relations, administering the customs and receiving foreign embassies. A faithful defender of the Talmudic school in Córdoba, he also established relations with the Jews in the Orient and continued his medical studies, assisting in the translation into Arabic of the works of the Greek physician Dioscorides.

During the caliphate of Córdoba, the sovereign was the absolute head of the government, even when he gained the throne through palace intrigue or revolt. His prime minister—known as a *hachib*—was at first a simple chamberlain, but, in the end, an indispensable official. The caliphs employed viziers, or ministers, to execute their orders. A consultative council of state composed of nobles, clergy, and high palace officials assisted the caliph. Occasional assemblies of officials, nobles, and other dignitaries were convoked to recognize the heir to the throne or to take an oath of allegiance to the sovereign upon his accession.

Six provinces were under Moslem control at the time of Abd-er-Rahman I, each of which was governed by an official, the wali, who had both civil and military duties. These governors were established in the provincial capitals of Toledo, Mérida, Saragossa, Valencia, Murcia, and Granada. Some other cities were also administered by walis, especially on the frontier, where a unified command was necessary. In the time of al-Mansur there were two frontiers: one in the Tagus Valley, with Toledo as the headquarters, and a second in the Ebro Valley, with Saragossa as the capital. An intermediary frontier was established at Medina Celi as a base for raids into Castile. There were also regional governors or caids, who enjoyed great authority and independence.

Moslem law was based on the Koran and had a religious character. Justice was administered in the name of the caliph, ordinarily by delegated special officials. The cadi, the chief judge and nearly always a man of distinction for learning, religion, or wealth, was an important official. He also administered state property and at times held high military office. Subordinate to him was the judicial scribe and the *mustaçaf,* whose police duties included supervision of the markets and public works and the enforcement of the law. The chief of the judicial police heard complaints against public officials and served as judge in criminal cases. There was also a criminal and police judge. After the disintegration of the caliphate some provinces and towns entrusted the direction of affairs to their alcaldes, who administered military, political, and judicial matters and attained great prestige in such cities as Toledo, Seville, and Valencia. Penalties ranged from fines to decapitation, the most severe punishments being reserved for those who abjured Mohammedanism or blasphemed Allah or the Prophet.

Moslem policy in regard to property consisted simply in the confiscation of all lands and houses belonging to the Visigothic state, the church, and those killed in combat or who fled before the Moslem advance. The state retained a fifth of the land taken, the *joms*, and their residents usually resided in the plains and paid a third of their produce to the treasury. The rest of the land was distributed among the conquerors, especially the Arabs, who received the preferred portion. In turn, the new owners let them to Spaniards, who paid them a third or a fifth of the harvest for the privilege of cultivating the land. The subjected mountaineers paid a capitation tax, and the conquered Spaniards also paid a territorial tax on their dwellings. Moslems paid a personal tax as well as the annual tenth of their produce.

Extraordinary taxes, customs, confiscations, and fines served to swell the public income. Usually fairly heavy, the exactions were light when compared to the extortion practiced by the walis, who regarded their offices as means of restoring or making their fortunes.

Moslem Spain, under the caliphate of Córdoba, came to be one of the richest and most populous regions in Europe. Demographically the Moslems always remained a ruling minority, even though in the ninth and tenth centuries the caliphate became one of the most densely populated areas in Europe. According to a census made in the reign of Hakam II, it contained six large cities, eighty others with considerable populations, three hundred smaller towns, and innumerable villages. After the reign of Abd-er-Rahman II, Córdoba was beautified with paved streets, public works, luxurious palaces and gardens, and many mosques. The most remarkable mosque was that of Abd-er-Rahman I, which had nineteen arcades from east to west and thirty from north to south, twenty-one doors, and 1293 columns. Córdoba had 200,000 houses. The public revenue rose to 300,000 dinars under Abd-er-Rahman I, to a million under Abd-er-Rahman II, and to five million in the time of Abd-er-Rahman III. The population probably increased steadily throughout the centuries of Moslem rule and reached its maximum under Hakam II and al-Mansur.

The principal wealth of Moslem Spain was agricultural, especially in the rich lands of the Guadalquivir Valley and the plain of Granada. The Arabs were excellent farmers, and they assimilated the knowledge of the Hispano-Romans. A numerous class of small proprietors, largely Mozarabs and Berbers, enjoyed better conditions than had existed under the Visigoths. The great latifundias were divided among their actual cultivators, especially in Valencia and Murcia, and the irrigation facilities of the Romans were expanded and improved. The Moslems introduced exotic products and plants, such as the fig, orange, lemon, palm, banana, sugarcane, melon, rice, and silk. They also perfected agricultural implements. As a result of their labor and industry, the plains of Granada, Murcia, Valencia, and Aragon prospered. They also raised stock on a large scale, moving their herds and flocks with the seasons to escape the heat or cold.

Mining continued to be one of the most important industries—some mines belonging to the caliph and others being owned individually. Other principal industries of the Moslems were textiles, ceramics, and steel. The silks and woolens of Córdoba, Granada, Málaga, Jaén, Seville, and Almería were celebrated. There were reported to be 13,000 weavers in Córdoba alone. Ceramics flourished in Badajoz, Denia, Seville, and the Balearic Islands. Almería, Murcia, Seville, Granada, and, above all, Toledo and Córdoba, became important centers for the manufacture of arms, especially armor and swords, delicately and exquisitely adorned. Leather, prepared and decorated in the most artistic fashion, became a characteristic industry in Córdoba and in Morocco.

Both internal and external commerce flourished as industry and agriculture expanded. Melons, fruits, figs, and olive oil were exported to the Orient. Eastern products came from Cairo along the sea coast through Tripoli and Kairwan to Tangier and across the strait. Seville, in time, became the principal port, with a population composed largely of renegades and dedicated to commerce—the commercial prosperity being partly due to the traffic in slaves and women for the troops and the harems of the caliphs. Almería had an important yard for the construction of ships. With the fall of the caliphate the material prosperity of the Moslem part of the peninsula declined. For a while, some of the cities retained their industrial activity, but the conquest of these areas by the Christians eliminated their commerce and industry.

Since participation in a holy war was one of the obligations for every good Moslem, the organization of the army was exceedingly important. While conversion of the infidel was the objective, the booty to be won also provided a powerful incentive. A fifth of it was always reserved for Allah, to be administered by the caliph for the aid of orphans, the poor, and pilgrims. At first the military organization was rather loose and informal. When a campaign was undertaken each tribe sent its available men under its own sheik and banner—there being two chiefs in each tribal division, one who led the troops to war, and a second who remained behind and replaced the first after three months. At the end of a campaign the soldiers were paid a salary.

The judicial police, a mounted police unit in the provinces, attained its greatest influence under the independent emirates. In some cities there were bodies of local militia whose chiefs, or alcaides, commanded expeditions and at times became frontier governors. The Moslems relied principally on cavalry for their rapid marches and devastating raids, but foot soldiers usually accompanied the horsemen. Spring was the time chosen for campaigns. The soldiers were called up for a definite time, but if the action was prolonged they might desert and the campaign would have to be postponed. On the whole the campaigns were little more than raids to destroy fields of grain, demolish fortresses, and collect captives. The Moslems used the same kinds of apparatus—catapults and battering rams—that the Romans and Byzantines used.

Abd-er-Rahman I was the first to reform the army, establishing a guard of Omayyad and Berber clients and Negro slaves. Abd-er-Rahman III increased the prestige of his slave guard, but al-Mansur, to counteract the increasing influence of the slaves, organized a guard and eventually an army of Berbers. In this fashion, a mercenary, standing army was created, greatly at variance with the old tribal organization, already weakened by the disappearance of the Arab aristocracy. The military power of the sheiks was ended, and slave and even Christian battalions, splendidly paid and equipped, formed the nucleus of the Moslem army.

Although the Arab conquerors of Spain were not mariners, they developed a navy—to counter the Norman raids—under Abd-er-Rahman II. Mohammed I ordered ships constructed for a Galician expedition, and Abd-er-Rahman III employed a powerful fleet, based at Almería, in the continuous struggle with the Fatimites.

Various languages were spoken by the heterogeneous population of Moslem Spain. Arabic was the official language, in spite of the fact that the Arabs and Berbers had difficulty in communicating in it. The Arabs tried to maintain the purity of their language and required that an officer of state use Arabic eloquently. As a result of their zeal they maintained a linguistic supremacy over the more numerous Berbers.

In daily usage a mixture of languages—indigenous dialects, those of the conquering races, and Latin—was spoken. The construction of the vulgar tongue differed from Arabic in both modulation and pronunciation. The Mozarabs considerably influenced the language spoken by the Moslems by the use of a modified Latin—Spanish—written in Arabic characters, called aljamia. Latin was also affected by daily contact with the conquerors. People spoke Arabic without forgetting the Latin, which, as time passed, developed regional characteristics. The clergy tried to maintain the Latin tradition. Since it was very difficult for Spaniards to express themselves in Arabic, many learned Arabs also spoke the vulgar tongue. Some members of the court even assumed Latin names and spoke the Romance tongue.

Education usually remained in private hands in Moslem Spain, though the caliphs brought learned men to the peninsula to give lectures. Hakam II endowed a number of schools to teach the doctrine of Mohammed to the children of the poor. Others followed his example and left legacies for the same purpose, and the Moslem clergy assisted religious instruction by teaching the maxims of the Koran and the Mohammedan traditions. As sects sprang up, the highly orthodox, very intolerant philosophy of Malik became dominant in the peninsula and restricted the activities of the teachers. The two grades in Moslem education were the primary and secondary. The Koran was read and copied and poetry and elements of Latin grammar were memorized. Reading and writing were usually taught by imitation. Most of the Spanish Moslems were literate, an advantage which people did not possess in other parts of Europe.

No organized plan was followed in higher education. Each master taught the subjects for which he was prepared by study and preference. Many of the classes were held in the mosques, where the only means of distinguishing the teacher from the students was his position in the center of the circle. No precise day or hour was arranged, yet persons came from the whole peninsula to listen to celebrated wise men. At the conclusion of a course of study the professors presented the students with licences, perhaps precursors of the modern academic diploma. The subjects studied included commentaries on the Koran, grammar, the dictionary, medicine, philosophy, and, especially, jurisprudence and literature. The teachers of the higher schools enjoyed great prestige and many of them gained important public offices because of their reputations in educational circles.

Literature, especially poetry, was greatly esteemed by the Moslems.

Each Arab tribe had a poet who sang of the victories, happiness, and despair of its members. Challenges, threats, and even declarations of war were issued in verse. Emirs and caliphs did not conceal their poetic efforts, and many among the literate public could understand and compose poetry. Popular poets wandered through the streets, or from palace to palace, and recited poems of heroism and love. At first the principal theme was war and the deeds of heroes, but amorous themes prevailed as the culture became more sophisticated. The reign of Abd-er-Rahman III was a great literary epoch, and many famous poets gathered at his court. Al-Mansur continued the patronage of poetry, and thousands of poems were written in praise of the powerful minister, including some that were satiric. While the Arabs cultivated history, biography, geography, and the novel, they never produced any dramatic literature.

Philosophy was highly valued among the upper classes, but all persons who cultivated it were unpopular with the people because they were regarded as heretics and the theologians stirred up antagonism to them. Some philosophical groups were organized as secret societies, fearful of giving publicity to their ideas; yet their interest contributed greatly to the fame of Moslem culture. Some of the learned men had studied Greek philosophy at a time when it was nearly unknown in western Europe. The pursuit accorded with the classical tradition of the Hispano-Romans, while the Jews had already introduced these studies into the peninsula for the second time. The Moslem philosophers were especially famous in the eleventh and twelfth centuries and had a notable influence on medieval science and in transmitting Greek learning to Europe.

Philosophy first became important in the tenth century during the reign of Hakam II; yet little of the early work has survived because of the hostility of the public and the theologians. One of the most celebrated philosophers was Ibn-Masarra (883–931), whose independent mysticism was considered orthodox in Spain. Born in Córdoba, probably to an indigenous family, he was educated by his father, who had traveled widely in the Orient and had become fascinated with philosophy. Ibn-Masarra became a hermit—asceticism being at that time a contemplative avenue for concealing heretical views—to whom students flocked. Exiled for a time, he died in Córdoba, venerated by his pupils, condemned by the wise men as a heretic, but respected by all. Ibn-Hazam of Córdoba (994–1064), another great philosopher, became vizier and intimate friend of Abd-er-Rahman V. After the adoption of a policy of greater tolerance which stimulated culture, teachers of the various subjects organized into schools, such as the celebrated one in Madrid founded by Maslama.

Astronomy also met with such popular opposition that the government at one time prohibited its study. Moslema-ibn-al-Kasim of Córdoba (904–64), for example, who devoted himself to astronomy, astrology, alchemy, and the occult sciences, was believed to be a magician—popular credulity being suspicious of a scientific approach. Azarquiel of Córdoba devised new and interesting theories of the fixed stars and the movement of the planets.

Mathematics was cultivated with greater freedom. The Arabs invented algebra and applied mathematics to the necessities of life. A famous geometrician, Abd-er-Rahman-ibn-Ismael, made a compendium of the *Organon* of Aristotle, and Moslem mathematicians also had a great influence on the revival of scientific thought in western Europe.

Medicine and the natural sciences, which were then largely pharmaceutical, owed much to Moslem Spain. When the Byzantine emperor sent an embassy to Abd-er-Rahman III, he included among the gifts a Greek copy of Dioscorides, with marvelously painted illustrations of the plants. As no one in Córdoba knew Greek, the caliph requested a translator. In 951 the emperor sent Nicholas, a monk, to translate the work. Yahya-ibn-Ishaq, another physician and surgeon of the period, composed a five-volume treatise on medicine. Probably the most notable physician was Abul Kasim (d.? 1013), who attained great fame as a surgeon in both East and West and wrote a medical encyclopedia, later translated into Latin. Rabbi Moses-ben-Maimon, or Maimonides (1135–1204), had great influence in the Western world. A native of Córdoba, he was forced to flee before the Almohad invasion and practiced medicine in Cairo. He was both a philosopher and scientist and wrote many notable treatises in Arabic. Averroës (1126–98), another philosopher and physician from Córdoba, also had great influence on succeeding Christian thought.

Despite the inferior legal position of Arab women, Moslem Spain had many celebrated female poets and scientists. Even the teaching of religious traditions was entrusted to women. Some of them went to the Orient to continue their studies and attended lectures with men. The culture attained by women was recognized to such an extent that one prince married a Negro slave because of her intelligence and wisdom.

Books were of wide influence among the people of Moslem Spain, partly because the population was highly literate, but also because books were cheap. The cursive character of Arabic writing and the use of paper made them less expensive to produce than the classical books had been, and they became the chief means of instruction. Manuscripts were copied extensively, and great libraries were collected to assist the studies of poor students. In addition to the celebrated library of Hakam II in Córdoba, the vizier of Almería, ibn-Abbas, collected a library of 400,000 volumes. One bibliophile of Córdoba sold his library for 40,000 dinars. Many individuals made a living from copying books, and great markets arose to meet the demand for them.

Moslem arts flourished amid the general prosperity. The Spanish Moslems gained universal acclaim for their contributions to architecture and the industrial arts. Sculpture and painting were not usually cultivated because of the religious prohibition of the representation of the human form, but there were some sects which tolerated animal and human forms. The latter were depicted in Medina Sidonia, and lions were roughly sculptured in the Alhambra at a later period.

Arab methods of construction differed from those of the Hispano-Romans. Moslem architecture had been influenced in both construction and adornment by the Chaldeans and Assyrians and, later, by the Byzantines. The Spanish Moslems developed a style which differed from its Oriental sources. The typical Moslem edifice, the mosque—the most famous example of which was in Córdoba—was fundamentally rectangular in plan, with a spacious entrance patio, surrounded by porticoes, and a fountain in the center for the ablutions of the faithful. A typical feature was the minaret, and from these slender towers the hours of prayer were announced. The temple proper had one or more naves and a mihrab or niche, oriented toward Mecca, before which the faithful prayed. The arch was fashioned in diverse forms, and the column was usually in Corinthian or near-Corinthian style. The Moslem architects broke the monotony of the superficial lines with geometric or schematic floral reliefs or arabesques. The mosques were not only used for prayer and meditation, but served also as general places of assembly, centers for the publication of the orders of the caliph, and as buildings for academic instruction.

Secular buildings followed the general plan of the mosque, modified according to the use for which they were designed. Ordinary houses had a central patio surrounded by arches with a fountain in the center. Palaces were large and luxurious, the one of Medina-Zahira, probably the best example of civil architecture, occupied approximately a hundred acres. In an age when cleanliness was far removed from godliness, public baths multiplied throughout the country.

In industrial arts the Spanish Moslems excelled in ceramics and in work in precious metals. The pottery of Valencia and Mallorca became famous. Delicately wrought lamps adorned the mosques, while the famous Toledan and cordovan swords were not only excellent weapons but were exquisitely ornamented with gold inlay and precious stones arranged in geometric designs. The luxurious furnishings of the palaces also were adorned with the rich fabrics from the Moslem looms.

Moslem love of music, as deeply rooted as the love for poetry, found expression in musical festivals, at which hired singers performed in the sumptuous palaces of the aristocrats. The Moorish transformation of Arab music made it more popular and thereby increased the popularity of poetry. Ibn-Moafa, a blind poet of Cabra, wrote songs in the Romance language which were very popular during the epoch of Omar-ibn-Hafsun. Other poets imitated him in the production of short, rhymed verses with varying measures. Musical instruments, including the harp, the zither, the oboe, and the flute, were manufactured in Seville and exported to Africa.

In spite of their culture, ferocity and a thirst for vengeance were distinctive characteristics of the Moslems in Spain. Execution being by decapitation, the streets of Córdoba and Toledo were often decorated with the heads of the victims. Although the upper classes lived in great luxury, the poor led miserable existences, in spite of the admonition of the Prophet that Moslems should provide alms and the efforts of the caliphs to fulfill their charitable obligations.

The Christians engaged in the reconquest of the peninsula not only raided Moorish Spain and carried on intermittent warfare with the Moslems, but by association and intermarriage influenced them in many ways. The Moslems adopted customs and usages which were in theory contrary to their religion. The Christian influence contributed greatly to the dignity which women attained among a people who customarily regarded them as inferior. In fact the culture of the Moslems was exotic and loosely rooted, and much of it quickly disappeared when they were expelled from the peninsula.

The Moslems, however, exerted great influence on the Christians, and many Spanish institutions reveal Moslem characteristics. There were Moslem enclaves among the Christians just as there were Christian enclaves among the Moslems, and the influence of the Moslems increased as the reconquest progressed. Along the frontier many Moslems knew the Romance language and many Christians knew Arabic. Bilingual members of both races served as guides and spies for the raiding army which paid them best. In military organization also the Christians adopted various Moorish offices.

Moslem influence also persisted in governmental institutions. The

Christians carefully tried to conserve the Moslem administrative machinery in the reconquered areas. They retained the customs duties, under the same official, and the position of cadi had great influence on the evolution of the office of alcalde, or judge. The most celebrated scientific works in Arabic were translated at the school in Toledo, which became a center for their dissemination throughout Europe. Alfonso X gave official protection to Arabic studies and endeavored to fuse the Islamic and Christian cultures. Moslem songs had much influence on the music and poetry of Christian Spain, and Moslem architecture was adapted to Spanish purposes.

From the invasion of Tarik in 711 until the final reconquest of Granada in 1492, a direct Moslem influence was brought to bear on the evolution of Spanish civilization. Spanish institutions, character, and psychology, as well as culture and language, were subjected to it. New traits were developed as that influence was absorbed, and its indelible impress was left on the peninsula.

CHAPTER VI

The Rise of the Christian States

For nearly eight centuries the Iberian Peninsula presented a scene of chronic warfare; the Christian states racked by feudal struggles, the Moslem states more deeply torn by anarchy, and the mutual hostility of the two groups never really ceasing. The effort to expel the Moors did not mean a steady advance of Christian arms, for the Christian monarchs had to deal with urgent internal problems of royal authority and to establish a clear line of succession to the throne while they confronted the Moslem forces. Moreover, they were often too jealous of each other to act harmoniously. At the outset they were baffled by the unity and strength of the determined Moors, and disconcerted by their swift military audacity. Only when the disintegration of the caliphate encouraged the rise of divisions within Moslem Spain did Christian arms make significant progress.

The southern frontier was important not only from the Spanish but the European point of view. Its defense was part of the Western struggle against the Mohammedan enemies of Christendom, who constantly threatened Constantinople in the East and dominated the southern Mediterranean. Although the Catholic Church launched a united attack by the Western Europeans, the southern frontier in the Iberian Peninsula existed long before the Crusades began, and the war continued there long after the divergent ambitions of the European monarchs had chilled their enthusiasm for a religious conflict. The reconquest of the Iberian Peninsula constantly attracted knights and adventurers from all Europe to help dislodge the common enemy and to bring Spain again into the current of Western Christian civilization.

Moslem garrisons dominated the greater part of the peninsula and a majority of the inhabitants had abjured Christianity by 716. Only a few Visigothic nobles continued to resist the invader. They joined the

Asturians in the Cantabrian Mountains to form the principal nucleus from which the reconquest spread. Pelayo, a fugitive from the court of Wittiza, had probably established himself by 718 in Asturias, where he organized the first Christian resistance to the payment of tribute to the Moslems. Forced to withdraw into the wild valley of Covadonga, he ambushed and defeated the pursuing expedition. It was the first victory of the reconquest and inaugurated the war of the southern frontier.

Other nuclei of resistance also appeared in the north. Garcí Jiménez in Sobrabre and Count Iñigo Arista in the Basque country collected their neighbors and the fugitives from the plains and extended the struggle with the Moslems. Alfonso I (739–57), the true founder of the kingdom of Asturias and the son-in-law of Pelayo, strengthened resistance to the Moslems by bringing the Cantabrians into the struggle. The evacuation of Galicia, León, and Asturias by the Berbers provided Alfonso with an opportunity to extend his territory.

By 757 the frontier line lay south of the Douro River. The Moslems defended a line running roughly from Pamplona to Coimbra through Guadalajara and Toledo. The area between the rival outposts was subjected to devastating raids and was usually deserted. Little by little the Christian frontier was extended by the victories of Alfonso's successors; yet the Christians were unable to mount a real offensive against the Moslems because their opportunities varied with the power of the emir or caliph who opposed them. Even in the most favorable periods the frontier never extended south of the Guadarrama Mountains.

Oviedo, founded as his capital by Fruela I (757–68), became the center of the kingdom of León. Between 808 and 814 the sepulcher and body of the apostle St. James was reported discovered in the kingdom, and the city of Santiago de Compostela grew around the sacred spot. Despite the raids of the Moslems and the anarchy of the turbulent nobility of Galicia, pilgrims flocked to the tomb of Santiago from all over Europe. Alfonso III (866–909) of León controlled most of the northwestern and north-central parts of Spain and brought the Basques under his rule by marrying Jimena, daughter of Count Iñiguez, but he lacked the power to insure the unity of his dominions. A conspiracy forced him to divide León, Asturias, and Galicia among his three sons.

As León expanded a new center of resistance appeared. Castile, so named for its numerous castles, and originally part of the duchy of Cantabria, had served as a refuge for fugitives from the invaders. Its counts gradually established their independence and Burgos became their most important center. In 931 Fernán González, count of Burgos, became count of Castile and Álava. Endowed with exceptional political and military ability and with the ambition usual in that age, he sought to establish his independence. Although once imprisoned for rebellion, Ramiro II of León (931–51) released him and arranged the marriage of his son and heir to the count's daughter, Urraca. By persistent intrigue González became the power behind the throne of León. Although the Navarrese captured him while their Queen Tota was allied with Abd-er-Rahman III, she refused to surrender him to the Moslems.

The Basque provinces and Navarre had also maintained a stout resistance against the Moslems, who never succeeded in penetrating the mountain areas and were exposed to guerrilla raids from Pamplona. The Franks were interested in the region and occupied Pamplona before their withdrawal and defeat in the Pass of Roncesvalles. Two other centers of resistance shortly appeared in the Pyrenees, the county of Ribagorza and the county of Aragon.

Iñigo Arista (835–57), the first king of Pamplona, defeated the Moslems and the Franks and united ancient Navarre with his realm. His successors struggled with the Moslems with varying fortune, extending their dominions to Nájera and Tudela, although Abd-er-Rahman III forced García I to flee to the mountains, defeated him and his ally, Ordoño II of León, at Valdejunquera (921), and destroyed Pamplona. Meanwhile, Aznar, an unknown chieftain, had taken the city of Jaca and the surrounding territory, assumed the title of count of Aragon, and allied himself with the kings of Pamplona. Later, Aragon was joined to Pamplona under the rule of García Sánchez I (925–70).

Sancho Garcés III (1000–1035) occupied Castile and León and united them with Navarre, Aragon, and the Basque country; he assumed the title "King of the Spains," and made Navarre the most important political center of the peninsula. At his death he divided his possessions among his four sons, who immediately became involved in a dynastic struggle, until Ferdinand I became king of Castile (1035–65) and León.

Originally, the territory between the Llobregat River and the Pyrenees had offered a haven for fugitive Spaniards as the Moslems moved northward. All of Catalonia was overrun except the recesses of the Pyrenees, which Louis the Pious, son of Charlemagne, crossed to conquer Barcelona, in order to establish a buffer against the Moslems and to control the independent leaders. He ended by dominating the entire region and establishing the Spanish March. The count of Barcelona became the marquis, or governor of the March, assisted by eleven subordinate counts. Wilfred I (874–98) won independence from the Franks and, as marquis, ruled six of the counts. Borrell II (947–92) had the mis-

THE IBERIAN
PENINSULA, c.1000
ATLANTIC OCEAN
Santiago
de Compostela
León
LEON
Burgos
Valladolid
Douro River
Pamplona
NAVARRE
Pyrenees
ARAGON
CATALONIA
Barcelona
Saragossa
Ebro River
Salamanca
Tagus River
Toledo
CALIPHATE OF CORDOBA
Córdoba
Seville
Guadalquivir River
Cartagena
Tarifa
Cádiz
Gibraltar
Ceuta
BALEARIC ISLES
MEDITERRANEAN SEA
Melilla
AFRICA

fortune to be a contemporary of al-Mansur, who checked the extension of the frontier and devastated Barcelona (986). When Borrell regained the city he denounced his nominal dependence on the Franks.

In 1002 the allied Christian forces of Navarre, León, and Castile won a decisive victory over the Moslems, and the anarchy within the caliphate after the death of al-Mansur in that year enabled the Christians to resume their advance, even though they were unable to maintain an offensive unity among themselves or stability within their kingdoms. After Ferdinand I crushed the rebellious nobles and consolidated his position in León and Castile, he turned on the Moslems, attacking the taifa kings one by one and raiding Seville and Coimbra. He thus extended his frontier from the Douro to the Mondego River.

Despite the separation of León and Castile at the death of Ferdinand I, Alfonso VI succeeded in reuniting them and in continuing the war against the Moslems. He concluded an alliance with the Moslem king of Toledo, forced the king of Seville to pay a double tribute, and advanced to the sea at Tarifa, exclaiming as he rode into the water, "This land is the tip of Spain, and I have trod upon it."

In 1085 Alfonso VI starved Toledo into submission, the city capitulating on condition that the lives and property of the citizens be respected: They could migrate if they chose, they would pay no more than a fixed tax, and they could continue to worship in a mosque in the city. Toledo became the base of operations against the Moslems and a center of Christian culture. It was also a point of contact between the two populations and had an important influence on the development of Christian culture, especially through the Mozarabs. The terms of the capitulation were not faithfully observed, for the conquerors soon converted the mosque into a Christian church.

All of the taifa states now offered Alfonso VI tribute in exchange for peace, but as he persisted in his offensive they called on the Almoravids for assistance. After the Christians were defeated at Zalaca (1086) the progress of Alfonso VI was checked, but it was not long before the Spanish frontier had been permanently advanced to the Tagus River.

One of the most colorful figures in Spanish history appeared in the reign of Alfonso VI—Rodrigo Díaz de Bivar, celebrated in legend, song, and history as the Cid Campeador. This knight first attained fame by a victory in single combat over a Navarrese warrior. He served Sancho II until exiled for an altercation with his sovereign. Although he was recalled, he was among the Castilian nobles to recognize Alfonso VI and soon won royal favor and the hand of Ximena, daughter of the count of Oviedo. His enemies curbed his restless ambition by accusing him of appropriating some of the royal tribute from Seville, and Alfonso VI sent him into exile.

The most striking period of the life of Rodrigo was thus inaugurated. As an exile and with few retainers, he sought wealth and honor in exchange for military service. While serving the Moslem king of Saragossa he failed to meet Alfonso VI as arranged, and the Castilian sovereign ordered the confiscation of his property and the imprisonment of his wife and children. In 1094 the Cid seized Valencia and lived there as an independent lord. He was typical of his era—no less warlike and ambitious and no more scrupulous in his appetite for wealth and power than his contemporaries. Taking advantage of the prevalent anarchy of the day, he made war on either Moslem or Christian, but never against his lord, Alfonso VI. After his death (1099) his widow held Valencia for a time against the attacks of the Almoravids, but was eventually forced to evacuate the city. The deeds of the Cid are recounted in the great Spanish epic, *Poema del Cid*.

Many foreigners served Alfonso VI in the war on the southern frontier. Among them was Count Raymond of Burgundy, who married Alfonso's eldest daughter, Urraca, and became count of Galicia. His cousin Henry married Alfonso's illegitimate daughter Teresa and was given the county of Portugal, consisting of the territory between the Minho and the Tagus rivers. Henry, a man of considerable ability and even greater ambition, took advantage of the struggle between his sister-in-law, Urraca, and her second husband, Alfonso I of Aragon, to follow a tenuous, vacillating policy in expanding his territories at her expense. His son, Affonso Henriques, continued the war against the Moslems, won a decisive victory over them at Ourique, and assumed the title of king of Portugal (1139).

The effort to unite Castile, Aragon, and Navarre through the marriage of Urraca to Alfonso I of Aragon produced anarchy instead, although Alfonso I extended the frontier southward to the Ebro and—as a religious crusade—made the war against the Moslems feasible. Alfonso VII (1126–57) united the thrones of León and Castile, but his succession to the throne of Aragon was disputed, and the union between Aragon and Navarre was dissolved. Ramiro II (1134–37), interrupting his monastic life to become king of Aragon, arranged the marriage of his infant daughter Petronilla to the heir of the Castilian king. This union would have reunited the two kingdoms, but the Aragonese recalled the unhappy results of the marriage of Alfonso I and Urraca and objected to their absorption into Castile. Instead, in 1137 Petronilla was betrothed to the count of Barcelona, Ramón Berenguer IV, who was then proclaimed prince of Aragon and regent, so that Ramiro II was able to renounce the throne and return to his monastery.

Although Alfonso VII failed to realize his pretensions to the Aragonese crown, the count of Barcelona and the king of Navarre recognized his sovereignty, and in consequence he convoked the Cortes of León and assumed the title of "Emperor of All Spain," empty as it was. He also had to defend himself against Navarre and was forced to recognize Affonso Henriques as king of Portugal by the Treaty of Zamora (1142). The ambitious designs of the Castilian king were undone by the division of his realm between his sons—Castile to Sancho III (1157–58) and León to Ferdinand II (1157–88). During the minority of Alfonso VIII (1158–1214) of Castile there was a period of civil strife in which both León and Navarre intervened. In 1170 the Cortes of Burgos declared this fourteen-year-old king of age, and he married Eleanor, daughter of Henry II of England, with the duchy of Gascony as her dowry.

Alfonso VII had led the Castilians in several successful campaigns against the Moslems. He raided Estremadura and Andalusia, capturing Córdoba in 1144, and three years later besieged and took Almería with the aid of Pisan, Genoese, and Catalan fleets. The Almohads recaptured Almería ten years later.

In the meantime, the Aragonese kings had also moved southward, capturing Huesca and Barbastro. Alfonso I captured Tudela and Saragossa (1118), thereby extending the frontier beyond the Ebro River. In 1125, with 4000 men, Alfonso led a raid deep into Andalusia and through Murcia to the Mediterranean Sea. Although he liberated no cities of importance, the Mozarabs in the areas through which he passed flocked to his standard and many of them returned with him to Aragon to repopulate the reconquered cities. Upon the accession of Alfonso II of Aragon (1162–96) the crowns of Catalonia and Aragon were united. He cooperated with Alfonso VIII of Castile in campaigns against the Moslems, founded the city of Teruel (1171), and repelled the Moslem raids into the province of Tarragona.

Ferdinand II of León defeated the Almohads at Ciudad Rodrigo (1173) and, four years later, led a raid to the gates of Seville. His nephew, Alfonso VIII of Castile, made the war against the Moslems one of his primary interests. With the aid of Alfonso II of Aragon he conquered Cuenca and in 1194 commanded an expedition which advanced to Algeciras, where he issued a challenge to the Almohad emperor, who answered by sending new troops to the peninsula.

Alfonso VIII then convoked a cortes to prepare for a decisive battle and sought aid from León and Navarre. Jealous of his growing power, their kings refused to cooperate, and Alfonso VIII was left to face the Almohad army at the disastrous battle of Alarcos (1195)—succeeding only in turning a rout into an orderly retreat. He succeeded in concluding a truce with Yacub, the Almohad emperor, who besieged Toledo, Madrid, Alcalá, and Cuenca, while the Christian states fought among themselves.

At the termination of the truce the Christians renewed their raids and the Almohads collected a large army. Alfonso VIII urged the pope to preach a crusade and called on the other Christian kings for assistance. Foreigners flocked to Castile from France, Germany, England, and Italy to join the army at Toledo, but deserted, tried to make themselves masters of Toledo, and committed many excesses on their return to the Pyrenees. Their defection was compensated for by the arrival of Pedro II of Aragon.

Through the assistance of an unknown scout the Christian army avoided a pass already occupied by the Moslems and encountered them on the plains near Jaén. The ensuing battle was a decisive victory for the Christians, who captured 60,000 prisoners and terminated the last Moslem threat to domination of the entire peninsula. Thereafter, the power of the Moslems gradually receded as Alfonso VIII and his cousin Alfonso IX of León extended the power of Christian arms southward.

Alfonso VIII also tried to unify the Christian states. The prosperity of Castile under his rule evoked the envy of the kings of Navarre, Aragon, and León, who formed an alliance against him in 1191, while he was resisting the Almohads. He faced the Moslems alone at Alarcos; Alfonso IX of León did not assist him because he was trying to recover territory which Alfonso VIII had wrested from him. In 1198 an effort to reconcile Castile and León—not entirely successful—resulted in the marriage of Alfonso IX to Berenguela, daughter of Alfonso VIII, who then attacked Sancho VIII of Navarre and incorporated the three Basque provinces into Castile. Until that time the Basques had retained their *de facto* independence.

There was no unity in Spain during the Middle Ages. The fundamental hostility between the Moors and the Christians split the peninsula in half, and, moreover, the Moors were as divided among themselves as were the Christians. On several occasions the Christian kings might have arranged a union, but their desire to divide their possessions among their sons led to disintegration and fratricidal strife. The ambitions of the Christian kings were as limited as their sovereignty.

Yet the foundation of a real unity was laid during these years of apparent anarchy. The easiest road to unity was through intermarriage—as in the case of Aragon and Catalonia. The petty kings of Spain were imbued with this psychology. The struggle with the Moors provided a second, common interest which often bound the Christian kings together, even though they were not loath to ally themselves with the Moslems or to withhold their forces from the joint effort.

The psychology of the Spaniard was profoundly influenced by these prolonged hostilities, which contributed to the creation of a new individualism in the peninsula, common to all of the states. Along the frontier the Castilian or Catalan was confronted with an individual who was just as fierce as he was but more sophisticated. All frontiersmen lived in constant dread of Moslem raids, and they developed a vigilance, a restraint of emotion, and a fatalism which enabled them to confront emergencies as they arose. While they had a profound respect for the military prowess of the Moslems, as Christians they believed themselves superior. They fought and ravaged the properties of a people whom they regarded as inferior in both religion and race. The cry of "Santiago!"—in honor of the apostle James, whose shrine was an object of veneration throughout Christendom—became the stimulus of their fighting spirit and the slogan of the crusade. The zeal and power of the Catholic Church in Spain came from the fanatical desire to rid the peninsula of the Moslems.

A significant basis for eventual unity was the vigorous conduct of the war of the southern frontier by León and Castile, as these kingdoms expanded from small beginnings in Asturias. Though in addition to liberating their own lands, Aragon and Catalonia conquered Valencia, the kings of Aragon were soon turning toward the Mediterranean as a route for expansion. León and Castile, on the other hand, reconquered New Castile, Estremadura, and much of Portugal and were poised to recover Murcia and Andalusia. As the conqueror and repopulator of the greatest amount of territory, Castile gained a dominant position in the unification of the kingdom.

The southern frontier attracted adventurers from all of Europe, some of whom hoped to better their fortunes in a land of opportunity, far removed from traditions of the past. Crusaders who returned to their native lands—loaded with booty or as broken warriors—they retained memories of the frontier which extended its influence throughout Europe.

Although actual warfare was intermittent, the frontier fighting had a far-reaching influence on military affairs. Christian armies were feudal—gathered for annual campaigns rather than for prolonged wars. Upon returning home the knights resumed their leisure and the peons returned to their ordinary occupations. In equipment and organization the armies of the southern frontier resembled any other feudal army, but their tactics were different. The ancient methods of guerrilla warfare, which had baffled the Romans, were employed by both antagonists. Surprise raids, ambushes, and the violations of truces were characteristic. These methods provided a training which was to bear fruit in the sixteenth century, when the Spanish soldier was supreme in a warlike Europe. Individualistic, self-reliant, and courageous, Spaniards were deployed with an effectiveness which baffled tradition-bound Europe and the aborigines in the New World.

CHAPTER VII

The Great Advance

The dual problem of expelling the Moors and uniting the several Christian states still confronted the Spanish sovereigns of the thirteenth and fourteenth centuries. The southern frontier was for a time pushed rapidly southward, but by the end of the fourteenth century this objective had been relinquished, as the struggle for supremacy among the Christian states within the peninsula became the primary preoccupation of their kings. That struggle had already begun in the earlier rivalry among the Christian kings, but it was accentuated. When not engaged in conflict with the Moslem kings of Granada, the kings of Aragon, Navarre, Castile, and Portugal intervened in the internal dissensions which frustrated their rivals, and, although too weak to dominate, they succeeded in weakening each other.

A new trend appeared in the peninsula in the thirteenth century. It was most apparent in Castile, but was also evident in the other kingdoms. Alfonso X of Castile seized upon the study of Roman law as a useful instrument for extending, consolidating, and centralizing the royal power. When ambitious nobles proved recalcitrant, he used other men who were willing to subordinate their own interests to those of the sovereign, selecting them from among the legal scholars of the universities. In no state did the magnates give up their prerogatives without a struggle, but by the beginning of the fifteenth century royal absolutism was well established, even if it was not completely recognized by the turbulent aristocrats.

After the Almohad invasion, the divided Moslems were subjected to a new Christian onslaught. At first Ferdinand III (1217–52) encountered opposition to his succession to the throne. After the dissolution of the marriage of his parents for consanguinity, Ferdinand had lived with his father, Alfonso IX, in the Leonese court, but on the unexpected death of his uncle, Henry I, Berenguela, his mother, succeeded in obtaining his recognition as king of Castile. Count Alvar Núñez de Lara, who with his partisans had long engaged in a feud with Henry I, led a rebellion which Ferdinand III had to suppress before he could consolidate his position on the throne. When the Laras were defeated in Castile they provoked the disappointed Alfonso IX to invade Castile and make an unsuccessful attack on his son.

Berenguela not only assisted her son in gaining the throne, but she also aided him in becoming a statesman as well as a military leader. She arranged his marriage with Beatrice of Swabia in 1219, and, through her sister Blanche, strengthened his relations with her brother-in-law, Louis IX of France. By the union of his son Alfonso to the daughter of James I of Aragon, Ferdinand also utilized marriage as a weapon of diplomacy.

Ferdinand devoted most of his energy to the reconquest, for his great objective was the humiliation of the Moor. The Castilians had lived at peace with the Almohads, following the truce of 1214, but the dissensions among the Moors which followed the death of Yacub in 1224 invited intervention. After preliminary raids and fruitless sieges Ferdinand took Priego, and raided the plain of Granada. On ascending the throne of León in 1230 and reuniting it with Castile, he renewed military action in Andalusia, forcing the surrender of Córdoba, where the great mosque was purified and consecrated to Christian worship.

During 1240 Ferdinand III conquered Osuna, Marchena, and Cabra, and in 1243 his son Alfonso occupied most of Murcia, whereupon its king offered to surrender his sovereignty. After he seized Arjona, Ferdinand besieged the strong city of Jaén, which he solemnly entered in 1246. In the same year he invested Seville, which had already been abandoned by the Almohads, and entered it after a long siege. He remained in Andalusia for the rest of his life.

Meanwhile, James I (1213–76) had ascended the Aragonese throne on the death of Pedro II. After a five-year regency torn by dissension, he attained his majority and inaugurated a new era in the evolution of his kingdom. Though confronted with a rebellious nobility, James won the sobriquet of "The Conqueror" because of his victories in both the peninsula and in the Mediterranean. The Cortes of Barcelona, resolving to improve the security of Catalan commerce by the conquest of Mallorca, still in the hands of the Moors, sent out the Aragonese fleet, which took the city of Mallorca in 1229 and a few years later also subjected Minorca and Ibiza. Soon after this achievement the conquest of Valencia—the most important event in the reign of James I—was undertaken. After three years of raids and sieges, he attacked the city in 1236, and it surrendered two years later. As he pressed on toward Játiva, he encountered Prince Alfonso of Castile, who was engaged in the occupation of Murcia. The rival conquerors nearly came to blows, but their differences were adjusted in a treaty which fixed the boundary between the two kingdoms: Murcia was reserved for Castilian arms and the province of Valencia was terminated at the Júcar and Segura rivers.

Alfonso X (1252–84), the Wise, the eldest of the ten children of Ferdinand III and Beatrice of Swabia, was thirty-three years of age when he succeeded his father. Although as Prince Alfonso he had been engaged in the conquest of Murcia and his reign opened with warlike enterprises, he had demonstrated an abiding interest in scientific and literary matters. He settled a disagreement with Alfonso III of Portugal over the Algarve by surrendering the disputed region as a dowry for his natural daughter, Beatrice, on her marriage to the Portuguese king. Alfonso also relinquished his claims to Gascony, but he forced the king of Navarre, Theobald II, to render him homage. Likewise, he soon settled the questions in controversy between himself and James I of Aragon.

As a descendant of the House of Swabia he was nominated emperor, and in the election at Frankfort in 1257 he received the votes of Saxony, Brandenburg, and Bohemia and accepted the imperial crown. Thenceforth, Alfonso's campaign for the diadem of the Holy Roman Empire became a constant preoccupation, but his dream of imperial glory found little popular sympathy either in Castile or Germany, and his own nobles used it as a pretext for rebellion. Rudolf of Habsburg was elected emperor in 1272, but Alfonso finally renounced his pretensions only on the promise of pecuniary aid for the war against the Moors.

After the deaths of Ferdinand III and James I, the extension of the frontier against the Moslems became less and less important to the kings of Castile and Aragon, and internal and international problems claimed their attention. Yet from the beginning of his reign, Alfonso X resolved to continue the wars against the Moors and realize his father's dream of carrying the war into Africa. In 1260 he made a raid on Morocco and took a great quantity of booty. Two years later he seized Cádiz in a combined land and sea action.

Although the Moorish king of Granada had recognized Castilian sovereignty, he instigated a general rebellion, with the cooperation of the Almohad ruler of Tunis, in Murcia and Andalusia. The rising was so extensive that Alfonso X barely escaped from Seville, but he began immediately to subject the rebellious cities in Andalusia, while James I of Aragon reconquered Murcia and generously restored it to his son-in-law. Granada continued to be a military problem until the termination of his reign.

A dynastic problem also troubled the last years of Alfonso X. The death of his heir, Prince Ferdinand de la Cerda, leaving an infant son, stimulated Ferdinand's brother, Prince Sancho, to aspire to the succession. Philip III of France aided the cause of the young prince and provoked a tension which threatened war with France. While trying to terminate the French intervention with diplomacy, Prince Sancho led an open rebellion, which in 1282, through a junta of nobles and high clergy at Valladolid, deposed Alfonso X.

Although his political activities failed, both in domestic and international affairs, Alfonso X was aptly called the "Wise" because of his cultural accomplishments. A poet and scholar in his own right, he was surrounded by a numerous group of Christians, Moors, and Jews who were active in literature and law. The king sought to build an absolute monarchy and restrain the feudal anarchy which had reappeared in Castile. His ideals of government, founded on the study of Roman law, then in great vogue in Western Europe, were embodied in an encyclopedic work entitled *Las Siete Partidas*. His political objectives were repugnant to members of the proud, intriguing aristocracy, and he was too indecisive and variable to press them firmly.

When Sancho IV (1284–95) succeeded his father on the Castilian throne, all of the nobles recognized him except Juan Núñez de Lara, who preferred exile in France to submission. Sancho was moderate and rewarded his recent adversaries with responsible positions, but his brother John remained constantly discontented and disloyal. Two parties in the Castilian court were at variance on foreign relations. One wanted to maintain a friendly accord with Aragon and resolve the problem of the Princes de la Cerda—the sons of Prince Ferdinand—who had been held as prisoners by Alfonso III of Aragon. The other faction preferred a French alliance in order to intimidate the defenders of the princes. Although at first inclined to an understanding with Aragon, Sancho IV concluded an agreement with Philip IV of France, hoping to gain support for a papal validation of his marriage with his cousin Maria de Molina.

In 1287 Sancho named Lope Díaz de Haro majordomo, and this Viscayan lord became the most powerful noble in Castile. Alvar Núñez de Lara placed himself at the head of the popular opposition aroused by this appointment. Maria de Molina also opposed Lope Díaz de Haro because he wanted to arrange a royal marriage with the daughter of Gaston de Bearne. On the advice of Denis, king of Portugal, that the power of the new favorite was prejudicial to his kingdom, Sancho soon began a dispute with Lope Díaz de Haro over an alliance with Aragon. Their friendship changed quickly to hostility, and Lope Díaz de Haro was killed in the royal chamber in Alfaro. The violent death of their lord brought on a revolt of the Basques. War was declared between Castile and Aragon, though actual combat was averted. In 1290 Philip IV conferred with Sancho at Bayonne, ratified the treaty which adjusted their differences, and then concluded matrimonial alliances for his family with Portugal and Aragon. Sancho carefully shaped his internal policy to free himself for the reconquest.

The Benimerins of Fez, disembarking in Tarifa in 1285, had committed horrible atrocities and besieged Jérez and Seville. Sancho had forced them to raise the sieges, sign a truce, and pay an indemnity for the damage committed. After the resolution of his international difficulties, he was able to renew the war with the Moors in 1292. Aided by the Aragonese and Genoese fleets, he captured Tarifa. By that time Sancho was already ill. He named Prince Ferdinand as his heir and died at the age of thirty-seven.

The last years of James I of Aragon were clouded with dynastic quarrels nearly as calamitous as those of his minority. The struggles between his heir, Pedro, and his bastard son, Ferrán Sánchez de Castro, invited aristocratic intervention, and the Moors of Valencia took advantage of the occasion to rebel. Weakened by infirmities, he abdicated at Valencia in 1276 in favor of his legitimate sons, Pedro and James—leaving the Balearic Islands to the younger.

Although James I directed Aragonese ambition toward the Mediterranean Sea, it was really Pedro III (1276–85) the Great who inaugurated the policy of expansion in that area. He made Aragon an important factor in western Europe and gave it a decisive influence on the destinies of southern Europe. After being crowned at Saragossa, he suppressed the rebellion of Valencian Moors at Montesa and restored order in Catalonia. He came into conflict with his brother James, who had inherited the Balearic Isles, the counties of Cerdagne and Roussillon, and Montpellier, and shortly forced him to recognize his sovereignty.

Pedro III proved himself an able diplomat. He used the Prince de la Cerda to force Castile to maintain good relations with Aragon and arranged the marriage of his heir with the daughter of Edward I of England. His relations with the Angevins were not so fortunate. Through his wife, Constance, daughter of Manfred of Sicily, he disputed the Angevin claims to Naples and Sicily, where the tyrannical government of Charles of Anjou had aroused great discontent in his subjects, who sent representatives to the Aragonese court. Pedro entered into a confederation with the Byzantine emperor and Pope Nicholas III against Charles and, feigning an attack on Tunis, set sail with fifty ships and 26,000 men against his unsuspecting enemies.

When the pope rejected the proffered sovereignty of Sicily, the crown was accepted by Pedro III in 1282. He defeated a Provençal fleet, quickly subjected Sicily, and invaded Calabria. Pope Martin IV, an ally of Charles of Anjou, thereupon excommunicated Pedro and placed Aragon under an interdict.

Upon his return to Aragon, Pedro faced the rising discontent of his subjects, who were angered by the heavy taxes imposed for the Sicilian war. The Aragonese Union formed in defense of their privileges forced Pedro to confirm the General Privilege at the Cortes of Saragossa and to concede a new constitution to the Catalans a year later. When Pope Martin IV, after deposing Pedro in 1284, invested Charles of Valois with the kingdoms of Aragon, Catalonia, and Valencia, the French at once invaded Catalonia and besieged Gerona. But the French fleet was defeated and an epidemic decimated the army, which was forced to withdraw. Pedro was on an expedition to punish his brother, King James of Mallorca, for betraying him to the French when he died. Like his father, James I, he was a man of great stature and an expert warrior. Usually cautious and always patient, he was resourceful and resolute when confronted with difficulties.

Alfonso III (1285–91) was in Mallorca, in command of an expedition against his uncle, James, when he inherited the throne. He quickly subjugated the island and Ibiza, subduing Minorca after his coronation, but the struggle continued on the Catalan frontier until he was forced to accept the humiliating Treaty of Tarascon with Charles of Salerno and Pope Nicholas IV. He had to go personally to Rome to remove his excommunication, pay the Church thirty ounces of gold, undertake a crusade to the Holy Land, and withdraw Aragonese troops from the service of his brother, King James of Sicily. In return, he was restored as king of Aragon and his sovereignty over Mallorca was recognized.

In Castile Sancho IV left a son nine years of age, Ferdinand IV (1295–1312), whose reign was one of the most turbulent in the history of the kingdom. The regency was entrusted to Prince Henry, but Prince John and the Haro, Lara, and Cerda families instigated disorder and rebellion. The kings of Portugal and Aragon intervened in Castile, and

Philip IV of France, anxious to extend his boundaries, tried to profit by the anarchy. The Castilian nobles, equally anxious to take advantage of a minor, shifted from party to party, expecting every act of disloyalty to be forgiven and every act of assistance to be rewarded with a generous grant.

Maria de Molina met all contingencies with ability and energy and defended the throne for her son during his minority. She won the townsmen with grants of liberal privileges, disarmed recalcitrant nobles with gifts of land, and separated her foreign from her domestic enemies. Yet, when Ferdinand attained his majority, he demonstrated his lack of gratitude for his mother's protection by demanding—on the advice of favorites only recently his enemies—an accounting of her use of public funds and by ignoring her advice.

After signing the Treaty of Córdoba, which recognized Castilian possession of Tarifa, Ferdinand took advantage of the discord among the Moors to renew the war against Granada. He concluded an alliance with Aragon by the Treaty of Alcalá de Henares, which divided Granada between Castile and Aragon, and besieged Algeciras, while James II invested Almería, which had been allotted to him. By 1310 peace was restored.

James II of Aragon (1291–1327) had already demonstrated his efficiency and energy as ruler of Sicily when he inherited the crown of Aragon from his brother. Although he wanted to retain the crown of Sicily and left his younger brother as his lieutenant in the island, he also recognized the necessity of compromise with Pope Boniface VIII and Charles of Salerno. In the Treaty of Anagni, James II renounced Sicily and was later invested with the crowns of Sardinia and Corsica by the pope (1295). His brother Fadrique, who was popular in Sicily, refused to consent to the surrender of the kingdom and stoutly defended Syracuse against his brother. The pope and the Angevins were forced to recognize Fadrique's rights to the crown of Sicily in 1302.

The political sagacity of James II is best revealed in his peninsular policy. As soon as he ascended the throne he concluded a marriage contract with the Princess Isabel, daughter of Sancho IV of Castile. When Boniface VIII denied a dispensation to remove the obstacle of their consanguinity, Isabel, after bearing the title of queen of Aragon for four years, returned to Castile. In the Treaty of 1291 with Castile James II reserved Algiers and Tunis for the crown of Aragon, as a zone of influence in North Africa. He cooperated with Sancho IV in the conquest of Tarifa, but intervened in favor of Alfonso de la Cerda against Ferdinand IV in an effort to obtain control of Murcia. In 1308 he participated in an expedition against Granada. He resolved an internal problem by referring the complaints of the Union to the Cortes of Saragossa, where the Justicia decided them in his favor.

In an adventurous epic of military prowess during the reign of James II, Roger de Lauria, a Templar, and Berenguer de Entenza, a Catalan noble, rallied to the appeal of the Byzantine emperor for aid against the Turks. They recruited 5500 men—idle and dangerous veterans of the Sicilian war—and sailed to Constantinople, where they defeated the Turks and were rewarded with titles. When one officer, Roger de Flor, was given the rank of Caesar, the jealousy of Michael Paleologus, heir to the throne, was aroused, and the leaders of the expedition were murdered. Reduced to 3500 men, the Aragonese defeated the Byzantine army and raided the countryside for provisions until they entered the service of Walter de Brienne, duke of Athens.

After recovering more than thirty towns with their aid, the duke tried to rid himself of these troublesome and independent mercenaries, but he was defeated and killed, and the Aragonese seized the duchy of Athens, which they offered to Fadrique of Sicily. He accepted the sovereignty of the duchy, and it was ruled by vicars from 1322 to 1379, when it passed to Pedro IV of Aragon until 1387. These stirring events occasioned great chronicles, such as that of Ramón Muntaner.

Under political pressure James II suppressed the Templars in his kingdoms, but replaced them with a new order of Montesa to combat the Moors on the frontiers of Valencia. In 1300 he founded the University of Lérida. His marriage alliances with Castile, designed to unify the peninsula, failed to produce the desired result.

The reign of Alfonso XI (1312–50)—who ascended the throne of Castile at the age of one year—was one of the most significant in Castile during the Middle Ages. By his stout defense of Tarifa he removed the danger of a Moslem counteroffensive and permitted Castile to play a role in international affairs. Castile was unusually turbulent during his minority. The four pretenders to the throne were named regents until the Cortes of Burgos approved Maria de Molina's custody of her grandson. The military energies of the kingdom were at once devoted to the reconquest—by intervention in the dynastic quarrels of Granada and by two victorious campaigns to its gates—but the rivalries of successive regents and the death of Maria de Molina had reduced Castile to complete anarchy when Alfonso XI attained his majority.

The king was confronted with the necessity of strengthening the royal power. Regarding the brotherhoods as instruments of municipal rebellion, he at once suppressed them, but he relied on the cortes as collaborators in his efforts at reform. As his advisers he selected men of merit. He then entered on a fifteen-year struggle with the nobility, who were led by Juan Manuel, Juan Núñez de Lara, and Alfonso de la Cerda, and at times supported by Portugal and Aragon. By 1337 the rebels were all subjugated.

Meanwhile, Alfonso had followed a defensive policy toward the Moslems, resisting the Moors of Granada, who were allied with the Moslems of North Africa. The Castilians lost Gibraltar, but, supported by Pedro IV of Aragon and Alfonso IV of Portugal, drove the invaders back to Africa, whence they never resumed the offensive. Algeciras was captured in 1344, and Alfonso died besieging Gibraltar.

Alfonso IV of Aragon (1327–36), the Benign, withdrew as an ally of Alfonso XI against the Moors in order to suppress a revolt in Sardinia—instigated by the Genoese—which continued until 1334. A year later Alfonso IV concluded a truce with Granada, which had attacked the Aragonese frontier and besieged Elche.

Alfonso IV confirmed the statute of James II, by which the kingdoms of Aragon and Valencia remained perpetually united to the county of Barcelona and could not be divided among the royal heirs. He also promulgated the Statute of Daroca (1328), which forbade the alienation of crown property for ten years. Despite these laws Queen Eleanor persuaded Alfonso to bestow some cities along the frontier on Prince Ferdinand, but the aroused nobles and Valencians forced the king to revoke the grants, a step which stimulated the queen's animosity toward her stepson Pedro, who had opposed the alienation of the crown property. The last days of the king were clouded by his separation from Queen Eleanor, who, fearing reprisals from Prince Pedro, fled to Castile and entered a nunnery. Alfonso the Benign was an affable and simple king who lacked the political and diplomatic ability to direct the destinies of his people.

Pedro IV (1336–87), the Ceremonious, was of a different temperament from his father. Where Alfonso IV was weak, he was energetic, firm, and even stubborn, always seeking a workable formula to resolve a problem or to excuse his acts. During his father's lifetime he had served as governor of the kingdom with great rectitude. Gifted in intrigue and a master of duplicity, domineering and arbitrary, he proceeded cautiously and was interested in enlightened legislation. In revoking the testament of his father he nearly became involved in a war with Alfonso XI of Castile, who intervened in behalf of Queen Eleanor and her sons. Actual conflict was averted by the threat of the Benimerins. Pedro sent a fleet to the aid of Alfonso XI and contributed to the capture of Algeciras. With cunning and a certain lack of scruple, he used the delay of James III of Mallorca in rendering homage and the pretext that he had circulated false money in his dominions as excuses for seizing Mallorca, Cerdagne, and Roussillon.

Because of his desire to leave his throne to his daughter Constance and thereby avert the succession of his brother, James of Urgel, Pedro proclaimed her as his heir. The count of Urgel then joined the Aragonese nobles in reviving the Aragonese Union in defense of the ancient privileges of the kingdom. With the Valencian aristocrats also against him, Pedro was forced to restore the count of Urgel as governor-general and revoke the proclamation of Constance as his heir. He did not intend to honor his concessions, having already declared them null and void in a secret constitution dictated at Perpignan; yet he feigned acquiescence to the demands of the Union. Suspected of poisoning the count of Urgel and besieged by the Aragonese, Valencians, and Castilians in Murviedro, Pedro again pretended submission to the demands of his enemies. The rebellious populace of Murviedro carried him to Valencia, where there was much rejoicing and some disorder until it was brought to a sudden halt by the outbreak of the plague, when Pedro seized the opportunity to escape.

The final phase of the struggle of Pedro IV with the Union was a bloody climax. While his partisans fought with the unionists, Pedro temporized, but the two factions finally met in combat at Epila (1348), where the unionists were defeated. Pedro was disposed to punish the rebels, but executed only thirteen of their leaders. The Privilege of the Union was abolished by the Cortes of Saragossa, and all books and documents referring to it were burned. The Justicia of Aragon gained his greatest authority in the cortes as the defender of Aragonese liberties.

War broke out between Castile and Aragon in 1356, when Catalan ships seized two Italian ships at Sanlúcar de Barrameda. In this protracted conflict Pedro utilized the White Companies of Bertrand du Guesclin against Castile. It was ended only temporarily with the assassination of Pedro I of Castile by Henry of Trastamara.

Although Genoa and Aragon were presumably at peace, the Genoese gave aid to a revolt of the seven Oria brothers in Sardinia. With naval aid from Venice and the Byzantine Empire, Pedro IV defeated the Genoese, and the Oria brothers feigned submission. Mariano de Alborea deserted the Aragonese cause and occupied most of the island. After Mariano's death his daughter married Brancaleón Oria, who had returned to the service of Aragon, and peace was finally restored. The

Aragonese obtained control of the towns they had held before the war, and Eleanor de Alborea gained control of the property formerly held by her father. Pedro IV also tried unsuccessfully to get the Sicilian crown.

The last years of the reign of Pedro IV were marred by internal dissension. He married Sybil de Forcia, a beautiful and ambitious woman who gained an ascendancy over the senile king. His son, Juan, who did not get along with his young stepmother, was dispossessed of his control of the kingdoms. At Pedro's death Juan was intent on vengeance against Sybil. Pedro IV was not a very sympathetic character. His wars and his Mediterranean expeditions exhausted his kingdom without any compensatory advantages.

Pedro I (1350–69), the Cruel, reigned in Castile when personal ambitions and private passions had reached their peak. He was only sixteen when Alfonso XI died, and his confidant, Juan Alfonso de Albuquerque, directed royal affairs. The favorite had been charged with the education of the prince during the latter years of Alfonso XI, when he was chief steward of Queen María of Portugal. At the beginning of Pedro's reign a crisis divided the court into two opposing factions. Juan Alfonso supported Prince Ferdinand of Aragon, nephew of Alfonso XI, as heir, while another faction aided a descendant of the princes of la Cerda.

Juan Alfonso committed error after error. He was judged responsible for the death of Eleanor de Guzmán, he made Samuel Levi treasurer of Pedro I, and he forced the death of Garcilaso de la Vega, thereby provoking an uprising by Henry of Trastamara, natural son of Alfonso XI and Eleanor de Guzmán. The revolt was easily subjected, but Henry remained an implacable enemy of Pedro I. Finally, Juan Alfonso introduced a very beautiful girl, Maria de Padilla, to Pedro, who became passionately interested in her. Her uncle, Juan Fernández de Henestrosa, soon became active in the royal court. When Juan Alfonso arranged Pedro's marriage with Blanche of Bourbon, the king at once abandoned her for his mistress. But the favorite was forced to flee to Portugal, Blanche was imprisoned in the alcazar of Toledo, and the alliance which had been contracted with France in the latter days of Alfonso XI was broken.

The incarceration of the queen caused another crisis. The citizens of Toledo rebelled and were soon joined by those of other cities, as well as many nobles, including Henry of Trastamara and Juan Alfonso. Pedro I became practically a prisoner until he fled from Toro and initiated the series of massacres which won him his sobriquet.

In 1356 Pedro I became involved in war with Pedro IV of Aragon. The Castilians assumed the offensive and occupied Tarragona. Pedro IV became an ally of Henry of Trastamara, then a fugitive in France, and both England and France soon intervened in the hostilities. Castile won the support of the English, the Aragonese allying themselves with France. The Peace of Ferrer (1361) ended the first phase of the war. Conquests were restored, prisoners were released, and most of the exiled Castilians, except Henry of Trastamara and some of his associates, were pardoned.

When both Blanche of Bourbon and Maria de Padilla died during the short truce, Pedro I took advantage of the opportunity to declare that he had been legitimately married to his mistress and recognized their son, Alfonso, as his heir. He assured himself of peace in Granada through the assassination of Mohammed IV and concluded the Treaty of London (1362) with Edward III of England. Thus, he appeared stronger than ever. But hostilities with Pedro IV were soon renewed. Pedro I besieged Calatayud and undertook a victorious campaign through Valencia, while dissension arose between Henry of Trastamara and Prince Ferdinand, whom the Castilians in the service of Pedro IV recognized as the true king of Castile. A new peace was concluded in 1363 at Murviedro.

In 1366 Henry of Trastamara was proclaimed king of Castile in Calahorra. Pedro I refused the opportunity to fight and withdrew to Toledo and Seville. Finally, he collected his partisans in Galicia and concluded an alliance with the Black Prince, the English governor of Aquitaine. Meanwhile, Henry of Trastamara had occupied the entire kingdom, but when he tried to block the advance of the English he was defeated at Nájera.

Pedro I then resumed his atrocities in an orgy of blood, while Henry returned to France to raise a new army. The Black Prince, disgusted with Pedro's crimes, withdrew to Aquitaine, while Henry reconquered Calahorra—Pedro having no force with which to resist him. Toledo was besieged, and when Pedro led his scanty forces to the relief of the city he was easily defeated by Henry and Du Guesclin and sought refuge in the castle of Montiel. In an attempt to escape, he was betrayed and led to the tent of Du Guesclin, where he was killed, probably by his own half-brother.

In the eleventh century, several of the Christian rulers of the north began to reconquer Spain from the Moslems. The only thing which these men and their warriors had in common was fierce pride in their religion. Otherwise, self-interest prevailed. When not battling the heathen, the Christian kings fought each other for power, and the warrior-nobles rebelled against their monarchs for the same reason. The situation was further complicated by the fact that most of the newly subjected Spaniards did not even share the religious beliefs of their masters.

Nevertheless, certain trends toward unity appeared by the fourteenth century. After generations of dynastic intrigue and political marriage, four kingdoms emerged from the welter of petty principalities: Aragon, Castile, Navarre, and Portugal. None was strong enough to dominate the others, but Castile did acquire the prestige of having taken the most Moslem territory.

CHAPTER VIII

Medieval Christian Civilization

Despite the diversity of social organization within the Christian states and the differences in the evolution of the kingdoms in the eastern and western parts of the peninsula, the common hostility to the Moslems affected all states. A basis for unity was laid in the extension of the frontier against the Moors. The effect on the psychology of the frontiersman has already been observed, but there was also an inevitable effect on institutions. The most obvious appeared in a new sense of democracy on the frontier. While the revival of Roman law was a factor in the development of absolutism and in the influence of the new men in the towns, these centers also participated in other developments which increased their importance.

In the intervals between campaigns the Christian kings tried to impose law and order on an otherwise lawless frontier. They arranged this by delegating their authority to the reconquered towns in charters, or *fueros*—confirmations of ancient privileges and guarantees of new ones. Perhaps a more pressing need was that of attracting people back to the towns, which had been fought over and left partly deserted, or of guaranteeing the rights enjoyed by the Mozarabs or the Moslems in the towns.

The towns also acquired importance in another way. The legislative body, the cortes, had followed the Visigothic tradition of approving the new sovereigns or the heirs to the throne. It was inevitable that the centers of population which had privileges of their own should be represented in these assemblies. Thus, the custom arose, even before the townsmen were represented in other dynastic states, of inviting some of the towns to send representatives to join the nobles and clergy in the cortes.

This custom was not necessarily a tribute to democracy, because although the towns were represented their powers were restricted. They could present grievances which might or might not be corrected in later decrees, but in no way did they restrain the development of the absolute power of the kings. The municipal representatives paid a tribute to tradition by swearing an oath of fealty to the new sovereign or by recognizing an heir. They even voted funds for specific purposes, but the kings were not dependent on them because they had income from royal lands and could levy taxes. The funds were voted for some common objective, such as a campaign against the Moors.

The trend was not democratic, for the *fueros* constituted a recognition rather of the collective rights of municipal entities—reminiscent of the ancient Roman municipalities—than of the individual rights of citizens. The people had no concept of individual dignity with which to oppose the increasingly absolute powers of the kings. In addition, the townsmen looked on their sovereigns as protectors against the nobility. The mass of the people was not considered and did not count, but the kings used educated members of the middle class as instruments against the aristocracy, and they proved selfless and loyal.

The nobles were ambitious—by the end of the Visigothic kingdom the idea of hereditary succession had not replaced that of elective succession—and many aristocrats hoped to acquire the crown for themselves. To restrain their ambition the kings took an oath to observe the privileges of the kingdoms, but they also required an oath from all representatives in the cortes to recognize the sovereign or his heir. While the kings utilized the nobles and their retainers in the reconquest, they also appointed new officials, the *adelantados,* on the frontiers to represent the royal authority and to restrain the defiant aristocrats.

Another factor for unity was the increasing tendency of the kings to codify legislation and to remedy omissions. At first some *fueros* were used as models for others. Ferdinand III, conceiving the idea of a code of laws applicable to the whole kingdom of Castile, ordered the *Setenario* drafted, but it was not promulgated during his reign. The confusion grew as ordinances requested by the cortes, royal decrees, and municipal *fueros* multiplied. Alfonso X issued the model *Fuero Real* to be used as a basis for later charters. He also published the *Setenario,* hoping to centralize authority through a broader application of Roman principles. The work on the *Siete Partidas,* or *Book of the Laws,* was undertaken in 1256 and completed nine years later. It was based on many sources and constituted an encyclopedic compendium of canon and Roman law. The principles which it revived modified the traditional Visigothic law and the *fueros*. The new code first gained acceptance among students in the universities, but Alfonso XI made obedience to it obligatory unless it was in conflict with the municipal charters, the *Fuero Real,* or the privileges of the aristocracy.

In Aragon the desire of James I for greater royal authority led to a compilation of the municipal charters. Bishop Vidal de Canellas drafted the *Compilation of Huesca,* which embodied the traditional law of Aragon, unadulterated by the influence of canon or Roman law. The work of codification was continued until under James II the ordinances of various communities and private documents were codified in the *Observancias.* Catalan law was not unified until 1413, when the *Usatges,* a general code of Catalan law, was compiled. Earlier, the customs of various communities had been codified. Valencians were subjected either to the Valencian *furs,* or charter, or to the severe restrictions necessary because of the numerous Moriscos who might be guilty of heresy or apostasy.

During the reconquest the population was scanty in the Christian kingdoms. At the end of the eleventh century there were not more than three million people in Castile and León. An increase in population by no means necessarily followed an extension of territory, but by 1480 there were between seven and eight million people in the peninsula, exclusive of Navarre and Granada, which were not yet included in a united Spain. Since the population had not kept pace with the land acquired, many of the older centers actually suffered a decline as reconquered lands were settled. This was particularly true of the northeastern kingdoms, where the epidemics which swept across Europe in the fourteenth and fifteenth centuries were deadly.

The population continued to be so heterogeneous that it provided no ethnic or religious basis for unity, and as the reconquest progressed an increasing number of aliens appeared. There were also three religions, whereas elsewhere in Europe the Church was dominant. In Castile a Jewish minority was prominent and in Aragon the *Mudejares,* or unconverted Moslems, were even more numerous.

Within the purely Christian population there was a lack of homogeneity, distinguished by differences in culture. In the north—Galicia, Asturias, and León—the original Hispano-Gothic population was dominant. The reconquest constantly added groups of Mozarabs. Only the Basque tribes remained free of foreign influences. The Hispano-Goths and the Basques moved southward with the reconquest and impressed their spirit and customs on the reconquered regions. Yet the Mozarabs retained their former ways of life and modified the customs of the conquerors from the north. In Toledo Alfonso VI granted a *fuero* based on Mozarab traditions, which the immigrants from the north had long since discarded.

A third Christian ethnic group consisted of the numerous contingents of Franks, including other foreigners, who had heeded the call of the crusade against the Moors or had remained in the peninsula after making the pilgrimage to Santiago de Compostela. Some of the Franks were notable men, but the majority were merchants, artisans, and traders who remained in the Castilian towns.

There was even less homogeneity in the eastern states of the peninsula. Although ruled politically by the crown of Aragon in a personal union, Catalonia, Aragon, and Valencia remained separate kingdoms with independent institutions. The Catalan problem was ever present, for the principality had a language, institutions, and traditions which differed from those of Aragon. The Catalans were also oriented toward the sea, while the Aragonese were landlocked and oriented toward the soil. They also had contacts with peoples across the Pyrenees who were from time to time brought under the crown of Aragon.

Institutions arose in Aragon which were peculiar to that kingdom. James I introduced the custom of associating the heir in the government, which led to the creation of the office of governor-general. An older office, the *justicia,* developed after the reign of Alfonso II, was charged with the cognizance of cases in which privileges had been violated or complaints directed against the authorities. While directly dependent on the king, the *justicia* became in time a moderative power between the kings and the nobility.

Navarre remained a peculiar area, populated largely by descendants of the Basques, who were independent culturally and linguistically. Only partly united to the kingdoms of Castile and León, the Navarrese were never assimilated culturally to either. Since Navarre straddled the Pyrenees, it was also influenced by the French.

There also appeared to be little unity in Spain in economic organization. Under the threat of constant frontier raids, ruled by their own charters in the towns, and isolated by the landed economy, the people were completely localized in their psychology. While the kings dreamed of uniting their feudal domains through conquest or intermarriage, their subjects followed their own private aims instead of the broader, royal objectives.

The social structure, which in feudal theory provided for mutual prerogatives and obligations, was thoroughly stratified—the three principal classes being the nobility, the townsmen, and the rural peasantry. The aristocrats had little in common with the burghers or rural peasantry whom they oppressed and for whom they felt only disdain. Pursuing their own conflicting private interests, the nobles were divided in status. The grandees—recipients of royal favors and possessors of extensive lands—formed the highest class and supplied the palace officials and the intimates of the kings. Partly dependent on the royal bounty, they also conquered lands on their own initiative in the war against the Moors. They held both personal and landed privileges and were a barrier to the establishment of centralized authority. They were exempt from taxation, and their principal obligation consisted of rallying to the king in the event of war. Combat was their principal vocation.

Less conspicuous than the grandees was a subordinate rank of nobles. Some of these were knights who could afford to equip themselves for war and to whom certain privileges were extended. Others were landholders called *infanzones de fuero,* collectively included in a concession of privileges to the inhabitants of a city. Like the knights they were dependent on the grandees, but were generally exempt from taxation and, as rural proprietors, formed the court of the local count. They came to be called hidalgos, persons of noble lineage, and were entitled to the honorable term of address of *Don.*

As the servile classes gradually obtained their freedom, they congregated in the towns, made the municipal councils an important political force, and increased the strength of the middle class. In general the towns contributed to the improvement of the rural classes and accelerated their emancipation. The class of free men ranked below the nobility and included small proprietors and workers in both rural and urban areas. Some of these had sought the protection of a grandee, and for this they relinquished some of their property, paid certain financial obligations, and undertook certain personal services.

The servile classes included personal servants and the serfs who cultivated the soil. The personal servants consisted of prisoners of war, usually Moors, slaves purchased from traders, and descendants of other servants. Serfs were the most numerous servile class. Bound to the soil and transferred with it, these descendants of the *coloni* of later Roman and Visigothic times cultivated their own land and contributed part of their produce or rendered personal services to their lords. They had the advantage of a certain security in an age of instability, but their lot was hard. In addition to those born serfs, some were forced into serfdom as criminals or prisoners of war, and some voluntarily sought it for a tenuous security. A serf might become a freedman through manumission, revolt, or flight. Because of religious influences manumissions were frequent and, in time, the freeman and the freedman constituted the great mass of the population.

Navarre, Catalonia, and Aragon differed in social structure from Castile in their larger foreign influence from across the Pyrenees. The Visigothic structure was modified by the Moslem conquest, the reconquest, and the influence of the Franks. Under Louis the Pious, the immigrating Franks were subject to their own laws and acquired all the lands not occupied. A feudal tendency was especially noticeable along the Frankish frontier, but a more democratic tendency appeared in the southern areas under Aragon. There the Moslems were displaced and communities developed under the domination of the townsmen. At first the Aragonese serfs enjoyed favorable conditions, but their marked dependence on their feudal lords later made their condition increasingly miserable and delayed their emancipation.

The clergy had great social influence because they possessed educational and cultural advantages denied the other classes. They enjoyed privileges which covered many abuses. Some of the popes tried to break the feudal dependence of the Church, but the kings of Castile always exercised their authority to establish sees, appoint bishops, convoke councils, and administer justice. Royal control was restricted only by the piety of a sovereign or the influence of the higher clergy. The monks of Cluny effected many reforms in the Church and worked to establish greater papal authority in Castile, but the kings successfully maintained the principle that, to be effective, the edicts of the Holy See required royal approval.

The Castilian bishops, under the leadership of the archbishop of Toledo, had as much influence as the grandees in the royal councils and also engaged in campaigns against the Moors or against internal rebellion. They extended their jurisdiction over the secular clergy, but the monks maintained their independence under their abbots, and the military orders were directly subject to the pope. As a result of royal concessions, pious bequests, and their own immunities, both secular and regular clergy acquired great wealth. Even the Cluniacs and the Cistercians degenerated into luxury and ostentation. But the ideal of poverty and humility was reborn in the Franciscans and Dominicans—St. Dominic being a native of Castile who founded his order principally to combat the Albigensian heresy.

As their wealth increased, abuses became more flagrant among the clergy of Castile. Some had wives and disposed of church property by testament, and many priests and monks suffered from the general ignorance of the times, even though among them were virtuous men of great learning. In general the prelates were recruited from the families of the grandees; they intervened in local politics and became as venal as their fellow lords.

The townsmen represented a new and alien tradition, primarily interested in industry, trade, and the accumulation of portable wealth in gold. They lacked the patriotic conservatism of landowners who had to defend their property to retain it, and they had little in common with the impoverished rural peasants who clung to their land and drudged upon it to survive.

While justice was a function of the kings, it was delegated to the alcaldes for civil cases and to judges and governors—*merinos* and *adelantados*—for criminal cases. In an age of disorder justice was not always effective, despite the severity of the penalties. Offenders were stoned, mutilated, burned, hurled over a precipice, buried alive, chained to die by starvation, hanged, drowned, or disposed of in any ingenious way that might discourage murder, rape, and banditry. By the end of the Middle Ages, the earlier judicial ordeals by hot water, the burning iron, and combat had fallen into bad repute, but torture was still used to extort a confession. The times were too disturbed, individuals too aggressive in asserting privileges, and officials too arbitrary to permit of real justice. The victims of injustice, especially if they were nobles, took matters into their own hands, while the nobility and clergy were exempt from penalties.

To protect themselves against the prevailing insecurity and the aggression of their aristocratic neighbors, the townsmen banded together in brotherhoods (*hermandades*) and formed an effective militia. The first brotherhood was confirmed in Toledo in 1300. The procedures adopted were summary, and the execution of the sentence imposed was quick. Such measures were well adapted to frontier communities where justice was frail and royal authority barely enforced.

Although the armies were feudal—consisting of the assembled nobles and their retainers—certain modifications in military organization were born of frontier needs. The tactics of the Christians, like those of the Moors, were guerrilla in character, and the weapons—such as lances, knives, and daggers—were those adapted to surprise attacks and ambushes. Sieges were rarely prolonged, and assaults on fortified towns, unless by surprise or treachery, were rarely successful. As the armies increased in size, the kings compensated the soldiers, and mutinies sometimes occurred when the royal treasury was unable to provide payment.

The crown of Aragon did not rely solely on the troops of vassals, for the kings took companies of military adventurers into their service as mercenaries. The hardiest were the mountain troops, the *almogávares*. The Aragonese usually opposed the formation of large armies because they were costly and the wars in which they were employed were at variance with the characteristics of Aragonese life. The nucleus of the Catalan army was formed by the municipal militia, under the control of the Catalan deputation, which was entrusted with the defense of the principality. As the militia was considered more important than the feudal contingents to maintain it, citizens were forbidden to enlist in the royal army.

One of the most important developments of the reconquest was the formation of military orders. The knights who entered them took vows to defend the Catholic faith and to wage ceaseless war against the Moors. The three principal orders in the Spanish area were Alcántara (1156), Calatrava (1158), and Santiago (1161). Since they were recognized by the Pope and placed directly under his authority, the orders acquired great influence in the peninsula. They were granted lands and towns and their elected masters became royal advisers whose offices were sought by many ambitious courtiers. Often defiant of royal authority, holding extensive possessions, and composed of ambitious aristocrats, the religious orders provided another obstacle to peace and internal unity.

The Castilians and Catalans differed in their attitude toward the sea. The latter demonstrated unusual maritime enterprise and made Barcelona a dominant commercial center in the western Mediterranean, whereas the Castilians, except along the Cantabrian coast, were more accustomed to the land. As Catalan commerce expanded it had to be protected against piracy. A Catalan navy soon appeared, consisting of royal ships built at royal expense or rented from other states, merchant ships, ships of the principality maintained for coastal defense, and ships of the city of Barcelona. Some feudal lords also possessed private navies.

The Castilian kings also tried to develop a navy. Alfonso X established an arsenal at Seville and organized a royal Castilian squadron of ten galleys. The Basques along the northern coast, with their ancient maritime experience, also had a profound influence on the improved organization of the Castilian fleet. In times of crisis Genoese ships were hired.

Both Castile and Aragon were poor in the early Middle Ages. Personal security was uncertain, and war was the principal occupation. Commerce and industry were first revived in those areas away from the frontier. Santiago de Compostela in Galicia became an early center of economic activity because of its proximity to the sea, the privileges which it had secured, and the hordes of pilgrims who congregated there. Commerce was exposed to the ravages of external enemies and internal anarchy as well as to royal duties and local exactions imposed by greedy lords.

Agriculture was encouraged both by the right conceded to those who broke the ground to appropriate it and the example of the monks. The principal products were grapes, millet, oats, beans, honey, wax, wheat, linen, and hemp, but harvests were often destroyed by Moorish raids or the farmers were discouraged by the outbreak of discord among the nobles. Famines were frequent, epidemics caused by malnutrition and lack of hygiene were widespread, and life was generally miserable. By the eleventh century the advance of the frontier stimulated agriculture in the interior, and the conditions formerly so frustrating to the farmer disappeared. Property was protected, serfs were emancipated, the towns created new markets, and the brotherhoods protected the farmers in their areas. As it was also in the royal interest to stimulate agriculture and repopulate the conquered areas, legislation was devised to accomplish these ends.

Stockraising early acquired importance in Castile because the animals could be moved from the hazards of war. The kings protected it, at times to the detriment of agriculture. Farmers and shepherds quarreled frequently over grazing rights, and stockraisers' associations regulated pasturage and provided guards and shepherds. Alfonso X elevated these associations into corporations, with judges who held special jurisdiction over their affairs. Alfonso XI authorized the consolidation of these corporations into a single formidable one, the *Mesta.*

There was little industrial development in Castile until the thirteenth century. Such manufacturing as existed was for current needs, and there was no surplus for exchange. A market for Castilian agricultural products was found in Flanders and Germany, and Santiago and Seville soon became important industrial centers with artisan guilds similar to the old Roman *collegia.* By the thirteenth century the guilds, organized as masters, journeymen, and apprentices, exerted an important influence on urban life. Many of the artisans were foreigners, Moors, or Jews. Seville became a center of the manufacture of linen textiles and ceramics, Toledo, Segovia, and Zamora produced good cloths, Aragon, Catalonia, Valencia, and Mallorca all made textiles in the thirteenth century. Iron was mined and worked in the Basque country.

As the frontier was extended to include the *mudejares,* who already had industries, Castilian manufacturing developed rapidly. The mining of precious metals, mercury, lead, and salt and the fisheries were converted into royal monopolies. Yet the progress of industry was not equally apparent in all parts of the peninsula. Castilian industry was still embryonic, even though the Jews and *mudejares* who controlled it reaped great wealth. When the state intervened excessively to prevent abuses, it thereby discouraged initiative.

Catalonia became the most important industrial center in Aragon. Since it was deficient in agricultural production, wheat and bread had to be imported. Industry was concentrated in Barcelona, where the mills along the rivers produced leather, textiles, and glass.

As agriculture and domestic manufacturing developed in Castile, commerce also flourished. The sailors of Galicia and the Basque provinces carried on trade with northern Europe and England, where Castilian wines were especially prized. After its recovery from the Moors, Seville became a commercial center. The stimulation of naval activity by Ferdinand III and the establishment of dockyards contributed greatly to the expansion of the merchant marine. Relations were particularly active with France and Flanders, whence cloth was imported in great quantities. Genoese merchants flocked to Castile and Lombard bankers made loans to Castilians at usurious rates.

Royal participation in commercial affairs was especially important in the extension of privileges for fairs and markets, tax exemptions, and the regulation of prices. The fairs at Medina del Campo attracted merchants from all Europe because they were freed from the payment of the sales tax. Royal commercial treaties and agreements concluded by the maritime towns protected the merchants, but royal customs duties and municipal impositions proved inescapable obstacles. The instability of the coinage and weights and measures defied royal efforts to alleviate the situation. Commerce really prospered as the result of individual initiative, aided by letters of credit and the consuls and special judges established in foreign centers.

Catalan trade flourished because it was favored by the *fueros*—which protected markets and guaranteed the security of merchandise—and because of its strategic maritime location. The Ebro became an artery of river traffic, while merchants attracted from all over the Mediterranean to Barcelona, settled there and gained influence. The conquests of James I stimulated commerce, which soon required a great deal of regulation. In imitation of Italian practices, consuls were established in foreign ports to stimulate and protect Catalan trade. The *Libro del consulado do mar,* a code of customary law observed in the Mediterranean, was compiled as a guide for these commercial representatives and reflected Catalan maritime development. Valencia also became an important port, and the merchants built a great commercial exchange there.

In the later Middle Ages, Catalans competed with the Italians in the Mediterranean carrying trade. Catalans also participated in the scientific development of navigation. Their cartographic work was superior to the Italian. The Catalans, confronted with more intense competition, favored a policy of protection so as to discourage foreign ships, protect the textile industry from competition, and retain a sufficient supply of domestic wheat. Thus, some cities were protected at the expense of others, and excessive regulations actually impeded the development of commerce.

A vigorous cultural development after the eleventh century was stimulated by the increasing importance of the Christian kingdoms, the increase in foreign contacts, and the influence of the Moslems. An Oriental influence was added to the traditional classical influence maintained by the Mozarabs and the clergy. Medieval cultural evolution reached its height in the thirteenth century, but even in the era of the most profound intellectual decay in Europe, the scientific and literary tradition did not completely disappear in the Christian areas of the peninsula. Lérida, Saragossa, and Toledo were centers of literary activity, where scientific works were translated and clerical libraries were accumulated. When universities first appeared in Europe in the twelfth century, Castilians went to Paris and Bologna for a higher education, but at the beginning of the thirteenth century Alfonso VIII established a center of general studies at Palencia to which he attracted scholars from France and Italy. This institution had an ephemeral existence, but about 1215 Alfonso IX of León founded the University of Salamanca. Sustained by royal patronage, it had rather a civil than a theological character. Another center of general studies was established at Valladolid, but a university was not founded there until 1346. James I, meanwhile, founded the University of Lérida (1300), and a second center of studies was established in Valencia.

Consequently, a true renaissance in classical studies began in the peninsula in the later Middle Ages. Kings not only facilitated cultural development, but also participated in literary activities. To the traditional curriculum, the trivium (grammar, logic, and rhetoric) and the quadrivium (arithmetic, geometry, astronomy, and music), were added Roman and canon law and theology. Alfonso X created an Arabic and Latin center in Seville, established a school in Murcia, and endowed chairs in medicine and surgery at Salamanca. Courses in Arabic language and literature, logic, and theology were established for the clergy, but some centers for advanced study were also opened to lay students. In Aragon the universities of Perpignan (1349) and Huesca (1391) were founded.

Ramón Lull (1233–1315) created an original form of primary education, which was more influential in Aragon than in Castile. A native of Palma de Mallorca, Lull was a distinguished writer, composing lyrics in Catalan. He became a Franciscan fired with zeal to convert the Moors. Devoting himself to a study of Arabic culture, he became a renowned authority on the subject and taught at Paris, Montpellier, and a Mallorcan college that he founded. He was also a philosopher and defended Christianity against the Moslems. His works are strongly mystical. Many towns in Aragon imitated his system of primary education, and many succeeding Aragonese and Catalan scholars became masters in foreign institutions.

Although Latin remained the official language in the medieval kingdoms, Castilian, Leonese, and Galician were well established by the twelfth century. Castilian became the typical language of the central frontier, modified by Mozarabic influences and developed later as a literary language. The Mozarabs also continued to use Arabic. In the eastern part of the peninsula the Catalans, in contact with the Franks and Provençals, developed a different language from that spoken in Galicia and Castile. While first restricted to vulgar usage, Catalan became a literary language through the poetry introduced by troubadours from Provence. By the time of James I a national sentiment had developed, and prose was written in Catalan. Ramón Lull used it, and even laws were drafted in it instead of Latin.

In Castilian literature three early formative influences were potent: the *mudejar* on the lyric and the popular dance, Provençal on language and poetry, and French, especially under Alfonso VI. Later, the classical and Italian influences became dominant. The earliest popular poetry was epic in character, celebrating the deeds of Christian warriors. Marcabrú, in the time of Alfonso VII, was the first troubadour, but Vidal de Besalú, under Alfonso VIII, was the most celebrated. The humble minstrels traveled among the people from castle to castle, chanting their strongly nationalistic verses to a musical accompaniment. Later, a new poetic school was stimulated by French influence. It differed from the more popular, heroic school in being concerned with religious and scholastic subjects and in being artificial in form. It appeared principally in universities and monasteries.

Lyric poets were particularly active in Galicia in the thirteenth and early fourteenth centuries. Their works were collected in anthologies of varied lyric and narrative compositions. These increasingly used Castilian, which gradually replaced Galician.

As the Galician influence declined, the classical Italian element became more prominent. The classics had been reintroduced in a somewhat adulterated form by the Moslems, and, reinforced by the new influences from Italy, they soon became popular in Castile, where the genuine Castilian lyric—in imitation of Dante—made poets contemptuous of popular verse. The works of the poets who flourished between 1369 and 1412 were collected in the *Cancionero* of Juan Alfonso de Baena, though the most brilliant period of the new mode occurred in the reign of John II of Castile (1406–54). The king composed verse, the marquis of Santillana (1398–1458) wrote sonnets in the Italian style, and Juan de Mena (1411–56) imitated the symbolism of Dante.

Gradually, Castilian became more popular in the eastern states because of its use in the education of the kings and the similarity of Aragonese and Castilian romances. Castilian nobles flocked to the court of Alfonso V and cultivated the language. Catalan also continued as a literary language, principally in imitation of the troubadours, a tendency strengthened by the influence of Provençal. It became conventional to mix mysticism with amorous sensuality and moral didacticism with satire. Ausías March (1395–1462), son of Pedro March the poet, was a famous troubadour who was also familiar with the classic spirit of Italy. He attained widespread popularity and had much influence on later poetry.

Dramatic literature also appeared in Castile, first in the *Misterio de los reyes magos* and then in two forms reflecting the current literary and social trends: the religious drama in which the mysteries were presented at the church festivals, and a more rudimentary type, with profane and grossly satiric themes, performed by jugglers in the streets and castles. The clergy tried to eliminate the profane elements, but the mimes and buffoons, whose presentations were usually comic and mixed with song, became increasingly popular.

Historical literature assumed great importance in Castile, first in the form of Latin and Castilian chronicles. Rodrigo Jiménez de Rada (1170–1247), a native of Navarre and the versatile tutor of the children of Ferdinand III, became bishop of Osma and archbishop of Toledo. He was the most notable historian before Alfonso X and the author of the *Crónica del Toledano* and other works. Lucas de Tuy (?–1249) was a great traveler who opposed the Albigensians and served as bishop of Tuy for ten years. His *Chronicon Mundi* in simple Latin, based on legends and earlier chronicles, has little historical value, but it was popular in his time and had a notable literary influence.

The personal interest of Alfonso X, who wrote—with the aid of collaborators—not only a universal history but one on Spain, was important in maintaining the popularity of historical literature. The best of the medieval historians of Castile lived in the fifteenth century when Pedro López de Ayala wrote chronicles of the times of Pedro I, Henry II, John I, and Henry III, and Fernán Pérez de Guzmán composed a series of biographical studies.

There were no scientific writers of importance in Castile until the fourteenth century, for earlier scholars had relied on Arab or European scientists. In the twelfth century many translators, such as Gundisalvo and Juan Hispalense, appeared. Arabic influence attained its height in the fourteenth century and from Spain was diffused throughout Europe. The leading writers were Moslems and Jews who imitated or translated the Arab philosophers. The exposition was usually encyclopedic and the approach dialectic, combined with superstition and ignorance, which produced extravagant theories. Alchemists, who searched for the philosopher's stone and were suspected of black magic, really laid the foundation for later chemical progress, while the science of astronomy owed a great deal to the earlier investigations of the astrologers.

The Catalans early demonstrated their interest in navigation and cosmography, which stimulated a corollary interest in mathematics and astronomy. Ramón Lull had numerous disciples, including Arnaldo de Vilanova (d. 1311), a versatile scholar, distinguished as a chemist, physician, philosopher, and theologian. Several influences stimulated the cultivation of the sciences in Aragon. A strong Oriental influence in Arabic and Hebrew led to the translation and imitation of Maimonides, Avicenna, and Averroës, until their medical and philosophical doctrines were diffused throughout the peninsula and western Europe. Other writers represented an anti-Semitic influence, revealed in controversial treatises. Finally, the Oriental influence was replaced by an Italian one originating in the court of Alfonso V in Naples, which gave rise to an extensive moral and political literature.

Medicine developed rapidly in Catalonia, and Bonpoac Bonfill of Barcelona translated both Galen and Hippocrates. Physicians were required to take examinations, anatomy was studied, hospitals were founded, and experimental research was stimulated. An asylum for the care of the insane was founded in Valencia in 1409.

After the decay of classical architecture in the Visigothic era, Christian architecture became more heterogeneous. The principal zone of Romanic architecture consisted of the Castilian and Leonese areas north of the Tagus River. The roofing of the churches was improved by the use of arched ceilings to reduce the danger of fire. This innovation demanded strengthened walls to support the increased weight of the ceilings. Pillars were enlarged and buttresses, erected on the outside, gave the necessary strength. Designs varied, but under French, Byzantine, and Moslem influences the pure Romanic was eliminated in military and civil architecture as well as religious. The churches of Galicia retained their Romanic features longer than did those of Castile.

By the thirteenth century Gothic architecture flourished in the peninsula. The pointed arches were raised, and the buttresses, which were joined to the wall by an arch adorned with a pinnacle, became more slender. The height of the churches increased, windows were introduced, the external walls became more angular, the use of decoration was extended, and the towers developed into spires.

The Gothic style was also marked by social influences. As cities became more populous and important, the middle class more numerous, and the secular clergy more prominent than the regular, greater space was necessary in the churches. All classes cooperated in the municipal enterprise of building a cathedral and worldly as well as religious themes were introduced. The cathedral of Toledo is genuinely typical of the period, while that at León, erected by an architect trained in France, represented an ultra-Pyrenaic influence.

Gothic civil and military buildings also rose. After the twelfth century the castle, formerly of wood, was constructed of stone and was largely defensive in design. It was surrounded by a moat and its walls were flanked by towers from which arrows could be discharged. Drawbridges and gates, also protected by towers, made the castles nearly impregnable, even to sustained sieges. Episcopal palaces and monasteries copied the defensive system of the castle, dominated the town and countryside, and perpetuated seigneurial independence and anarchy. In the narrow, tortuous streets of the towns, the guilds and private individuals built elegant and comfortable houses, great halls were included among the administrative buildings, and bell towers summoned the citizens or the militia.

A new type of architecture arose from the influence of the *mudejares* in the Christian kingdoms, which combined Moslem and Christian features in a simplified Gothic form. Wooden ceilings in the brick buildings were richly ornamented, and arched windows were divided by columns. In the Aragonese and eastern areas Romanic architecture became lighter under an Italian influence. The cathedrals of Lérida and Tarragona reflect Gothic influences, but Catalonia fell under the classical influence and failed to acquire a true Gothic spirit.

Sculpture, painting on glass and parchment, and metalwork also flourished in Castile. The artists at first imitated earlier models, but the work became more lifelike. The French influence on Castilian sculpture is especially noticeable. The introduction of the Gothic style made sculpture even more important for its decorative values, but it always remained secondary to architecture. The classical influence was revealed in sacred or allegorical compositions in low relief or in statuary. Some of the altar images of wood covered with silver or gold leaf were imported from France.

Although painting was not very important in early, medieval Castile, the illumination of manuscripts and painting on glass were popular. The art of the illuminator declined as painting on wood and murals became more popular. By the time of Sancho IV there were palace painters, and the Italian school of Giotto was influential in the courts of John I and John II. A Flemish influence was more apparent than the Italian in the fifteenth century. Jan van Eyck visited the peninsula and painted a portrait of the Princess Isabel of Portugal. Later, the Flemish school became popular in both Andalusia and Castile.

Many Flemings and Germans painted in Barcelona. Luis Dalmau, a disciple of van Eyck, was active in the court of Alfonso V. He was sent to Flanders, and when he returned to Barcelona he was entrusted with the painting of the altar in the chapel in the council hall. The painter Jaime Baco attended Alfonso's court; he was known as Jacomart when he died in Valencia.

Liturgical hymns provided nearly the only vocal music of the early Middle Ages. The sacred music harmonized many voices, whereas the popular song was written for a single voice and evolved with Provençal and Galician poetry. Some of the kings of the fifteenth century were patrons of musicians and poets.

In the evaluation of medieval Christian institutions in the Iberian Peninsula, the influences which produced them must be constantly recalled. In an age of frontier warfare and internal anarchy, institutions had the primary object of providing security and the necessities of life through the cooperation of the protectors and the protected. Vices common in all ages were prevalent, but were gradually modified by the Christian effort to make all men better. This could be done less by legislation and reform than by indirect means, making men aware of their worth and dignity as human beings. In the later Middle Ages, the ideal of national solidarity under a strong sovereign gradually began to replace the prevailing particularism, and culture began to mature, stimulated by foreign influences and the interest of the aristocracy.

CHAPTER IX

Progress Toward Spanish Unity

By the mid-fifteenth century, the Castilian house of Trastamara achieved a dominant position not only in its home territory, but also in Aragon. Two Trastamara cousins, Isabel of Castile and Ferdinand of Aragon, married in 1469. They had only distant claims to their respective crowns, but the deaths of the immediate successors eventually led Isabel to the Castilian throne and Ferdinand to the Aragonese. The two kingdoms, while retaining separate administrations, were nevertheless joined through the personal union of the monarchs. Although no one could have foreseen it at the time, that event marked the beginning of Spain's greatest era.

Ferdinand and Isabel worked hard to strengthen their power internally as well as internationally. Under the leadership of Ferdinand himself, the Spanish army captured Granada, the last Moslem outpost, in 1492. The king and queen wholeheartedly supported the Church in the spiritual reconquest of their subjects. In fact, their reputation as defenders of the faith stood so high that the pope had no choice but to allow them to retain control over the Spanish clergy. Ferdinand and Isabel kept the nobility and the bourgeoisie firmly in their places. They continued the work of centralization which their ancestors had begun by promoting royal government and justice, and by stimulating trade and industry.

The monarchs were responsible for making Spain a notable international power. Ferdinand waged victorious campaigns against the Moslems in North Africa, forcing them to pay tribute. More important, he frustrated the French kings in their attempts to take Naples away from the house of Aragon. Finally, in 1512 he conquered Navarre and annexed it to Castile. Isabel, too, helped to increase Spain's international prestige. Her contribution was ultimately more significant than her husband's, for she financed Columbus' expedition to the New World.

When Henry II (1369–79) ascended the throne over the corpse of his half-brother—Pedro I—the first step toward the political unification of the Iberian Peninsula was taken. He was a bastard and a usurper, but he had acquired a more cosmopolitan view of the peninsular situation than that held by his predecessors. While he developed a policy of reconstruction in Castile, he sought also to defend his throne against internal and external enemies. The situation at his accession was desperate. His former allies, including Aragon, were united with traditional enemies against him. Some cities and areas in Castile, such as Carmona, Zamora, and Galicia, remained faithful to Pedro I. Moreover, Henry II was perplexed by difficulties stemming from the Hundred Years' War. The English hoped to neutralize the Castilian fleet, and the French wanted to use it to interrupt English communication with the continent.

Henry II undertook the offensive before his enemies could unite. Forcing Ferdinand I of Portugal to a truce he gained time to defeat the Moors and subject Carmona. A year later he made peace with both Portugal and Aragon, and their kings referred their differences with him to papal arbitration. Castile had been an ally of France since 1368, but there was a more decisive reason for his intervention in the Hundred Years' War. John of Gaunt, duke of Lancaster, who had married Constance, Pedro's eldest daughter, claimed the Castilian throne and sought peninsular allies. After defeating an English fleet at La Rochelle, Henry attacked each of his enemies separately. He invaded Portugal, occupied Viseu and Almeida, and joined the nobles opposing Ferdinand I, forcing them to conclude the Treaty of Santarem (1373), by which his two natural sons married two daughters of Ferdinand I and the Portuguese fleet was to assist the French.

Turning to Navarre, Henry II compelled Charles II to conclude the Peace of Briones (1373), by which Charles restored the towns he had occupied and approved the marriage of his heir to the Princess Eleanor of Castile. Aragon remained the principal enemy in the peninsula; Pedro IV was the ally of John of Gaunt, who was preparing to land at Calais and invade Castile from Bayonne. The French assailed his army as it left Calais, and when John arrived in Bayonne he had only a handful of men. Although Henry II's siege of Bayonne ended in failure, he was able to invade Aragon and force Pedro IV to the Peace of Almazan, which stipulated the marriage of Prince John of Castile to Princess Eleanor of Aragon. Peace was restored in the peninsula, and Henry II had successfully defended his throne against his foreign enemies.

Despite his foreign difficulties Henry II accomplished much in Castile. He established a permanent junta of prelates, nobles, and municipal representatives to reform the government and assist him in the consolidation of his position. To assist in the maintenance of order he reconstituted the brotherhood as a body of permanent militia. The cortes was in nearly continuous session to solve his economic problems and approve his extension of privileges to those who had aided him in the civil war.

John I (1379–90) had already become familiar with the problems of government in Castile through the foresight of his father. His reign was profoundly significant because it marked the definitive tenure of the throne by the House of Trastamara. John I was forced to reorganize the government and to restrict the privileges his father had so lavishly bestowed. He also was confronted with the Hundred Years' War, which required a foreign policy placing an additional strain on Castile, and his subsequent misfortunes may be attributed to circumstances rather than to lack of capacity.

The beginning of his reign was triumphant. His wife had borne an heir, Prince Henry, and the future appeared secure. The two principal problems were the Great Schism in the Church and the Hundred Years' War. John convoked the Assembly of Medina del Campo to examine the rights of each of the papal pretenders, and influenced perhaps by his French allies, after months of investigation he accepted the claim of Pope Clement VII of Avignon, thereby aligning Castile with the French. He was victorious with his ally in the conflict with the English—burning Gravesend—until the death of Charles V of France abruptly ended the offensive.

John of Gaunt had not given up his claim to the Castilian crown. With Ferdinand I of Portugal as an ally, he was soon at war with John I, whose natural son rebelled at the same time, but the Castilian king forced his son to submit and then invaded Portugal, where he won victory after victory. At the Peace of Yelves (1383) the heirs of the two kingdoms were pledged in marriage, but on the death of his wife John I married the Portuguese heiress. Ferdinand I died later in the year, and a Portuguese rebellion headed by John, master of Aviz, broke out against John. Unwilling to relinquish his right to the Portuguese crown, John undertook a great expedition against Lisbon and was disastrously defeated at the battle of Aljubarrota (1385). This was the signal for John of Gaunt to attack. He landed at La Coruña (1386) and occupied part of Galicia. John I waited for French aid, followed a scorched earth policy, and tried to negotiate. The English invasion of Castile solidified the adherents of the crown; and the desperate resistance forced John of Gaunt to withdraw to Portugal and accept the Peace of Bayonne. The duke of Lancaster gave up his pretensions to the Castilian crown, and Prince Henry married Catherine of Lancaster, the granddaughter of Pedro I, thus uniting the rival claims.

Meanwhile, a John I (1387–95) had also ascended the throne of Aragon. As he was already seriously ill and had little interest in government, he named his brother Martin, duke of Montblanch, as his lieutenant. In 1380 their father, Pedro IV, had arranged the marriage of his grandson Martin the Younger with Maria, queen of Sicily. The ceremony was celebrated in 1390, but Louis of Durazzo was also proclaimed king of Sicily. Although confronted by a rebellion Martin the Younger was able to rule the kingdom. This enterprise extended Aragonese influence in the Mediterranean, which was elsewhere challenged. John I was unable to quell a rebellion in Sardinia, and in 1390 Catalan dominion in Greece was terminated with the loss of the duchy of Athens.

Martin I (1396–1410) succeeded his brother as king of Aragon, although he had to contend with other aspirants to the throne and was not crowned until 1399. His immediate attention was devoted to two expeditions against the Barbary pirates, who had attacked the coast of Valencia. No more of a statesman than his brother, he was unable to contend with the internal anarchy or the complications of the succession. Although his son Martin the Younger was recognized as heir, he died in Sardinia while completing the reconquest of the island. On the death of Martin I in the following year, without an heir, the line of the old counts of Barcelona was extinguished.

Henry III of Castile (1390–1406), known as the Sufferer, was only eleven years old at the death of John I. Although already married to Catherine of Lancaster, a regency had been provided by the will of his father. A series of anti-Semitic riots instigated by the preaching of the archdean of Ecija caused much bloodshed in 1391, especially in Seville. Henry's reign was marked by struggles to maintain order and restore the economy of the kingdom. He succeeded in eliminating the two principal causes of aristocratic intrigue against him by sending Eleanor of Castile back to her husband in Navarre and by burning the nearly impregnable town of Gijón, where his natural uncle, Alfonso Enríquez, had established a base of opposition. His most forceful measures to restrain the nobility were the establishment of the office of *corregidor* to strengthen royal control in the cities and the revocation of many grants of crown land made during the regency.

The Castilian king also maintained a strong policy toward the papacy. He placed an embargo on the export of gold and silver by the holders of ecclesiastical benefices in Castile and also delayed recognition of Benedict XIII. A ten-year truce concluded with Portugal after a two-year war was generally unfavorable to the Portuguese. Despite increasing tension, embittered by a series of incidents, the truce with Granada had been maintained because Henry III had been preoccupied with other problems. In 1406 the Moors invaded Murcia and captured Ayamonte, but they were defeated near Baeza just before Henry's death.

Henry's policy was unexpectedly vital, considering the state of his health. He attempted to end the raids of Moslem pirates on the coasts, clearing the strait of pirate ships and destroying their refuge in Tetuán. An initial step in the overseas expansion of Castile was also undertaken. The Canary Islands had been discovered in 1341, but no European state had formally claimed them. The definitive conquest and colonization was begun in 1402 by Jean de Béthencourt, who took an oath of allegiance to Henry III in return for his support.

Anarchy reigned in Aragon because of the many pretenders to the throne at the death of Martin I. The count of Urgel, James of Aragon, based his claim on being the grandson of Alfonso IV and husband of Isabel, daughter of Pedro IV. Martin of Sicily had a natural son, Fadrique, count of Luna, who had been legitimatized by Benedict XIII. The House of Trastamara also had a claimant to the Aragonese throne in Prince Ferdinand, a nephew of Martin I. The other pretenders were not seriously considered.

The count of Urgel had the greatest number of partisans in Aragon, but his arrogance had aroused a great deal of antagonism in the kingdom. Martin I had favored his grandson, the count of Luna, or his nephew, Ferdinand of Antequera, who had an enviable record as one of the regents of Castile and a powerful following in Aragon. While the representatives of the three eastern kingdoms deliberated, the count of Urgel constantly intrigued, and Ferdinand of Antequera, whose accession would unite the two kingdoms under a single family, sent 1500 horsemen to the frontier to support his claim in case of difficulty. The archbishop of Saragossa, a partisan of Ferdinand, was assassinated by followers of the count of Urgel, an act that strengthened the cause of the Castilian prince.

It appeared that force might decide the issue until in 1412 it was agreed that the deputies in the three assemblies would elect three persons of accepted probity from each of the three kingdoms to act as arbiters. These nine met in the Castle of Caspé, where a majority of six made the final decision. When the votes were cast Ferdinand of Antequera received the three from Aragon, two from Valencia, and one from Catalonia. Thus, the dynasty of Trastamara acquired control of two of the four Christian kingdoms, but Ferdinand I, aided by his Castilian friends, had to defeat the count of Urgel to consolidate his position in Aragon.

Ferdinand I had a large family which controlled extensive lands in Castile. He had named his second son, John, lieutenant-general of Sicily, but Alfonso V (1416–58) incorporated Sicily into Aragon and recalled Prince John and married him to Blanche of Navarre, widow of Martin of Sicily, while his sister married John II of Castile. Thus, with their sovereigns first cousins, and each married to the sister of the other, Aragon and Castile were closely united. In addition, King John of Navarre, a third member of the dynasty, was consort of Blanche, daughter of Charles III of Navarre. It appeared that the union of the Christian kingdoms was as real as it could be under individual sovereigns.

John of Navarre and his younger brothers Henry and Pedro were princes of Aragon, but they also wanted to protect their landed interests in Castile. They intrigued as rivals of Alvaro de Luna, confidant of John II of Castile. Weak and indecisive, John II, who was more of a poet than a statesman, was engrossed with literary activities and public spectacles and ill-fitted either by aptitude or taste for kingship. Among the grandees who sought his royal favor was Alvaro de Luna, natural son of an Aragonese family which had followed Henry of Trastamara to Castile. Alvaro de Luna rose through character and intelligence from his position as page to the child king until he gained a complete ascendancy over him and became the arbiter of policy.

The princes of Aragon and John of Navarre became leaders of the parties hostile to the royal favorite, and the neighboring kingdoms of Aragon and Navarre were drawn into the rivalry. John II remained loyal to Avaro de Luna and named him constable of Castile and master of Santiago. In the intermittent civil war which followed, the nobles were divided between the two factions, but by the victory of Olmedo (1445) Alvaro de Luna, although previously exiled three times, appeared to have consolidated his power. But he was soon confronted with treachery among the sycophants who surrounded him. In arranging the second marriage of John II of Castile to Isabel of Portugal, he underestimated the character of the new queen and created not an ally but a rival who resented his domination of the king. Then, he sought to avenge himself on those who had betrayed him and not only terrified them but, in murdering Juan Pérez de Vivero, committed an act which gave them an opportunity to arrest and try him. The antagonism to his efforts to build a strong personal, if not truly central, authority and the intrigues of his enemies led to his execution in 1453. Yet Alvaro de Luna had demonstrated that a turbulent nobility might be restrained by a strong central authority. He fell when he lost the confidence of a fearful king.

One of the objects of Alfonso V was to safeguard the possessions of Aragon in the Mediterranean. He led an expedition to Sardinia, where he subjected the rebellious cities, and he undertook the conquest of Corsica, but he was defeated in a naval battle by the Genoese. At this time Joanna II of Naples, whom Louis III of Anjou had besieged, asked Alfonso V for aid, adopting him as her son and heir and naming him duke of Calabria. The Aragonese king welcomed the opportunity to extend his influence and to combat Louis III of Anjou, an ally of Genoa. He entered Naples in 1421 and was received as a liberator. Joanna II proved inconstant, however, and, fearing the loss of her throne to Alfonso, appealed to his rivals and named Louis III as her heir. Leaving his brother Pedro as his lieutenant in Naples, Alfonso returned to Barcelona.

In 1432 Alfonso V was again in Italy, preparing an attack on Naples. His cause was desperate until the deaths of Louis III and Joanna II left the Neapolitan throne vacant. He besieged Naples in 1435, but was defeated by the Genoese fleet and captured, with his brothers John and Henry. John of Navarre and Alfonso were released by the duke of Milan, and John returned to Aragon as lieutenant-general of the peninsular kingdoms, while Queen Maria ruled the principality of Catalonia. Alfonso captured Naples in 1442 and was recognized as king by Eugenius IV and the other Italian powers, except Milan. Despite petitions for his return to Aragon, Alfonso remained in Naples until his death, preferring that city, where he had no cortes to contend with and could patronize Italian art and literature. He became so absorbed in the splendor of his court that he refused to participate in an expedition to avenge the fall of Constantinople. Although he created an Aragonese empire in the Mediterranean, there was little enthusiasm for his policies in Aragon, where his absence led to turbulence.

It was already evident when Henry IV (1454–74) ascended the throne of Castile that he would be as inept and indecisive as his father had been. The Castilian grandees renewed their intrigues and pursued their own ambitions. The fall of Constantinople marked the collapse of the eastern frontier before the Moslem Turks, but the western frontier was still held, unweakened though static as a result of the struggle for union among the Christian kingdoms. While the Ottoman Turks pressed forward in the Balkans, Castile remained the guardian of the southern frontier, a staunch defender of Christendom and with the latent power to resume the attack. The internal evolution toward unity was progressing, because by dynastic marriages the House of Trastamara dominated three thrones—Castile, Aragon, and Navarre.

CHAPTER X

Conquest of the Moslem Kingdom; The New World

When John II (1458–79) ascended the throne of Aragon the union of the Christian kingdoms was not as remote as it appeared. The Nazrid kings of Granada were engaged in fratricidal strife, and only a sustained attack by a determined Christian sovereign was necessary to incorporate Granada into Andalusia. No longer a threat to the frontier, that kingdom was only a barrier to territorial and racial unity. Henry IV of Castile, who was incapable of winning either the loyalty of the aristocracy or the affection of his people, could not unite the kingdoms. Thus, the surviving son of Ferdinand of Antiquera, John II of Aragon, became the true architect of a united Spain. He did not seek to unite the Christian kingdoms under his own rule, but through the marriage of his son Ferdinand with Isabel of Castile.

Neither Ferdinand nor Isabel were direct heirs to the thrones of Aragon and Castile, and their succession appeared improbable. Isabel had an older half-brother, Henry IV, whose progeny would take precedence over her. She also had a younger half-brother, Prince Alonso whose primacy as a male would entitle him to succeed Henry IV. Isabel was only seven years old at the accession of John II of Aragon, and his plans had ample time to evolve. The possibility of Ferdinand's accession to the Aragonese throne was even less certain. A year younger than Isabel, he had three older half-brothers and sisters. It appeared that Prince Charles of Viana would inherit the thrones of both Navarre and Aragon on the demise of John II, or one of his sisters would succeed in Navarre and thereby separate the two kingdoms.

Henry IV's incapacity and licentious revels with his Moslem courtiers gave John II of Aragon an opportunity to intrigue against him among his rebellious grandees. The Castilian king was married to Blanche of Navarre, John II's daughter, in a union the issue of which might well have united Castile, Aragon, and Navarre, but they had no children. In 1452 Henry IV divorced Blanche on the grounds that their marriage had never been consummated. Three years later, he married Juana of Portugal, a princess of great beauty and sister of Alfonso V, but after six years they too had produced no children. Then, in 1462 Juana gave birth to a daughter.

Some of the grandees, led by Juan Pacheco, marquis of Villena, the unscrupulous confidant of the king, and his uncle, Alonso Carrillo, archbishop of Toledo and a willing tool of John II, charged that the infant princess was not the daughter of Henry IV and called her "Juana la Beltraneja," after her supposed father, Beltrán de le Cueva. They objected to her succession, deposed Henry IV at Ávila, and recognized Prince Alonso as king in 1465. The loyal nobles rallied to Henry IV and defeated the rebels at the second battle of Olmedo (1467). The rebellious nobles suffered another severe reverse in the sudden death of Prince Alonso, popularly believed to have been poisoned—probably because of the contemporary custom of shooting poisoned arrows at fish, of which Alonso had eaten. The crown was offered to Isabel, but she refused it while Henry IV was alive. The rebels then agreed to submit if Henry IV recognized Isabel as his heir, an arrangement ratified in the Treaty of Toros de Guisando (1468).

Considerable dissension also arose concerning the marriage of Isabel. After the marquis of Villena had failed to wed her to his brother, Pedro Girón—because of the timely death of the aged bridegroom—he proposed that she marry Alfonso V of Portugal. It was also proposed that she marry the duke of Guienne, brother of Louis XI, while Alonso Carrillo supported a union with Ferdinand, son of John II of Aragon. Thus, there was a possibility of the union of Castile through Isabel with either Portugal, France, or Aragon.

In the meantime, John II had quarreled with his eldest son, Charles of Viana, who died suddenly. It was rumored that he had been poisoned by his stepmother, Juana Enríquez, daughter of a Castilian partisan of the Aragonese union and a woman of strong character, who wanted to see her son ascend the Aragonese throne. It appeared that the marriage of Isabel and Ferdinand would unite Castile and Aragon in a personal union, but Henry IV favored the marriage with Alfonso V. Isabel was inclined toward her cousin Ferdinand, but she dutifully promised Henry IV that she would not marry without his consent. Then, while Henry IV was in Andalusia, aided by the archbishop of Toledo and John II of

Aragon, Ferdinand slipped into Castile and was married to Isabel in Valladolid in 1469.

Although the death of Charles of Viana removed an obstacle to the succession of Ferdinand in Aragon, a majority of the Catalans retained their affection for their dead prince. At the same time the serfs of Catalonia rebelled against their lords. The plight of John II was desperate. He was not only at war with Henry IV and Louis XI, but was in dire financial straits. Pledging the income of Cerdagne and Roussillon to France for aid, he succeeded in defeating the rebels in successive battles. Then he named his twelve-year-old son Ferdinand lieutenant-general (1464).

Barcelona, the center of resistance to John II, chose Henry IV as its count, and when he deserted named Pedro, constable of Portugal, as his successor. Louis XI occupied Cerdagne and Roussillon, but John II, blinded by a cataract at the age of seventy, concluded a series of alliances with Naples, Milan, England, Burgundy, and Brittany. He had his cataract removed with a red-hot iron and marched triumphantly on Barcelona, forcing it to capitulate in 1472. He then obtained the surrender of Cerdagne and Roussillon by Louis XI and repaid him for the aid he had received in the Catalan war. The war dragged on until 1478, when a new truce was adjusted with France, but the problem of Cerdagne and Roussillon remained.

The territorial union of the Christian kingdoms was not yet accomplished. The heirs to the largest kingdoms were married, but Navarre and Portugal were not included in the potential union and the Moors still controlled Granada. When Henry IV died in 1474 Isabel was crowned queen of Castile; John II of Aragon lived until 1479 and Ferdinand then inherited his throne.

Meanwhile, Juana la Beltraneja, daughter of Henry IV, became the principal obstacle to the accession of Isabel to the Castilian throne. Henry IV had been so enraged by the defiant marriage of Isabel that he recognized his daughter as his heir. Although there is little reason to suspect his physical condition justified his sobriquet of "the Impotent," the nobles seized upon his admission of impotency with Blanche of Navarre as a justification for their rebellion. To legalize their claim to the throne, Ferdinand and Isabel organized a battery of publicists to charge that Juana la Beltraneja was not actually his daughter.

Yet before they could assume the throne of Castile, Ferdinand and Isabel had to defeat the supporters of Juana la Beltraneja. In addition to the strong aristocratic support for Juana, there was also another problem. Ferdinand pretended that he was the legitimate heir of the crown of

Castile as the nearest male heir of the House of Trastamara. The problem was compromised by an agreement by which the rights were divided equally between the Catholic Kings.

War shortly broke out with the followers of Juana la Beltraneja. She was betrothed to her uncle, Alfonso V of Portugal, and they invaded Castile. Ferdinand and Isabel had no resources for the war until money was supplied by the Cortes of Medina del Campo (1474). While Isabel established herself at Tordesillas to attend to the supply of the army, her husband assumed personal direction of the military operations and won a decisive victory at Toro (1476), whereupon she was recognized as queen by the Cortes of Madrigal and made a triumphant progress through Estremadura to Seville.

The Castilian army won a bloody victory at Albuera and Princess Beatrice of Portugal, Isabel's aunt, intervened to restore peace. Conquests along the frontier were restored, Alfonso gave up his claims to the Castilian crown, and Ferdinand and Isabel relinquished their claim to that of Portugal. An amnesty was extended to the Castilian nobles who had supported Juana la Beltraneja. She entered a convent, where she lived as "the excellent lady" until 1530. Finally, to cement the peace, Alfonso, the grandson of the Portuguese king, was betrothed to Isabel, eldest daughter of the Catholic Kings.

Although, with the accession of Ferdinand to the Aragonese throne in 1479, Castile and Aragon were united in the persons of their sovereigns, each retained its separate cortes and independent administrations. The Catholic Kings administered justice jointly or individually and signed their letters jointly, but in Castile Isabel retained control of fiscal affairs, and her approval was required for all municipal and ecclesiastical appointments. Ferdinand's participation in Castilian affairs was largely personal, while Isabel exercised even less influence in Aragon.

The sovereigns who ruled Castile and Aragon were well adapted by nature and disposition to solve the problems which confronted them. Both were of medium stature and attractive physique. Ferdinand had dark hair and flashing eyes, Isabel was a blonde with greenish-blue eyes. Both were shrewd and calculating. Ferdinand was affable and persuasive —of "good-understanding"—and very temperate in eating and drinking and deliberate in his movements, since "neither anger nor pleasure made a great alteration in him." Isabel was also temperate in character and action. She never drank wine and rarely revealed the emotions which moved her. Beneath Ferdinand's imposing exterior lurked a mind of singular cunning and ingenuity, for he was a skilled diplomat, undaunted by either truth or falsehood. Isabel, a devout Catholic, was more rigid and demonstrated an unwavering piety. While she was as intelligent as Ferdinand, she was rather more tenacious and regarded her position as one which entailed strong obligations of duty. Having inexhaustible spiritual energy, she was sharp, discreet, and extremely industrious in the affairs of government.

Ferdinand was a good horseman, skilled in handling weapons and an excellent jouster, for he had been trained in military exercises from his youth. Isabel was well educated for her sex and position. She knew enough Latin to read and understand it. She liked ceremony and "wanted to be served by great and noble men," but her humility exceeded her pride. Ferdinand and Isabel were, in short, a royal pair each of whom complemented the other. Ferdinand was a product of the training of John II of Aragon in foreign affairs. He was cautious and persistent, perhaps a bit parsimonious, but he had been forced to conserve the scanty resources of Aragon under his father's tutelage and was not blessed with an abundance of treasure when Isabel ascended the throne of Castile. Rarely frank and generous, he used all the devices of intrigue and subterfuge. He not only measured lies with Louis XI but served as a model of Machiavellian royalty.

At times Isabel's piety degenerated into intolerance, but tolerance was not regarded as a virtue in the age in which she lived. Where one of the Catholic Kings was weak, the other was strong. Ferdinand has usually been held in less esteem than Isabel, but he was not a native of Castile and was more available as a whipping boy to the victims of his political manipulations than was Isabel, who had stirred the patriotic fervor of Castilians. Ferdinand was the more worldly of the two, although both survived many changes of fortune with fortitude.

The most important problem which confronted the new sovereigns was the overweening ambition of the grandees, veritable sovereigns in their extensive domains, who had defied Henry IV. Those who opposed the succession of Ferdinand and Isabel were forgiven, and they returned to court somewhat chastened. As the most powerful class in Castile the great nobles had to be treated with tact. While Isabel controlled them, she also used them as a foundation for royal power. Yet the prevailing anarchy had to be terminated, and they could not be permitted to defy royal justice. There were two areas in which the nobles were most impatient of royal restraint. They had always been restive in Galicia, and Andalusia was the frontier—dominated by haughty grandees. Even in Castile many alcaldes had defied royal authority behind the walls of their cities. Throughout Castile many castles—built for frontier security but converted into bases for lawlessness and banditry—were now seized or destroyed.

One of the most prized offices in Castile was the mastership of one of the military orders, which provided its possessor with prestige, wealth, and an independent army. Civil war nearly broke out in the struggle for the mastership of the Order of Santiago, vacant since the death of Juan Pacheco. In 1476 Isabel intervened. She persuaded the thirteen electors and the knights to choose Ferdinand and gained papal approval for the selection. In the end Ferdinand was named master of the three principal orders, thereby eliminating a source of discord and bringing needed treasure to the crown.

Seville had been reduced to a state of anarchy by the turbulent grandees, largely as a result of the feud between the Guzmans and the Ponce de Leons. After the victory at Toro, Isabel went to Seville and forced both families to submit, surrender their strongholds, and remain in exile. These steps guaranteed the peace of the city. She held a public audience for those who had been oppressed or injured in the struggle. Few in Seville were innocent of crimes, of aiding criminals, or of profiting from them. Isabel was so severe that 4000 persons fled the city, but she later proclaimed a general amnesty. Justice was energetically rendered throughout Andalusia and in the Canary Islands.

Quarrels among the nobility and clergy had long created grave commotions in Galicia, where some of the aristocrats had been tenacious partisans of Juana la Beltraneja and others had defied royal authority. In 1480 the Catholic Kings decided to suppress the disturbances there. They established a court, invited the cities of Galicia to present their grievances, and negotiated to determine what fortresses should be destroyed—forty-six castles were razed, taxes were collected and properties seized from the churches and monasteries were restored. Banditry, the levying of tribute, and private warfare were suppressed. Those who resisted royal justice were either exiled or executed. Although their privileges were sharply curtailed and they were forced to recognize their obligations to Isabel, the grandees continued to provide the principal support for the throne. The Catholic Kings did not wish to eliminate them, but only to ensure their loyalty and subordination.

Both the pious Isabel and the shrewd Ferdinand wished to renew the crusade against the Moors, to drive them from the peninsula, and to unify the nation territorially. The war of the reconquest had degenerated into intermittent campaigns and truces. Abul-Hasan, emir of the capital city of Granada since 1466, a man of impetuous disposition, cherished a special animosity toward Christians. In 1476 he took advantage of the civil war in Castile and refused to pay tribute, exclaiming that the mints of Granada "coined no longer gold but steel." His brother az-Zagal and his son Boabdil had already rebelled against him.

In an effort to restore his popularity Abul-Hasan broke the truce with Castile and seized Zahara (1481). Instead of applauding his act the people of Granada feared reprisals, and the Catholic Kings did undertake to retaliate. Ferdinand sent an expedition from Seville under the marquis of Cádiz to seize Alhama (1482). The Moors besieged the city, but it was relieved by the duke of Medina-Sidonia, and the two ancient rivals were reconciled in the service of their kings. Using Alhama as a base, Ferdinand assumed command in Andalusia and besieged Loja, but failed to capture it because his supplies were inadequate. Ferdinand's untrained army was poorly provided with artillery and inspired with little crusading zeal. The withdawal to Córdoba was disorderly and might have degenerated into a rout had it not been for the cool leadership of Ferdinand. Fortunately for the Castilians, new dissensions broke out among the Moors, as a result of which Boabdil was proclaimed ruler in Granada.

Meanwhile, in Córdoba, great preparations were being made to resume the campaign in the spring of 1483. Ferdinand and Isabel were still desperately short of funds. In addition to their continuous military operations, they had to equip a fleet to patrol the Strait of Gibraltar so as to prevent the Moors in Morocco from aiding those in Granada. The Santa Hermandad, which had been expanded on a national basis by Henry IV and adopted as a nucleus of their armed forces by Ferdinand and Isabel, provided men and supplies. The sum of 100,000 ducats was obtained from the ecclesiastical revenues of Castile and Aragon, and the pope issued a *Bula de Cruzada* granting indulgences for bearing arms against the Moslems and commuting military service into monetary payments to support the war. Considerable sums were also borrowed from some of the Castilian grandees.

Although the Castilians were ambushed and decisively defeated at Ajarquia, Boabdil was defeated and captured. Aisha, his mother, ransomed him, and he was released as a vassal of the Spanish sovereigns. In return, he granted rights of passage to the Castilian troops, agreed to pay an annual tribute of 12,000 gold doubloons, and surrendered 700 Christian captives without ransom. Abul-Hasan at once charged Boabdil with treason, but the Moors in Granada rallied in Boabdil's favor.

By this time Ferdinand and Isabel had rekindled the enthusiasm for a crusade against the Moors. They made the war a religious cause while their continued presence among the soldiers kept a militant spirit alive.

Ferdinand shared all the discomforts of military life with his soldiers in order to restore order and discipline. Volunteers and adventurers flocked to the army from all over Europe, and their reports of its prowess did much to raise Spanish prestige. The Spaniards, who had hitherto employed guerrilla tactics nearly exclusively, now learned much of the art of war from the foreigners, especially from the Swiss mercenaries. Gonzalo de Córdoba, one of the Spanish captains, became familiar with conventional European methods and evolved the tactics which made the Spaniards the ablest soldiers in Europe.

The war against Granada enabled the Spanish kings to complete their plans for military reorganization. Spanish recruitment had been largely feudal until the expansion of the Santa Hermandad provided the basis for a permanent standing army. The reorganization was not concluded until after the fall of Granada, but important changes were made in methods of combat before that time. Since the mountains of Granada were unfavorable for cavalry, infantry and artillery became important in a war of sieges to which guerrilla tactics were with difficulty adapted.

New tactics were combined with the old. Spanish horsemen systematically ravaged the countryside and cut off the supplies for the besieged. Engineers were recruited in Spain and in foreign lands, the artillery was increased in both number of guns and efficiency, heavy guns to fire large balls of stone and iron were cast, and powder was imported in large quantities. Francisco Ramírez of Madrid, who had extensive military experience, developed a train of artillery unequaled elsewhere in Europe. Although the Moslems were expert marksmen with the arquebus and crossbow, they were deficient in artillery. Ferdinand and Isabel also displayed unprecedented interest in the welfare of their troops. Provisions were collected at Córdoba and forwarded to commissaries in the combat areas. Surgeons and medical supplies were also assembled, and the wounded were placed in special tents, the first military hospitals.

Spanish progress was slow because the Moors were well-fortified, tenacious in battle, and desperate in their resolve to defend their castles. The war assumed a new character only gradually and the early campaigns were undertaken, as in the past, on an annual basis. The campaign of 1485 culminated in the fall of Ronda. In the same year az-Zagal, now leader of the party which had supported the old emir, forced Boabdil to flee to Córdoba and was proclaimed emir in Granada. With the Moors divided into two hostile factions, the wily Ferdinand concluded a treaty with Boabdil, making him a grandee of Castile with the title of duke and marquis of Guadix. az-Zagal also tried to negotiate with the Spaniards, but he was too stubborn and the Castilian ambassador too proud to permit an agreement. After taking Loja the Castilians besieged and captured Vélez Málaga in the spring of 1487. Ferdinand then attacked and took Málaga.

Undaunted by a fruitless campaign in 1488 Ferdinand assembled a powerful army at Jaén in the following spring, which moved on Baza. Isabel visited the Spanish camp and tried to inspire the troops. To sustain the siege she pawned her jewels to merchants in Barcelona and Valencia. This showed courage, for Ferdinand wanted to withdraw, and the jewels were not wholly redeemed until 1495. When Baza continued to resist, Ferdinand resorted again to diplomacy, and the city was surrendered as a result of bribery. az-Zagal also gave up Almería and Gaudix and became a vassal of the Spanish Kings in a small district near Málaga. He rebelled later, but surrendered his domain for a money indemnity and migrated to North Africa, where the Berbers stripped him of his treasure and he ended his life in misery.

Ferdinand now demanded that Boabdil surrender Granada, but the people forced their leader to continue the war. When Ferdinand besieged Granada in 1491, the whole aspect of the conflict changed, for he prepared for a prolonged siege instead of a short raid. Although Granada was formidably defended, the Moors soon became alarmed as the Spaniards erected the city of Santa Fé to complete the encirclement. The surrender of Granada was arranged through secret negotiations, which proved more effective for the Spaniards than heroic feats of arms. Boabdil tried to hold out, but the situation had deteriorated and starvation was threatened. By the terms of the formal capitulation, signed January 6, 1492, the lives and property of Moslems and Jews were assured. Boabdil received 30,000 gold Castilians on the day of the surrender and retained La Alpujarra and some villages. He later sold his properties to Isabel and withdrew to the Moslem court at Fez.

The Catholic Kings made their triumphal entry into Granada in January 1492, named a military governor and appointed Fray Hernando de Talavera, Isabel's confessor, bishop of Granada. But they did not respect their promises of tolerance and humanity to the Moors. In 1499 the bishop succumbed to the influence of Francisco Jiménez de Cisneros, archbishop of Toledo, who demanded a more aggressive policy in the conversion of the Moors. Ferdinand and Isabel had recommended temperate measures, but the zeal of the archbishop caused him to try to extirpate both the writings and the "paganism" of the Moors. The Inquisition was extended to Granada and many Moslems, under harsh compulsion, were superficially converted to Christianity.

As a result, revolt broke out in Granada and spread to the rural areas.

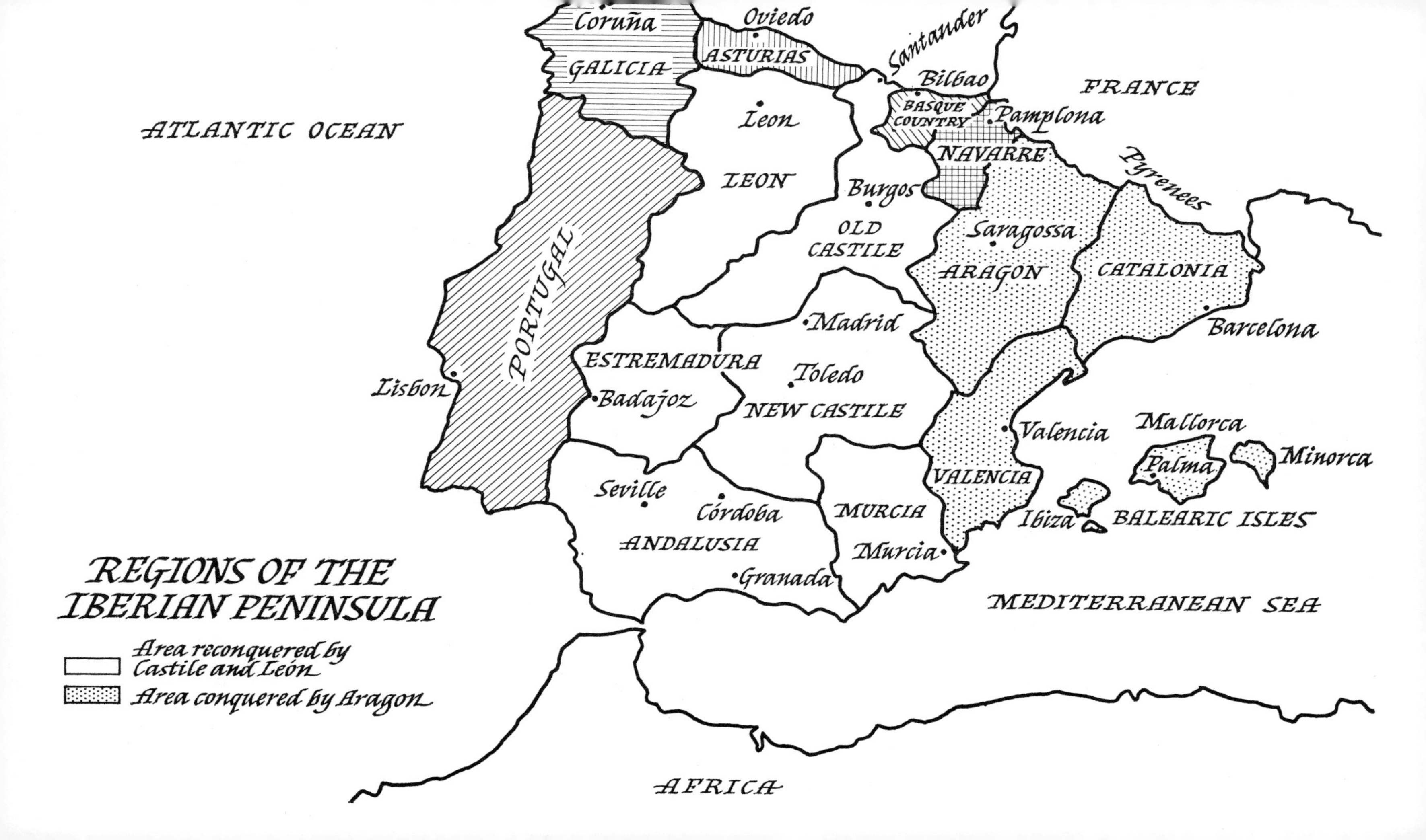
REGIONS OF THE IBERIAN PENINSULA
Area reconquered by Castile and León
Area conquered by Aragon
ATLANTIC OCEAN
FRANCE
Pyrenees
MEDITERRANEAN SEA
AFRICA
Coruña
GALICIA
Oviedo
ASTURIAS
Santander
Bilbao
BASQUE COUNTRY
Pamplona
NAVARRE
Leon
LEON
Burgos
OLD CASTILE
PORTUGAL
Lisbon
ESTREMADURA
Badajoz
Madrid
Toledo
NEW CASTILE
Saragossa
ARAGON
CATALONIA
Barcelona
Valencia
VALENCIA
Seville
Córdoba
ANDALUSIA
Granada
MURCIA
Murcia
Mallorca
Palma
Minorca
Ibiza
BALEARIC ISLES

Partially suppressed, it was renewed in 1501. Ferdinand was not convinced of the need of fanatical retaliation against the Moors, but Isabel was stubborn in her determination to rid Castile of all remnants of the non-Christian population. By the edict of expulsion, published in 1502, all unconverted, adult Moors were ordered to leave Castile and León within three months. Those who remained and rejected conversion came under the jurisdiction of the Inquisition. By the new policy toward the Moors in Granada—a reaction against Henry IV's leniency toward his Moslem favorites—the development of a fanatical intolerance was accelerated, fostered by Isabel's piety and the uncompromising spirit of Cardinal Cisneros.

Isabel had been too preoccupied with the conquest of Granada and too short of funds to heed the suit of Christopher Columbus (1451–1506) for assistance in the search for a westward route to the Far East. This Genoese sailor absorbed the maritime lore of Portugal as well as of his native city, two of the principal naval powers of the fifteenth century, and pondered it well. When he was unable to obtain the support of John II of Portugal for his venture, he sent his brother Bartholomew to obtain the aid of Henry VII of England or Charles VIII of France, while he went in person to enlist the patronage of Isabel. As the conquest advanced and as some of her astute advisers pleaded with her, Isabel agreed to assist in financing the project. The siege of Granada was progressing satisfactorily, and she expected to acquire the treasure of the Nazrid kings of Granada.

In the Capitulations of Santa Fé (1492) Columbus was named admiral over all lands "discovered or acquired by his labor and industry." He was ennobled with the title of "Don," a dignity prized by a common sailor and a foreigner, and named viceroy and governor-general of the lands he acquired. He was given a tenth of the profits accruing from the voyage in precious metals or produce of the new lands. His price was high, but he was offering the Catholic Kings the opportunity of pioneering in the new realm of imperialism, and while they reaped the main portion of the riches, he earned his share by braving the dangers involved.

With three small ships, the "Santa María," "Niña," and "Pinta," manned by ninety men and boys, Columbus sailed from Palos on his first voyage on August 3, 1492, and persisting in his course despite the discouragement and near mutiny of some of his companions, he landed at San Salvador (Watlings Island), in the Bahamas, on October 12, 1492. Although he searched for Cathay and Cipango and labored under the mistaken belief that he had actually reached the Far East, he succeeded only in sailing through the Bahamas, landing in Cuba, exploring a part of Española (Haiti), and founding the little colony of La Navidad on that island with the thirty-nine men who could not be accommodated on the ships after the wrecking of the "Santa María."

On his return voyage, Columbus sailed into the Tagus and landed at Restello (later Belém) near Lisbon, on March 4, 1493. John II heard the account of his success with some annoyance. When Columbus landed in Spain on March 15, Ferdinand and Isabel were holding court at Barcelona, 800 miles across the peninsula. With a few men whom he had engaged as servants and six Indians from Española, Columbus crossed the peninsula to Barcelona, where he was fittingly received by Ferdinand and Isabel.

Columbus not only returned with a fairly clear assurance of great wealth to be derived from the lands he had discovered in the name of Ferdinand and Isabel, but he held the promise of relieving a situation which was giving Ferdinand and Isabel some anxiety. Spain was a poor country, with meager resources for the support of her eight million inhabitants. The Spanish sovereigns were trying to restore order in the peninsula, yet the conquest of Granada left thousands of border fighters, who had existed by raiding their Moorish enemies, unemployed. They were rough, self-reliant individualists, whose poverty and restlessness would present a problem to any sovereign desiring peace. The discovery of the New World provided an outlet for the unemployed of Spain. The alacrity with which the voyages of Columbus were followed by those of other mariners and the swiftness of the Spaniards in exploring and occupying the New World provide evidence of their vigor and enterprise in overseas expansion.

In three subsequent voyages Columbus returned to Española with colonists and supplies, touched the northern coast of South America, and followed the shores of Central America. He never found the Great Khan or Cipango and died in 1506 in dire poverty. The New World was named after Amerigo Vespucci, a representative of the Florentine house of Medici, who received better publicity for his voyages. Ferdinand had little regard for the poor mariner who before Isabel's death in 1504 had given Castile the footholds which Spanish valor and energy were to expand into one of the greatest empires in history. He was already engrossed in his Italian venture.

CHAPTER XI

Spain as a European Power, 1475–1515

Under Ferdinand and Isabel, Spain slowly but indisputably accomplished a transition from medieval disunity to modern centralization and homogeneity. It became a nation with lineaments recognizably akin to those which it bears today. It also became the center of an empire expanding rapidly on the islands and continents beyond the Atlantic. That ocean, so recently a stormy barrier, became the bridge to a golden future. The primary ambition of Ferdinand, however, did not lie overseas but in Europe. His hopes and fears were those that preceding rulers of the thirteenth and fourteenth centuries would have thought entirely proper to his position. He wished first of all to give Aragon a position of supremacy in the Mediterranean. Once this goal was won, he desired to achieve for his state a dominant place in European affairs. He would bring Spain into a leadership it had never before exercised.

This meant that Spain embarked upon a double course of evolution. The importance of Barcelona in the western Mediterranean, and the expansion of Aragonese power into the Balearic Islands, Sardinia, Corsica, Naples, and Sicily involved Aragon in policies that looked eastward, whereas Castile was interested in expansion to the west. The ambitions of both kingdoms had imperial scope. But if the westward movement had a larger freedom, the policies of Aragon involved her in the European balance-of-power struggle and plunged her into a century of warfare in Italy. The restless men who were left without employment by the disappearance of the Moorish frontier were soon needed, if they had not migrated across the Atlantic, in the Italian conflicts.

The principal obstacle to the ambitions of Ferdinand V lay in the strength of the French monarchs. A direct collision came when Charles VIII of France was drawn into Italian affairs in a way which threatened to place him in control of Naples. This at once aroused Ferdinand to action. A cousin whose position he valued sat on the Neapolitan throne.

If the French gained possession of Naples they would threaten the integrity of Sicily, in which Aragon had a direct interest, and he regarded this as intolerable. He prepared to take up arms against Charles VIII and the French forces to protect the Neapolitan throne, defend his cousin, and sustain his own interests.

The prospective antagonists sought alliances. Ferdinand tried to win the support of the Aragonese Pope Alexander VI for the king of Naples. To free himself for the Italian venture Charles VIII ceded Cerdagne and Roussillon to Ferdinand in the Treaty of Narbonne (1493). Although primarily a compact between France and Spain, it was stipulated that this treaty did not cover an attack on the pope. As Naples was a fief of the Holy See, Ferdinand thus hoped to free himself of the engagement if the French attacked Naples.

In 1494 Charles VIII invaded Italy with a brilliant army and with the aid of several Italian princes. The struggle with Granada was ended, and Ferdinand V, although he preferred diplomacy to war, was able to devote himself to a foreign venture. When Alfonso II of Naples appealed for his aid, Ferdinand V demanded the cession of part of the kingdom. The Neapolitan king abdicated in favor of his son and fled from the city before the approach of the French, whose king Charles VIII triumphantly entered Naples in 1495.

Ferdinand V then organized a Holy League to resist the French and to defend the papal dominions. Charles VIII had not anticipated war with Spain, Austria, Milan, Venice, and Pope Alexander VI and had overextended his line of supply. He returned to France, leaving half of his troops in Naples. On the way north he defeated the Italians and forced Milan to withdraw from the Holy League. Gonzalo de Córdoba, the Spanish commander, who had already won distinction in the war against Granada, landed at Messina with a small force of Spaniards. He invaded Calabria with brilliant results. By 1498 the Great Captain—as Gonzalo was later known—had driven the French from Calabria, captured Ostia, and returned to Spain.

Ferdinand V also attacked the French through Roussillon, but a truce was concluded and negotiations were in progress for a permanent peace when Charles VIII died (1498). The king of Spain also hoped for an opportunity of obtaining Naples and opposed the investiture of Frederick III as its king.

By the Treaty of Granada in 1500, Louis XII and Ferdinand V agreed to divide Naples, since Frederick III had endangered Christendom by seeking Turkish aid. Louis XII assumed the title of king of Naples and Jerusalem, and Ferdinand V took that of duke of Apulia and Calabria. The treaty was approved by Pope Alexander VI, and French troops immediately entered Naples. Louis XII appeased Frederick III with the duchy of Anjou, while Gonzalo de Córdoba subdued Calabria. But hostilities broke out between the French and the Spaniards, and the alliance was broken. Archduke Philip of Austria, son-in-law of Ferdinand V, intervened. Pro-French in sympathies, he concluded a pact with Louis XII at Lyons in 1503 that provided Charles, infant son of Philip, should marry Claudia, daughter of Louis XII, and become king of Naples and duke of Calabria. Until the marriage was consummated, the division of Naples would continue and the areas in dispute would be mediated.

Louis XII wished the war suspended in Naples, but the Great Captain had no orders to terminate hostilities. He defeated the French and triumphantly entered Naples in 1503. Louis XII accused Ferdinand V of perfidy in breaking the treaty, demanded an indemnity, and prepared three armies for an attack on Spain. One army invaded Navarre, a second attacked Roussillon, and a third, under Marshal Trémouille, invaded Lombardy. After sharp skirmishes, the reinforced Spaniards won a decisive victory over the French at the Garigliano River. When Gaeta surrendered in 1504, Spanish dominion in Naples was assured and the French withdrew.

The Great Captain returned to Naples as the hero of the Italian campaign. He reorganized the government and suppressed a mutiny caused by a delay in pay, but his liberality in the distribution of honors and estates to his Italian allies aroused Ferdinand's suspicion. By the Treaty of Blois (1505), Aragon retained Naples, and Gonzalo de Córdoba remained as governor of the areas conquered in Italy. The Spanish sovereign expected his overseas possessions to meet their own expenses and yield revenue for Spain. Neapolitan prosperity declined.

Like all dynastic monarchs of the sixteenth century, Ferdinand and Isabel were intent on the expansion of their dominions and influence. They used their diplomacy to that end, but Navarre presented them with a difficult problem. It was an enclave on the flank of Aragon and Castile and a constant threat because its dynasty acknowledged French sovereignty. Magdalena, sister of Louis XI and widow of Charles of Viana, had placed her two children under the protection of the French king because Navarre was torn by strife between the Agramonts and the Beaumonts, who favored the Spanish cause.

In 1476 Ferdinand intervened in Navarre to end civil strife and forestall a French invasion. The Treaty of Tudela was the first step in the establishment of Spanish protection. Francis Phoebus, son of

Magdalena, ascended the throne in 1479 and was succeeded by his sister, Catherine, four years later. The Catholic Kings were anxious to contract a matrimonial alliance with Navarre that would eventually bring Navarre into the united Spain. They proposed their son, Prince John, as the husband of Catherine, but, unintimidated by Spanish pressure, Magdalena arranged the marriage of her daughter to Jean d'Albret —a triumph for French diplomacy.

Since the conclusion of peace with Portugal in 1479, the Spaniards and the Portuguese had lived in amity. The Portuguese heir had been betrothed to Isabel, eldest daughter of the Catholic Kings, and although the treaty was annulled in 1483, the marriage of Prince Alfonso and Isabel was celebrated in 1490. A few months later the Prince was killed in a fall from his horse and Isabel returned to Castile.

John II of Portugal, somewhat annoyed that Columbus had made a successful voyage under Castilian patronage, was not satisfied with the line of demarcation arranged by Alexander VI and undertook negotiations to protect the colonial interests of Portugal more effectively. As a result, the Treaty of Tordesillas was concluded in 1494, and the line of demarcation between the empires of the two states was established 370 leagues west of the Cape Verde Islands. Portuguese rights to Guinea and other territories already possessed were recognized.

Manuel I, who succeeded John II in 1495, asked for the hand of Isabel in marriage. Political considerations overcame the reluctance of the princess to accept the union. Portuguese sailors had rounded the Cape of Good Hope (1486), promising an eastern route to the Indies by sea. The dynastic prospects of the Catholic Kings were also critical. John, their only son, was unmarried and childless. As the eldest daughter, Isabel might produce offspring who would be in line for the succession to a united Spain and Portugal. So, Isabel was persuaded to marry Manuel I in 1497.

Throughout his reign Charles VIII of France was engaged in a continuous battle of diplomacy with the crafty Ferdinand. The king of Aragon, wishing to recover Cerdagne and Roussillon as essential to Spanish unity, adopted a policy of rapprochement toward both Austria and England. When Henry VII proposed a close political and commercial alliance, the marriage of Arthur, Prince of Wales, and Catherine, youngest daughter of Ferdinand and Isabel, was arranged by the Treaty of Medina del Campo (1489). Although Charles VIII was absorbed with the problem of Brittany and preparations for the Italian campaign, he took notice of the Anglo-Spanish treaty and agreed to restore Cerdagne and Roussillon.

The struggle in Brittany had presented Ferdinand an opportunity to encircle France. The Emperor Maximilian I of Austria had married Mary of Burgundy, heir of Charles the Bold. Upon her death Maximilian I became regent in the Netherlands for their son, Philip the Handsome. Although the emperor had not been very reliable as an ally, a double marriage was arranged by the Catholic Kings with the powerful House of Habsburg. Juana, second daughter of the Catholic Kings, sailed to Flanders to marry the Archduke Philip, and the same fleet brought Margaret of Austria back to Santander in 1497 to marry Prince Juan of Asturias.

Isabel died in 1504, leaving the Castilian crown to Juana, with Ferdinand as regent. The Archduke Philip of Austria already had a following among some of the more discontented aristocracy, and a party favoring the immediate accession of Juana and Philip was formed, encouraged by Flemish intrigue. The tension increased when Philip requested that Ferdinand retire to Aragon. The suspicion of Ferdinand concerning the loyalty of Gonzalo de Córdoba, viceroy of Naples, was also aroused. The Great Captain was a Castilian and owed his appointment to Isabel as much as to his own military prowess. It was rumored that Philip and Maximilian I were trying to undermine Gonzalo's loyalty and gain Naples for the archduke, and the rumors were fanned by courtiers, jealous of the viceroy.

To forestall the Habsburgs, Ferdinand negotiated with Louis XII. Philip had arranged the marriage of his five-year-old son Charles to the daughter of Louis XII. Ferdinand married Germaine de Foix, heiress of his half-sister, Eleanor of Navarre, niece of the king of France, in 1506. Although this marriage tended to neutralize the encirclement of France, so greatly feared by Louis XII, it also stimulated division within Spain.

Ferdinand, Philip, and Juana agreed to rule Castile jointly, but after his marriage to Germaine de Foix the grandees abandoned Ferdinand, who had to resign his regency in favor of Philip and Juana, retaining only the income assigned to him by Isabel's will and the administration of the military orders. Philip I thus became king of Castile, for it had long been recognized, even by Isabel, that Juana was incapable of governing. Ferdinand did not give up easily and drafted a protest, promising to recover the government when he could.

Philip I, known as "The Handsome" because of his regular features, long, flowing hair, and well-proportioned physique, was not very intelligent. Rash and impetuous, and born to expectations of grandeur, he had an intemperate ambition and was impatient of advice. He was indolent, sensuous, and fond of pleasure. He enjoyed only a brief reign as king of Castile. The Cortes of Valladolid declared Castile the possession of Juana, recognized Philip as her consort, and named their son Charles as her successor. Yet Philip assumed sole control of the government and was appointing Flemings to official posts and evicting their former incumbents when he was seized with a fever and died in six days (1506).

Juana was reputed to be mentally unstable, subject to fits of jealousy over her husband's inconstancy. When Philip openly made advances to a lady in her suite, Juana assaulted the hapless female and ordered her hair cut. Although Juana was lucid at times, she clad herself in black and refused to participate in the festivities prepared for her at Valladolid. Philip tried to keep her in seclusion, but she was supported by some of the nobles. The townsmen and lower classes became indignant when Philip declared that she was incompetent, but her father, her husband, and her son kept her confined for fifty years while they controlled Castile.

After the death of Philip, a provisional regency was established. Ferdinand was in Naples, and the faction which had supported Philip I intrigued in behalf of the infant Charles, the Emperor Maximilian I, or some other monarch. But Ferdinand began to eliminate his opponents as soon as he returned to Spain. He had restrained his vengeance until he was sure of the loyalty of the people of Castile, but he now exiled or imprisoned the adherents of the late Philip I. Although Gonzalo de Córdoba was permitted to withdraw to inactivity on his own estates, his nephew was imprisoned and heavily fined. The archbishop of Toledo was rewarded for his loyalty with a cardinal's cape, and Juana was persuaded to take up quarters at Tordesillas, where she remained for the rest of her life. Then Ferdinand took the oath as administrator of the realm in the name of Juana and as guardian of Charles I.

As a result of the proximity of the Moroccan coast and the threat of the Barbary pirates in that area, Ferdinand had considered expansion in North Africa for some time. He was also interested in consolidating his position in the Canary Islands. The Portuguese had recognized Castilian jurisdiction there in return for a free hand on the west coast of Africa. By 1500 the entire archipelago was under Castilian sovereignty, although the Herreras administered the four smaller islands until the eighteenth century. A Spanish expedition had also conquered Melilla on the Moroccan coast.

Cardinal Jiménez de Cisneros wished to continue the crusade against the Moors, but he also hoped to exterminate the Barbary pirates who raided the Mediterranean coast of Spain. Though the death of Isabel had interrupted an expedition to conquer Oran, the project was renewed, and Cisneros financed it. An expedition had captured the fort of Mers-el-Kebir, the key to Oran, but the garrison had been left to shift for itself until the threatened loss of the fort provoked a renewal of Spanish activity. With Cisneros again providing the funds, Pedro de Navarro captured the island and town of Vélez de Gomera in 1508. After protracted negotiations over this territory in the Portuguese sphere of influence, Spanish possession of the African coast opposite the Canary Islands was confirmed, and with the excuse for delaying the attack thus removed, the expedition captured Oran.

Cisneros, as regent, hoped to found a Spanish empire in Africa, attract Spanish colonists, and establish permanent posts, but Pedro de Navarro, the commander of the expedition, was a professional soldier interested in booty rather than the broader plans of his patron. The Spaniards took Bugía in 1510 and Tripoli in 1511, and some of the tribes recognized Spanish sovereignty, but the Barbary coast could not be permanently held by isolated garrisons. Ferdinand had found the cardinal's intervention in administrative affairs in the peninsula somewhat irritating and wanted to keep him occupied in Africa without actually undertaking further conquests. When Cisneros returned to Spain, a bitter quarrel developed with Ferdinand over the cardinal's rights in the new territory.

Ferdinand V was also occupied by war in Italy, where Louis XII, resentful at the loss of Naples, again sought to extend his power. On the pretext that Venice might seek compensation for her losses to the Turks in the peninsula, the League of Cambrai—including France, Spain, the Empire, and five Italian states—was organized to despoil Venice of her possessions on the mainland. Ferdinand's share of the spoil included the five Neapolitan cities pledged to Venice for sums advanced during the recent war.

Ultimately, after the states had shifted sides—pitting Spain against France in the Holy Alliance formed by Pope Julius II—the situation of the French became increasingly precarious. Their generals quarreled among themselves; Milan, Genoa, and Este rebelled against them; and the remnants of their army withdrew across the Alps. After the victory of Novara of the Swiss (1513), the viceroy of Naples occupied Milan and bombarded Venice, Louis XII concluded a truce, and the Italian wars came to an uneasy halt. The Spanish possessions outside the Iberian Peninsula had been considerably expanded, and Spain was supreme in Europe as a military power.

The Catholic Kings had tried to unite the peninsular kingdoms through marriage alliances, but as far as Portugal was concerned the diplomacy seemed ineffectual. After the death of Isabel the Albret dynasty in Navarre—as vassals of Louis XII—was in a difficult position, for it remained within the Spanish sphere of influence. The concern of the Albrets was increased when Ferdinand married Germaine de Foix, and they further embittered the Catholic King by concluding a treaty with Philip I. Louis XII demanded their expulsion and the recognition of Gaston de Foix as king of Navarre during his interview with Ferdinand at Savona, but the death of Gaston at Ravenna ended this threat to Spanish interest.

During the second phase of the Italian wars, the English and Castilians prepared to invade Guienne. When Ferdinand, to reassure himself regarding the attitude of his nephew, Jean d'Albret, demanded free passage for the invaders through Navarre and a guarantee of Navarrese neutrality, the Albrets concluded an alliance with Louis XII. Ferdinand sent the duke of Alba into Navarre and Jean d'Albret fled to France. With the kingdom subdued, Ferdinand published a papal excommunication of the Albrets and assumed the title of king of Navarre (1512).

The death of Louis XII (1515) altered the foreign policy of Ferdinand. Francis I ascended the French throne and invaded Italy with an imposing army. Defeating the Swiss at Marignano, he entered Milan. Julius II joined France and Venice. Ferdinand, old and ill, turned to his son-in-law, Henry VIII of England, and concluded an alliance with him (1515). Within a year he was dead. He had failed in many of his undertakings, but it could be said with truth that he had given Spain the leadership that he coveted.

And as he passed from the stage, a greater figure stepped upon it. His successor as ruler of Aragon and Navarre, and as regent in Castile, was identified by Ferdinand in his will—the son of the crazed Juana, Charles of Ghent, who was to become famous in history as Charles V.

CHAPTER XII

The Institutions of the Catholic Kings

The Catholic Kings made Spain the first power in Europe, but they had first to create a nation. Although in administration the kingdoms remained separate, Castile dominated the others. It covered the largest part of the peninsula—the economically poor, central plateau—and was strategically located to influence the other regions. In addition, the Catholic Kings maintained their court in Castile, and the other kingdoms became appendages of the royal, international policy of Castile. Spain continued to be a federation of regions and the complete unification was never more than superficial, except as the regions expressed patriotic enthusiasm for an absolute king. Thus, the personal popularity of the monarchs stimulated a national feeling which temporarily obscured regional tendencies.

In centralizing the administration and extending Castilian policies, Ferdinand and Isabel were not innovators. While they introduced some new ideas, in general they merely adapted and improved on older traditions. They held the political power in Castile, and their authority increased as they advanced the prestige of the nation abroad. At first they used the nobility and later the clergy as instruments of their policy, but both classes were subordinated to the royal sovereignty.

Although the aristocratic hierarchy remained the same, the principal noble houses attained greater splendor as they reflected the increased prestige of royal authority. The nobles held the important offices in court and reared large families to support their prestige. The duke of Nájera, for example, had twenty-seven sons. The old pomp of the Castilian court disappeared, and the extravagances of John II and Henry IV were restrained by sumptuary laws, yet the ceremony was preserved. The nobles retained the *juegos de cañas,* but Isabel lost her interest in bullfighting in which men and horses were often killed. The Florentine ambassador, Guicciardini, was astonished by the extreme simplicity in which the Spanish kings lived.

In accord with the precedent set by the Order of Santiago, Ferdinand assumed the masterships of the three principal orders and, much later, in 1523 a bull of Adrian VI incorporated the orders in the crown of Castile. This policy not only removed a cause of rivalry, but added new wealth and authority to the crown. The need for military orders in an age when the frontier had disappeared was no longer evident, but they retained their landed interests and social prestige.

In Castile, as the nobles were converted into courtiers, members of the middle class were admitted to important offices. Lawyers in administrative posts were already inclined toward absolutism, and some of them were elevated to create a new nobility, dependent on the monarchs. Although complaints were raised concerning abuses committed by the *corregidores,* they were appointed in increasing numbers. The town councils were also regulated to permit royal appointment of the municipal officials and to exclude aristocratic influence. The old particularism of the regime of *fueros* in the towns was replaced by the will of a single patron—the sovereign.

The cortes, which had met frequently during the previous reigns, was convoked only nine times in twenty-five years (1475–1503). It approved the internal reforms early in the reign, but from 1482 to 1498, while Granada was being conquered, the New World discovered, the Inquisition established, and the Jews expelled, it was not convoked once. Its real importance declined as it became more dependent on the royal council.

With the development of absolutism, the Catholic Kings used dependable administrative officials of their own. The Royal Council of Castile, formerly composed of nobles, was dominated by the lawyers by 1480, and the royal control was complete. As bureaucracy developed, other councils, such as those of the Inquisition, the Military Orders, the Indies, a new Royal Council, and an extraordinary Council of Justice, were created to act independently of the Council of Castile. The royal secretary exercised decisive influence; the royal chancellor, vested in the archbishop of Toledo, was indicative of the increasing influence of the clergy; and the constable of Castile was vested in the House of Velasco. The numerous palace officials subjected the transmission of documents to detailed regulations, and the financial administration required a large staff of scribes and other officials.

Ferdinand and Isabel were especially interested in the administration of justice in order to extend royal authority and to ensure impartial justice to all citizens. The Royal Brotherhood, based on the Holy Brotherhood of Henry IV and the earlier medieval brotherhoods, was adapted and extended by the Cortes of Madrigal (1476). Each locality maintained militia who relentlessly pursued criminals within its jurisdictions and exacted severe penalties. The brotherhood succeeded in reestablishing security, but the local tax required for its support became a burden, its severity was unpopular, and in 1498 it was modified, continuing only in rural districts.

The ordinary courts had meanwhile been reformed and strengthened. Three regional courts were established at Valladolid (1489), Ciudad Real (1492—moved later to Granada, 1505), and in Galicia. The judges in each court were named annually by the king and had cognizance of civil matters. The Council of Castile was the court of final appeal.

After the conquest of Granada, a new military policy was proclaimed. One man out of every twelve between the ages of twelve and forty-five was required to serve in the royal army and was paid by the crown for his service. New tactics were introduced in the use of artillery as a protection for the infantry and in the use of long pikes, with short swords, javelins, and arquebuses, to equip the foot soldier to meet the horseman on equal terms. The organization of the infantry was also improved. The company of 500 men was too small to be effective, and a regiment finally evolved composed of twelve companies, with an additional 300 heavy and 300 light cavalry. Each brigade of two regiments had sixty-four pieces of artillery. By 1505 the Spanish army consisted of twenty regiments.

Spanish tactics struck terror into the hearts of the enemies of Spain. The pikemen and men with short swords were formed in squares, with the pikemen on the outside. The arquebusiers and artillery were disposed so as to shoot to the best advantage, the cavalry being used in scouting or pursuing the defeated foe. The charges of the enemy horse, thinned by fire of the artillery and arquebusiers, were usually unable to penetrate the pikemen, but if they did, the men with the short swords finished them. The Spanish regiment also had greater fire power and flexibility than other continental armies.

Spanish naval power also increased. It was based on three maritime centers, the Cantabrian coast, Andalusia, and Catalonia, and played an important role in the war with Alfonso V of Portugal, the conquest of Granada, and the expeditions to North Africa. The new weapons were not fully utilized, since the Spaniards continued the older tactics of ramming and boarding the enemy. The Catalan fleet became less important after the reign of John II of Aragon, as emphasis shifted to the Atlantic seaboard, with the need for great colonial fleets.

Financial reform was essential for the larger role Spain was playing in the later fifteenth century. The Cortes of Madrigal (1476) attempted to end financial abuses by the aristocracy and establish an orderly collection of taxes. The grants of Henry IV were revoked, interior customs duties were suppressed, private coinage was forbidden, and a minute inventory of royal finances was undertaken. The Cortes of Toledo (1480) continued the work of reform.

The three types of revenue—stamp tax, sales tax of 10 percent, and customs dues—emphasized by Ferdinand and Isabel proved insufficient for the continuously increasing expenses of the state, and it was necessary to invent new sources of income. The first was the sale of indulgences, originally used for the war against the Moors, but converted into an ordinary tax and productive of many abuses. After the Catholic Kings secured ecclesiastical tithes for the war against the Moors, they also used them for other purposes, even for the Italian wars. Ferdinand and Isabel frequently borrowed money, and the national debt mounted rapidly. At the death of Isabel it was 127,000,000 *maravedis,* and five years later, in 1509, it was 180,000,000.

As a result of Isabel's piety and the clerical influence in royal affairs, the Catholic Kings were loyal to the pope and advanced the interests of the Church in their dominions. In return they demanded control of the Spanish clergy and firmly upheld the idea of a national church under their authority. They had a powerful collaborator in Cardinal Pedro González de Mendoza, archbishop of Toledo, who was known as "the Third King of Spain" until his death in 1495. Pope Alexander VI, formerly Cardinal Rodrigo Borgia and a member of a powerful Aragonese family, was also very cooperative in ecclesiastical policies. The pope conceded Ferdinand and Isabel the nomination of candidates for the most important benefices, with the understanding that they would be approved by the papacy. The less important benefices later fell under political control. In Granada and the New World the Catholic Kings were given complete control over Church appointments as a reward for their services to Christendom.

Although Ferdinand and Isabel prevented papal intervention in ecclesiastical affairs, the clergy acquired a spiritual ascendancy in Spain. Isabel protected their property and privileges from aristocratic usurpation, and the Church was wealthy and possessed an influential voice in temporal affairs. The pope may have had ulterior motives in the concessions he made, for he recognized the political influence and prestige of the Catholic Kings. He needed their support in Italy and granted what he could not well refuse. In 1494 Alexander VI conferred on them their proud title of "The Catholic Kings," both as a reward for past services and as an inducement to support him against Charles VIII in Italy. As a skillful diplomat Ferdinand also exalted the papal authority when it was politically useful. Moreover, the Catholic Kings rendered great service to the Church by reforming the monasteries, restraining immorality in the clergy, and stimulating priests to active zeal.

Ferdinand and Isabel also used the Church to unify Spain racially and religiously. They revived the crusade in the war against Granada, which accentuated the intolerance of the Spanish spirit. Although in the past they had tolerated the Moslems, they later expelled those who rejected the Christian faith. The basis of expulsion was more than religious, for the unconverted Moslems maintained relations with their coreligionaries in North Africa and offered a constant threat to the security of the Mediterranean coast of Spain. However unjust and cruel the expulsion may have been, there were sound reasons for it.

A useful instrument for the unification of the nation was available in the revived Inquisition. The popular hostility which had risen in Castile against the Jews had produced attacks on them despite the royal protection they had enjoyed. The Church had condemned them, and some of the clergy were uncompromising in their attitude toward them. The Catholic Kings wished to unify Spain and remove all threats to national security and internal peace. Isabel, as a devout Catholic, did not believe that Christians could coexist with persons of another faith without grave danger of contamination. In addition, many of the converted Jews had attained political and economic influence in Spain and aroused the envy of others less fortunate.

The first measures against the Jews were taken at the Cortes of Madrigal (1476) and the Cortes of Toledo (1480). A bull of Sixtus IV in 1484 revived and confirmed the old restrictions on their dress and relations with the Christians, but since the Jews had some influence and played an important role in the supply of the army they continued to enjoy many privileges and a certain amount of royal protection. When Granada was finally conquered a decree for the expulsion of the unconverted Jews from Castile and Aragon was promulgated under penalty of death and the confiscation of all their property. They were given three months in which to arrange their affairs. All who rejected the Christian faith began their exodus. Some went to Portugal and Navarre from Castile, only to be expelled from Portugal in 1496 and from Navarre in 1508, as the rigorous policy pursued them. They also migrated to Italy and North Africa. It has been estimated that 165,000 Jews emigrated, 50,000 were baptized, and 20,000 died.

The expulsion of the Jews, including many scientists and literary men of value to the national culture, did not solve the problem. The converted Jews avoided the restrictions and prospered in Spain. Some of them became sincere Catholics and even attained high ecclesiastical office. Fray Hernando de Talavera, Isabel's confessor and later archbishop, was reputed to be of Jewish blood. Others continued to practice Judaism secretly, and this apostasy was viewed by zealous Catholics as a threat to the unity of Spain and the purity of its faith. The discovery of heresy and religious crimes increased the popular prejudice, stimulated, no doubt, by members of the clergy.

A papal bull, issued at the request of the Catholic Kings in 1478 by Sixtus IV, authorized them to name inquisitors to search out heretics. The Spanish Inquisition thus established was an independent, national institution, subject to the Catholic Kings. Isabel was inclined toward clemency and hoped to reclaim those guilty of apostasy, but the Inquisition began to function in Seville two years later, utilizing the traditional procedures and penalties against heresy. Many *conversos* fled, but they were condemned forthwith and their property was confiscated. In the next eight years 700 were executed and 5000 were condemned to prison for life or to other rigorous punishment.

Originally, the Inquisition was directed against apostasy, but it was expanded to include all cases of heresy. The zeal of the inquisitors, fired by a fanatical intolerance, was excessive, and, however carefully the regulations issued in 1488 sought to provide a fair trial, many irresponsible accusations were made and many innocent victims were condemned. Although Archbishop Hernando de Talavera was accused, his influence as confessor to Isabel led to his exoneration. Protests were directed to the Holy See, and Alexander VI censured Torquemada, the first inquisitor general. He was replaced by Fray Diego de Deza in 1498, and Cardinal Cisneros assumed the office in Castile and the bishop of Vich in Aragon in 1507. Under Torquemada, from 1485 to 1498, some 8000 persons are reported to have been condemned to death in Castile, although more restrained estimates indicate that only 2000 were executed between 1480 and 1504.

When the Inquisition was extended to Aragon it was confronted with problems different and more varied than those in Castile. Due to the influence of the *conversos,* outbreaks occurred and there was strong opposition to it in the prosperous, commercial center of Barcelona on the ground that there were no Jews or Moslems there. The Catalans, reluctant to accept Castilian officials and either civil or ecclesiastical authority, delayed the establishment of the Inquisition for three years. Although the number of victims appears to have been smaller in Aragon than in Castile, the persecution did stimulate the extensive migration of Jews from Barcelona.

Abuses in the procedure of the Inquisition arose from the resort to torture to obtain confessions and from the secrecy of the trials. The prisoner was held isolated and was not permitted to know the names of his accusers lest he seek vengeance. When a victim confessed, he was expected to denounce his accomplices. After the trial the sentence was read at an auto-da-fé, usually celebrated with a procession of inquisitorial officials, members of the regular clergy, and the victims. Those condemned either abjured publicly or were turned over to the civil authorities for the execution of the sentences. The Inquisition also established tests of purity of blood as necessary conditions to the exercise of public office or the acceptance of honors. In their zeal for racial and religious unity the Spaniards devised an institution which became a terrible weapon of intolerance and tyranny. Suspicion, cast on the innocent by secret accusations, was often sufficient to condemn the unfortunate, prejudged victims.

The reign of the Catholic Kings was also marked by much economic and social legislation, reflecting the conditions of the era. They were pioneers in dynastic nationalism as they were in imperialism. They wished to assume complete control of the state in economic as well as social affairs, and they evolved policies which later became known as mercantilist, because they had realized that gold was wealth and they endeavored to control the gold supply to their advantage. Some of their measures were unfortunate, but they were trying to amass sufficient capital to assist in the development of Spain from an agricultural to a commercial state. At the same time they were endeavoring to defend both the pastoral system and the agricultural system of large estates. The prosperity of one system was not possible without the ruin of the other. In fact, Ferdinand and Isabel were trying to make a poor country prosperous, and they used the precedents that were available.

The grandees possessed most of the land, though the Castilian meseta offered little opportunity in agriculture for wealth except in the raising of sheep. Labor in the fields was regarded with contempt because of the low status of the agricultural workers, who were regarded as social outcasts and political nonentities. The northern ports exported wool to Flanders and woolen textiles constituted the only industry of any importance in Castile. Consequently, the Catholic Kings stimulated sheep-raising by increasing the privileges of the *Mesta* and placing a royal delegate over the Council of the *Mesta* (1500). This guild of sheep-herders, although closely regulated by the crown, was near enough to the throne to gain favor. It rapidly became a political force, strong enough to defend itself against the hostility of both the aristocracy and the townsmen. In turn, the crown was rewarded with increased revenue from the *montazgo,* or tax paid by the *Mesta.* The result was catastrophic for agriculture, which continued to decay. The expulsion of the Moors, who were one of the most industrious and enterprising elements of the population, assisted in depopulating many rural areas.

Famine appeared in Castile and Andalusia, caused by the plague, floods, and poor harvests. The Catholic Kings tried to regulate the price of grain, but renewed droughts defeated their efforts and Ferdinand was forced to authorize the import of foreign wheat. Yet in 1509 a magnificent harvest so reduced the price of grain that many merchants and farmers were ruined. Throughout the reign fields were left uncultivated, and only the fertile, well-watered areas, such as Andalusia, provided agricultural products for export. Most of Castile, situated on the dry meseta, defied the most favorable combinations of climate and labor to make it productive. There was also a scarcity of labor in the agricultural areas, since, after 1480, the serfs were granted the right to migrate, and many of them sought more respected work in the cities. Ferdinand and Isabel also tried to stimulate agricultural production and the distribution of agricultural products, but the nobility was too strongly entrenched to permit the improvement of the oppressed status of the peasantry.

In industry Ferdinand and Isabel tried to stimulate old industries and create new ones by avoiding foreign competition. The import of certain manufactures, such as silks, and the export of raw materials needed for the national industries were prohibited. On the other hand, the export of iron, leather, salt, wine, and oil was encouraged, and an effort was made to stimulate the textile industry, which failed, for Spanish textiles could not compete in the foreign market either in price or quality. The immigration of skilled, foreign labor was encouraged by granting the laborers tax exemptions. The guild system was fostered to ensure quality and facilitate state control. Despite the odds—poor communications, the scarcity of skilled labor, and the lack of capital—appreciable results were obtained. Seville manufactured ceramics, tiles, arms, silver work, leather, silks, and velvet; Toledo produced silks, ceramics, hats, and arms; Saragossa, Valencia, and Barcelona made glass; Granada was a center of silk; and inferior textiles were produced in many centers.

In commerce the protective policy found expression in dubious mercantilist measures. The exportation of merchandise in foreign ships was prohibited whenever space was available in Spanish ships. Consulates, modeled after the Catalan offices in the Mediterranean, were established in many places to stimulate and regulate Spanish commerce. They were also established in Burgos (1493) and Bilbao (1511) to regulate the export of wool and cloth. Actually, until the trade with the New World developed, the northward shift of commercial gravity, combined with piracy, the decay of Catalan industry, and foreign competition, caused a decline in the Mediterranean trade. Barcelona, Valencia, and Mallorca especially felt this.

The scarcity of capital in Spain attracted many foreigners to the coastal towns. Germans, Flemings, Genoese, Florentines, and Frenchmen founded banks and mercantile enterprises in Spain. Their activity soon aroused protests. In 1515 the cortes requested that foreigners not be permitted to conduct business in Spain for more than a year. Ferdinand declared that they were indispensable, even though they had already been subjected to certain restrictions to avoid the exportation of money.

The unification of Spain territorially favored internal commerce, as it suppressed customs barriers, expanded the potential market, and maintained its security by eliminating the anarchy which had prevailed during the fifteenth century. The era of Ferdinand and Isabel was a period of transition from a national to an imperial economy. While the effects of the discovery and conquest of the New World were not yet evident, the way was prepared for imperial regulation and control in the establishment of the *Casa de Contratación* at Seville (1503).

Despite the anarchy during the reigns of Henry IV of Castile and John II of Aragon, Spanish culture had developed and under the stimulus of new foreign influences, it was further advanced under the Catholic Kings. They not only had literary interests of their own, but they also encouraged cultural growth through purposeful, governmental policy. Prince Juan was carefully educated as the heir to the throne, and Ferdinand and Isabel also tried to improve the educational opportunities for the younger nobility. Peter Martyr and Lucio Marineo Siculo were persuaded to migrate to Spain from Italy, where they had acquired scholarly reputations, and introduce liberal scholarship. Spanish scholars resident in Italy, such as Nebrija, were encouraged to return to their native land.

To encourage literary endeavor, all books imported into Spain were exempt from duty. Printing, which popularized books and expanded the reading public, was introduced into Spain some twenty years after its invention, either in Saragossa in 1473 or in Valencia in 1474. Within a few years printers in Seville, Salamanca, Toledo, Burgos, and nearly all of the important cities were publishing books by native authors, and the revival of the classics was being hastened by the publication of translations.

Colleges and monastic schools, some of which became universities, were founded in Castile, and centers of liberal studies were created through the private initiative of the clergy. Although neither Ferdinand nor Isabel founded an educational institution, Isabel took a special interest in the college founded at Ávila. The University of Salamanca won distinction by the learned men on its faculty, and foreigners as well as natives were attracted to it until its student body increased to 7000.

Cardinal Cisneros created the greatest institution of the period in the University of Alcalá, established in 1508. He desired to have a center dedicated to the humanistic studies, the classical languages, Hebrew, and philology. Scholasticism was strongly entrenched at the older institutions, and the new studies were not well received by them. Some twenty-two professorships were established at Alcalá in the ancient languages, rhetoric, and philosophy. Many foreigners and the best Spanish humanists gathered there, and under the cardinal's direction the Polyglot Bible was undertaken in 1502. Edited by nine scholars, it was a monumental work in Hebrew, Greek, Aramaic, and Latin, which was not completed until 1517.

There was less activity in the Aragonese universities than in those of Castile. The University of Barcelona, founded in 1450, did not develop into a true seat of learning until Ferdinand expanded its privileges in 1491, when it became more active. An institute of liberal studies at Valencia was encouraged by papal approval in 1500.

Many Spaniards went abroad in search of a classical education, especially to Italy. Some of these became patrons of literature. In general, Italians were scornful of Spanish culture, for education continued to be an aristocratic privilege in Spain and the mass of the people remained illiterate.

A literary renaissance continued in Spain with an emphasis on the classics. Ferdinand and Isabel did not initiate the movement, for it had already started in the courts of John II of Castile and Alfonso V of Naples. John II was a poet, scholar, and something of a musician, who honored the men of letters visiting his court, and Alfonso V's conquest of Naples facilitated the transmission of the humanistic spirit to the peninsula. As the Italian influence in literature and art increased, that of France became weaker.

Among the poets who cultivated and imitated the classic writers was Juan de Mena (1411–56). His allegorical poem *El Labarinto* made him the national poet of the court. He tried by his poetic works to improve the literary language, which he hoped to make more refined than the vernacular. He combined the familiar poetry of the *cancioneros* with allegorical tendencies and produced his most significant works, such as *Laberinto de Fortuna,* in this style. The marquis of Santillana (1398–1458) was not only a warrior and prominent politician, but also a typical representative of the early Renaissance in Spain. A humanist who created a splendid library, he subsidized the translation of the *Iliad,* the *Aeneid,* and the tragedies of Seneca and was both a literary critic and a poet. His verse was influenced by Italian as well as French and Catalan poetry.

Satire flourished in the *Coplas de Mingo Revulgo,* of which Henry IV and his favorite, Beltrán de la Cueva, were the subjects. A moral tone in these severe and elegant verses also set forth precepts for good government.

Most of the best poetry before the era of the Catholic Kings consisted of the numerous romances inspired by the frontier struggle with Granada. Gómez Manrique (1412?–90?) and his nephew, Jorge Manrique (1440–79), are the two outstanding poets of the court of Henry IV. The former, a nephew of the marquis of Santillana and primarily a politician, was always modest concerning his literary accomplishments. A great part of his work was court poetry, demonstrating technical facility but lacking in poetic substance. Jorge Manrique composed a short *cancionero* of amorous poetry and also wrote burlesque poetry, following the allegorical tendencies of his age. His reputation rests principally on his *Coplas por la muerte de su padre Don Rodrigo,* one of the most beautiful compositions in Spanish literature.

Two important chroniclers were contemporaries of Henry IV. Alonso de Padilla (1423–92), a publicist, rallied to the support of the Catholic Kings and violently attacked Henry IV in his *Crónica de Enrique IV.* Diego Enrique del Castillo (1433–1504?) was chaplain and adviser to Henry IV and faithful to his patron. His *Crónica del Rey don Enrique IV* demonstrates his allegiance.

During the era of the Catholic Kings Spanish literature evolved from the medieval and became more abundant. It was marked by the complete triumph of humanism and the Italian influence and revealed the victory of Castilian as a literary language, cultivated even by Catalan, Aragonese, and Valencian poets. Interest in the older romances also continued, popular themes were imitated and rephrased, and old forms were adapted. Former models, springing from the national spirit, were cast aside with the old techniques, which began to appear archaic and vulgar. As literature became more artistic and refined, more studied and artificial, it also grew less intelligible to the people. The new art was accessible only to the initiates, chiefly noble dilettantes and those patronized by them.

One of the principal interests was the translation and imitation of classic authors. Antonio de Nebrija, probably the greatest of the Spanish humanists, taught at Salamanca and Seville, and as a protégé of Cardinal Cisneros assisted in the work on the Polyglot Bible. He had an encyclopedic knowledge of the Scriptures, linguistics, and science and translated a number of the classic authors. Hernán Núñez de Toledo (1475?–1553), another humanist of distinction and a famous Greek scholar, also worked on the Polyglot Bible. He taught rhetoric at the University of Alcalá and Greek at Salamanca and was best known for his critical texts of classic authors.

In poetry new techniques were used in the adaptation of the Castilian romances to new forms. Although the greater part of it was still allegorical and moral, novelty appeared in the spirit of the poetry, where the popular was often combined with the erudite. Musical techniques were improved and popular Castilian songs were adapted from the lyric poetry. Juan de Padilla (1468–1522?) wrote one of the last allegorical poems—*Laberinto del Marqués de Cádiz.* In other works he was more realistic, but he never challenged the Dantesque expression of Juan de Mena. Many erotic lyrics were collected in the *cancioneros* of the period. The old regional poetry continued to flourish in both Catalonia and Valencia, but with less vigor than in the middle of the fifteenth century. Valencia was the principal center of poetry in Catalan and of a bilingual literature. Castilian poetry flourished also in Naples and even in Rome in the colony of Spaniards gathered there under the patronage of Alexander VI.

The prose of the era of the Catholic Kings escaped the artificial trends popular in the poetry. History, especially, became more personal and literary. The authors followed classic models and their work lost some of its naive charm, but they were inspired by the heroic character of the age. Among the outstanding historians were Andrés Bernaldez (d. 1513), chaplain of the archbishop of Seville. He followed the example of the Castilian chroniclers in his *Historia de los Reyes Católicos don Fernando y doña Isabel.* Hernando de Pulgar (1430?–93?), secretary and ambassador for the Catholic Kings, enjoyed extraordinary prestige at court and composed his chronicle in imitation of Livy, placing long discourses in the mouths of his characters to give his work a literary and dramatic touch. His *Claros varones de Castilla* was his most important work. Diego de Valera (1412–86), a political adventurer, wrote a *Crónica de los Reyes Católicos,* other chronicles, and many letters. Christopher Columbus also wrote letters and a memoir of his voyages in a simple but dramatic fashion.

Diego de San Pedro published two sentimental novels in prose. The second, *Cárcel de Amor* (1492), had a great vogue, with thirty editions in Spanish and twenty in foreign languages. A vague and expansive novel, with chivalric characters inspired by Dante and Boccaccio, it had many imitators. In 1508 the four books of the *Amadis de Gaula* were published in Saragossa. Rodriguez de Montalvo confessed to having adapted the first three volumes and of being the author of the fourth. This famous book had been popular in Portugal earlier. The knightly society of the fifteenth and sixteenth centuries delighted in the love story and marvelous adventures of Amadis.

Although the old mysteries connected with religious festivals were continued, they developed more dramatic techniques with the gradual introduction of new forms of dramatic dialogue and prepared the way for the later drama. Juan del Encina (1468–1529) was the first writer of Spanish comedy. He wrote various religious and secular works, which were presented in private houses for the entertainment of the nobility. His comedies combined medieval and renaissance characteristics and succeeded in secularizing the medieval mysteries.

The most authentic dramatic masterpiece of the period was *La Tragicomedia de Calixto y Melibea,* popularly known as *La Celestina,* first published in 1499. Fernando de Rojas (1475?–1537?) is reputed to be the author of the later acts. The first act was written by Rodrigo Cota or Juan de Mena. The authors who contributed to this drama created a classic which was also an immediate success. Bartolomé Torres Naharro (?–1524?) was the best Spanish imitator of the Italian comedy of manners, reproducing the atmosphere of Spanish society in Italy.

As Spanish culture flowered, the interest in philosophy and the natural sciences was likewise stimulated. Juan Luis Vives (1492–1540), the great philosopher of the Spanish Renaissance, was a friend of Adrian of Utrecht and Erasmus, a reader to Catherine of Aragon in England, and a tutor of the Princess Mary. A Platonic philosopher and an adversary of scholasticism, he represented in his criticism of the prevailing philosophic trend the spirit of the age and foreshadowed conclusions of later philosophers. In many respects, like his friend Erasmus, he was ahead of his time.

Francisco López de Villalobos (1473?–1549), one of the most important figures in medicine, enjoyed great favor at court. He was something of a medical genius, writing *El Sumario de la medicina* (1498), as well as a humanist, translating and commenting on various classical authors. Julian Gutiérrez de Toledo also served as physician to the Catholic Kings and wrote medical treatises. The work of these royal physicians indicates the progress of medicine during the era. In 1483 Ferdinand approved dissections of cadavers to improve the study of anatomy, and seven years later, Antonio Amiguet established a school of surgery in Barcelona. Physicians were required to undergo examinations, and many hospitals and asylums were founded.

Nautical and geographical studies were much stimulated by the establishment of the *Casa de Contratación*. Juan de la Cosa published maps and geographical and mathematical treatises, and marine currents and the deviations of the magnetic needle were studied as a basis for the modification of nautical instruments and the determination of longitude from a definite point.

A classical revival in Spanish art, springing from the same Italian influence that prevailed in literature, was strengthened by political contacts between the peninsulas. Italian art was imported, and many Spanish artists made pilgrimages to Italy, while aristocratic patrons encouraged Italian artists to come to Spain. The Spanish grandees, fired with the zeal of the classic revival, tried to reflect in their own houses the artistic atmosphere with which they had come in contact in Italy. They also sought to emulate the luxury of the Burgundian court. The age of Ferdinand and Isabel was a period of artistic transition, in which the northern influence from France and Germany mixed with the classical influence from Italy.

In architecture the fusion of the Gothic and Renaissance techniques is best revealed in the plateresque style, so-called because of the exuberant decoration characteristic of the later fifteenth and early sixteenth centuries. It was marked by a free and varied combination of Gothic with classical elements in the adornment of buildings. A third influence, the Isabelline style, coincided with the attainment of unity after the conquest of Granada and flourished from 1475 to 1525. It was marked by a happy combination of German and Moslem influences. The pure Moorish style, which triumphed in the Alhambra, the royal residence in Granada, passed to Andalusia from Granada and was also stimulated at Toledo by the *Mudejares.*

Many northern architects came to Spain. Hans of Cologne, for example, brought German art to Burgos. His son Simón fell under the influence of Moslem architecture and in a sense nationalized it. A sculptor as well as an architect, he composed many beautiful façades. His school at Burgos was influential throughout Castile. The cathedral at Astorga was supervised by Juan Gil Hontañón, who was succeeded by his son, Rodrigo Gil Hontañón, and by Juan de Álava. In New Castile Juan Guas, a native of Lyons, became the leading architect of the Isabelline style, his most popular and expressive monument being the Franciscan church of San Juan de los Reyes, founded by Ferdinand and Isabel at Toledo. Enrique Egás combined the plateresque with Isabelline architecture in the hospital of Santa Cruz in Toledo.

The earliest examples of Renaissance architecture in Spain were foreign in both form and spirit. Lorenzo Vásquez of Segovia built the first important Renaissance building, the College of Santa Cruz in Valladolid, between 1487 and 1491. Vásquez adapted elements of classical style to the Gothic with great originality. Although the plateresque was the first version of Italian architecture in Spain, the Isabelline style had already prepared the way for it. The architects who developed it were more interested in ornamentation than in resolving complicated problems of construction and succeeded in combining the grandeur of the Gothic with the classical Renaissance style. One of the most skilled designers in combining classical with Gothic ornamentation was Francisco of Cologne, Simón's son, who was born at Burgos about 1470, and who was both decorator and architect. Juan de Alava, who built the cathedral of Palencia, also adopted the plateresque style. Rodrigo Gil Hontañón became the most representative architect working in it and produced some of its most expressive monuments.

The Isabelline and Renaissance styles were also combined to form the Cisneros style, a national type which blended Gothic, *Mudejar,* and Renaissance elements. The best example of it, the cathedral at Toledo, was built under the direction of Enrique Egás between 1504 and 1512. This style spread throughout Castile from Toledo. Gradually, the classical replaced the earlier styles, largely as the result of the influence of Lorenzo Vásquez and Alonso de Covarrubias (1488–1570).

Varying influences were also evident in sculpture, especially Italian, Gothic, and Moorish. The best sculpture of the period is found in the retablos, or altar decorations, and in the funerary statuary. As in earlier times, the most persistent foreign influences originated in Burgundy and Italy, whose artists and sculptors were brought to Spain by Spanish patrons.

In painting the Italian Renaissance had increasing influence. As a bountiful patron of painting and the plastic arts, Isabel merely reflected the devotion to art shared by some of her subjects. Spanish artists followed Italian models more and more, even though many painters also came to Spain from northern Europe. Much of the art was religious in character, such as the murals and frescoes in chapels, but many finely illustrated codices of a secular nature were also produced.

Fernando Gallegos, who adopted the Flemish style, was the principal leader of a school of painting at Salamanca, and in a rival school at Seville, Bartolomé Bermejo also spread Flemish methods. He was a talented disciple of Jan van Eyck, whose work was greatly admired during his visit to Valencia. Bermejo, who worked in a naturalistic but thoroughly Spanish style, became the most influential artist in Aragon, where Jaime Huguet and the Vergós family were also notable contemporary painters. Another artist typically Flemish in technique was the Cordovan painter Alejo Fernández Alemán.

Italian influence was more evident in Valencia, to which Paul di San Leocadio, a Lombard, and Francisco Pagano, a Neapolitan, were induced to migrate by Cardinal Rodrigo Borgia, while he was archbishop of Valencia. Rodrigo de Osuna, a third protégé of the cardinal active in Valencia, was completely Italian in style. Hernando Yañez de la Almedina, who worked in Cuenca, has been regarded by some critics as the greatest artist of the Spanish Renaissance. He had studied with Leonardo da Vinci.

The northern influence in Castile was stimulated in the middle of the fifteenth century by Jorge Inglés, but the dominant artist in the Castilian school was Pedro González Berruguete (1450–1508?). Although he first painted murals in Toledo, most of his surviving work is in the cathedral at Ávila. Juan of Burgundy, a student of Ghirlandajo, and the artist most responsible for popularizing the Italian style in Castile, worked principally at the cathedral of Toledo, but he also collaborated with other artists in the decoration of the University of Alcalá. Later, he founded a school at Salamanca. He painted twelve pictures for the cathedral at Palencia. Isabel was his special patron.

Music enjoyed great favor at the Castilian court, and many poets composed music for their lyrics. Popular music was based on the romances, in the longer of which the melody was repeated incessantly, with enough variation to prevent its becoming monotonous. The guitar became the most popular Spanish instrument, as it was easily adapted to the variations of popular music and the regional characteristics.

The age of the Catholic Kings was an era of ferment in Spain. Traveling into all parts of the nation and interested in every phase of national activity, they laid the foundations for Spanish domination in Europe. By the end of their reign Spain had already emerged as the principal dynastic monarchy in Europe, with an empire which included dominions in both the Mediterranean and the New World. The union of Castile and Aragon joined two currents of varying orientation and produced a dynamic nationalism equally enthusiastic for the achievements of a Columbus or a Gonzalo de Córdoba.

CHAPTER XIII

The Reign of Charles V

The sixteenth century was literally the "golden age" of Spain. For the Spanish monarchs used the gold from the New World to build the greatest army of Europe; and that army enabled them to dominate European political affairs. Under Charles V the Spanish forces earned the respect of other nations. They defended western Christendom against the Turks, fought the German Protestants to a draw, and checked the territorial ambitions of the French. Charles's son, Philip II, used Spanish wealth and military power to make his kingdom supreme in Europe.

Nevertheless, Philip's policies paved the way for the decline of Spain. He mismanaged the nation's finances, so that he left Spain heavily in debt. He overburdened his subjects with an inefficient bureaucracy, and he stifled individual enterprise. His long and wasteful wars against the Netherlands and England injured Spanish prestige abroad. Since Philip's successors had neither the ability nor the means to handle this situation, Spain steadily lost in power and reputation. The seventeenth century was to belong not to Spain, but to France.

During the reign of the grandson of Ferdinand and Isabel a transformation took place in the attitude of the Spanish people toward political affairs. Once they had been primarily interested in the peninsula, but now they were drawn into the vortex of world politics. They had reluctantly begun to think in national concepts and they were now burdened with imperial affairs. Although they were at first suspicious of their young sovereign and his foreign advisers, it was not long before they became proud of his leadership in world affairs. They opposed his coronation as Holy Roman Emperor, but they took delight in the empire he consolidated. While the power of Castile greatly increased from the extension of Spanish authority in the New World, the policy of Aragon in the Mediterranean was sustained in the struggle with their most persistent enemies, the French. However much the expansive policies and imperial problems of Charles V drained Spanish resources, they also aroused Spanish pride and a national and imperial consciousness.

Charles V (1516–56) was born in Ghent, on February 23, 1500, the son of Princess Juana and the Archduke Philip. He was recognized as the heir to the Castilian crown after the death of Isabel (1504) and the official acknowledgment of the increasing neuroticism of his mother. Ferdinand V became regent on the death of Philip I and, despite his proposal that his grandson be educated in Castile—to prepare him better for the responsibilities he would assume—Charles was brought up in Flanders. His brother, Ferdinand, born in 1503, was really the favorite of his grandfather, but the aging king, however wavering his intent, finally named Charles as his successor in Aragon. In Flanders, Charles was reared by his aunt, Margaret of Austria, and his tutor, Adrian Dedel, a native of Utrecht and dean of Louvain. His chancellor and preceptor in political affairs was William of Croy, lord of Chievres, a statesman of great administrative capacity and some prestige among Flemings.

Francisco Ximenes de Cisneros, confessor of Isabel in 1494 and later archbishop of Toledo and cardinal, was named regent of Castile, León, Granada, and Navarre by Ferdinand in his last testament in 1516. Ferdinand had no real authority to name his successor in Castile, except that which arose from the incapacity of Juana, but the Council and the grandees confirmed Cardinal Cisneros as regent for the second time. He had previously served in that position at the death of Philip I.

Some difficulties arose when both Adrian of Utrecht and the supporters of the young Prince Ferdinand wanted to control the regency, but Charles tactfully confirmed the cardinal and named Adrian of Utrecht as his representative in Spain. Adrian soon complained of the omnipotence of the austere cardinal, and William of Croy tried to strengthen the Flemish party at the Spanish court. The Flemings continued to intrigue, but the firmness of the cardinal foiled their plots.

Although it was desirable for Charles to proceed to his Spanish domains, he had pressing problems in the Netherlands, including the task of restoring good relations with France. In 1515 he and Francis I concluded the Treaty of Noyon, which settled problems relating to Naples and betrothed Charles to Francis' daughter Louise. Spanish leaders wanted him to come to Spain as soon as possible, for it was important that he gain an understanding of the people he was to rule. His father had always been a foreigner in Spain, suspected by Spaniards and suspicious of them. The only men who had supported Philip I were ambitious Castilian grandees, who hoped to satisfy their cupidity by condoning Philip's extravagance and resented the strong hand of Ferdinand. Some of them remained in the Flemish court, where they tried to turn Charles against his grandfather. After the death of Ferdinand other Spaniards went to Flanders to try to turn the alien Fleming into a loyal Spaniard and derive what profit they could from the situation.

The cardinal had long hoped to create a permanent army, and he now arranged for the cities of Castile to raise, equip, and drill military forces in proportion to their population. He hoped they would always be ready to serve the king. In time of peace the towns bore the cost, but when the troops were brought into royal service in time of war, the crown bore it. Two facts caused the abandonment of the plan. The nobles were jealous of their military prerogatives, and the cities opposed any increase in taxation and feared any threat to their cherished *fueros*. Cardinal Cisneros had been granted broad authority by Charles, and he worked in the public interest, proving to be an excellent financial administrator, removing many unworthy officials, and thwarting all conspiracies formed against him.

Cisneros did not wish to proclaim Charles as king because he believed this would be premature and even illegal while Juana was alive, but he finally obeyed the royal order. Prince Ferdinand proved to be a danger in the hands of the intriguing grandees, but the cardinal dismissed those who became too ambitious and sent Ferdinand to Flanders. Alonso of Aragon, a natural son of Ferdinand V, also caused some anxiety. He had been entrusted with the government of Aragon and hoped to proclaim his nephew Ferdinand king. Such a step would have separated Castile and Aragon, and Cisneros patriotically discouraged it. Two other areas demanded the vigilance of the regent. He had to be constantly alert for a threat from Portugal or an attack on the Italian dominions by Pedro de Navarro, the renegade Spanish general who had deserted to the French. Cisneros staunchly defended the integrity of the dominions which had been entrusted to him. In general, he adopted a policy later followed by Charles V, for he was suspicious of the French, and cultivated English friendship to counteract Francis I.

The cardinal still hoped to build a colonial empire in North Africa. After Haruc Barbarossa, the Berber corsair, captured Algiers (1516), Cisneros defended Bugía against him and sent an expedition to the relief of the Rock of Algiers. It was disastrously defeated, and as the strength of Barbarossa increased, the cardinal sent assistance to his opponents. Meanwhile, in the New World, the humane efforts of Father Bartholomé de las Casas to protect the Indians against the *encomen-*

deros raised a serious problem which the cardinal tried to solve by sending a group of Jeronimite friars to investigate.

Although Sicily, ruled by Hugo de Moncada as viceroy, was outside the jurisdiction of Cardinal Cisneros, he was nevertheless concerned with a revolt in Palermo, provoked by Hugo's avarice, cruelty, and extravagance. The viceroy was expelled, and after a period of anarchy the aristocracy established a provisional government. In appointing the unpopular count of Monteleone as an official, Hugo stimulated the townsmen to a second revolt. Again the aristocracy restored order. Charles V learned from this experience that a disaffected nobility could be a menace, but a loyal nobility a bulwark of great strength against a popular revolution.

The eighty-one-year-old cardinal was most anxious to have Charles come to Spain and tried to hasten the journey, which was finally undertaken in the fall of 1517, just as Cisneros became ill at the convent of Aguilera. At the instigation of Flemish rivals of the cardinal, Charles sent him a cold letter, expressing appreciation for his services and relieving him of his responsibility, but Cisneros died without learning its contents. When Charles went to Tordesillas to see his mother, it was in reality to improve his own interests rather than because of filial affection.

At sixteen Charles was not a prepossessing figure. He was of medium height, well proportioned, but still adolescently thin. His eyes bulged and his protruding lower jaw, a typical Habsburg feature, caused his mouth to hang open and gave him the appearance of an imbecile. He was unable to chew his food properly and digestive disorders gave him an unhealthy pallor. His speech was hesitant, broken by continual stammering; he was so ill-educated that he was reserved and withdrawn; and he had no real intimates. Many observers concluded that he was a nonentity. In fact, he had a decided will of his own and in time demonstrated ambition, ability, and independence of judgment.

Charles I took his oath at the Cortes of Valladolid (1518), but the grandees soon found reason for displeasure with him. Those who had joined his court in Flanders, with a host of Flemish advisers and favorites, accompanied him to Spain. Young and inexperienced, he lacked firmness in managing them. He was not only surrounded by ambitious foreigners, but was unfamiliar with the Castilian language. It was soon rumored that he had inherited the malady of his mother. He chose his principal counselors from among his old associates. He named the lord of Chievres senior accountant of Castile, Jean de Sauvage, another Fleming, grand chancellor, and Adrian of Utrecht archbishop of Toledo.

The appetite of the Flemings for high office appeared insatiable, and they obtained appointments in spite of the petitions of municipal representatives, requesting that places be withheld from foreigners.

The Flemings, who tried to appear antagonistic among themselves, skillfully played on the dissensions among the Spaniards. William of Croy became leader of the adherents of Ferdinand V, while Jean de Sauvage gained control of the former partisans of Philip I. The Flemings were alarmed by the popularity of Prince Ferdinand among the Spaniards. He was suddenly relieved of his Spanish servants and sent to the Netherlands with a Flemish retinue before the news of his departure was released in Spain. Jean de Sauvage died and was replaced as chancellor by Mercurino de Gattinara, a former Burgundian official of Italian birth and great ability.

In 1519 Charles I was advised of the death of his grandfather, Maximilian I, which raised an immediate question of the imperial succession. The Flemings wanted Charles to succeed to the imperial throne, while the Spaniards in general opposed this. Charles was attracted by the glamor of the position as well as by the opportunity it offered of increasing his resources for the defense of Europe against the advancing Turks. William of Croy directed the campaign for the imperial crown against Francis I and Henry VIII. It was an expensive project. Pope Leo X opposed the candidacies of both Francis I and Charles, as a threat to the independence of the Holy See. Finally, after the duke of Saxony had declined it, the seven electors unanimously offered the crown to Charles. It has been estimated that the diadem cost Charles V 100,000 gold florins, borrowed from the Fuggers of Augsburg.

The rising discontent in Spain was revealed at the Cortes of Santiago, when Charles asked for new subsidies. The 200,000 ducats a year for three years voted by the Cortes of Valladolid had not yet been collected. William of Croy had increased the taxes and tried to impose them on the previously exempt grandees. He had also obtained papal approval of the payment of a tenth of the income of the clergy to the king for three years. The Flemings were collecting coin and jewels to send to the Netherlands, and money was becoming scarce. Toledo took the lead in protesting the financial exactions, and its residents rose to the cry of "Long live the King and death to his evil counsellors," as Charles passed through the city. He and William of Croy were forced to flee to Tordesillas.

At Santiago Charles requested 400,000 ducats for the expenses of his imperial coronation. Many petitions were presented, demanding that the king should marry, that he should not leave the kingdom or permit gold and silver to be exported, and that he should not name foreigners to office. By intimidation and bribery, William of Croy broke the resistance of the representatives, but, because of the hostile atmosphere in Santiago, the cortes moved to La Coruña, where the subsidy was approved. Then Charles V made a fatal mistake. He named his old tutor, Cardinal Adrian of Utrecht, a kindly but weak man, as governor of the kingdom of Castile; Juan de Lanuza, former ambassador to Flanders, as captain-general of Aragon; and Diego de Mendoza as viceroy of Valencia. This accomplished, he embarked for his coronation in Germany in 1520.

The departure of Charles V lighted the fire of revolt. His imperial policy, his favors to foreigners, the greed of the Flemings, and his subordination of Spanish to international interests were more than the peninsular-minded Spaniards could endure. The general discontent was directed against the unfortunate representatives who had opposed the subsidy. In Segovia the people rose and hanged Rodrigo de Tordesillas. The Royal Council sent the hated Rodrigo Ronquillo, who was both just and severe, to Segovia to punish the rebels. When he was denied admission, he established himself in Santa Maria de Nieva and attacked the city, hanging all the citizens he could arrest. Juan Bravo assumed the leadership of the rebels at Segovia and in July, 1520, notified the other cities of what had occurred.

Meanwhile, the rebellion had spread to other cities. Zamora had burned its agents in effigy and chosen the restless Bishop Antonio de Acuña as its leader. Burgos deposed its corregidor, and Ávila, Toro, Madrid, Guadalajara, Alcalá, León, Soria, Salamanca, Ciudad Rodrigo, and Cuenca joined the movement. The rebellion followed no social lines, but included persons of every class. On July 29, 1520, the representatives of the cities met at Ávila, constituted themselves a Holy Committee, and chose Pedro Laso de la Vega as president and Juan Padilla as military leader. The complaints of the rebels, or *comuneros,* were simple at first. They asked the king not to appoint foreigners to public office or permit the export of gold and silver, and the mutinous nobles resented the loss of their exemption from taxation. The Junta at Ávila broadened its program to include the regulation of the royal household and its expenses, the nomination of ecclesiastical dignitaries, the amortization of properties of the church and monasteries, and other popular demands.

Juan de Padilla of Toledo and Juan Zapata of Madrid went to the assistance of Segovia and forced Ronquillo to flee to Arévalo. The Council of Regency, under the vacillating and pacific Adrian of Utrecht, determined to suppress the rebellion by force of arms, sent Antonio de

Fonseca to Medina del Campo. Warned by the Toledans, the citizens of Medina, who had hitherto held aloof from the rebellion, attacked the troops as they entered the city and most of it was burned. It was important as a market center and the loss affected the agricultural and commercial classes throughout the area. This unfortunate incident, for which both Fonseca and the Council refused to take responsibility, served to increase the spirit of revolt. Cardinal Adrian of Utrecht recognized the gravity of the situation, but, lest he aggravate the people further, he ordered the dissolution of the royal army.

Charles V had arrived in Germany and was advised of the situation. He called a council composed of Flemings, Germans, Italians, Castilians, and Aragonese. The Flemings accused the Spaniards of infidelity to their king, while the Spaniards blamed the Flemings for their rapacity and bad government. Charles named Adrian, Admiral Fadrique Fadriquez, and Constable Iñigo de Velasco as governors of Castile and ordered the rebels to return to immediate obedience.

After relieving Segovia, Juan Bravo and Padilla had taken Tordesillas and interviewed the queen, who was confined there. She was in command of her senses and listened to the complaints of the *comuneros,* but she, as a virtual prisoner of her son, was unable to do anything about them. The cardinal had already urged her to sign a statement condemning the *comuneros,* but she had refused. In their conference with her the rebel leaders were respectful and were well received, but she would sign none of the documents presented to her. This was the critical point in the revolt. Had she signed the nomination of a delegation of the Junta to keep her informed of its proceedings, she would have publicly signified her adherence to the movement. The admiral and the constable wanted to pacify the rebels by acceding to their petitions, and the wealthy merchants of Burgos urged the *comuneros* to submit. They, in turn, tried to justify their conduct to the emperor.

On the whole, enraged by the nomination of the committee of three governors, the *comuneros* remained firm. After accusing Padilla of inaction they named Pedro Girón to command their troops. Padilla had entered Valladolid and forced Adrian and the members of the Royal Council to flee to Medina de Rioseco. Padilla then retired to Toledo. While the negotiations to induce the rebels to lay down their arms were unsuccessful, the royalists succeeded in taking Tordesillas. Then, the nobles, including Pedro Girón, began to desert the rebel cause. Originally political in character, the movement had now become popular and opposed to the very things for which most of the nobles supported the crown. There were disturbances, jealousy and discord, but Padilla and the bishop of Zamora assembled their troops and entered Valladolid with 2000 Toledans, where Padilla was again named military leader.

In February 1521 Padilla took Ampudia and captured Torrelobatón, but discord appeared in the ranks of the *comuneros*. Men such as Pedro Laso de Vega wanted to negotiate a truce and others like Padilla wanted to force the outcome with arms. Charles issued a decree from Worms, declaring the *comuneros* traitors and naming 249 who were guilty. In the meantime, Bishop Acuña of Zamora had seized the see of Toledo, recently vacated by the death of the archbishop.

Padilla remained inactive in Torrelobatón until April, awaiting reinforcements for the recovery of Tordesillas. The contingents from Zamora, led by Juan Bravo, and from Salamanca, led by Franciso Maldonado, were the only ones to arrive. When the imperial troops appeared the rebels had consumed their supplies. Padilla tried to withdraw to Toro, but his army was pursued by the imperial cavalry. He made a disorganized stand at Villalar and then sought death in battle with the horsemen but was wounded and captured with Bravo and Maldonado. The three leaders were condemned by a summary trial and beheaded the following day. María Pacheco, widow of Padilla and daughter of the count of Tendilla, continued to resist in Toledo, but the city was forced to capitulate in October 1521, and the valiant María fled to Portugal to save her life.

In 1522 Adrian of Utrecht was elected pope and Charles returned to Spain. He disembarked in Santander, accompanied by his Flemish advisers and 4000 German troops. He had granted a general amnesty to the rebels, from which nearly 300 persons had been excluded. Despite appeals for clemency, many were executed and imprisoned. The bishop of Zamora was hanged from the wall of the castle of Salamanca in 1526 for having killed his jailer.

The revolt of the *comuneros* represented a popular protest against the rapacity of the foreigner advisers of Charles which developed into a revolt against the absolute power of the monarch. All classes participated in it: nobles, clergy, and the middle class of the towns. Many nobles probably took advantage of the situation to attain private objectives, but when they were confronted with the imperial threat of treason they deserted. The townsmen, left to suffer the consequences, were so thoroughly suppressed that they were no longer a threat to absolutism.

A rebellion of a somewhat different character had occurred in Valencia and Mallorca. There, the fertility of the soil and the wealth of the landlords had produced profound differences between the aristocratic, wealthy classes and the more numerous class of poor laborers.

Moreover, the absenteeism of the lords, who congregated in the cities to enjoy urban security and pleasures, had produced bitter feeling against them. The laborers were armed and had been organized in Valencia, by authority of Ferdinand, to enable the brotherhoods to resist Turkish and Berber raids on the coast.

In 1519, when an epidemic broke out in Valencia, the authorities and many nobles abandoned the city. The people formed a committee, composed of thirteen artisans, under the leadership of Juan Lorenzo, a carder, and the young but intelligent Guillén Castellvi or Sorolla. They armed themselves under the pretext that they feared a Moslem raid and then declared themselves openly against the nobles. Játiva and Murviedro followed the lead of Valencia, and popular brotherhoods were formed, whence the name of *Germanias,* applied to the revolt. Germs of the rebellion were already latent when Charles went to Germany. He had named Diego Hurtado de Mendoza, count of Mélito, as viceroy of Valencia. The count proved incapable of maintaining order and even provoked the events which followed by his inadequate measures. When the people chose two plebeian juries to investigate complaints the viceroy fled to Játiva and thence to Denia. The nobles rallied there, but other cities organized popular movements. The discontent now flared into open rebellion. Bloody fighting began, and it was not until some 12,000 people had been killed that the revolt was quelled—with the nobility still clinging to their privileges and persisting in their abuses.

The rivalry of Francis I and Charles V is one of the fundamental facts of the sixteenth century. Charles V was the great grandson of Charles the Bold, with a pretension to the Duchy of Burgundy which Louis XI had taken from the House of Habsburg. The French still coveted the Duchy of Milan and the hegemony of Italy. Additional causes for enmity were created by the rivalry of the two sovereigns in Flanders and Artois and for the imperial crown and control of Genoa. Both aspired to exercise their hegemony in Europe and, in the struggle which ensued, the Italian venture of Ferdinand was expanded into a struggle which involved the encirclement of France by the House of Habsburg.

During his trip to receive the imperial crown Charles had disembarked at Dover and held a happy interview with his uncle, Henry VIII. Chievres and Gattinara obtained English acquiescence to the coronation of Charles by promising aid to Cardinal Wolsey in gaining election as pope. In Flanders, Charles assembled the estates and was immediately granted funds for the expenses of the coronation in a reception quite different from that accorded him in Spain. After Henry VIII and Francis I failed to reach an understanding at the Field of the Cloth of

Gold, in June, Charles and Henry conferred in Calais, a month later. Then Charles V was crowned at Aachen in October in a brilliant ceremony.

The Protestant movement had already been inaugurated in Germany by Martin Luther, and Charles was called upon to intervene. He convoked the Diet of Worms to hear Luther and settle other matters of grave importance. It was inevitable that he should oppose the Lutherans. The unity of both Spain and the Empire was based on that of the Catholic world. A threat such as that posed by Luther attenuated the very foundation of his authority; yet, he tried to be judicious and avert an open break. At the Diet of Worms, Charles condemned Luther and a month later ordered the publication of the ban of the empire against him and his adherents. Ferdinand was named lieutenant and vicar general of Charles in Germany. The marriage of his sister to Louis II of Hungary and of Ferdinand to Anna, the sister of Louis, was also arranged. In addition, he was forced to ask for funds to recover the territories in Italy.

Hostilities had already begun with France. Francis I encouraged Henry of Albret, pretender to the throne of Navarre, to invade that kingdom. Robert de la Marck, duke of Bouillon, was protected by the French in his attack on Luxemburg to recover the castle of Aimeries. In their first invasion of Navarre, the French reached Logroño, but were forced to withdraw (1521). In the second expedition, the French captured Fuenterrabia, and the Spaniards were unable immediately to dislodge them. In northern France, Charles V's general, the count of Nassau, occupied the Duchy of Bouillon, capturing Tournai, and invaded Champagne. Francis I and the duke of Alençon attacked Flanders. When in 1522 Charles turned his Austrian dominions of the House of Habsburg over to his brother Ferdinand, the Netherlands were placed within the Spanish orbit, as a Spanish outpost in northern Europe against France.

Meanwhile, the alliance between Charles V, Leo X, and Henry VIII had been concluded. Prospero Colonna led an imperial army into the Duchy of Milan and forced the French under Lautrec to evacuate the city. The French were defeated near Pavia and at Bicocca. The conquest of Milan and the restoration of Parma and Piacenza to the Holy See were followed by the death of Pope Leo X. Pope Adrian VI, despite his former relationship to Charles, remained neutral in the conflict. At this time, Charles was forced to return to Spain by the pressure of the internal situation, but first he held his conference with Henry VIII to strengthen the alliance.

The struggle now became more general. The constable of France, Duke Charles of Bourbon, abandoned the French cause in 1523 and fled to Franche Comté. His marriage was arranged with Eleanor, sister of Charles V. The dismemberment of France was agreed with the duke, who controlled large domains in southern and central France. Henry VIII entered the alliance and revived his pretensions to the ancient Plantagenet possessions in France. Charles V needed resources for the war and convoked the Cortes of Valladolid. After acceding to some eighty petitions of the municipal representatives, he was granted 400,-000 ducats. Death terminated Adrian VI's short tenure of the papacy, and Cardinal Julius de Medici succeeded him as Clement VII. He was opposed to alien domination of Italy and tried to prevent any foreign power from becoming too strong there.

The English invaded France and were within eleven leagues of Paris before they were halted by La Trémouille. The Germans invaded Champagne, where they were checked by the duke of Guise, while the Spanish attack on Béarn was stopped by Lautrec. The French resumed the offensive, intent on recovering Milan. A powerful French army under Admiral Bonnivet invaded Italy and captured the city. In 1524, after a sustained siege, the Spaniards under the admiral of Castile, Iñigo de Velasco, recaptured Fuenterrabia. Then the tide turned against the French. They were defeated in Italy. Charles of Bourbon, the marquis of Pescara and the marquis of Vasto penetrated Provence and besieged Marseilles. The siege was finally raised when the imperial army, short of supplies, had to abandon Toulon and withdraw to Lombardy. Encouraged by this success, Francis I again occupied Milan and besieged Pavia. The imperial army was still short of supplies and money, so short in fact that the imperial leaders pawned their jewels and estates and asked the Spanish soldiers not only to serve without pay but to assist in the payment of the foreign soldiers in the army. Nevertheless, in the battle of Pavia, the flower of French chivalry was killed and Francis I was captured (1525).

Louise of Savoy, regent while Francis I was a prisoner in Madrid, negotiated for the release of the royal prisoner. Charles V was firm. Francis I fell ill and was forced to sign the Treaty of Madrid (1526), by which he renounced Naples, Milan and Genoa and agreed to restore the estates of Charles of Bourbon. He agreed to marry Eleanor, sister of Charles and widow of Manuel of Portugal. Although he left his two eldest sons as hostages, Francis I declared the treaty void as soon as he was released, because it had been forced upon him while a prisoner.

The pressure of other problems had meanwhile demanded the attention of Charles V. He had not only been confronted with popular rebellions in two parts of his dominions, but the threats of the Protestants in Germany and the Turks in Hungary and the Mediterranean were increasing. While the peasants, encouraged by the preaching of Martin Luther, sought the alleviation of their abuses in Germany, the Moriscos also rebelled in the kingdom of Valencia. The emperor had ordered that they should be baptized, but the lords had secretly urged them to remain faithful to their religion, as they would thus be more content with servitude. Many of them fled to the mountains around Segorbe, and it was necessary to subjugate them in Valencia, Aragon, and Granada by force of arms.

As soon as he was released, Francis I began to search for allies. He found them in Henry VIII and Clement VII, both of whom feared the increasing power of Charles V. The Holy League was formed in 1526, including Milan, Venice, Genoa, and the Swiss. Charles, as usual, was short of funds. In 1527 he convoked the Cortes of Valladolid. The nobles declared that they would assist him with arms but not with money, since they considered themselves exempt from taxation. The cities were unable to vote new subsidies because they had not yet paid for the royal wedding of Charles to Isabel of Portugal. Ferdinand collected troops in Germany and Charles of Bourbon, who had been invested with the Duchy of Milan, led troops to Italy from Spain. His army was composed of a heterogeneous body of mercenaries who devastated the countryside. They had not been paid and Charles of Bourbon had no money to pay them. When the Lutheran commander, George Freundsberg, was suddenly stricken with paralysis, the soldiers mutinied and marched on Rome. The Italians were unable to stop them and the constable was killed in the assault on the city. The imperial soldiers, leaderless and uncontrolled, sacked Rome, forcing Clement VII to seek refuge in the Castle of St. Angelo where he remained, practically a prisoner, for seven months, until he surrendered Parma, Piacenza, and Modena and paid a ransom of 400,000 ducats. Charles V had ordered the advance on Rome but not the final assault on the city. He ordered the release of the pope and, with his court, dressed in mourning, did penance for the sacrilege.

The domination of the imperial forces in Italy produced a rapprochement between England and France, which led to an offensive and defensive alliance in the Treaty of Westminster (1527). After the sack of Rome, they concluded the Treaty of Amiens. While one object was to obtain the release of the sons of Francis I and the pope, their principal aim was to reduce the imperial power in Italy. They were joined by Florence and Venice. In 1528 Lautrec led another powerful French army into Italy where, with the aid of Andrea Doria, he seized Milan, Genoa, and Pavia, and besieged the remnant of the imperial army in Naples. The city was saved by the shortage of French supplies and the plague, which swept away three fourths of the besieging army and forced the French to capitulate. Another French army was defeated at Landriano in 1529. Then Andrea Doria deserted the French alliance. Charles gave him the government of Genoa for life, made him supreme commander of the Spanish fleets, and paid him a subsidy of 60,000 ducats a year to provide fourteen galleys for the imperial fleet.

Francis I was now obliged to seek peace. Margaret, the aunt of Charles V, who governed the Netherlands, intervened as mediator. Charles had already come to terms with Clement VII for the pacification of Italy and the repulse of the infidel. Peace was concluded at Cambrai in 1529. Francis I ceded his claims to Milan, Naples, and Artois and married Eleanor, sister of Charles V. His two sons were released for two million gold escudos. Both parties to the conflict were exhausted economically and militarily. Charles V had obtained great sums through loans from the banks of Genoa and Antwerp. The possession of Italy, however, was necessary to him to ensure communications among his several dominions.

In August 1529, Charles V went to Italy to contract a new alliance with Clement VII, the king of Hungary, Venice, Milan, and Savoy. Two months later he won a personal triumph when he was crowned emperor by Clement VII at Bologna (1530). On the death of Francisco Sforza in 1535 Milan became a fief of the empire and was occupied by imperial troops. The move reawakened the jealousy of Francis I, who needed only a pretext to renew hostilities in Italy. Paul III, who had succeeded Clement VII, favored neutrality, but Francis I entered into negotiations with Suleiman the Magnificent of Turkey and the Protestant princes in Germany to assemble allies for the impending conflict with Charles V. Then, without a previous declaration of war, he invaded Savoy and despoiled Duke Charles III, a brother-in-law of the emperor through his marriage with Beatrice of Portugal.

Following a plan cherished previously by the Constable of Bourbon, 70,000 imperial troops under Antonio de Leyva invaded Provence. The French were able to resist long enough to devastate the country. Deprived of supplies and plagued with dysentery, the troops of Charles V soon withdrew after advancing to within sight of Marseilles. Through the mediation of Eleanor of France and María of Hungary, the sisters of the emperor, a ten-month truce was concluded in 1537, followed a year later by a ten-year truce arranged by Paul III.

Constantly in need of funds, Charles V had convoked a cortes in Valladolid and Monzón in 1537. The petitions presented reiterated the old themes, an indication of the consistent failure of Charles to reform the abuses attacked. Charles proposed the establishment of a tax called the *sisa*, which consisted in the reduction of the weight or measure of foodstuffs without changing the price. The clergy agreed, but the nobles opposed. Charles had a violent altercation with the constable of Castile. The latter, when threatened by the emperor with being thrown out of a window, exclaimed, "Think it over! Although I am small, I weigh a great deal." The cortes was dissolved.

The last war with the French arose over the assassination of two French envoys who had been sent to arrange an alliance with Venice and the Turks. One of them was Antonio Rincón, who had migrated to France from Spain and become a diplomatic agent. He was murdered, with the Genoese, César Fregoso, on the Po River by masked men. Francis I protested, charging the governor of Milan with the crime. He also seized George of Austria, bishop of Liége and recently named archbishop of Valencia, a natural son of Maximilian I. Then he declared war and attacked with five armies in Luxemburg, Roussillon, Brabant, the Netherlands, and Piedmont in 1542. The Turks, as his allies, continued their advance in Hungary. The army of the dauphin posed the most serious threat in Roussillon, but the French invasion was halted.

It was now Charles V's turn to search for allies. Paul III refused to enter an alliance, but Charles concluded one with Henry VIII, who was to invade France simultaneously with him. In 1543 Charles V went to Italy, where he secured a loan of 150,000 ducats from Cosimo de Medici. Then in Germany he invaded Gueldres and forced the duke of Cleves, who at the instigation of Francis had sought to seize the city, to surrender. In July the Turkish squadron of Barbarossa joined the French under the count of Enghien at Marseilles, after burning Reggio in Calabria. They attacked Nice, which was relieved by a Milanese army under the marquis of Vasto. In the east, Suleiman marched toward Vienna.

In the agreement with Henry VIII, simultaneous attacks were to be launched in Champagne and Picardy with Paris as their objective, while the marquis of Vasto was to invade southern France through the Piedmont. Francis of Bourbon, young count of Enghien, defeated the imperial forces at the plain of Cerisoles and frustrated the southern invasion. In the north, however, Henry VIII fulfilled his commitment and besieged Boulogne and Montreuil. Charles penetrated the Champagne and reached Château-Thierry, within twenty-four leagues of Paris. As winter was approaching and Charles was unable to spend that season in a hostile and devastated country, he concluded the Peace of Crespy, 1544.

It was agreed that the conquests made since the truce of Nice should be restored. The two sovereigns formed an alliance against the Turks. The duke of Orleans was to marry either Maria, with Flanders as a dowry, or the daughter of Ferdinand of Austria, with Milan as a dowry. Charles V renounced his claims to Burgundy and Francis I gave up his pretensions to Naples and Sicily and his sovereignty over Flanders and Artois. Francis I further promised to give no aid to the pretender to the Navarrese throne. The English, however, continued the war. The Council of Castile was disposed to surrender Milan rather than Flanders, but the unexpected death of the duke of Orleans disposed of that problem. Milan became a Spanish duchy and Italy a Spanish dependency. Charles was worn with the pressure of constant problems and travels and campaigns which had broken his already feeble health.

During his struggle with Francis I, Charles had also been engaged in a bitter struggle with the Moslems. Suleiman the Magnificent had built a formidable power in the east. His troops had dominated Hungary and had become the terror of the Danube. In 1529 he had besieged Vienna with a large army. Charles was forced to send an army under the marquis of Vasto to raise the siege. Andrea Doria then seized Coron and Patras and two strong forts at the entrance to the Strait of Lepanto. He devastated the coasts of Greece (1533). Under Suleiman the Turks not only controlled the eastern Mediterranean, but began a further advance along the coast of North Africa.

While the Spaniards had been unenthusiastic over the Italian wars, they were greatly interested in a continuation of their crusade against the Moslems. Here their attitude coincided with that of Charles V. As Holy Roman Emperor he was the designated leader of Christian Europe against the threat of Islam. His dynastic interests were threatened in the Danube Valley as well as in the Mediterranean, where the famous Moslem pirate, Keirreddin Barbarossa, appeared. A native of Mitylene like his brother Haruc, he was of Greek and Christian origin. The brothers had fought the Spaniards on the North African coast since 1515, engaging in piracy from the Dardanelles to the Strait of Gibraltar. Haruc had extended his power as king of Algiers, but after his death

Barbarossa placed his dominions under the protection of the sultan of Turkey. In 1533 he was named admiral of the Turkish fleet and in the next two years he recovered Coron, sacked the coasts of Italy, and took possession of Tunis. The Turkish fleet was master of the Mediterranean Sea.

After the establishment of peace in western Europe at Cambrai, Charles V was free to deal with the Turkish problem. Andrea Doria's entrance into Spanish service had provided him with adequate naval forces. Petty raids were immediately launched against the piratical ports in North Africa. Charles determined to take Tunis and, in 1535, with Andrea Doria, the papal, and Portuguese squadrons, he proceeded to attack the city. He had coined money for the enterprise with gold from the New World. Barbarossa fled to Algiers, and Muley Hassan was restored to his throne in Algiers, with the understanding that he would release 16,000 Christian captives, refrain from capturing subjects of Charles or Ferdinand, no longer protect pirates or rebellious and fugitive Moriscos, and consent to the erection of Christian churches.

Barbarossa had escaped from Tunis and remained a threat. When Francis I concluded his alliance with the Turks, Charles formed a new Holy League with Venice and Pope Paul III against them. In 1538 at Prevesa, near Corfu, a naval battle remained indecisive when a storm arose to separate the combatants. The Turks gathered 100,000 men in Albania to attack Italy the next year. Barbarossa, with seventy galleys, landed near Otranto to cooperate with the French, but Francis I concluded the truce of Nice and the Turks lost their Christian allies. Charles V tried to negotiate with Barbarossa to lure him from his service with Suleiman, but was frustrated when Antonio Rincón, the French envoy, discovered the plot and revealed it to the Turkish sultan. The pirates raided Gibraltar in 1540, but were pursued and defeated by the Spaniards.

Then Charles V determined to capture Algiers, the seat of Barbarossa's activities. Andrea Doria advised against the project, but Charles was adamant. The weather proved adverse, and Charles was able to avert a disaster only by his timely departure when a storm threatened the destruction of the fleet (1541). Barbarossa died (1546) leaving his conquests and his treasure to his son. The real heir to his power in the Mediterranean, however, was Dragut, an Anatolian who had entered his service and who continued to ravage the Italian coasts after the death of his chief. He had served for four years as a galley slave and was filled with a desire for revenge against the Christians. Establishing his headquarters on the coast of Africa, twenty-eight leagues from Tunis, he captured Tripoli (1551) and Bugía (1555) and was still a threat at the end of the reign of Charles V.

One of the most pressing problems of the reign of Charles V was the Protestant revolt in Germany. It was important in Spanish affairs not only because of the drain on Spanish manpower and treasure which it produced, but also because of the ideological and political consequences. The participation of Spanish mercenaries in the struggles of Germany had a bad effect there as well as in Spain, where the people were opposed both to the absence of their ruler and the use of Spanish soldiers in foreign wars. Nevertheless, the Spaniards were staunch in the Catholic faith and the rise of Protestantism in Germany alarmed them and served to fortify their loyalty.

Charles V tried at first to avert the break, but when the movement began to spread, he resolutely placed himself on the side of the pope against the heretics. Although at the Diet of Speier he tolerantly agreed not to molest Lutherans for their faith, for he hoped to pacify the country, the Diet of Augsburg, under his presidency, condemned the Lutherans (1530). Both parties then prepared for an armed conflict. Charles was confronted with the threat of the Turks to Vienna and signed the Peace of Nuremberg (1532). As the revolt spread he decided, after the failure of the religious conference at Regensburg, to resort to arms to suppress it.

In 1544 Charles called upon Paul III to summon a general council of Christendom. If the Lutherans refused to attend, he would be absolved of his promise to tolerate them. If they attended they would be outvoted and their submission might be gained without a war. The Lutherans, however, refused to fall into his trap. After that war was inevitable. The Council of Trent was assembled in 1545. War raged in Germany while it deliberated. Spanish soldiers formed a good part of the imperial army in Germany, but they only served to represent to the nationally aroused Germans the oppression of their conquerors.

Charles V was ever desirous of finding a means to restore peace in Germany on his terms. The Interim peace of Augsburg in 1548 made some concessions to the Protestants, but subjected them to the Roman Catholic Church. In 1547 the Council of Trent had been moved to Bologna, where Paul III could better supervise it. It provided evidence of the growing distrust between the emperor and the pope and of Paul III's fear of Habsburg power in Italy. Fourteen Spanish and Sicilian bishops continued the sessions at Trent, an indication of the extent to which the Spanish church had been nationalized and subjected to the imperial rather than the papal authority. The Protestants had protested against unjust treatment by the Interim of Augsburg, and after a new war the Peace of Passau, ratified in the Diet of Augsburg, guaranteed them religious liberty and equality in rights.

María, Charles V's sister in the Netherlands, constantly warned him that there was danger of an alliance between Henry II of France and the German Protestants. Charles trusted in the Catholicism of the French king, but in 1552 Henry II gave support to the Protestant princes of Germany to preserve the balance of power. The hope of retaining Catholic unity had vanished, and Lutheranism was bound to be recognized. Therefore, Charles left the settlement at Passau to Ferdinand, and after unsuccessfully besieging Metz he returned to the Netherlands. The war was not concluded with Henry II until 1556.

While Charles V was struggling to maintain the unity of Christendom, a veteran of his army founded the Society of Jesus to defend and extend Catholic influence. Ignatius Loyola was a Basque, born in a petty noble family in the province of Guipúzcoa in 1491. Early in his life, as a protégé of the high treasurer of the Catholic Kings, he was devoted to amorous and military pursuits. When war began between Francis I and Charles V he entered the military service and had risen to the rank of captain when he was wounded at the siege of Pamplona in 1521. During his long and tedious convalescence, he was given the life of Christ and the lives of some saints to read.

His shattered leg made it impossible for him to continue in the military service. His reading had awakened him to a new area of activity. Therefore, he decided to devote himself to the service of religion as a soldier of Christ. For a while he led an austere existence, fasting, scourging himself, and submitting to severe penances. Gradually, he abandoned his self-inflicted punishment and recognized that he would have to acquire learning in order to prepare himself to influence the lives of men. He evolved a plan for the foundation of a company of traveling missionaries, akin to the military orders, with Jerusalem as headquarters. As he meditated, he added another objective, the reclamation of heretics.

Loyola was not an educated man. He knew only Spanish and it was necessary to prepare himself for the role he hoped to fill in the attack on heresy. After he was thirty he began his academic career. He studied at Barcelona, the University of Alcalá, and the University of Salamanca, and, finally, went to the University of Paris. There in 1528 he was associated with students from many countries and became the spiritual leader of a small group of them, six of whom were later associated with him in the foundation of the Society of Jesus. At Montmartre they dedicated themselves to the service of the Church.

Upon leaving Paris, Loyola went to Venice, where his companions joined him in 1537. They proceeded to Rome for permission to make a pilgrimage to Jerusalem. A war between Venice and the Turks prevented their departure for the Holy Land. Consequently, they returned to Rome to consider the work they might accomplish in Europe in behalf of the Church. By 1539 they had decided to establish the Society of Jesus, a company of soldiers of Christ ever ready to support the Church. They had already taken the vows of poverty and chastity, and now they took a vow of obedience. In 1540 a papal bull sanctioned the new order. A year later, Loyola was chosen the first general of the Jesuits.

The inner circle and leaders of the Society of Jesus vowed special obedience to the pope to undertake any missionary activity he might require. Loyola's aim was to develop a disciplined body of men to recover the ground that had been lost to the heretics. This objective required an active rather than a contemplative life. It was necessary for them to accomplish their work not in solitary contemplation in a convent but by energetic activity in the world to win converts to the Catholic Church.

The Jesuits gained an enormous influence as preachers, confessors, teachers, and missionaries in the empires which were being created among non-Christian populations. From the beginning, the Spanish government regarded them with suspicion as special emissaries of an alien pope. The Dominicans viewed them with jealousy as potential rivals. Yet by insinuating their influence over the pious nobility as confessors, they gained greater power in Spain than even in Italy. At the death of Loyola in 1556, although the society was not large, seven of its thirteen provinces were in Spanish and Portuguese territory, where it wielded increasing influence as a vested interest.

Throughout his reign Charles was occupied with the problem of the succession. In 1531 he had invested his brother Ferdinand with his Austrian dominions, as king of the Romans. He tried to arrange his son Philip's succession to the imperial throne, and with this in view, he sent Philip to Germany in 1550 and brought Maximilian, the son of Ferdinand, to Spain. Ferdinand, however, was opposed to this project and Maximilian quickly returned to Germany. The two brothers agreed that Ferdinand would become emperor and Philip would succeed him as king of the Romans. Then, at the death of Ferdinand, Philip would become emperor and Maximilian would become king of the Romans. This arrangement was wrecked by the attitude of the German princes and the renewal of the war with the Protestants. Charles V, therefore, renounced his plans to obtain the imperial crown for Philip, although he named him vicar of the empire in Italy. He also had other plans which did not materialize, such as the establishment of the ancient possessions of the House of Burgundy as a northern buffer against France.

Like his grandparents, he was a firm believer in marital diplomacy. Early in his reign he arranged the marriage of his sister, Eleanor, to Manuel of Portugal, whose two previous wives had been her aunts. She was later married to Francis I by the Peace of Cambrai. In 1524 his daughter Catherine was married to John III of Portugal, and two years later he married John's sister, Isabel, who was his cousin. Charles V had been successively committed to a series of diplomatic engagements. He was engaged to Claude and later to Louise of France. In forming the English alliance, he was engaged to Mary, daughter of Henry VIII. The Portuguese marriage, however, had many advantages. It pleased the Spaniards, continued the policy of peninsular consolidation inaugurated by Ferdinand and Isabel, and was also financially advantageous, because John was rich and Isabel's dowry was 900,000 ducats. Charles married his natural daughter, Margaret, first to Alessandro de Medici and later to Octavius, son of Pier Luigi Farnese. His sister Isabel was married to Christian II of Denmark.

Philip, his heir, when duke of Milan, was married to his first cousin, Princess Maria of Portugal, but she died two years later. When there appeared a danger that Mary Tudor, also a cousin of Charles, would be deprived of the succession in England by Lady Jane Grey, Charles was stimulated by a further threat to the family alliances of the Habsburgs. When Mary became queen he suggested that Philip marry her and thereby insure Habsburg supremacy in England. Negotiations for a second Portuguese marriage for Philip were broken off, the matter was broached to Mary Tudor, and she finally agreed to it. Charles V wanted to protect the Netherlands and unite with England against France. Mary's primary interest was in the restoration of Catholicism in England. In 1554 the marriage was consummated, but since there was no heir, the union failed of its purpose.

Meanwhile, the war with the French in the Netherlands had dragged on. The accession of Giovanni Pietro Caraffa as Paul IV, a fanatical zealot and a bitter enemy of the House of Habsburg, was a severe blow to the aging emperor. The integrity of Spanish dominions in Italy was threatened. Finally, at Brussels, tired and ill, Charles V abdicated in 1556. The states of Flanders, Brabant, Spain, and Naples, with the dominions in the New World, were given to his son Philip. Two years later the imperial government and his Austrian dominions were passed to his brother Ferdinand. Charles retired to the Hieronymite convent of Yuste in Estremadura in 1557 and died a year later.

The reign of Charles V brought extensive changes in the administration of his Spanish dominions. He was conscious of being neither Castilian nor Aragonese. In place of a personal union there was a union of the governments in his person. Although he did not seek to fuse his several Spanish kingdoms, he did seek to unite them. As a dynastic sovereign he regarded Spain as only one unit in the possessions of the Habsburgs, yet he kept the German possessions separate from the Spanish and perhaps gave a preponderance of appointments to the Spaniards. Spain was not only the source of supply for his empire, it also became the center of his dominions. It was the chief support of the Italian wars, and the threat of the Turks and the pirates focused his attention there. Finally, the wealth of the Spanish possessions in the New World demonstrated the importance of Spain as the principal foundation of his power.

Although Charles retained absolute power, he let the councils organized by Ferdinand and Isabel delude themselves with a display of authority which they did not actually possess. He permitted the grandees in the Council of State to discuss imperial affairs, but they had no real power, because he used the council merely as a means of conferring social distinction, and the decisions continued to be made by Charles and his chief ministers. The Council of Castile had a reputation for great power, but Charles retained most of the authority in his own hands. The presidency of the Council was in the hands of reliable ecclesiastics, such as the archbishops of Santiago, Granada, and Seville and the bishop of Pamplona successively.

The cortes of Castile met some fifteen times during the reign of Charles V. The general cortes of Aragon met six times, the cortes of Catalonia twice, and those of Aragon and Valencia once each. While the popular representatives thus had the opportunity of occasionally airing their grievances, the chief purpose in convoking the cortes was to provide money for the imperial and military projects and to transfer to them, in part, the responsibility for increasing taxation. Charles was careful to avoid conflict with the ancient traditions of Castile and even more of Aragon. He listened patiently to their grievances and petitions. He even sanctioned legislation of which he disapproved. In the end, however, the cortes lost authority steadily during his reign. He had virtually the right of arbitrary taxation in Castile, but he sought in yielding to the *encabezamiento* or general tax on individuals to distribute taxation more equitably without interfering with the privileges or exemptions of the nobility, which he was unable to moderate, and to delegate to the municipalities the problem of obtaining the funds.

In 1544 the Castilian cortes requested that it not be summoned more than once every three years because of the expense involved in more frequent meetings. This step marked a complete surrender of traditional rights and authority in the control of taxation. The members might have tried to restrict royal authority and perhaps gain more effective control of legislation. Their petitions were presented less frequently and, even when Charles acceded to them, they could the more easily be relegated to the oblivion of the unenforced measures which became traditional in the nation. The principal abuses of which the representatives complained were delays in the administration of justice, clerical abuses, the grant of benefices to foreigners, and the impoverishment of the realm through the economic policy of the crown.

During the reign of Charles the *corregidores* reached the zenith of their power, although they continued to petition for an elevation of the qualifications for the office and for life appointment because of the expense of legal studies. They were seldom reappointed. The *residencias* or investigations were unsatisfactory because the investigating officials took overlong in their inquiries. The concentration of power in the crown, on the other hand, strengthened the independence of the secular courts and the power of the ecclesiastical courts waned as conflicts of jurisdiction increased. In Aragon, the *Justicia* was subordinated to royal authority, but the shift in the center of gravity in the nation to Castile left the traditions of Aragon antiquarian relics of the past. The *Justicia* was in fact subordinated to lieutenants appointed by the crown, although appeals to the royal *audiencia* were permitted.

Spanish national resources were subjected to a terrific drain by the foreign responsibilities and wars undertaken by Charles V. He endeavored to develop and centralize the collection and administration of the royal revenue by naming a committee of six to superintend the work. This committee inevitably developed during the next reign into the Council of the Treasury. As a result of its work, royal revenues were greatly increased. The heaviest burden fell on Castile, where the general tax on individuals provided the principal service voted by the cortes to replace the sales and other taxes.

Charles, however, had independent sources of income which further freed him from reliance on the cortes. The military orders, which were finally granted to the crown by the bull of Pope Adrian VI in 1523, provided an annual income of 75,000,000 *maravedis*. Much of this income, as well as the revenue derived from the quicksilver mines at Almadén, was pledged to the Augsburg banking house of the Fuggers, to repay loans used in bribing the imperial electors and as security for future loans. Leo X also granted Charles a tenth of the clerical income and raised his share to one-fourth in 1532. The clergy voted him one-half of their income for 1540–42. The revenues from taxes on Spanish industries, raw materials, and the movement of cattle and commodities within the realm were also increased. These were so difficult to collect that they were usually farmed out to agents, with disastrous results for the economic welfare of the kingdom. Finally, rights, privileges, and offices were now sold throughout the realm more lavishly than ever before. The sale of patents of nobility, the legitimization of natural children, and sinecure posts of influence and authority brought in additional funds. Annuities out of state revenues, conferred by the king as a mark of favor, were sold for many times the annual yield. The purchaser received the right to collect a high rate of interest from the tax collector before the sums were even turned over to the royal treasury. By 1539, despite plans proposed to end such speculation on the national credit, there were ninety-nine holders of such annuities.

Many loans were also contracted with the great financial houses of Florence and Genoa. By the time of Charles's abdication the Fuggers controlled much of the revenue of Castile. Each loan resulted in the mortgage of another source of royal revenue. Royal credit became less and less secure, so that the rate of interest rose to 14 percent. By the end of his reign, according to good estimates Charles owed the Fuggers alone some two million ducats and at least five million to other banking houses. Despite the financial plight to which he reduced the kingdom, Spanish expenses were not materially increased. The money was expended outside of Spain. Yet Charles found it impossible to meet his obligations. Payments to his troops were constantly in arrears.

Since Charles used Spain to raise revenue for his imperial ventures, most of his economic measures were adapted to that aim. He favored the herdsmen at the expense of the farmers, with results disastrous for Spanish agriculture. Land lay uncultivated and crops were both inferior and inadequate. The *Mesta* received the protection of the crown and attained the zenith of its prestige because it was more productive of funds than were farmers.

While Ferdinand and Isabel had tried to foster national industries by a restriction on imports, Charles tried rather to encourage the importation of foreign manufactures so that he could collect customs duties from the trade. As a result Spanish industries suffered. The quality of Spanish textiles could not meet the competition of the cloths of the Flemish towns. Charles ordered cheaper cloths manufactured when prices began to rise in the latter part of his reign, but Spanish weavers still could not compete with the inferior fabrics from abroad. Not only was the importation of foreign silks permitted but duties on the exportation of raw silks and goods from Granada to Castile were increased so steeply that the Genoese traders could obtain the raw material more cheaply than could the Spaniards. Consequently, an economic decline took place under Charles V. The silver and gold of the New World passed through Spain to Germany and Italy and left a notable lack of currency in Spain.

The reign of Charles V was brightened by the successes of Spanish arms. The reorganization of the army under Ferdinand and Isabel now produced its most brilliant results. National military service had been established in 1496 and improved by Cardinal Cisneros in 1516. Yet in his foreign wars Charles relied on mercenary soldiers. He enlisted many Germans and Italians, who did not like the Spaniards, but who sometimes broke down the peninsular isolation of the Spaniards and broadened their point of view. The *tercio* emerged as a new military unit. It consisted of twelve companies of 250 men each, to which only Spaniards were admitted. As has been indicated, the fact that the armies of Charles V appeared to be constantly in arrears in pay and deficient in supplies meant a heavy drain on financial resources.

In the New World, this era was rendered illustrious by the exploits of the Spanish conquerors, who in small groups overthrew the aboriginal empires of the Aztecs, Incas, and Mayas of several million inhabitants each. The conquistadores were men who had grown up along the Spanish frontier and were endowed with its rugged self-reliance—men like Pizarro, De Soto, and Cabeza de Vaca. As they extended their suzerainty over the aborigines, a mass of wealth in precious metals flowed into Spain, sending the price of bullion plummeting downward and enabling Charles V to assume a role of influence to which he could not have otherwise aspired.

Spanish administrative institutions were rapidly transplanted to the New World, where they were adapted to novel conditions. In Spain these possessions were governed by the Council of the Indies, which was fully organized by the end of the reign of Charles V. The *adelantado* became an important official on the American frontier during the conquest, but when he threatened royal authority and when full control over the conquered areas had been established, his powers were revoked. Two viceroyalties were established in New Spain (1529) and Peru (1542). Wherever the Spaniard migrated he founded municipalities similar to those in Spain, with their councilmen and alcaldes.

CHAPTER XIV

The Age of Philip II

Despite the dissipation of Spanish resources by Charles V in imperial enterprises in Europe, the impetus given to Spanish development under Ferdinand and Isabel was so great that Spain went forward to reach the zenith of her power in the second half of the sixteenth century under Philip II. Although still confronted with imperial problems, he was truly Spanish in outlook and sought to consolidate Spanish power in Europe and the New World. Under his prudent direction Spain achieved the dream that Charles V had cherished and became, for a time, the arbiter of European affairs. As champion of the ideal of Catholic unity, she was the leader in the effort to restore that unity, but the spirit of individualism awakened in Europe during the Renaissance was too strong to be crushed. Spain was forced into a duel with England to maintain her hegemony. The English were more vigorously imbued with the new spirit and were more flexible. Spain, under clerical domination, was already feeling the effects of the continuous strain on her resources required by the effort to maintain her supremacy and support a bureaucracy saturated with inefficiency.

Philip II was as Spanish as his father had been Flemish at the beginning of his reign. He was born in Valladolid in 1527. His education was supervised by a professor from the University of Salamanca, Juan Martínez. Later, he studied the humanities, religion, mathematics, fine arts, and the sciences and became fluent in Portuguese and Latin, but he never learned French and Italian well.

Philip was of less than medium height, but the elegance with which he dressed gave him a grace and dignity which made him appear taller than he was. He had blue eyes and light hair and beard, which he wore "short and pointed, after the Spanish fashion." His Habsburg ancestry was revealed by his protruding underjaw and lip. He was slow in speech, probably because he preferred to write his thoughts and orders rather than communicate them orally. Although he was taught the use of weapons, hunting, and riding, he was sedentary in habit and seldom engaged in any form of exercise. He had a weak stomach, suffered from asthma and gout, and was melancholy and possessed by a hypochondriacal fear of dying as a result of some accident.

Reading and writing most of the day, weighed down by the responsibilities of his royal position, he tried to keep every corner of his farflung dominions under constant observation. He took his duties seriously, but in trying to direct every detail himself, he never gave full confidence to his ministers, however faithful they might be. He was submerged in reports throughout his reign. He was patient and restrained, kindly and conscientious, but he judged his dominions through the eyes of his observers and never really understood them for himself.

Philip II was more attentive to the affairs of Spain than was his father, for he was more Spanish and had not been forced to assume the imperial burden that had consumed the energy of Charles V. He was just in his approach to Spanish problems and determined to see that justice prevailed in his kingdom. By nature kindly and prudent, he was not inaccessible to his subjects, despite his love of solitude, and heard all supplications with courtesy and inscrutable reserve. In his simplicity he marked a reaction from the luxuries of his father's Burgundian favorites to the days of Ferdinand and Isabel. Perhaps he was simple in his tastes because of his frugality, for he permitted only those ceremonies necessary to maintain his dignity as a sovereign. If he wasted Spanish resources on ill-conceived projects, it was for the service of Spain and not for himself.

Yet Philip II was not indifferent to the lighter aspects of life. He derived his recreation from listening to the jokes of professional buffoons. He played cards, loved music, and enjoyed playing the guitar. He was an enthusiast of art both as a patron and as a connoisseur. Though he had a number of mistresses, his amours did not influence his statecraft. His greatest pleasure was derived from the affection of his family. His first wife, María of Portugal, died when he was eighteen, at the birth of Prince Carlos. His second marriage—to Mary Tudor—was a union of political expediency. His third wife was Elizabeth of Valois, daughter of Catherine de Medici. His eight happy years with her gave him two daughters, Isabel and Catherine. In 1570 he married Anna of Austria, daughter of his cousin, the Emperor Maximilian II. She bore four sons and one daughter, but only Philip lived beyond his eighth year.

At the age of sixteen, Philip II had been charged with the regency of the Spanish kingdoms. He had taken his oath as heir to Castile in

1528, and as heir to Aragon in 1542, and later he served as regent during the absence of his father from Spain. In 1549 he was recognized as the heir to Flanders, and three years later was sworn as heir to Navarre. Thus, because of the preoccupation of his father with imperial problems, Philip had the opportunity of familiarizing himself with the problems of government long before he ascended the throne of Spain.

His ability to handle the problems of statecraft was immediately put to the test. He had inherited not only extensive dominions from his father, but wars and enmities as well. Henry II of France broke the truce of Vaucelles in 1556 by sending an army of 20,000 men into Italy under the duke of Guise to conquer Naples and aid Paul IV, who had continued his attempts to dislodge the Spaniards from Milan and Naples. Paul IV announced that he had deprived Philip II of the kingdom of Naples, whereupon Philip ordered the duke of Alba, viceroy of Naples, to invade the papal dominions. The duke took Ostia and arrived before Rome. Philip II went to England to obtain aid from his wife, Mary Tudor. With a heterogeneous army recruited in Flanders, Hungary, Germany, and England, Filibert, duke of Savoy, besieged Admiral Coligny in Saint-Quentin. The Constable Montmorency was decisively defeated when he tried to relieve Coligny, and Henry II was forced to recall Guise to defend France. The loss of French assistance then forced the pope to withdraw from the league.

When the duke of Guise returned to France, he immediately attacked and captured Calais—the last English stronghold on the continent—and then Thionville and Dunkirk. The Spaniards were deficient in resources, but with the aid of the English fleet they won the battle of Gravelines in 1558. Both Philip II and Henry II, however, were becoming alarmed at the rapid spread of Calvinism in France, and negotiations for peace were initiated. The death of Mary Tudor eliminated the question of the restoration of Calais. By the Peace of Cateau-Cambresis, signed in April 1559, all conquests were mutually restored, and both sovereigns agreed to support the Catholic Church against heretics. To consolidate the concord, Philip married Elizabeth of Valois, daughter of Henry II. Filibert of Savoy married Henry's sister Margaret and received the territory of Savoy, conquered by the French, as a dowry, thereby creating a strong buffer state between France and the Spanish possessions in Italy. Henry II was wounded in a tourney held during the celebration of the marriages and died soon afterward. Paul IV also died in 1559. With the disappearance of the persons who had been most intent on maintaining hostilities between France and Spain, between Habsburg and Valois, the ancient enemies united to meet new problems created by the diffusion of Protestantism. Thus, a new phase was inaugurated in European affairs.

In 1559 Philip II returned to Spain for the rest of his life. He had Prince Carlos recognized as heir to the throne at the Cortes of Toledo and chose Madrid as his residence, thereby converting the royal villa into the capital of the monarchy. A formidable revolt immediately called his attention to the Moriscos. In accord with a request of the cortes in 1560, the enslavement of the Moslems in Granada had been prohibited, but various restrictive measures were imposed on them at the same time. The Moriscos in Valencia were disarmed in 1562, and a year later, those in Granada were prohibited from bearing arms without the permission of military authority, but many of them hid their weapons. In 1564 the Moors were denied the right of asylum in the villages of their lords or in the churches, which brought them under ordinary judicial authority, and many of them fled to the mountains, where they lived as outlaws. In 1566 they were forbidden to use Arabic or their customary dress and baths and were obliged to surrender their Arabic books and keep their houses open for inspection. Finally, it was ordered that Morisco children should attend schools for instruction in Christianity and the Castilian language.

The Moriscos were indignant at these restrictions. The flame of revolt was lighted when the popular Farax-ben-Farax, a dyer, entered Granada in 1568 at the head of a numerous band of mountaineers. Although the Moriscos in the city failed to support him and he had to withdraw, the mountaineers became conscious of their strength. They chose as their leader young Ferdinand de Córdoba y Valar, a descendant, they claimed, of the Ommiad caliphs. He assumed the name of Muley-Mohamed-aben-Humeya, king of the Moriscos, and named Farax-ben-Farax as his military commander. He also requested aid from the Berbers of North Africa. The rebellion took the Spaniards by surprise, and the Moriscos captured, tortured, and killed 6000 Christians in six days.

In 1569 the marquis of Mondejar, with 2000 soldiers, undertook an expedition into the hills to subdue the rebels. Reinforced with militia as he proceeded, he subjugated the mountaineers in a bloody campaign. He had brought Aben-Humeya to the point of negotiating for surrender and groups of rebels held out only in the most inaccessible recesses of the mountains, when the Council of Granada, annoyed at his conciliatory policy, asked Philip to relieve him of his command. Philip appointed Don Juan of Austria, natural son of Charles V and Barbara of Blomberg, as commander, and aided him with Italian veterans.

The Moriscos sent an embassy to the Turks, who promised their cooperation. Aben-Humeya assembled 5000 men, and they renewed the struggle with great energy. The Moriscos were further angered when all those in Granada between ten and sixty years were ordered to assemble for transportation to neighboring provinces. A body of Moslems from Algiers arrived, and the rebel forces rose to 18,000 men.

Don Juan undertook his campaign against them in 1570. He captured Galera and Guejar, but was surprised and defeated at Serón. Recovering the fort, he entered into secret negotiations with El-Habaqui, the Morisco leader, to whom he proposed favorable terms. The Moriscos were to be permitted to dwell only in the plains and they were to be disarmed, but their lives were to be respected. Their new king, Aben-Aboo, declined to accept the terms and had El-Habaqui killed. The Spaniards thereupon renewed the campaign and gave no quarter. Prisoners were hanged, women and children were sold as slaves, and the Moriscos of Granada were ordered deported to Castile. The revolt ended only when Aben-Aboo was assassinated at the instigation of the Spaniards. Although the kingdom of Granada was slowly repopulated by Christian colonists, the problem was not completely solved.

The Turks still threatened Spanish security in the Mediterranean. They were not only a constant menace to commerce, but they aided the rebels in Granada. In 1565 the Turks besieged Malta and captured the fort of San Telmo. Philip sent aid to the island, and the Turks withdrew after losing 20,000 men, including Dragut the pirate.

Various reasons led Philip II to build an alliance to break the Turkish power once and for all. Venice was declining and could no longer bear the brunt of the war against the Turks. Pius V was anxious to end the Turkish threat, and Philip also had a strong desire to prove himself the champion of Christendom. It was necessary to destroy the accord between the sultan and the North African pirates who harassed the coasts of Italy and at times descended on the Levantine coast of Spain. An occasion was presented when the Turks attacked Cyprus.

Philip II agreed to enter a league with Venice and the pope in 1570. The emptiness of the Spanish treasury was an obstacle to any expedition against the Turks, for the war in Flanders in the preceding five years had consumed not only the ordinary income but the treasure from the New World as well. But the subsidy from the Spanish clergy, amounting to 500,000 ducats a year, and the bull of the crusade, which amounted to even more, were given to Philip II as an inducement to enter the league.

The negotiations for the league were difficult to arrange, since the purposes of the three participants were at variance. The Venetians wanted to destroy the Turkish fleet and restore the peace necessary for continued commerce with the Levant. The pope wanted to recover the Holy Land. Philip was in agreement with the pope, but, in addition, wished to extend Spanish conquests on the North African coast and extirpate the pirates. Venice wanted a temporary league, while Philip and the pope wanted a permanent one. In the end an alliance against the Turks, Algiers, Tunis, and Tripoli was formed. Spain assumed half of the expenses, Venice two-sixths, and the pope one-sixth. Selection of the commander of the expedition presented one of the most difficult problems, but Don Juan of Austria was finally chosen, with Marco Antonio Colonna, constable of Naples, as the papal representative and Augustino Barbarigo as the Venetian commander.

Meanwhile, Nicosia, the capital of Cyprus, had been besieged by 100,000 Turks and forced to capitulate. While the Turks continued their effort to take the island, the fleet of the Christian league—300 vessels, carrying over 80,000 men—assembled at Messina in August 1571, and began to seek the Turkish fleet of 240 vessels and 120,000 men. Both adversaries appeared reluctant to attack and maneuvered for the advantage. When the Turks moved out of the Gulf of Lepanto the issue was joined on October 7, 1571. In a three-hour combat the Christians won a decisive as well as famous victory. Some 40,000 Moslems were killed, 8000 were captured, and 12,000 Christian slaves were freed. Miguel Cervantes Saavedra was wounded in the left hand while fighting in Doria's galley. Uluch-Ali-Bey of Algiers led the remnants of the Turkish navy to Constantinople, where the Turks immediately began to construct a new fleet.

Disputes at once arose among the members of the league over the division of spoils and plans for future campaigns. The pope still insisted on the conquest of Turkey and the Holy Land, the Venetians wanted to destroy the new Turkish fleet, Spain was intent on North Africa, but also suggested an attack on the Balkans, with the idea of creating a buffer state for Don Juan of Austria to use as a base for defending Europe against the Turks. Meanwhile, there were good reasons for the inactivity of the Spanish fleet in addition to a shortage of funds. France had joined Turkey in an effort to destroy the league, and a powerful French fleet was assembled in Bordeaux under the command of Strozzi. No one knew its destination. Turkey had offered Algiers and Bizerte to the French. Admiral Coligny had invaded the Netherlands, taking Valenciennes and besieging Mons. There was ample reason for Philip to keep the fleet near enough to defend Spain in case of need.

The Venetian and papal envoys had protested Spanish inactivity. The Venetians—even threatening to ally themselves with the Turks to attack Don Juan—concluded a separate peace with the Turks. When he learned of the treaty Philip impassively remarked that while the Venetians worked only for their own interests, he worked in behalf of Christendom and for the benefit of the Venetians.

At this moment the massacre of St. Bartholomew's Day in France provoked a renewal of the struggle between the Catholics and the Huguenots and removed the French threat. Philip ordered Don Juan to proceed from Sicily to Africa where he captured Tunis and Bizerte and left Muley Hassan as tributary king in the first city and a Spanish garrison in the second.

At the time of the Morisco revolt an incident occurred which deeply embittered Philip and yet revealed his deep concern for the future welfare of his dominions. The heir to the throne, Don Carlos, had so warped a mind that it was necessary for Philip to avert his accession to the throne and a consequent disaster to Spain. From an early age Carlos had demonstrated a cruel and choleric disposition, delighting in the torture of animals and of those who contradicted his caprices. Of feeble intelligence, he was raised by his aunts, María, wife of Maximilian of Austria, and Juana, the widowed queen of Portugal. In 1556, when he was eleven, his marriage had been arranged with Elizabeth of Valois, daughter of Henry II, but for political reasons she had become his stepmother instead. Various other marital alliances were considered for him—with Mary Stuart, widow of Francis II, with Margaret, daughter of Catherine de Medici, and with Anne of Bohemia—but his mental condition prevented the realization of any of them.

Four years after Don Carlos had been recognized as the heir to the throne he was given an independent establishment and began to attend the meetings of the council. While attending the University of Alcalá de Henares in 1561, his injury in a fall downstairs necessitated trepanning of his skull by the famed surgeon Vesalius. As a result either of the operation or of the fall, his character became more violent and abnormal than before.

The attacks of Don Carlos on members of the court and his rumored plans to leave Spain led Philip to consult with some of his advisers. Don Carlos had ordered horses prepared for his flight and had threatened Don Juan of Austria. He was summarily imprisoned in his room. The record of his trial has disappeared and the reasons for it are obscure. It may have dealt with his incapacity to succeed his father or some political or religious charge, but, before the sentence was pronounced, he died (1568). According to trustworthy testimony, his death was a result of overeating or heavy drinking, but it is still surrounded in mystery. Philip II has been accused of ordering the death of his son, and many legends have arisen, but whatever the cause of his death, Don Carlos was evidently a degenerate and his removal as heir to the throne was a blessing to the Spanish people.

During the period following Philip's visit to Flanders at the abdication of Charles V, the situation in that country had deteriorated into open rebellion. Philip had made an unfortunate impression on the Flemings. They were as much opposed to the domination of the Spaniards as the Spaniards had been to the Flemish advisers of Charles V. Spanish rule had not improved the economic condition of the Netherlands, where the people were ruined by taxation for distant projects from which they received no tangible return. Local privileges and liberties of the Flemings and their cities were endangered by the centralized absolutism of Philip II. The spread of Lutheranism was another cause of misunderstanding. The Flemings did not merely seek freedom of conscience, but in their own land persecuted the Catholics, whose champion Philip II aspired to be. There was also a sharp division within the Low Countries between the Germanic northern provinces, commercial and Lutheran, and the southern provinces, dominated by the Walloons, industrial in economy and Catholic in religion.

Perhaps the strongest motive for the revolt may be found in the character of Philip II, who was never popular in the Low Countries and whose stubborn defense of the integrity of Catholicism, nomination of governors distasteful to the inhabitants, and maintenance of Spanish troops among them gave fuel to the flame of dissatisfaction. Philip was determined to establish his authority in the Netherlands, to Hispanicize them as far as was possible, and to subvert their liberties without changing their ancient political organization. An immediate reason for dissatisfaction was provided by the appointment of fourteen new bishops, in addition to the six already there, and the naming of Cardinal Granvelle as primate. Philip II nominated the bishops, instead of permitting their election by the chapters according to Flemish tradition, and assigned them the income of the richest abbeys. Their very presence was distasteful to the Calvinists and Lutherans.

The leaders whom the revolt brought into conflict were William the Silent, prince of Orange, and Antonio Perrenot, Cardinal Granvelle, a native of Burgundy. William had been governor of Holland, Zeeland, and Utrecht and had been honored by Charles V. He was wise, energetic, persevering, and also ambitious to rule his native land and to end Spanish rule and Catholic domination. Cardinal Granvelle, bishop of Arras, was the son of a devoted secretary of the emperor. He had considerable ability and felt great loyalty to those to whom he owed his advancement, and he had the full confidence of Philip II. Count Egmont and the count of Hoorn supported William of Orange. Margaret of Parma, natural sister of Philip II, was governor of the Low Countries. She had been married to Alessandro de Medici and Ottavio Farnese, grandson of Paul III, and was hard-working and methodical but unattractive. While she was officially vested with the authority over the Low Countries, she had to obey secret instructions from Philip.

When the Spanish troops were withdrawn from Flanders in 1560, the Flemish nobles felt greater freedom to protest without fear of retaliation. The complaints against Cardinal Granvelle increased. Although in 1562 Philip II denied that the Inquisition would be established in Flanders, the nobles demanded Granvelle's dismissal. When that was refused, they withdrew from the council of Margaret of Parma and did not return until Cardinal Granvelle was removed. Then, the promulgation of the decrees of the Council of Trent, already accepted in Italy and Spain, raised the possibility that they might be enforced in Flanders. Count Egmont went to Madrid, where he was affectionately received, but Philip II refused to have the decrees suspended in Flanders and the die of revolt was cast.

The Flemish nobles, led by William of Orange, held secret meetings to organize their protest. In April 1566 some two hundred armed nobles met and formulated the Compromise of Breda, which they presented to Margaret of Parma. In this memorial they formally requested the suspension of the Inquisition and the decrees of the Council of Trent in Flanders.

The turmoil in Flanders, however, had passed the point of restraint. In outbreaks in Antwerp, Ghent, Tournai, and other places, images were destroyed and churches were sacked and burned. Margaret of Parma became practically a prisoner of William of Orange and Count Egmont. Although an edict of Philip II was published, authorizing the suspension of the Inquisition and extending a general pardon, the situation was too far advanced to permit the rebels to retreat. More than four hundred churches and convents were attacked, and friars and nuns were shot in the streets. When the council of Margaret of Parma split in two, she turned to the old party of Cardinal Granvelle for support. There were rumors of imminent invasion by armed Protestants from France and Germany.

The council in Madrid was also divided. Some members favored conciliatory measures, but the duke of Alba supported severe ones, and when the news of the outrages arrived, his view prevailed. Philip II was too preoccupied with other pressing matters to give the decision the prudent consideration it deserved. In 1566 Margaret of Parma announced the imminent arrival of a Spanish expeditionary force in Flanders under the duke of Alba, and the prince of Orange withdrew to his estates in Germany.

Ferdinand Alvarez de Toledo y Pimental, third duke of Alba, had been a trusted general of the emperor. As governor of the Spanish dominions in Italy, he had demonstrated both prudence and energy. He was harsh, indefatigable, and fanatically loyal to his king and his Church. He arrived in Flanders by land, crossing northern Italy, Switzerland, and Lorraine with some 10,000 Spanish veterans and instructions which were as severe as they were secret.

One of the new governor's first acts was to seize Count Egmont and the count of Hoorn. He hoped by rigorous measures against the leaders of the revolt to bring the Flemings to rapid submission. The Tribunal of Blood had been established five days earlier to ascertain the identity of those responsible for the previous disorder and punish them. It was an investigative court of seven magistrates, and the duke reserved the right of passing sentence to himself. Margaret of Parma retired to her estates, recommending clemency, yet Count Egmont and the count of Hoorn were condemned and beheaded and their property confiscated (1568). The event sent a wave of anger through the Protestants of the Low Countries.

Early in 1568 the young count of Buren, son of William of Orange and a student at the University of Louvain, was seized and taken to the University of Alcalá as a hostage. Meanwhile, William of Orange and his brothers, Adolf and Louis of Nassau, had invaded Flanders, an event which had hastened the execution of the two counts. Louis of Nassau was victorious in the battle of Heiligerlee, but the duke of Alba took the field, defeated Louis in two battles, and forced William to withdraw to Germany, while the duke returned in triumph to Brussels.

The rebellion appeared to be completely subdued, when economic circumstances forced the Spaniards to levy new taxes on the Flemings. Elizabeth of England had seized the funds being carried by two Basque ships to the duke of Alba when they were forced to seek refuge in English ports. In retaliation English ships in Spanish and Flemish ports were seized, but this action did not restore the treasure. In 1569 the States General was convoked in Flanders to impose a 10 percent sales tax on all personal property and a 5 percent tax on the sales of real property. Hitherto unknown in Flanders, these taxes produced angry discontent in a land where industry flourished and trade was brisk.

The Council of Blood had also been active in punishing rebels, and the newly appointed bishops began to hunt out heretics. In 1570 the duke of Alba issued a general amnesty for those who repented and abjured their errors. Many hastened to reconcile themselves with the Church, but the Council of Blood found new victims. By this time, the duke considered that he had attained his primary object in suppressing the rebellion. He was ill and tired and asked to be relieved.

At the very time the Peace of Saint-Germain (1570) temporarily ended the religious warfare in France, it was rumored that the rival parties had united to invade Flanders. This threat delayed the retirement of the duke of Alba. His need for new funds was pressing, and the collection of the sales tax, which had been suspended in 1569 in return for the grant of two million florins a year, was resumed. Both Catholics and Protestants, including even the councilors faithful to Spain, firmly opposed the measure. When businessmen and merchants began migrating to neighboring countries, the duke ordered some of them hanged at the doors of their shops.

As a result, rebellion again broke out in the Low Countries, beginning in Holland and spreading to other provinces. Louis of Nassau seized Mons and Valenciennes with French aid. William of Orange came to his brother's support, but the duke of Alba won a victory at Jemappes, forced William back into Germany, and sacked the towns he had captured. When the duke of Medinaceli arrived to replace Alba, the latter was unwilling to relinquish his command. As the rebellion continued, factional discontent appeared in the Spanish party. The soldiers were unpaid and mutinied after the fall of Haarlem. The duke of Alba tried to obtain loans from various merchants and, despite his financial need, was forced to suspend the collection of the hated taxes.

As it had become evident that the duke of Medinaceli would be unable to cope with the situation when the duke of Alba left the Low Countries, the governor of Milan, Luis de Requeséns, was designated the duke's successor in 1573. He was an expert soldier, affable and kindly in character, and gained a quick appreciation of the situation in Flanders. The duke of Alba had believed that religious differences were fundamental in the rebellion. Requeséns concluded that the revolt was based rather on economic motives, but was increased in fierceness by the atrocities of the foreign troops in Flanders. He proposed the extension of a wide amnesty and the suppression of the Council of Blood.

Meanwhile, the hostilities continued. The Spaniards lost their last citadel in Zeeland when the rebels took Middelburg. But the defeat of Louis of Nassau at Mook (1574) frustrated the plan of William of

Orange for penetrating Brabant to Antwerp and broke the military power of the rebels. Just as all Holland seemed ready to submit, the Spanish troops mutinied over their failure to receive their pay, and they were prevented from sacking Antwerp completely only by the appearance of Requeséns. In 1574 the desired amnesty was proclaimed, although 292 persons were excluded from the pardon extended to those involved in the rebellion since 1556. The much-hated Council of Blood was abolished.

Indeed, as Requeséns undertook slow negotiations with William of Orange, the military phase of the rebellion became more intense. The Flemings resisted heroically at Leiden, opening the dikes and flooding the surrounding land to defend themselves. When the Spaniards captured several cities in 1575, the States General of the rebel provinces authorized William to seek foreign aid. The sovereignty of the rebellious provinces was offered to Henry III of France and to Elizabeth of England, but neither wished to break openly with Spain. Elizabeth suggested the creation of the kingdom of Flanders for Don Juan of Austria, but Philip II was loath to give up the rich country, even to his half-brother. The French Huguenots recommended the duke of Alençon as king of Flanders, but Henry III was jealous of his brother.

In the midst of the negotiations Requeséns died (1576). Funds were so low that his body lay unburied for three days. As the States General continued its efforts to obtain foreign intervention to force Philip II to alter his policy, William of Orange renewed his campaign, slowly crushing the scattered Spanish garrisons. Spanish troops were concentrated in Antwerp, and when a conflict broke out there between them and the soldiers being raised by the States General, the Spaniards ruthlessly sacked the city and killed some 2000 inhabitants in the so-called "Spanish Fury." Their atrocities awakened general indignation throughout the Netherlands, and kindled a spirit of resistance so bitter that the days of Spanish rule were clearly numbered.

Although Don Juan of Austria had been named to succeed Requeséns, the States General continued negotiating with William of Orange—the popular leader of the Low Countries. In November 1576, they concluded the Pacification of Ghent. It was agreed that the Spaniards should be expelled by an armed alliance of Catholics and Protestants. The question of religion would be settled by the States General. Meanwhile, the edicts against heresy were suspended, prisoners condemned by the Council of Blood were liberated, and confiscated property was restored. It was further stipulated that only natives should hold Flemish offices and that the States General would name its own foreign representatives.

Finally, the States General resolved that it would force any new governor to accept this agreement. Never had Spanish authority been so low.

Don Juan was loath to accept the difficult post, lest he lose the bright military laurels he had already won at Lepanto. On the other hand, he was attracted by the possibility that he might be victorious in a struggle with Elizabeth of England, that he might win Mary Stuart in marriage and that he might even gain the English throne—all as a sequel to the pacification of Flanders. Wild dreams! He was impetuous and obstinate, capable both of explosive hatreds and deep affection, and an expert soldier and artilleryman. He lived luxuriously, spoke French, and understood German, Flemish, and Italian. He was in Italy when he received the nomination to the Flemish post, but he went at once to Madrid, consulted Philip II, crossed France, and arrived in Flanders in November.

Don Juan gave evidence of his desire to obtain peace in the Low Countries. He ordered the Spanish troops to suspend hostilities and took a conciliatory attitude toward the council and the provincial estates. He regarded the States General as illegally convened without the requisite royal authority. Philip II had authorized him to grant the measures desired, such as the withdrawal of Spanish troops, but he was ordered to maintain royal authority and respect for the Catholic Church. Even William of Orange was included in the general amnesty.

In the calm which followed Don Juan's arrival, divisions among the people of the Low Countries became more apparent. By 1577, they had split into two groups and were unanimous only in demanding the withdrawal of the Spanish soldiers. The people of the southwest were intent on the establishment of Catholicism, while those of the north, led by William of Orange, wished to establish Protestantism and overthrow completely the authority of Philip II. Don Juan was astute enough to take advantage of the break in the ranks of his opponents. He endeavored to widen it by making concessions. In the "Perpetual Edict" he approved the withdrawal of Spanish troops. They were to depart by sea, if possible, but when the northern provinces refused the use of their ports, they were forced to march southward toward Italy. The concessions he had made were forgotten in the quarrels which developed over the evacuation of the troops.

Don Juan was formally welcomed in Brussels in 1577, but the States General agreed to recognize him as governor by a majority of only one. Both that body and he were suspicious. Don Juan shortly withdrew from Brussels, seized the fortress of Namur, and requested Philip II to send

Spanish troops back to Flanders so that he could regain the initiative. He wished to retrieve his fortunes by the use of force.

In the meantime, William of Orange had reorganized the rebels and tried to obtain effective foreign aid. The estates, in December 1577, had rejected Don Juan as governor. In 1578 they signed a treaty with England for assistance in men and supplies to promote the candidate John Casimir, count of the Palatinate, for the position of hereditary sovereign of the Low Countries. In the hope of dividing the Catholics, William of Orange had initiated negotiations with the duke of Alençon, brother of Henry III of France, and the Archduke Mathias, brother of Emperor Maximilian II. To counteract the influence of Henry III, who irritated Philip II by the support he gave his brother, Philip entered into secret negotiations with Henry of Bourbon, chief of the French Calvinists. Mathias arrived and assumed the position of count, with the reluctant William of Orange as his lieutenant. The international politics of the situation became more intense as the several powers intervened in behalf of their candidates. At this juncture, Don Juan died (1578).

At the death of Don Juan only three of the seventeen provinces of the Low Countries remained faithful to Spain. Don Juan had designated his cousin, Alexander Farnese, as his successor, and Philip II confirmed the appointment. The duke of Alençon and the count of the Palatinate withdrew to France and Germany. Alexander Farnese, taking advantage of the division in the rebel ranks between Catholics and Protestants, besieged and captured Maestricht, in the sack of which thousands of citizens perished. As a result, Artois, Hainault, and French Flanders submitted to his authority. In the Convention of Arras, in return for the withdrawal of Spanish troops, they accepted the reestablishment of the government as it had been in the time of Charles V, the protection of Catholicism, and the confirmation of the Perpetual Edict (1579). In turn, William of Orange organized the Union of Utrecht, including the seven northern provinces, which recognized the Protestant religion and rejected the authority of Philip II. Henceforth, the two groups in the Low Countries were mutually hostile.

In 1580 William announced the end of Spanish sovereignty in Antwerp and the States General proclaimed the duke of Alençon as governor and liberator of Flanders. The duke raised the siege of Cambrai in 1581 with 16,000 men, but retired at once to France. The war continued indecisively until Spanish policy was revitalized with the arrival of Cardinal Granvelle. He originated the idea of placing a price on the head of William of Orange, since he considered peace impossible while the Dutch prince lived. In 1581 the States General of Holland and Zeeland accepted the sovereignty of William. The duke of Alençon died in June 1584, and a month later a Burgundian, Balthasar Gerard, succeeded in assassinating William. The States General in Antwerp gave Maurice of Nassau, second son of William, the title of admiral and the government of Zeeland, Holland, and Utrecht.

Alexander Farnese, who was both a soldier and a statesman, tried to maintain an active military campaign and at the same time conciliate the rebels by offering to forget the past if they would be loyal to the king and Catholicism. He issued titles of nobility and distributed confiscated property. Bruges and Ghent surrendered, and Antwerp was captured after a heroic resistance. Then Brussels and all Brabant capitulated. These events led Elizabeth of England to decide finally to intervene in the struggle. Robert Dudley, earl of Leicester, with an English force of 5000 men, was sent to the aid of the Protestants in 1585. The Flemings had placed their hopes in this gallant but imprudent gentleman, who was given great authority, but soon aroused opposition by the prohibition of trade, a blow to Flemish economic activities. He withdrew to England in 1587, and the Flemish named Maurice of Nassau as their leader in the defense of the rebellious provinces. Alexander Farnese became ill, retired in 1589, and was replaced by Count Charles of Mansfield.

While Philip II had become the champion of Catholicism, Elizabeth of England, his former sister-in-law, became the defender of Protestantism. The rivalry of England and Spain found expression in all of their relations. Antagonism was evident not only in Scotland, France, and the Low Countries, but on the high seas as well, where English seamen preyed on Spanish commerce. Philip II had married Mary Tudor in the hope that their offspring might rule England and the Netherlands and promote Spanish and Catholic interests. Philip II also proposed marriage to Elizabeth of England, but she was too prudent, too shrewd, and too patriotic to permit England to be subordinated to Spanish interests. The struggle in England developed around Mary, queen of Scots, who was Catholic and in the line of succession to the English throne.

After a period of embittered relations Philip sent Bernardino de Mendoza as Spanish ambassador to London in 1578. Elizabeth, who had been secretly encouraging the rebellious Flemings, had demanded that Philip II conclude peace with them. The selection of Mendoza was an indication that Anglo-Spanish relations especially concerned the Low Countries. He was instructed to attempt to conciliate Elizabeth but England and Spain remained on bad terms. The Jesuits also had a mission in England, headed by Edmund Campion and Robert Parsons, whose objective was the subversion of Elizabeth's throne. Although Philip II disapproved of the order and was at odds with the pope who dispatched it, he was the acknowledged head of the forces of the Counter Reformation. Therefore, the Jesuit intrigue, which was regarded as Catholic in its inspiration by Englishmen, reflected its odium on Philip II. He was also believed to be inciting rebellion in Ireland.

There were active indications of English antagonism toward Spain. From 1577 to 1580 Sir Francis Drake, during his voyage around the world, had raided Spanish settlements in the Caribbean. Elizabeth not only refused to surrender any of the plunder he had obtained, but even offered some of it as a bribe to Mendoza to ease relations with Spain. She had encouraged Antonio of Portugal in his pretensions to the Portuguese throne. In short, neither Elizabeth nor Philip II wanted an open break which might lead to war, but each was anxious to balk the policies of the other.

The Low Countries had long been regarded as a strategic possession of Spain in relation to England. It was essential for Elizabeth to keep the Netherlands revolt alive to protect English economic relations with those provinces and safeguard England from possible invasion. Elizabeth had tried to use France to promote the revolt and even encouraged the duke of Alençon in his pretensions for her hand. As time passed, however, it was evident that she would have to oppose Philip II more openly.

Jesuit intrigue among Catholics in England was believed to extend even to plots for the murder of Elizabeth. In 1583 evidence was obtained that Mendoza was involved in the intrigue, and he was ordered out of England. Two years later, by the end of 1585, Philip II was converted to the idea of an attack on England. Hoping to bring England back into the Catholic fold without war, he had dabbled in Catholic plots around Mary, queen of Scots, to ensure her succession to Elizabeth. The English expedition under the earl of Leicester to the Low Countries and the depredations of Sir Francis Drake in the West Indies and the Cape Verde Islands convinced Philip that he should attack England directly.

Preparations were made for the construction of a powerful fleet to descend on England with an army of invasion. The task was hampered both by the attack of Drake on the harbor of Cádiz and the death of Cardinal Granvelle, who had been leader of the war party in the council. The only man in Spain capable of directing the vast enterprise Philip II had undertaken was removed. The situation was further complicated by the fact that Mary, queen of Scots, had been imprisoned since 1568. Although she had been the center of many conspiracies, Elizabeth was resolved that Mary or her son, James, should succeed her. When James accepted Protestantism, Mary disinherited him and indicated that she believed Philip the heir to the English crown. Her execution in 1587 removed a cause for the postponement of the attack on England and the delay of war, for it eliminated the last hope of a peaceful restoration of Catholicism in England. In Philip's eyes, at least, it made him lawful king of England. Pope Sixtus V, despite his fear of Spanish preponderance, concluded an alliance by which he promised a subsidy of a million scudi for the expedition against England (1587).

The original chief of the Spanish Armada was an expert mariner, Alvaro de Bazán, marquis of Santa Cruz. His death, however, left the command to Alonso Pérez de Guzmán, duke of Medina-Sidonia. He was the richest peer in Spain, son-in-law of the Princess of Eboli, but unfamiliar with naval affairs. Sailing from Lisbon on May 30, 1588, the squadron consisted of 130 vessels, with 3000 sailors and 18,000 soldiers. To it were to be added the troops of Alexander Farnese in the Netherlands. Elizabeth had entrusted the defense of her kingdom to the earl of Leicester, with Lord Howard as admiral and Sir Francis Drake as vice-admiral, assisted by John Hawkins and Martin Frobisher.

As the Invincible Armada rounded Cape Finisterre a severe storm forced it to take refuge at La Coruña. The duke of Medina-Sidonia was bound by minute instructions, even as to his tactics. The transportation of the veterans of Alexander Farnese in the Low Countries was considered essential for the invasion of England, but Philip II failed to recognize that the Dutch Sea Beggars had blockaded Alexander Farnese and that the element of surprise which was essential to the success of the invasion had long since been lost.

Another storm scattered the Armada at the mouth of the English Channel. The English, fearful of being caught in a narrow harbor, had put to sea and eluded the Armada. The first contact of the two fleets occurred outside Plymouth. The English ships, although fewer, were better constructed than the Spanish galleons, which were high and designed for boarding. The English were excellent sailors and possessed long-range artillery, while the Spanish had traditionally used their guns at close range, preparatory to boarding. Philip had taken this into consideration in his instructions to the Spanish commander. The Spaniards were to fight at close quarters. The English, however, with their superior sailing ability and their long-range guns, poured a deadly fire into the galleons and kept them at a distance. The fleets sailed back and forth in this manner for a week until the Spanish Armada sailed into Calais with the English in close pursuit.

Alexander Farnese was ready to invade England in accordance with his promise to Philip II, but he refused to put to sea until the fleet could protect him. With the English fleet waiting for the Spanish Armada in the channel, that was obviously impossible. Then the English forced the Spaniards out of their anchorage with fire ships. In the confusion which followed, the duke of Medina-Sidonia was able to gather only fifty ships to fight the battle of Gravelines. The English followed their customary tactics and the plight of the Spaniards became hopeless. A storm broke up the conflict and forced the Armada into the North Sea. As they dared not pass through the English Channel again, they sailed around Scotland and Ireland to Spain. Their return voyage was beset by storms and the remnants of the Armada did not reach Santander until September 22. The Spanish threat to England had been decisively beaten and only sixty-six ships, about half of the number that had sailed on the expedition from La Coruña, ever straggled back to Spanish ports. Although the duke of Medina-Sidonia retired to his estates in Andalusia in disgrace with his compatriots, Philip II stood loyally by him.

This was the supreme disaster of Philip's reign. The Spanish navy had been defeated, and Spain learned that she could be deprived of her dominion of the seas, so essential to her colonial communications. The immediate effect, however, was a moral one. The Spaniards remained formidable on the high seas for many years after the defeat of the Invincible Armada. The English had merely demonstrated that they could be repulsed. In 1589 Sir Francis Drake raided La Coruña and threatened Lisbon, burning Vigo on his return to Plymouth, but he lost thirty ships and thousands of men in the raid. For the next few years the English were content to let their seamen harry the Spanish colonies and attack the Spanish treasure fleets. The Spaniards, in turn, made a futile raid on the Cornish coast. In 1595 the English again attacked Spain directly. Cádiz was practically defenseless and the onslaught compelled the Spaniards to burn their ships in the harbor and stand passively by while the English sacked and burned the town. Philip II launched a new armada against England, but it was also struck by a storm and lost a third of its ships with 2000 men. The English retaliated in 1597 with an unsuccessful attempt to invade Spain. A year later Philip sent still another imposing fleet against England, but it was again dispersed by a storm.

Meanwhile, in the Huguenot wars in France Philip II had taken the side of the Catholics. He consistently aided the faction led by the duke of Guise and the cardinal of Lorraine. Henry III had protected the duke of Alençon in his efforts to govern Flanders and aided Antonio de Crato in his expedition to the Azores. On the death of the duke of Alençon in 1584, Henry III agreed to recognize the aged cardinal of Bourbon as his heir, in opposition to Henry of Bourbon, the leader of the Huguenots. The duke of Guise, who was popular in Paris, was acclaimed as a popular leader in 1588, and Henry III, accused of compliance toward the Protestants, had to flee. Then, by order of Henry III, the duke and his brother, the cardinal of Lorraine, were assassinated. Before his own assassination in 1589, Henry III named his ally against the Guise faction, Henry of Bourbon, as his heir. Henry of Bourbon defeated the Guise faction in two battles and besieged Paris. Philip II at once ordered Alexander Farnese to raise the siege (1590).

After the defeat of the Armada, the English aided the Flemish rebels openly. During the absence of Alexander Farnese in 1590, Mansfield had lost several towns. Others were lost in the following year, including Zutphen and Deventer to Maurice of Nassau. The Spanish troops mutinied again for lack of pay. When Alexander Farnese tried to raise the siege of Nimwegen by Maurice of Nassau, he was ordered by Philip II to go to the assistance of Rouen, which Henry IV of France had besieged. Alexander Farnese defeated Henry IV in the battle of Aumale (1592), but was forced to return to the Low Countries, where he died.

Philip II was alarmed by the policy of the popes, who favored a reconciliation with Henry IV. He intervened in the French struggle by supporting a candidate for the French throne. His daughter, Isabel Clara Eugenia, had a claim to the French crown through her mother, Elizabeth of Valois, but it was weakened by the exclusion of females from the French succession under the Salic Law. The abjuration of his Protestant faith by Henry IV and his triumphant entry into Paris (1594) practically ended Philip's hopes. The war continued for a time with varying fortunes. When the Spaniards captured Amiens, Henry IV quickly recovered it and slowly won the support of the French Catholics, including the duke of Mayenne, leader of the Guise faction. Philip II was therefore forced to conclude the Treaty of Vervins in 1598, a few months before his death. Providing for the mutual restoration of conquests the treaty gave scanty advantages to Spain for the half century of intrigue, expense, and bloody warfare in which the country had been involved.

Relations with Portugal became of great importance during the reign of Philip II, and gave him one of the most striking of his triumphs for

Spain—a triumph, however, of temporary character. One natural effect of the discovery of America had been a vigorous display of Castilian interest in the Canary Islands and in northwestern Africa. Since the Portuguese had given great attention to the exploration and colonization of these areas, the Spaniards came into rivalry with them. Fortunately, a peaceful road out of their jealousies was found. In a series of treaties between 1480 and 1509, the Portuguese recognized the validity of the claims made by Castile to her holdings. In 1494 the Canary Islands came under definite Spanish control and were held chiefly as stepping stones on the route to the New World. Almost simultaneously, the Spaniards took determined action to obtain a post on the Atlantic coast of Africa, to be used as a base for keeping the Moslems and their corsair fleets in check. Before the fifteenth century ended the Spaniards took possession of Melilla and converted it into a port useful for both trade and defense. These actions laid a foundation for a rapprochement between Spain and Portugal.

Then in 1578 the death of Sebastian of Portugal in his ill-fated African expedition produced a problem of succession to the Portuguese throne. A bachelor, he left no issue. His uncle, the aged Cardinal Henry, was proclaimed king, but the pope refused to release him from his religious position and duties. At once a weird variety of claimants for the crown appeared. They included Philip II, the duchess of Braganza, the prior of Crato, Catherine de Medici, and the dukes of Parma and Savoy. Philip II had the support of many of the Portuguese noblemen, his prestige as king of Spain, and the advantage of the fact that many of the Portuguese longed for Iberian unity. On the other hand, some leaders in France and England feared that the addition of Portugal to Philip's dominions would give him an excessive augmentation of power. They favored the prior of Crato, the most popular and turbulent of the claimants. Though illegitimate, the prior was in the direct line of succession from King Manuel. The pope and most of the clergy supported him.

But Philip had advantages which in the end counted decisively. His mother had been a quite legitimate daughter of King Manuel. He employed a special ambassador of great astuteness, Cristobal de Moura, to press his demands. In a move as shrewd as it was tactful, he announced that if Portugal were brought under his control, he would regard it as a political body quite separate from Spain and would respect its rights of self-government. The result was that in 1580 the Portuguese cortes voted to accept Philip as sovereign. Some disorders broke out as he prepared to take control, and he had to move armed forces—which he had kept in readiness—into the country, under the duke of Alba, who easily suppressed the opposition offered by the prior of Crato, with a minimum of offense to the Portuguese people. Philip had given strict orders that any breach of discipline, or any outrages or excesses, would be severely punished. The troops respected these commands. In an atmosphere of general good will, therefore, another Portuguese cortes in 1581 ratified the accession of Philip to the throne, and with solemn ceremonies he assumed the duties of king. He swore not to confer any Portuguese offices on Spaniards.

Portugal thus became a part of the Hispanic union, and the peninsula was for the time being an integral whole. The new union was not as perfect as that of Aragon and Castile, for long independence had given the Portuguese a strong nationalist feeling, but it seemed to offer great promise. The Portuguese dominions in Asia, Africa, and above all South America, where Brazil held the richest potentialities, promised a great augmentation of the power and wealth of the peninsula which Philip II ruled. If only Portugal could be held long enough to permit the real welding of the closely related peoples! Philip II tried hard to foster a fraternal feeling. He had to garrison some Portuguese cities to hold the restless followers of the prior of Crato in restraint, but he kept his promise not to appoint Spaniards to Portuguese offices and otherwise behaved with moderation. Lisbon continued to be the capital of the Portuguese colonies and to hold control of the sea-route around Africa to the Orient. Philip was able to bequeath suzerainty over Portugal to his successors, Philip III and Philip IV, but these successors proved weak—unable to stem the decline of the nation. Fresh causes of friction arose, and the year 1640 found Portugal in arms against the Spaniards under a new ruler of its own, John IV. The union that had promised so much and that represented one of the most statesmanlike policies of Philip II lasted only sixty years. Thenceforth, Spain and Portugal were to remain parted.

The last years of Philip II were unhappy for him and tragic for Spain. Long a victim of the gout, he became afflicted with dropsy and other diseases. His final days were full of suffering, stoically endured. Foreign affairs offered him constant anxiety. The Turks, still bitter rivals of Spain in the Mediterranean, offered constant threats to Italy and to Spanish commerce. The stubborn revolt in the Low Countries against Spain, so vividly described in the pages of John Lothrop Motley, continued throughout Philip's entire reign, with a steady drain on Spanish manpower and finances. Threats of an extension of the Spanish Inquisition to the Netherlands united the people, Protestant and Catholic alike, in the fiercest opposition. Indeed, the principal seat of rebellion in the Low Countries was quite as much in the Catholic South as the Protestant North. Eventually, the struggle involved Spain in open war with England under Elizabeth and with France, with the result that warships of these countries successfully raided the Spanish ports, attacked Spain's communications with Latin America, and preyed on her overseas commerce. The struggle continued for a half century after Philip's death, ending, as all students of the development of liberty know, in the independence of the Protestant Netherlands—their achievement of freedom being a great landmark in history.

Philip II had removed to the Escorial, as the world has always called the great monastery of St. Lawrence, with a vast palace and church attached, which he had begun building in 1563. For the last fourteen years of his life, which closed in September 1598, he ruled his domains from this gigantic building of 120 miles of corridors and 1200 doorways. Thirty miles from Madrid, it has been one of the most impressive sights of Europe. Here he lies buried side by side with Charles V, and all about them are disposed the tombs of later kings, with the queens who bore monarchs. This edifice, designed and built by Juan de Herrera, may indeed be called the most famous structure reared by Christian Spain.

The reign of Charles V, however promising it appeared at its beginning, had been unfortunate for Spain. It raised, against the wishes of the Spanish people, the illusion that imperial grandeur was a proper objective. To achieve that grandeur and to dominate Europe, Spanish manpower and wealth were drained away on the battlefields of Germany and Italy. In a sense, the grandiose schemes of Charles V were marked by failure. He failed to win permanently the hegemony he desired in Europe. His hold on Italy was tenuous. His native Flanders was left as an isolated appendage of Spain, hostile to Spanish control and indefensible against France and England. The Turks remained a threat to Europe on the continent and in the Mediterranean. Europe, at the end of his reign, was divided into two hostile camps religiously instead of possessing the Catholic unity which Charles had valiantly and constantly sought to defend.

Indeed, Charles V and Philip II were victims of events rather than masters of them, and Spain was the unfortunate heir of their failure. During their reigns Spanish dominions under Habsburg control were extended in both Europe and the New World, but the increased tendency toward royal absolutism checked the national enthusiasm which had developed under the Catholic Kings. Castilian domination of the peninsula was consolidated. The eyes of the Spaniards were turned permanently from the Mediterranean to the Atlantic. Nevertheless, bureaucracy began to present an obstacle to the sturdy individualism of the past. Had Charles and Philip developed the empire in the Americas with the resources they wasted in Europe, they might have left their successors an even greater heritage than they did.

Philip II was to blame, however, for the financial mismanagement of his reign. He had inherited a debt estimated at twenty million ducats from his father, who had recklessly mortgaged the future of Spain. The cortes of Castile continued to vote him annual subsidies of 150 *cuentos,* maintaining in theory its power to approve all new taxes. The Aragonese cortes contributed some funds, but they were insignificant in view of Philip's heavy expenditures. While Philip inherited financial problems, his conduct of affairs also increased them. He retained the ruinous imposts then in effect and defied the reluctant legislature by adding many new ones. Municipal offices were multiplied so that they could be sold for profit. Large sums were borrowed at exorbitant rates of interest from foreign bankers. In the end, by continuing to mortgage the future for an always elusive victory, he increased the national debt fourfold.

Many new forms of revenue were introduced to balance the budget. In 1558 Philip extended the sales tax to New Spain and New Castile. He levied duties on the exportation of Castilian wool and established other new charges on the customs. He ordered all gold, silver, and quicksilver mines and salt pits incorporated into the royal domain. He established royal monopolies. He increased the tax on individuals. He obtained subsidies from the pope. Yet by 1573 the debt had risen to fifty million ducats, and the ordinary income of the realm had been spent five years in advance.

The levying of taxes, even if the approval of the cortes was sought, was easier than their collection. The Castilian cities refused to accept an increase in the head tax and paid the old sales tax instead. Philip finally became unable to meet his financial obligations. German and Genoese bankers flatly refused to arrange new loans, especially after he suspended payments in 1575. Spanish credit in Europe was so nearly ruined that it took Philip two years to reestablish it. He issued fresh pledges to his creditors, in place of the old, promising them interest out of regular crown revenues. When for a time he was able to borrow money again, he merely mortgaged the future even farther in advance. He reached the lowest ebb of his fortunes with the defeat of the Invincible Armada. That expedition cost him ten million ducats. In 1590 the cortes voted a direct contribution of eight million ducats, but the money had already been spent. A second decree suspending payments was published in 1596.

The population of Spain, in 1594, had been estimated at just over nine millions. At least two-thirds of the people lived in the Castiles and León, with a density of sixty per square mile. In Andalusia and Murcia, where there were over a million and a half persons, the density was thirty-nine. In Aragon it was only twenty-one. The inhabitants preferred the pasture lands of the central meseta to the fertile valleys—an indication of the continued decline of agriculture.

The Spanish army was not modified in basic organization under Philip II. The revolt of the Moriscos revealed the need for an increase in the available forces within the kingdom. Finally, in 1590 the council approved a plan which was put into operation. The army, in effect, declined, for Philip was not a military man. He never liked military men and was usually unable to pay them. The army also suffered from a lack of skilled leadership. The duke of Alba, who was in constant demand, was the last of the great Spanish soldiers of imperial days. Yet the prestige of Spanish arms remained high, and the Spanish army was generally regarded as nearly invincible until the end of Philip's reign.

As a result of the defeat of the Invincible Armada, however, the Spaniards lost their control of the seas. The naval forces were temporarily paralyzed. A new fleet was constructed, but Philip never really understood the importance of the control of the sea to his empire. He neglected all appeals to preserve it and risked it in one ambitious attack foredoomed to failure. He preferred to purchase his ships abroad and to hire foreigners and their ships for his service, for it required a smaller original investment and he did not have money. There was also a shortage of sailors and sea captains. Alvaro de Bazán was the last of the great Castilian seadogs, and no foreigner of the ability of Andrea Doria appeared to replace him. Philip preferred intrigue and diplomacy to the use of force in gaining his ends.

One of the strongest influences of the Church in Spain lay in its control of education, learning, culture, and art during the period of the Counter Reformation. Dominicans and Jesuits controlled the universities. They regulated their curricula and the methods of teaching. Yet there was a great zeal for scholarship, and the age of Philip II marked the beginning of the golden age of Spanish literature.

The greatest scholarship of the reign was produced in history, theology, and law. The greatest historians were Ambrosio de Morales (1513–91) and Jerónimo de Zurita (1512–80). Philip II made Zurita his secretary and a councilor of state. Subsequently appointed chronicler of Aragon (1563), he traveled through Spain, Sicily, and Italy. His six-volume *Anales de la Corona de Aragon,* published from 1562 to 1580, was considered a work of great importance even in his own day. He may be regarded as one of the founders of critical historical scholarship in Spain. The Jesuit Juan de Mariana (1535–1624) also accomplished most of his work during the reign of Philip II, although it was published later. He has been estimated as "a paragon of learning, and a master of Spanish prose."

The outstanding theologians were Jesuits, Luis Molina (1535–1600) and Francisco Suárez (1548–1617). The latter in 1597 was appointed to the University of Coimbra. He was the last of the old scholastic philosophers and taught that the same doctrine may be held by science and faith. He held in *De defensione fidei* that earthly power is properly held by the body of men and that kingly power is derived from them. This doctrine so enraged James I of England that he had the book burned by the hangman. Nevertheless, this doctrine became the basis of subsequent Catholic teaching on democracy. Hugo Grotius held Suárez in high esteem because in *Tractatus de legibus* he distinguished between natural law and international law, which he declared was based on custom. The most learned legal writer of the day was Diego de Covarrubias y Leyva (1512–77), professor of canon law at Salamanca, who wrote on many legal topics as well as on the Council of Trent.

In poetry as well as prose the religious influence also prevailed. The works of Saint Teresa of Ávila, Saint John of the Cross, Luis de León, and Fray Luis de Granada are the most significant examples of this influence. Fernando de Herrera in *Canción a Lepanto* and *Perdida del Rey Don Sebastián y su Ejército* commemorated the triumphs and defeats of the Christians in fighting the Moslems.

The great names of Spanish literature of the age of Philip II, however, are Lope de Vega and Miguel Cervantes de Saavedra. Felix Lope de Vega Carpio (1562–1635) did not publish his first work until the year of the death of Philip II, but he was molded by his experiences and adventures during Philip's reign. He was not highly educated, and his early life was marked by a series of escapades—he was banished from Madrid for libel. Then he eloped with Isabel de Urbina and served in the Invincible Armada. He finished his epic *La Hermosura de Angélica* in the intervals of fighting the English. His *La Dragontea,* published in 1598, was an attack on Sir Francis Drake and his *La Corona trágica* was a defense of Mary, queen of Scots. The founder of the national Spanish drama, his plays were distinguished by wit, brilliant dramatic effects, and fine portrayal of character. He had a profound influence on the European theater.

Miguel de Cervantes Saavedra (1547–1616), who was born in Alcalá de Henares, also grew up in the age of Philip II. He fought in the battle of Lepanto, where he was wounded and lost the use of his left arm. While returning to Spain he was captured by the Moslems and taken to Algiers as a galley slave. Finally, in 1580 he was ransomed by his family, which was financially ruined in the process, and returned to Spain. His ensuing life was a constant struggle against debt, for which he was sometimes imprisoned. His first published work was *La Galatea* (1585), a pastoral romance. In the next three years he wrote and produced more than twenty plays. He was fifty-eight years old when the first part of his masterpiece, *Don Quijote de la Mancha,* was published (1605). Like Lope de Vega he knew his native land at the height of her power and on the eve of her decay.

During Philip's reign architecture, sculpture, and painting were almost completely dominated by the clergy and the Church. Philip II took great interest in the fine arts and the Escorial reflected his deep religious feeling and his somber outlook. His influence led to the disappearance of the plateresque style during this age and was strongly felt in much of the painting and sculpture. Philip showed special favor to Alonzo Sánchez Coello (1531–90). This Spanish-born Portuguese portrait painter, who succeeded the Fleming court painter, Antonio Mor, his master, painted portraits of Philip II, Prince Carlos, and Princess Isabel. He caught in their somber dignity the characters of the Spanish court. He also produced numerous religious pictures. With his pupil, Juan Pantajo de la Cruz (1551–1609) and Antonio Mor, who came to Spain in 1552, he painted most of the members of the royal family and most of the courtiers and warriors of the day.

The great artist of the age, however, was El Greco, Domenico Theotocopoulos (1548?–1614?). He studied under Titian in Venice and painted in Rome. In 1577 he was in Toledo at work on the altar of the Church of Santo Domingo el Antiguo. He painted St. Maurice as an altarpiece for the Escorial for Philip II, but the work did not please the king. In Toledo he achieved such masterpieces as his famous "Burial of the Count of Orgaz." The Italian, Federigo Zuccaro, had more success in pleasing Philip II. He painted Elizabeth and Mary Stuart in England and was brought from Rome to Spain to decorate the Escorial.

Philip II was more interested in the representation of sacred subjects than he was in pictures of secular life. Luis de Morales (1509–86), his most characteristic religious painter, lived and worked in his native Badajoz. Profoundly Spanish in his harsh and melancholy realism, he painted vivid pictures of the suffering of saints and was very popular. Few paintings were inspired by the imperial achievements of Spain. The religious atmosphere was too somber under Philip to permit the luxury of daily enjoyment.

The reign of Philip II was also a golden age in music. Tomas Luis de Victoria (1540–1611) was the most popular Spanish composer of the age. He studied in Rome for the priesthood and later succeeded Palestrina as music master of the Collegium Romanorum. About 1594 he returned to Spain to serve as chaplain and choirmaster for the Empress María, sister of Philip II, in whose memory he composed his last and greatest work. He wrote only sacred compositions, but used a polyphonic technique to express his passionate mysticism. Secular melodies were also popular, and every gentleman learned to play the guitar.

Charles V left Philip II an overwhelming heritage. Philip sought conscientiously to discharge his responsibility, but he was not a man to delegate it. The empire became burdened internally by the bureaucracy that his desire for absolute control of every detail of his dominions demanded. In fact, his stubborn desire to be king in every sense of the word and his sturdy defense of the Catholic status quo in an age of transition served to increase the problems that perplexed him. It cost him part of the Netherlands, and he spent much Spanish blood and treasure to retain them. Philip was Spanish, he was Castilian. He was more inclined to diplomacy than to war, but he did not hesitate to use both to seek his ends. He made Castile supreme in Spain and Spain continued to be supreme in Europe, but he left her weaker in both prestige and power than when he began his reign. In a real sense he was the champion of traditions that were becoming obsolescent in Europe. In seeking to perpetuate them and make them dominant in his realm, he retarded the nation's development and paved the way for its decline.

CHAPTER XV

The Decline of the Spanish Habsburgs

The successors of Philip II had neither the understanding nor the vision to assume their inheritance. In the years which followed his death Spain steadily lost prestige in Europe, as her rulers showed themselves either unwilling or unable to cope with urgent problems both at home and abroad. Philip II himself had no illusions as to the abilities of his son and successor Philip III (1598–1621): "God, who has given me so many kingdoms, has not blessed me with a son capable of governing them. I fear they will govern him." His fears were soon justified. The new king had scarcely come to the throne when he gave power to an old gambling and drinking companion, Francisco de Sandoval, marquis of Denia. Sandoval, soon made duke of Lerma, was a member of a coterie of young courtiers who had become impatient with the prudent policy of Philip II. Replacing the experienced Cristobal de Moura, he surrounded the king with ministers devoted to bolder policies, men too often working in their own interests rather than the king's.

Despite the serious financial and social problems which Philip inherited—a shortage of coin, rising prices, a growing discontent among many of the lower classes—he encouraged by his personal behavior a new era of extravagant spending among the aristocracy. His marriage at Valencia to Margaret of Austria was celebrated with lavish splendor. The new cortes certainly thought it excessive when very reluctantly they granted the 18,000,000 ducats which the king demanded. Other cortes too made large grants: at Saragossa, in return for a general amnesty to the recent rebels, Philip received 200,000 ducats for himself, 10,000 for the queen, and 6000 for the duke of Lerma. The cortes of Valencia, too, supplied 400,000 ducats to the royal treasury. The eastern kingdoms, however, were not as submissive as Castile: there were demonstrations in Valencia and protests in both Aragon and Catalonia against the transgression of their *fueros*. On his way back to Madrid Philip showered titles on undeserving courtiers to fill the coffers of the duke of Lerma and to conciliate his partisans.

Abroad, as at home, Philip III was faced with a tangle of unresolved difficulties, as the war against the confident, expanding power of England was bedeviled by the struggle with his own Flemish subjects.

War was continued in the Netherlands without either party gaining a positive advantage. In 1600 Maurice of Nassau captured some forts in Gueldres, when the Spanish troops mutinied and the Archduke Albert was defeated in the battle of the Dunes. The Spanish army was reinforced from Italy and Maurice of Nassau, with aid from Henry of Bourbon, Elizabeth of England, and the German princes, threatened Brabant with a fleet and 30,000 men. But Elizabeth died and James I did not have her personal animosity against Spain. In 1602, with the Italian *tercios,* the Archduke Albert besieged Ostend in an effort to retrieve some of the waning Spanish prestige, and the city capitulated after a lengthy and famous siege. Ambrosio Spinola, the great Genoese general who had entered the service of Philip III, continued to gain advantages over Maurice of Nassau.

The Spanish treasury could not well bear the strain of the war, and both the Flemings and the Dutch were exhausted with the long struggle. A truce was negotiated in 1609 for twelve years between Spinola and Jan van Olden Barneveldt, despite the opposition of the military party of Maurice of Nassau. Spain recognized the *de facto* independence of the United Provinces, guaranteed freedom of commerce with them, and suspended hostilities on the basis of the status quo.

Taking advantage of their increasing control of the sea, the English also assumed the offensive against Spain, attacking the treasure-laden galleons from the New World, interrupting Spanish commerce with the colonies, and even attacking Spain. In 1599 a powerful English fleet attacked La Coruña, the Canary Islands, and the Azores. In retaliation the duke of Lerma sent a fleet of forty ships to invade England, but it returned, battered by storms, without having made contact with the English. A year later Philip III tried to aid the rebellious Irish Catholics, who had recognized his sovereignty. A fleet sailed from Lisbon and landed Spanish troops at Kinsale and Baltimore, but they were soon forced to capitulate.

After the accession of James I, a treaty of peace was signed at London in 1604. Philip III sent an able series of ambassadors to England in Pedro de Zuñiga, Alonso de Velasco, and the count of Gondomar. The count, who became an intimate friend of James I, even demanded and secured the execution of Sir Walter Raleigh. He negotiated the marriage of the Prince of Wales with the Princess Maria and succeeded in maintaining peace with England during a crucial period.

Although the Treaty of Vervins (1598) had concluded peace with France, Spain was skillfully opposed by French diplomacy and secret aid to the rebellion in the Netherlands. The duke of Sully tried to obstruct the peace with England, but the duke of Lerma foiled him with skillful bribery—keeping advised of intimate details in the French court and even learning Henry IV's secret cipher. Spanish agents instigated conspiracies in France, while the French aided the German Protestants against the Habsburg armies. War was again imminent in 1610, but Henry IV was assassinated, and the situation changed in favor of Spain. Marie de Medici, who became the regent of France, was soon under the influence of Iñigo de Cardenas, the Spanish ambassador, and Sully was forced to withdraw from the court. As a result, in 1615 a double marriage was concluded. The prince of Asturias married Elizabeth of Bourbon, daughter of Henry IV, and Louis XIII married the daughter of Philip III, Anne of Austria.

Charles Emmanuel of Savoy, a restless, intelligent, and ambitious enemy of Spain, seized Montferrat in 1613 and announced himself as the liberator of Italy. He was defeated at Asti by the Spanish viceroy of Milan, and in 1617 peace was concluded at Pavia by which Montferrat was restored to the duke of Mantua. Spanish hegemony in Italy had so declined that the three Spanish viceroys followed personal policies. When Venice supported Savoy, the viceroy of Naples defeated the Venetian fleet at Gravoso, repudiated the Peace of Pavia, and with the viceroy of Milan and the Spanish ambassador in Venice, the marquis of Bedmar, turned the whole Spanish force in Italy against the Venetian Republic. They were accused of the treacherous design of destroying the city and proclaiming the duke of Osuna, viceroy of Naples, as king of that city. Both the duke of Osuna and the marquis of Bedmar were recalled as a result of their conspiracy.

By the end of Philip III's reign, Spain was also involved in the Thirty Years' War. Philip II's policy of protecting the German Habsburgs had been continued, and once again Spanish manpower and economic resources were wasted on enterprises of little direct value to them. When Frederick V was proclaimed king of Bohemia, the Catholic League supported Ferdinand II of Habsburg. Spinola, with 30,000 men, crossed the Rhine into the Palatinate and his aid was responsible for the imperial victory at Prague in 1620.

At the same time, the Berber pirates, aided and stimulated by the Turks, continued to raid the Mediterranean coasts of Spain, Italy, and the Balearic Islands. The Spaniards retaliated by raids on Malta and Tangier, and in 1618 a Neapolitan captain even seized ships in the Dardanelles. Meanwhile, castles were erected to defend the Andalusian coast and Cádiz and Gibraltar were fortified. Although the Moslem threat in the Mediterranean was contained, some of the Spanish outposts in North Africa were abandoned or lost.

At home in Spain the Morisco community was a continuing social, economic, and religious problem. Hated by many Spanish Christians, envied for their wealth and industry, feared because of their rising numbers, the Moriscos were protected only by those lords who profited from their work or by those members of the clergy who hoped for their ultimate conversion. But increasingly there were alarming reports of projected uprisings, of help to the French, and intrigue with the Berbers. In 1609 Lerma struck at them: the Moriscos were to leave the country within three days. They must take only what they could personally carry, leaving only enough older men to train new laborers and children under six years old born of Christian mothers. Exploited, many of them robbed or even killed on the way, the Moriscos fled from Spain, all too often to fall victims to the Moors in Africa. About 150,000 are estimated to have left Valencia; 64,000 went from Aragon, many more from Andalusia and Murcia. In Estremadura and Castile, where many had become converts or had married Christians, their position was often especially tragic. The expulsion of the Moriscos, while popular at the time, was a serious economic blow to the community, doing little to resolve the social or economic problems of the country as a whole.

Apparently oblivious to the problems which threatened his dominions, Philip III devoted himself either to religious exercises or to frivolous pastimes and left matters of state to his favorite, the duke of Lerma. While the entertainment of an extravagant court bore heavily upon the nation, Lerma and his associates enriched themselves at public expense. However, many high officials were brought to trial for bribery and corruption, as was, for example, Alonso Ramirez de Prado, a councillor, whose heirs were obliged to surrender 400,000 ducats. The unpopular Pedro Franquesa, a man of humble origin who became secretary to the duke of Lerma, was found to have appropriated even greater plunder. He was exiled after being forced to pay an enormous fine. Another secretary, Rodrigo Calderón, was tried in a famous case of corruption, which led to the formation of a powerful party of young noblemen against the duke of Lerma. This aristocratic cabal, including the count of Olivares, succeeded in driving the old

SPANISH NETHERLANDS
FRANCHE COMTÉ
FRANCE
MILAN
PORTUGAL
SPAIN
BALEARIC ISLES
SARDINIA
NAPLES
SICILY
Melilla
SPANISH POSSESSIONS IN EUROPE, 1648
TO SPAIN

duke from the court, and he was replaced by his son, the duke of Uceda.

Philip IV (1621–65), an even weaker king than his father and only sixteen years old at his accession, followed his father's habit of leaving affairs of state to sycophants and favorites. All effective power was very soon taken over by the count-duke of Olivares, a royal favorite who, after a successful career at the University of Salamanca, had joined the retinue of Prince Philip in 1615. Olivares, though himself as guilty of corruption as his predecessors, began by announcing revolutionary reforms, stringent economies in the royal household, and sumptuary laws to suppress luxury. The cortes of the kingdom, favorably impressed by this decisive beginning, made grants to the king, with only the eastern kingdoms showing apprehension of the apparent trend toward centralization.

In foreign affairs Olivares was a more adept diplomat, with more definite policies than the duke of Lerma, but he was unfortunate in having as his chief antagonist a statesman of the ability of Cardinal Richelieu. Olivares was determined to continue the war in Flanders, despite the desire of the Archduke Albert and Spinola for peace. Although Cardinal Richelieu supplied financial aid to the Dutch, Spinola captured Breda after a ten-month siege, a feat of arms which astonished Europe and was immortalized by Velazquez. The Dutch war became merely an episode in two broader rivalries, the Thirty Years' War between the Catholics and the Protestants and the struggle between Bourbons and Habsburgs.

As a result of the renewal of the Thirty Years' War in 1625, Spain consumed resources that would have been more usefully devoted to other objectives. The victories of Tilly and Wallenstein for the Catholic party were countered by the triumphs of Gustavus Adolphus, and after his death at Lützen, Cardinal Richelieu became the active ally of the German Protestants. Richelieu formed a league against Spain and invaded the Valtelline, but after a brief war, peace was concluded at Monzon (1626). It was agreed that the Valtelline would remain Catholic, but the sovereignty of the Swiss was recognized, the fortresses were surrendered to the pope and dismantled, and Spain was forbidden to keep troops in the territory. On the death of the duke of Mantua, Charles Emmanuel of Savoy proposed a joint invasion and the division of Montferrat to Olivares. Richelieu was then preoccupied with the siege of La Rochelle, but he checked the invasion, captured Pignerol, the key to the pass into Italy, and retained it by the Treaty of Cherasco (1631).

Spanish leaders in the Netherlands proved to be incompetent, and

Philip IV named his brother, the Cardinal-Prince Ferdinand, as governor. He went to Flanders with an army of 18,000 men. Under his command the Spanish infantry won a great victory over the Swedes at Nördlingen and captured Treves. Cardinal Richelieu then intervened and declared war on Spain and Austria in 1635. The climax of the war —in 1640—was disastrous for the Spaniards. The French captured Arras and invaded Flanders, separatist movements sprang up in Portugal and Catalonia, and the cardinal-prince found his activities restricted. In revenge he allied himself with the French opposition—the Cinq Mars conspiracy—but Richelieu discovered and executed the traitorous French nobles.

By this time the war had spread from the East to the West Indies. The Dutch destroyed a Portuguese fleet, and, after ascertaining the route to the East Indies, conquered Ceylon in 1628. Commerce was so interrupted by the extension of the war that Spain was nearly isolated economically. Richelieu had won the advantage in the struggle between the Habsburgs and the Bourbons, and Spain was forced to remain on the defensive.

Relations with England did not improve. Philip III had entered into negotiations to marry his daughter Maria to Prince Charles, heir to the English throne. In 1623 the prince of Wales visited Madrid incognito, accompanied by the duke of Buckingham. They were graciously received and entertained for six months, and the count of Gondomar worked faithfully to advance the match in England. Although the prince and princess were apparently pleased with one another, the two nations were separated by religious and commercial rivalry, and the marriage plans were broken off. When Charles I ascended the English throne two years later, he dispatched a fleet against Cádiz. The expedition failed, but the English became more friendly with the Dutch and continued their attacks on Spanish commerce.

The strong policy of Olivares had meanwhile provoked rebellion in Spain. He hoped to reduce the whole peninsula to Castilian domination. The first resistance was offered by the Basques, who had been alienated by the salt monopoly, the forced levy of troops, and the subsidies. A revolt was quickly suppressed and the leaders executed. The Catalans were especially jealous of their privileges and traditions. The Catalan cortes had resisted the extraordinary war subsidies and the forced levies of soldiers for foreign service that Olivares attempted to impose on them. The Italian and Castilian soldiers stationed in Catalonia were regarded as foreigners, and disagreeable incidents arose over quartering. The industrious and sober Catalans also resented the licence and frivolity of the royal court. They were already exasperated by the neglect of matters they considered important, when Olivares ordered that the Catalan *fueros* should not be respected in a conflict with the royal service and announced a new levy of soldiers.

A new viceroy arrested two of the Catalan leaders who complained of the atrocities of the Spanish soldiery. This precipitated a riot, the Castilians were attacked, and the viceroy was seized and killed. The Catalans rose throughout the principality. Some of the royal counselors favored conciliation, but Olivares was resolved to deal severely with the rebels. The citizens of Barcelona resisted and the city was besieged. When the defiant Catalans proclaimed their independence and hailed Louis XIII as count of Barcelona, Cardinal Richelieu sent two French armies to overrun Roussillon and relieve Barcelona. The prince of Condé quickly subdued Roussillon, and in 1642 Spain lost that frontier province forever.

As the antagonists sought to excel each other in reprisals, the war became increasingly savage. Philip IV led an army into Catalonia, where the French defeated him at Saragossa and overran a great part of the principality before the attitude of the Catalans changed. Finding the French to be just as arbitrary as Olivares they renewed their allegiance to Philip IV. In 1657 the Castilians captured Tortosa and, after a siege of fifteen months, starved Barcelona into submission. The Peace of the Pyrenees ended the struggle in 1659.

The Catalan revolt was also the signal for trouble to break out in Portugal, where discontent had been mounting steadily ever since the death of Philip II. His successors had failed to follow his policy of scrupulous regard for Portuguese institutions: many of the clergy resented what they considered a too lenient policy towards Portuguese Jews; Olivares, wanting to centralize the government of all the peninsular states, even wished to unite the cortes of Portugal and Castile. The worst sources of dispute, however, were taxation and trade. Olivares levied a 5 percent property tax and aroused hostility by his attempts to make the Portuguese pay for their own defense. The war, too, was intensely unpopular, disrupting the lucrative Portuguese trade with the Dutch, who were increasingly active in Portuguese possessions in Africa, the East Indies, and the New World. The Dutch held Bahía in Brazil, and in fifteen years had seized 540 Spanish and Portuguese ships.

The position of Margaret of Savoy—Philip IV's aunt and, without other qualification, the viceroy of Portugal—was seriously weakened when Portuguese garrisons were sent to Catalonia and Flanders. Resistance hardened around the duke of Braganza, who, spurning Olivares' offer of the viceroyalty of Milan and an invitation to accompany the expedition to Catalonia, retired to his estate, where he could rally 80,000 Portuguese. Richelieu at once sent an agent to provoke trouble in Lisbon and offer French help to the rebels. When the Catalans rose in arms, the Portuguese, under Braganza's steward, João Pinto Ribeiro, attacked the Castilian guard of Margaret of Savoy and imprisoned her in the fortress at Lisbon. The duke of Braganza was solemnly proclaimed John IV in 1640: Spain's enemies recognized him at once, hailed Portuguese independence, and hastened to offer their friendship and alliance.

Although a conspiracy, initiated by the marquis of Ayamonte, to make the duke of Medina-Sidonia king of Andalusia was foiled, Spain appeared confronted with disaster on every hand. Nevertheless, the round of palace festivities continued in Madrid, and the theater at the Buen Retiro consumed treasure which might have better been devoted to the reconstruction of Spain. Slowly the prestige of Olivares, author of so many disastrous policies, began to decline. Popular hostility was most evident in the writings of the humorist and satirist, Francisco Quevedo, who was imprisoned for his audacity. Olivares alienated the queen by his objection to the intervention of women in politics, and she also blamed him for the illicit affair of Philip IV with Maria la Calderona. The royal family became suspicious of the efforts of the omnipotent minister to keep them away from court.

Olivares accompanied the king to Catalonia, still hoping to isolate him from the nobility, but the queen utilized his absence to win the support of his numerous enemies. The situation had become so desperate when Philip IV returned to Madrid that his loyal queen insisted that he had to dismiss Olivares or face disaster. The count-duke resorted to his customary stratagem and requested that he be allowed to retire. To his surprise the king approved the request, and he withdrew to Faro, where, still awaiting his recall, he died in 1645.

After the fall of Olivares, Philip IV began to take a greater interest in public affairs. The death of Richelieu had removed his most formidable enemy, but Cardinal Mazarin, who had begun his career in the Spanish service, adopted the policy of his predecessor, even though Anne of Austria, regent of France, was a sister of Philip IV. The proposal for the marriage of Philip IV's daughter to the dauphin seemed to give some hope of peace.

In 1641 the count of Azumar had become governor of the Spanish Netherlands and had won a number of victories, but when he besieged Rocroi, the duke of Enghien won a brilliant victory, relieving the city in 1643. The terror of the invincible Spanish pikemen was dissipated, and thereafter successive viceroys were unable to check the French. The exhaustion of both combatants hastened the peace negotiations, which had been initiated at Hamburg in 1641 and were concluded in 1648. In the Treaty of Westphalia Spain at last recognized the independence of the United Provinces.

Meanwhile, there were revolts in Italy, caused by the financial exactions of the Spaniards, the use of Italian soldiers in foreign wars, and the abuses of Spanish officials. After outbreaks in Sicily and Milan had been suppressed, a more serious revolt occurred in Naples. Fearing a French invasion, the viceroy laid a tax on fruit, a principal item in the diet of the populace, whereupon Masaniello, a fish vendor, led a revolt marked by many atrocities. The viceroy was forced to capitulate, but the sovereignty of Philip IV was restored in 1648.

The war with France continued until the French besieged Dunkirk in 1658 and defeated the Spanish army sent to relieve it. Spain lost all of maritime Flanders and part of Brabant, just as negotiations for peace were renewed. In the Treaty of the Pyrenees of 1659, Anne of Austria was able to offer her brother better terms than the precarious Spanish position in Flanders justified. María Teresa was betrothed to the future Louis XIV with a large dowry, on the condition that she renounce her claim to the Spanish throne. While the French restored most of their conquests in the Spanish Netherlands and Franche Comté, the English retained Dunkirk, and Spain ceded Roussillon and Artois to France.

During the later years of his life Philip IV fell under the influence of a female counselor, a venerable abbess with whom he carried on an extensive correspondence. The queen had died in 1644, and five years later Philip married the fifteen-year-old Archduchess Mariana of Austria. When he died in 1665 Spain had lost her hegemony in Europe, partly because of Philip's disastrous reign, and was fast becoming an impoverished satellite of France.

On the death of Philip IV Mariana of Austria became regent. The new king, Charles II (1665–1700), was a four-year-old boy whose accession to the throne was a bitter blow to Spain. Suffering from the worst features of inheritance of continuous close intermarriage he was too retarded both physically and mentally ever to speak or eat like an adult; he was unable to learn even the rudiments until he was nine. Spain was inflicted with a king and ruler who all his life was to have the tastes and concepts of the nursery.

Mariana was assisted in the regency by counselors of conflicting personalities and attitudes. Her natural stepson, Juan José of Austria, had been well educated but had little political judgment. Mariana hated him, and he hated her in return, blaming her for the indifference toward him of Philip IV during his later years. Their antagonism was increased by the appointment of the regent's Jesuit confessor, John Everard Nithard, as inquisitor general, which admitted him to the Council of Regency. A naturalized citizen from the Tyrol, he was cordially disliked as a foreigner; the nobles envied him for his influence and the citizens of Madrid blamed him for the prohibition of theatrical presentations.

Peace was finally concluded with Portugal when Spain recognized her independence in 1668. For the moment Spain was then at peace, but a wise minister would have been wary of France. Although he had been warned of French treachery, the ingenuous Father Nithard suspected nothing. Even though Leopold I, anxious to ally the two branches of the Habsburgs, proposed cooperation with England, Sweden, and Holland to counteract the intrigues of Louis XIV and protect Spain, the regent and her advisers ignored such suggestions.

Despite warnings of probable French aggression, the regency remained apathetic until an army of 50,000 Frenchmen invaded Flanders, claiming the fortresses in the name of the wife of Louis XIV. The War of Devolution began as a triumphal march for the French. Within a year Franche Comté had been overrun, and England, Holland, and Sweden had joined in the Triple Alliance to resist the threat to the balance of power. By the Treaty of Aix-la-Chapelle in 1668, Louis XIV returned Franche Comté but retained his conquests in Flanders. The French ruler had already concluded a secret agreement with Leopold I which envisaged the future partition of the Spanish dominions.

Don Juan now found the time propitious to intrigue against the regent, for Father Nithard's handling of foreign affairs had completely discredited him. Don Juan refused command of the Spanish army, and soon placed himself at the head of the discontented nobles. When one of his intimate companions was charged with an attempt to assassinate Father Nithard and executed, Don Juan fled to Catalonia. The two factions engaged in a furious war of pamphlets. In 1669 Don Juan approached Madrid with an escort of 500 soldiers, and Father Nithard was forced to leave the city in a coach, which was stoned by the people as it passed through the streets. Withdrawing to Guadalajara, Don Juan submitted a program to the regent, demanding an honest administration of justice, a decrease in taxation, and economy in expenditures. He was temporarily reconciled by his appointment as viceroy of Aragon and finally submitted to Mariana, who at this time raised a royal bodyguard to strengthen her position.

Another favorite soon succeeded Father Nithard. He was Ferdinand de Valenzuela, a Neapolitan, with sufficent charm and versatility to rise from obscurity as a page to the viceroyalty of Sicily. He gained the ear of the regent by reporting court secrets to her and made it his duty to please everyone when he became first minister. He provided public works and food for the populace of Madrid, distributed offices among the grandees, and entertained the young king with bull fights, festivals, and theatrical presentations. Although Don Juan was placed in honorable exile in Sicily as viceroy, the grandees were finally aroused to direct a manifesto to the king, demanding the dismissal of Valenzuela. He fled to the Escorial as Don Juan entered Madrid with 12,000 men. Inspired by vengeance, Don Juan seized the favorite, annulled the royal gifts to him, exiled him to the Philippines, and sent Mariana to Toledo. Charles II, at fifteen, had just attained his majority.

The ill-formed child had developed into a misshapen man. His enormous chin protruded so that, like his great-grandfather, Charles V, he had difficulty in eating. His tongue was so abnormal in size that he could hardly speak intelligibly. He was known popularly as "Charles the Bewitched" because the religious melancholy and mysticism of his progenitors had bred in him a superstitious fear of everything he could not understand, and he understood little. His legs were so frail that he had been treated as an infant until he was ten years of age. In the end his own fragility overwhelmed him, and "he died of senile decay when most men are hardly in their prime."

While Spain was torn by court intrigue, Louis XIV had divided his recent opponents and attacked the Dutch. As they were nearly isolated, they sought aid from Spain. In 1672 three French armies invaded Holland, and William III of Orange formed a defensive alliance with Austria, the German states, and his old enemy Spain. Turenne, the great French general, conducted a brilliant campaign in the Palatinate, while other French armies overran and occupied Franche Comté. The Catalans tried to recover Roussillon, but were forced to withdraw. The campaign of 1676 was equally disastrous for the Spaniards. By the Treaty of Nimwegen in 1678, Spain finally relinquished Franche Comté and important strongholds in the Netherlands. This treaty, which marked the zenith of the power of Louis XIV in the domination of European affairs, made evident the continued decline of Spanish power.

Although prodigal in promises Don Juan disappointed his adherents by accomplishing very little after he made himself first minister. The exile of his aristocratic opponents, the insistence on etiquette to flatter his own vanity, the shortage of food, and the loss of territory in the Peace of Nimwegen cost him his former popularity. He became preoccupied with counteracting the intrigues of Mariana, who wished to secure the Spanish succession for the Austrian Habsburgs. Earlier, Don Juan had determined to arrange the marriage of the young king to Marie Louise of Orleans, niece of Louis XIV, but the outbreak of hostilities blocked that union. The Emperor Leopold I offered a marriage with his daughter, but after the Peace of Nimwegen, Don Juan tried to perpetuate his own power by selecting a French princess and hence again arranged the marriage of Charles to Marie Louise of Orleans. This marriage was finally celebrated after the death of Don Juan and the return of Mariana to the palace.

The duke of Medinaceli, who succeeded Don Juan as the principal adviser of Charles II, was an indolent, affable minister, popular with his peers because he lacked the firmness to resist their appeals for subsidies. The economic situation, which had deteriorated throughout the reign, grew steadily worse. Prices rose as production decreased, and strikes, desultory outbreaks, and demonstrations against bad government continued.

Then the aggressive policy of Louis XIV embroiled Spain in a new war in 1681. When the Sun King tried to justify his occupation of Casale in Italy and Strasbourg in Germany, and claimed Alost in Flanders, William III renewed his alliance with Sweden, Spain, and Austria. The French invaded Catalonia and besieged Gerona, captured Luxemburg, bombarded Genoa, and forced the Dutch and the emperor to accept the Treaty of Ratisbon, to which Spain, abandoned by her allies, was finally in 1684 forced to adhere. Spain lost Luxemburg by the treaty.

The duke of Medinaceli was now held responsible for the economic woes of the nation. Commerce was paralyzed, treasure ships from the New World were the prey of rival shipping in increasing numbers, and the treasury was exhausted. As prices rose to excessive heights, the troops in Flanders went unpaid, and the plague ravaged the crowded cities. In 1685 Medinaceli retired, his place being taken by the count of Oropesa, an anxious, intelligent, and able administrator, who suppressed unnecessary offices and expenses and hopefully undertook some governmental reforms.

New French aggression now forced Spain to enter the League of Augsburg, with Sweden and Holland. While Louis XIV tried to separate the allies with promises and threats, French ships attacked the Spanish fleet in the Bay of Cádiz and seized a great amount of treasure. Open warfare was begun in 1688, in which William III, who had just become king of England, also joined.

Queen Marie Louise, staunchly French and disliking anything Spanish, did little to conciliate her subjects and succeeded only in increasing the hostility between the two nations. When she died in 1689 a center of French intrigue was removed from the court. Leopold I, still anxious to increase Austrian influence in Spain, proposed Anna of Neuburg, his sister-in-law, as the new queen. Mariana, the queen mother, approved the marriage, but this diplomatic rebuff led Louis XIV to declare war again on Spain. The French were at first victorious in the Spanish Netherlands, Italy, and Catalonia, where they captured Barcelona in 1697. When the able French general, the marshal of Luxembourg, died the allied armies began to recover the initiative. Louis XIV then concluded the Treaty of Ryswick (1697), so moderating his demands that he restored Catalonia and all conquests since the Treaty of Nimwegen.

Anna of Neuburg, who proved to be imperious and avaricious, gained complete domination over the unfortunate Charles II, and her intrigues forced the count of Oropesa to retire. Power now rested with Anna's Capuchin confessor, her governess, Baroness Berlipsch, and her secretary. The baroness, a greedy woman, was the soul of the triumvirate. In the scramble for preferment and profit which disrupted the government, the duke of Montalto became first minister. His measures, both economic and military, aroused protests and the financial situation of Spain became precarious. The health of Charles II also grew more delicate. His physical weakness and attacks of convulsions led to the rumor that he was bewitched. The problem of the succession became imminent, and numerous candidates for the throne appeared.

Three principal contenders sought the throne of Spain for their progeny. Louis XIV based his claim principally on the rights of María Teresa, his wife and the sister of Charles II, although she had renounced her right to the throne in the Peace of the Pyrenees. Louis XIV's mother, Anne of Austria, was also a Spanish princess, the sister of Philip IV. Louis XIV chose as his candidate to the Spanish throne his grandson Philip of Anjou, and a French party, including a number of Spanish nobles offended by Anna of Neuburg's overweening pride, was formed at the Spanish court. Hoping to take advantage of this resentment, Louis sent the able count of Harcourt as ambassador to Madrid.

Anna of Neuburg, leader of another clique, supported the candidacy of her nephew, the Archduke Charles, second son of Leopold I, whose claim was based on his marriage to a younger sister of Charles II. Mariana favored her own great grandson, Prince Joseph of Bavaria. Both the Dutch and the English favored his candidacy because the aggrandizement of a state like Bavaria would not disturb the political equilibrium of Europe.

Although Mariana's death in 1696 deprived the Bavarian party of its strongest advocate, Charles II signed a will in favor of Prince Joseph, but Anna of Neuburg forced him to destroy it. Recognizing her power over Charles II, Louis XIV tried to attract her to the cause of the duke of Anjou by proposing her marriage to the dauphin after the death of Charles II. In 1697 the Austrian ambassador obtained a letter from Charles II in which the Archduke Charles was recognized as the heir to the Spanish throne, but the French party grew stronger and the Austrian party gradually lost ground as the two ambassadors vied for the queen's favor.

To avert a renewal of a general war, France, Holland, and England concluded a treaty of partition of the Spanish dominions in October 1698, by which the electoral prince of Bavaria was to be awarded the throne of Spain, the Indies, the Spanish Netherlands, and Sardinia. Anjou was to receive the Two Sicilies, Tuscany, the Marquisate of Finale, and the Province of Guipúzcoa, while the Archduke Charles would receive the Duchy of Milan. Such a treaty aroused general indignation in Spain—as well as in the Emperor Leopold—against those who sought to dismember the monarchy without considering the desires of its people. Charles II then declared Prince Joseph his heir (1698), but the boy died a year later.

In a second treaty of partition concluded between France, Holland, and England the Archduke Charles was to receive Spain, the Indies, the Spanish Netherlands, and Sardinia, while Anjou would receive the same territories promised him in the first treaty. This agreement also aroused Spanish resentment. Moreover, Leopold I still wanted the whole Spanish empire, while Louis XIV was willing to take all he could get.

As the intrigues intensified, it was suggested to Anna of Neuburg that she marry the Archduke Charles after the death of Charles II. This suggestion irritated the failing king, and in 1700 he was finally persuaded—partly by the desire to prevent the dismemberment of his dominions—to name Philip of Anjou as his heir. Less than a month later, Charles II died.

The later Habsburgs were unable to maintain the hegemony of Spain in a wartorn Europe. Isolated from the actual details of government in a frivolous court where intrigue flouted royal authority, they left the direction of the government to unworthy favorites. They had inherited the enmity of the Bourbons, and as Louis XIV emerged as the new master of Europe Spain was reduced to the position of a pawn in European politics, dependent on a French monarch with whom it was nearly constantly at war. With her commerce paralyzed and communications with the New World threatened, with profligate ministers wasting her resources, and with sovereigns who were interested only in themselves, Spain was left with but a fraction of her former strength.

CHAPTER XVI

Political and Economic Problems of the Seventeenth Century

Throughout the seventeenth century many important changes in Spanish government and society affected the relation of Spain to its dependencies, of the central government to the provinces, and of different social groups and interests to one another. The power of Spanish arms, the prosperity of Spanish trade, and, indeed, of Spain's whole economy was seriously impaired: weakness and vacillation at the head of Spanish society was partly a cause, partly a symptom of a more serious, much more widespread malaise.

One significant failure of the Habsburgs, as of all Spanish rulers, was their inability to overcome the strong, centrifugal forces in Spanish culture, society, and the whole political tradition of the country.

The principal unifying influence was Castilian, but the other regions had no common national aspirations and not only retained their own organs of government, but also the old separatist spirit, an attitude which survived in the Catalan revolt of 1640. The component states of the Spanish empire were governed by viceroys, who were regarded by their subjects as foreigners. Olivares tried to reduce the *fueros* and extend the legislation and influence of Castile as a remedy for the diversity. He also hoped to remove traditional antagonisms and build a sentiment of national solidarity by transporting people from one region to another, but in the end he hesitated to exasperate the regional sentiment further. He could Castilianize only so far, as the revolt of the Catalans proved.

Nevertheless, certain unifying influences continued, such as Catholicism and loyalty to a common monarch. Absolutism also had an important effect—the political institutions representing local aspirations lost much of their vigor either to defend their *fueros* or to perpetuate their own traditions. Even in Castile the cortes, which represented only eighteen privileged cities in the sixteenth century, continued to decline. Although the members presented numerous petitions, they never used their right to grant financial assistance in order to win political concessions in the popular interest. The municipal representatives never developed the patriotic political interests of their class, but instead, usually sought their positions for private purposes. In 1660 the crown assumed greater authority in the selection of municipal representatives, and they lost their independence. When the cortes was no longer allowed to approve grants to the crown (1665), the only motive for convocation disappeared, and it did not assemble until 1700, even to consider the problem of the succession.

In spite of the decline in prestige and authority, however, the Castilian cortes retained a certain constitutional function as the principal reason for its existence: it always recognized the new sovereign. Although the cortes of the subordinate regions were more vigorous, they met no more frequently than did the Castilian cortes. Even when they stubbornly resisted giving approval to taxes, their resistance was fruitless, for the methods and threats of absolutism were devious. Royal intervention in municipal life through the nomination of the local officials paralyzed municipal resistance in the cortes. The municipal councils, dominated by the nobles and powerful bourgeoisie, lost their political importance. More and more isolated from the people, the councils became effective instruments for centralization and for absolutism. To obtain financial resources the kings sold public offices, increasing their number beyond actual need. This further subordinated the municipal government and the municipal representatives in the cortes to the royal will.

Despite the influence of royal favorites, who controlled both the government and the kings, the prestige and importance of the Royal Council increased. Although the several secretaries became tools of the favorites, the council, which could promulgate laws by a two-thirds vote, came to be the judicial representative of the king as an appellate court. Since it also had extensive administrative functions in interpreting laws and supervising subordinate officials, in 1608 it was divided into four chambers—one for administration and three for judicial affairs.

Subordinate judicial officials continued to function as established by the Catholic Kings. The Royal Council supervised sixty-eight magistracies in Castile alone. Three new audiencias, or high courts, were created after 1505 in Seville, the Canary Islands, and Mallorca. In time a judicial bureaucracy of alcaldes and corregidores was created. Special tribunals also administered matters relating to the Inquisition and the

Santa Fe
ATLANTIC OCEAN
VICE-ROYALTY OF NEW SPAIN
St. Augustine
FLORIDA
Habana
CUBA
ESPAÑOLA
PUERTO RICO
Mexico
Santiago
San Juan
BELIZE (Br.)
JAMAICA
Santo Domingo
Porto Bello
Caracas
Panama
PACIFIC OCEAN
Lima
VICE-ROYALTY OF PERU
BRAZIL (Port.)
Buenos Aires
SPANISH EMPIRE IN THE NEW WORLD
c.1600

military orders. Among the many municipal officials, the corregidor became the most important. The influence and authority of this magistrate varied, but the power of the office was expanded. He not only had the right to nominate members of his council and extensive staff, but he usually supervised public works and customs and administered justice. His principal and most difficult task was to maintain the royal influence in the municipal council.

While the alcaldes retained their medieval judicial and administrative functions, they were restricted in judicial matters by the audiencias. In some towns alcaldes were elected, in others they were chosen by lot, in many the king named them. In numerous communities local officials were appointed for life, their positions became hereditary, and the offices even became the property of important families. Yet even as the right to election was lost, authority was increased, and these offices retained their traditional prestige because they provided the fundamental administrative positions in the kingdom. The royal agents might have difficulty in dominating local factions, but the municipal councilors were fully familiar with local prejudices and antagonisms.

By 1700 the military and diplomatic expenses incurred in extending Spanish dominion, winning military glory, and maintaining Spanish hegemony in Europe had proved disastrous for the public treasury. The effort was not accompanied by increased prosperity, an improvement in the general welfare, or commercial advantages. The nearly continuous warfare drained the revenues and left the financial situation of the nation steadily more precarious. Peace was purchased temporarily by the duke of Lerma, and the more sensible policies adopted by the count-duke of Olivares reduced expenses, but taxes could not be kept down and new and more onerous financial burdens replaced the old ones. Even though articles of basic necessity were taxed, the deficit continued to increase and abuses in the collection of taxes and the debasement of the coinage persisted.

As the expenses of an extravagant court rose, the cortes protested, but the peculations of the favorites continued. Military expenses increased under both Philip III and Philip IV, though the zenith of Spanish military glory had passed. Much of the time the soldiers were unpaid, and to prevent mutinies the generals often had to compensate them from their own resources. It became impossible to balance the budget, especially when loans were increased and the habit of compromising anticipated revenue continued. As ordinary appropriations became insufficient to meet the deficit, new taxes were devised, but an effort to tax the classes formerly exempt was vigorously resisted. Taxes on the consumption of merchandise were extended, and a royal monopoly on tobacco was established by Philip IV. To compensate the treasury for the loss of revenue occasioned by the expulsion of the Moriscos, new taxes were imposed on the tenants who replaced them. Philip IV created a stamp tax in 1636, and nobles were taxed on the transmission of their titles and in place of providing soldiers. Those who obtained the honorific title of "don" had to pay two hundred reales for its use, four hundred reales if it were granted for life, and six hundred reales if it were granted in perpetuity.

Since it was more difficult to raise money in the eastern kingdoms, the Castilians had to bear the heaviest financial burden. The loss of the United Provinces deprived Spain of considerable revenue, while the flow of treasure from the New World was uncertain and beset with piracy and storms. The increased taxes were imposed on only part of the population—the nobles, clergy, and some professional men were exempt from ordinary taxes. The expenses of the financial administration of the taxes became excessive as the number of employees of the centralized bureaucracy multiplied.

It was impossible, however, to produce wealth where there was no basis for it. Spain was impoverished, and the effort to bleed her for taxes only made the plight of the inhabitants worse. Castile, which bore the heaviest part of the burden, suffered a loss of population, which in 1623 was estimated at six million. Many people had been swept away by war, famine, plague, or expulsion, although the population increased slightly during the second half of the century in some areas. The total population of Spain was estimated to be seven to eight million people at the end of the seventeenth century.

The declining population reflected the demographic situation in Castile. As the meseta lost its privileged position and power was centralized, the population of Madrid increased. At the same time, the concentration of property in a few hands led to the decay of agriculture and to the urban migration, which brought its quota of rogues, vagabonds, and beggars to the cities. Both nobles and clergy became more numerous. At the beginning of the reign of Philip IV it was estimated that there were 125,000 monks and nuns, 478,000 nobles, and 276,000 persons who served them.

Under the house of Austria the Spanish nobility was transformed into a class of royal dependents, residing at court. Those who remained in the obscurity of their rural properties had little social or political influence. As the courtiers became more dependent on the king for offices and favors, competition among them filled the court of the later Habsburgs with intrigue and corruption. As a class, nobles enjoyed many privileges in addition to their opportunities for political preferment and influence. They held certain privileges in criminal cases, could not be imprisoned for debt, and were exempt from many taxes.

One reason for intrigue at court was the economic position of the nobles. Wealth had been transformed from land into commodities, and the landholding nobles were comparatively less wealthy than the industrial and commercial classes. Although the system of entail kept the wealth of the aristocrats intact, it also restricted the number of heirs and led to the concentration of land in fewer hands. Younger sons were thus forced to seek military or ecclesiastical careers at court and, finally, constituted an inferior class within the ranks of the nobility. The opposition to the entail increased in the seventeenth century, resulting in the recognition of several heirs. This practice partly removed the threat of the increased power of the aristocrats.

Another factor which led to the concentration of land was the price inflation resulting from the influx of precious metals from the New World. Smaller proprietors were led by the high prices to sell their lands, and the larger ones were encouraged to expand their holdings. Despite attempted reform of the situation, absenteeism increased during the reigns of Philip IV and Charles II. Neither the landed nobility nor the Council of the Mesta would tolerate any reform which would undermine their privileged positions.

With the increase of commercial wealth a rich bourgeois class was created, which imitated the nobility and tried to enter it. The bourgeois were affected by the national decline more than were the nobles. The miserable situation of the lower classes, especially in the rural areas, was reflected in the frequent revolts. Personal servitude was perpetuated by the sale of captured Turkish and North African pirates as slaves. Some 2000 Moslems and Turks, sold at Cádiz at the end of the century, were concentrated there as oarsmen in the galleys and as dockworkers. By 1654 there were also some 1500 Negro slaves in Cádiz, and a special police force was organized to prevent revolts among them.

Guilds, already numerous in Spain, were greatly expanded in the sixteenth and seventeenth centuries. As a result of the growth of the industries in which they were already organized and their establishment in new crafts, the guilds were subject to increasing regulation by the central government. Formerly, they had been under municipal supervision, but the royal government soon began to regulate them on a national basis, and a uniform body of law was formulated after a codification of the regulations in 1604. Centralized control became complete in 1679, with the establishment of the Board of Commerce and Money to approve the ordinances. By this time the guilds had lost their autonomy, but the towns retained some control over them, and they also played an important role in municipal government. In time guilds became closed bodies, opposed to individual enterprise and jealous of their exclusive privileges. They maintained a rigid separation between apprentices and masters and were instrumental in the perpetuation of an economic caste system. Thus, sales were restricted and production limited, but guild members were provided with social security.

Important changes also took place in the structure and effectiveness of the Spanish army. In the decisive defeat at Rocroi (1643), it lost its reputation for invincibility and its domination of the battlefields of Europe. Earlier, it had been possible to recruit a mercenary army in the extensive dominions, but the army also included many volunteers of Spanish origin, among them nobles, knights, and gentlemen of the military orders. Since it was not limited to a single campaign or a fixed period, the service of the volunteers varied from that of the foreign mercenaries, who formed a corps of veterans, proud of their victories and despising those who did not follow a military career.

In the second half of the seventeenth century, military spirit declined with the decay of the Spanish empire. The army became undisciplined and mutinous when the soldiers were not regularly paid; the military force was unable to sustain the empire. One of the fundamental causes of the military collapse lay in the attitude of the kings. Charles V was a warrior-king, but Philip II, who used, but did not admire, his soldiers, was not. Philip III did not even pretend to military qualities, and Charles II completely neglected the armed services. Sully, perhaps, suggested the real reason for the decline of Spanish arms when he declared that Spain had long maintained an army out of proportion to her resources.

Recruiting to the army proved difficult, despite the large contingents of volunteers. Royal agents enlisted men interested only in the pay and the clothing, who sometimes took leave as soon as they had received these. Many of the conscripts also deserted. In general, the militia—called to arms in emergencies—replaced the contingents of aristocrats. In 1666 Spain's entire regular army was reduced to 113 companies of some 6200 men commanded by 600 officers. The younger members of the nobility were unwilling to serve as simple soldiers. Even when they entered the army, they were more intent on careers at court, which were more lucrative than the study or practice of the art of war. Only in moments of crisis for the monarchy did the aristocrats rally to the flag.

Earlier, the tercio consisted of twelve to fifteen companies of 250 to 300 men under a commander whose name the unit bore. Each tercio was made up of three groups of soldiers: pikemen, arquebusiers, and musketeers, but eventually the musketeers, with the superior weapon, predominated. The tercio was replaced by the regiment at the end of the seventeenth century. The infantry continued to form the backbone of the Spanish army, although each unit was accompanied by one hundred light cavalry and artillery, which constantly improved in effectiveness. But the failure to adjust to the continuing innovations in warfare explains in large measure the decline of the Spanish army.

Despite the loss of control of the seas, the Spanish kings were still able to assemble considerable fleets. They were formed by renting foreign ships, as well as by shipbuilding and purchasing or seizing merchant ships, but they were not as large as in the days of Philip II. Some nobles had private fleets. The duke of Lerma maintained a squadron of four galleys for which he received a perpetual grant, and the squadron of the duke of Osuna, better organized and administered than the royal fleet, rendered notable service in the Mediterranean between 1611 and 1624, when the duke was imprisoned for using his ships in piracy.

The galley, which had been abandoned in the fifteenth century, recovered some of its prestige when it was needed to combat the oared ships of the Turks in the Mediterranean. With three to five banks of oars, some of the galleys were luxuriously equipped. Finally, they were used as transports in the Mediterranean. Caravels with sails were used for navigation in the oceans, and Alvaro de Bazán designed the galleon, which could mount many guns.

Admiral Diego Brochero improved the technique of construction without varying the types of ships, and in 1642 he introduced fire ships, which had already been used effectively by the Dutch and the French. The size and capacity of the ships were so increased in the seventeenth century that some were of more than 2000 tons and carried an armament of 120 guns. The castles in the poop and the prow were lowered and the ships were lightened and covered, until the frigate was developed. The number of guns also increased and their use was perfected. Battle tactics, on the other hand, were slow to change, for the Spaniards preferred to board their enemy and capture the ship rather than sink it. Artillery was used at close range in preparation for that maneuver, instead of at long range as the Dutch and English preferred. The sailors and soldiers on the ships used crossbows and arquebuses until the musket and carbine were introduced.

The religious unity of Spain and the methods used to preserve it brought their own problems, not only religious, but social, intellectual, administrative and economic. The clergy not only enjoyed great social consideration but nearly monopolized intellectual activities. They were employed as intimate and influential advisers by the kings, and the less important among them were the spiritual directors of the Spanish people, either as educators, confessors, or counselors. The Church's increased wealth from pious donations, bequests, and foundations awakened many envious critics who wanted it returned to circulation. It has been estimated that the income of the clergy in the sixteenth century was five million ducats. The higher prelates had an average of twenty thousand ducats a year, but the archbishop of Toledo had three hundred and fifty to four hundred thousand ducats a year. The economic and social power of the Church was greatly increased, although much of its wealth was used in charitable works.

It was natural for the Habsburgs to support the Counter Reformation and try to maintain the religious unity of Spain. The works of heretics and critics of the Church were denied admission, and the reading of the Bible in the vernacular was prohibited. Yet the reputation of, for example, Erasmus won him popularity in Spain, and his books were read surreptitiously, even in monasteries, until his writings were prohibited and his admirers persecuted. There were never many Protestants in Spain. The Inquisition was always energetic, and Lutheran propaganda was driven underground in Seville and other cities. The seventeenth-century kings were not as rigid as Charles V and Philip II had been in the persecution of heresy. Catholic unity had become so solidly established that there was little to fear from the Protestants. Philip IV was somewhat tolerant, and restrictions on religious worship were so relaxed that the protests of the archbishop of Granada against the celebration of Protestant ceremonies in the British embassy were ignored. Catholic France rather than Anglican England was becoming the threat to Spain, and political considerations took precedence over religious ones.

By the end of the sixteenth century the Supreme Council of the Inquisition had gained complete juridical independence and cognizance of all appeals from lower courts, though its pretensions to extend its jurisdiction to include matters not properly ecclesiastical were resisted. The Catalans and Aragonese insisted that the council be restrained from proceeding against crimes subject to civil jurisdiction and foreign to heresy. The revolt of the Catalans against Philip IV forced him to relinquish his cherished plan of extending the jurisdiction of the Inquisition to the eastern provinces, but at the end of the reign of Charles II the Inquisition still had great power, the protection of successive kings, and the general support of the people.

Despite its rapid expansion and its activity in converting heretics, the Society of Jesus was never universally popular in Spain. Many of the clergy, both regular and secular, were jealous of Jesuit success. The Dominicans, who controlled the Inquisition, regarded the Jesuits as rivals, and even Charles V was suspicious of an organization dedicated to the defense of papal prerogatives, though Philip II recognized their value as allies in the struggle to maintain religious unity. The rivalry with other religious orders continued throughout the seventeenth century, quickened by theological differences, conflicts in jurisdiction, and disparities in education. Although Philip IV and Olivares supported the Jesuits, a Dominican friar in Toledo kindled an uprising by attacking them from the pulpit. The favoritism shown Father Nithard by Queen Mariana led to a reaction against the society. The Franciscans, who had controlled the post of confessor to the queen, joined the Dominicans in opposition. Despite this hostility the Jesuits consolidated their position in Spain. Benefited by papal support and increased prestige when Ignatius Loyola was canonized (1622), they attained the height of their power in the seventeenth century.

The later Habsburgs continued to resist the extension of papal authority in Spain, and papal bulls were frequently denied publication there in the seventeenth century. Charles V had established a Spanish court to regulate appeals to the Roman curia, but it soon created opposition, as it was considered a threat to both civil and royal authority. The people regarded the nuncio as a foreigner who interfered in national affairs and committed other abuses; his court was therefore subjected to royal supervision, and his position became difficult. Philip IV temporarily closed the office by restricting the bull naming the incumbent, when Spanish litigants complained of his rapacity and Spanish bishops protested his intervention in their jurisdiction.

Throughout the century the royal policy was intended to restrict the independence of the national clergy, especially in regard to their immunities. They were exempt from ordinary taxation, and the property they held was inalienable. Philip IV tried to restrict the tax exemption of the clergy, while the cortes petitioned that the Church be prohibited from accumulating estates and demanded their sale. The king and the clergy opposed such a drastic attack on the landed wealth of the Church, but the king had few scruples against the seizure of clerical property by papal authorization. In a sharp conflict between ecclesiastical immunity and the civil authority, ecclesiastical privileges were reduced and an effort was made to correct the abuses in ecclesiastical tribunals.

During the sixteenth century, the increase of private capital in Spain produced some industrial development, especially in Castile, which became the principal beneficiary of the commerce with the New World. Seville, an important textile center—with 130,000 workers employed in 15,000 shops—was one of the principal producers of crude silk in Western Europe. In Toledo 50,000 worked in the silk industry. Despite increasing numbers of textile workers in Toledo and La Mancha, their production was insufficient to meet the demand, and the manufacture of woolen hats was so active in Toledo that all of the residents of one parish were engaged in it. The hats of Seville were much esteemed and even exported to Turkey and North Africa. Saragossa, Barcelona, and Valencia were also important textile centers.

Yet Spain did not evolve as rapidly industrially as did her competitors. The ships carrying wool to the Netherlands brought back textiles which found a ready market, for Spanish cloth was inferior. Spain failed to obtain productive independence and remained principally an exporter of raw materials. Domestic production of textiles never developed enough to produce a surplus for export or even to satisfy national and colonial demands. The balance of trade was constantly unsatisfactory, and an increasing national debt was the avenue to national insolvency. Industry gradually declined under Philip III, recovered momentarily under Philip IV, and collapsed completely under Charles II—ruined by heavy taxes, foreign competition, and excessive regulation.

On the Cantabrian coast the fishing industry continued to be important. In the ancient fishing centers along the Mediterranean coast tuna were caught and dried, and not content with the spoils of the coastal waters Spanish fishermen also sailed to Ireland and Newfoundland, where the Basques carried on a losing struggle with the Dutch and English for fishing rights during the sixteenth century. In the following century the Basques tried to recover their share of the Newfoundland fisheries, but the French demanded freedom of commerce in the New World in return.

Mining declined, discouraged in part by the abundance of precious metals imported from America. Philip II incorporated the mines in the crown, which permitted free exploitation under certain conditions, but production remained unimportant. The Fuggers took advantage of the scarcity of capital in Spain to gain control of the mercury mines of Almadén and the silver mines of Guadalcanal.

The situation in agriculture did not improve in the seventeenth century. It was not accorded the protection given to industry and stock-raising. The number of workers and domestic animals declined, and the miserable existence of the laborers drove them to the cities or colonies. The shortage of agricultural labor was aggravated by the expulsion of the Moriscos, and the only measures for the benefit of agriculture were for the personal protection of the workers and to encourage irrigation. In some areas there was a short-lived prosperity. Sugarcane was successfully cultivated around Valencia, and vineyards flourished in central Spain and around Seville. Most of the land was depopulated and held by absentee landlords. Some attempts were made at colonization, but neither the treasury nor the colonists were able to compensate the landlords.

Commerce was active, but not usually for the benefit of Spaniards. The principal commercial centers were Seville, Cádiz, Medina del Campo, and the Mallorcan ports. Seville became the important mercantile center of Spain, largely because of its monopoly of the trade with the New World. Merchants engaged in that commerce grew wealthy, married their daughters to aristocrats—and even these did not disdain commercial transactions. There was also trade with Flanders, North Africa, and Italy. Philip III conceded many privileges to the Flemish and German merchants congregated in Seville, as the customs duties were important to an impoverished royal treasury. The Genoese controlled banks in several cities, and most of the ships engaged in the Spanish carrying trade were foreign.

By the middle of the seventeenth century even commerce had begun to decline—hastened by Portuguese independence, the Catalan rebellion, and losses in shipping. Foreigners benefited more from the commerce with America than did the Spaniards, either by raids or by the contraband trade. Finally, sandbars blocked the Guadalquivir River. Cádiz, on a nearly perfect harbor, became the heir of the commerce of Seville, and the House of Trade was moved there. Medina del Campo, the commercial center of the north, continued to hold fairs twice a year, attended by both Spanish and foreign merchants until the early seventeenth century, when Burgos became the center of commerce in Castile and the fairs at Medina del Campo began to decline. Despite the advantages held by the Atlantic ports and the threat of raids by Moslem pirates, a considerable commerce developed along the eastern coast. Even at the end of the seventeenth century Barcelona extended increased privileges to its merchants and spent huge sums on the reconstruction of the port.

Although Spain was the pioneer in mercantilist theories, the government followed no consistent public policy and often promulgated contradictory measures. While there was an earnest endeavor to protect the interests of Spanish merchants and manufacturers, the increasing demands of the public treasury and the inconsistency in its administration and policies rendered ineffectual the measures designed to favor commerce. At times, for example, special assistance was given to foreigners on whom the kings relied financially.

In the seventeenth century the general interests of the nation were overlooked, compromised by ministerial indiscretion or sacrificed for political convenience. In 1603 the duke of Lerma dealt a severe blow to commerce and provoked reprisals by prohibiting trade with the Dutch and by placing a 30 percent tax on all ships failing to prove they were not Dutch. At the same time, in the search for allies, political necessity arranged commercial treaties which provided for freedom of commerce, thereby contradicting the policy of protection.

Some effort was made to stimulate internal commerce, but, although internal customs were abolished, the movement of certain products from one region to another was prohibited. The religious communities of Madrid were permitted to open taverns for the sale of their wine. This privilege was so abused and so many additional articles were sold in the taverns that they were temporarily closed. The government was always preoccupied with the suppression of contraband trade, for Spanish individualism was ever defiant of commercial restrictions in both hemispheres, and officials often cooperated in the illegal trade.

The cortes presented petitions for improvements of bridges and roads, but usually these were carried out through local initiative or to facilitate the transport of military supplies or the passage of a royal procession. Some attempt was made to improve waterways, but conflicting interests impeded progress in the construction of canals. The effort to improve irrigation met with little more success. The Imperial Canal, completed in Aragon under Charles I, was in a bad state by 1564, but could not be repaired for lack of money. Many canals were planned, but few were completed.

It was impossible for Spain to retain her hegemony over Western Europe, or even in her own empire, because of the poverty of her resources and the rivalries which she encountered. That she was able to dominate Europe for a century was largely a result of the vision of the Catholic Kings and the gold from the New World that flowed through her coffers onto the battlefields of Europe. The later Habsburgs were unable to maintain the imperial pace of their predecessors and let control drift into the hands of favorites. By the end of the seventeenth century Spain was drained economically and socially of her reserves of power.

CHAPTER XVII

The End of the Golden Century

The period of Spain's declining power in Europe, the years of crisis for her economy and of humiliation for her rulers and her armies, was, paradoxically, a time of unparalleled intellectual and cultural achievement. Spain's universities continued to flourish and her rich men patronized painters and poets, dramatists, musicians, and architects. In an age of religious conflict Spanish mystics expressed their revelations in serene, sensitive, highly sophisticated prose and verse. In an age which all too often had little of glory for Spain there were Spaniards of enough ability and skill to do justice to the highest and noblest achievements. Unsuccessful Spanish kings, insignificant Spanish statesmen were immortalized—though sometimes satirized—by Spanish painters and poets of genius.

During the sixteenth century the universities were developing rapidly, and many new institutions were established. They had already contributed to the cultivation of Roman and canon law and the creation of a new class of legal administrators, who transformed the evolution of public administration and judicial activity. The universities, of which there were thirty-two in 1619, attracted thousands of students to Spain from foreign countries. The most famous were the universities of Salamanca and Alcalá, the opinions of whose faculties were sought from many parts of Europe. Alcalá was renowned for the scientific activity of its faculty and notorious for the conduct of its students. In the middle of the sixteenth century Salamanca had 7800 students, but by 1700 the number had declined to 2000. Attendance at Alcalá declined from 2060 to 1637 during the same period. There were sixty professors at the University of Salamanca and forty-two at Alcalá, and the two centers of learning became rivals in attracting professors as well as students. The University of Valladolid, a third intellectual center in Castile, was especially important for the study of Roman law. A principal cause of the decay of the universities was the Spanish reaction to the Protestant Reformation, by which intellectual activity and public support were restricted. Ideas which had formerly been popular were persecuted, and as the larger institutions became dominant democratic organization and freedom disappeared.

By the middle of the seventeenth century the Jesuits had become the principal educators of Spain. In 1625 Philip IV founded the Imperial College, or Royal Studies of San Isidro, which soon began to compete with the universities. It was directed by the Jesuits and was designed to educate the elder sons of the nobility. Despite a protesting memorial from the University of Alcalá, which recruited its students from the aristocratic class and was especially affected, the new institution continued to enjoy the patronage of Philip IV and Olivares and obtained great influence at court. The universities received only one concession—the Royal Studies of San Isidro could not grant degrees or give academic courses. Other institutions, too, were created by the Jesuits for the education of their own members. The Jesuit College of Gandia (1546), for example, also admitted laymen.

Primary instruction was neglected during these centuries and failed to develop in the same way as did secondary or higher education or to provide a broad base for a literate public. Some municipalities provided for a teacher in their budgets, but most of the primary schools were ecclesiastical. The Franciscans were especially active in establishing such schools, but they did not usually admit all children. Some convents also provided for the training of girls.

During the sixteenth century printing was widely diffused in Spain, and although the publication of books was greatly restricted, they were more abundant in the seventeenth century. The Escorial, built by Philip II as a residence, monastery, and church, contained an art collection and a library, which became, like the library of Ferdinand Columbus in Seville, one of the largest in the sixteenth century. Members of the clergy and nobility also collected extensive libraries. The count of Gondomar, for example, had more than 15,000 volumes, later incorporated into the National Library. Philip II also conceived the idea of dedicating the fortress of Simancas wholly to an archive. Built in the fifteenth century, this castle became the temporary residence of the Catholic Kings. Ferdinand de los Cobos, Charles V's illustrious minister, began to deposit the papers of the crown of Castile there, and by 1545 Philip II completed the renovation necessary to convert the castles into an archive.

Spanish mysticism, after Ramón Lull, had a national development.

At first ecclesiastical authorities rejected the mystical approach and prohibited any investigations of it; when suspicion faded, this literature became abundant. Among Spanish mystics, Saint Teresa (1515–82), who excelled in her command of clear, vivid prose, acquired a world-wide reputation. Born in Ávila of a noble family, she became a Carmelite in 1534, and in 1562 founded her first reformed convent in Ávila. She came into conflict with both civil and ecclesiastical authorities and her autobiographical *Life* was even denounced to the Inquisition. She was also an incomparable letter writer. Saint John of the Cross (1542–91) was one of the great mystics. From a humble family, after studying with the Jesuits he entered the Carmelite Order in 1563 and attended the University of Salamanca. Later he was associated in the reform of Saint Teresa and founded a number of monasteries. In addition to his prose writings on mysticism, he was an exquisite poet in the traditional style, and he also produced some of the purist lyrics in Spanish literature.

The practical application of philosophy also developed a school of moralists, among whom was Baltasar Gracián (1601–58), a precursor to some extent of Schopenhauer, who translated his classic *Oráculo* into German. Gracián first studied with the Jesuits and then entered the society in 1619. He taught in various Jesuit schools, but by 1651 he became disenchanted with the society, as indicated by the publication of his *Criticón,* a *roman à clef,* without the permission of his superiors. An analytical and objective critic of his contemporaries, he wrote in the highly mannered style known as Gongorism, after the Spanish poet Luis de Góngora.

Interest in jurisprudence and politics continued because of the typical problems which confronted imperial Spain. Preoccupation with the practical as well as the theoretical aspects of administrative affairs led to philosophical and logical considerations. Spaniards were particularly interested in canon law and international law as a result of the ecclesiastical problems and the wars which confronted them. This concern began with Charles V's election as emperor and became more intense in the seventeenth century. Penal law also received more than passing attention because of the controversies which developed around the procedures and penalties of the Inquisition.

Spanish economists, principally concerned with the national wealth, the importation and consumption of foreign products, and the state of Spanish finances, tried to propound general economic theories to solve their problems. A forerunner of Adam Smith, Martinez de la Mata believed that work was the only source of wealth. Alvarez Ossorio prepared a plan of government for Charles II which dealt with the fundamental political and economic problems of his day, and other economists defended government intervention in the production and distribution of wealth.

The seventeenth century produced worthy successors to the official chroniclers of the preceding century. Much progress was evident in the methods of achieving objective history. Historians such as Father Juan de Mariana (1535–1624) and Antonio de Herrera (1559–1625) were still active. Mariana, one of the representative Jesuit writers, studied at Alcalá and devoted himself to education and preaching. Of a critical spirit, he was veracious and dedicated to research. He was intensely national in his point of view, depicting the greatness of Spain and the glorious deeds of its people. His *Historiae de rebus Hispaniae,* which concludes with the Spanish Kings, was published between 1592 and 1605. Antonio de Herrera studied in both Spain and Italy, where he served as secretary to the viceroy of Naples. Among his several histories were *Historia general del mundo en tiempo del rey don Felipe II* (1601 and 1612), which covered the history of Europe from the Spanish point of view, and *Decadas* or *Historia general de los hechos de los castellanos en las islas y tierra firme del Mar Océano* (1601), an account of the New World from the discovery to 1554, written after he had been named chronicler of the Indies.

Works on the natural sciences, physics, and mathematics were not as popular as those on history and philosophy. Although Philip II had founded an academy of mathematics, it was closed in 1624, and mathematical studies generally declined during the seventeenth century. Some excellent maps were published, but geographical works were neither as numerous nor as varied as in the past, and cartography declined as a science. A number of medical societies were founded in imitation of the Royal Society of Medicine of Seville (1697).

The "Century of Gold" was one of splendid achievement in literature. The increasing popularity of the theater alarmed some of the clergy and magistrates, who feared its effect on religion and morals. After some agitation they succeeded in obtaining from Philip II a decree to suppress it just before his death. The accession of Philip III saved dramatic presentations. Some theologians condoned them and many hospitals, which were then the impresarios, depended on the income of the theaters. A number of cities, therefore, requested that the theaters be reopened, and although this was authorized in 1600, the charges against them were repeated. In 1644 theatrical presentations were suspended because of the death of the queen and suppressed two years later. Yet, five years later, drama was revived in the royal palaces and elsewhere in Madrid. When Philip IV married Mariana of Austria, who was devoted to dramatic presentations, the theater attained a popularity of which Lope de Vega had never dreamed. The royal theaters were enlarged, improved, and well staffed. Productions grew more magnificent, often lasted throughout the night, and included poetry, music, dancing, and magic.

Pedro Calderón de la Barca (1600–1681), the master dramatist of his age, wrote 110 plays and 70 *autos* (one-act religious plays) and originated the zarzuela, a brief theatrical sketch combining recitation and singing. *Loas,* or prologues, were also introduced for his comedies, and dancing was presented during the intermissions. Many of his plays were commissioned by the court. He became a priest in 1651, but continued writing plays, being at work on one at the time of his death.

Despite the campaign of the moralists against the theater, the number of dramatic companies increased. Both Cervantes and Lope de Vega continued to write plays well into the seventeenth century, and the theater was one of the most active interests of the later Habsburgs. Other dramatic authors also contributed distinction to the theater. Father Gabriel Téllez, better known as Tirso de Molina (1584?–1648), wrote with vigorous realism and originality. Ruíz de Alarcón y Mendoza (1581–1639) imitated the French theater of Corneille. Francisco de Rojas-Zorilla (1607–48) and Agustín Moreto (1618–69) wrote graceful high comedy, and a succession of brilliant playwrights continued to exercise an influence on the drama elsewhere in Europe.

The novel, especially the popular, picaresque type more or less initiated by *Lazarillo de Tormes,* was best presented by Mateo Alemán (1547–1614?), whose *Guzman de Alfarache* (1599) attained a popularity and a number of editions without precedent among Spanish classics. Other writers also imitated Alemán with picaresque tales of adventure. Vicente Martínez Espinel (1550–1624), who was also a musician and poet, in his *Vida del Escudero Marcos de Obregón* (1618) produced a work which the French author Lesage imitated in entire episodes in his *Gil Blas de Santillane.*

In poetry the Italian influence which had triumphed in the sixteenth century was still important. One of the principal and most vigorous poets was Luis de Góngora (1561–1627). His works were not published but circulated in manuscript. He first became widely known in 1605 by his use of the complicated and artificial style called Gongorism. Another school of poetry, conceptism, founded by Alonso de Ledesma Buitrago (1562–1633), was more philosophic; its principal exponent was Francisco de Quevedo y Villegas (1580–1645). Educated by the Jesuits and at Álcala, he became involved in the political activity of both Philip III and Philip IV. Although he won attention as an incisive literary critic, it is as a satiric and comic writer in both poetry and prose that he is known in world literature. Baltasar Gracián also composed allegorical and philosophical verse characterized by its moral tone.

In heroic poetry some writers imitated Italian models, others composed burlesque versions, but the principal themes were based on contemporary events and historical incidents. Bernardo de Balbuena (1568–1627), who spent most of his life as bishop of Puerto Rico, wrote a long epic poem, *El Bernardo,* or *La Victoria de Roncesvalles.* Cristobal de Mesa (1561–1633) produced an epic on the battle of Las Navas de Tolosa (1594) which is heavy and uninspired. A better work of his is *La Restauración de España* (1607), which records the deeds of Pelayo, the Asturian king, at the victory of Covadonga.

The Castilian language had spread throughout the peninsula in the fifteenth century, but Catalan and other regional languages persisted. The Catalan religious drama was active until the prohibition of the mysteries halted its development, though a number of Catalan religious plays were produced in the seventeenth century. Castilian companies began to produce secular plays in Barcelona after 1579, and instead of discouraging the Catalan dramatists, the example aroused interest in plays in the regional tongue. Father Antoni Barat was a dramatist of the period who wrote in Catalan. However, the increasing influence of Castilian, French, and Italian models smothered a renaissance of regional dramatic literature. Valencia, where Guillén de Castro (1569–1631) wrote *Las Mocedades del Cid,* also had a regional theater.

In both the sixteenth and seventeenth centuries there was a steady diffusion of Spanish culture abroad. Spanish scholars taught in French universities and secondary schools and in Flanders, Germany, Bohemia, Italy, and Poland. The educational influence of the Jesuits was pronounced throughout Europe, and Spaniards were esteemed as professors and men of science. Translations of Spanish literature emphasized the influence of Spanish culture, though the trend was most apparent in such Catholic countries as Italy and France in the seventeenth century.

The decline in literature in the latter part of the seventeenth century can largely be attributed to the bad taste and intellectual exhaustion of the period, though other factors were the Inquisition and the Index prohibiting publications which contradicted Catholic dogma and expurgating even orthodox works. All persons suspected of heterodox opinions, regardless of their status, were persecuted. Even though there were few heretics and most works were orthodox, the threat of accusation by the Inquisition hung heavily over Spanish writers.

In architecture the plateresque style, which developed radical regional variations, dominated Spanish construction until 1700. Juan de Herrera, however, introduced new influences which completely changed the trend of peninsular design. The Escorial inspired other architects by its simplicity and majesty, but later architects imitated its severity rather than its grandeur. Under Philip III and Philip IV this style declined. Juan Gómez de Mora, director of public works of the kingdom, was the last architect to remain faithful to the principles of Herrera. Crescenzi, who came to Spain from Rome in 1617, introduced the new baroque style. His most typical work, the court jail—today the Ministry of State—was tentatively baroque. The style immediately became popular with Spanish architects, who were already prepared for it by the ornate plateresque.

The Jesuit architect Francisco Bautista adapted the style freely with classic forms, in transition from the severity of Herrera. The Church of San Isidro el Real in Madrid (1626–51) is his best work, but his chapel of Cristo de los Dolores in Madrid is the most typical and beautiful representative in the city of the era of Philip IV. Later, Francisco de Herrera Henestrosa (1622–85), named royal painter and palace architect, introduced additional Italian architectural principles. Francisco Rizi, a native of Madrid, also a royal painter, spread the baroque through his decoration of the Buen Retiro theater. This variation of baroque style did not affect principles of construction, but remained purely decorative and superficial. Called churrigueresque, after its most celebrated cultivator, José Churriguero, the new flamboyant style became dominant after the accession of Charles II and marked the triumph of fantasy over reason. Composed of elements which violated every functional principle, its lines were irregular, its ornamentation obscured the construction with imitations of cloth, shells, flowers, and clouds, and it had neither the grandeur of the Italian baroque nor the grace of the French.

Spanish sculpture was marked by two influences in the Golden Century. The church and the people remained faithful to the dramatic style introduced by the Flemings, French, and Germans who worked in Castile during the fifteenth century, whereas the court and the nobility preferred the more seductive Italian models. In general, Spanish sculpture lost the simplicity which had characterized it during the two preceding centuries. Its two most illustrious masters were Juan Martínez Montanés (1561–1649) and Gregorio Fernández (1576–1636). Juan de Juni had populated Castile with theatrically expressive, but tortured and convulsed images. Fernández, on the other hand, was placid and serene, producing altar pieces and polychrome images for many cities, and Montanés developed polychrome sculpture into an imaginative and glorious art.

A disciple of Montanés, Alonso Cano (1601–67), also an architect, founded a third school in Granada. He had a remarkable plastic ability and a profound sense of form. He found a strong sculptural tradition in Granada, the result of the work of Diego Siloé, but he surpassed the work of Siloé and his pupils, producing the masterpieces of the school. Pedro Roldán (1624–1700) and Pedro de Mena (1628–88) were his able disciples.

During the seventeenth century the great Spanish masters, Velázquez, Murillo, Zurbarán, and Ribera, attained international fame. Among the many other excellent artists were Jaime Huguet, Maestro Alfonso, Bartolomé Bermejo, and Pedro Berruguete. Before this period much work considered Spanish was in reality imitative of Flemish, French, or Italian. Although the art of the seventeenth century was truly Spanish, it attained universal validity, and greatly influenced the art of other countries. Several tendencies characterized the Spanish school during this century. The art was naturalistic, and the canvasses were often somber. Ribera and Zurbarán conceived their work in large, dramatic canvasses with a pervasive power discernible in few masters of the Spanish baroque. The result was a genuinely religious art.

Baroque religious art also revealed an increasing secularization, though never to the extent reached in the Flemish or Italian schools. The worldliness of Spanish painting reflected an intimate relation with the national literature and a reaction against the Italian school. Italian formalism had some influence in Spain, but the Spanish artists tended to regard it as secondary. Despite the great Flemish influence in Spanish naturalism, the Spanish masters sought to incarnate and translate plastic effects in their pictures. Their former enthusiasm for color persisted, and they zealously studied to associate the exaltation of the Flemish with the beauty of Venetian art. They never submerged their own individualism, but developed independently. Many Venetian pictures were gathered into royal and private collections, young artists were inspired by them, and the effect was wholesome for the majority of Spanish artists. Flemish influence was even more direct. Rubens, whose reputation was supreme, often visited Spain, and many of his works were collected and copied there. Van Dyck also had Spanish disciples and imitators.

The founder of the Valencian school, Francisco Ribalta (1551?–1628), was one of the patriarchs of Spanish baroque painting. He developed a naturalism combined with a mystic quality of remarkable sensitivity. José de Ribera (1591–1652) developed the technique evolved by Francisco Ribalta and became the greatest artist of the Valencian school. His pictures are realistic, vigorous, and show a sense of humor. He was extraordinarily successful as an engraver. Taken to Naples by the duke of Osuna, he remained there until his death. Luca Giordano was among his many imitators. Jerónimo Jacinto Espinosa (1600–80) continued the Ribalta tradition in Valencia, where he was especially preoccupied with religious compositions. Pedro Orrente (1570–1644), known for landscapes and animal paintings, also had an important role in the evolution of Spanish painting. He traveled continuously. While not an eminent painter, he was one of the first artists to come under Valencian influence and to carry it to other parts of Spain.

Seville occupied a predominant place in Spanish seventeenth-century art, and Juan de Ruelas (1558?–1625) was one of the precursors of the baroque school there. Under the influence of Tintoretto he subverted the dramatic and savage characteristics of the Valencians. Other Sevillian artists learned from Ruelas, but none of them could equal his grave mystical sense. Juan de Castillo (1584–1640), best known as the teacher of Murillo, was greatly influenced by Ruelas, and Pablo Legate (d. 1671), a native of Luxemburg, settled in Seville as a young man and studied the works of Ruelas and Ribera to great advantage.

Francisco de Zurbarán (1598–1664?), a staunch advocate in Spain of the style of Caravaggio, was regarded as an intruder by some of the artists of Seville, although he became the official painter of the city. He attained his greatest success in Madrid, where Philip IV entrusted him with the decoration of the Palace of the Buen Retiro. The tranquility and simplicity of his pictures account for the special demand for his work in monasteries. His work reveals the influence of Ribera. He painted many famous pictures of friars.

In his art, Bartolomé Estebán Murillo (1618–82) best expressed the religious character of Spain, for he associated a sensual exaltation with a jubilant faith. His national inspiration is revealed in his depiction of roguish children and beggars. Most of his life was spent in his native Andalusia, but in his early work in the Franciscan monastery in Madrid he gave an indication of the principal inspiration of his later art, the association of naturalism with sweetness. A devout Catholic, he served as first president of the Academy of Painting of Seville, founded in 1660. No artist of the seventeenth century was as industrious and productive as Murillo. He painted easily and quickly. His last work was the embellishment of the Church of the Capuchins in Cádiz. While working there he fell from a scaffold and was killed. Among his numerous disciples, the ablest was Miguel de Tovar (1678–1758).

Although there was a school of painting at Córdoba, its proximity to Seville and the greater attraction of Madrid restricted its development. The influence of Seville was especially decisive in the work of the Córdovan artists, of whom Antonio de Castillo (1616–68) was one of the most significant. This school included Antonio García Reynoso (1623–77), Juan de Alfaro (1640–80), and the Carmelite friar, Juan Santisimo Sacramento (1611–80). Granada also developed a local school of some importance, but its activity was restricted, and external influences prevented the development of a true regional character. The most representative artists of this school were Pedro de Moya (1610–74), his disciple, Pedro Atanasio Bocanegra (d. 1669), and Juan de Sevilla (1623–95). Toledo and Madrid were the chief centers of Castilian painting. Although the influence of El Greco was strong, his successors in Toledo converted his unearthly effects into a more impressionistic style. Many of the Castilian artists were under the influence of Caravaggio. Luis Tristán (1586–1640) and Bartolomé González (1564–1627) were among the Toledan painters.

Diego de Silva y Velázquez (1599–1660) won recognition almost immediately upon his appearance in the capital, where he enjoyed the artistic leadership for nearly forty years. Trained in Seville by the elder Herrera and Francisco Pacheco, he went in 1622 to Madrid, where his portrait of Góngora won immediate admiration. In 1629 he went to Italy, where through Rubens he gained an appreciation of the Venetians—especially Titian and Tintoretto. When he returned to Madrid, he won acclaim with his painting of the young Prince Baltasar Carlos, in which was revealed the development of a new style, richer and more pictorial in detail. His later years were devoted to marvelously observed portraits of the royal family and the court buffoons. He also drew upon mythological themes with superb taste and subtlety. He had many disciples, including his son-in-law, Juan Bautista Martínez del Mazo (1612–67), Juan de Pareja (1607–60), and José Leonardo (1605–56).

The seventeenth century was a period of decline in music, after the golden age of the sixteenth century, when Spanish musicians attained international fame and performed in the artistic centers of Europe. However, there were some important composers of religious music, such as Sebastián Vivanco, Sebastián Aguilera de Heredia, and the Catalan, Juan Antonio Pujol. The principal innovation in the last half of the century was the introduction of the dramatic lyric, or zarzuela.

The true keynote of Hispanic culture in these centuries was universality—based on the existence of the Spanish empire in Europe and the New World. Patronage by the court and the nobility gave arts and letters an opportunity to flourish as they never had before. The kings, the Church, and the aristocracy spent lavishly on the construction and decoration of palaces and churches, and they protected the artists and encouraged and subsidized their work. The very forces that seemed to produce the political and economic decline of Spain—pride in conquest and extravagance—worked in the cultural sphere for a richer expression in literature and art.

CHAPTER XVIII

The Reign of Philip V

During the eighteenth century the Bourbon rulers of Spain took their direction from the more powerful Bourbons of France. Gallic influence was especially evident in the foreign policy of Spain. Philip V, the first Bourbon to take the Spanish throne, intrigued against Louis XIV, but the Sun King soon reduced his grandson to submission, and Philip's armies joined the French forces in two wars against Austria.

As the century began and men looked back on recent years of defeat, disaster, and declining power, many in Spain still found, as they thought, good reason for optimism, still hoped for a new period of greatness and prosperity for Spain. The main source of their hope was the duke of Anjou, named by Charles II as his successor, who came to the Spanish throne as Philip V (1700–1746). Grandson of Louis XIV and great-grandson of Philip IV, the new king might, it seemed, put an end to the centuries-long rivalry between France and Spain and weld the two nations in a new unity bringing unprecedented power and glory to both. Louis XIV urged his grandson to be a good Spaniard, but always to remember that he was born a Frenchman. The Spanish ambassador rejoiced in the new links between France and Spain: "What joy! There are no longer any Pyrenees! They have sunk into the earth and we form only one nation." The rejoicing, unfortunately, was premature and unjustified. Anjou's succession brought a major war even before he arrived in Spain: the French connection, which many in Spain applauded, bred suspicion, fear, and hatred abroad, as Spain became not a partner but a dependent under her first Bourbon ruler.

The new king, who went to Spain in 1701, organized his government under Cardinal Portocarrero, a statesman already in the service of Louis XIV, who lacked both ability and tact. Opposition to Anjou's accession was quick in gathering. Leopold I of Austria and the maritime powers of England and Holland opposed it, for the union of France and Spain under the influence of Louis XIV upset the balance of power in Europe. The three powers united against the Bourbons, and Louis XIV, who had already anticipated such a move, prepared for the War of the Spanish Succession. He allied himself with some of the petty German princes, the duke of Savoy, and some of the Italian states. However, despite his efforts to woo the Portuguese to his side, they remained staunch in their traditional friendship with the English, alienated by the Bourbon desire to restore Iberian unity.

Each of the three powers to support the pretensions of the Archduke Charles to the Spanish throne had individual reasons for opposing Philip V. The Habsburgs were disappointed over the loss of the Spanish crown to their ancient dynastic rivals; the Dutch were fearful of the increased power of the French to threaten the United Provinces through the Spanish Netherlands; England, ruled by William III, was ever sensitive to the extension of French influence and its effects on British commerce in the New World and on colonial expansion. The three powers signed the Grand Alliance at The Hague in 1701.

In Spain parties were developed in support of the various candidates for the Spanish throne. Opinion was divided, especially because of the traditional hostility to France, and there was unanimity only for the maintenance of the integrity of the Spanish empire. The Catalans, Aragonese, and Valencians, who most strongly opposed the French, were also strongly intent on the preservation of their *fueros*.

If Louis XIV had ever intended to respect the autonomy of Spain, that intention remained unfulfilled from the moment his grandson arrived in Madrid; Philip V was reduced to a monarch in name only. The count of Harcourt, succeeded a little later by Marsin and Blécourt, was installed at the court not only as French ambassador but also as adviser to the king. Louis XIV arranged the marriage of his grandson with Maria Luisa of Savoy, intervened in the administration of the Spanish Netherlands, and exercised a considerable influence in the distribution of Spanish offices. Cardinal Portocarrero subsequently strengthened the position of the French party by arranging with Louis XIV to appoint a financier capable of solving the acute economic problems. The agent chosen, Jean Orry, was able and industrious, but his harsh manner and indifference to hallowed customs in Spain soon aroused general hostility. Louis XIV believed that Aragon should share in the expenses hitherto borne exclusively by Castile, that the Church should contribute to state expenditures, and that the abuses in the administration of the colonies in America should be rectified. Orry endeavored to carry out this program and was expelled from the court three times because of his efforts to reform Spanish economy.

The French party was also aided by the Princess Orsini, who entered the royal court as a lady-in-waiting to Queen Maria Luisa. She had married the prince of Chalais, who fled from France as a result of a duel and died on his way to Rome. There his widow married the wealthy Flavio Orsini, duke of Bracciano, a grandee of Spain.

Princess Orsini was a tall, handsome woman. Intelligent and born to intrigue, her experience was invaluable to the fourteen-year-old queen from Savoy. She discarded the rigid etiquette isolating the Spanish kings from their people and made the French court her model, but she never failed to respect Spanish sentiment or Spanish pride. In the end, however, her influence over the royal couple aroused the hostility of many aristocrats and finally even alienated Louis XIV.

The War of the Spanish Succession began in 1702, when Prince Eugene, commander of the imperial forces, attacked the French in northern Italy, besieging Mantua and Cremona and capturing Marshal Villeroi. Philip V hastened to Naples, where Austrian intrigue had instigated a revolt which the duke of Medina-Sidonia had difficulty in suppressing. He arrived at Naples with a fleet of twenty-eight French vessels in April 1702 and marched northward to his duchy of Milan, where with the duke of Vendôme he defeated Prince Eugene near Luzzara in August. Meanwhile, the duke of Marlborough was sent with an English force to the Rhine. Although William III, Louis XIV's principal opponent, died in 1702, his sister-in-law, Queen Anne, carried on his engagements.

The enemies of the Bourbons were also busy in Spain. When grandees in contact with the allies proposed that the English and Dutch fleets surprise Cádiz, Sir George Rooke, with fifty ships, sailed into the bay in July 1702 and demanded that the city submit to the Archduke Charles. Maria Luisa, who shamed her mediocre advisers into action by threatening to go to Andalusia to arouse the people in defense of Cádiz, even offered her jewels and valuables for the national defense. The English, learning that a Spanish silver fleet of thirteen galleons convoyed by twenty-three ships had taken refuge in Vigo, forced an entrance into the harbor, captured nine silver-laden galleons, and sank or captured the convoy.

On this audacious attack Philip V returned to Madrid. An incipient rebellion was brewing in Catalonia, and dissension between the Princess Orsini and the proud French ambassador, Cardinal d'Estrées, seriously compromised the Bourbon cause. The princess, however, outwitted the diplomats and even defied Louis XIV until he requested that she continue in her favored position. Thus, she became supreme in Spain and almost independent of Louis XIV. Under her capable direction the financial situation of the country was improved, the administration of justice was reformed, and many beneficial measures were introduced.

The War of the Spanish Succession had become a European war, as the international hostility to the Bourbons grew more resolute. Louis XIV induced the elector of Bavaria to conclude an alliance by offering him the Spanish Netherlands, but Portugal joined the Grand Alliance against the Bourbon kings. The Archduke Charles, with his cause thus strengthened, landed in Lisbon in 1704 and was proclaimed king of Spain. Philip V had in the meantime completely reorganized the Spanish army and with the duke of Berwick and 40,000 men successfully invaded Portugal until he was forced to withdraw to summer quarters.

The unstable duke of Savoy had joined the allies, but they were defeated at Höchstädt, and an army of Hungarian rebels was at the gates of Vienna. The archduke's cause was desperate, but Prince Eugene and Marlborough united to retrieve victory from apparent defeat. Advancing up the Danube in 1704 they completely routed the Bavarians and the French at the battle of Blenheim, drove the French out of Germany, repelled the Hungarians, and forced the Bavarians to submit.

Admiral George Rooke convoyed the prince of Hesse-Darmstadt, ex-viceroy of Catalonia, to Barcelona, where the Austrian party expected to find support. Although the revolt did not materialize and Barcelona remained loyal to Philip V, on his return voyage Rooke attacked Gibraltar, which had been so neglected by the Spaniards that there were only sixty soldiers in the garrison. After resisting for two days the defenders surrendered in August 1704.

On the loss of Gibraltar the ministry was reorganized, and the new French ambassador, the duke of Grammont, became a member of the ruling junta. By using the influence of Maria Luisa, the Princess Orsini soon regained her position in the Spanish court, whereupon Louis XIV decided to govern Spain through her. A new royal ministry was formed, dominated by José Grimaldi, who was generally esteemed for his diligence and honesty.

In August 1705 the English fleet sailed from Lisbon with the Archduke Charles for Barcelona, where the Habsburg cause had many sympathizers. Although the bulk of the fleet proceeded to Barcelona, some ships were detached to encourage a revolt in Valencia. The Bourbons suffered a serious reverse when Barcelona was forced to capitulate, and the archduke, proclaimed as Charles III, solemnly entered the city on November 7, 1705.

Lord Galloway had invaded Spain from Portugal and forced the duke of Berwick to retreat. Amid accusations of treason in the Bourbon camp, the allied forces advanced on Madrid, which the archduke entered in 1706. Saragossa had joined the Austrian cause, and the rest of Aragon soon rallied to Charles. Undaunted, Philip V continued the struggle and recovered Madrid, where he reestablished his court and waited for the following spring to renew the conflict.

Military events outside the Iberian Peninsula were not as favorable to the Bourbons. In 1706 Marlborough defeated Marshal Villeroi at Ramillies. Dutch and German troops overran Brabant, Antwerp fell, and the Spanish withdrew to Mons. Prince Eugene won the battle of Turin in Italy, forced the French army to withdraw across the Alps, and the Austrians occupied the Piedmont. In 1707 the Bourbons lost both Milan and Naples. Only a decisive victory could restore their cause. Berwick defeated the British and Portuguese at Almansa. While Philip V overran Granada, the combined armies of Berwick and Orleans captured Saragossa and Lérida, overran Aragon, and carried the war into Catalonia. Philip V then avenged himself on the Catalans for their lack of loyalty by abolishing at one stroke of the pen the privileges that Philip II had not dared to attack openly. Philip V was determined to emulate his grandfather by centralizing the control of the Spanish regions and establishing the absolutism of the Bourbons in Spain. He further reorganized the army, created inspectors and intendants, and prepared the way for a Bourbon victory in the peninsula.

When in 1708 the French were defeated at Oudenarde and, with the loss of Lille and Ghent, Artois and Picardy lay defenseless, Louis XIV decided to negotiate with his enemies. Although he was unable to persuade his grandson to renounce the Spanish throne, he did persuade the British and the Dutch to consider peace on the basis of the dismemberment of the Spanish empire. When confronted with this threat Philip V resolved to free himself from French domination and was supported by the majority of his Spanish advisers. The Princess Orsini was persuaded to head the conspiracy while the French were too preoccupied elsewhere to interfere. Amelot was replaced by Blécourt and a government of Spaniards, in which the princess retained her influence, was established.

Louis XIV was disposed to abandon his Spanish allies until a demand that he surrender the Spanish fortresses he held led to a renewal of the war. The allied armies captured Tournai and Mons and won the bloody battle of Malplaquet (1709), but the Bourbon forces in Spain, determined to defend the integrity of the Spanish dominions, contained the imperial threat in Portugal by winning the battle of Gudina. The Spanish were forced, however, to evacuate Balaguer and Catalonia.

Philip V was not dispirited by his reverses, but resolved to make 1710 the decisive year and, using gold from the New World, raised a new army. Although the archduke defeated the Spaniards, he remained in Saragossa, and when he failed to advance on Madrid at once, Maria Luisa, again regent, was able to evacuate the city with her court and take refuge in Valladolid. The measures of the Archduke Charles were ill-received, and the Spaniards resorted to guerrilla tactics against the imperial forces, which, being predominantly Protestant, aroused a great deal of religious animosity. When the Austrians advanced from Madrid to join the Portuguese, Philip V forced them to abandon the city and withdraw to Aragon, where, in close pursuit, he defeated them at Brihuega and Villaviciosa. By 1711 the Bourbons had overrun the greater part of Catalonia, and the dejected Archduke Charles returned to Vienna.

The death of the Emperor Joseph I altered the balance of power in Europe. The British, now governed by the Tories, who were anxious for peace, feared the extension of the power of the archduke as both emperor and king of Spain as much as they did that of Louis XIV. Consequently, negotiations were renewed with the French. Louis XIV excluded the Spanish plenipotentiary and insisted on representing his grandson. Philip V had refused to dismember his empire, but Louis XIV undertook the operation without his approval.

After the coronation of the archduke as Emperor Charles VI, the formal congress to redraw the map of Europe was convoked at Utrecht (1712). The English, alarmed at the possibility of Philip V's accession to the French throne following the death of the dauphin, demanded that the Spanish king renounce his rights to the French crown, while the duke of Orleans, regent of France, relinquished his Spanish pretensions. Philip V also issued a law of succession, overriding Spanish tradition by giving preference to his male descendants over the females.

By the Treaty of Utrecht, imposed on the Spaniards by Louis XIV in the summer of 1713, Philip was recognized as king of Spain and the Indies, but he agreed that the crowns of France and Spain should not be united. His Italian possessions of Naples, Tuscany, and Milan, the Spanish Netherlands, and Sardinia were ceded to Charles VI. Prussia received Spanish Gueldres, and Savoy received Sicily, to be exchanged later for Sardinia, with the royal title. Great Britain retained Gibraltar and Minorca and obtained the commercial privilege of the asiento. This secret treaty granted the English South Sea Company a monopoly of the slave trade with Spain's American colonies and the right to send a merchant ship of five hundred tons a year to trade with the colonies. The Princess Orsini was rewarded with a Flemish principality, but Charles VI, in ratifying the treaty, refused to consider its cession to her. He also denied recognition of Philip V as king of Spain, until the Treaty of Rastatt (1714), which restored peace between Austria and Spain.

The Catalans, although abandoned by the allies, determined to resist Philip V. It was agreed in the peace negotiations that they would enjoy a general amnesty and the rights of other Spaniards, but, dissatisfied with the loss of their autonomy, they declared war in July 1713. The duke of Popoli, viceroy of Catalonia, occupied Manresa and besieged Barcelona, while the Catalans resorted to their time-honored guerrilla tactics. In a final attack on Barcelona in September 1714, the Catalans resisted desperately from street to street and house to house, but were finally forced to surrender to prevent the burning of the city.

Although she had been an active agent of Louis XIV, the Princess Orsini had retained the confidence of Philip V. Few Spaniards had enjoyed any political power, for the real minister was Jean Orry, who executed the plans of the princess. After the death of the queen (1714), the influence of the princess grew, and she distracted Philip's melancholy and protected Orry, who was intent on the reform of the Spanish administration. Meanwhile, an Italian had appeared in court who soon gained control of the government. Giulio Alberoni, an Italian priest and steward of the archbishop of Plasencia, so delighted the duke of Vendôme with his conversation and culinary ability that he accompanied the duke to Flanders, to Paris, and finally to Spain, where he became the intermediary between the duke and the Princess Orsini. On the death of Vendôme, Alberoni returned to France, became an agent of the duke of Parma, and was chosen by Louis XIV as an adviser to Philip V. Alberoni continued his friendship with the Princess Orsini and, on the death of Maria Luisa, they proposed the marriage of Philip V with Elizabeth Farnese, daughter of the duke of Parma. The Princess Orsini was less astute than Alberoni, believing that she could retain her control over Philip, since the Italian queen would be indebted to her for the marriage. Alberoni deliberately encouraged this illusion, picturing the young lady as a simple child with little ambition. When the princess learned that Elizabeth had quite a different character, it was too late. Alberoni met Elizabeth Farnese as she entered Spain and warned her to beware of the princess. The new queen angrily dismissed the princess when they met. The "old fool," as Elizabeth called her rival, was forced to go to France, where she met a frigid reception. She hoped to be recalled to the Spanish court, but Philip V, inclined to forget her past services, abandoned her. Elizabeth Farnese, who immediately gained an ascendancy over the weak will of Philip, became the real ruler of Spain. She soon became unpopular with the Spaniards, but she retained her mastery over the king.

Behind the scenes Alberoni was quietly gaining an influence over both Elizabeth and the king. Soon the dominant force in the court, he adopted a policy designed to reduce the French influence. Louis XIV had died (1715), and his nephew, the duke of Orleans, had become regent of France. Philip V still hoped to gain the French throne and resented the obstacle posed by the duke. Alberoni undertook negotiations for more amicable relations with Great Britain and Holland, but succeeded only in concluding a commercial treaty to the advantage of Great Britain. It also implied the recognition of George I as king, although until then, Spain had supported the Stuart pretender. Alberoni also conciliated the Dutch and the pope and sent six galleys to aid the Venetians against the Turks. He became principal adviser to Philip V and his influence over Elizabeth Farnese was increased after the birth of Prince Charles (1716). In 1717 he was made a cardinal. The duke of Orleans sent the marquis of Louville to counteract Alberoni's influence and restore French prestige in the Spanish court, but Philip V refused to receive him and he returned to France, leaving the cardinal in a stronger position than before. In 1716 and 1717 Philip was suffering from melancholia, and the real government fell into the hands of Elizabeth.

In November 1717 a Spanish force occupied Sardinia. France had emerged from her isolation by concluding the Triple Alliance with Great Britain and Holland to ensure the execution of the Treaty of Utrecht. Neither Great Britain nor France wished to support Charles VI, fearing an increase in his influence, but the Quadruple Alliance was finally concluded with Austria. Charles VI recognized Philip V as king of Spain, agreed that Sicily should be exchanged for Sardinia, and recognized the infant Prince Charles as heir to Parma. He was the third in the line of succession to the Spanish crown, for his elder half-brothers preceded him, but Elizabeth Farnese was determined that he should have a throne even if it was only a duchy.

Spain was also invited to adhere to the Quadruple Alliance, but Alberoni was not satisfied with the advantages offered. He wanted to restore Spanish control in Italy. In July 1718 a Spanish expedition overran Sicily, immediately causing international complications. In August, Admiral Byng annihilated the Spanish fleet at Cape Passaro, off Syracuse. Alberoni rejected an ultimatum of the allied powers and resorted to reprisals, expelling the British consuls from Spain and confiscating British ships. War was inevitable, and Great Britain broke relations with Spain in December 1718. France became a British ally two months later, when a vast conspiracy, in which Alberoni was involved, was discovered against the duke of Orleans.

A Spanish fleet was sent to aid the Old Pretender in Scotland, and Alberoni tried to organize a second expedition against France, but both were frustrated. In April 1719, 30,000 French soldiers overran the Basque provinces and captured San Sebastián. In the midst of adversity Alberoni continued his intrigues and sought allies, but the French invaded Catalonia and an English army landed in Galicia and captured Vigo. Great Britain and France required the dismissal of Alberoni as a condition of peace and, abandoned even by Elizabeth Farnese, he was given three weeks in which to leave Spain. In the peace negotiations which followed, Philip V demanded the surrender of Gibraltar and Minorca by the British. This demand was rejected, and Philip V had to agree to surrender Sardinia to Savoy and again renounce the crown of France, for which he had conspired against the regent. The imperial provinces in Italy were restored, and Charles VI abandoned his claim to Spain. In return, the succession of the children of Elizabeth Farnese to Tuscany and Parma was recognized.

Philip V was at peace for the first time in his twenty-year reign. The marquis of Grimaldi, who assumed control of Spanish foreign relations, was firmly convinced of the necessity of collaboration between the two Bourbon houses in European affairs. In 1721 a defensive treaty reconciled Philip V and the duke of Orleans, and a double matrimonial alliance was arranged with France. Prince Luis of Asturias was betrothed to Louise Elizabeth of Orleans, and Louis XV was betrothed to the infant daughter of Philip and Elizabeth Farnese. The child was sent to France to be educated as the future queen, the marriage of Luis was celebrated in 1722, and the union of Prince Charles and another daughter of the Regent was arranged.

Philip was usually in a state of melancholy, secluded from the world in his sumptuous palace, San Ildefonso de la Granja, built in 1721 to remind him of Versailles. Desiring to be relieved of the burden of government, in 1724 Philip abdicated in favor of his son Luis, thereby fulfilling a vow made in 1720. If Luis died without heirs, the succession would fall to his brother Ferdinand and then to the sons of Elizabeth

Farnese. In reality Philip V continued to rule, for the sixteen-year-old Luis was in bad health and submissively obeyed his father's orders. His ephemeral reign lasted until August 1724, when he died, leaving his father as his heir.

During the second reign of Philip V, Ferdinand was the recognized heir, and the principal goal of the royal administration was to find better thrones for Prince Charles and Prince Philip. A new minister emerged to serve as the instrument of the ambitious queen. For some months a Dutch adventurer, Baron Jan Willem Ripperda, became master of Spain. Although born into an aristocratic family of Groningen, he was of Spanish blood. Changing his religion to improve his chances for worldly success, he became a deputy in the States General and Dutch ambassador to Spain. At the conclusion of his mission, he settled in Spain, where to ingratiate himself with Philip V he returned to the Catholic faith. He was soon rewarded with the position of superintendent of the factories of Guadalajara. Although Alberoni discharged him, he was named superintendent of all the factories of the kingdom after the cardinal's dismissal.

Ripperda well knew of the ambition of Elizabeth Farnese for her sons. He proposed that Philip send him on a secret mission to Vienna, where he would use his supposed friendship with the emperor and Prince Eugene to obtain the recognition of Prince Charles and Prince Philip as the heirs of the Italian duchies of Parma, Plasencia, and Tuscany. The moment was propitious, for neither France nor Great Britain was disposed to dispute the rights to the duchies. Since Elizabeth was willing to negotiate for the support of Charles VI to advance her dynastic interests, Baron Ripperda was sent to Vienna incognito.

Meanwhile, the duke of Bourbon had succeeded the duke of Orleans at the head of French foreign affairs. Louis XV was in poor health, and the new minister wanted him to marry quickly, produce an heir, and block the accession of the rival house of Orleans. Maria Anna, the affianced Spanish princess, being too young to bear children, was returned to Madrid with little ceremony, and Louis XV married the daughter of Stanislas Leszczyński. The indignant Spanish sovereigns ordered Ripperda to obtain an alliance with Austria, and he returned with the Treaty of Vienna in 1725.

Three treaties were concluded between Spain and Austria. In a treaty of peace Charles VI finally recognized Philip V as king of Spain on condition that he renounce his claims to the French throne. Philip V acknowledged the Italian duchies as fiefs of the empire, but Prince Charles's right of succession to them was also recognized, and in the meantime he could garrison them with Spanish troops. In the commercial treaty Philip V promised to protect the trade of the Ostend Company against the attacks of the Dutch and British privateers. The emperor, in return, agreed to urge Great Britain to restore Gibraltar and Minorca and arranged the marriage of his eldest child, Maria Theresa, to Prince Charles.

Despite the disadvantages in the treaties of Vienna the Spanish sovereigns rejoiced at the success of the negotiations and Ripperda was made a duke and grandee of Spain. The other European powers were alarmed. Great Britain, France, and Prussia concluded a defensive alliance. When Ripperda returned to Madrid and was named prime minister, he immediately revealed his imprudence. He threatened Great Britain with invasion unless Gibraltar and Minorca were restored, but his efforts to reorganize the army and navy were thwarted by the lack of resources. He sent agents to England, intrigued with the Jacobites, and actually planned an invasion of England. War appeared imminent.

The irresponsible policy of Ripperda raised a public outcry against such diplomatic activities. He was forced to resign in 1726, sought asylum in the British Embassy, and finally fled to The Hague, where he became a Protestant for the second time. He then went to Morocco, became a Mohammedan, and led an attack on Ceuta. He died in Tetuán, while planning to go to Rome to seek a papal pardon for his religious vagaries.

Elizabeth Farnese wanted war. José Patiño, an able organizer and administrator, had succeeded Ripperda as principal minister. In February 1727 the Spaniards unsuccessfully besieged Gibraltar for four months. Louis XV becoming dangerously ill and Philip V or one of his sons being in line of succession to the French throne, Elizabeth began to intrigue for the crown of France for Prince Charles, since her stepson, Prince Ferdinand, would inherit the throne of Spain. In 1729 peace was concluded in the Treaty of Seville among Great Britain, Holland, France, and Spain. Elizabeth was indignant with the emperor for refusing Prince Charles as a husband for Maria Theresa and not admitting Spanish garrisons to protect his rights in Tuscany. By the treaty, French and English commercial privileges with Spain and Spanish America were renewed, and 6000 Spanish troops were admitted to three Italian strongholds to protect the rights of Prince Charles.

It was easier to negotiate the Treaty of Seville than it was to fulfill it. The maritime powers wanted to prevent a close union between Spain and France, and Cardinal Fleury of France tried to maintain a balance of power. The emperor refused to admit the Spanish garrisons to Parma and Tuscany, but the death of the duke of Parma precipitated events. A second Treaty of Vienna (1731), which the British and the Dutch guaranteed, provided that the emperor admit Spanish garrisons into the Italian duchies and recognized the rights of Prince Charles, who proceeded to Italy, where he was placed under the protection of the grand duke of Tuscany and the duchess of Parma, both of whom recognized him as their heirs. The duchess of Parma took possession of Parma and Plasencia in his name.

France was isolated, and Patiño recommended an alliance with the Bourbons, to whom Elizabeth was more inclined, now that her son was established. Charles VI stimulated the rapprochement by raising obstacles to the immediate investiture of Prince Charles as ruler of the Italian duchies. France needed the Spanish alliance, for Cardinal Fleury had to protect the interests of Stanislas Leszczyński, father-in-law of Louis XV, in Poland on the death of Augustus II, king of Poland and elector of Saxony. Patiño, recognizing the strength of his position, demanded the abrogation of the Treaty of Utrecht. The French government acceded to this demand, and the Treaty of the Escorial was signed in 1733. It concluded the Family Compact between the two branches of the House of Bourbon and cemented the alliance between France and Spain.

In the Treaty of the Escorial, France guaranteed possession of the Italian duchies to Prince Charles, together with any territory acquired in the impending war with Charles VI, and agreed to protect Spain against a British attack and to assist in the recovery of Gibraltar. Spain also agreed to aid France in the war against the Austrians.

Prussia, Austria, and Russia supported Augustus III's pretensions to the Polish throne, while France supported Stanislas Leszczyński. Spanish intervention in such a war was foreign to her previous policy, but Elizabeth Farnese seized the opportunity to obtain Naples and Sicily for Prince Charles. In the war the French army rapidly overran Italy, while the Spanish fleet supported the conquest of Naples and Sicily. Prince Charles was crowned king of the Two Sicilies at Palermo in 1735, a position formally recognized in the treaty which was shortly concluded. The duchies of Parma and Plasencia were restored to the empire, although Elizabeth wanted them for her younger son, Prince Philip; however, she finally accepted the fait accompli.

Despite the hostility of Philip V, the able José Patiño ruled Spain for ten years without the title of prime minister—a worthy rival of his contemporaries Sir Robert Walpole and Cardinal Fleury. As a good economist he had tried to rebuild Spanish naval power, and he increased the army to 80,000 men. He favored and stimulated commerce, suppressed abuses in taxes, protected Spanish industry, and created commercial companies to advance trade. He was succeeded by the marquis of Villadarias, an honest, slow, and cautious Viscayan. It appeared that a new era of peace had opened for Spain. Although still in poor health, Philip recovered his faculties except for occasional periods of melancholy. Yet the unpredictable passion of Elizabeth Farnese lurked beneath the apparent calm of the court. Charles was king of Naples and Sicily, but he was unmarried, and Elizabeth hoped to expand his dominions. The emperor had rejected him as a son-in-law, but he was finally betrothed to Marie Amelia, daughter of Augustus III. Luis, the third son, had become archbishop of Toledo and a cardinal. Prince Philip had yet to be established and in 1737, he was married to Marie Louise, eldest daughter of Louis XV, but he still had no throne.

By 1738 a conflict with Great Britain again appeared imminent. Trade and colonial rivalry in the New World had long been a source of irritation between the British and Spaniards. The British constantly sought to extend their commerce, either legally or through contraband activities, and the colonial rivalry between the British in Georgia and the Spaniards in Florida led to further discord. A strong war party in England, headed by the duke of Newcastle, was eager to provoke hostilities, even though both Philip V and Sir Robert Walpole desired peace.

When the Spanish authorities insisted on the inspection of British ships in American waters the situation became critical. In 1739 the British agreed in the Convention of the Pardo to pay an indemnity of 95,000 pounds, but when the Spanish government urged the payment of claims against the South Sea Company, public clamor in England led to the opening of hostilities. Popular opinion had been inflamed by the publicity given to a Captain Jenkins' missing ear, allegedly cut off by Spanish officials when he was caught smuggling. The French rallied to the aid of Spain, and the war began auspiciously for the Spaniards, who seized many British ships. Admiral Vernon sacked Porto Bello in November 1739, but he failed to capture Cartagena and Santiago de Cuba. A squadron of British ships tried to blockade El Ferrol, but the Spanish fleet slipped through and sailed to reinforce the Indies.

In 1740 when the Emperor Charles VI of Austria died, the war spread across Europe. The question at issue was the recognition of the Pragmatic Sanction by which Maria Theresa was guaranteed accession to the Austrian throne. Again, Elizabeth Farnese used the opportunity to find a throne in Italy for Prince Philip, the son-in-law of Louis XV, whose aid she now hoped to obtain. Cardinal Fleury was unable to restrain the war party in France, and the French became the allies of Prussia in 1741, even though they had approved the Pragmatic Sanction. The Spanish government, with a new and able minister, José del Campillo, in office as a result of the preparations for war, supported the elector of Bavaria for the imperial throne in order to gain French assistance in Italy. Although the British Mediterranean fleet tried to guard the route to Italy, the Spanish fleet evaded it and landed Prince Philip and 14,000 men in Genoese territory, while the duke of Montemar, with a second force, marched through France. Charles Emmanuel of Savoy, who had supported Maria Theresa so as to check the extension of Spanish influence in Italy, blocked Prince Philip's advance. The French failed to send the promised reinforcements, but Montemar's army united with that of Naples. In the meantime, King Charles of Naples and Sicily had been forced by the threat of an English bombardment to sign a declaration of neutrality, and his army had to withdraw. Prince Philip tried to undertake the offensive in Savoy, but was driven back across the frontier. The Treaty of Breslau in 1742 placed Spain in a difficult position, for Prussia and Poland withdrew from the war, and the victorious Austrians forced the Spanish army in Italy back into Naples. In Spain, Campillo was succeeded by Ensenada, a protégé of Patiño and a distinguished administrator.

Charles Emmanuel conducted a double set of negotiations to gain possession of Lombardy. When Maria Theresa signed the Treaty of Worms by which she abandoned her claim to Milan, and Savoy received parts of Pavia and Piacenza, France declared war on Austria and drew closer to Spain. The second Family Compact, signed at Fontainebleau, in October 1743, provided for an offensive and defensive alliance, with the primary purpose of establishing Prince Philip in Milan, Parma, and Piacenza. France promised to declare war on Great Britain at the propitious moment and to restore Gibraltar and Minorca to Spain. Preparations were also made for Prince Charles Edward Stuart to invade Great Britain. The English were defeated in a naval engagement in the Mediterranean, but the expedition to assist "Bonnie Prince Charlie" failed. Although King Charles broke his pledge of Neapolitan neutrality, the invasion of Italy from France was futile, and the Franco-Spanish army was obliged to withdraw.

When the marquis of Argenson became foreign minister of France, he had to maintain the alliance between the two Bourbon courts, despite his antagonism to Spanish aspirations and the dynastic ambitions of Elizabeth Farnese. As the death of Charles VI had changed the international aspect of the relations between France and Spain, Elizabeth feared France might conclude peace with Austria. Then Louis XV's army won the victory of Fontenoy in Flanders, and the Franco-Spanish forces took Piacenza and Pavia. The allies defeated Charles Emmanuel of Savoy, advanced to Asti, and entered Milan in December 1745.

Francis of Lorraine, husband of Maria Theresa, being elected emperor, Argenson was disposed to peace, even at the sacrifice of Elizabeth Farnese's ambitions. The Austrians, alarmed at Frederick the Great's victory at Kesseldorf, offered Parma and Pavia to Prince Philip, but this peace proposal was rejected by the Spaniards. Argenson then undertook negotiations with Charles Emmanuel, who began an offensive in Italy with Austrian support. The Franco-Spanish allies lost city after city, and the Austrians recovered Piacenza after a bloody battle. A few weeks later Philip V died.

At the beginning of his reign, the first Bourbon to rule Spain proved himself to be a valiant soldier, but he soon relinquished the government to others. Owing to the melancholy which beset him he allowed the inordinate ambitions of his wives to direct his indolent will. Instead of keeping the peace he plunged into ruinous military adventures.

CHAPTER XIX

The Sons of Philip V

With the accession of Ferdinand VI many Spaniards were glad to welcome a king born on Spanish soil, but the new king, as all realized, came to the throne at a most difficult time. Abroad, the war was still going badly and at home Ferdinand inherited all the problems of his predecessors. No one, fortunately, wanted the war to continue. Ferdinand himself wanted peace and was able to use his wife, Barbara of Braganza, to work through Portugal to negotiate with Great Britain. Negotiations, of course, were not easy. At the Congress of Aix-la-Chapelle—opened in November 1747—none of the allies could agree. Maria Theresa distrusted Charles Emmanuel, France was jealous of Spain. The English and Dutch were not on cordial terms. It was not until 1748 that the definitive treaty was agreed on. Prince Philip and his heirs were established in the duchies of Parma, Piacenza, and Guastalla. England claimed the privilege of the asiento with Spain and the right of trade through its single ship for four years, as an indemnity for the years she had not enjoyed the privilege.

The new king, like his predecessors, had his favorites; however, two ministers really governed Spain. The marquis of Ensenada, who had already served Philip V very ably, retained the confidence of the new sovereigns, as did José de Carvajal y Lancaster. The latter had served as a diplomat and was charged with the ministry of State on the recommendation of Ensenada. Inclined to a reconciliation with Great Britain, he knew that the British needed Spanish friendship and preferred Spanish neutrality to an amicable policy with France. He wished to give Spain time to recover from her military reverses and free her from attacks on the high seas and in the colonies. He believed that the interests of Great Britain and Spain did not really conflict, for the British only desired supremacy on the high seas and in commerce. Spain could build up her military power and depend on the naval power of Great

Britain to defend her colonial empire. As a prerequisite for such an alliance, however, Carvajal demanded the surrender of Gibraltar and Minorca to Spain.

Ensenada, on the other hand, preferred France because of his hatred for the British. All of his measures aimed at strengthening Spain against Great Britain, whom he blamed for Spanish decadence. Ferdinand VI restrained both tendencies firmly. He desired peace and preferred a free course to an alliance to serve either French or British interests. To Ensenada, however, was due the reconstruction of the Spanish navy and army. He reorganized the treasury to increase the revenue, which left a reserve of 60,000,000 ducats at the death of Ferdinand VI.

Despite his policy of neutrality, Ferdinand VI was a double first cousin of Louis XV. In his policy of rapprochement with Austria, the ancient rival of the Bourbons, Ferdinand indicated his divergence from his two half-brothers, the duke of Parma and the king of Naples. In the end, he concluded a defensive treaty with Austria in Italy in 1752. This drove his half-brothers into closer relations with France.

The intrigue in the courts of London and Versailles to influence Ferdinand VI continued. Carvajal resisted the French, who wished to renew the Family Compact, and negotiated with the Portuguese for a treaty concerning the colony of the Sacramento, which he proposed to exchange for certain territories in Paraguay. John V of Portugal had been converted to the proposal, but his successor did not wish to continue the negotiations. Then Barbara of Braganza used her influence to obtain her brother's approval of the treaty (1750). Ensenada, however, intervened to prevent the fulfillment of the treaty. Richard Wall, an Irish Catholic in Spanish service, was recalled from the London embassy to become minister of State. Ensenada advised Charles of Naples of the treaty, and he protested its fulfillment. When Keene, the English ambassador, discovered a plan concocted by Ensenada with the French to attack the English settlements in the Gulf of Mexico, he joined with Wall to bring about the political ruin of Ensenada, who was exiled to Granada.

At the start of the Seven Years' War the British hoped to win Spain to more friendly relations, but despite the continued intrigues of the ambassadors of both nations Ferdinand VI remained firmly neutral. After the French had captured Minorca (1756) they redoubled their efforts to attract the Spanish, even offering to assist Prince Philip in obtaining the Polish throne. Spanish opinion was aroused by the attacks of the British corsairs on their American commerce, the contraband activities of the British, and their expansion in the Gulf of Honduras and on the Mosquito coast. When the war was unfavorable, William Pitt offered a plan to restore Gibraltar in return for an alliance and Spanish aid in recovering Minorca.

Then in 1758 Barbara of Braganza died. Ferdinand VI, who had no heir, was at once urged to remarry, but it was too late. His health, too, was rapidly deteriorating. He suffered from intense depressions, cut himself off from everyone, and began to show signs of increasing insanity. He died the year after his wife. Twelve days later he was succeeded by Charles of Naples, whom he had named as his successor, who became king as Charles III.

Few changes were made in the Spanish ministry. Leopoldo de Gregorio, marquis of Squillaci, became minister of Finance and Richard Wall remained as minister of State. France and Great Britain were still engaged in the Seven Years' War. Charles III tried at first to adhere to the neutrality established by his brother, but his obvious preference for the French made him resent more than ever the grievances which the Spanish suffered from English contraband trade. The English occupied the coast of Honduras and refused to share the Newfoundland fisheries with the Spaniards. He was perturbed when the British landed in French Santo Domingo in 1759, until he was assured that they had no designs on the Spanish half of the island.

As relations became more embittered with Great Britain, the French continued their efforts to win Spain as an ally, until the third Family Compact was concluded in 1761. It was an offensive and defensive alliance. Spain would declare war on Great Britain and France would sustain Spanish pretensions in regard to Newfoundland and Honduras. At the conclusion of hostilities Spain would cede Dominica, St. Vincent, Santa Lucia and Tobago to France in return for Minorca. Portugal would be forced to close her ports to British commerce. The mutual guarantees were extended to the Bourbon duke of Parma and the Bourbon king of the Two Sicilies, who also adhered to the pact.

The treaty, however, was more advantageous to France than it was to Spain, who soon suffered the consequences of her folly. The French were already in a precarious military situation, and the Spaniards became victims in a war for which they were not prepared. Their forces were disorganized and their American colonies were unprotected except for such defense as they could provide themselves. The British, already victorious on land and sea, were a formidable enemy.

Spain declared war, in January 1762. Portugal, given an ultimatum to join the alliance, announced her intention of remaining neutral, thereby revealing her subordination to Great Britain. The French ambassador then announced that allied troops would cross the frontier not to conquer territory but to prevent the British from occupying Portugal. An army of 40,000 men under the command of the marquis of Sarria invaded Portugal, but the campaign was futile.

On the high seas, Great Britain was now far superior to the Spaniards. A British fleet captured Habana and the British quickly occupied Manila. As compensation for their losses, the Spaniards occupied the Portuguese colony of Sacramento in the Plata River area.

In the negotiations for peace Charles III refused to consider territorial concessions to Great Britain until Choiseul by the Treaty of Fontainebleau ceded Louisiana to Spain as compensation for the losses to Great Britain. The Treaty of Paris was signed on February 10, 1763. Great Britain returned Manila and Habana to Spain in exchange for Florida. Portugal was evacuated and Sacramento was returned to the Portuguese. Further, the British were conceded the right of cutting logwood in Honduras, provided the fortifications there were destroyed. Charles III relinquished the Spanish pretension to fishing on the Newfoundland banks. Spain had lost a great deal of national prestige as the bitter fruit of the Family Compact.

At home the principal directors of Spanish policy were the marquis of Grimaldi and the marquis of Squillaci, the unpopular minister of Finance, known as Esquilache. A Sicilian, he was unpopular because he was a foreigner and because of a series of changes introduced by him —a monopoly of bread and olive oil, for example, which raised their prices. A demonstration against him in 1764 led to the killing by the Walloon guard of a number of civilians. Finally, in March 1766 rebels in the streets of Madrid demanded Esquilache's removal. The king in the end had to give in to their demands and send him to Italy.

The insurrection in Madrid was not an isolated incident. There were outbreaks throughout the country over the high cost of living. Charles III was forced to make changes in his ministry—the count of Aranda becoming president of the Council of Castile, with the task of restoring order in the kingdom. The king was reluctant to return to the capital, but Aranda won the support of the guilds, the nobility, and the municipal council against the fulfillment of decrees wrested from him by violence.

It was believed that the outbreak was not as spontaneous as it appeared. The rebels, it was said, consumed much wine and ham and paid well for it; many of them had fine linen or silk underneath their humble clothes. An investigation was undertaken, and in June 1767, Campomanes presented a report in which the Jesuits were accused of responsibility for the outbreak. Spain had been hostile toward the Jesuits long before the Esquilache incident: the majority of the secular and regular clergy attributed to them an undue influence which had made them arrogant, the universities were jealous of the success of their educational institutions, which attracted many students, and finally, the politicians were royalist and did not like their influence in Spain and in the court. Jesuits were charged with exceeding their authority in Paraguay, accused of responsibility for the loss of Manila, and charged with aspirations for universal monarchy. In 1767, when the Court of the Council of Castile reported to the king, it not only formulated reasons for the expulsion of the Jesuits, but presented the details of the plan. Aranda was given unlimited power to execute the royal will. The Jesuits were expelled and their houses in Spain and the New World were closed.

Aranda, the new president of the Council of Castile, was the real author of the expulsion of the Jesuits which followed the revolt over Esquilache. He was a Spanish anticlerical who had been influenced by the Encyclopedists in France. Charles III was jealous of his authority and prerogatives and was also hostile to the pretensions of the Holy See. The Jesuits controlled secondary education in Spain and were annoyed by the treaty of 1750 which sacrificed their colonies. They had been expelled from France by Choiseul in 1764, from Portugal by the marquis of Pombal in 1759, and from Naples in 1767. A clique in the Spanish government had been hostile to them, and their position became more precarious in Spain. The representatives of the Bourbon family in Parma and Naples also expelled the Jesuits. In 1773 the pope issued a bull suppressing them. Clement XIV died in a few months, and his successor, Pius VI, was silent in regard to the Society of Jesus.

Grimaldi was a staunch defender of the Family Compact and favored the commercial pretensions of France. In 1768 he concluded a treaty giving the French the same advantages which Great Britain enjoyed in the peninsula. Relations with the British grew embittered over the Falkland Islands. The Spaniards claimed that the English, in occupying the archipelago, had violated the Treaty of Utrecht. Choiseul timidly supported the Spanish position, but the dispute became critical when the governor of Buenos Aires, Bucarelli, expelled the British from Port Egmont. The indignation aroused in London was increased by the restrictions which Charles III placed on British commerce.

For a time war appeared imminent. Grimaldi tried to avert it and called on France to support the Spanish position under the Family Compact. The count of Aranda advised war, while Spain could rely on her allies in Vienna, Florence, Naples, and Versailles, but the state of Spanish preparedness imposed a decree of caution on Spanish policy. After the fall of the Choiseul ministry in France, Louis XV refused to support the Spanish position. Finally, Charles III, abandoned by his allies, accepted the British demands and Port Egmont was restored to England. This incident demonstrated the weakness of the Family Compact and the inability of France to fulfill her obligations under it. It also produced the fall of Aranda.

Meanwhile, negotiations had been undertaken with the Sultan of Morocco, Sidi-Mohamed-ben-Abdallah, which produced a treaty of friendship in 1767. Seven years later, the sultan decided to expel the Spaniards from the territory they occupied in Morocco. Incited by the dey of Algiers, he besieged Melilla with 13,000 men, but was unsuccessful in the face of the stout defense of the city. Charles III decided to attack Algiers, a haven for pirates, to protect Mediterranean commerce. Alexander O'Reilly was placed in command of an expedition of 20,000 men. Through leaks in the Spanish cabinet the dey of Algiers was forewarned, and the attacking force was repelled in 1775 with heavy losses. Public opinion, aroused against those responsible for the disaster, brought about a widespread conspiracy to overthrow Grimaldi, but he was maintained in office by the loyalty of Charles III.

Relations with Portugal were also less than cordial as a result of the Treaty of 1750, which had not been fulfilled. The Portuguese marquis of Pombal, depending on British support and manifesting the most friendly intentions, secretly instigated attacks on the Plata settlements. Grimaldi was accused of timidity, but two fleets were dispatched, one to Lisbon and the other to Buenos Aires. On the death of Joseph I of Portugal, Pombal fell. The Princess Maria Francisca, daughter of the deceased monarch, ascended the throne, and in 1777 a treaty was concluded establishing a boundary in the disputed region, and the Spanish agreement to evacuate the island of St. Catherine. The marital ties of the Spanish royal family had averted a struggle between the two peninsular kingdoms.

When the American Revolution began neither France nor Spain could view it with indifference. Vergennes, the French premier, was for war, and Aranda, the Spanish ambassador at Versailles, favored an attack on England. Both Spain and France were eager to avenge their losses of 1763. They also were in agreement that aid to the rebel British colonies would weaken British power. Both powers sent secret agents to the colonies.

Meanwhile, Grimaldi, weary of the continuous intrigues against him, decided to retire (1776). He was succeeded as secretary of State by the count of Floridablanca. At the same time American agents in Paris received financial assistance from the Bourbon courts through Rodriquez Hortalés and Company, negotiated by Beaumarchais. Munitions were also forwarded to the Spanish authorities in Louisiana to be distributed to the American revolutionaries. Benjamin Franklin, Silas Deane, and Arthur Lee formed the triumvirate of American agents seeking European aid against Great Britain, but the Spaniards refused to consider an immediate alliance. Charles III was anxious to undermine British power, but he feared British retaliation on the exposed Spanish colonies in the New World. Consequently, Spanish policy was tortuous and vacillating.

In 1777 Arthur Lee arrived in Burgos, where he held a conference with Grimaldi. Despite Grimaldi's explanation that Charles III had no intention of breaking with Great Britain, Lee waited in Vitoria for a response from the king. When Floridablanca was advised of the interview he tried to accomplish a double objective: to keep Lee content and to get him out of the country before his presence proved embarrassing. Finally, Lee returned to Paris satisfied with the promise of financial aid and supplies.

Benjamin Franklin had meanwhile been authorized to conclude an alliance with Spain, and the Spanish ambassador had difficulty in dissuading him from going to Madrid. The defeat of the British at Saratoga caused the French to believe the moment for an alliance was propitious, before the British should effect a reconciliation with the colonists. Although Aranda was of the same opinion, Floridablanca opposed it, and consequently, Spain did not adhere immediately to the Franco-American alliance concluded in 1778. Instead, Charles III offered his services in the role of a mediator. The offer, however, was rejected, and Spain concluded a treaty with France to attack the British Isles (1779).

The war with England was popular in Spain. Even beggars contributed some of their alms to the cause. Aranda, restless and bellicose and with an inveterate hatred of the British, criticized Floridablanca and drafted plans for campaigns. In July 1779 the Spaniards blockaded Gibraltar with 8000 men and a fleet, but a British fleet under Admiral Rodney defeated an inferior Spanish squadron (1780), and reached Gibraltar.

José Gálvez, minister of the Indies, planned that a Spanish fleet should unite with the French in the West Indies and attack Florida. Hostilities had already begun in the New World. The Spaniards attacked British settlements in Campeche, while Bernardo de Gálvez captured Mobile (1780) and took Pensacola (1781). There was also fighting in the Gulf of Honduras and along the Mosquito coast.

The British, now confronted by a war in both Europe and America, were anxious to divide the allies. Floridablanca let the English agent know that Spain could make a separate peace, but insinuated that the surrender of Gibraltar was a necessary prelude to its consideration. Shortly after this interview, John Jay arrived in Madrid as the American representative. The Spaniards had continued to aid the Americans with money and arms, but because of the scruples of the court of Madrid, the aid was not rendered openly. John Jay requested more aid, and his petitions were usually satisfied despite the financial difficulties of the Spaniards. For the recognition of the independence of the United States, however, the Spaniards required a settlement of the various border controversies with the Americans.

In 1781 the Spanish government prepared secretly for the recovery of Minorca. Caught by surprise, the British were forced to surrender to the Franco-Spanish expedition in 1782. This success inspired the Spaniards to convert the blockade of Gibraltar into a siege. In Great Britain the Rockingham ministry replaced Lord North, and definitive negotiations for peace were undertaken. A Scotch businessman, Oswald, was sent by Lord Shelburne to initiate the preliminary conversations. The uncompromising attitude of Spain in demanding Minorca and Gibraltar embarrassed the proceedings, but the British countered with a demand for the restoration of all Spanish conquests and the exchange of Puerto Rico for Gibraltar. Finally, Vergennes offered to renounce Gibraltar if Spain were permitted to retain Minorca and the Floridas. By the treaty of Paris, finally signed in September 1783, the Spaniards acquired Minorca and East and West Florida. The Bahamas were restored, but Honduras was freed from the British, who were permitted to cut dyewood in a prescribed area. Spain had had an important role in the liberation of the North American colonies from British rule. She not only diverted the war efforts of the British but also loaned nearly 8,000,000 reales to the rebels and advanced other sums which were never recovered.

In the latter part of the reign of Charles III, Floridablanca tried to establish a lasting peace with the Moslems. In 1780 a treaty was concluded with Morocco, but it did not end the contraband trade with Gibraltar. The dey of Algiers refused to negotiate with Spain without the consent of the sultan of Turkey. Then Charles III concluded a treaty of alliance and commerce with Turkey which permitted the establishment of Spanish consuls in Turkey and allowed Spanish subjects to visit the holy places. A treaty was also negotiated with Tripoli. Force was required to persuade Algiers to negotiate. The city was bombarded in 1783 and 1784 and in the following year a peace was concluded. Efforts to convert a truce with the dey of Tunis into a definitive peace were futile because of the dey's commercial demands.

In 1787 the enemies of Floridablanca united against him. Aranda, restless in his honorable exile as ambassador to France, returned to Madrid, and attacked Floridablanca with his customary violence. Floridablanca, tired of the satires and libels to which he was subjected, asked that Charles III accept his resignation, which Charles refused to do.

The last days of Charles III were saddened by deaths in his family. Finally, in 1788 he himself caught a fever and died within two days. Coming late to the throne, he had shown his ability in Naples and had proved to be an honest, conscientious ruler. A sincere reformer, he had chosen men of ability and loyalty as his ministers. Both he and his brother Ferdinand VI had been kings genuinely committed to the good of Spain and the interests of the Spanish people. Charles was succeeded by his second son, who was forty when he ascended the throne as Charles IV.

CHAPTER XX

Spain and France, 1788–1808

The position of Charles IV and his minister, the count of Floridablanca, was complicated from the very start of the reign by developments in France. Floridablanca had some advanced ideas and had shown a willingness to introduce limited economic reforms, but the revolution in France was on quite a different scale from anything previously seen. It struck at the very roots of monarchy and aristocracy and challenged the whole traditional structure of European society. Spain, of course, by virtue of the Family Compact, was in a peculiarly difficult position.

Floridablanca was not an enthusiastic proponent of the Family alliance, but events on the other side of the Pyrenees demanded his attention. With the fall of the Bastille, the abolition of feudal rights, and the royal family's imprisonment by the people, the first emigrés entered Spain. He was anxious to avoid the revolutionary virus. The cortes were quietly dissolved, a rigid censorship was imposed on French publications, and foreigners were forbidden to reside in Madrid unless they could provide an adequate reason for their presence.

As Spain was an ally of France, Floridablanca was in a delicate position. Should he declare for the old regime of the Bourbons or the newly and popularly constituted French government? French officers in the Spanish army made common cause with the emigrés. Although Floridablanca was sympathetic with the old regime it was necessary for him to proceed cautiously while Louis XVI was a virtual prisoner. When the French court asked for a loan of three million piastres the Spanish deficit was already eighteen million pounds, but Charles IV handed two-thirds of the sum requested to the marquis of Belamazán and half a million piastres were sent to France. This liberality aggravated the financial plight of Spain. As a result of inflated labor costs, public works were suspended, food prices rose, and taxes became more onerous.

Although a Frenchman from Bayonne, Paul Peret, made an attempt to assassinate Floridablanca, events in France justified the minister's prudence. The French evidently condoned the revolutionary events in Paris on Bastille Day, 1790. When the Nootka Sound controversy developed it proved a means of testing the attitude of the French Constituent Assembly toward Spain. The Spaniards seized two English ships at Vancouver—where the English had established a fur trading post—claiming prior occupation of the sound, and both Great Britain and Spain prepared for war. When Floridablanca invoked French aid under the Family Compact Louis XVI promised assistance, but the French Assembly referred the matter to a commission.

The Nootka Sound incident was adjusted when the British ships were returned and an indemnity paid. Yet, while the negotiations were in progress, the French Assembly abandoned Spain. Floridablanca, irritated, began to persecute those Frenchmen in Spain who were zealous in voicing their revolutionary opinions. Spanish troops were sent to the frontier, and French emigrés were benevolently received in Spain. As the orators in the Assembly in Paris denounced Spain, relations became strained. However, Floridablanca continued to temporize in regard to the attitude to be adopted toward the new regime.

After the flight of Louis XVI to Varennes the policy of Floridablanca became more antirevolutionary. In a note delivered to the Spanish ambassador in Paris, he exhorted the Assembly to respect Louis XVI and ordered four ships armed in Cádiz. When the Assembly rejected his communication, Floridablanca had foreigners classed as resident and transient: the former had to be Catholic and recognize Spanish sovereignty, the latter could reside in the court only with his permission, and their admission was restricted. The French emigrés regarded these measures as persecution, and many returned to their native land. Floridablanca negotiated with the French to obtain the liberation of Louis XVI—demanding that the French king be carried to a neutral state—but when the Assembly met in the fall of 1791, it again rejected his request.

During this time the number of emigrés in Spain had increased. There were 2000 French refugees in Catalonia alone. Floridablanca favored them and maintained vigilant guard of the French frontier. By 1792 Jean Francis de Bourgoing, the new French ambassador in Madrid, pointed out to Charles IV that the policy of Floridablanca made the position of Louis XVI more, rather than less, precarious. As Charles was anxious to protect his French cousin, the pressure of the French, added to the continued hostility of Aranda and the intrigues of Maria Louisa to advance the career of her favorite, Manuel de Godoy, caused him to dismiss Floridablanca.

The government was again entrusted to the count of Aranda, who hoped to liberalize the policy of Floridablanca and lessen the hostility of the French Assembly. His friendship toward the French revolutionaries, it was anticipated, would help to restore amicable relations. Bourgoing was officially recognized as the representative of France, and the tricolor of the revolutionary party was permitted to be flown in Spain.

Events in France, however, did not soothe the anxiety of the Spanish court. War had begun between France and Prussia and Austria. The people of France invaded the Tuileries in June and assaulted the royal palace in August 1792. The authority of Louis XVI was suspended and the National Convention was convoked. Aranda consequently became less sympathetic toward the revolution. Then the monarchy was abolished and a republic proclaimed. The September executions had already alienated Spanish opinion, and Aranda was considering a declaration of war on France, when the victory of the Republican army at Valmy led him to change his belligerent attitude. He thereafter followed a policy of prudent neutrality. Nevertheless, the vacillation of Aranda had discredited him, and in November 1792 he was replaced by Godoy, the court favorite who had risen swiftly to power—largely, it was said at court, because of his intimacy with the queen.

Meanwhile, Charles IV had requested the Convention to permit Louis XVI to seek refuge in Spain, proposing Spanish neutrality and mediation in return for the life of the dethroned French king. When this note was read to the Convention in January 1793, its leaders wanted to declare war on Spain. Neither Aranda nor Godoy had recognized the republic in France, and it was not the right time for the least Spanish intervention on behalf of Louis XVI. His execution produced both grief and indignation in Madrid. Citizens flocked to the ceremonies in his memory, and the French were jeered at in the streets.

Godoy demanded the security of the French royal family and the cessation of French revolutionary propaganda in other countries. When Bourgoing rejected these demands, he was handed his passports and left Spain. Even though Aranda continued to propose neutrality, hostilities appeared inevitable, and in March the Convention declared war on Spain. The war against France was popular, and all classes and regions rallied to the call to arms. It became a crusade to sustain the Catholic and monarchist ideals against the excesses of the Revolution.

Three armies were formed to invade France, the largest of which was in Catalonia. Smaller armies were organized in Aragon, Navarre, and Guipúzcoa. The Catalans quickly invaded France, and their victory at the Mas-Deu River produced panic in Perpignan. They captured Bellegarde in June 1793. Two reverses at Peyrestortes and Vernet were followed by the victory of Trouillas. Then the French were reinforced, and the Catalans withdrew to defend their camp and shorten the front. Meanwhile, Spaniards captured Hendaye, overran the Sarre Valley, and in 1794 broke the French lines, capturing the system of fortifications along the Ciboure River. In the central part of the frontier the prince of Castel-Franco maintained the defensive. When Toulon rebelled against the Convention, the British, who had concluded an alliance with Spain in May 1793, cooperated with a Spanish squadron in occupying the city, but the republicans forced the allies to evacuate it. Many of the citizens accompanied the allied armies as they withdrew.

In 1794 the problem of the continuation of the war was considered in the Spanish Council of State. Although Aranda opposed it, Godoy, who had become duke of Alcudia, and just been named captain general of the Spanish armies, demanded that the war be waged until it could be ended honorably. When Aranda threatened the favorite, he was rewarded with exile in Jaén and eventual imprisonment in the Alhambra.

Hostilities were renewed. The Catalan army was forced to withdraw by the reorganized French forces under General Dugommier. Bellegarde was lost, and the French invaded Catalonia and occupied Figueras. In the western Pyrenees the French invaded the Basque country and captured Fuenterrabia and San Sebastián. The deputies of Guipúzcoa tried to negotiate with the French, but Guipúzcoa was treated like a conquered country, which soon provoked a revolt against them by the Basques. The French entered Navarre, but as General Moncey feared to advance with an army before him and the people in arms around him, he withdrew to San Sebastián and St. Jean Pied de Port.

Meanwhile, revolutionary propagandists had been active in Spain. Secret republican committees were organized in various provincial cities. Even in Madrid young aristocrats planted the tricolor, and a conspiracy was discovered which aimed at the proclamation of a republic. These revolutionary symptoms quickened the desire of the government to negotiate a peace.

In the following year, 1795, the Catalans won a victory at the Fluvia River and drove the French from Puigcerdá and Bellver. The campaign was less fortunate in the west, where the French occupied Bilbao and Vitoria. Godoy had already undertaken negotiations for peace at Basel in July 1795, although Great Britain, also a belligerent, was determined to continue the war. He had originally demanded the restoration of Louis XVII and the withdrawal of the republicans to American territory, where they might found a republic which Spain would recognize, but the successes of the French in the Basque country forced him to reduce his demands. The Peace of Basel restored to Spain the areas conquered by the French and the prisoners of war. In return Spain ceded the Spanish part of Santo Domingo to France. Charles IV also agreed to serve as mediator in the general restoration of peace. Godoy was awarded the title "prince of the peace" for his success in preserving the territorial integrity of Spain.

With peace restored Godoy decided to strengthen the ties of friendship between Spain and France. The organization of the Directory had given a degree of legality to the French government in Spanish eyes. Furthermore, a Franco-Spanish alliance seemed to be in Spain's best interests because of the continued grievances of Spain against the British. Emmanuel Sieyès, on the part of the French Directory, was especially desirous for such an alliance, which would protect the frontier at the Pyrenees and give France naval aid against Great Britain. One difficulty arose. General Perignon, the conqueror of Catalonia, was sent as French ambassador to Madrid. Many French monarchists had fought against him in the Catalan army and Barcelona was reputed to have more than 6000 emigrés, in addition to the expatriated clergy, who numbered 15,000. Perignon demanded restrictive measures against the expatriates as a preliminary step to an alliance.

Godoy, anxious to renew the Family Compact, compliantly ordered French clergy in Spain to withdraw from the ports, capital, and royal residences. Although the Treaty of San Ildefonso (1796) provided for an offensive and defensive alliance between Spain and France against Great Britain, Spain remained neutral toward the other nations with which the Directory was at war. Charles IV, complacently allying himself with those who had decapitated his cousin, made Spain again a French satellite and placed the Spanish fleet at the disposition of the French. Secret clauses prohibited any French emigré from service in the Spanish navy, obliged Spain to declare war on Great Britain, and provided for the surrender of Louisiana to France when Gibraltar was secured. However, the conduct of Charles IV toward the emigrés remained ambiguous. He supported his Bourbon relatives, and the emigrés not only served in the army and navy but enjoyed great regard in the court and in Madrid society.

In 1796 Spain was again at war with the British. General Bonaparte rapidly overran Italy, but the Spanish fleet of twenty-five ships was defeated at Cape St. Vincent by a British force of fifteen ships. The Spaniards recovered sufficiently to resist Nelson's bombardment of Cádiz and attack on Tenerife. In the West Indies the British captured Trinidad, but were repelled in Guatemala and Puerto Rico. When the Directory negotiated a peace with Great Britain, its Spanish ally was ignored and lost Trinidad without even a demand for the return of Gibraltar.

Although this betrayal of Spanish interests by the Directory shocked Spain, the government remained subservient to French demands and in 1798 expelled the emigrés. When one of Godoy's agents was compromised in Paris, even the queen failed to defend her favorite with her usual ardor. Dismissed as head of the government and replaced as chief minister by Francisco Saavedra, he continued his intrigues at court. Yet the new minister was even more under French influence than Godoy had been. Emigrés were forced to register and French nobles were extradited.

When Napoleon invaded Egypt and a British fleet captured Minorca, an army of Ferdinand IV of Naples overran the Papal States, but was soon defeated and the French entered Naples (1799). Charles IV disapproved of his brother's policy and wanted the Directory to recognize his rights to the throne of the Two Sicilies. But there was a strong Anglophile party in Spain, and Godoy became its leader. Great Britain represented the hope of the royalists. By the end of 1798 England, Russia, Turkey, Naples, Tuscany, Austria, and Portugal, alarmed by the French victories in Italy, had formed a strong coalition against France. Urquijo had now become chief minister, but he was not popular with the French Directory.

Napoleon's coup d'état of 1799 substituted the Consulate for the Directory in France. Charles IV was pleased at the advent of the Consulate, believing that it was a step toward the restoration of the monarchy. And Napoleon, who wished to win Spanish support, at first flattered Godoy, the queen, and the Spanish ministers with presents. He proposed an expedition to recapture Minorca and captivated Maria Louisa with the idea that he would find territorial concessions in Italy for the prince of Parma. His victory at Marengo won him further support in Spain. Since he needed Spanish assistance in expelling the British from the Mediterranean and in evacuating his army from Egypt, as well as naval cooperation in the New World, he sent General Berthier to Madrid in 1800 to negotiate the Treaty of San Ildefonso, signed in October.

Spain ceded Louisiana to France and provided Napoleon with six ships in exchange for the promise of a kingdom for the prince of Parma, whose wife was the daughter of the Spanish sovereigns.

The situation in Spain was deplorable. Yellow fever swept Andalusia in an epidemic in which 80,000 died. The French demanded financial assistance even though the Spanish treasury was impoverished. Irritated when the Spanish fleet was ordered to proceed to Cádiz from Brest, Napoleon sent his brother Lucien to Madrid. When Godoy advised Urquijo to oppose the nomination of Lucien Bonaparte as ambassador, Napoleon, further annoyed, demanded the dismissal of Urquijo, who was replaced by a relative of Godoy. Lucien, at the conclusion of the Peace of Lunéville, signed an accord completing the cession of Louisiana and arranging for the prince of Parma to rule the kingdom of Etruria.

France wanted to force Spain into war with Portugal to compel her to withdraw from the English alliance. Godoy, who dreamed of a kingdom for himself, was a willing tool. In 1801 a convention was concluded by which Spain would declare war on her neighbor. When General Leclerc arrived with 20,000 men, they were joined by 60,000 Spaniards, and Godoy was placed in command of the allied forces. War was declared in May 1801 and a month later Portugal was forced to sue for peace. She agreed to pay a heavy indemnity and exclude British ships from her waters. Although Lucien Bonaparte signed the treaty for France, Napoleon did not like it. During his sojourn in Spain Lucien had accumulated 20 paintings and 100,000 escudos in diamonds in return for the creation of the kingdom of Etruria, and as a result of the Portuguese peace he received 100,000 francs as a pension and Charles IV sent him his portrait and five million in diamonds. After the conclusion of a treaty between France and Portugal with additional clauses, Napoleon ordered French troops withdrawn from Spain and Lucien went back to Paris. The final Peace of Amiens (1802) returned Minorca to Spain, but Great Britain retained Trinidad.

Relations with France became less cordial after Napoleon decided to send an expedition to Santo Domingo to crush the revolt there. The Spaniards, loath to collaborate, sent a small squadron to observe the enterprise. Godoy, whose position was stronger than ever following his appointment as supreme commander of the army in 1801, wanted to conclude a separate peace with Great Britain. At this time, however, he made a mistake and an enemy in opposing the marriage of the prince of Asturias. But Charles IV had resolved on it, and the negotiations for a matrimonial alliance with the Neapolitan Bourbons were completed in 1802. Princess Maria Isabel married the heir of the king of Naples, and

Ferdinand, prince of Asturias, married Maria Antonia of Naples. Napoleon was displeased by both marriages.

As the Peace of Amiens was threatened and war again appeared imminent, Napoleon wanted to reassure himself concerning the attitude of Spain. He asked Charles IV to obtain the renunciation of the French throne by the Bourbon count of Provence, but Charles did not wish to undertake the disagreeable task. The Spaniards also protested the sale of Louisiana to the United States.

Pierre de Beurnonville, the new French ambassador, increased his demands: the recognition of the French alliance, the prohibition of British merchandise, and the censorship of English publications attacking Napoleon. But the Spanish government was indecisive, hoping to maintain neutrality in the new war. Talleyrand demanded a subsidy of six million reales a month as the price of neutrality. Charles IV declared that the deplorable state of the Spanish treasury, the plague, and the succession of bad harvests made it impossible for Spain to make such a contribution. Napoleon threatened Godoy with ruin unless he acceded to the demand. At this crisis the British seized two French ships in Spanish waters.

Napoleon tried to carry out his threat and sent a letter to Charles IV charging Godoy with using his relations with the queen to obtain his elevation to power. Maria Louisa and Godoy persuaded Charles not to read the letter. However, the convention of neutrality was signed. In accordance with it the governors of Málaga, Algeciras, and Cartagena were dismissed because they had not fired on the British to prevent their seizure of French ships, which were thereafter guaranteed security in Spanish ports.

Since Spain was actively aiding the enemy of Great Britain, Spanish neutrality was suspect. When William Pitt the Younger became prime minister he demanded that Spain desist from its armament work at El Ferrol. Relations were further strained when the British captured four Spanish galleons carrying gold and took them to England. After other British attacks on Spanish shipping, in December 1804 Charles IV declared war on Great Britain, even though his treasury was exhausted, the harvests had been poor, and plague stalked through the peninsula.

Napoleon was anxious to employ his naval resources for an invasion of England. But with their superior naval power the British blockaded the French at Brest and the Spaniards at El Ferrol, leaving Lord Nelson master of the Mediterranean. Napoleon had instructed Admiral Villeneuve to feign an attack on the British West Indies so as to draw Nelson away from the Mediterranean. Nelson learned of the plans through the

Neapolitan court, and, after crossing the Atlantic twice in sixty days, he intercepted the Franco-Spanish ships at Cape Finisterre. The two fleets met four leagues from Cape Trafalgar, on October 21, 1805. Nelson, with lighter vessels, outmaneuvered the allied fleet and decisively defeated it. Spanish naval power, as well as the French, was finally broken, sacrificed to the ambition of Napoleon.

In December the French won the battle of Austerlitz and Napoleon concluded the Peace of Pressburg. Only England remained hostile to him. He thereupon decided to have a firmer ally in the Neapolitan kingdom. As Queen Caroline, who was unfriendly toward the French, had imprudently broken Neapolitan neutrality, Ferdinand IV was dethroned to make way for Joseph Bonaparte. Charles IV was helpless, but vainly tried to claim his right of succession to the kingdom of the Two Sicilies for the benefit of the king of Etruria.

Around Prince Ferdinand and the princess of Asturias there arose a strong party of Fernandists. They were discontented nobles who favored Great Britain and desired to free Spain from her humiliating subjection to France. The directing genius of the party was Juan de Escóiquiz. Ferdinand had been educated by Escóiquiz, an admirer of Godoy who was both ambitious and involved in intrigue. When Godoy had been dismissed, this tutor tried to obtain for Ferdinand the privilege of attending the council. Although he was exiled to Toledo for his impertinence—and never forgave either Charles IV or Godoy—he retained his influence over the prince. Maria Antonia of Naples, princess of Asturias and the daughter of Caroline of Naples, shared the enmity of Escóiquiz for both Godoy and Maria Louisa.

Godoy admired Napoleon and corresponded with him through an agent, with the object of recovering Gibraltar. He flattered the emperor, promising him money and men and insinuating that he might be considered as a candidate for the Spanish throne if Charles IV died. He also denounced the Princess Maria Antonia for her intrigue against France. When Napoleon requested Godoy to state his ambitions more clearly, he asked for an independent sovereignty between Spain and Portugal. In 1806 Maria Antonia died, and rumors of poison were circulated.

Then, suddenly, Godoy changed his policy and secretly entered a coalition against France with the Russian ambassador, Baron Strogonoff. He was preparing for war when Napoleon's victory at Jena occurred. He immediately expressed unlimited fidelity to Napoleon and tried to explain his military preparations. Napoleon pretended to believe him and sent a new ambassador to Madrid, Francis de Beauharnais, brother of the Empress Josephine, to exploit the existing enmity in the Spanish royal family. Suspicious of Godoy's attitude he demanded that Spain adhere unconditionally to the continental blockade against Great Britain. Charles IV agreed. He then asked that a Spanish force be sent to Hanover, and in 1807, the marquis of Romana arrived in Germany with 20,000 men. Spain was defenseless, deprived of her best troops, and helpless against any action the French emperor might take.

In the meantime Godoy had received new indications of the regard of Charles IV and had been named president of the Council of State. His conceit was so great that he proposed Prince Ferdinand's marriage to his sister-in-law. Ferdinand refused. He was not only an enemy of Godoy but he also became a rival for the favor of the emperor, now the supreme arbiter of European affairs. Assisted by Maria Louisa, Godoy was active in persecuting the prince. Some of his servants were tried and condemned, and it was even rumored that while Charles IV was gravely ill, Godoy and the queen had contemplated establishing a regency and excluding the prince of Asturias. Yet the unpopularity of Godoy reached its height when he was named military chief for the king. The Fernandists rallied for the struggle to dominate the nation. Escóiquiz even intrigued with the French ambassador, an enemy of Godoy, to arrange the marriage of Ferdinand to a member of the imperial family.

Napoleon, indignant that Portugal would not participate in the continental blockade against Great Britain, decided to conquer Portugal and partition her dominions. He had occupied Etruria and it was necessary to compensate the queen of that state, who was a daughter of Charles IV. Beauharnais proposed a secret treaty against Portugal to the Spanish ministry, and a pact was signed at Fontainebleau in 1807. The sovereigns of Etruria would receive Lusitania, the northern part of Portugal—but under Spanish sovereignty—as compensation for the loss of their kingdom. The southern part of Portugal would constitute an hereditary state for Godoy, while the central part, between the Douro and Tagus rivers, would be assigned when peace was concluded. The Portuguese colonies would be divided between France and Spain. Napoleon would send 28,000 men through Spain—to be joined by an equal number of Spaniards—to conquer Portugal. An additional force of 40,000 men, concentrated at Bayonne, would follow the first French army if needed.

The dissension in the Spanish royal family gave Napoleon a pretext for the conclusion of his design. Talleyrand had already advised the dismemberment of Spain. The rivalry and counter intrigues between the factions surrounding Godoy and Prince Ferdinand became more intense, and Godoy openly spoke of his succession in the event of the death of Charles IV. The Fernandists arranged a ministry to oppose Godoy's plans. In October 1807 the prince was accused of a plot to dethrone his father and poison the queen. While Godoy feigned illness, Maria Louisa was decisive. Ferdinand was interrogated for three days. In the end he weakened, asked for forgiveness, and was pardoned. His increasing popularity in contrast with the hatred for the favorite, Godoy, restrained the sovereigns from opposing public opinion.

Meanwhile, Marshal Junot with 20,000 French soldiers and General Juan Carrafa had invaded Portugal. They entered Lisbon in November 1807. Napoleon sent an agent to become familiar with the route from the Pyrenees to Madrid and to ascertain whether Spanish opinion was favorable to Ferdinand or to Godoy. A second French force under General Dupont established itself at Valladolid, while a third army of 30,000 men entered the peninsula in January 1808. Marshal Joachim Murat, brother-in-law of the emperor, was named his lieutenant in Spain. By March the French army had occupied the citadels of Pamplona and Barcelona and entered San Sebastián. There were 100,000 French soldiers in Spanish territory.

The occupation of the frontier strongholds by the French produced consternation in the court. Godoy recognized his error too late to rectify it, and Napoleon now made his plans explicit. He demanded the provinces north of the Ebro River. The royal family considered following the example of the Braganza family of Portugal and fleeing to its American dominions. Godoy insisted on going to Seville, but Ferdinand opposed this. Charles IV denied any intention of leaving Madrid and tried to calm the public in a proclamation.

People of all classes had been congregating in the capital, infuriated against those who had betrayed Spain. At Aranjuez they broke into Godoy's palace and burned and sacked it. Charles now surrendered to his advisers and dismissed Godoy, who was forced by thirst to leave the garret in which he had hidden. Although Charles ordered his son to protect Godoy, he was wounded and bruised when he reached the barracks. As the king and queen feared for their own safety, Charles finally called Ferdinand to him and before the courtiers handed him his abdication (March 19, 1808). Then he sought the protection of Murat, who had offered him safety in the name of the emperor.

Charles IV had ascended the Spanish throne in the most critical period of the national history. He was kindly but of scanty intelligence and completely dominated by Queen Maria Louisa. He tolerated the behavior of his favorite beyond the limits of endurance. Of a weak and irresolute will, he never succeeded in governing, but let his authority be exercised by those who were unworthy of it, and so compromised Spain, his throne, and himself.

CHAPTER XXI

The Defiance of Napoleon, 1808–1814

As a result of the outbreak at Aranjuez, Godoy had fallen, Charles IV had abdicated, and Ferdinand VII had ascended the Spanish throne. Spain was occupied by a foreign army, but the people had not yet awakened to the reality of the situation. They believed that the French army intended to support Ferdinand VII in the overthrow of Godoy. The supporters of Ferdinand were enthusiastic.

Napoleon, however, had other plans for Spain. His alliance with Alexander I of Russia had given him the opportunity to expand his empire in the west without fear of retaliation on his eastern frontier. When the mutiny at Aranjuez occurred, he immediately took advantage of the opportunity which it provided. He declared that the Spanish throne was vacant and offered it first to his brother Louis, king of Holland, and then to Jérôme, king of Westphalia. Both refused it. Meanwhile, Napoleon's lieutenant in Spain, Joachim Murat, intervened in Spanish affairs to implement the arrangements of the emperor. He advised Charles IV and Maria Louisa to protest the legality of their abdication. Charles IV accepted the suggestion and declared he had been forced to abdicate in order to avoid greater evils and bloodshed.

Ferdinand VII had already assumed control of the government and named his ministry. His first measures were beneficent and promising, in response to the enthusiasm his accession had aroused. He suppressed the sales tax on wine, permitted the hunting of dangerous animals on royal estates, and announced his intention of undertaking such public works as roads and canals. He also ordered the suspension of the tax on ecclesiastical property, which further increased his popularity with the clergy. In reality, however, his position was precarious. Beauharnais had withdrawn from the capital, and Murat was reserved, carefully avoiding any act which might be interpreted as approving of the new regime.

Murat entered Madrid on March 23, 1808, welcomed in silence by the curious populace of the capital. Ferdinand made his public appearance in Madrid on the following day and was enthusiastically received. His most cherished desire was to win the sympathy of the imperial representatives and to strengthen the ties of amity with France, but his efforts proved futile. Murat did not recognize him and refused to accept the credentials presented by Ferdinand's ambassador. Napoleon had already instructed Murat to recognize only Charles IV as king of Spain. In April Napoleon arrived in Bayonne, where he had already invited Ferdinand to meet him. After nominating a Junta to govern in his absence Ferdinand left Madrid for the frontier, assured by the emperor that there would be no inconvenience in recognizing him as king of Spain.

Ferdinand crossed the Bidassoa on April 20 and entered Bayonne. Napoleon, after receiving him cordially and arranging a small dinner in his honor that evening, sent Savary to announce his resolution to relieve the Bourbons of the Spanish crown. Later, Ferdinand appeared on a balcony, feebly waved a handkerchief, and shouted, "I have been betrayed." Some two hundred Spaniards who had gathered before his residence offered to liberate him, but French troops arrived to break up the crowd and provide a guard. When Ferdinand refused to accept the sovereignty of Etruria and marriage with an imperial princess in exchange for renunciation of the Spanish crown, Napoleon broke off negotiations and would deal with no one but Charles IV.

In the meantime Murat had assumed control of Madrid. He ordered the liberation of Godoy and escorted him to Bayonne, despite the opposition of the Junta. He also demanded the recognition of Charles IV as king, which the Junta evaded under the pretext of awaiting the outcome of the meeting at Bayonne. Charles IV and Maria Louisa, on April 22, undertook the journey to France, after Charles IV had reclaimed the crown. Murat had been instructed to stimulate the belief that Spain was without a sovereign. Napoleon directed Ferdinand to return the crown to his father, but Ferdinand wanted to return to Spain, assemble the cortes, and have the restoration approved. The emperor refused this condition. He then dictated a letter to Charles IV in which the old king denied his son's authority to return a crown which had never been legally his.

The people of Madrid had been astounded by the liberation of Godoy, the departure of the royal family, and the arrogant attitude of the French troops occupying Madrid. Hostility to the foreigners increased steadily. Murat occupied the palace of Godoy instead of Buen Retiro, which had been assigned to him. Drunken French officers killed a

Spanish merchant, and French soldiers broke into the Casa de Campo and seized the rifles stored in Madrid. Thereupon, Spanish officers conspired against the French.

On the morning of May 2 groups of armed Spaniards assembled before the palace as the queen of Etruria and her sons, Prince Antonio and Prince Francisco, were preparing to leave for Bayonne. A locksmith entered the palace and reappeared crying, "Treason! They have taken the king from us and they want to take all the royal family from us! Kill! kill the French!" The shouts of a gentleman on one of the balconies of the Alcazar further excited the mob, which broke into the royal palace and made a demonstration of loyalty before Prince Francisco. Murat sent an aide to the palace who was attacked and would have been killed but for the intervention of French soldiers. When a battalion of grenadier guards arrived and fired on the multitude the Second of May had begun.

The citizens of Madrid rapidly organized resistance to the French and attacked them in all parts of the city with any weapons at hand. Women assailed the cavalry of Caulaincourt in the Puerta de Toledo, and citizens bravely resisted the attacks of the Poles and Mamelukes in the Puerta del Sol. The captain general of Madrid had ordered the Spanish troops to remain in quarters, but 4000 soldiers and 600 officers joined in the attack on the foreigners. The Park of Monteleón was the scene of bloody fighting.

At noon Murat ordered the Council of Castile to use its influence to appease the wrath of the mob. Then he organized a military court which, without trial, condemned to death the prisoners taken in the struggle. The Prado and many other places were red with blood. On May 3 Murat issued a proclamation establishing the death penalty for anyone bearing arms.

Important events had also been taking place in Bayonne. In a cold interview between Charles IV and Maria Louisa and their son, Charles exclaimed to him: "You are too strong! Have you not vexed my white hairs enough?" Ferdinand, however, did not want to renounce the crown and would only consent to surrender it before a duly assembled cortes. Napoleon dictated a letter for Charles to Ferdinand: "My son, the perfidious counsel of those who surround you has placed Spain in a critical situation. Only Napoleon can save her!"

When the news of the rising in Madrid arrived, Napoleon held another interview with the Spanish royal family. Charles IV blamed Ferdinand for the events, Maria Louisa hurled abuse at her son, and Napoleon ended the interview by threatening to treat Ferdinand as a rebel unless he recognized his father as the legitimate king. Under this pressure and in fear of the emperor Ferdinand renounced the crown and Charles IV surrendered it to Napoleon. The only conditions attached to the transfer of authority were the preservation of the integrity of the empire and the recognition of the Catholic faith. The other Spanish princes agreed, and on May 12 the royal family was taken to Fontainebleau.

Napoleon now held the crown of Spain, which he immediately transferred to his brother Joseph, king of Naples, who gave up a peaceful kingdom for one on the verge of rebellion. Joseph I was proclaimed king on June 6, guaranteeing the integrity of his dominions. Joseph Bonaparte, the elder brother of Napoleon, resembled the emperor, but lacked his prudence and intelligence. He was insatiably ambitious. Though he tried to be affable, in an effort to attract the Spaniards, the method of his accession had aroused "twelve million" Spaniards against him, and those who served him sought only their own advancement.

Following the suggestion of Murat, Napoleon convoked a general deputation of 150 persons at Bayonne for June 15. The majority of the deputies did not appear, but Napoleon and Murat filled their places. Sixty-five deputies were present at the initial session and ninety-one at the closing one. Joseph appeared in Bayonne on June 7 and was ceremoniously recognized as king of Spain. On June 20 a constitutional project was presented to the deputies which contained some positive juridical advantages for the Spanish people, but had the great disadvantage that it was imposed by a usurper. It was published in the *Gaceta de Madrid* on July 27. A week earlier, after having organized his ministry, Joseph I had entered Madrid.

The Spaniards, refusing to accept a foreigner imposed by Napoleon, had already declared war on the French. On May 9 Asturias was the first region to raise the cry of independence. Cartagena also launched a popular movement against the French, and the rebellious contagion spread throughout the nation. The people themselves had assumed the task of driving the invaders from Spanish soil. No central government was able to do this, for the Junta left by Ferdinand VII to govern the kingdom had already capitulated. The representatives of central authority were concerned for their own careers and were not inclined to resist the French. In many cases they became victims of their own timidity and the popular reaction they provoked. The first to offer allegiance to the French were the very monarchs whom Napoleon had dispossessed.

The Catalans, however, remembering the previous French occupations, rose en masse against the invaders. The resistance was organized in Lérida and the civilian militia won the first victory of the war for independence in a surprise attack on the French troops, which forced them to withdraw to Barcelona.

The popular attacks were not always successful, however. General Gregorio de la Cuesta was defeated disastrously at Cabezón, and the French entered Valladolid. The Spaniards also lost 4000 men in the battle of Rioseco, which led Napoleon to exclaim jubilantly that the victory had placed Joseph on the throne of Spain. The marquis of Lazán failed in his efforts to prevent the French march upon Saragossa at Tudela. That city was besieged and bravely defended by Palafox and the citizenry until the news of the victory of Bailén forced the French to raise the siege.

The position of the French in Madrid was untenable. Murat controlled the government, but he could not combat the popular indignation. Gradually, he came to understand the people whom he thought he had intimidated on May 2. A rapid extension of the war throughout the peninsula had been the reply of the Spaniards to his barbaric massacre of the prisoners of Madrid. Murat had dreamed of being king of Spain, but the reaction of the Spanish people and his failure to realize his regal desire led to his illness, and he was replaced by René Savary, shortly named duke of Rovigo.

Inspired by their victories and undaunted by their defeats the Spanish people had completed their organization of resistance to the French. They had created provincial juntas, chosen in the capitals of each province. They had taken the sovereignty abandoned by their king and leaders to themselves and had exercised it. They had raised troops, imposed taxes, dictated laws, and entered into relations with foreign powers. Asturias sent an embassy to England. Galicia entered into close relations with Canning, the English minister. Seville named representatives to the British government. Other provinces also negotiated with the British to obtain munitions for use in the war against the French. Seville obtained a million pesos, a British consul in Cádiz, and the aid of the British in returning to Spain some 10,000 Spanish soldiers whom Napoleon had sent to Denmark.

Most of the provincial juntas acted independently. Only the Junta of Seville, under British inspiration, wanted to establish its superiority over the others, but failed to extend its authority over Andalusia. The very necessities of war, combined with the spirit of unity which animated the old region of Spain and which was inspired by a common animosity toward the French, led inevitably to the concentration of power in a central junta.

While the war was being waged in northern Spain, General Pierre

Dupont de l'Etang, one of the principal leaders of the French army and a veteran of many victories, led an army of 14,000 Frenchmen into southern Spain with the intention of conquering Andalusia and aiding the French squadron anchored at Cádiz. He entered Córdoba triumphantly on June 7 and sacked the city, but the mobilization of the Spanish force in Andalusia caused him to withdraw toward Andújar. He was then reinforced by the arrival of divisions under the command of Vedel and Gobert.

The Spanish army under Francisco Javier de Castaños, of some 27,000 men, advanced to Bailén, crossing the Guadalquivir at Mengíbar, where Gobert was defeated and killed. Vedel had abandoned Bailén lest the Spanish guerrilla forces block his retreat through the passes of the Sierra Morena. Dupont, unaware that the Spaniards had occupied Bailén, withdrew at night toward that city and found the Spanish army blocking his path. The battle lasted until Dupont, whose troops were weary from the long march and who despaired of aid from Vedel, asked for a suspension of hostilities on July 19. When Vedel arrived, the army had already surrendered. The battle proved that the legions of Napoleon were not invincible. The prestige of French arms had received its first reverse.

The moral effect of the battle was great, and it also had immediate fruits. The French raised the siege of Saragossa, Joseph I evacuated Madrid, and the French forces withdrew from the rest of the peninsula to concentrate in the northern part of Spain. As the Portuguese rebelled against Marshal Junot, an English force under Sir Arthur Wellesley disembarked in Portugal. He quickly defeated the French in successive victories at Rorissa and Vimeiro. Junot was forced to sign the capitulation of Sintra on August 30; whereupon the French troops were evacuated from Portugal and transported to France in English ships.

It was necessary to unite the several provincial juntas under a single government so as to concentrate the total efforts of these isolated bodies against the French invaders. The local juntas proposed a central government or the convocation of a cortes to direct the resistance. Those of Valencia and Seville favored a federation which would leave them autonomous in local and domestic affairs. Various Bourbon princes also aspired to the regency of Spain or to an American kingdom.

As there was no supreme authority to convoke a cortes, in September the representatives of Aragon, Catalonia, Valencia, and Asturias assembled in Madrid, while those of other juntas met in Aranjuez. Finally, on September 25 the matter was resolved by the establishment of a supreme Central Junta at Aranjuez. It was composed of thirty-five members, who chose the count of Floridablanca as interim president. Although it wasted some time on matters of etiquette and titles, this junta succeeded in organizing the army into four corps and in creating a militia.

From the first the Council of Castile claimed that the Central Junta was illegal and proposed the convocation of a cortes to choose a regency. Two factions at once appeared in the Central Junta, one led by Floridablanca, a bitter partisan of the old regime, and the other by Jovellanos, who wanted to establish a regency. For the most part the Central Junta was ineffective. Its orders were ignored by the generals, and it was impossible to maintain contact with them. Early in November Napoleon crossed the Bidassoa River into Spain, and his rapid advance forced the Central Junta to leave Madrid. Badajoz was chosen as its destination, but the decision was changed and in December it established itself in Seville. Admiral Apodaca remained in London as the ambassador of the Central Junta.

Since the personal intervention of Napoleon constituted a threat which demanded British military as well as financial assistance, Sir John Moore sailed from England with 35,000 men and disembarked at La Coruña. Napoleon had concentrated an army of 300,000 men in Spain and was prepared to subject the peninsula. The Spanish forces, too weak to hold the extensive frontier, were defeated in successive engagements. Napoleon declared many Spanish nobles traitors, confiscated their property, and advanced on the Spanish capital. The Spaniards, heavily outnumbered, tried to hold the pass of Somosierra with artillery but were overwhelmed.

On December 1 the emperor reached Madrid, hoping to enter without resistance, as he had done in all the capitals of Europe. The citizens prepared to defend themselves, but capitulated when the city was bombarded. Napoleon remained in Chamartin de la Rosa and entered Madrid only once, when he visited the royal palace and declared that Joseph was better lodged than he was. He was somewhat irritated by the indifference of the populace as he passed through the streets. Treating Spain as a conquered country, Napoleon dismissed the members of the Council of Castile, abolished the Inquisition, reduced the number of monasteries by a third, and suppressed internal customs duties and feudal rights.

Meanwhile, the English army under Sir John Moore had moved out of Portugal with the object of cutting the communications between Madrid and France and blocking Napoleon's retreat. The English army of

18,000 men reached Valladolid, where Moore changed his plan, and withdrew toward Galicia, expecting to embark his forces at La Coruña. Napoleon entrusted the pursuit of the English to Marshal Soult and returned to Paris. Soult caught up with Moore at La Coruña, where a bloody but indecisive battle was fought in January 1809. Moore was fatally wounded, but his army succeeded in embarking.

Following the victory at Tudela, the French had besieged Saragossa, which capitulated on February 21. The situation of the French in Barcelona was critical, because of the rebellious attitude of the inhabitants, until Saint-Cyr invaded the Ampurdán and made himself absolute master of the city. In February 1809 the French besieged Gerona a third time and subjected it to a terrible bombardment, but the Spanish commander refused to capitulate. The inhabitants were forced to reduce their rations and eat their horses, and after a siege of seven months the city surrendered.

Marshal Victor, on the central front, defeated the Spanish forces at Uclés on February 19. Following this victory, Joseph solemnly entered Madrid. In the north, Marshal Francisco Ballesteros organized resistance along the Cantabrian coast, and the marquis of La Romana entered Galicia with 9000 men. Marshal Soult, who had been ordered by Napoleon to invade Portugal, reached Santiago on February 3, defeated the rearguard of La Romana, and entered Portugal. Marshal Ney, who replaced Soult in Galicia, invaded Asturias and sacked Oviedo, forcing La Romana to take to sea at Gijón.

Sir Arthur Wellesley's army became the principal target of Napoleon. The French might defeat the Spaniards, but after one victory they were confronted by a newly improvised army. Fighting the English was a more familiar problem for the emperor. Soult had taken Chaves and captured Pôrto. Wellesley advanced northward from Lisbon, advised by spies of discontent in the French camp and a conspiracy against Soult, who withdrew hastily to Orense, thence to Lugo, where he joined Ney. The conquest of Portugal had failed.

Wellesley believed that Soult's army was ineffective, and with his Spanish allies marched rapidly on Madrid. Joseph I confronted the allies at Talavera, where they won a moral victory against heavy odds, and Wellesley prudently withdrew to Portugal.

After successive Spanish defeats the heart of Andalusia lay open to the invaders. Meanwhile, Napoleon had conquered Austria and sent new reinforcements to his brother Joseph in Spain, who now had nearly 400,000 men. The French occupied Andalusia, Joseph I entered Córdoba and Seville, and Granada and Málaga were occupied. Cádiz was saved from capture by the arrival of the duke of Albuquerque with 9000 men a few hours before Marshal Victor appeared.

Napoleon now determined to expel the British from the peninsula. Marshal Massena, with 100,000 men, was sent against Portugal in April 1810. Taking Ciudad Rodrigo, Astorga, and Almeida, the French advanced on Bussaco, where they unsuccessfully attacked the entrenched English. On the following day the duke of Wellington, as Wellesley had now become, withdrew to the heavily fortified lines of Torres Vedras, blocking the advance on Lisbon. Massena remained in Portugal for five months, but, unable to surprise the English, he began to withdraw toward Salamanca. Soult, who had advanced to aid Massena, took Badajoz and was ready to march on Lisbon when he learned that Massena was withdrawing. The Anglo-Spanish force besieged Badajoz, and Soult, who went to the aid of the city, was defeated at La Albuera (May 16, 1811).

The war had continued with varying fortune in Aragon and Valencia, which the emperor was especially anxious to capture. Marshal Suchet finally besieged the city, which capitulated in January 1812. As a result, Alicante, Peñiscola, and Denia quickly fell to the French.

In 1812 Wellington undertook the siege of Ciudad Rodrigo. When it fell, the cortes gave him the title of duke of Ciudad Rodrigo. Following up his victory, Wellington took Badajoz by assault and advanced on Salamanca in June. Joseph I was forced to evacuate Madrid and withdraw to Valencia.

In August 1812 the Anglo-Spanish forces triumphantly entered Madrid. In danger of being isolated, Soult raised the siege of Cádiz and abandoned Andalusia, while Drouet withdrew from Estremadura. An Anglo-Sicilian expedition landed at Alicante on August 9, 1812, and in September Wellington entered Burgos. Four days later he was named commander-in-chief of the allied armies. Destroying the fortifications in Madrid, he retired to Portugal, while Joseph I, anxious to avenge his reverses, reentered the city on December 3.

Meanwhile, the Central Junta had been active in Seville. Its most important task had been the convocation of a cortes. Ferdinand VII, from Bayonne in 1808, had urged the reunion of the cortes to obtain the necessary subsidies for the defense of the kingdom. The local juntas favored such a move, and Jovellanos supported the reestablishment of the ancient tradition in the Central Junta.

It was finally agreed to restore the ancient cortes in its legal representation. The Central Junta continued its administrative tasks. Martín de Garay, from Estremadura, exercised the most important influence in it as secretary. The marquis of Astorga, successor to Jovellanos, paraded through the streets of Seville, surrounded by a civic guard. The problem of the establishment of a regency was resolved in November by the appointment of an executive committee, which expedited the convocation of the cortes and provided for the representation of the transoceanic colonies.

When the French invaded Andalusia in 1810, the Central Junta fled to the Isle of León. It incurred a good deal of popular animosity as a result of the misfortunes suffered by the Spanish armies and the charges of peculation leveled at its members. When an independent junta was created in Cádiz, the Central Junta resolved to create a regency of five members, which undertook its task while Cádiz was besieged by Marshal Victor.

The Regency delayed in convoking the cortes, under the pretext that its members were ignorant of the details of the work of the Central Junta. Nine provinces sent representatives to demand the immediate assembly of the cortes, but the Regency delayed for further consultation. Then it issued the call for the cortes, which was to assemble in a single chamber on September 24 on the Isle of León.

The Cortes of Cádiz opened solemnly. The regents and 105 deputies swore to preserve the Catholic religion, the integrity of the nation, and the rights of Ferdinand VII, recognized as the legitimate king. The cortes declared that the national sovereignty resided in it. For the time being, the executive power was declared to reside in the regents and the legislative power in the cortes.

As the debates proceeded two parties appeared in the cortes, the liberals or *reformistas* and the *serviles* or *antireformistas.* The former were imbued with the ideals of the French Revolution and believed in a constitutional rather than an absolute monarchy. The *serviles* supported the traditions of the nation and unlimited royal power. The so-called "American" party, led by José Mejía, alternate for Santa Fé de Bogotá, a brilliant orator, followed an intermediate policy. Before withdrawing from the Isle of León to Cádiz, on February 9, 1811, the cortes decreed the equality of the residents of America and Spain and suppressed some of the privileges of the nobility.

The most important work of the Cortes of Cádiz was the constitution of 1812, which was promulgated on March 19, 1812. It declared that the Spanish nation included Spaniards of both hemispheres and that it was not the patrimony of any family or person. Sovereignty resided in the nation, which had the exclusive right to formulate its fundamental laws.

Its government was vested in a moderate, hereditary monarchy. Spaniards, however, had certain responsibilities, including the payment of taxes, military service, fidelity to the constitution, obedience to and respect for the laws, and, after 1830, the ability to read and write. Individual rights, such as personal security and the inviolability of the home and property, were guaranteed. Freedom of the press and the right of petition were also provided. A Council of State of forty members was created as a consultative body. The cortes was constituted by a single chamber, with one deputy apportioned for each 70,000 persons, indirectly chosen by the cities, to serve as the legislative organ. While the person of the king was regarded as sacred and inviolable, the principle of ministerial responsibility was established. The king sanctioned the laws with a suspensive veto. He conducted foreign relations, commanded the army and navy, and exercised the right of pardon. The order of succession was fixed on the basis of primogeniture and females could succeed.

There was continuous discord between the Regency and the cortes. A definite rupture developed over the suppression of the Inquisition in February 1813. The measure produced an immediate reaction among the clergy, who refused to proclaim the decree, but the cortes proceeded further with anticlerical measures. The regents were then provisionally replaced by a new group of three councilors of state. The first ordinary cortes was convoked for October 1, 1813.

In the resistance to the French invaders, the Spanish people resorted to their long familiar tactics of guerrilla warfare. They assembled and dispersed to avoid pursuit. They placed flight ahead of valor as a military virtue, and, in making surprise attacks, kept the French constantly off balance. One of the principal guerrilla leaders was Juan Martin Díez, known as "El Empecinado." A shoemaker, he had served in the army and before the Second of May had intercepted French mails. He was most active along the Douro River, where his band of followers served for the booty they could collect. He stopped convoys, surprised careless detachments, and raided the areas around Burgos, Soria, and Segovia. His followers dressed fantastically in imitation of the French. After the battle of Bailén, he seized a lady of the family of General Moncey, with her coach, baggage and jewels, leaving her escort unaware of the abduction. Sometimes he participated in battles and was entrusted with important missions.

El Empecinado was responsible for cutting the communications between Madrid and Aragon. After operating in Guadalajara and Cuenca, he withdrew to Aragon in 1811 and was defeated at Valderas. With his brothers, Manuel, Damaso, and Alonso, he cooperated with the regular troops around Salamanca. Finally, he was defeated and wounded at Pedrosa del Rey near the end of the war in February 1813. The Central Junta recognized his contribution by making him a general. Another guerrilla leader, Jerónimo Merino, a curate of Villoviado, collected 300 horsemen and maintained his vigil on the road between Burgos and Valladolid. El Empecinado supplied him with arms at first, but he was soon able to capture all he needed. On one occasion he shot sixteen Frenchmen in retaliation for the execution of members of the Junta of Burgos.

Catalonia was never completely subjected because of the organization of its corps of volunteers, who retired to the mountains of Manresa and harried the French. In Valencia, José Romeu was another successful guerrilla leader. The most famous guerrilla, however, was Francisco Espoz y Mina, called "King of Navarre" by the French. Beginning with a small band of seven men, he increased his forces and was named commander-in-chief of the guerrillas of Navarre by the Junta of Aragon. He became the terror of his enemies. He gave no quarter and, in fierce reprisals, shot his prisoners. The Junta of Valencia sent him a general's uniform. Some of Mina's attacks were famous. He fell on the column of Baron Deutzel, who had already avoided one ambush prepared for him, capturing a thousand prisoners and a hundred carts, and he surprised a Polish regiment of seventeen hundred infantry and captured the royal secretary. He constantly invented new atrocities to terrify the enemy.

On May 22, 1813, Wellington advanced eastward from Portugal to cut the route from Madrid to the French frontier. Joseph I had already withdrawn from Madrid to Valladolid in March, and the French garrison evacuated Madrid, arriving at Burgos on June 9. They were routed at the battle of Vitoria and retreated across the Pyrenees, retaining only the cities of San Sebastián and Pamplona. Suchet also controlled Catalonia, Aragon, and Valencia. San Sebastián fell to the Anglo-Spanish forces on August 31, and Pamplona was captured November 1.

Wellington, learning of Napoleon's defeat at Leipzig, invaded southern France and captured Ascain, Sare, and St. Jean de Luz. Soult entrenched himself at Bayonne, but after suffering reverses at Orthez on February 27, withdrew to Toulouse, where Wellington defeated him. The allied forces continued to advance and captured Paris. On April 11, 1814, Napoleon abdicated. Soult and Suchet had already withdrawn from Spanish territory, and the remaining strongholds in French hands were surrendered. The war of independence was concluded.

Napoleon's overthrow was in large measure to be attributed to his intervention in the Iberian peninsula. He underestimated the resilience of the Spanish people. He could defeat their armies, but he could not conquer them. They harassed his lines of communications, they intercepted his convoys, and when one guerrilla band was scattered another appeared to replace it. With the arrival of the British, under the able leadership of the duke of Wellington, the Spaniards had the generalship and the moral and material support they needed to drive the invader from their soil. Had Napoleon been able to concentrate his total power on the Iberian peninsula, he might have succeeded in conquering it. His lines were too extended, his ambition too vast, and in any event, it is difficult to believe that he would have permanently succeeded in subjecting Spain and Portugal. Nevertheless, he unleashed the liberal forces in Spain against the Bourbon absolutism, and in this he left a permanent imprint on Spanish history.

CHAPTER XXII

Political and Economic Stagnation

The Bourbon kings of the eighteenth century carried on the centralizing process which the Trastamaras and the Habsburgs had started. They subordinated local government to royal, reformed national finances, and reorganized the armed forces. Taking a paternal interest in public welfare, they attempted to improve agriculture, stimulate commerce and industry, and establish a better educational system.

On the whole, the Bourbons were successful in stabilizing Spain under their rule, but they could not stop the forces of liberalism. Influenced by French and English liberals, more and more Spaniards were thinking of themselves as individuals with inalienable rights. They were beginning to resent royal despotism, benevolent though it was under the Bourbon monarchs.

After their accession to the throne the Bourbons completed the work of the Habsburgs in the development of absolutism in Spain, influenced by the example of Louis XIV in France. Philip V was a Frenchman, reared in the atmosphere of the court of Versailles, and Louis XIV had instructed him carefully: "Kings are absolute lords and the full and free disposition of all property belongs naturally to them for use as discreet administrators, that is, according to the necessities of the State." Philip V was an apt pupil and a willing tool of his grandfather in applying his ideas and advice in various ways.

At the beginning of the eighteenth century the cortes had long since ceased to meet at regular intervals, and it assembled only four times in Castile during the century—and then only to acquiesce in matters of special interest to the king. Charles III convoked them only to recognize his heir (1760), and Charles IV merely revoked the change introduced by Philip V in the succession (1789). The Aragonese and Castilian cortes were assembled even less frequently and, in the end, were fused with those of Castile. Only Navarre retained independent cortes, which had little influence in public affairs.

As the Bourbon absolutism intensified, the influence of Castile as the dominant kingdom of the Spanish nation was extended. As the eastern kingdoms had rallied to the support of the Archduke Charles in the War of the Spanish Succession, in 1707 Philip V revoked the *fueros* of Aragon and Valencia. A series of royal decrees then imposed new taxes and regulations until the ancient liberties of the Catalans were nearly totally suppressed by 1716, although they succeeded in retaining their penal law and judicial procedures, their civil and mercantile laws, and certain economic privileges. Mallorca suffered the same restrictions imposed on the other eastern kingdoms. In 1715 the Audiencia of Palma was created under a captain general with local officials named by the king. The Basque provinces were the only region of the nation which retained their *fueros*.

The centralizing tendency of the Bourbons was most patent in the administrative regime. They did not believe provincial administration was logical when it might oppose the central authority. They followed two principles—centralization and uniformity—in reorganizing the territorial structure of the kingdom. It was, in effect, a federation, with its roots antedating the formation of the personal union of Ferdinand and Isabel. There were thirty-two provinces in Spain, unequal in status and with strange anomalies existing among them, quite at variance with the uniformity desired in a thoroughly centralized nation. There were varying administrative districts and various types of villas, depending on their allegiance to the king, a lord, an abbey, or one of the military orders. Some localities had overlapping jurisdictions. The high officials to whom the regional governments were entrusted varied in title and authority.

Audiencias were created in Valencia, Saragossa, and Barcelona, similar to those of Valladolid and Granada, and under the presidency of captains general, who commanded the troops and supervised the administration. Their old financial attributes were relinquished to a new official, the intendant, modeled after the French official of the same title, with duties largely economic in character. For a while the Audiencia of Barcelona was permitted to function without appeals from it to the central authority, but after 1740 appeals were allowed to the Council of Castile. In Navarre the viceroy continued to be the supreme representative of royal authority.

Nevertheless, the Bourbons, including Philip V, were somewhat more humane than were the kings of the House of Austria. The rigid palace etiquette was modified. Their counselors, especially under Ferdinand VI and Charles III, participated more effectively in the government—not as favorites who usurped the royal prerogatives under the later Habsburgs, but as true ministers. They were permitted, for example, to remain seated while consulting the king, whereas formerly they had been required to kneel. Charles III represented the ideal of enlightened despotism in Spain, and all of the Bourbon kings were interested in problems related to the improvement of economic, social, and cultural conditions. This attitude worked a revolution in policy. As much attention was given to the public welfare as to the personal desires of the sovereigns. It was a revolution imposed from above, designed to strengthen the national resources.

French influence remained strong in Spain. Liberal and revolutionary ideas penetrated the Pyrenees and were diffused among the cultivated classes. Some Spanish politicians corresponded directly with the encyclopedists and liberal leaders of France, while French agents were active in extending revolutionary propaganda. Institutions appeared in which liberal ideas were discussed and propagated. Book shops were opened. Secret societies were organized. Newspapers propagated the ideas of the French liberals.

Spanish officials made an attempt to restrain the liberal and revolutionary contagion. They tried to prevent agitators from entering Spain, and edicts were issued against prohibited books, such as the *Encyclopedia*. Customs officials were alerted. In 1805 a special jurisdiction of printing, independent of the Inquisition and Council, was organized, but it was impossible to restrain the influence of ideas. Restriction was too indecisive and too many public officials were tolerant of the liberal ideas, which, in opposition to the government, became popular. Spaniards began to regard themselves as free men who should dedicate themselves to the protection of their liberties. Liberals spoke with admiration of England, where freedom of thought, freedom of press, and freedom of speech prevailed.

The centralizing policies of the Bourbons were extended to the *municipios*. All of the Bourbons tried to make the local officials dependent on the central authority. At the same time they hoped to make the citizens more active in municipal government, but conciliar offices had been sold by the crown in times of financial pressure, and the purchasers considered them as inalienable adjuncts of their estates. In the Basque provinces and Navarre the people in the smaller villages intervened directly in the administration of their affairs through the *concejo abierto*. As the municipal power in the rest of the nation was exercised by the *ayuntamientos,* members of the local governing boards, who had already become less democratic by the sale of their offices to hereditary holders, the policy of restricting the transmission of offices by requiring official approval of the heirs was adopted.

One of the most urgent problems was economic. Efforts at reform—to restore and conserve the financial resources of the nation—were undertaken early in the reign of the Bourbons. Orry tried to correct the deficit in the Spanish treasury, which had increased as a result of the recent war of the succession, but he aroused much opposition. His principal contribution was in the centralization of the treasury under a general official and the regularization and increase in the collection of taxes. Amelot, another Frenchman sent by Louis XIV, succeeded in reorganizing and improving the administration of the army. From 1726 to 1754, after the failures of Alberoni and Ripperda, the ministers were exclusively Spaniards. José Patiño improved and paid the army, enlarged the navy, modernized financial policies, and stimulated commerce and colonial interests. Campillo and La Ensenada continued the reforms of their predecessors.

Charles III not only improved the finances, but as a typical enlightened despot he also continued the other economic reforms. He had gained much practical experience during his reign in Naples, and had a series of able ministers to collaborate in the reformation of the Spanish economy: the count of Aranda, his successor and rival the count of Floridablanca, and Pedro Pérez y Rodríguez (Campomanes). Under Charles IV new ministers appeared: Jovellanos, who enjoyed a short tenure because of Godoy's enmity, Saavedra, and Godoy. The reformers encountered a great deal of opposition in their efforts to improve the economic condition of the nation. They had to combat vested interests and the ancient traditions of Spain as well as accomplish their reforms in spite of the apathy and general ignorance of the people. They were also impeded by the continuous warfare in which Spain was engaged and which neutralized their efforts and drained the resources they conserved. While the deficit fluctuated from time to time, the national debt steadily increased from a billion reales in the time of Philip V to seven billion reales under Charles IV. Despite the efforts to equalize the tax burden it fell ever more heavily on the poorer classes, and abuses persisted in the collection of taxes.

Some progress was made in regularizing municipal administration, but at the cost of a centralization of authority. Greater progress was made in sanitation and the policing of the towns. Streets were paved, and public lighting was installed in some cities. Hospitals increased in number and capacity. Postal service was regulated and regularized. Nevertheless, even this progress was not accomplished without unusual effort on the part of the ministers. The traditional rules of etiquette provoked continual conflicts over the most insignificant matters. Every effort at reform became involved in a maze of political documents and red tape.

The Spanish army was still constituted by voluntary recruitment. Under Charles III the *quinta*—a system by which one out of every five men was selected for the army by lot—was introduced and immediately met resistance. It led to a mutiny in Barcelona in 1773, and its enforcement was suspended. The Basques refused to accept it, the Navarrese protested it, and it was never adequately enforced in Castile. Many persons were exempt from its application, and the selectees were often replaced by vagrants, deserters, and other undesirable persons. Only those who could exercise no influence whatever served in the army.

Although Philip V was responsible for the reorganization of the army and the reawakening of the Spanish military spirit, Charles III published the great reform of the army, which had been in preparation for twenty years, largely the work of Alejandro O'Reilly. The royal guard was organized and expanded with the creation of the Walloon Guards in 1704. The army was then organized into three arms: the infantry, the cavalry, and the artillery. A fourth arm, the corps of engineers—previously part of the artillery—was created by Philip V in 1711. In 1703 new weapons were introduced by Philip V, who wanted to reorganize the army in the French fashion: muskets, arquebuses, and pikes were replaced by the latest small arms. A year later the *tercio* units were converted into line regiments of a single battalion and twelve companies.

For many years Spain continued to employ foreign soldiers, especially Irish, although later, French émigrés, Swiss officers, and German soldiers, as well as other foreigners, were enlisted. There was a reserve formed by the provincial militia, created in 1704. By 1766 this reserve consisted of forty-two regiments of two companies each. At the beginning of the century there were only 20,000 soldiers in the army, all badly armed and equipped, but the continuous warfare of the eighteenth century considerably enlarged this number. By 1761 the army contained 80,000 soldiers, and by 1808 it had been increased to 109,000. Its effectiveness, however, was inferior to its numbers. Morale was bad, training indifferent, and the armament deficient.

Greater progress was made in the development of the navy than in the army, since the ministers hoped to neutralize the naval power of

Great Britain by uniting the naval forces of France and Spain. New ships were constructed and arsenals were built at El Ferrol and Cartagena. The principal craft, the warship which replaced the old galley, had already demonstrated its superiority in the seventeenth century. Most warships had two decks with sixty to seventy cannon or three decks with eighty to one hundred pieces. Galleys were already falling into disuse except in the Mediterranean; the last one was built in 1794. The Spanish navy, despite efforts to improve it, remained inferior to the English and even to the French. One of its principal defects was lack of trained personnel for artillery and maneuvers, a deficiency which was the natural result of the depopulation of the coastal areas and the decay of the fisheries and merchant marine, which had hitherto supplied the navy with capable personnel.

The reformers also turned their attention to the Church, an institution even less susceptible of reform than the army or navy. Many thought, with good reason, that the Church's wealth and power were excessive. By the end of the eighteenth century its income from property alone was estimated at about 564,621,400 reales. In 1787 there were 3148 communities under ecclesiastical jurisdiction. Tithes and firstfruits—some of which admittedly were paid to the king—amounted to about 648,000,000 reales a year. Mass stipends and church fees added something like 136,000,000 reales. The Church's total income, in short, was in the region of a billion reales.

It was impossible to avoid the Church's influence. Clerics were everywhere: they virtually controlled education, they influenced politics at all levels, they affected—sometimes favorably, often adversely—the whole cultural, intellectual, and scientific development of Spain. In 1787 the population of Spain was about 10,409,879; it has been estimated that twenty years earlier, in 1768, there were about 149,805 ecclesiastics. Olmedo, with a population of 2000, had seven churches and seven convents.

Some of the fiercest attacks were turned against the Inquisition. Even in the seventeenth century complaints against the jurisdictional excesses of the Inquisition and the impediments which it placed in the ordinary judicial processes had arisen. These protests increased in the eighteenth century, strengthened by the prevailing theory of absolutism. The Inquisition was accused of exceeding its competence; it was said to abuse its power by using its religious influence for political purposes. Its critics said that it published decrees contradictory of royal orders, that it had condemned books arbitrarily and expanded its jurisdiction in an excessive manner. The Inquisition, it was alleged, was no longer a servant of the political policies of the king and had to be subjected; the increasing sense of tolerance was not sympathetic to religious persecution.

The first conflict with the Inquisition occurred under Philip V, when it publicly condemned a memorial of Macanaz. The Princess Orsini—an enemy of the inquisitor general, Giudice—with the minister, persuaded the king to order the inquisitorial edict withdrawn. Macanaz, who was entrusted with the reform of the Inquisition, in the end was attacked by the institution as "seditious," "heretical," and "schismatic." Ferdinand VI believed that the Inquisition was still useful in preserving the purity of the faith, but Charles III followed a policy of reforming and subjecting it to the state. By the end of his reign it had been forbidden to execute any order of the Roman court without permission of the Council of Castile or to intervene in ordinary judicial administration, and it was ordered to permit authors whose writings were condemned to defend themselves.

Most of the clergy, despite some outstanding examples of learning, were ignorant and credulous, and their wealth was not evenly distributed. There was considerable agreement in the government on the necessity of reforming the clergy, but some officials believed that the pope should undertake this task. In 1723 Pope Innocent XIII published rules for the instruction and discipline of the clergy, restricted the persons admitted to the religious orders to the number which could be normally sustained, and reduced the number of benefices.

Members of the nobility were not as influential under the Bourbons as they had been under the House of Austria. As many of them had opposed Philip V, the Bourbons resolved to restrain their political ambitions and excluded them from all positions in which they might threaten the royal power.

The higher nobility included the grandees and titled aristocrats, who enjoyed economic privileges and jurisdictional authority and remained covered before the king. The Spanish Bourbons tried indirectly to force the nobility to sustain their public responsibilities, though Philip V abolished the archaic right of life and death held by the nobles of Aragon. The lower nobility, the caballeros and simple hidalgos, enjoyed traditional exemptions and powers and some, for example, controlled the nominations to municipal offices. The desire to be a hidalgo persisted, and the petitions for the title increased to such an extent that the pretenders were required to pay 30,000 reales when their ancestry was traced to the fourth or fifth generation. In 1754 Ferdinand VI declared all Viscayans nobles. Later, in 1785, the title of "hidalgo" was conceded only for personal merit. In 1789 there were 119 grandees, 535 noble titles of Castile, and more than 500,000 hidalgos, the majority of whom, however, retained only the honors, the empty vanity, and the estate of their ancestors. Nobles occupied the palatine offices in the court, held commands in the army, and discharged the offices of viceroy or ambassador.

The middle class consisted of members of the liberal professions, merchants, and manufacturers, and small landowners. The importance of the middle class increased socially, although the suppression of the cortes restricted its political influence. The kings tried to break the barriers between the nobility and the middle class. Those who had risen by wealth or talent were generally assimilated into the nobility, while those in more modest circumstances were accustomed to mingle with the lower classes. The middle class provided the most effective source for recruiting men valuable in the direction of the affairs of the nation and in its industrial and commercial advancement. Its members sympathized with the liberal ideas of France and were willing to accept innovations and the reforms of the enlightened ministers.

In 1783 an effort was made to dignify labor by declaring that it did not demean the family or the person who performed it. The urban workers were in a better condition than the workers in the country, though the laborers in the large cities opposed changes as well as the influx of foreigners. The Bourbons had encouraged French immigration to stimulate industry, and the Spanish workers resented the competition and the successful new methods.

In the tenure of property a concerted effort was made through legislation to reduce the number and size of the entailed estates (*mayorazgos*). The practice of entailing estates to the eldest son was the principal reason for the preservation of the great estates, which had multiplied throughout the country and impeded the distribution of wealth. The owners were empowered to alienate their property and invest the proceeds in government enterprises bearing 3 percent interest, while the state sought to break up the large estates by incorporating them in the properties of the crown or by distributing them in small parcels among the farmers and laborers. These measures proved unsuccessful because of the opposition to them of the provincial aristocracy—both the nobility and the members of the middle class, who controlled the municipal governments. The lower classes who received the small parcels of land had neither the capital nor the vision to utilize them. Some estates disappeared, but the majority of the nobles retained their lands intact.

Most people lived in misery and ignorance at the beginning of the century and strongly resisted efforts to improve their status. At least 140,000 vagrants wandered Spain, many of whom were fit for work but could not find it. The ministers of Charles III vainly tried to solve the problem by providing a living for the women able to work, placing the aged and infirm in hospitals, and enlisting the men in the army and navy. As a preliminary step to the solution of the plight of the miserable the reformers, assisted by societies and individuals of the upper classes, sought to acquaint the masses with the state of economic affairs and awaken their interest in reform. The crown created model factories, importing workers from other countries to instruct the Spaniards in new techniques. Uncultivated areas were colonized in an effort to stimulate agricultural production. These innovations proved futile, for the clergy were opposed to them; much of the land was unsuited to intensive cultivation without the expenditure of more funds than the treasury could afford, and the Spaniards were suspicious of foreigners who came to educate them in new methods. Nevertheless, some progress was made. The privileges of the *Mesta*—the organization of cattle-raisers—so long an impediment to the farmers, were restricted, and the conditions of the renters of land were improved. Essential raw materials were admitted free, and free transit was provided for indigenous products. Four great highways were planned during the reign of Charles III to link Madrid with Barcelona, Valencia, Cadíz, and La Coruña.

One of the most determined efforts of the reformers was to revitalize the decadent industry of Spain. Philip V was inspired by Colbert's success under Louis XIV and wanted to introduce French practices in Spain. Minute regulations were adopted. At first the legislation undertook to protect and regulate industry, and manufacturers were conceded privileges and exemptions from military service and taxation. Yet at the end of the century industry was still burdened with a multitude of taxes, both direct and indirect. The theories of Colbert succumbed to those of Adam Smith and the Physiocrats. In 1790 the king began to award prizes for manufactures and exports. Regulations were relaxed, model factories were reestablished under royal patronage, and foreign workers were again assisted in entering Spain, but the model factories usually cost a good deal more than they earned. Technically, however, Spanish methods improved considerably. Textile industries, especially, developed markedly during the century and flourished in Valencia, Catalonia, Aragon, and Galicia, where linen and hemp were manufactured. Barcelona was the principal manufacturing region in Catalonia, while the metallurgical industries were important in the

Basque country, Catalonia, Navarre, and Galicia. Mining also progressed in the eighteenth century, largely as a result of the relaxation of the legislation in regard to its exploitation. Various stones, both precious and industrial, were exploited in great quantity. Iron was mined in Aragon and the Basque provinces, copper in Minas de Ríotinto, lead at Linares, and tin in Galicia.

Fishing declined. England had opposed the Spanish pretensions to the Newfoundland fisheries, and the Spaniards had to pay a tax to acquire the cod they consumed. Whale fishermen were still active along the Cantabrian coast, but the most successful fisheries were those for sardines along the Galician coast, for anchovies in Catalonia, and those along the African coast.

The renaissance in industry, unfortunately, was short-lived. The general scorn for manual labor was not overcome, while the deficiency in techniques was another obstacle. Consequently, despite the abundance of some raw materials in Spain, the nation was dependent on foreign commerce, and although efforts were made to protect national industries, the balance of trade was always in favor of the foreigners. The retention of the sales tax and of municipal privileges made distribution difficult and favored contraband. Economic policy was so uncertain and the multiplicity of taxes so great that commerce was seriously restrained. Commerce had become important enough to be well organized, with both official and private bodies to stimulate it. The highest governmental organization was the General Board of Commerce, which had its own jurisdiction and could override any *fuero* opposing it.

Despite their regulatory aims the administrators also recognized the value of private interest and initiative in commercial affairs. Early in the century legislation sought to stimulate the restoration of commerce through individual effort. Although every merchant was obliged to become a member of a guild, official recognition was also extended to those who associated freely to stimulate and defend their interests. Companies of merchants were formed independently to purchase raw materials and manufactured goods in quantity. Some were created expressly to conduct the trade with the New World.

Foreigners became increasingly active in Spanish commercial life. Several factors stimulated their enterprise: the decadence of Spanish industry favored the importation of foreign products, official efforts to restore economic activity led to the introduction of foreign personnel and the imitation of foreign agencies, French influence increased, especially as a result of the accession of the Bourbons, and after the War of the Spanish Succession, both Spain and France had to submit to the commercial demands of Austria and her allies, the Dutch and the English.

Colonies of foreigners were established in Spain. Cádiz was the principal center of French commercial interest, with over 2700 Frenchmen resident there in 1791, in a total of nearly 9000 foreigners. The Italians, especially the Genoese, continued to be important in Spanish trade—more than 5000 Italians were in Cádiz. The English, also numerous, wielded great influence, with twenty English commercial houses in Cádiz. The silver mines of Guadalcanal, which had been abandoned in the seventeenth century, were reopened by the English in 1728, and the cobalt mines in Aragon and those of Almadén were operated by Germans.

The reformers of the eighteenth century recognized the necessity of improving the educational system. The existing institutions had declined, and the people were illiterate and ignorant. Elementary education, largely directed by the clergy, left much to be desired. The condition of the teachers was precarious. Paid by the towns, their salaries were small and their positions insecure. Instruction included Christian doctrine, reading, writing, arithmetic, and Castilian grammar and spelling. The leaders of Spain were greatly concerned with diffusing knowledge as well as with improving the educational standards, and Spanish traditions encouraged much of the revived interest in education. But the lay spirit of the century was new. The reformers desired to found educational institutions, secular in origin and without clerical control, to neutralize the Church influence even in religion. Thus, the disciples of the Encyclopedists and the supporters of absolutism worked together to secularize education.

Primary education was especially backward, as there were not enough schools. Despite the fact that criticism persisted throughout the century, much was done to improve and expand the facilities for education. The law of 1780 organized education on such an exclusive basis that teaching by persons not members of the guild of teachers was prohibited. It also laid down minute regulations, stipulating the sites of schools, their objectives, and the texts. A novelty at the end of the century was the introduction of the ideas and methods of the Swiss educator Pestalozzi, by a Swiss captain, for the children of poor soldiers. Godoy became interested in the Pestalozzi methods and established the Royal Pestalozzi Institute. Afterward, the movement spread throughout the peninsula, but the disciples of Pestalozzi and the memorial presented to Godoy in 1793 had little practical influence. Godoy suppressed the Royal School in 1808.

After the expulsion of the Jesuits, secondary education was improved. Until their expulsion the Jesuits had controlled the field. They provided the best training and had the best instructors, so that after they were expelled it was necessary to replace them. New lay schools were founded, and the old municipal, conventual, and private schools were subjected to regulations designed to avoid abuses and improve their work.

The twenty-four Spanish universities had also declined in importance. They were inadequately endowed, had few students, and their influence had been restricted. Some were closed for lack of funds, while the smaller universities suffered particularly when the larger ones, because of declining standards, refused to extend credit for work taken in the smaller schools. Only wealthy students were admitted to the larger institutions, and they looked with contempt on poor students. They were a turbulent group on the whole and frequently indulged in outbreaks. The routine studies were little adapted to the demands of the age, and the faculties were not abreast of current scientific progress. Not only were the natural and physical sciences neglected or poorly taught, but even theology and philosophy were moribund.

The reformers immediately undertook to improve higher education through official intervention in university life. The institutions lost their ancient autonomy and were centralized under state control. The real reform began in the period of Charles III, who in 1769 assumed the nomination of the director of each university and subjected all of them to inspection. A new curriculum was introduced, and the study of medicine was especially improved. Not only did the ministers proceed to reform the universities, but they also subjected them to royal legislation.

Since the efforts to reform the traditional institutions proved difficult and largely sterile, the reformers also tried to create new institutions to carry out the ideas of the times. Teachers were imported, colleges of medicine were established in Madrid, Barcelona, and Cádiz, of mathematics at Barcelona and Valladolid, and of jurisprudence in various cities. Technical and professional institutions and libraries were also founded. The royal archives were reorganized, and the Archive of Simancas was further improved by Campomanes. In 1785 the Archive of the Indies was founded at Seville, including all sources relating to the New World. Philip V created the Royal Library, which was opened to the public in 1714 and said to contain 200,000 volumes.

The reformers hoped to establish a nucleus of Spanish studies as a basis for further progress. Consequently, they not only invited scholars from foreign lands to come to Spain, but they also provided subsidies to encourage Spanish students to study abroad. Students were sent to

France, England, and Holland. Of the numerous periodicals established during the century—after French and English models—some were created by private initiative while others were supported by the state.

There were insuperable obstacles to the accomplishment of the aims of the reform. The people were not only ignorant but happy in their ignorance. The problem was the conquest of indifference, and this could only be accomplished gradually; the results achieved were small in proportion to the energy expended. The reform movement was further impeded by the strength of the existing traditions and the suspicion of the clergy toward the purposes of the reformers. Prejudice was an almost insuperable obstacle. Women were not usually admitted to the Royal Library. Many books were prohibited lest they infect the Spanish people with even more radical and revolutionary ideas. The clergy, in defense of their position and vested interests, urged the public authorities and the Inquisition to be vigilant not only against books which were suspect, but also against any novelty which appeared dangerous. Whatever success was achieved was due to the initiative of the reformers and their support by men in official positions.

Scientific interest was a fundamental characteristic of the rationalism of the eighteenth century. Some of the professors of the University of Salamanca held that "wisdom was the useful application of truth to the necessities and order of civil life." Jovellanos had found powerful support among scientists for his educational reforms. Consequently, the tendency toward practical studies produced an intensive cultivation of experimental science or scientific principles. Biologists studied, classified, and described the life of the known world, established botanical gardens, and collected and experimented with plants. Naturalists also worked in museums and translated and wrote natural histories. The Museum of Natural History in Madrid assembled all the existing collections in Spain and added many new items brought from America by order of the king.

There was some progress in the physical sciences. Ignacio Ruiz de Luzuriaga experimented with magnetism and electricity. Other scientists demonstrated considerable ability and imagination in experiments with gases and mechanics and invented machinery that was useful in the textile industry. Two professors of Vergara discovered wolfram. New alloys were produced. Chemical principles led to new medicines, and foreign chemists brought to Spain made useful discoveries.

At the beginning of the century anatomy and surgery were in a state of decay in Spain. But the experimental spirit was extended to medicine. Colleges of surgery were founded, dissection was revived, and diseases were studied. Francisco Javier Balmis accompanied ten other physicians and surgeons in an expedition to carry smallpox vaccine to the American and Asian colonies. The Royal Academy of Medicine was created in Madrid in 1734, and auxiliary medical societies were established in the principal cities.

Jorge Juan y Santacilia (1713–73), educated in the Jesuit College of Alicante, traveled in 1735 to South America as a member of a French scientific commission. The publication of the results of his investigation increased his reputation, and he was sent to England to make a study of English types of ships. On his return to Spain he was charged with the construction of Spanish ships and the direction of the arsenals. He invented a new type of boat which became a model for the Spanish navy, directed the construction of the astronomical observatory, and in his later years was director of the Royal Seminary of Nobles in Madrid and the Board of Commerce and Money.

Antonio de Ulloa (1716–95), another important marine scientist, studied mathematics, accompanied Jorge Juan on his trip to South America, and made a second trip to Peru in 1755. Ulloa brought from London the first ideas of electricity and magnetism to Spain, made many scientific observations, and was responsible for great advances in the art of printing and binding. He established the first Museum of Natural History in Madrid and the first metallurgical laboratory.

As Spanish colonial power declined the number of publications devoted to geography decreased. Yet, in addition to the scientific travels of Jorge Juan, Ulloa, and Felix de Azara (1746–1811), other Spaniards were credited with geographical discoveries on the northwestern coast of America and along the coast of Venezuela, Chile, and Peru. The Hydrographic Center, created in 1797, published notable maps of North and South America. Ethnographic studies of the Chilean Indians and many maps and charts were published.

In historical literature the critical spirit initiated in the seventeenth century was strengthened. Existing traditions were revised as a result of numerous investigations, and there was much polemical writing as a result of the political and religious struggles which absorbed the government. Interest was aroused in the history of Spanish jurisprudence, and the critical ability of Spaniards was concentrated especially on the errors introduced by credulous writers in regard to ancient, medieval, and ecclesiastical literature. Sound principles of historical investigation were established as Spanish historians reviewed their past. The new Academy of History collected and published documents of great service to historical writing. Old works were reedited and reprinted and extensive bibliographical data were collected. Historical scholars also investigated more recent historical problems and produced an extensive literature on modern history and biography. The great work of historiography of the eighteenth century was the celebrated *España Sagrada* by Father Enrique Flores (1702–73). This worthy historian, a native of Villadiego, entered the Augustinian order in 1718. His work was an enduring example of erudition and critical evaluation and provides an inexhaustible source for modern investigators.

Literary history appealed to those who desired to reply to foreign critics, for Spanish writers of the eighteenth century had to combat the reaction inspired by the decline of Spanish literature since the seventeenth century. Strengthened by the necessity of combating the bad taste of the later Habsburgs, writers analyzed and censured their recent literature in satires and detailed critiques and produced new and original theories of poetry and literary taste. This reform movement was neoclassical and strongly under French influence. French writers enjoyed great popularity in Spain and numerous translations of Corneille, Racine, and Voltaire were made.

Some authors extolled the literature of the sixteenth and seventeenth centuries, especially the drama, and the older works were collected and reprinted. Also, French models were imitated. The public never lost interest in the national theater, and Spanish plays were presented in Madrid and the provinces throughout the century. Many scholars, both Spanish and foreign, maintained the interest in the classic literature of Spain. The works of Cervantes, especially *Don Quijote,* increased in popularity, until he became the most celebrated author in the eighteenth century. Calderón de la Barca, whose greatness as a dramatist was equaled only by that of Lope de Vega, enjoyed an expanding reputation in Germany, where his works were translated, edited, and imitated. The heroic poetry of Spain also attracted attention abroad. The servile subjection to French literary tastes was diminishing by the end of the century.

Creatively, the eighteenth-century literature was sterile in comparison with that of preceding centuries. The most significant poets were Juan Meléndez Valdés, Nicolás and Leandro Moratín, and Manuel José Quintana. Meléndez Valdés (1754–1817) wrote pastoral and erotic poetry in imitation of Garcilaso and others, and his odes entitle him to a place among the best Castilian poets. Nicolás Fernández de Moratín (1737–80) wrote the *Fiesta de toros en Madrid* in imitation of Lope de Vega. He was thoroughly Spanish and won great popularity. His son, Leandro Moratín (1760–1828), a better poet than his father, composed graceful lyrics. Quintana (1772–1857) was representative of the lyric poetry at the end of the century. He was a disciple of Meléndez Valdés, and, if not original, won acclaim through his appeal to liberalism and patriotism. Two authors won great popularity for their fables. Felix María de Samaniego (1745–1801) and Tomás de Iriarte (1750–91) deserve attention not only for their merit, but for their originality in developing a new literary genre which had not previously appeared in Spain.

As a result of the efforts of the strict moralists, to whom drama appeared dangerous, most of the Spanish theaters were closed at the beginning of the eighteenth century, and plays were presented only in the great capitals. French influence, however, revived dramatic presentations. The theater was not only a favorite diversion for the public, but new dramatic forms were invented. Musical comedies appeared in 1768.

Vicente García de la Huerta wrote a tragedy, *La Ráquel,* combining traditional Spanish with French techniques, which proved popular throughout the peninsula. Leandro Fernández de Moratín imitated Molière and became the leading representative of the French school. A partisan of Joseph Bonaparte, he was obliged to leave Spain, but Ferdinand VII pardoned him. Ramón de la Cruz y Olmedillo (1731–94), introducing themes which had not hitherto been dramatically presented, drew on the proletarian life of Madrid. Juan Ignacio del Castillo (1763–1800), who wrote on similar subjects, was his rival in popularity.

There was little interest in the novel in the eighteenth century. The only important work produced was Father José Francisco de Isla's *Fray Gerundio de Campazas,* which ridiculed the preaching of the clergy. The publication of the first part of it in 1758 produced such violent debates that the Inquisition confiscated it and prohibited discussion of it. Isla (1703–81) became a Jesuit and died in Bologna after the expulsion of the Jesuits. He also made a famous translation of Lesage's engaging *Gil Blas de Santillana.* Another Jesuit, Father Montengón, also wrote novels, one in imitation of Rousseau's *Emile.*

During the eighteenth century the same influences which had dominated architecture in the seventeenth century persisted. At first, a variety of baroque—churrigueresque—after José de Churriguera (1665–1723), was the most popular style. It was followed by the classical reaction, spreading from Italy through France. Ventura Rodríguez (1717–85) devoted himself during a distinguished career to the neoclassical style. His nephew, Manuel Martín y Rodríguez, designed the building for the Spanish Academy. Juan Villanueva (1739–1811) built the Prado, the Observatory, and the entrance to the Botanical Garden. The Catalan, Soler y Fonseca, built the Bolsa de Barcelona, considered by some as the most elegant building of the century in Spain.

Spanish sculptors continued to work in painted wood during the greater part of the eighteenth century, but this popular form was already a decaying art. The retablos of this epoch were baroque and large, richly decorated in stone and metal. This ecclesiastical use of sculpture did not satisfy the tastes of the neoclassicists. French and Italian sculptors also came to Spain to adorn the parks and palaces with statuary, and Spanish sculptors were trained in the new style either directly in Italy or by their foreign masters in Spain.

Spanish art also reveals the influence of foreign painters in the eighteenth century. The classic period of Spanish art was at an end. Philip V brought French painters to Madrid, and Italian and German painters also appeared. Of the foreign masters Anton Rafael Mengs (1729–79), a German, was the most important. He ambitiously undertook to unite the art of Raphael with that of Michelangelo, Correggio, and the Venetian school. He was highly regarded by Charles III and was the idol of Spanish artists and the arbiter of the Academy. His disciples, however, lacked originality. The renowned Giambattista Tiepolo of Venice also came to the court of Charles III in 1762, and during his eight years there painted ceilings in the Royal Palace. Francisco Bayeu (1734–95) was also a distinguished painter, but the most highly regarded artist of the period was Luis Menéndez (1716–80).

Francisco José de Goya y Lucientes (1746–1828) was the great exception in an age characterized by mediocrity and lack of originality. He was born of humble parents near Saragossa. During his youth he led a tempestuous existence while pursuing his artistic studies at Saragossa, Madrid, and Rome. In 1775 he returned to Madrid, engaging for a time in painting a series of tapestry designs in oil for a royal factory in the province of Huelva. He depicted popular scenes that were gay, free and altogether charming. The brilliance of the work brought him to royal attention. He became court painter in 1786 under Charles III and remained a favorite of Charles IV and Maria Louisa, producing paintings of the notables both candid and realistic. In the ten years after 1790 he executed his caprichos, a series of etchings containing a great deal of social satire. Other series followed, especially the *Los Desastres de la guerra,* a realistic and terrible document on the horrors of the war of independence. He retained favor during the changes in regime and at seventy retired to his villa, the Quinta del Sardo. The last years of this genius were spent in voluntary exile in Bordeaux.

In music there was considerable rivalry between the Italian school and the more regional and popular native forms. Italian opera, introduced by a company presenting Italian music in the Theater of the Buen Retiro in 1703, became immediately popular in the court, and Italian singers—including Carlos Broschi, long a favorite—enjoyed favor under Philip V and Ferdinand VI. Many Spanish musicians adopted the new mode and composed operas in the Italian style. Vicente Martin y Soler (1754–1806), a Valencian, called *lo Spagniolo* in Italy, wrote many operas. Manuel Vicente García of Seville, the father of two celebrated singers—Maria Malebran and Paulina Viardot—also attained renown for his compositions.

Meanwhile, the zarzuela continued the popular Spanish operetta tradition cultivated by many native musicians and preserving the characteristics of the national music. The *tonadilla,* which was dramatic and comic, continued to be sung by the comedians at the beginning and end of the performances and between the acts. Esteve, the official *tonadillero* of the theaters of Madrid, composed some very celebrated satires. One, sung by "La Caramba," María Antonia Fernández, alluded to the duchesses of Benevente and Alba and brought persecution on the author. Finally, in 1799 a royal order sponsored by Count Aranda prohibited the presentation of any songs not in Castilian. This appeared to indicate the triumph of native music, but in the more intellectual circles the Italian school continued to enjoy favor.

The eighteenth century was one of continued cultural decline, following the collapse of the Habsburg economy, despite the valiant effort of reformers in all fields. There were, nevertheless, influences penetrating Spain, largely from France, which were to revolutionize Spanish society. Spain, no longer the dominant nation in Europe, was striving to maintain her place in the world in competition with nations more richly endowed with resources. Where Spain had once influenced and often dominated her neighbors, she was now subservient in many respects, imitating movements originating abroad.

CHAPTER XXIII

The Reaction of Ferdinand VII

The Spanish liberals were sadly mistaken in believing that Ferdinand VII would support the new constitution. Immediately upon taking office, he suspended constitutional government in favor of the old monarchical absolutism. But his harsh treatment of the liberals and his capricious administration soon produced a revolt. Military officers, together with the liberals, forced Ferdinand to restore the constitution in 1820. For three years the country was in turmoil: the liberals split into moderate and extreme factions, and the royalists continued to plot against them. Meanwhile, the other European powers decided to intervene. A French force invaded Spain in 1823 and rescued Ferdinand from his virtual imprisonment. Although the French had hoped that the king would instigate moderate constitutional rule, he returned to his earlier repressive policy against the liberals. Ferdinand persecuted them until the day of his death.

During the struggle of the Spanish people to free the peninsula from the invader, Ferdinand VII had been in Talleyrand's castle at Valençay. This was a pleasant retreat and Talleyrand a polished urbane host. He assembled a small court, treated the Spanish princes with solicitude and respect, and rigidly observed palace etiquette. The exiled Spanish king was deeply preoccupied with fears concerning his possible fate at the hands of the emperor. The death of the duke of Enghien by Napoleon's order haunted him, and he humiliated himself as the most submissive and fervent of the emperor's admirers. Napoleon, on the other hand, treated his captive with the greatest contempt and was irritated when the dispossessed Spanish king called him his cousin. He was guarded with great vigilance, lest a conspiracy free him.

Meanwhile, the Spanish patriots were bravely defending their national independence and the throne of Ferdinand. Everything contributed to make him the model of royal virtue in Spanish eyes. Forged letters, attributed to him, were circulated in a desire to stimulate resistance. "Noble Asturias," he was supposed to have written, "I am surrounded on all sides, I am the victim of perfidy." In short, Ferdinand's captivity provided an opportunity for execrating the emperor and eulogizing the king.

Confronted with defeat and anxious to relieve himself of the Spanish affair, Napoleon preferred to negotiate with his prisoner rather than with the Spanish people. He, therefore, ordered Count de La Forest, his former ambassador to Spain, to arrange a peace with the captive Ferdinand. At first Ferdinand was fearful and mute, but in a second interview in November 1813, he displayed greater astuteness, prudently replying that it was necessary to consult the Spanish authorities. Napoleon also released the duke of San Carlos and persuaded him of the advantages to be derived from an accommodation between Napoleon and Ferdinand. The duke went to Valençay and overcame Ferdinand's scruples in regard to Spanish obligations to England. Consequently, on December 11, 1813, a treaty was concluded at Valençay and signed by La Forest and the duke of San Carlos. Ferdinand was recognized as king of Spain on the condition that he restore the rights of the pro-French faction, provide a pension of thirty million reales for Charles IV and Maria Louisa, and arrange a treaty of commerce with France. Napoleon at first proposed, as a condition, the expulsion of the British from Spain, but Ferdinand was unwilling to agree to this stipulation.

The Regency refused to ratify the treaty because Ferdinand was a prisoner, and the Cortes of Cádiz supported the regents, declaring that the king would not be recognized until he had subscribed to the oath provided in the Constitution of 1812. Even before the return of *"El Deseado,"* there was a division of opinion between him and his subjects. It was already evident that the conservatives were anxious to suppress the Constitution of 1812.

Desiring to relieve himself of the Spanish affair completely, on March 7, 1814, Napoleon sent passports to Ferdinand VII, who left Valençay and entered Spain on March 22. He was enthusiastically received, and through the intrigues of the royalists at court was led to believe that the absolute government could be restored. The king held a meeting with his companions to determine the most discreet royal policy to be adopted toward the constitutional reforms which, in theory at least, had transformed Spain. He was already inclined by the adulation of his reception toward a restoration of absolutism. On April 16 he went to Valencia, where he reviewed the troops and obliged Cardinal Borbón, president of the Regency, to kiss his hand. Already a conspiracy had been hatched to restore the absolute monarchy, with Francisco Javier Elío, captain general of Valencia, as the principal leader.

The reaction moved swiftly. General Elío handed Ferdinand VII the baton of military command, and in accepting it Ferdinand exercised authority before taking his constitutional oath. He reviewed a division on the plains of Puzol and was rendered the honors due to royalty. Meanwhile, in Madrid, the conspiracy also progressed, under the leadership of the duke of San Carlos. The *persas,* sixty-nine royalist deputies, issued a reactionary manifesto. With this encouragement Ferdinand decided to abolish the constitution, thereby destroying the limitations on his power and eliminating the necessity of taking the oath. Troops were concentrated in Madrid, and on May 4, 1814, the king signed the decree which restored absolutism and suspended the constitution. To protect himself against the possible reaction of the liberals, Ferdinand ordered the imprisonment of all liberal deputies and entrusted the command of the provinces to loyal generals. In a respectful letter of April 25 the cortes invited Ferdinand to assume his position as chief of the nation.

Francisco Ramón Eguía y Letona, secretly named captain general of New Castile, executed the order for the imprisonment of the liberal deputies. The palace in which the cortes was meeting was assaulted and destroyed by a fanatical mob demanding the return of absolutism. The Stone of the Constitution was wrenched from its place, broken into pieces, and the fragments were placed in a basket and dragged through the streets. There was no resistance on the part of the duly constituted government, and Ferdinand VII, with the opposition reduced to impotency, made his triumphal entrance into Madrid on May 13.

Despite the promise he had made to pardon the francophiles, Ferdinand inaugurated his restoration by expatriating the adherents of Joseph I. All of the institutions created by the Cortes of Cádiz were abolished, while the Royal Council, the Council of State, the monasteries, and the Inquisition were reestablished. A coterie of private advisers of the king began to dismiss ministers and make appointments. Ferdinand, annoyed at the delays in trying the liberals, sentenced them without trial.

Gradually, the abuses produced a reaction. The militia was discontented because it had not been compensated for its recent services to the nation. The partisans of the Constitution of 1812 began to organize and conspire. In March 1815 Ferdinand VII created his Ministry of Police and Public Security, and in April the publication of all newspapers and reviews was prohibited, except the *Gaceta.* Masks were banned, some theaters were closed, and in May the Society of Jesus was reestablished. Even the friends of Ferdinand were not immune from the royal caprice.

Masonic societies with political objectives had meanwhile appeared, and many officers were affiliated with them. Juan Díaz Porlier, a valiant guerrilla leader, tried to stimulate a revolt in La Coruña, but was betrayed by his secretary and imprisoned. He directed a second attempt from prison in which the Constitution of 1812 was proclaimed in La Coruña. Released, he marched on Santiago with a thousand men, but was captured in bed by some Galicians, imprisoned, and hanged.

The atmosphere of the court of Madrid produced flattery and intrigue for royal favor. Ferdinand was called "the best father of his vassals" by his servile adherents. But new conspiracies were born. General Luis Lacy, who had been overlooked in promotions despite his services during the War of Independence, plotted with Francisco Milans. The intrigue was discovered and Lacy was captured, sentenced to death, and shot.

Spain was poorly represented at the Congress of Vienna, and her mediocre envoy, Pedro Gomez Labrador, could accomplish little in negotiations dominated by Prince Metternich and Talleyrand. The Spanish were already allied with the British by the treaty of July 5, 1814. Alexander I of Russia had been alienated from England, while Talleyrand tried to effect a rapprochement with the traditional enemies of France, the English. While Ferdinand was in Valençay, the question of his marriage to the sister of Alexander, the Grand Duchess Anna, had been raised. The rapprochement with Russia aimed at securing assistance in subjecting the rebellious American colonies as well as Russian support in recovering the kingdom of Etruria.

The revolutionary spirit in Spain had not, however, been eradicated. The Masons were especially active and had expanded after 1814. Spanish officers, such as Rafael Riego, who had been a prisoner in France, founded lodges in the military strongholds, and lodges were established in Granada, Barcelona, La Coruña, Madrid, and even in Alcalá de Henares. The most active lodges, however, were in Andalusia, Seville, and Cádiz, where ardent partisans of the constitutional regime had congregated. It was a particularly strategic area, as the troops destined to suppress the insurgents in the New World were concentrated there for embarkation. The central lodge in Cádiz met in the home of Francisco Javier Istúriz and many officers attended its meetings, but to stimulate Masonic activity it was decided to establish an executive group to direct the activities of the regimental societies.

Antonio Alcalá Galiano was the founder of the new lodge and the leading spirit of the new revolutionary movement. His activity secured the cooperation of merchants, nobles, intellectuals, and even members of the clergy. The conspirators chose Colonel Antonio Quiroga as leader of the movement, but he was already under arrest. On January 1, 1820, Colonel Rafael Riego, commander of an Asturian battalion, proclaimed the Constitution of 1812 before his soldiers and was at once joined by the battalion from Seville. However, the loyal troops prepared the defense of Cádiz and repulsed the advance of the revolutionists.

The revolt had been undertaken even though some of the most optimistic participants were depressed at its failure to achieve immediate success. La Coruña rebelled, followed by Saragossa, Barcelona, Pamplona, and other cities. Even the restless General Enrique O'Donnell led a revolt in Ocaña with the forces which had been placed under his command to suppress the *pronunciamiento.* Meanwhile, the Spanish government named General Manuel Freire to suppress the movement. Riego was defeated in Algeciras, Málaga, and Córdoba. When the people of Cádiz congregated to celebrate the restoration of the Constitution of 1812, General Freire fired on them. In Madrid, too, the people rebelled when they received news of what had occurred.

Ferdinand and his ministers were intimidated by the rapid spread of the movement, and on March 6 they announced the convocation of the cortes. Popular excitement had increased and even extended to the doors of the palace. The king took his oath to the constitution, and on March 10 issued a manifesto which concluded with the well-known phrase: "Let's proceed frankly, I the first, by the constitutional path." A constitutional period followed, characterized by a constant struggle between reactionary absolutism and the temporarily triumphant liberals. The king was supported by the Junta, the Regency, and the royalists. The liberals, unfortunately, were divided into two groups—*doceañistas* and the extremists. While the liberals were enthusiastically confident in their program, they were forced to persecute those who had recently been their persecutors and eliminate the most uncompromising of their opponents in an effort to consolidate their power. Freedom of the press, however, was restored, and the Supreme Court, the Council of State, and the constitutional ayuntamientos were reestablished.

When the cortes had been convoked, those who had refused to take the oath to the Constitution of 1812 were condemned to exile and loss of honors. On the other hand, the consultative Junta permitted the francophiles to return to their homes, as some had already done. Others returned to occupy positions of authority. The *doceañistas* who had escaped the persecution of 1814 were the leaders who had contributed to the success of the revolution by calling in the military to redress their civil wrongs. Some of them were very advanced in their ideas. The extremists—usually affiliated with the Masonic lodges—were enthusiastic democrats and bold in their political opinions. There was little republican enthusiasm, since those who favored an absolute government, defeated momentarily, were not resigned to their loss of political control, but had already begun to organize their intrigues.

Patriotic societies and the revolutionary provincial juntas were constantly active in their efforts to influence public opinion and the decisions of the consultative Junta. The most outspoken groups gathered at the Cafe of Lorencini in Madrid and at other centers. The most famous was "the Friends of Order," who had their headquarters at a cafe called the Fontana de oro, where Alcalá Galiano was usually to be found. The meetings opened and closed with patriotic poetry and songs, such as the hymn of Riego. The moderates, under the Prince Anglona, Martínez de la Rosa, and the count of Toreno, were less effective. Well intentioned, but vaguely idealistic in their program, they sought to combat the other parties as well as the government. When the cortes opened in July 1820, two parties immediately appeared, the extremists and the moderates. Harmony was further dissipated by the attitude of the American deputies, who favored the emancipation of the colonies. A serious crisis arose over the dissolution of the army on the Isle of León, which had led the revolution. Riego was called to Madrid. He had been promised the captaincy general of Galicia, but he immediately quarreled with the ministers and aroused a public demonstration in his honor, after which he was ordered to Oviedo. Some deputies defended him in the cortes. The government defended itself successfully, but the division between the *doceañistas* and extremists was final.

A new crisis was provoked by the suppression of the monastic orders. Ferdinand refused to approve the decree, until he was intimidated by the threat of a popular outbreak. He then abandoned Madrid for the protection of the Escorial where, without the approval of his ministers, he named José Carvajal as captain general of Madrid. The political societies took to the streets and demanded the convocation of an extraordinary cortes. The Permanent Deputation agreed to ask the king to dismiss his private advisers and return to the city. Ferdinand promised to convoke the cortes and returned to a hostile capital. When Ferdinand appeared on a balcony the citizens sang patriotic hymns and exhibited the young son of General Lacy, shouting "Long live the son of Lacy! Long live the avenger of his father!"

The bishops of Pamplona, Barcelona, Valencia, and Orihuela issued angry pastoral letters against the government. Political passion increased —the royalists hurled filth at the Stone of the Constitution and the *doceañistas* wore a green ribbon on their hats, emblazoned with the slogan, "Constitution or death." The moderates in the nation were caught between the radicals of both extremes, whom Ferdinand encouraged in order to discredit the constitutional regime.

The liberals had also proclaimed the Spanish Constitution of 1812 in Naples and Piedmont. Since this revolutionary action was not in accord with the reactionary desires of the Holy Alliance to maintain absolutist monarchs, Austria was delegated to restore absolutism in Naples and Piedmont by armed force. The liberals fled to Spain, where they increased the general confusion. Louis XVIII was anxious that Spain have a charter like the one he had granted the French. While England followed a vacillating policy, Pius VII encouraged the absolutists and Czar Alexander condemned the constitutional regime.

The extraordinary cortes had, meanwhile, made some progress in theoretical reforms. As disorder spread throughout the country—in December and January—the navy was reorganized, public charity was provided, provisions for the freedom of the press were established, and the nation was divided into fifty-two civil provinces and thirteen military districts. At the end of February 1822 Martínez de la Rosa was charged with the formation of a new government, and the ordinary cortes convened under the presidency of Riego. While the liberal factions engaged in futile political debate in that legislative body, the royalist guerrillas were active in their disturbance of public security.

Francisco Martínez de la Rosa had served as a professor in the University of Granada and during the War of Independence represented his native city in the provincial junta. He became a friend of Alcalá Galiano and was a member of the cortes of 1813. He acquired a reputation for integrity, and his skill as an orator increased his popularity. He was recognized as chief of the majority in the chamber and became the idol of the liberals. During the years of reaction he was imprisoned, but at thirty-five he was the chief of a ministry; he was no longer the revolutionary of 1814. The *doceañistas* accused him of being reactionary and of cooperating with the royalist faction. Anxious to reform the Constitution of 1812, he had been inspired toward conservatism by the spectacles of public disorder.

Nevertheless, Martínez de la Rosa was deceived by Ferdinand, who had accepted the constitution only for reasons of political expediency, while he tried to stimulate the royalist factions, well aware that a considerable part of the Spanish people retained their sympathy for the old regime. He invited the great powers to intervene in Spain in his behalf. Louis XVIII promised him aid, with the understanding that he would not intervene to restore absolutism, but wanted a temperate constitutional monarchy in the French style. French troops were then ordered to the Pyrenees frontier. Mozo Rosales had promised the secret agents of Louis XVIII that the royalists would conquer a stronghold where a regency could be established. The royalists consequently seized the Seo de Urgel on June 21, 1822, and massacred the garrison.

The stage was set for revolution. An occasion presented itself on June 30, 1822, when the king was returning to the palace after closing the cortes. The people hurled insults and stones at the guards, who charged with bayonets fixed. The crowd retreated, and when a liberal officer, Mamerto Landaburu, reprimanded his grenadiers he was bayoneted. The royal guards, on the other hand, were in open rebellion, and forty deputies suggested the establishment of a regency unless Ferdinand ceased supporting the rebels. To restrain the rebellious guards the government negotiated with them. The king refused to accept the proffered resignations of the ministers, who, with the secretary of the Council of State and the governor, were imprisoned in the palace.

Ferdinand's situation was critical. When the moderate ministry of Martínez de la Rosa, believing it had no authority to continue to rule the country, resigned, the extremists—inspired by their recent victory over the guards—forced Ferdinand to name a radical ministry under Colonel Evaristo San Miguel. The absolutists, on August 15, established a regency at Urgel to rule "during the captivity of Ferdinand VII." Headed by the marquis of Mataflorida, the regency was uncompromising in its desire to reestablish an absolute monarchy instead of following the desire of the French for a constitutional charter.

In Madrid the government became more radical, its principal victim being General Elio, who was hanged in Valencia on September 4. Royalist bands devastated Catalonia, and guerrilla bands operated in Navarre, Castile, and León. The regency of Urgel, lacking money and arms, urged foreign aid to restore Ferdinand VII to his former position of authority.

General Espos y Mina was ordered to suppress the royalist factions in Catalonia. The regents were forced to abandon Urgel, and the fortress was taken on February 3, 1823. The liberals were merciless, burning towns and shooting their prisoners without pity. The remnants of the regency army fled to France and were disarmed. Ferdinand convoked an extraordinary cortes, and the deputies, who assembled on October 7, shaken by recent events, enacted extreme measures in their anxiety to strengthen the government. Resolutions were approved which violated personal rights in order to suppress conspiracies directly or indirectly against the constitutional regime. Despite the success of the liberal leaders in Catalonia and Navarre, the royalists there were encouraged by the prospect of aid from France.

Meanwhile, the nations of the Quintuple Alliance were considering the dangerous threat to legitimacy posed by events in Spain. Only Great Britain was reluctant to intervene in Spain, as she was benefiting from the commerce of the rebellious Spanish American colonies and was unwilling to establish a precedent for their reincorporation into the Spanish Empire. Metternich of Austria opposed French intervention in Spain, since it would increase her influence in European affairs and disturb the power equilibrium. Alexander of Russia, however, was hostile to anything that threatened the political stability of European sovereigns. Ferdinand VII and the royalists were particularly anxious for the French to intervene.

Louis XVIII hoped to establish a temperate constitutional monarchy in Spain. Disgusted with the excesses of the regency of Urgel, the French abandoned it and came to an understanding with the Junta of Bayonne, which adopted a deceptive constitutional policy. A secret treaty between the intervening Great Powers was signed November 22, 1822, by which France was entrusted with the military expedition to Spain to restore the situation which had existed before March 9, 1820. The Powers demanded the abolition of the Constitution of 1812, the freedom of the king, and the repression of anarchy. Russia demanded the restoration of absolutism. France and Austria preferred a moderate monarchy. Prussia was silent on the matter. The Spanish government and the cortes were indignant. In January 1823 Louis XVIII had announced a declaration of war on Spain in the opening session of the French assembly. He declared that one hundred thousand Frenchmen were ready to march to "conserve the throne of Spain for a descendant of Henry IV, avoid the ruin of that beautiful kingdom, and reconcile it with Europe."

The Spanish government was in great difficulties. It had not only to resist the French invasion, but also suppress civil war within Spain, overcome the opposition of Ferdinand, inspire its vacillating generals with enthusiasm for the constitution, and provide resources for the war from a nearly empty treasury.

Although the French liberals continued to oppose the Spanish campaign, Chateaubriand was determined that the French Bourbons should derive some glory from it and unite their people behind them. In April the duke of Angoulême led 90,000 French soldiers across the Bidassoa River, easily defeating the few liberals who tried to stop them. The French, who were joined by 35,000 Spanish royalists, were received as liberators by the people, and on May 24 they entered Madrid, where the fury of the opponents of the constitutional government was unleashed. The Stone of the Constitution was broken, Riego's effigy was burned, and the picture of Ferdinand VII was triumphantly carried by the crowd in the streets.

The duke of Angoulême immediately occupied himself with the creation of a regency. The Junta of Bayonne, which had been converted into the regency of Oyarzún, was moved to Madrid. Meanwhile, on April 23, the cortes was reconvened in Seville. Ferdinand VII was forced to sign a decree declaring war on France, and a new ministry of radicals was formed. As the French approached the city and Ferdinand refused to leave it, Alcalá Galiano baldly proposed that the cortes should declare Ferdinand insane and name a regency. Three regents were appointed. On June 12 Ferdinand and the royal family moved to the Isle of León.

The Madrid regency began the proscription of the constitutionalists and the liberal deputies. The duke of Angoulême had issued a manifesto, prohibiting the imprisonment of anyone without the prior authorization of the French command and ordering the imprisoned political leaders and militia to be released. He was anxious to demonstrate to the Spaniards that French intervention had as its sole object the establishment of a moderate system of government, conciliating the crown with the people and inaugurating an era of peace, order, justice, and good administration.

As the French army continued its victorious march through Andalusia, General Ballesteros tried to offer resistance at Campillo de Arenas, but was defeated. General Morillo, in Galicia, disapproved of the suspension of royal authority by the cortes and concluded an understanding with the French. General Quiroga resisted in La Coruña, but was forced to surrender on August 21. General Mina, aided by a legion of foreign liberals, held out in Catalonia until the end of the invasion. Riego, on the other hand, left Cádiz and disembarked in Málaga, where he sought to revive the energy of the constitutional cause, but he was captured and turned over to the French as a military prisoner.

In August the duke of Angoulême—ambitious to capture the city which had resisted the marshals of Napoleon—decided to force the surrender of Cádiz. To protect Ferdinand VII he demanded his release, but the constitutionalists declared that the king would remain in the city, where he was protected by the loyalty of his subjects. Nevertheless, the defense of the city was useless before the superior strength of the besieging army, and the cortes authorized the release of Ferdinand to the custody of the French. After Ferdinand had solemnly promised a general amnesty, the royal family was permitted to leave the city. There was general rejoicing at his release. When the duke of Angoulême advised the extension of the amnesty, Ferdinand smiled and invited the French prince to listen to the cries of "Long live the absolute king" raised by the people in the street.

As soon as he was freed from constitutional restraints Ferdinand VII resumed his reprisals against the liberals. On the day of his liberation he issued a decree annuling all of the acts of the constitutional government since March 7, 1820. He ordered that no deputy or official of the recent regime should be within five leagues of his route during his journey to Madrid. The three members of the regency established in June were ordered to be hanged. Riego had already been executed in Madrid, before Ferdinand had returned. Throughout Spain the persecution of the liberals was intensified.

Victor Sáez, Ferdinand's confessor and principal adviser, had been named secretary of state on October 4. The last strongholds of the liberals had been forced to surrender and the war concluded. Louis XVIII had advised Ferdinand to be lenient and benign, but the admonition was useless, for Ferdinand was supported by an uncompromising party. On November 1 the duke of Angoulême left Madrid to return to France. Some 45,000 French soldiers remained in Madrid, however, as Ferdinand was unwilling to risk another revolution, and the occupation was prolonged until 1828 at his request.

Francisco Tadeo Calomarde (1773–1842), a protégé of Godoy, was active in supporting the regency of Madrid and became the most important person in the reaction of Ferdinand VII. He retained his influence until 1832. Ferdinand was enmeshed in the political struggles of the moderates and the *apostólicos,* and Calomarde was ever willing to support the latter party with which his absolutist ideas were sympathetic. He inspired restrictive measures through his decisive influence in the government. Military commissions were created to try liberals who had "conspired, spoken, or written in favor of the constitution of 1812." In the cabinet the ministers spied on one another for the benefit of the king.

In 1825 the liberals were subjected to even more rigorous persecution. The police threatened with severe penalties any one who criticized the government or received antigovernmental political material. Educational institutions were purged, and secret societies were prohibited. The more moderate ministers believed that Aymerich, minister of War, was responsible for the repression and finally succeeded in overthrowing him. After his dismissal the military commissions were suppressed. The Apostolic party, supported by Calomarde, continued to be more royalist than the king himself. In September 1825 Ferdinand created a consultative junta to propose reforms considered necessary.

Despite the continued activity of exiled liberals in stimulating rebellion or in exhorting the king to change his policy, Ferdinand was determined to proceed with his reactionary course. In 1826, when Calomarde became minister of State and chief of the cabinet, the royalists were even more intent on reaction than were Ferdinand and his ministry. The *apostólicos* recognized Carlos as their real leader, as he was more typical of their concept of absolutism.

In May 1829 Queen Amelia died. Ferdinand, who had no heir, immediately began to consider remarrying. He chose his niece, Maria Cristina de Borbón, daughter of Francis I, king of Naples, and was married in December 1829. The arrival of the new queen gave promise of better relations among the Spanish factions. The supporters of Prince Carlos were bitterly disappointed by the marriage, for if Ferdinand were now to have an heir the prince would not succeed his brother. While a son would assuredly hope to succeed his father, a daughter did not have the same certitude. To avoid any dispute in regard to the succession Ferdinand published his pragmatic sanction of March 27, 1830.

Philip V had introduced the Salic law in 1713, which excluded females from the throne. In 1789 the cortes had reestablished the ancient law of the *Partidas,* but Charles IV had not promulgated the change. Ferdinand drafted a will in which he declared that his sons should succeed him by order of primogeniture. He also declared that if the heir were a princess she also should succeed him. Prince Carlos and his followers protested the decree on the ground that neither his father nor his brother could deprive him of his legitimate inheritance. Carlos held that when he was born, the Salic principle of Philip V was still effective. Ferdinand, however, specified in his will that Maria Cristina should govern as regent until his own son or daughter attained the age of eighteen. In October 1830, a princess, Maria Luisa Isabel, was born, who, according to her father's decree, had the legal right to inherit the throne.

At this juncture, an important event occurred in France which affected Spanish affairs. The French liberals overthrew Charles X and established the democratic monarchy of Louis Philippe of Orleans. Ferdinand VII was reluctant to recognize the new king, and in retaliation Louis Philippe not only gave aid to the liberal exiles in France, but permitted the arming of expeditions to stimulate revolt in Spain. Most of the Spanish émigrés had sought sanctuary in England, where General Mina led a faction of Masons and moderates of aristocratic origin, and General José Torrijos commanded a second faction. A junta was formed in London to direct the reconquest of Spain. While the majority of the liberals concentrated in southern France, members of the junta, under English protection, moved to Gibraltar to launch an attack from the south. General Mina organized the plan of attack at Bayonne, but the movement was doomed from the first because of internal discord. The émigrés invaded Navarre and Catalonia, but the effort was futile and superior forces forced them to withdraw to France. Meanwhile, the Spanish ambassador in Paris, the count of Ofalia, had persuaded Ferdinand to recognize Louis Philippe. As the French no longer had any excuse for protecting the liberals, they prohibited the use of southern France as a base of operations for the invasion of Spain. This compelled the liberals to depend on an attack from the south.

In January 1831 Torrijos, with two hundred companions, attempted a landing, but was forced to return to Gibraltar. Salvador Manzanares, expecting an abortive conspiracy in Cádiz to materialize, was cut off in the mountains and killed. The indefatigable Calomarde restored the military commissions, and many liberals were imprisoned and some were executed. Torrijos was still a threat, however, and a stratagem was devised to capture him. Vicente González Morino, governor of Málaga, pretending to be a liberal conspirator, inveigled Torrijos into disembarking, whereupon he was captured with fifty-two companions and shot.

Calomarde was still the directing genius of the Spanish cabinet. He had maintained his influence by flattery, but he was forced to choose the party to which he was most inclined. The adherents of Prince Carlos were discontented, but Maria Cristina gained the support of the moderates, the army, and even of the liberals. When the royal family and the court moved to San Ildefonso for the summer, Ferdinand VII was stricken with gout. The queen proved an excellent nurse, but she had other problems. The Carlistas believed that their hour had arrived. Calomarde, who now revealed his real character, declared to the queen: "The kingdom will declare itself for Don Carlos. The army and 200,000 royalists love him and want him." Since it would not be possible to sustain the direct succession to the crown without Calomarde's aid, it seemed best to negotiate with him and reach an understanding.

As Ferdinand appeared to be on the point of death, Maria Cristina was intimidated and offered Prince Carlos a place in the future council of regency, which he refused. The accommodation which Calomarde had suggested was impossible, and throwing aside his former servility he declared for Prince Carlos. Maria Cristina, convinced of the necessity of annuling the pragmatic sanction, persuaded Ferdinand to sign a codicil in the form of a decree which reestablished the exclusion of females under the Salic law. He thereby disinherited his daughter and provided for the succession of his brother.

It had been agreed that the new decision would be kept secret until the death of the king. Unfortunately for the Carlists, however, Ferdinand recovered. The codicil was destroyed, and Calomarde was dismissed and exiled to Aragon, from where he fled in disguise to France.

Ferdinand now issued another decree undoing the one which had been destroyed and reestablishing his pragmatic sanction. His health was still in a precarious state, and Maria Cristina was entrusted with the government. Surrounded by devoted followers who had the national welfare at heart, she issued a series of beneficent decrees. The universities which had been closed by Calomarde in 1830 were reopened. An amnesty ending the nine-year persecution of the liberals was granted to all except those who had voted for the removal of the king at Seville. In January 1833 Ferdinand was able to assume again his responsibilities as king, and he approved of the work accomplished by Maria Cristina.

The Carlists, however, not resigned to the obvious blow to their hopes for Prince Carlos' accession, redoubled their activities. Volunteer groups of royalists were formed in León and Barcelona, and intrigues against Ferdinand were abetted. When the cortes assembled in July to witness the oath of Princess Isabel as princess of Asturias, Prince Carlos refused to attend. In March he had moved with his family to Lisbon. Ferdinand recognized the imprudence of allowing his brother to go to Portugal where, inspired by Miguel the absolute king, he could conspire with greater freedom. He ordered Carlos to go to the Papal States and even sent a ship to Lisbon to carry him there. When the prince again refused to comply with the royal request Ferdinand died, stricken with apoplexy.

It has been charged that the principal weakness of Ferdinand VII was cowardice. First he feared Godoy, then he cowered before Napoleon, finally, he was afraid lest the liberals take his crown. The absolutists used this fear for their own purposes. Fear bred duplicity in Ferdinand; he joked lightly with his victims before condemning them. He had more intelligence than the other Spanish Bourbons, but he was weak of will. He loved literature and art. He understood the role of royalty better than did his Bourbon predecessors, but he never gave up a belief in absolutism. While his career was changed somewhat by the French Revolution he was never influenced by its ideals, as many of his subjects were. Therein lay the tragedy.

CHAPTER XXIV

The Disputed Succession

On October 24, 1833, the three-year-old daughter of Ferdinand VII was proclaimed Queen Isabel II, with her mother, Maria Cristina, as regent. Her succession was disputed from the start. France and Great Britain recognized the infant queen, but Austria, Prussia, and Russia remained ominously silent. Sardinia and the kingdom of the Two Sicilies recognized Prince Carlos, and the Holy See, too, failed to recognize Isabel, probably because of the influence of Pedro Gómez Labrador.

The first minister, Zea Bermúdez, failed to survive the crisis and was replaced by Francisco Martínez de la Rosa. The treasury of the nation was exhausted at a time when the rebellion of the followers of Don Carlos—the Carlists—demanded men and money. Negotiations were undertaken with France to secure a loan of 200,000,000 reales. In February the national militia was organized as an urban guard and a levy of 25,000 men was ordered. The amnesty was expanded to include many who had previously been excepted. The property of ecclesiastics who joined the Carlists was confiscated, and the monasteries of which a sixth of the members had joined the Carlists were suppressed. The Council of State was replaced by a Royal Council.

In addition to this work of reconstruction and defense, the principal contribution of the ministry was the Royal Statute. The purpose of this was to give the nation a representative system which both restrained popular participation and permitted the crown to regulate the parliamentary mechanism. It was a charter conceded by the queen as a simple restoration of the ancient laws of the Spanish monarchy, lest the liberals be offended. It was an extremely conservative document, marking a reaction against the radical innovations of the Constitution of 1812. While it pleased the Moderates, the extreme liberals did not like it and at once inaugurated a violent campaign in behalf of individual rights and national sovereignty.

On April 25 the government adhered to the Quadruple Alliance with Portugal, France, and England. The Portuguese government agreed to expel Prince Carlos from Portugal, and Spain promised to support it against the rebellious Prince Miguel of Portugal. England would cooperate with her navy to support these measures and France would assist when necessary. Negotiations were also concluded with the Rothschilds to advance the Spanish government 15,000,000 francs for a commission of 2 percent and an interest of 5 percent. In exchange the debts incurred from 1820 to 1822 were recognized and the House of Rothschild was named the "Banker of Spain." The restoration of the legislative organ of the government appeared to have satisfied the most pressing demands of the liberals. The upper chamber was a docile instrument in the hands of the ministry, and only the duke of Rivas, who aspired to be leader of the opposition, proposed more extensive reforms.

Prince Carlos had found a haven in Portugal where—in the interest of absolutism—he cooperated with Prince Miguel both in the Carlist war and in Miguel's struggle with the child queen of Portugal, Maria de la Gloria. The Quadruple Alliance, however, had approved armed intervention in Portugal, allowing the queens of both Iberian nations to unite their forces to compel Carlos and Miguel to withdraw from Portugal. In April 1834 England promised to supply naval contingents, Maria offered the supporters of Prince Miguel amnesty, and Maria Cristina offered a subsidy befitting his rank to Prince Carlos for his voluntary acceptance of exile. The French later promised not to aid the Spanish insurgents.

Meanwhile, General Rodil invaded Portugal from Ciudad Rodrigo, forcing Prince Carlos to flee finally to Évora. Prince Miguel, unable to sustain himself against the combined forces of Spain and Portugal, renounced the throne, although Carlos refused to surrender his claim to the Spanish throne and was taken to London on the British ship "Donegal" in June. He took a house near Kensington Gardens, but eluded his protectors and entered Spain in July.

The natives of Navarre had risen in the cause of Carlos. The guerrilla Zumalacárregui was proclaimed leader of the rebels, including those of Vizcaya and Guipúzcoa. As a result of the military talent and persistence of this exceptional guerrillero, the war did not proceed happily for the government troops. Zumalacárregui organized his bands of guerrilla soldiers into a small army, after successive initial reverses, and not only infused confidence in them but also imposed an iron discipline. Without artillery and confronted with the necessity of using his munitions sparingly, he defeated successive generals sent to subdue him.

Quesada assumed command of the government's military operations in February 1834 and initiated a new strategy, while at the same time he sought to enter into negotiations with his former subordinate, Zumalacárregui. When these failed, the royalist general became irritated. The war assumed a savage character. Zumalacárregui was tenacious, and the fruitless pursuit of his guerrilla bands not only wore out the soldiers of Quesada but also reduced their morale and made the hope of eventual victory more remote. Quesada tried to terrify the rebels into submission by the ferocity of his punishments. Prisoners and defenseless noncombatants, including women and children, were shot. Zumalacárregui retaliated with fierce reprisals. He offered battle only when the advantages of the terrain and his numerical superiority assured him of victory. His reputation for invincibility increased as he won battle after battle.

The war increased in fury, but the Carlists appeared invincible. The destruction of their property served only to increase their savage reprisals. No quarter was given. The loyal generals had hitherto followed a strategy based on a system of fortified positions, from which they sought to capture the elusive guerrillas. Now they adopted the plan of concentrating their forces, taking as their first step in the new strategy the abandonment of fortified positions, which the Carlists immediately occupied.

The civil war also raged in Catalonia, Aragon, and Valencia, where the Carlists raided the lowlands from their mountain strongholds. Manuel Carnicer had been defeated in April 1834 at Mayals, but his dispersed forces were reorganized by Ramón Cabrera, who quickly attained great prestige as a Carlist leader in Catalonia. He had served under Carnicer and Zumalacárregui, and Prince Carlos named him second in command of the Aragonese rebels. After the death of Carnicer, who was surprised by the liberals, Cabrera became the principal Carlist leader in the east.

In Burgos and Soria the old guerrilla leader Jerónimo Merino was active. The Carlist bands in Asturias and Galicia lacked cohesion, and their leaders did not constitute a serious threat. After April 1835 the Elliot agreement, initiated by England, modified somewhat the savagery of the fighting. Prisoners were protected and the wounded or ill who were captured in hospitals and villages were no longer executed.

Prince Carlos did not fully appreciate the value of the services of

Zumalacárregui—envious perhaps of his success and popularity—and this attitude so affected Zumalacárregui that he offered his resignation, which Carlos refused. Then the Carlists undertook the siege of Bilbao, either to establish a royal court or to facilitate a promised loan by capturing a city of importance. The city was defended by 4000 soldiers under the count of Mirasol, and the preliminary assault was murderously repelled. Zumalacárregui was wounded in the leg when he appeared on a balcony to direct the placing of a battery and soon died. The siege continued, but the city was bravely defended and was relieved by Generals Latre and Espartero.

On June 8 the count of Toreno was called upon to constitute a ministry. His views were doctrinaire and his ministers reflected his attitude. To ingratiate himself with the radicals, however, he proposed a series of anticlerical measures. In July 1835 he suppressed the Jesuits, confiscated their property, and abolished many undermanned convents and monasteries. This action only served to arouse further anticlerical sentiment and attacks on religious houses. Toreno was unable to sustain himself against his many opponents, and Juan Alvarez y Mendizábal was asked to form a ministry.

Mendizábal, known as "Juan and a half" because of his stature, was an enthusiastic liberal and had collaborated in the overthrow of Prince Miguel in Portugal. His financial speculations had been successful and he had amassed a fortune. Regarded as a Jewish financier by his enemies, in office, as leader of the Progressives, he displayed patriotism, indefatigable energy, and a certain ability. He immediately introduced a program of reform—opposing foreign intervention and suggesting that the war be concluded with national resources. The urban militia was converted into a National Guard, and the provincial deputations were reestablished. On October 11 all religious corporations, except those devoted to the education of invalid children or assistance to the sick, were suppressed.

The new premier was popularly regarded as the savior of Spain. He was expected to resolve the financial problem as well as he had reestablished public order. If he could restore the national credit, a loan could be obtained to increase the army and secure munitions, and the Carlist threat could be terminated. Mendizábal undertook the task, trusting in his foreign contacts and his knowledge of finance. He did not realize that his oldest friends would be his greatest adversaries. Through Villiers, the English ambassador, he tried to obtain a loan on the basis of a permit for the sale of English cotton, but France intervened to stop the negotiations. The Spanish government needed 100,000,000 reales and failed to get them; it needed 100,000 men and only 46,983 were raised—sent to the northern front ill-equipped and in a deplorable condition. Mendizábal offered to save the nation from bankruptcy without increasing taxes, borrowing money, or alienating state property.

Unimpeded by political opposition in the cortes, he revealed the secret of his financial plans. It was called *desamortización*—the dissolution of the property of the church and the creation of a new bourgeois class devoted to its benefactor, the Progressive party. Commissions were established to take over the property of the religious orders, who had consistently supported the Carlists and absolutism. The few friars still in Madrid were expelled, and a commission was named to study the disposition of the property obtained from the suppressed monasteries. The properties were immediately placed on sale on liberal terms and at such prices that the reduction of the debt was not attained. Many individuals took advantage of the opportunity to enrich themselves. Politically, however, the operation was a success, for new proprietors were created, whose existence depended principally on the continued tenure of the Progressives and the establishment of liberal institutions.

When the new cortes was convened in March 1836, Mendizábal was confronted with a new enemy, Istúriz, who soon replaced him as premier. Francisco Istúriz was the son of a wealthy merchant of Cádiz, who had been a fellow conspirator of Mendizábal in 1820. He spent ten years in exile in London and never learned English because he was preoccupied with plans for the Spanish revolution. Since the Istúriz ministry represented a reaction, its position was precarious. While the Progressives formed a purely constitutional party, the Moderate party appeared to be subject to the caprices of the crown. The Progressives believed that the liberal desires of the country had not been satisfied, although Mendizábal was more conservative, hoping to reconcile the people with the crown. Once out of power, however, the Progressives used every means at their disposal to fight Istúriz, who hoped to convoke constituent cortes to formulate a constitution which would meet popular demands. The elections were favorable to him, but violence had already broken out. The more liberal Spaniards were ready to overthrow the cabinet by revolutionary methods.

General St. Just and the count of Donadío, the civil governor, were assassinated in Málaga and the Constitution of 1812 proclaimed. The revolutionary movement, undoubtedly directed by the Progressives, spread rapidly into other provinces. The Progressives conspired with the sergeants of the Royal Guard—in an effort to oblige the queen regent to reestablish the constitutional regime—at La Granja, where the court had moved. While most of the officers were attending the opera in Madrid, the leaders of the mutiny formed the regiment of Royal Guards in the esplanade before the royal residence. Two sergeants demanded that Maria Cristina reestablish the Constitution of 1812. Threatened with mutiny, the queen ordered its publication until the cortes should draft a constitution.

When Istúriz learned of the mutiny at La Granja, he tried to restore the loyalty of the guards, but though he was popular, he was forced to submit to the dictates of the rebels, who demanded that the oath to the Constitution of 1812 be taken. General Quesada, who was hated by the militia and who had offered to lead the garrison of Madrid to liberate the queen, was assassinated. José Calatrava then became premier, and the new ministers persuaded the rebels to return to Madrid, where they were joyously welcomed.

The Carlist war remained a series of raids and indecisive battles in the north as well as in Catalonia, Aragon, and Valencia. It was as savage as ever. The most famous of the Carlist raids was that made by Miguel Gómez, which blazoned the weakness of the government forces. In June 1836 Gómez left Amurrio with 2700 infantry and 180 horsemen. Although pursued by General Baldomero Espartero, he entered Oviedo and Galicia, where he captured a convoy carrying 8000 duros to pay the royalist troops. He entered Santiago before Espartero caught up with him, continued to elude his pursuers, and passed through León and Palencia. After threatening Segovia he even alarmed Madrid. During this raid the mutiny of La Granja occurred. General Córdoba, discouraged by the attacks of the press and unable to prosecute the war with the necessary resources, resigned, recommending that Espartero be named commander of the army of the north.

The first measures introduced by the new Progressive ministry of Calatrava were radical, in fulfillment of their promises. All property which had been abandoned was confiscated, and all sales and transfers of property by Carlists were declared void. Officials and government employees who did not support the government program were dismissed. Finally, the property of the religious orders was sold. Preparations were also made to press the war against the Carlists with greater vigor. A draft of 50,000 men by lot was ordered, and a forced loan of 200,000,000 reales was approved. In addition, a decree provided for the mobilization of the National Militia.

One of the primary purposes of the cortes which convened on October 24, 1836 was the revision of the constitution. Even the most ardent *doceañistas* had recognized that the Constitution of 1812 did not meet the demands of the times. Although the constitution prescribed that a regency for a minor should consist of three to five persons, the Progressives confirmed Maria Cristina as queen governor. It was important to formulate a constitution which would ensure cooperation and concord between the Moderate and Progressive parties.

The Constitution of 1837 consecrated individual rights and provided for the establishment of the Catholic faith as the religion professed by all Spaniards. The cortes with the king made the laws, the king executed them, and the courts applied them. The cortes was organized as a bicameral body, including the Senate and the Congress of Deputies. The king named the senators, of whom there would be three-fifths as many as there were deputies, on the proposal of the electors in each province in proportion to its population. Deputies were to be elected directly, apportioned on the basis of one to each 50,000 persons. Senators had to be forty years of age with sufficient income to make them independent. Deputies had to be twenty-five years of age and were elected for three years. At each election the Senate would be renewed by a third, following the order of seniority. The king's person was sacred and inviolable, but ministerial responsibility was established. In succession, the rule of primogeniture was established, although females were entitled to inherit the throne if there was no available male heir. The Constitution of 1837 was moderate in content and democratic in form. It was hoped that it would reconcile the two parties into which the Spanish liberals had divided. Nevertheless, the Moderates and Progressives were more subject to the stimulus of ambition than to theories of compromise and the demands of the public interest. Their political rivalry continued, and the new constitution provided little basis for cooperation between them.

While the Progressives were elaborating their program of reform, revising the electoral law, and unifying the contributions for the support of the clergy, the Moderates were active in intrigue. The revolutionary societies took advantage of every opportunity to increase their influence and conspire for the control of the government. In August 1837 General Baldomero Espartero was called to the capital to protect it against the daring attack of the Carlist leader Zaratieguí. When Espartero established his headquarters in Madrid, the Moderates expected him to be sympathetic with their activities, but he was unwilling to compromise himself. He was offered the post of minister of War and the presidency of the government, but he refused to assume political authority. He had increased his prestige by refusing to combine military and civil authority, and his efforts to restore discipline in the army further added to his standing. In September 1836 he was named to succeed García in command of the Army of the North.

The liberals believed that the conclusion of the Carlist war was only a matter of weeks and urged the military leaders to initiate final operations. They planned a convergent attack by General Sarsfield, the English under Evans Lacy, and Espartero. The Carlists, led by Prince Sebastián, an able commander, defeated Evans Lacy's division at Oriamendi. Sarsfield was forced to withdraw to Pamplona, and Espartero retired to Saragossa, from where he launched an attack on the Carlist towns adjacent to the French frontier, capturing Hernani, Oyarzun, Irún, and Fuenterrabia, in May 1837. Meanwhile, Cabrera, who combined mobility with strategic ability and knowledge of the terrain, moved his Carlist forces rapidly from one part of Aragon and Valencia to another, upsetting the strategic planning of his enemies.

Prince Carlos invaded Castile and advanced on Madrid with 12,000 infantry and 1600 cavalry. In May he defeated the royal troops at Huesca and Barbastro. His troops were defeated at Gra, but after a raid on Manresa they united with Cabrera. Although defeated at Chiva by General Oráa, Prince Carlos reorganized his forces and continued toward Madrid. The government hurriedly called on Espartero. Another Carlist leader, Juan Antonio Zaratieguí, invaded Castile, capturing Segovia. Espartero forced him to withdraw, but he was able to join Prince Carlos at Valladolid. The Carlists crossed the Tagus River and in September appeared before Madrid. Carlos expected his absolutist partisans in the capital to rally to him, but found little support when he reached Madrid and had to withdraw, pursued by Espartero.

By this time the financial situation was desperate. The floating debt had risen to 351,000,000 reales in addition to 50,000,000 of the 200,000,000 forced loan. With other obligations the total deficit was 500,000,000, and the minister of Finance was authorized to negotiate a loan for that sum.

Ominous rivalries developed. General Narváez, charged with the organization of a reserve army, was antagonistic toward Espartero, who had already won his military reputation. Espartero, too, was jealous of Narváez, who had not succumbed to the attentions of either the Progressives or the Moderates, although the latter, as the party in power, had more to offer him. The two generals differed finally in politics. Espartero was a Progressive, and his followers represented Narváez as an instrument of the government in sinister, antiliberal projects. The captain general of Madrid offered his resignation, but it was refused. When Narváez offered his resignation it was accepted. Then General

Córdoba, involved in a conspiracy in Seville, called General Narváez to his assistance. Compromised in a rebellion which was quickly suppressed, Córdoba fled to Portugal, and Narváez sought refuge in France.

It was an opportune time to take advantage of the discord which prevailed in the councils of Don Carlos. The differences between the intransigent and absolutist *apostólicos* and the moderate royalists developed into a real hatred after the return of the pretender from his expedition in 1837. The *apostólicos* had gained ascendancy over him and had adopted violent measures against generals whom they suspected of disloyalty. Carlos, on the advice of an ardent *apostólico,* José Arias Tejeiro, had named General Guergué as commander of his forces.

Guergué demonstrated his ineptitude as a general and was defeated at Peñacerrada when he tried to relieve the Carlist stronghold, which Espartero captured. Don Carlos then entrusted the command of his armies to Rafael Maroto, a man of moderate ideas and proved military experience. Although General Maroto reorganized the Carlist armies and strengthened his defenses, the exhaustion of the Carlist forces and the corruption of some of the Carlist counselors indicated that the time had come to terminate the struggle.

The government in Madrid had worked secretly to accelerate such a solution for the war. It had stimulated intrigues in behalf of peace and had succeeded in demoralizing the Carlist forces. As discord increased among the Carlists, Maroto learned of a rebellion planned by Guergué and others. Acting rapidly and with energy, he intimidated his critics by exemplary punishment.

Carlos dismissed Maroto and declared him a traitor. Maroto, however, had won the support of the soldiers and forced Carlos to exile his most uncompromising advisers. These differences placed the Carlist cause in a precarious plight. Defeated in successive battles, Maroto was forced on the defensive. Although he wanted peace at any price, he hoped to obtain the greatest number of advantages possible for the Carlists. He restricted his pretensions to two essential points: respect for the ancient Basque *fueros* and recognition for the ranks of the Carlist officers.

The Carlists could count on no foreign assistance. While the French had followed a benevolent policy of neutrality favoring the liberals and the English supplied them with an expeditionary force, Austria, Prussia and Russia had given little real aid. They had withheld recognition of Isabel II, but their effective aid was restricted to words.

Despairing of obtaining the mediation of King Louis Philippe, Maroto was forced to reveal to Carlos that he had undertaken negotiations leading to peace. When the prince reviewed his troops at Elorrio he was greeted with shouts in support of peace and of Maroto. Carlos was indignant, but he could not halt the negotiations. Maroto then held a conference with Espartero near Durango. Although they were unable to find a solution to the problem of the *fueros,* the Convention of Vergara—restoring peace—was ratified in Vergara on August 31, 1838. Under the conditions of the convention Espartero agreed to recommend to the government that it fulfill its promise to propose to the cortes the concession of the *fueros* or their adaptation to the fundamental institutions of the monarchy. The officers of the Carlist army were confirmed in their ranks for service in the Spanish army provided they recognized the Constitution of 1837, Isabel II, and the regency of Maria Cristina. All Carlist arms and equipment were surrendered to Espartero, who further agreed to recommend consideration by the government for the widows and orphans of the Carlist soldiers.

With his army no longer in existence Prince Carlos withdrew to France to await better times. He issued a proclamation declaring that the real Carlists had been sold for foreign gold and the self-preservation of some of the Carlists. The Basque provinces and Navarre were pacified, and peace was restored in Galicia, Asturias, Estremadura, and La Mancha, although Cabrera still kept the field in the east.

Baldomero Espartero, now duke of La Victoria and the hero of the war, exercised the decisive influence in Spanish political affairs. He had the confidence of Maria Cristina, but she favored the Moderate party and Espartero was an avowed Progressive. The two parties still struggled for the control of Spain, and when legal means failed the defeated faction resorted to revolution.

The Progressives were victorious in the election of a new cortes, which immediately undertook consideration of the Basque *fueros*. Those of the Basque provinces and of Navarre were confirmed, but without prejudice to the constitutional unity of the monarchy. The conciliatory attitude of the parties, however, was not permanent, as the Progressive majority continued to oppose the government and the hostility of the two parties was accentuated.

In the elections, the Moderate party obtained the majority in the cortes, leading the Progressives to resort to the strategy of opposing the seating of the Moderate deputies on the ground of electoral abuses. When the congress was constituted in March 1840, the debate on the organization and powers of the ayuntamientos was begun. The government followed a policy of centralization, while the Progressives were more generous in their encouragement of self-government. The proposed law gave the king the right to nominate the principal officials in the provincial capitals and the political chiefs of the provinces the right to nominate the officials of the communities of more than five hundred citizens.

In Catalonia, at this time, the Carlist cause was completely discredited when Cabrera was defeated, and he and his followers were interned in France. Espartero now strongly opposed the policy of Maria Cristina's government regarding the law of ayuntamientos. She offered him the presidency of a new ministry, but he rejected the post unless she refused to sanction the law relating to ayuntamientos. When she arrived in Barcelona, Antonio Van Halen, captain general of Catalonia, threatened her with revolution unless she altered the ministry. Despite Espartero's protest, however, Maria Cristina sanctioned the law, and he at once resigned his command.

The revolution of 1840 had begun. Espartero entered Barcelona triumphantly on July 13 and was loudly acclaimed by the crowd, which demanded the fall of the ministry. In August Maria Cristina organized a new Moderate cabinet. This produced a revolution in Madrid, where the ayuntamiento established a revolutionary junta under the presidency of Joaquín María Ferrer. When Maria Cristina learned of the revolt in Madrid she urged Espartero to march on the capital to reduce the insurgents. He refused, declaring that the disturbance was not to be attributed to anarchists but to "the Liberal party, which, vexed and fearful of the return to despotism, has taken up arms." The revolution then spread from Madrid to other provinces.

Espartero went to Madrid to form a government and to devise a political program in collaboration with the local junta. The only discrepancy to develop was the demand of the local rebels for a new regency, but Espartero defended Maria Cristina's rights. The new government announced its new program: the annulment of the law of ayuntamientos, the dissolution of the cortes, the enforcement of the principle of ministerial responsibility, and the queen regent's promise to fulfill the constitution and approve the acts of the juntas until the next cortes could assemble.

Maria Cristina restrained her indignation at the proposal of a coregent and took an oath to support the ministers, but postponed discussion of the program until the following day. She invited Espartero to remain after the other ministers left and told him her intention of renouncing the regency and leaving Spain. Espartero, who would immediately become responsible for public policy, tried to dissuade her, but she drafted her abdication (October 12, 1840). Before embarking at El Grao de Valencia she signed the decree dissolving the cortes. The departure of the queen regent for France did not solve the primary problem of Spanish political affairs. Her abdication was an episode which left party strife as bitter as ever. However, the Moderate party had suffered a defeat in the fall of Maria Cristina.

Although the Progressives emerged triumphantly from this phase of the party struggle, they were confronted with extremists in their own ranks. The more radical politicians wanted to suppress the Senate and extend the revolutionary juntas; some wanted to restore the Constitution of 1812; others wanted to reform the Constitution of 1837. Meanwhile, on January 1, 1841, the government convoked the cortes, suppressed the secret police, and constituted the ayuntamientos on the basis of universal suffrage.

The Progressives had an overwhelming majority in the new cortes, since the Moderates had withdrawn from the electoral contest. Yet, since the Senate was renewed only by a third, the Moderates still retained a respectable influence. The most crucial problem which the cortes had to resolve when it assembled in March, was that of the regency. The personal followers and friends of Espartero were the principal proponents of a single regent. The conservatives held the balance of power in the dispute. Espartero's victory, however, was due to the fact that twenty-five Moderate senators voted in his favor by order of Maria Cristina. He became regent in May 1841. Antonio González, hitherto an insignificant figure, was named premier. This choice and the fact that three of the six ministers were generals led many to realize the political ineptitude of the new regent.

The problem of the guardianship of the princesses was immediately raised. Maria Cristina pretended to exercise it from exile. The government proposed that guardianship be exercised by a council of five in her name. When Maria Cristina protested the nomination of the tutor as a violation of the will of Ferdinand VII, the government issued a badly conceived manifesto and the moderate opposition rallied to the support of the exiled queen mother. Thus, many of the conservative generals participated in the conspiracy of Leopoldo O'Donnell at Pamplona in September 1841. Only a part of the garrison supported him, forcing him to retire to the citadel, but the Royal Guard left Saragossa to aid him, and General Piquero rose in Vitoria, the center of the movement, where a junta was formed. Revolts also occurred in Bilbao and Vergara.

Even though Madrid was a stronghold for the regent, the conspirators believed that a coup in the capital was necessary, but their attempt to seize the queen and Princess Luisa Fernanda was repelled by eighteen guards, who defended the stairway of the palace. The reprisals were bloody, and several generals were shot. The Basque provinces also paid dearly for their sympathy for Maria Cristina. Local authorities were subject to the central government, whose decrees were extended to the Basques without any restriction. The failure of the conspiracy only served as a pretext for the radical wing of the Progressive party to demand more extreme measures. A junta was established in Barcelona which ignored the central authority and acted with full autonomy, and the citadel of Barcelona, built by Philip V as a threat to the rebellious spirit of the Catalans, was demolished. Espartero disapproved of these excesses and the government had to declare martial law in Madrid, Barcelona, and other cities.

Three factions of the cortes had joined to overthrow the government. Although Espartero, trying vainly to hold his party together, offered the presidency to General Rodil, opposition to the regent increased. The Moderates conspired, aided by Louis Philippe, who was sympathetic toward Maria Cristina, then in Paris, and Republican factions also became active in various sections of the country. Espartero was accused of prolonging the minority of the twelve-year-old Isabel II.

Another revolt in Barcelona in November 1842 was led by José María Carsy, editor of *El Republicano,* supported by the militia and many citizens. Espartero marched on Barcelona and ordered its bombardment. His troops reentered the city, but for this severity he received a cool reception when he returned to Madrid.

Paris now became the center of Moderate activity. Narváez had been appointed the director of the conspiracy by Maria Cristina, but he relinquished his position to Leopoldo O'Donnell. The Moderates had the support of the French and even the British cabinet was cool toward the regent. The conservative press began to attack him while the Moderate leaders in Spain conferred with the dissidents in the Progressive party. In January 1843 Espartero dissolved the cortes, having failed to find the support he expected. In the elections for the new cortes the regent received the support of only seventy deputies. Although he momentarily considered renouncing the regency, he was dissuaded by his friends, and another revolution was thus initiated. Espartero, who had formerly been the idol of the masses, was now execrated. His imprudent policy, his strict partisan spirit, and his subjection to the advice of his intimates had alienated the nation. The first region to revolt was Andalusia. Málaga rebelled in May 1843 and Granada, Almería, and Seville followed her example. Espartero sent General Van Halen to suppress the uprising. Then Colonel Juan Prim rebelled in Reus. Barcelona, still bitterly hostile to the regent, established a junta, and Valencia, Cuenca, and Valladolid joined the revolt.

The conspirators in France lost no time. Generals Narváez and Concha disembarked in Valencia, while Generals Serrano and González Bravo organized a ministry in Barcelona. Espartero hastened to Andalusia, where Van Halen ordered the bombardment of Seville. Madrid had been the center of Espartero's popularity, but General Aspiroz, who had rebelled in Castile, and Narváez, who had been in Aragon, entered Madrid on July 23. On the following day Colonel Prim arrived with his Catalan division. When Espartero received the news of the occupation of Madrid, deserted by his troops and accompanied only by his personal escort, he issued a fulmination against the rebels and embarked for London.

CHAPTER XXV

The Reign of Isabel II

Baldomero Espartero, duke of La Victoria, had been overthrown by a heterogeneous combination of parties, formerly bitter rivals for political power. His fall had been made inevitable by the defection of members of his own Progressive party, who damaged the morale of their own party and turned against their acknowledged leader when they joined their ancient political enemies, the Moderates. Espartero had undoubtedly abused his authority in bowing to the caprice of his advisers, and he broke his party into factions. Alliance with the Moderates was dangerous, for they had the opportunity of winning the support of the neutral mass of the nation, largely interested in the pursuit of private, individual objectives and long opposed to innovations or changes in the constitution. The aristocrats had been hostile to the Progressives, and the conservatives generally were ready to heed the grievances of the persecuted Moderates.

Most of the Progressive military leaders had supported the exiled Espartero, but General Ramón Narváez had become the real arbiter of Spanish political affairs. The duke of Bailén was named tutor to Queen Isabel II, and the provisional government immediately considered anticipating the declaration of her majority because of fear of the attitude of the populace in Barcelona and Saragossa, who demanded a central junta.

In spite of the fact that the proposal to declare Isabel II of age was an obvious infraction of the Constitution of 1837, General Narváez, accompanied by General Prim, kissed the hand of the queen at a palace ceremony and then appeared before the troops to acclaim the constitution, the queen, and the provisional government (August 1843). Although the Catalans rebelled, the fact that there was no general conspiracy organized against the government made it easy to restore order.

Both Moderates and Progressives continued their alliance in the elections in defense of the Constitution of 1837. A new party also appeared, small but active. Called "Young Spain," it was led by González Bravo, an opportunist politician disposed to support either of the parties that would best advance his interests.

When the cortes opened on October 15, the government introduced the proposal to declare Isabel II of age, and the senators and deputies by a vote of 103 to 16 (November 1843) approved the law declaring that she had attained her majority at the age of thirteen. The youthful queen took her oath to the constitution, whereupon the provisional government resigned. Salustiano Olózaga, a liberal who had been persecuted under Ferdinand VII, was named premier. The existing alliance between the Progressives and the Moderates could not endure. Olózaga's announcement of his program was the signal for the Moderates to attack the man who sought to reunite the Progressives. It was impossible for him to govern as the cortes was constituted, and he recognized that it was necessary to dissolve it. Isabel II signed the decree. On the following day she told Narváez, who had resigned as captain general of Madrid, that Olózaga had forced her to approve the decree. A declaration of the queen was read in the cortes stating that Olózaga had not only grasped the royal hand to make Isabel sign the decree, but had closed the doors of the chamber so she could not escape. Olózaga, relieved of his position, emigrated to Portugal and thence to England. The Moderates had obtained their long-desired political authority.

As soon as the Progressives were in opposition they began to conspire, but González Bravo was able to repress their plots for a time. The national militia was disarmed and the press was gagged. Some of the leading Progressives were arrested, and on the advice of Narváez and some of the aristocratic leaders the Civil Guard was created. González Bravo also assumed the initiative in bringing Maria Cristina back to Spain. She returned to Madrid in April 1844. The ministry of González Bravo, however, was only a "bridge by which the Moderates might pass to the bank of command," and when Maria Cristina's influence was restored, she used it to replace González Bravo with Ramón Narváez.

The Progressives refused to participate in the elections and Narváez obtained an overwhelming majority in the constituent cortes. A new constitution was promulgated in May 1845, which suppressed the democratic principles contained in the Constitution of 1837, eliminated the principle concerning national sovereignty, and replaced the direct election of the upper chamber with nominations from the crown. The sovereign was permitted to absent himself from the kingdom and to marry without the permission of the cortes. The ministry completed the constitutional revisions with a restrictive modification of the organic laws of the nation. Decrees were vested with the authority of laws approved by the cortes, and centralizing policies were introduced into local and provincial administration. The liberty of the press was curtailed. The clergy were so liberally endowed that the question was raised as to whether the measure provided mere state support or an indemnification for the seizures of Church property.

Even in exile Espartero, the Progressive leader, sought to overthrow the established order, and other exiles gathered around him in London. There was also revolutionary activity in Paris and Lisbon. Alvaro Gómez Becerra presided over a revolutionary junta in Madrid. From December 1843 to December 1844, 214 persons were executed for political crimes.

The problem of the marriage of the youthful Isabel II divided the Moderate party. Her mother favored the count of Trápani. National opinion in general, however, was opposed to the Italian prince, largely because he was the brother of the queen mother. The powers which had not recognized Isabel II—Austria especially—hoped to obtain a marriage which would terminate the dynastic strife in Spain. After the Carlist pretender had ceded his claim to his son Carlos Luis, count of Montemolín, in 1845, more conservative Spaniards also favored this candidate.

As the marriage became of international interest, France and England expressed concern. Louis Philippe was anxious to contract an alliance with Isabel through a marriage with a prince of France. The British defended the freedom of Spain to contract any marriage desired except with a French prince. Both powers, however, favored the marriage with the Italian count of Trápani, who in no way aroused their mutual jealousy, and they succeeded in obtaining recognition of Isabel II by the king of the Two Sicilies. In September 1845 France and England agreed that Isabel II should marry a descendant of Philip II. Narváez was not only unable to advance the candidacy of the count of Trápani, but he also annoyed Maria Cristina by his refusal to support the conspiracy to enthrone one of the sons of the second marriage of Maria Cristina as king of Mexico. Maria Cristina now approached the House of Coburg to obtain Prince Leopold as a consort for her daughter, but this aroused French opposition. With the potential candidates thus reduced, the most likely remaining ones were Isabel's cousins, Prince Francisco de Asís, duke of Cádiz, and Prince Henry, duke of Seville, the sons of Prince Francisco de Paula. Lord Palmerston had preferred

Leopold of Coburg but, with his elimination, favored Prince Henry because of his sympathy toward the Progressives.

The Moderates, however, were alienated by the very reason which had led the English to favor Prince Henry: he had published a manifesto containing progressive ideas in 1845, and not long thereafter he defied the governing party by his implication in the Galician revolt. This left Prince Francisco de Asís as the only candidate. The French approved of the union with Prince Francisco on the condition that the duke of Montpensier marry Isabel's sister, the Princess Luisa Fernanda. The marriages thus arranged and celebrated in October 1846 were a diplomatic victory for the French, but they alienated the English.

With the solution of the dynastic problem the reactionary faction in the government attained greater prestige, strengthened by the influx of many former Carlists into its ranks. Although some uncompromising Carlists renewed their hostility to the government of Isabel II, they did not constitute a formidable threat. The Progressives, on the other hand, were discredited, broken by the split in their own ranks and outmaneuvered by their political opponents. While Narváez was no more cultivated than Espartero, he surpassed the latter in political vision and his understanding of people. Yet schism in the moderate ranks was inevitable. Narváez was unscrupulous, and many Moderates refused to support his policies, while others were repelled by the spectacle of a military leader exercising civil authority. As a result a Puritan faction led by Joaquín Francisco Pacheco appeared, which consisted of the most decided adversaries of the ministry.

General Serrano Domínguez, who because of his handsome appearance, gallantry, and successful career exercised a marked influence over the queen, was a member of the new faction. The government sought to reduce his influence by appointing him captain general of Navarre, but Isabel II refused to sign the decree. Then the government entrusted him with military duties in the Basque provinces, but he excused himself because of his responsibilities as a senator. When the government tried to bring him to trial, he sought sanctuary in the British embassy. The ministers depended on their majority in the cortes and the opposition between them and the crown increased. The queen was isolated.

Joaquín Francisco Pacheco assumed the presidency of a new ministry, conservative-liberal in character, which inaugurated an era of tolerance. Olózaga was granted an annuity, and González Bravo was appointed to the Royal Council. But the private differences between Isabel II and her consort offered greater difficulties than did normal political problems. The royal couple had moved into separate residences, and with the dissolution of the cortes the government devoted all its energies to a reconciliation. José de Salamanca, a lawyer from Málaga who had used his Andalusian charm and talent to grow rich in the salt monopoly and to become the financial arbiter of Spain, was chosen to bring the queen and Francisco de Asís together again. Although Isabel seemed willing to reach an understanding, Francisco opposed any compromise.

The political factions tried to take advantage of the royal disaffection to advance their own interests. The Progressives rallied around the queen, expecting much from Serrano. The Moderates, who disliked the general intensely, intervened to influence the prince to participate more actively in politics than he had done as a mere consort. Consequently, Salamanca's efforts to reconcile the royal pair failed, and the ministry found itself attacked by both reactionaries and Progressives. Narváez constituted a cabinet in October 1847 and after sending Serrano into honorable exile as captain general of Granada, succeeded in temporarily reconciling the queen and her consort.

In Catalonia the Carlists had proclaimed the count of Montemolín, the son of Carlos, king. General Pavía captured Tristany, one of the Carlist leaders, and executed him, but the war spread. Cabrera reappeared with a thousand men, but he was no longer the ferocious leader of old. With only scanty resources and few arms, he sustained himself for a while by his military skill. By the end of November 1849 Catalonia was pacified. During the nine months of his dictatorship Narváez used his energy to save Spain from the revolutionary movement. He deprived Prince Henry of his honors as a punishment for his revolutionary manifesto from Perpignan and expelled the British ambassador.

Within the Moderate party there were some intellectuals who had grown discontented with the continued intervention of generals in politics. Bravo Murillo, who became premier in January 1851, was in that group. After preparing for an ecclesiastical career he dedicated himself to the law and became a professor at the University of Seville. Especially astute in financial matters, he served as deputy in 1837 and 1840, although during the Espartero regime he emigrated to France. Even though the several moderate factions were the declared enemies of the new government, the military were Murillo's most formidable adversaries. Despite the intrigues against him the policies of his ministry were successful. Austria and Prussia finally recognized Isabel II and sent representatives to Madrid. Murillo's economic reforms, however, were more important. He presented a proposal on the public debt which was finally approved in both chambers of the new cortes in July 1851. He was unsuccessful, on the other hand, in uniting the factions in the

Moderate party. The Progressives, too, were divided into factions, including the democratic party on the extreme left which bordered on republicanism.

Two events led Bravo Murillo to adopt an equivocal policy: Louis Napoleon was successful in his coup d'état establishing himself as emperor in France in December 1851, and two months later as Isabel came out of the Royal Chapel, where she had given her thanks for the successful birth of Princess Maria Isabel, she was attacked and wounded by an assassin. Since Bravo Murillo wanted to override the cortes and legislate by decree, the attempt on the queen's life produced a reaction which was propitious for his plans. His fundamental error, however, was to attempt to modify the Constitution of 1845 in a more restrictive and conservative sense, whereupon the Progressives united with the Moderates to overthrow him. The generals had joined in opposition to "the lawyer" who had tried to correct the abuses of parliamentary rule and terminate military intervention in civil affairs. Although Bravo Murillo struggled vainly to maintain his position, Maria Cristina also opposed his reform and advised Isabel to change ministries. The opposition persisted against the ministry of the count of Alcoy during the next four months. Generals O'Donnell and Narváez were closely united by fear of the restoration of Bravo Murillo and the desire to regain their own authority. Their campaign was financed by the concessions of railways, in which Salamanca, the banker, had participated. As the projected railway lines had been forced to depend on financial assistance from the state, many applications for unsound concessions were presented, and once approved, the funds were devoted to speculation rather than to the construction of railways. A new law was passed making every concession the subject of a special law (March 1853).

From threats the opposition proceeded to violence. The most formidable of the generals had been given posts outside the peninsula. General Leopoldo O'Donnell, the chief of the coalition, had been ordered to Santa Cruz de Tenerife, but had remained in hiding in Madrid. Antonio Cánovas del Castillo, a friend of O'Donnell and editor of *Las Novedades,* hurled sharp and incisive criticism at the government in the *Athenaeum*. The rebellion was set for June 13, 1854, and when the necessary troops were collected, they marched to Alcalá de Henares. O'Donnell issued a manifesto, explaining the reasons which moved them to resort to arms as "the repeated and scandalous infractions of the constitution, the persecution of the press, and the venality of the ministers, as especially demonstrated in the railway concessions, in the sale of public offices" as well as in the discharge of business affairs.

Isabel II returned hastily from El Escorial to Madrid, hoping to win the loyalty of the rebels with words, but Luis Sartorius, who had become head of the ministry, preferred military action. He placed Madrid under martial law and removed the rebel generals, while Isabel II reviewed the loyal troops. Meanwhile, the rebels had marched to Vicálvaro, where an indecisive battle was fought and the loyal army withdrew in disorder to Madrid.

As Cánovas del Castillo was anxious to give the movement a civil character and to make it more than a mere military coup d'etat, he left Madrid and conferred with the rebels at Manzanares. When the manifesto was proclaimed in Madrid the Progressives joined the rebellion. Isabel II was advised to withdraw to Aranjuez, but she heeded the words of the French ambassador: "The king who abandons his palace in times of revolution does not usually return to it."

Another general now emerged as the strong man of Spain, Leopoldo O'Donnell. He was of Irish ancestry, the first O'Donnell, Hugo, having come from Ireland in 1602. General O'Donnell had forced the Carlist guerrillero Cabrera to raise the siege of Lucena and been rewarded with the title of count of Lucena. Courted by the political leaders, he became an opponent of Espartero, a Moderate, and one of the outstanding generals among the conservatives. In temperament O'Donnell was serene and phlegmatic, and although impelled by ambition he was incorruptible. He had few political ideas of his own, and when someone remarked to Cánovas del Castillo that the general was an idol, Cánovas replied: "Yes, an idol, I know it well because I talked many times through him."

The revolution which had been inspired by the Moderates against a moderate ministry resulted in a victory for the Progressives. It was logical to call upon the general who had led the movement, but Maria Cristina resentfully advised Isabel II to call Espartero to power. On entering office again Espartero imposed certain conditions before he would undertake the government of Spain. His popularity had been reestablished and the queen accepted his program. He entered Madrid on July 28 and was enthusiastically received, after which he called Leopoldo O'Donnell and embraced him publicly, and the breach between the Moderates, who had led the revolution, and the Progressives appeared to be healed. O'Donnell became minister of War in the new cabinet.

One of the first acts of the Espartero government was to convoke a constituent cortes in November 1854. A violent campaign had been launched, defaming Maria Cristina, and she was secretly escorted to Portugal. The elections for the cortes witnessed the birth of a new party, the Liberal Union, of which the majority of the new deputies were members. It was formed of Moderates and temperate Progressives who had grown weary of revolution, but met difficulty in maintaining harmony between the partisans of O'Donnell and Espartero.

In the debate on the new constitution there were a few votes against a monarchical form of government, but the ultraconservatives were more aroused by the proposed law which ordered the immediate sale of all the properties belonging to the state, charitable and educational institutions, the municipalities, and the clergy. Although the law was approved by the cortes, it was an infraction of the concordat of 1851 with the Holy See, which recognized the right of the Church to acquire title to property and to hold ownership securely. Therefore, Joaquín Francisco Pacheco was sent to Rome to negotiate on the delicate matter. Espartero and O'Donnell had persuaded the queen to sign the law in April 1855, but she was reluctant to comply. The pope was adamant in refusing to accept the new law and decided to break relations with Spain. Monsignor Franchi, the papal nuncio who had tried to keep Isabel from signing the law, asked for his passport and Pacheco returned from Rome.

After the approval of the basis for the new constitution, Espartero desired to retire, but some of his friends, including O'Donnell and the queen, succeeded in dissuading him. The struggle between the pure Progressives and the members of the Liberal Union had aroused jealousy between Espartero and O'Donnell. The former was impatient at the violent attacks on him in the moderate press. In addition, the militia members were dissatisfied. They recognized Espartero as their leader and were anxious for a more definitely progressive program with ultraliberal reforms.

When the constituent cortes again assembled in October 1855, the pure Progressives tried to break the alliance between Espartero and O'Donnell. With the Democrats they staged a demonstration by the guards against the reactionary deputies and in behalf of a republic. Espartero broke up the tumult. During January 1856 the constitution was finally approved, but it was never promulgated because the pure Progressives wanted to submit it first to the sanction of the queen.

The breach between the parties widened. The Moderates accused O'Donnell of weakness in facing the socialist disorders in Castile, while the extreme Progressives became more hostile toward Espartero. Although the clerical faction supported Isabel II in an effort to forestall the promulgation of the constitution, Espartero depended on the loyalty of the queen and believed she preferred him to O'Donnell. The latter, however, became stronger each day, and Espartero, despite warnings that Isabel planned to form a conservative ministry under O'Donnell, refused to heed the advice to dismiss him and his military colleagues.

A crisis was reached in July 1856. The violence and arson rampant in Castile could no longer be tolerated, but Espartero and O'Donnell disagreed on the measures to be adopted to restore order. Escosura, minister of the Interior, an intimate adviser of Espartero, resigned when Isabel II supported O'Donnell. Espartero rose and took the arm of Escosura and said, "Wait and we will go together." The queen exclaimed, "Then O'Donnell will not abandon me." Espartero was eliminated from the coalition.

The fall of Espartero produced a reaction among the Progressives and drove them into an alliance with the radical Democrats. The conservative faction, however, had the support of the clergy, aggrieved by the repressive measures taken against them in the persecution of the Jesuits, the prohibition of processions, the expulsion of the nuncio, and the exile of a number of bishops. The hostility between the Moderates and the Progressives appeared once more in the repression inaugurated by O'Donnell. The constituent cortes was disbanded and the Constitution of 1845 was restored, although modified somewhat by an additional act of September 15, 1856.

Isabel II had used O'Donnell to dissipate the progressive threat, but she had not forgotten his complicity in the recent revolution. She was, in fact, anxious to restore Narváez, who had freed the throne from the difficulties of 1848. On the occasion of her birthday she offended O'Donnell and he resigned, whereupon Narváez returned to power.

Under Narváez a reaction began against the revolutionary principles that had recently been in vogue. The concordat of 1851 was restored intact. The law relating to the sale of Church property was suspended. The progressive legislation relating to the deputation and municipalities was annuled. Although the Constitution of 1845 was restored, it was further modified by Nocedal's law of July 1857. The additional act of O'Donnell was abrogated, and the press was again restricted. Narváez arbitrarily sentenced many unfortunate persons to prison who were guilty of no crime. While his drastic methods restored order, they also aroused discontent. Isabel reacted against his authoritarian measures, and when Narváez became aware of her attitude he resigned.

It was evident from the failure of successive ministries that the throne of Isabel II was in a precarious state. The Liberal Union was the only party that could withstand the tide of revolution. The old Progressive party, now called the Liberal party, no longer tried to defend the obsolete

Constitution of 1812, but advocated a constitutional regime of the European type. In their eagerness to establish a government of law, its members devoted most of their energy to opposing the ultraconservatives, who were complete reactionaries. The Moderates became the Conservative party. They aided the revolution against Espartero, but their ideology was restricted to the effort to impede the reforms of the liberals. The radicals of this party were constitutionalists. The center was larger, but its principal objective was despotism of the kind personified by Narváez. Bravo Murillo led a more conservative group, which, while sustaining civil authority, tolerated infractions of the constitution and appeared to support absolutism. The third party was the Liberal Union. Organized by O'Donnell, it consisted of the temperate liberals, alarmed by the excesses of Espartero. They were joined by the liberal conservatives of the Moderate party, who opposed both reaction and absolutism. O'Donnell, who represented a central position, was hated by the extreme liberals because of his complicity in the revolution of 1854. He did not form a stable party, but it was a tactical victory to form the center against the extremists of the right and left. It also attracted those who believed in national order and desired to end the revolutionary disturbances. Although the Liberal Union gained an overwhelming majority in the cortes which convened in December 1858, thereafter it continued to lose support. O'Donnell was anxious to maintain order, but lack of unity in the government produced a series of crises and ministerial changes, until finally O'Donnell proposed the dissolution of the cortes. When the queen refused to accept the proposal, O'Donnell regretfully relinquished power.

The territory Spain still held in Morocco was under constant attack by local chieftains. The continued Moroccan aggression against Melilla, Ceuta, Alhucemas, Chafarinas, and Vélez led to Spanish complaints to the sultan of Morocco. An agreement was signed in August 1859 for the extension of Spanish jurisdiction around Melilla, but at the very same time the Moslem raiders attacked Ceuta. The Spanish government demanded the punishment of those responsible for the attack and guarantees for the future restraint of the tribesmen. As Great Britain was alarmed at the danger of the extension of Spanish power at the Strait of Gibraltar, the Spanish government hastened to quiet British suspicion with the assurance that Spanish military operations were intended only to guarantee the termination of attacks on her strongholds and that Spain would not occupy permanently any point the possession of which would endanger the freedom of navigation in the Mediterranean. Ceuta, the port of debarkation for the expeditionary force, was ten leagues from Tangier and seven leagues from Tetuán, the objectives of the expedition.

O'Donnell was named commander-in-chief of the expeditionary force. The Spaniards landed in Ceuta during November and December, and at the beginning of January 1860 they assumed the offensive. The impetuous General Juan Prim, in the vanguard, was attacked in the Valley of Los Castillejos and was saved only by his own bravery and by timely aid, after losing more than seven hundred men. The army continued its march, and after a battle before Tetuán the city surrendered. For his heroism Prim was awarded the title of marquis of Castillejos. When an attack was then launched against Tangier the Moslems, discouraged, opened negotiations for peace, and the Treaty of Tetuán was concluded in April 1860. The emperor of Morocco ceded to Spain all the territory between the sea and the Sierra Bullones to the Valley of Aughera. In addition, he promised to confirm an agreement of the preceding year, ceding a strip of territory at Santa Cruz la Paqueña for a fishing colony and agreeing to pay an indemnity of 400,000,000 reales. The city of Tetuán was to be occupied by Spain until the sum was paid.

During the government of the Liberal Union, Spain also became involved in hostilities with parts of its old empire in America. In 1861 the natives of Santo Domingo were still struggling with the Negroes of Haiti in a war which had been in progress since the surrender of the Spanish half of the island to France by the Treaty of Basel. The inhabitants of Santo Domingo, tired of the war and of French domination, expressed their desire to reunite with Spain. O'Donnell welcomed the proposed annexation, and in March 1861 the Spanish banner was raised in the island; however, the era of Spanish sovereignty was short-lived, for Santo Domingo again became an independent republic.

Intervention in Mexico—also in this year—involved Spain in various projects of European diplomacy. For many years Spain had demanded indemnification for the damages suffered by Spaniards during the war for the emancipation of Mexico. Additional claims for damages to Spanish interests had arisen during the civil strife between the Mexican Reformists and Conservatives. Just as the Reformists succeeded in gaining power and expelling foreign diplomats in October 1861, the governments of London, Madrid, and Paris reached an accord to oblige Mexico to pay her debts. A Spanish expedition was prepared in Habana and took possession of Vera Cruz. In an ultimatum to Mexico in January 1862 the representatives of England, France, and Spain declared that conquest was not their intention, but that it was necessary for Mexico to meet her obligations.

Meanwhile, Napoleon III was hoping to find an empire in Mexico for his protégé, the Archduke Maximilian of Austria. General Prim, who was in command of the expeditionary force, soon became aware that the French planned to act independently. When this became clear, England and Spain prepared to withdraw from the expedition, while Napoleon III continued with his aim of enthroning Maximilian. Prim was accused by the French representative of opposing the candidacy of the archduke because he hoped to obtain the crown of emperor of Mexico for himself, whereupon he indignantly issued orders for the return of the Spanish troops to Habana.

The last international episode of the reign of Isabel II was the War of the Pacific in 1865–66. The relations of Spain with Peru and Chile had been precarious ever since 1853. Peruvians had maltreated Spanish citizens and in 1863 had killed several Basques. Spain sent a squadron under Admiral Pinzón to demand explanations. When he occupied the Chinchas Islands to guarantee a redress of the grievances, Chile supported Peru by depriving the Spanish squadron of fuel. Although the Peruvian government promised the required indemnity and the Chinchas Islands were evacuated, relations with Chile grew more embittered, and the Spanish schooner "Covadonga" was seized in November 1865. A Peruvian revolution at this time elevated General Prado to the presidency, who—in alliance with Chile—declared war on Spain. The Spanish bombardment of Valparaiso in May 1866 produced general indignation in America. The Spanish then bombarded Callao, where the armored batteries of the city seriously damaged their vessels. At this point the intervention of the United States, France, and England put an end to the conflict.

Narváez's return to power represented the triumph of the forces of reaction. The Progressives, convinced that they could not proceed by legal means because of the nature of the new ministry, chose Juan Prim as their leader and prepared for revolution. Maria Cristina, who had returned from abroad, was prudent and experienced enough in politics to recognize the danger from the Progressives and advised that they be attracted to the monarchist camp. Her words were unheeded and the political situation deteriorated rapidly.

Narváez intended to adopt a liberal policy, and he wrote to González Bravo that he was "going to be more liberal than Riego." He published an amnesty for all crimes charged against the press, but his efforts to attract the members of the Liberal Union and the Progressives were futile. Although the ministry put down several attempts at revolution, when a demand was made for its dissolution Isabel asked O'Donnell to restore the government of the Liberal Union. By this time the crown had exhausted its resources. The Moderates were a danger rather than a support for the throne, as their attitude and program provoked revolution. Since the Progressives were intent on revolt, the Liberal Union was the only party which could oppose the hostility to the throne. O'Donnell tried vainly to effect a reconciliation with the Progressives by offering hostile editors ministerial positions.

In January 1866 General Prim attempted a revolution in Madrid, demanding a constituent cortes. But his reinforcements failed to arrive, and General Zavala pursued him to the frontier of Portugal, after which he continued to direct revolutions from Paris. The conspiracy included the Progressives and the Democrats and was based on the discontent of most of the sergeants of artillery in the nation. In June 1866 the sergeants at San Gil seized the officers, five of whom were shot, but as the rebels had no military leader they were soon suppressed. Juan Prim had come to Hendaye, but returned to Paris when he learned of the collapse of the insurrection.

Narváez again replaced O'Donnell at the head of the government and immediately adopted a policy of repression, which increased both the discontent and the opposition. The Progressives became more active as revolutionaries and found allies in the intellectuals of the Democratic party. Narváez's aim was to obtain a truce in revolutionary activity, but the Progressives, under Prim's leadership, continued to formulate their plans. The alliance of the Progressives and Democrats was confirmed at Ostend. They established their headquarters in Brussels, with another revolutionary center in Paris. They intended to substitute a provisional government for that of Isabel II and then convoke a constituent cortes.

The prestige of Narváez was still the principal support of the throne. The Liberal Unionists were beginning to be attracted by the idea of revolution, but an alliance between the Unionists and the Progressives was doubtful as long as O'Donnell was alive, since he opposed any break with the queen. His death in 1867, however, clarified the situation. The court rejoiced, with little realization of the fact that one of the staunchest supports of the monarchy had disappeared.

The cortes which assembled in December 1867 was submissive to the government and prepared the legislation recommended: the reform of the law of public order, the organization of a Rural Guard, a penal law on vagrancy, modification of mining legislation, and a new law on public education. When Narváez died in the following spring, another staunch supporter of the toppling throne disappeared. González Bravo attained his ambition of being elevated to the position of premier, while Carlos Marfori, the queen's favorite, became colonial minister.

González Bravo now inaugurated a civil dictatorship which he believed invulnerable, but the situation was more precarious than he realized, for the revolutionary coalition between the Progressives and the Unionists had been forged at a conference in Bayonne. Serrano had become chief of the Liberal Union party on the death of O'Donnell, though some of the members of the party, led by Cánovas del Castillo, did not want to commit themselves to revolution. However, even the publication of the news of the alliance of the Unionists, Progressives, and Democrats did not awaken the government to a realization of the dangers surrounding it. The measures taken were repressive, and several generals were imprisoned or exiled.

With the opposition to the throne united, the preparations for the overthrow of Isabel II were begun. Sagasta established relations with Carlos and Cabrera in an effort to obtain the support of the Carlists, but the negotiations failed. The duke of Montpensier, who hoped to replace Isabel II on the throne, was sympathetic with the movement, but he had been removed to Lisbon. Prim also concluded an understanding with Prince Henry, brother-in-law and cousin of the queen. He had been active in many revolutionary movements.

The court remained oblivious of the danger. The queen, surrounded by sycophants, relied on González Bravo because of Marfori's confidence in him. On August 8 she went to San Sebastián, where the royal family was accustomed to escape the heat of Madrid, but the date of the uprising which had been set for August 9 was postponed until September. Revolutionary activity continued nearly in the open and was known to exist in Seville and Cádiz. The Unionists were especially strong in Andalusia. Prim, who had been taking the waters of Vichy, returned to London, assured by Napoleon III that France would not intervene if Prim promised not to support the candidacy of the duke of Montpensier to the throne. Prim agreed in order to relieve any threat on the northern frontier.

On September 12, Prim, Sagasta, and Ruiz Zorrilla boarded the "Delta" at Southampton and arrived at Gibraltar on September 17. The "Buenaventura," chartered for the rebels by the duke of Montpensier, sailed for the Canary Islands to bring the exiled generals to the peninsula. Prim crossed to Cádiz, where Admiral Juan Bautista Topete, the commander of the revolutionary naval forces, had signed a proclamation.

Prim had not met Topete before he boarded his frigate, the "Zaragoza." The admiral, an adherent of the duke of Montpensier, told Prim he wanted to proclaim a constitutional monarchy under Princess Maria Luisa Fernanda, sister of Isabel II and wife of the duke. Prim replied that the meeting at Ostend had agreed to leave the matter to a constituent assembly.

The authorities at Cádiz had meanwhile been warned of the proposed uprising, and Prim and Topete decided that to postpone it any longer might endanger its success. The fleet arrayed itself in order of combat before Cádiz on the morning of September 18. General Serrano had not arrived, and it was agreed that Prim should assume command. He presented himself to the sailors and Topete addressed them. The "Zaragoza" fired a twenty-one gun salute. The citizens of Cádiz rose in arms, and the revolution spread throughout Andalusia. Prim and Topete disembarked and published a manifesto. On the following day Serrano arrived, and the leaders of the movement issued a proclamation entitled "Spain with Honor."

González Bravo was surprised by the gravity of the revolution, despite the constant threat of such a pronouncement. His government resigned and advised Isabel II to form a military cabinet. He then fled to France, and the marquis of La Habana assumed control of the loyal forces. Meanwhile, the revolution had gained momentum. Serrano with an army and Prim in the frigate "Zaragoza" proceeded along the coast kindling rebellion. Some of Isabel's advisers recommended that she abdicate in favor of Alfonso, her son, which would have been an acceptable solution to Serrano and might have ended the revolt. Marfori, however, was appalled at the thought of losing his influence and authority. General Concha then suggested that Isabel return to Madrid, but Marfori again demurred, and another possible solution was abandoned.

General Pavía led the loyal forces out of Madrid on September 20, 1868. Serrano, meanwhile, had concentrated his forces, which were superior in number, at Córdoba. The two armies met in an indecisive battle on September 28 at the bridge of Alcolea, but the rebels won a moral victory, since the royal forces had not forced the bridge.

The following days were full of anxiety for the court. General Concha, who was blindly optimistic, refused to consider the removal of the royal family to France. When news arrived, however, of the rising of Madrid on September 30 and of the spread of revolution throughout the nation, Isabel boarded a train for France. She went to Biarritz, where she was affably received by Napoleon III and the Empress Eugenie. From Pau, Isabel issued a protest against her violent overthrow and a declaration of her rights to the throne. On October 3, 1868, the victorious rebel leader, Serrano, entered Madrid.

The crown of Isabel II had never rested easily on her head. Her uncle had disputed her accession during her minority, and when she was finally old enough to ascend the throne her own weakness prevented her from being successful. Her troubles were in part to be attributed to the political disintegration of the country, caught in the tide of democratic aspiration, but Isabel's private life had not been a happy one. She would, perhaps, have preferred to wed Prince Henry rather than his brother Francisco de Asís. The royal couple lived apart, and Isabel's private life under such circumstances gave rise to scandal. Many rumors were circulated about her which did not add to the prestige or the strength of her reign. Perhaps her happiest days were spent in France after her exile.

CHAPTER XXVI

Spanish Civilization in the Early Nineteenth Century

The early nineteenth century marked the beginning of the reaction against absolutism, largely as the result of the penetration of the ideals of the French Revolution into the peninsula. French ideology had already penetrated the intellectual atmosphere of Spain and the popular will found some expression in the Constitution of 1812—which in its elaboration was genuinely Spanish—approved by the Cortes of Cádiz. Despite the strong French influence on the deputies to this cortes, they remained especially Spanish in their devotion to the traditions of the nation. In a sense, they hoped to restore the emergent democracy which, they believed, had flourished on the Spanish frontier and in the *fueros* during the Middle Ages. They based their declaration of national sovereignty on the *Fuero Juzgo,* in contradiction to the centralizing tendencies contained in Roman law.

The Royal Statute of April 1834 was the work of Martínez de la Rosa. Like other Moderates he hoped to avoid the dangerous extremes sought by the radicals in 1820 and yet establish a moderate monarchy. As soon as the Progressives obtained power they elaborated a new constitution in 1837, which was conservatively democratic, consecrating individual rights, but maintaining a system of checks and balances in the separation of powers. However liberal the Constitution of 1812 in regard to the individual and the restriction of absolutism, it centralized the government in imitation of the French. Spanish democracy had hitherto been based on local and regional autonomy, since Spain, until the advent of the Bourbons, was more a confederation of states than a unitary monarchy. Although in the Constitution of 1812 hereditary and royal intervention in the nomination of the members of the municipal council was replaced with their free election, local variations were eliminated.

The councils were regulated by fixed and uniform rules and were presided over by the political chief, or, in his absence, the alcalde, and their duties were uniformly prescribed.

The situation changed with the reaction of Ferdinand VII and the restoration of the Constitution of 1812. At the end of Ferdinand's reign there was a great variety in municipal government, which proceeded from the old regime. Then Maria Cristina restored the uniformity of 1812. Free elections were necessarily continued, but a centralizing tendency was apparent in the dependence of the alcaldes on the governors. In addition, the queen was authorized to name *corregidores* for Madrid and the provincial capitals.

The province in Spain was partly based on geography, partly on history, but in general it was fashioned for the convenience of the governor. Its capital was the political and administrative center, serving as the seat of the deputation, a council of seven representatives of the district under the presidency of a political chief. The Constitution of 1812 established thirty-one provincial deputations. Meanwhile, Joseph I had divided Spain into thirty-eight prefectures. Ferdinand VII reestablished the old provincial organization, but the revolution of 1820 restored that of the Constitution of 1812. In 1822 a new organization was provided by which Spanish territory was divided into fifty-two provinces.

Judicial organization, too, was transformed by the Cortes of Cádiz. That function was assigned exclusively to the courts. Neither the king nor the cortes could administer justice. Although the liberals did not yet dare establish trial by jury, they did provide that no Spaniard could be judged by any commission except a competent court. In the communities the alcaldes administered justice, with courts of higher jurisdiction in the territorial audiencias and the supreme court, and new audiencias were created in Madrid, Valladolid, Granada, and Pamplona to supplement the nine existing ones. Judicial independence was also provided in the Cortes of Cádiz by the establishment of the principle of the irremovability of judges.

After the French invasion of the peninsula, the class which lost the most prestige was the nobility. The ignorance of the nobles prevented them from comprehending the threat posed by the French Revolution, but the liberals, already imbued with French ideals and inspired by the magic word "equality," soon demonstrated that the threat was real. The Cortes of Cádiz was convened without recognition of class distinction. By a decree of August 1811 the jurisdiction of nobles over their estates was abolished, together with their privileges. Although they lost their political authority they nevertheless retained their economic power, since their old serfs were merely converted into tenants. A new class rose triumphantly out of the wreck of the old social order. The members of the middle class could aspire to all official positions, regardless of whether they possessed an escutcheon or a tonsure. They were the directing force under the national sovereignty. The people, on the other hand, whose sovereignty had been loudly proclaimed, remained ignorant and uncultivated. Their prejudices were easily aroused by clerical or demagogic activity. They expected to be redeemed either through absolutism and the generosity of their sovereigns or by the establishment of democratic institutions. Thus, as they shifted in their allegiance from one faction to another, the relative instability of the parties or the ambitions of their leaders kept the nation in a tumult.

Economically, Spain was devastated by war from 1808 to 1814. Attempts at reconstruction were further interrupted by the Carlist War and the pronunciamentos which followed the War of Independence. Men were diverted from economic pursuits to fight in the defense of the nation and then of the party. Death and famine added their toll to losses in war. Between 1797 and 1822 the population declined by a million and a half as a result of war, famine, and yellow fever. In addition, over one hundred thousand Spaniards went to the New World either through voluntary emigration or as members of military expeditions. An official census in 1833 estimated the population at 12,286,941. As a result of the scarcity of laborers during the War of Independence, production declined. There was a shortage of bread, and wheat had to be imported from abroad. The loss of the American colonies also produced a depression in the monetary market, as the importation of precious metals from the New World ceased. It became necessary to stimulate agriculture and dedicate more land to cultivation after the Napoleonic wars. Spanish wines and fruits continued to be exported, and olive oil remained a particularly important product of Seville. Honey was produced in Cuenca and silk in Murcia. While agriculture had generally languished during the wars, stock raising greatly increased.

Industry had likewise suffered from the hazards of war, but was greatly stimulated by a minister of Ferdinand VII, Luis López Ballesteros. To him were due many improvements and, in general, the revival of the national industrial energy. Catalan manufacturing, especially of threads and textiles, revived after 1814. With the advent of steam power, mechanical devices were introduced by José Bonaplata in Barcelona, whose company established a factory utilizing textile machinery. Barcelona and the surrounding Catalan region enjoyed great industrial prosperity. Steam was applied to the milling industry, and the Molino de Irujo in Cádiz was able to turn out 2000 fanegas of flour daily. Gas illumination was also introduced in 1807 in Cádiz and Granada, and in 1826 to 1829 it was installed in the Lonja in Barcelona; in 1832, on the birth of Princess Maria Luisa Fernanda, the illumination of the Puerta del Sol in Madrid was undertaken.

One of the most disastrous factors in the decline of Spanish commerce was the loss of the colonial empire, which deprived Spain of a valuable income with which to balance its trade. As a result trade increased with the colonies which remained under Spanish rule. Sugar and cacao were imported from Cuba, and the Philippines and Puerto Rico also furnished valuable products.

Public works were paralyzed by the constant wars. The sums appropriated for the building of roads were small in comparison with those needed, and the internal political vicissitudes, which caused the emigration of some of the better-trained personnel, were as great an impediment to public works. In 1828 the government also tried to renew the construction of the Canal of Castile, but little was accomplished. The problem of irrigation received earlier and more favorable attention. The Canal of Castaños was undertaken in 1817 to irrigate the left bank of the Llobregat, and from 1817 to 1822 the chamber of commerce of Barcelona renewed work on the Canal of Urgel, but was forced to give up the work because of difficulties in the terrain.

The plight of the Spanish treasury was already desperate at the end of the reign of Charles IV. Joseph I was unable to sustain himself financially without the aid of his brother, the Emperor Napoleon. He resorted, however, to extraordinary financial means, confiscating the silver of the churches and the jewels of private individuals, yet he lacked money to pay his troops. Meanwhile, the Central Junta, despite the financial situation, promised to reduce taxes, but was also forced in the end to confiscate the gold and silver jewels of the churches as well as the properties of the pro-French bishops. It also resorted to forced loans, established a tax on coaches and carriages, and created a direct tax on salaries and capital. The Cortes of Cádiz increased taxes on rents and income and even turned to lotteries in an effort to meet expenses. Salaries were reduced and a direct property tax was imposed. New taxes were introduced throughout the period or were substituted for unduly onerous ones, yet expenses always exceeded income. The War of Independence cost twelve billion reales, and there was always a deficit.

The financial situation deteriorated with the restoration of Ferdinand VII, who tried to revive the old system but was confronted with imminent bankruptcy, and army and state employees could not be paid. With the restoration of the Constitution of 1812 hope arose for an improvement in national finance, but it was futile. Although, under Ferdinand VII, López Ballesteros proved to be an able minister of Finance, increasing the income and introducing economies, the debt increased from twelve billion reales to eighteen billion in 1826.

Yet the financial position of Spain was not quite as desperate as these facts suggest. The national economy had been transformed and production had been increased. The Cortes of Cádiz had abolished the restrictive measures maintained by the guilds; although they were reestablished in 1815 the monopoly of the guilds was broken, and freedom of industry was established. The suppression of the feudal rights and the policies ending civil and ecclesiastical entailment increased the circulation of wealth and gave hope for greater prosperity in the future.

The Spanish Church had faced a crisis following the introduction of liberalism into Spain. It opposed the liberal trend, but the measures taken by Joseph I in despoiling the churches of their wealth, suppressing the military orders, the Inquisition, and ecclesiastical immunity and abolishing the religious orders, caused the clergy, many of whom were killed by the French in the war, to join the national cause with enthusiasm. In succeeding years the Church suffered from the vicissitudes of politics. Ferdinand VII restored the old religious regime, and reestablished the Jesuits. After the Revolution of 1820 the Inquisition was again abolished and its prisoners were liberated. The Jesuits were later readmitted, but Ferdinand refused to sanction the reestablishment of the Inquisition. At the death of Ferdinand VII the clergy, unable to restore their power under his rule, were largely sympathetic with the Carlists. Pope Gregory XVI, for example, refused to recognize Isabel II. When Mendizábal's policy involved the confiscation of clerical property, the papal nuncio withdrew, and consequently the government became even more hostile to the Church. Meanwhile, the alienation of clerical property had continued. The income of the Inquisition was applied to the public debt. The property of nine hundred suppressed convents, however, was confiscated and sold for trifling sums.

The events in Spain produced embittered relations with the Holy See. Gregory XVI not only refused to recognize Isabel II but withheld recognition of the bishops nominated by the government, and many bishoprics remained vacant. The conflict became sharper, and Espartero ordered the expulsion of the apostolic representative. Meanwhile, the mass of the Spanish people had remained staunchly Catholic. Holy Week, for example, was celebrated with all its ancient splendor at

Seville, and religious processions filed through the streets of Barcelona and Valencia.

The disturbances of the first third of the nineteenth century were disastrous to Spanish culture. Important archives were despoiled, as when Napoleon ordered many of the papers of Simancas carried to Paris, and the English burned the episcopal archives of Astorga. In 1807 Charles IV had suppressed the eleven lesser universities, and the Cortes of Cádiz in 1810 closed all of them. At that time they were deserted anyway, since most of the students were in arms. The University of Salamanca, however, was reorganized in 1814, and the reformers also proposed the creation of a Central University in Madrid, pensions to enable students to study within or outside Spain, and competition as the sole basis for selection as a university teacher.

With the return of Ferdinand VII a radical change took place in educational plans. In 1818 a decree established the conservative plan of 1771. After the Revolution of 1820 the plan of 1807 was restored, and the Central University at Madrid was created in the Imperial College, from which the Jesuits had been expelled. Once again the vicissitudes of politics changed the situation. In 1824 Calomarde established the plan bearing his name. Twelve universities were recognized, and a new university was created in the Canary Islands. Higher education was divided into three periods above the first stage—the bachelor's degree, the licentiate, and the doctorate.

Secondary education continued to be very deficient. In 1809 Jovellanos published a plan for public education in which he stressed secondary education as a necessary complement of primary instruction. Quintana had already suggested that secondary education should be preparatory for later specialization, and he proposed provincial universities. After the reaction a new regulation in 1825 created provincial secondary and normal schools.

Primary education was neglected at the beginning of the war with the French. The Institute of Pestalozzi had closed. The Constitution of 1812 provided for the establishment of schools in all communities—an aspiration that has not yet been fully realized—and Quintana's report of 1813 recommended a free, general, uniform, and unified primary system. In 1825 four categories of schools were established: in Madrid and provincial capitals, in district communities of over 1000 citizens, in communities of from 500 to 1000 citizens, and in communities of from 50 to 500 citizens.

A number of historians were active during this period. Diego Clemencin (1765–1834), an erudite Murcian, became a minister in the cabinet of Martínez de la Rosa under Ferdinand VII. In addition to valuable translations, he wrote *Comentario al Quijote* and *Elogio de la Reina Católica Doña Isabel.* The count of Toreno (1786–1846) wrote *Historia del levantamiento, guerra y revolución de España,* an able history of considerable literary merit. Antonio Alcalá Galiano (1789–1865), his contemporary, was the author of *La Historia de España desde los tiempos primivitos hasta el reinado de Isabel II.* Sebastian Miñano (1779–1845) satirized the Constitution of 1812 and wrote an eleven-volume geographical and statistical dictionary of the peninsula for which he was severely attacked.

Such philosophers as existed were strongly under foreign influence. Outstanding among them was Jaime Luciano Balmes (1810–48). He founded *Pensamiento de la nación.* A dedicated teacher, he wrote many philosophical works and attained an international reputation as the greatest of the Catholic philosophers of contemporary Spain. The cultivation of the exact sciences received a new impetus during the constitutional period. The academies of engineers and artillery stressed mathematics, and numerous treatises were published.

Romanticism was the great vogue of the period in literature. It entered Spain through France, introduced, perhaps, by political émigrés. French classicism also had its followers, one of the notable being Manuel José Quintana (1772–1857), who outlived his age as a master of the lyric. An ardent liberal, he served as secretary to the Central Junta and fell under the displeasure of Ferdinand VII. Center of a literary circle, director of education (1821–23), and tutor of Isabel II, who made him a senator, from 1837 to 1857 he lived in retirement as a famous literary figure. He composed odes and cold, declamatory dramas. Alberto Lista y Aragon (1775–1848) was another whose poetry was classic in its coldness and affectation.

Angel Saavedra y Ramirez de Baquedano, duke of Rivas (1791–1865), was a native of Córdoba. Wounded in the War of Independence and persecuted as a liberal, he went into exile. His talents as a dramatist surpassed those of all his contemporaries. His famous work, *Don Álvaro,* was the most characteristic of the romantic plays. He not only used the motifs of the classic theater, but also introduced into Spain the contemporary romantic tendencies. Perhaps the leading essayist and dramatist of the period—a man with a European reputation—was Mariano de Larra (1809–37), widely known under his pseudonym "Figaro." His works were satirical and embittered. José Zorrilla (1817–93), one of the leaders of the Romantic movement, wrote the still popular play *Don Juan Tenorio* (1844) on the theme of Don Juan. Manuel Briton de los Herreros (1796–1873), the director of the National Library and secretary of the Spanish Academy, produced 175 works. A suave satirist, his comedies of manners were realistic and humorous. Antonio Gil (1796–1861) and Ventura de la Vega (1807–65) were also important dramatists. Zarate was a neoclassicist. Ventura de la Vega's major work was *El Hombre del mundo,* a precursor of the high comedy which later came into vogue. José de Espronceda (1808–42) was a revolutionary as well as the most significant of the romantic poets. His *A Jarifa en una orgía* is a somber, turbulent, lyrical work. The noble *El Diablo mundo,* inspired by the legend of Faust, remained incomplete.

Catalan literature also enjoyed a revival during the early nineteenth century. Most of the Catalan authors wrote in Castilian, but Buenaventura Carlos Aribau (1798–1862) greatly stimulated the renaissance of Catalan as a literary language. He also encouraged work in classic Castilian and was founder of the famous *Biblioteca de autores españoles.* In 1834 he published in Catalan his famous *Oda a la patria.*

José Alvarez (1767–1827), perhaps the most notable sculptor of the period, followed the style of Canova. One of his most notable works was "Ganymede," and others included statues of Maria Luisa and Maria Isabel de Braganza. José Ginés (1768–1823) was a baroque sculptor who outlived the vogue of that style. Damian Campeny (1771–1855), a pupil of Canova, became director of the School of Noble Arts and was named sculptor to Ferdinand in 1819.

Romanticism also influenced Spanish painting. In the reaction and protest against neoclassicism, Vicente López (1772–1850) was the most important of Goya's successors. He became court artist for Ferdinand VII in 1815 and painted well-known portraits of Ferdinand VII, Calomarde, and most of the royal family.

Some painters revealed the deep impression that Goya had made on his contemporaries. The Valencians Asensio Juliá and Leonardo Aleuza y Nieto (1807–43) were both under his influence. The first Romantic painter in Spain was Jenaro Pérez Villamil (1807–54), who became court painter in 1850. Two other romantic artists who acquired reputations that have persisted are Antonio Maria Esquivel (1806–57) and José Gutiérrez de la Vega.

Spanish music became more subject to foreign influences, as the tonadilla decayed and the popularity of Italian melodies increased. Patriotic hymns were characteristic of the revolutionary period. The "Hymn of Riego" was composed in 1820 by José María de Reart y Capons and Ramón Carnicer composed a "Hymn to Liberty." Juan Crisóstomo de Arriaga (1806–26) was a precocious musician of Bilbao, called the Spanish Mozart. He studied with his father and at the age of eleven had already completed several compositions. In 1822, he emigrated to Paris, where Cherubini acclaimed him as one of the most inspired musicians he had known. Ramón Carnicer y Batlle (1789–1855), who gained renown as an orchestra conductor, composed a symphony and several operas.

CHAPTER XXVII

The Failure of Amadeo and the First Republic

After the deposition of Isabel II in 1868 the revolutionaries still had to consolidate their victory. On October 8 the revolutionary junta transferred its authority to the duke of Torre to organize a provisional government, and the constituent cortes were convoked for February 1869. Already there were signs of disagreement, though this was papered over by the manifesto to the voters on November 2, which preserved the fiction of revolutionary solidarity. But some of the Democrats, for example, insisted on a republic and refused to sign the manifesto, which they considered too monarchic in tone. The dissident Republicans issued their own manifesto and held a separate meeting, at which Emilio Castelar urged the immediate establishment of a republic. In several places there were republican revolts.

Despite all this, the elections, when they came, were relatively peaceful. The Progressives obtained the greatest number of seats and the Unionists constituted the strongest minority, with the Republicans forming the opposition.

The revolutionaries were optimistic when the constituent cortes assembled. Confronted with a difficult task, they had to extend an amnesty for penalties imposed on the press. A loan of 100,000,000 reales was necessary to permit the government to function, and although they had promised to abolish the draft, they needed 25,000 men in the army, a decision which aroused violent opposition. Finally, they had to draft a new constitution, and a commission was appointed to undertake the task, which, twenty-five days later, presented a document to the cortes on March 30, 1869. It was approved, after a torrent of eloquence, on June 1, by a vote of 214 to 55.

The Constitution of 1869 consecrated individual and political rights, and the mixed rights of freedom of thought, assembly, association, and petition. It established a monarchy based on national sovereignty. A bicameral legislature was provided, with both chambers elective. The king was inviolable, but his ministers were responsible to the cortes. Judicial unity was established but the ayuntamientos and provincial deputations were extended greater independence.

Debate on the religious issue became impassioned. The Democrats proposed freedom of religion and the separation of church and state but the factions on the right were staunch in their defense of religious unity. The religious article provided that the nation would maintain the Catholic faith, and the public or private exercise of their faith was guaranteed to all foreigners and to any Spaniards who professed a religion other than Catholicism.

The deputies had approved of a monarchy, but there was immediate discord over the designation of the monarch. Carlism had reappeared in Navarre, and the supporters of the duke of Montpensier opposed the exclusion of all branches of the Bourbons. General Serrano, named regent in June 1869, appointed Prim, who had strong support in the chamber, as premier. He had been a power in the revolution, a pacifying force in the constituent cortes, and was now the most important political figure in Spain; to consolidate his influence he had appointed a dozen military men to high offices. As a result the Unionists accused him of establishing militarism, fearful that the Progressives would reach an understanding with the Republicans.

There were disturbances in Málaga, Seville, and Alicante. Republicans had greatly increased their influence, which inclined toward a federal republic, advocated by them in the constituent cortes. Now they began to conclude pacts in the various regions. This activity inspired a good deal of violence from Catalonia to Andalusia. Federalism was proclaimed in a number of places. When the constituent cortes reassembled in October 1869, the government proposed the suspension of the constitutional guarantees and martial law. Prim maintained stability in the government with an iron will; he knew where he was going. While the Unionists continued to support Montpensier and the Republicans proposed the exclusion of the Bourbons, Prim maintained a strict neutrality, and Spain remained a monarchy without a king.

The candidate of the Unionists, based on the claims of his wife to the throne, was Antonio de Orleans, duke of Montpensier, who had participated in the revolution of 1868 and was warmly supported by Admiral Topete and General Serrano. But both Prim and Napoleon III opposed his choice as king, and his hopes for the throne were finally wrecked by a duel which he fought with Prince Henry and in which the latter was killed. Both Carlos and Prince Alfonso, son of Isabel II, were potential candidates for the crown, but they were unpopular with the revolutionaries.

General Prim had his own candidates for the throne. Inspired with the ideal of Iberian unity, he became interested first in Ferdinand of Coburg, consort of the late queen of Portugal. In July 1870 Prim offered him the crown, but he did not appear greatly interested in it. Prim was anxious to find a royal family sufficiently liberal to arouse the sympathy of the revolutionaries and invited Amadeo of Savoy, duke of Aosta, to accept the throne, but he refused. Thomas of Savoy, duke of Genoa, also had warm support, but his mother feared for her son's life in a country as unruly as Spain and exerted every effort to dissuade him from accepting the crown.

Espartero, duke of La Victoria, was extremely popular as a candidate. His selection was urged in the press and in demonstrations by his partisans, but the government was not very enthusiastic. Prim was cautious. He did not reject Espartero as a candidate, hoping, perhaps, to use him if the other candidates disappeared. He asked the old duke if he would accept if the constituent cortes chose him as king. Espartero replied simply: "My many years and my lack of health would not permit me to discharge the duties of the office."

The most celebrated candidate was Prince Leopold of Hohenzollern-Sigmaringen. Bismarck inspired the German press to urge the candidacy of this prince, though Napoleon III had indicated his opposition to a Prussian prince for national and patriotic reasons. Prim entrusted a young Spanish diplomat with the task of ascertaining the attitude of the prince, his father, and William I, king of Prussia. The negotiations, conducted in great secrecy, were known to but few people. Bismarck sent two agents to Madrid to propose an alliance of Prussia and Spain against France. The Spanish cabinet rejected the proposal. Then, after continued consultations, Bismarck, with the aid of the crown prince of Prussia and the Portuguese wife of Leopold, succeeded in persuading him to accept the Spanish crown.

Prim had kept the French ambassador in ignorance of these negotiations, but when he could no longer dissimulate, the alarm of Napoleon III increased. In Prim's absence his agent announced Leopold's acceptance to Rivero, minister of the Interior, thence it was finally reported to José Ignacio Escobar, editor of *La Época*. The secret was out. Prim exclaimed, "Lost labor and God grant that it may not be more," in announcing to the cabinet that the Hohenzollern prince had accepted the crown. He then convoked the cortes for July 20 to elect the German candidate.

Napoleon III immediately tried to prevent the choice of Leopold as king of Spain, but Leopold renounced his acceptance on July 12. The consideration of the candidacy of Prince Leopold was used by Bismarck to provoke the Franco-Prussian war. Bismarck had insisted that Leopold be a candidate. Prim was unaware of being an instrument in the hands of the German chancellor to force Napoleon III to demand the assurance of the king of Prussia that the German prince would not again be a candidate. When the demand was refused, Bismarck so altered the text of the Prussian sovereign's telegram that it appeared a refusal to receive the French ambassador, Benedetti. The national pride of France was offended and the Franco-Prussian war resulted.

Nevertheless, the failure to find a king in Germany was shortly compensated by the acceptance of the Spanish crown by Amadeo of Savoy in October 1870. Prim was jubilant. In November the cortes proceeded to vote on the candidates. Amadeo received 191 votes, Montpensier 26, Espartero 8, Alfonso of Bourbon 2, and 60 deputies cast their ballots for a federal republic. A commission was sent to Florence to offer the crown to Amadeo. The prophecy of a Progressive who had declared "We will have a king when Don Juan wishes and the one he wants" had been fulfilled.

Meanwhile, the revolution and the search for a Spanish monarch had revived the Carlist cause. Carlos Maria Isidro and the princess of Beira had three sons. Carlos Luis, count of Montemolín, renounced the throne and ceded his claim to his brother Juan, who had married the Archduchess Beatrice, daughter of Francis IV of Modena. Juan had two sons, Carlos de Borbón y Este, later known as Carlos VII, and Alfonso. Juan de Borbón had advanced ideas and led an errant existence, annoying even the princess of Beira.

After the unfortunate attempt at revolution at San Carlos de la Rápita, Carlos Luis, count of Montemolín, again renounced his pretensions to the Spanish throne, but shortly thereafter he and his brother Ferdinand withdrew their renunciations. Juan, however, refused to surrender his hopes. He tried to present himself as a democratic and constitutional king of Spain. In 1860 Carlos Luis (known to Carlists as Carlos VI), Ferdinand, and Maria Carolina died, a blow to the Carlist cause, since Juan de Borbón was the antithesis of the traditional absolutist program.

The real leader of the Carlist cause was now Maria Teresa of Braganza, princess de Beira. She was masculine in her vigor despite her age.

In 1864 she directed a letter to the Spanish people which concluded with "Long life to Carlos VII," then sixteen. Juan de Borbón later conferred with his son in Paris and abdicated in favor of Carlos VII in October 1868. Carlos now assumed the leadership of the party. In July, he published a manifesto to the Spanish people, but the government was able to thwart every Carlist conspiracy.

On December 27, as Prim was on his way to the Ministry of War, several men fired on the coach in which he was riding. He was wounded in the left arm and died on December 30, 1870. Amadeo of Savoy, who was en route to undertake the rule of Spain at the age of twenty-six, landed at Cartagena in January 1871 and went immediately to Madrid, where he took the oath to the Constitution of 1869 and appointed his first ministry, under Serrano. The king then went to Alicante to meet Queen Maria Victoria, who was young and attractive. His political strength was provided by the generals who supported him, for he was generally disliked by the populace because of his father's recent seizure of the Papal States from Pope Pius IX.

Two parties now appeared in Spanish politics. The Progressive party disappeared, and its right-wing members formed the Constitutional party with the Unionists. This party defended the Constitution of 1869 and recognized the duke of La Torre as its leader and Sagasta as its political chief. The left-wing Progressives and the monarchical Democrats formed the Radical party under the leadership of Ruiz Zorrilla. The Republicans, the Carlists, the moderates, and the Alfonsists opposed the Constitutional party and the Radical party, which supported the government.

Amadeo's government was based on a coalition of Progressives and Unionists. His principal opponents were the Carlists and the Republicans, united only in their desire to overthrow the dynasty. In the elections for the cortes the coalition obtained a majority, with the Carlists forming the most numerous minority. In his first address to the cortes, Amadeo I outlined a program of government to which he loyally adhered. He promised to rule Spain as long as he retained the confidence of the people, and he subsequently tried to maintain a neutral position in the party strife which surrounded him.

Two political leaders were important in the reign of Amadeo I. They had been friends and political colleagues for many years, but the partisan leadership converted them into implacable enemies. Ruiz Zorrilla inclined to the left. Sagasta, on the other hand, remained a Progressive. Ruiz Zorrilla always remained a liberal. As a deputy in 1858 he formed an intimate friendship with Sagasta, and in 1864 he became a revolutionary as an ardent champion of the Progressives. A brilliant orator and a partisan of a democratic monarchy, he was entrusted with the formation of a short-lived ministry after the resignation of Serrano. His government proved beneficial for Spain, but the politicians were either Zorrillistas or Sagastinos and were irreconcilably divided.

Amadeo I had two personal advisers at that time. One was Morliani, a Spanish senator, sent with him to Spain because of his familiarity with Spanish politics. Morliani advised that the radicals be called to power, but the other intimate of Amadeo, Dragonetti, his secretary, favored the Liberal Union. Consequently, Sagasta then accepted the responsibility of government, although opposed by the Democrats.

Amadeo urged all factions to formulate a program, but they were interested in politics more than they were in ideals, covering their personal ambitions with vacuous proposals and sonorous phrases.

The next ministry was formed by Serrano, duke of La Torre, but the Radicals and Republicans uncompromisingly withdrew from the chamber, and fearing revolution, the government asked for the suspension of constitutional guarantees. Amadeo refused, Serrano resigned in June 1872, and Ruiz Zorrilla, who had led the opposition, was forced to undertake the last ministry of Amadeo I.

The Carlist pretender, Carlos VII, had protested the selection of Amadeo as king of Spain, and the leader of his followers in the cortes, Cándido Nocedal, a former minister of Isabel II, was anxious to advance Carlos' interests by legal means, but the militant faction in the party urged civil war. During the winter of 1871–72 the Carlist plans failed, and the military faction in the party persuaded Carlos, now titled duke of Madrid, to resort to violence to gain the throne. In April 1872 the Carlists in Navarre, Aragon, Vizcaya, and Guipúzcoa rebelled. What they lacked in arms and money, they made up in enthusiasm. They had no military commanders as in the old days, but the Basques, the Navarrese, and the Catalans sustained their cause. The duke of La Torre had led two divisions into Vizcaya, where, fearing the superior forces of Serrano, the Carlists negotiated the Agreement of Amoribieta in May 1872. The terms of the convention were honorable for the Carlists, and the Deputation of Vizcaya was granted the right to assemble under the oak of Guernica according to *fuero* to arrange payment of the expenses of the war.

This convention, however, proved to be only a truce, for the Carlists continued the war in Catalonia, Navarre, and Guipúzcoa and their guerrilla bands operated in other provinces. By January 1873 the Basque provinces and Navarre were again in revolt.

With the Carlist menace still poised in northern Spain, the Republicans more aggressive, and the Alfonsists increasing their adherents among the upper classes, Amadeo I's position daily became more insupportable. The very parties which had invited him to occupy the Spanish throne were divided into factions and were more interested in their own political advantage than they were in the national welfare. Indeed, the Carlists were not really strong and the Alfonsists were just beginning to win their influence, but it was necessary for both parties to attack Amadeo to prepare for the restoration of either branch of the Bourbons.

Both the Sagastinos and the Unionists opposed the cabinet of Ruiz Zorrilla. The Republicans, allied with the radicals, awaited their opportunity to seize control of the nation and destroy the monarchy. The government sought to regenerate the country by the further extension of liberty, but this served only to stimulate the popular clamor. On July 18, as Amadeo I returned to the palace about eleven o'clock in the evening, an attempt was made to assassinate him. Fortunately, only a carriage horse was wounded. The assailants, who were arrested, proved to be Republicans. Amadeo, however, was undismayed by the attempt on his life and made a trip through the northern provinces, where he was warmly received.

The elections for the new cortes were held in August 1872, and the resulting new Congress was markedly *Zorrillista* in character. Ruiz Zorrilla, strengthened by the support of the cortes, proposed the dissolution of the Corps of Artillery. Amadeo refused to sign the decree, acceding only when he was urged by the government. Finally, on February 11, 1873, Amadeo I relinquished the Spanish crown.

He had ruled Spain for two difficult years. During that time he had tried sincerely to fulfill his obligations as a constitutional monarch. His supporters, however, had been unable to demonstrate the same abnegation of their own personal ambitions. The antidynastic forces accused Amadeo I of being a foreign king, but they forgot that Spain had not had a truly national sovereign since Ferdinand and Isabel. The king was assailed for the very traits with which he might have won the affection of the Spanish people. His modesty and simplicity were ridiculed, and his amorous adventures were severely condemned by politicians who had conveniently converted themselves into moralists.

Amadeo had been chosen as king by Juan Prim. The death of the general removed a powerful counselor and was a severe blow to the stability of the throne at a time when his support was most vital. Indeed, Amadeo was inexperienced. He understood neither political intrigue nor the customs of his people. He tried to remain loyal to the constitution, but his position was rendered insupportable by the volatile personal politics and the individual ambition of both his friends and his enemies.

The two chambers of the cortes met in a single assembly and by a vote of 258 to 32 approved the following proposition: "The National Assembly reassumes all the powers and declares the Republic as the form of government, leaving to the constituent cortes the organization of this form of government."

Estanislao Figueras presided over the first republican ministry, which had been established by a cortes with a monarchist majority. Two powers struggled for control of Spain, the government and the assembly. While the monarchists who had accepted and served the republic supported Martos, who had been elected president of the Assembly, the old Republicans were led by Figueras, Pí y Margall, and Castelar and controlled the cabinet. The policy of the "Republic for the Republicans" was approved by the assembly, and those who had long professed republican ideals were given the responsibilities. A new government strongly republican and still under the presidency of Figueras was organized.

Francisco Pí y Margall as minister of the Interior held the decisive position to restrain the radicals and avert the attacks of Martos. He was a Catalan, of a family of modest means, and a staunch devotee of federalism. He acquired a profound influence in his own day and many later disciples reflected his views.

The constituent cortes assembled on June 1. A week later, the deputies approved a democratic federal republic, whereupon Pí y Margall was elected president of the executive power and minister of the Interior. Many problems confronted him. The civil war increased as a threat in the northern provinces. The Alfonsists were intriguing. The Cantonalists were preparing to disown the authority of the central government, and the country was in an anarchic state. The impatient Federalists tried to establish their system of government before the constitution had been approved. Regional movements were developing in Barcelona, Málaga, and Seville, and the Anarchists were active in Alcoy, where they shot the Republican alcalde. Under these circumstances the cortes ordered the government to proceed with energy against those who disturbed public order and dishonored the republic.

Nicolas Salmerón y Alonso was elected president when Pí resigned. Salmerón had held a chair of philosophy in the Central University. He soon became affiliated with the Democratic party, and when the revolution of 1868 began, he became a member of the revolutionary junta. He was a member of the cortes of 1871 and 1872, where he won a reputation as an orator of great ability.

As president Salmerón was energetic. He was determined to restore order both among the Republicans and the Carlists. Revolutions had occurred in Valencia, Castellón, the greater part of Andalusia, and in Toledo, Salamanca, and Bejar. The canton at Cartagena had organized a committee of public safety, later replaced by a cantonal cabinet. Salmerón therefore sent General Martínez de Campos to restore order in Valencia, while General Pavía was ordered to restore the authority of the central government in Andalusia. Pavía took Córdoba, and shortly thereafter Cádiz, Loja, and Granada submitted. In Castile, Salamanca and Bejar were restored to normalcy, and even the Carlist attacks were repelled.

Only Cartagena continued to resist. The frigate "Vitoria" was sent to Alicante, while at Torrevieja the funds of the customs office were seized. Meanwhile, General Contreras undertook another piratical foray. Leaving Cartagena with the frigates "Vitoria" and "Almansa" he bombarded Almería in July 1873 and then proceeded toward Málaga. The Prussian man-of-war, the "Frederick Karl," forced the release of the crew members of the "Vigilante," as well as stopped the frigates of Contreras and temporarily detained him. The frigates were surrendered to the English and taken to Gibraltar. In the meantime, the rebels had undertaken an expedition through Murcia, where they collected considerable booty in Orihuela. Contreras then organized a force of 2000 men and marched toward Chinchilla, where he was decisively defeated by the government troops under General Salcedo.

Sentences of death were imposed on the captive rebels. Although popular opinion supported the extreme penalty, Salmerón had defended its abolition. He was firm in his resolve and refused to sign the order for its imposition. As a result, he resigned the presidency.

Emilio Castelar, a representative of the extreme right wing of the Republican party, was named president of the executive power in September. He had abandoned a legal career to devote himself to literature. For several years he wrote for reviews and newspapers. After serving as professor of history in the Central University of Madrid, and founding *La Democracia,* an openly antidynastic newspaper—defending an individualistic republicanism—he was persecuted for his views and lost his professorship. When the revolution of 1866 was suppressed, he was condemned to death and fled to Paris, where he resided until the revolution of 1868. Upon returning to Spain he undertook active propaganda on behalf of republican ideals, continuing to be a unitary republican, but he had to subordinate his own views to prevent a schism in republican ranks. Salmerón had already indicated that the right wing of the Republican party was the only one which could save the regime. Although Castelar was determined to exercise a kind of dictatorship which would reestablish peace and restrain the excesses of the demagogues, he was confronted by a gigantic task. He had to restrain local disturbances, suppress the cantonal dissension, and continue the struggle against the Carlists, and these goals could only be reached with the cooperation of the conservatives.

The revolutionaries in Cartagena could not maintain their independence with their own resources alone, but they continued their piratical raids. They attacked Torrevieja and Aguelas and bombarded Alicante. Finally, Rear Admiral Lobo blockaded Cartagena. The rebels, however, evaded the blockading fleet, attacked Valencia, and returned with much booty to Cartagena in November 1873.

The talent of Castelar as a statesman was soon tested in the Virginius affair, in which Castelar's tact and decisive action avoided a conflict with the United States. The Spanish warship "Tornado" seized the filibustering steamship "Virginius," which contained a number of rebel Cubans. Joaquín Jovellar, captain general of Cuba, ordered thirty-seven members of the crew and twelve passengers of the "Virginius" shot (November 1873). The American minister, General Dan Sickles, protested that American citizens had been seized and shot. Castelar resolved the diplomatic incident by agreeing that the "Virginius" would be returned, Spain would salute the American flag, a judicial investigation would be undertaken, and the matter of indemnity would be resolved by arbitration. It was agreed that if the ship had no right to fly the American flag or had been active in sustaining the Cuban revolt, the United States would make reparation to Spain.

Meanwhile, the Republicans of the left and center had been indignant at the strong policy of Castelar. The three former presidents began to attack him, and when the cortes reassembled in January 1874, General Pavía, fearing the defeat of the government, proposed that the cortes be suspended. General Pavía, a Republican devoted to Castelar, now contemplated a coup d'état. However, Castelar did not approve of military intervention in civil affairs and rejected this proposal. The session of the cortes was tempestuous. Castelar, attacked by the Federalists, eloquently defended his policies. Nevertheless, he was defeated by a vote of 120 to 100, whereupon he presented his resignation.

Pavía was aware that the elements of the left had agreed to elect

Eduardo Palenca as president. He sent an armed force to the congressional hall, and his civil guards cleared the chamber of the protesting deputies, forcibly dissolving the last genuinely republican assembly. The First Republic had ceased to exist.

The Carlist cause had been stimulated by the proclamation of the republic. The liberal army was undisciplined and even Martínez de Campos was unable to restore order in it. In July 1873 Carlos VII appeared in the Basque country and took an oath to observe the *fueros* of Vizcaya at Guernica. The Carlists raided the Basque provinces and Navarre at will. They blockaded Bilbao and threatened Vitoria. Then General Moriones was restored to the command of the liberal armies and reanimated their spirit. The Carlist troops, inspired by the presence of Carlos, fought bravely and the battles were bitterly contested. The liberal forces on the Catalan front had continued to be plagued with lack of discipline, but finally Castelar found in General Turón a man capable of restoring discipline, just as dissension appeared in the Carlist ranks. In Aragon, Valencia, and Murcia, the Carlists were favored by the appearance of cantonalism. They occupied Segorbe and Sagunto and raided Alicante and Murcia.

The party supporting the Bourbons appeared to be extinguished by the revolution of 1868, but its leaders patiently awaited their hour. Isabel II had protested her loss of the crown in a manifesto from Paris and throughout 1869 her supporters conspired in Biarritz. Maria Cristina believed that Isabel II should abdicate and tried to persuade her daughter of the necessity of that step, but she hesitated to make that decision and established herself in Paris. Finally, Isabel decided to abdicate and to transmit her claims to the Spanish crown to her son Alfonso, prince of Asturias.

Prince Alfonso, born on November 28, 1857, was only eleven years old when his mother was dethroned. He had accompanied her into exile and had witnessed the discord between his parents. Maria Cristina had tried to reconcile her two daughters and to invest her son-in-law, the duke of Montpensier, with the leadership of the Alfonsist party, but the duke had been a candidate for the Spanish throne and was not popular with the supporters of Alfonso. Nevertheless, after tedious negotiations, Maria Cristina succeeded in having Montpensier chosen as chief of the party, and he was established as regent during the minority of the prince. Alfonso was pledged to wed his cousin Mercedes, the duke's daughter.

Alfonso, the hope of the legitimist party, was of medium height and intelligent in appearance. He had studied in Paris until the city was threatened during the Franco-Prussian war, when he moved to Switzerland with the royal family to continue his preparatory education; the Theresianum in Vienna was chosen for his advanced education. There he became acquainted with his cousin, Mercedes, daughter of the duke of Montpensier, in 1872. His regard for her explains his acquiescence in the duke's leadership of his party.

By the end of 1872 the breach between Isabel and her brother-in-law, Montpensier, had widened. She finally decided to entrust the leadership of the Alfonsist party to an émigré, Antonio Cánovas del Castillo, despite her personal antipathy to him. He was granted full authority in August 1873.

General Pavía had effected his coup d'état as a result of the cooperation of the constitutionalists and the radicals and with the patriotic intention of restraining both extremes and restoring order in the nation. The republic had, in effect, already perished, but the constitutionalists and radicals alone formed the new ministry under the presidency of Serrano and retained the name and form of a unitary republic. It had to resort to dictatorial methods to govern. Constitutional guarantees were suspended and the Law of Public Order of April 1870 was invoked.

Although the cantonal dissidence had been suppressed, the Carlist threat was daily increasing. General López Domínguez had subjected Cartagena, and the rebels had fled in the frigate "Numancia." Carlos VII, however, was determined to capture Bilbao, an important city and port. With the enthusiasm that had led them to try to take Bilbao before, the Carlists again besieged the city. The liberal forces rushed to the aid of the beleaguered city, in which the civilian population suffered severely when it was bombarded by the Carlists. In this crisis Serrano hastened north to replace General Moriones. The battle raged four days around the heights of Somorrostro. The liberal fleet moved into the creek of Bilbao to support the land forces, but they failed to pierce the Carlist lines and the siege continued.

A new army was formed by the government under the command of General Manuel de la Concha. Unable to withstand the combined forces of the liberals, the Carlists retired on May 1 and the republican army entered Bilbao. The Carlists were then forced on the defensive. A furious battle was fought at Montemuro, in which Concha was mortally wounded. Encouraged by this success the Carlists besieged Pamplona, where they suffered defeat on December 10. The liberal forces, however, had lost Olot to the Carlists in Catalonia. On the central front the Carlists had captured Albacete and Liria and made raids into the province of Cuenca before returning to Valencia.

The plans for the restoration of Prince Alfonso were being carefully laid meanwhile by the patient Cánovas del Castillo, whose greatest obstacles were raised by members of his own party. Since it was necessary to obtain the support of a military leader of some prestige, though Cánovas did not like the traditional Spanish militarism, he tried cautiously to arouse military sympathy. He still, however, counted more heavily on the political and legal activity of civilian leaders, but intrigue was active in the court of Isabel II and served only to impede his preparations. Marfori believed that Francisco de Asís should intervene. Alfonso had concluded his studies in Vienna and returned to Paris, where Cánovas visited him in August 1874. The prince traveled during that summer, visiting London, Belgium, and Germany, and in October entered the Royal College of Infantry and Cavalry at Sandhurst, as Cánovas had advised him to become familiar with the civil freedom and constitutional government of England. He issued a manifesto from Sandhurst, thanking his admirers, discussing constitutional government, liberty, and justice and declaring "whatever may be my fate, I will neither cease to be a good Spaniard nor, like all my ancestors, a good Catholic, nor, as a man of the century, truly liberal." Drafted by Cánovas, this manifesto constituted his governmental program.

Although Cánovas was opposed to a pronouncement several generals, including Arsenio Martínez de Campos and Luis Dabán, without his knowledge conspired to proclaim Alfonso. In Sagunto, on December 29, 1874, Martínez de Campos addressed the troops, proclaimed Alfonso king, and the soldiers responded with *vivas* for Alfonso XII. Martínez de Campos advised Joaquín Jovellar, commander of the central army, of the events at Sagunto. The garrison of Madrid already sympathized with the restoration, and the army of the north was little disposed to defend the republic. Cánovas del Castillo, annoyed at the turn of events, was forced to take advantage of his opportunity. The idea of a Bourbon restoration gained momentum and new adherents. Primo de Rivera, captain general of Madrid, obtained the resignations of the ministers and took Cánovas to the Ministry of the Interior, where he was faced with the problem of selecting a cabinet. He chose a ministry regency, which was established on December 31, but he retained its guidance as president. Martínez de Campos was rewarded with a promotion to lieutenant general.

These events were not immediately communicated to Alfonso XII, who was on vacation in a London hotel, in a modest room on the third floor. On December 30 he arrived in Paris, and after dinner prepared to go to the theater. Before he left he received a note which said, "Sire,

Your Majesty was proclaimed King yesterday by the Spanish army. Long live the King." When he returned to his hotel he heard the details of the proclamation. Cánovas del Castillo telegraphed Isabel the following day and congratulated her and Alfonso on the triumph which had been "attained without a struggle or the shedding of blood."

On January 5 Alfonso XII declared to a London *Times* correspondent, "I am not King of a party. The ministry is composed of men of all opinions. It is liberal and constitutional, as they have taught me to be, and I am really liberal and constitutional." Alfonso was joyfully received in Madrid on January 14.

Spain had restored the rule of the Bourbons after having been unable to make either a truly constitutional regime or a republic effective. The fault lay in the lack of experience in the practical application of constitutional government. Each nation has to adapt its government to the political experience of its people. The Spaniards had been inspired to imitate the French for over three-quarters of a century. They had learned to follow leaders and principles, but both leaders and factions were too individualistic to subordinate their own political principles to those of a more impersonal party. They took their principles literally and in their desire to implement them resorted to bullets rather than ballots.

CHAPTER XXVIII

The Reign of Alfonso XII, 1875–85

During the ten-year reign of Alfonso XII, some stability returned to Spain, largely due to the work of Alfonso's prime minister, Cánovas del Castillo. He managed to effect a coalition between his own Conservative party and the Liberals, and together the two parties built up support for the government. Although enemies of this moderate administration continued to conspire against it, Cánovas kept them in restraint.

The dominant personage in the restored regime, Antonio Cánovas del Castillo, had directed the Alfonsist party and attempted to place Alfonso XII on the throne without the intervention of the army. He remained the leader of the party and became the first minister of Alfonso XII. Born in Málaga in 1828, Cánovas in 1845 went to Madrid. Through a nephew of Leopoldo O'Donnell, he met the general, who wanted someone to arrange his papers, and the two men soon formed a close friendship. Cánovas joined the Puritan faction of Joaquín Pacheco, participated in the overthrow of Espartero, and composed the manifesto of Manzanario. As a reward for his revolutionary services, he was named the principal official in the secretaryship of state and was sent to Rome, where he remained from 1855 to 1857.

When he returned, he was named civil governor of the province of Cádiz, and two years later he was made subsecretary of the Ministry of the Interior. He served as minister of Colonies in 1865–66, and after the revolution of 1868 was elected to the cortes, where he built the nucleus of the future Conservative party. Cánovas has been accused of being doctrinaire, but neither his erudition nor his theories paralyzed his realism in decisive moments. His greatest errors were committed in later years when his faculties were less keen. He held that the failure to recognize historical reality was "the greatest infirmity that politicians could suffer."

Although Alfonso XII had assumed the crown, Spain was still in the throes of civil war. Carlos, who had refused to accept the restoration, was confident of ultimate victory. He was supported by many Spaniards, and his successes had increased his confidence. His Bourbon relatives flocked to his assistance. The most important of these was Alfonso of Bourbon, count of Caserta, brother of the last Neapolitan king, who left his haven in the Papal States to support his cousin. And many others sought to restore their fortunes through the triumph of the Carlists. Carlos VII had a modest court at Estella, where his adherents assembled. Alfonso XII, however, was encouraged by the defection of Cabrera, who entered into negotiations with him in 1875, although the mass of the Carlists did not follow Cabrera. The Carlist leader was recognized as count of Morella and marquis of El Zer and given the rank of captain general, but he died in Paris without enjoying these advantages or ever returning to Spain.

The government concentrated 200,000 men against the principal Carlist center in the north, and Alfonso XII joined the army in January 1875. The Carlists made a supreme effort in the attack on Lacar and fought with such spirit that the Alfonsists were demoralized and forced to retreat. In February the Alfonsists decided to suspend hostilities, and Alfonso XII returned to Madrid. Carlos VII took the oath as king before the Vizcayans under the tree of Guernica in July, and two days later swore to observe the *fueros* of Guipúzcoa. His attitude toward the traditional liberties of the Basques explains in large measure their loyal support of the Carlist cause. They had not forgiven the advocates of a unitary form of government for the suppression of their ancient *fueros*.

Martínez de Campos now sought to attract the Carlists to the liberal cause, and to effect such a policy, reprisals were abandoned and negotiations were undertaken to reduce the outrages of the Carlists against prisoners. Finally, the government decided to bombard the Basque ports held by the Carlists, but the maritime campaign to intimidate the Basques was futile, although the Alfonsists were encouraged in June by the victory of Treviño. An indecisive battle was fought at Castellón de la Plana, but the Carlist leader, Dorregaray, still predicted that if he had 10,000 rifles, he would guarantee to be in Madrid in a month and a half. In Catalonia Savalls negotiated with Martínez de Campos. The details of their interview were never divulged, but Martínez de Campos marched through Catalonia without being attacked. To stimulate the Carlists, Savalls promulgated the *fueros* of Catalonia. Lizarraga was besieged in the Seo de Urgel by Martínez de Campos and, after a spirited resistance, was forced to capitulate.

The government determined to end the Carlist war once and for all.

Two great armies were organized under Generals Quesada and Martínez de Campos. Carlos VII also prepared for a decisive engagement and named the count of Caserta as the commander of his forces. The Carlists were defeated at Peñacerrada on October 23, and dissension increased among their leaders. During the winter the Carlists were repeatedly defeated, and in February 1876 Quesada reached Bilbao. Martínez de Campos had conducted a difficult campaign on the Batzán River and Primo de Rivera captured Estella, the Carlist stronghold. In mid-February Carlos VII had assembled his generals to discuss measures of resisting the enemy and averting a catastrophe. The Carlist forces rapidly began to disintegrate, and on February 28, 1876 the Pretender—with some 10,000 followers—crossed the frontier at Arneguy. Three weeks later Alfonso XII made a triumphant entrance into Madrid.

Colonial problems had also complicated the task of the government of Cánovas del Castillo. The first sparks of revolt had flared in Puerto Rico, in 1851 and 1852. They had been suppressed, but the movement for secession had gained momentum as secret societies conspired for independence. The situation in Cuba was more serious. There the conspirators initiated a general revolt against Spain at what seemed the propitious moment, since they were familiar with the revolutionary atmosphere in Spain and hoped to take advantage of it. In 1868 Carlos Manuel de Céspedes, the father of Cuban independence, issued a call for revolution in a manifesto and soon afterward proclaimed the abolition of slavery, in order to rally the Negroes of the island to the cause of independence. Early in 1869 General Dulce arrived in Cuba to take command of the Spanish forces. He was a revolutionary and hoped to resolve the Cuban problem by the extension of liberties, but was handicapped by dissension in his own ranks. The Spanish volunteers would not support a policy of independence or one reflecting on Spanish authority. Dulce offered the Cubans the liberties consecrated in the Constitution of 1869, but the negotiations broke down, destroying the last hope of conciliation.

Operations against the rebels had been directed by the count of Valmaseda and General Valeriano Weyler. Céspedes, who commanded the rebel army and had organized a junta of government, now sought the recognition of Cuban independence from the United States. A constitution was formulated for the Cuban Republic, and the assembly which had gathered in Camagüey elected Céspedes president and Manuel Quesada commander of the rebel forces.

When Dulce was replaced by General Caballero de Rodas, an ardent patriot, the campaign was immediately favorable to the Spanish troops, the rebels being defeated at Jiguani, Manzanillo, and Bayamo. Thomas Jordan, an American, succeeded Quesada as commander of the rebels, and Céspedes and the Cuban assembly took refuge in Oriente. Céspedes and his government led a fugitive existence, enduring many privations. Dissension in the rebel ranks soon brought his downfall, and Salvador Cisneros Betancourt, marquis of Santa Lucía, was named president.

Failure to quell the rebellion led to the replacement of one Spanish general by another. Although reinforcements were requested, the Spanish government was too busy with the Carlists to spare them, and Spanish resources were exhausted.

General Martínez de Campos, an able diplomat, as had already been demonstrated in the Carlist wars, was sent to Cuba to direct operations against the rebels. The Cubans were ready to negotiate, since they, too, were exhausted by the prolonged struggle and the continuous dissension among their leaders.

When Vicente García became president of the Cuban Republic, he concluded the Convention of El Zanjón with Martínez de Campos in February 1878. This conceded to Cuba the same political and administrative privileges enjoyed by the Puerto Ricans. The slaves were liberated. The rebel forces surrendered and were allowed to live in peace. Although Antonio Maceo continued the war until May when he finally accepted the terms, the Cubans were not reconciled, and the Maceo brothers revived the revolt, which was not finally suppressed until 1880.

Cánovas del Castillo was premier of Spain from the restoration until February 8, 1881. The old parties were reorganized. The Moderates, under Claudio Moyano's leadership, remained as a vestige of the past, clinging loyally to the ideals of the Constitution of 1845. Cánovas presided over the new Liberal-Conservative party, and the old Constitutionalists slowly formed the Liberal party under the leadership of Práxedes Mateo Sagasta. The antidynastic parties included the recently defeated Carlists, but their reputation and influence were much reduced. Salmerón and Castelar led one faction of the divided Republicans, which supported liberal tendencies and gradually drew closer to the Liberal party of Sagasta. The other faction, the Federalists, led by Pí y Margall, had enthusiastic and vocal support. Ruiz Zorrilla, who had supported Amadeo I, was implacable in his opposition to the Bourbons and was gradually converted into an ardent Republican.

Confronted with the task of the reconstruction of Spain—divided by the trend of recent events, revolution, and civil war—Cánovas del Castillo found his program to restore order rendered somewhat easier by the exhaustion of the opposition and of the country in general. Ruiz Zorrilla and three generals who went to bid him farewell were exiled. The premier came to an understanding with Sagasta in regard to the electoral program and the constitution of the two dominant parties. Moreover, Romero Robledo manipulated the elections with the cunning and knavery that had already won him a reputation for political legerdemain. The policy of the government was outlined in a few decrees. In February 1875 the law of civil marriage was annulled as the exclusive law and replaced by two forms—canonical marriage for Catholics and civil marriage for non-Catholics. The principle of universal suffrage was adopted.

The first elections after the restoration were held in January 1876. The Liberals under Sagasta adopted a program supporting the Constitution of 1869 and the monarchy of Alfonso XII. Both Conservatives and Liberals profited from the electoral tricks of Romero Robledo, minister of the Interior, who was so confident in his control of the electoral machinery that when the king asked him if many Republicans would gain seats, he declared, "I promise Your Majesty that none will be elected." Two Republicans, including Castelar, a friend of Cánovas del Castillo, were elected.

One of the primary tasks of the new cortes was the formation of a new constitution. Largely the work of Cánovas del Castillo, it was approved in June 1876. It established the principle of religious toleration instead of religious liberty. It was also more liberal than that of 1845 and reproduced nearly literally some of the provisions of the Constitution of 1869. Individual rights were guaranteed, but it was less liberal in political rights than the Constitution of 1869. The power of making the laws was lodged in the cortes with the king, while the king had the responsibility of enforcing them. The legislature was bicameral. Ministers could attend either chamber even though they were not members of one of them, and deputies were elected in the proportion of one for each 50,000 persons.

During the summer of 1876 the Republicans began to reorganize. Ruiz Zorrilla and Salmerón concluded a political agreement in Paris, but Castelar refused to join them. Some two hundred adherents of Ruiz Zorrilla were imprisoned for conspiring. In 1877 Alfonso XII traveled throughout the nation and with the reluctant approval of Cánovas, married his cousin Mercedes, daughter of the duke of Montpensier, in January 1878. Five months later she died.

Ruiz Zorrilla was not reconciled to the strong new regime in Spain and continued to plot in Paris. A revolution in behalf of a republic was launched in August 1878, but the participants were imprisoned. In October an unsuccessful attempt was made on the king's life by Juan Oliva Moncasi, a communist.

When General Martínez de Campos returned from Cuba he was named premier. Although he was a popular hero as a result of the conclusion of the Cuban war, he had little political aptitude and was dominated by Cánovas. To provide the succession to the crown Alfonso was advised to remarry, and he made Maria Cristina of Habsburg, daughter of the Archduke Charles, his queen in November 1879.

Sagasta became the official leader of the Liberal party. With the adherence to it of Martínez de Campos at this time, it won the confidence of the crown. On a ministerial division over the conversion of the debt Sagasta was named premier.

During the revolution of 1854 Práxedes Mateo Sagasta served as president of the revolutionary junta in Zamora, became a deputy to the cortes, and won a reputation as a debater. He fought in the streets during the counterrevolution of 1856 and became an ardent revolutionary and a Mason. In 1858 he again became a deputy as well as editor of *La Iberia.* In 1866, again a revolutionary, he was condemned to death, but escaped to France. After the revolution of 1868 he became minister of the Interior and president of the government under Amadeo. He then joined the opposition to the First Republic and recognized Alfonso XII.

When Sagasta assumed the presidency of the Ministry in February 1881, the constitution of the parties varied little. The strongest party, which had long enjoyed power under the leadership of Cánovas, was the Liberal-Conservative. The Constitutionalists, now united with the Centralists, formed the Fusionist party. The Moderates, an anachronism from the period of Isabel, were steadily declining in importance. The Carlist party was the strongest in the dynastic opposition. Among the divided Republicans, Castelar defended the idea of a unitary and conservative republic, and some of his allies wanted only his permission to join the Liberals. Salmerón and Ruiz Zorrilla led the Revolutionary Republicans, and the Federals were still staunch in their support of Pí y Margall.

The popular reaction to the first measures of a Liberal government was encouraging. A general amnesty was conceded for crimes of the press, and many followers of Ruiz Zorrilla were won to the Liberal party. Castelar proclaimed his support of the new government. In the elections for the new cortes in August 1881, Venancio González, minister of the Interior, demonstrated his aptitude for political manipulation. Like Romero Robledo, he was a prime example of the policy of maintaining political stability through electoral corruption.

By 1882 the Republicans accused Sagasta of being more of a Monarchist than Cánovas. While the cortes devoted attention to economic matters, political intrigue increased. A more radical Dynastic party led by Serrano, Lopez Domínguez, Montero Rios, Martos, and Moret demanded constitutional reform, trial by jury, and universal suffrage. The Carlist party was divided. Many of its adherents, annoyed by the autocratic methods of Cándido Nocedal, formed the Catholic Union led by Alejandro Pidal y Mon. A collectivist group of extremists, organized in "The Black Hand," attacked property and individuals in Andalusia. Martos was the real leader of the Dynastic Left. Although he remained a Republican, he advised his friends to support the monarchy, and they attacked the Fusionists in the cortes.

Just at this time Alfonso XII was involved in a slight international incident. Invited to observe the German military maneuvers he met William I in Hamburg. When he returned through France he was received with hostility, for the French were indignant that Alfonso had accepted the title of colonel of a regiment of uhlans serving in a garrison in Alsace. The Parisians shouted, "Down with the uhlan! Long live the Republic!" This outbreak, however, served to increase the warmth of Alfonso's reception when he returned to Madrid.

As a result of the attacks of their political enemies the Liberals now controlled only 222 deputies in the cortes. Posada Herrera was entrusted with the presidency of the government, and the new ministry was markedly influenced by the Dynastic Left. The existence of the new government was precarious, and the differences between the Left and the Fusionists increased. Posada Herrera tried to unite all of the liberals, and Sagasta, president of the congress, was accused of duplicity because he had been consulted in the drafting of the message which his followers had attacked. The only solution for the political crisis was to dissolve the cortes and recall the Conservatives to power.

Cánovas del Castillo, who preferred not to preside over the new government, wanted Romero Robledo to become premier, but his colleagues insisted that he take the helm again. Romero Robledo, however, remained important in his capacity of ensuring the election of those candidates who had the party approval. He favored the Dynastic Left at the expense of the Liberal party candidates.

The never robust health of the king began to preoccupy the Monarchists. The physicians recommended relaxation and avoidance of all mental or physical fatigue for him, and Cánovas usually consulted him alone. In May 1884 the king vomited blood, which confirmed the alarm and indicated the nature of the ailment. In July he was taken to Betelú, but his health did not improve and the rumors regarding it increased. Other anxieties added to the problems of the government. An epidemic of cholera appeared in Alicante, and students rioted in the Central University and in the provinces. The Liberals, in coalition with the Federals, won a resounding victory in March 1885 in the municipal elections. This event produced a union of the Fusionists with the Dynastic Left. By June the cholera had spread to Valencia and Murcia, and a few cases appeared in Madrid. Alfonso XII visited Aranjuez, where the epidemic became most violent. By August it had spread throughout the nation.

An international imbroglio developed in 1885 in the Caroline Islands, when the German gunboat "Iltis" slipped into the Bay of Yap and raised the German flag while two Spanish ships were in the harbor. The Germans claimed that no power exercised effective sovereignty over the islands. The Spanish public was indignant and the Spanish press began a patriotic clamor that threatened war. In August some 50,000 persons demonstrated in Madrid, and Martos and Becerra of the Dynastic Left made warlike speeches. Alfonso XII prudently opposed any resort to arms, but a crowd assembled in front of the German legation, tore down the coat-of-arms, and dragged it through the streets. A similar incident occurred at the German consulate in Valencia. Germany declared that the commander of the "Iltis" had acted without authority and recognized the rights of Spain. This calmed the public, but Sagasta assembled his liberal leaders, and they favored a declaration of war on the German Empire. Pope Leo XIII then assumed the role of arbitrator between the two governments on the proposal of Spain. The sovereignty of Spain was recognized over the Caroline and Palau islands, but the Spanish government was obliged to establish a regular administration in the islands, with a force sufficient to maintain order and its rights. Germany received freedom of commerce, navigation, and fishing in the islands, and the right to establish a naval and coaling station. Germans were also guaranteed the right to establish plantations in the islands on an equal basis with the Spaniards.

Meanwhile, however, Spain mourned her king. His illness had become worse during the summer, and an effort was made to carry him to Sanlúcar de Barrameda in the hope that he would recover, but he was unable to undertake the journey. He died on November 26, 1885, at the age of twenty-six.

Spain enjoyed political stability during the reign of Alfonso XII largely as the result of the political perspicacity and manipulation of one man, Antonio Cánovas del Castillo. All the opposition to the regime was still active. The Carlists continued to oppose the government, while the Republicans, still as divided as ever, continually conspired. Cánovas del Castillo, however, found able lieutenants in maintaining his control of Spain, and gradually won the cooperation of his political rival, Sagasta, in building a two-party system in support of the dynasty. Despite the vacillation in crushing the revolt in Cuba, there seemed hope for the development of an orderly democracy. But the foundation of the system was frail. It was based not on intelligent decisions, but on the cupidity of the electorate. As long as Cánovas was able to vitalize the program of the Conservative party, stability could be maintained, but the domination of some able leader was necessary to restrain the personal ambitions of the particularistic leaders seeking political authority.

CHAPTER XXIX

The Regency of Maria Cristina

Just before the death of Alfonso XII, Antonio Cánovas del Castillo conferred at length with Práxedes Mateo Sagasta. They agreed in the so-called Pact of the Pardo that when the queen became a widow she should be named queen regent. Since she was pregnant, neither of her two daughters could be named as successor to Alfonso XII. Both Cánovas and Sagasta were loyal to the throne and wished to spare the young and inexperienced queen unnecessary anxiety over governmental affairs.

Cánovas called upon all Monarchists to restrain their private ambitions, support the regent, and terminate party strife. He then resigned and was succeeded by Sagasta in November 1885. Only a few intransigents regarded the transfer of power to the Liberals as a betrayal of the Conservative party. It was unified and disciplined and any deviation from the party line arose from personal ambitions or frustrations rather than from ideological disagreement.

On May 17, 1886, Maria Cristina bore a son, who was proclaimed Alfonso XIII. The regent was discreet and conscientious and rarely intervened in the actual government of the country, preferring to respect the restrictions imposed on her by the Constitution of 1876. As Cánovas had been the man of the restoration, so Sagasta was the man of the regency.

Although partisan strife was reduced by the restraint shown by Cánovas and divisions among the Republicans, a rebellion occurred in September 1886, when General Villacampa issued a republican pronunciamiento. The Liberals were not prepared for the crisis. The conspiracy, carefully planned by the Military Republican Association, involved forces stationed in Madrid and Alcalá. Instigated by the restless Ruiz Zorrilla, the rebellion did not gain the expected support, and the rising was suppressed. Brigadier Villacampa was captured and condemned to death, but later pardoned.

The principal problems of the government of Sagasta were created by members of his own party. Only private rivalries threatened ministerial stability. When Cánovas spoke at the Barcelona Exposition in October 1888, he attacked the economic policy of the government, supporting a policy of tariff protection, which was popular in industrial Catalonia, against the free-trade tendencies of the government. Following this, the Conservatives abandoned their benevolent attitude toward the ministry and became more vigorous in their opposition. The Liberals retained power long enough to secure the adoption of a law on universal suffrage (1890), but Sagasta was forced to resign and Cánovas was recalled to the premiership.

Many problems clamored for solution. One of the primary aims of Cánovas was the resolution of the economic problem. He favored a protective tariff to stimulate national industry, and as soon as he became premier, he abolished the provision of the law of 1869 which permitted the gradual reduction of duties. The minister of Finance negotiated a loan of two hundred and fifty million pesetas to meet Spain's financial obligations and also negotiated with the Bank of Spain to regulate the circulation of money. The bank was permitted to issue fifteen hundred million pesetas in paper money and its existence was extended to 1921. In return, it granted a loan of one hundred and fifty million pesetas to the government without interest.

A second problem lay in Cuba, where the colonists were still restless following the Ten Years' War. Cánovas recognized that Cuban problems were intimately related to the economic situation, but he insisted on trying to assimilate the Cubans instead of giving them autonomy. His determination was unfortunately expressed when he declared, "We will use the last man and the last peso in the island of Cuba, if it is necessary." Another aspect of the problem was the necessity of countering filibustering expeditions which were only aimed at the renewal of the civil war.

Spanish colonial policy was in a critical state. In general the average Spaniard saw the colonial problems in the light of the past, based on pride in the empire prior to the decline of Spanish resources, and the colonials, stimulated by the example of their neighbors, sought autonomy if not independence. The Cubans were not their only restless colonials. The natives of Ponapé in the Caroline Islands and the Moros of Mindanao in the Philippines also rebelled. The Cubans were aroused by charges of corruption in the colonial administration, exaggerated for political reasons. The refugee Cubans in New York, Tampa, Jamaica, and Santo Domingo plotted constantly to renew the war for independence and were responsible for filibustering expeditions and propaganda in the foreign press. Within the island, raids by bandits were frequent. American investors in sugar plantations were the victims of the raids and added their influence to the demand for reform and order.

When Romero Robledo became colonial minister he tried to reduce administrative expenses in Cuba by dividing the island into three departments and suppressing some courts and schools. General Polavieja, captain general of Cuba, resigned, protesting that he was responsible for the maintenance of order in the island. Romero Robledo was charged with creating the three departments as a means of rewarding his friends. Cuban trade was so disrupted that its customs receipts were reduced by thirty million pesetas in 1892.

In Spain in 1891 the government extended a generous amnesty to both civil and military men who had been implicated in previous revolutions, and many politicians returned from exile. Thus protected, the Republicans were triumphant in several cities in the municipal elections of that year, their greatest victory being in Madrid, where they won twelve seats.

Regionalism was still vigorous. In March 1892 the General Assembly of the Delegates of the Catalan Union, under the leadership of Enrique Prat de la Riba, met in Manresa and formulated the Bases of Manresa for a Catalan regional constitution. They provided for Catalan autonomy in internal affairs, the official use of Catalan as the only language, and restriction of public offices to Catalans. In military affairs Catalans were to contribute only volunteers to the national army and navy, and the reserve should constitute a regional force of conscripts.

In Morocco, where Spain held Melilla and Ceuta, there were constant skirmishes with the Rifs. The government was forced to resort to retaliatory raids to restore order, which the Moroccan government was impotent to maintain. When new forts were built to protect Melilla, the Moroccans requested that they be moved away from a native cemetery, but as the Spaniards failed to heed the request, they were attacked and forced to retire.

Charges of administrative corruption were constantly raised against the Cánovas government. When Villaverde investigated some of the activities of the city government of Madrid, especially those of Alberto Bosch, alcalde of the city, Romero Robledo tried to defend Bosch. Cánovas augmented the scandal by supporting Romero Robledo, and the government was confronted by a popular demonstration in the capital. The ministry was forced to resign and Sagasta became premier.

So many outstanding men were members of the new government that it was called the "Cabinet of Notables," but little unity prevailed among the distinguished ministers. Despite the Liberal majority, their efforts at reform were vigorously resisted by those whose interests were prejudiced. Antonio Maura tried to extend autonomous concessions to both Cuba and Puerto Rico, but succeeded only in arousing the animosity of the Conservatives in both Spain and the colonies.

Terrorism became common. In San Sebastián, when the municipal band refused to play a patriotic Basque song, the hotel in which Sagasta was lodged was stoned, and the police fired on the demonstrators. In Barcelona acts of violence were committed by the anarchists. Two dynamite bombs were hurled under the horse of Captain General Martínez de Campos during a military parade, and an anarchist hurled two bombs into a theater, killing eighteen persons.

The Sagasta government slowly organized reinforcements to send to Morocco to restore Spanish prestige. General Margallo, in command at Melilla, renewed the construction of the fort, but was attacked and killed when he tried to break through the besieging forces. New contingents soon brought the force at Melilla to eighteen thousand men. Meanwhile, negotiations had been initiated with the sultan of Morocco, who admitted that he was unable to restrain the Rifs, although he promised to punish them. In November 1893 General Arsenio Martínez de Campos was named to direct operations in Africa, with twenty-five thousand men in his command. He concluded a pact with the Moroccans by which the construction of the fort was continued and the rebel leaders were surrendered to the sultan for punishment. Early in 1894, Martínez de Campos concluded a treaty with the sultan in Marrakesh, establishing a neutral zone between Melilla and the Moroccans; the aggressive Rifs were punished, and the sultan agreed to pay an indemnity of twenty million pesetas.

In spite of Sagasta's promise to extend reforms to Cuba, the government was confronted with a renewal of the rebellion. In February 1895 the Cubans rallied to the "Cry of Baire" and again resorted to arms. Some of them had been appeased for a time by the concession of local government, but the separatists refused to abandon their agitation or trust Spanish promises of reform. The local government had been established under a very rigid formula. The provincial council was retained and a Council of Administration was organized, of thirty members, half of whom were nominated by the crown and half elected in Cuba. Nevertheless, when the separatists issued their call to arms, there was an immediate response. The Spanish soldiers in Cuba were not very enthusiastic in suppressing the legitimate aspirations of the Cubans or in defending centralist theories and commercial monopolies. When the Madrid press condemned their attitude as unworthy, thirty young officers assaulted the editorial offices of the most provocative newspaper, *El Resumen.* Then, a second newspaper, *El Globo,* attacked the officers, whereupon they wrecked its offices. The Civil Guard, the police, and the military leaders rallied to the defense of the officers, and Sagasta was forced to resign.

Cánovas, aging and no longer able to solve political problems with his former resolution and dexterity, had to constitute a government in a critical period. His lieutenant, Francisco Silvela, disappointed at his failure to obtain a cabinet post, continued to engage in partisan politics as the empire tottered. Cánovas, to enable the conservatives to govern Spain, conferred with Sagasta and they agreed to cooperate.

While Spain was paralyzed into political inaction by personal politics and acts and charges of political corruption, events moved swiftly in Cuba. General Martínez de Campos arrived in Santiago with six thousand infantrymen and a battalion of marines, but his forces were inadequate to cope with the insurgents. Cuban exiles had flocked to the rebel standard. In March 1895 José Martí and Máximo Gómez issued the Manifesto of Montecristi from exile in Santo Domingo, declaring war on Spain. Martí was recognized as supreme leader of the rebels, with Gómez in command of their forces.

Martínez de Campos was familiar with Cuban tactics through long colonial experience with guerrilla warfare. He hoped to attract the rebels by prosecuting the war and yet sparing the wealth of the island. He succeeded in reconciling the Cuban pacifists, but his efforts were ineffective against the zealots who wanted complete independence. He tried to localize the war by establishing three military districts. The death of José Martí in an early encounter was a loss to the cause of the rebels, but they were encouraged when the Spanish general was defeated at Peralejo, and Gómez invaded Camagüey. Martínez de Campos had hoped to drive them eastward, but their mobility gave them the advantage, and they evaded or defeated his columns and even threatened Habana. Martínez de Campos resigned.

By this time Spain had more than one hundred and sixty thousand men in Cuba to suppress the forty thousand insurgents. The nation could not endure the sacrifice of men and money, but the Spanish people were little acquainted with the real facts of the war. Spain had become involved through the proud intransigence of the politicians, and the press loyally supported the government. The old Federalist, Pí y Margall, was one of the few politicians to urge autonomy for Cuba, for which he was charged with lack of patriotism.

The veteran General Valeriano Weyler, a rigorous and inflexible disciplinarian, arrived in Habana in February 1896. To carry out his policy of devastating the land and sternly suppressing the rebels, he immediately instituted a military regime to restrain saboteurs and to prevent aid to the insurgents. To complete his control of the civilian population he ordered the concentration of the inhabitants in camps under military supervision. This policy, which condemned those so concentrated to misery and possible death from the unsanitary conditions in the camps, was especially censured in the United States. The American press—already sympathetic toward the rebels and seeking sensational news—dubbed Weyler "The Butcher." His purpose was to prevent noncombatants from giving aid and assistance to the rebels, but he failed to recognize the propaganda value of his inhumane measures.

Cánovas won the expected majority in the general elections and called on the entire nation for support in the resolution of the Cuban problem. The crisis had sharpened with the mounting interest of the United States in the rebellion, for American statesmen and businessmen had come to regard the revolt sympathetically. The Congress of the United States approved recognition of the belligerency of the Cubans in 1896, but President Cleveland disregarded the resolution and offered American mediation, which Spain rejected.

The difficult problem could only have been resolved with the recognition of Cuban independence. Spain did not have naval forces strong enough to blockade the island and so to prevent the passage of filibustering expeditions and supplies. Blinded by his egoism Cánovas rejected all friendly offers to extricate him from the situation. Although he was prepared to make legislative concessions, Spanish pride stopped any thought of Cuban autonomy.

General Weyler continued the attempt to subdue the insurgents province by province. He succeeded in defeating both Maceo and Gómez, but they escaped. Finally, in a decisive campaign against Maceo, the Spaniards won a decisive battle at Rubí, and Antonio Maceo was killed at Punta Brava in December 1896. His death, however, did not end the campaign as Weyler had hoped.

In Spain the condition of the treasury, drained by the Cuban war, was desperate. New and arbitrary taxes were imposed. Terrorist activity, organized by the anarchists—who had made numerous adherents among the southern migrants—in Barcelona, impelled the cortes to pass a law to restrain such outrages. Moreover, Spain was also having difficulties in the Philippines, where the Tagalogs and mestizos of Luzon were in rebellion. In 1891 the Tagalogs organized the Philippine League under the leadership of José Rizal, who hoped for independence. He was exiled, but the Filipinos, led by Andrés Bonifacio, established a *Katipunam,* a secret society like the Masons, to extend the spirit of separatism throughout the archipelago. In Spain they established the Hispanic-Filipino Association, which demanded representation in the cortes, the reduction of the number of priests, the reform of the administration, facilities for primary education, and the admission of Filipinos to half the administrative posts.

The rebellion broke out in the islands in August 1896. The secret societies had been discovered through the confession of a repentant conspirator, but several provinces rebelled and two thousand rebels tried to penetrate Manila. They committed many atrocities, burned convents, and murdered the occupants. Emilio Aguinaldo and Andrés Bonifacio emerged as the leaders. Although General Blanco was defeated in several engagements, he captured Talisay and succeeded in pacifying the province of Laguña. Late in 1896 General Camilo Polavieja landed in Manila with thirty thousand men to replace the listless Blanco. The rebels controlled the provinces of Cavite and Batangas, but after defeats in several engagements the rebellion was quelled in most of the provinces by 1897. Many rebels were executed, including José Rizal, whose death seriously damaged the Spanish cause. He was shot in December 1896 in the mistaken belief that he was implicated in the rebellion.

The rebellion continued under the leadership of Aguinaldo, and Polavieja resigned and was replaced by General Fernando Primo de Rivera. The Spaniards were now confronted by twenty-five thousand rebels, but General Primo de Rivera recovered Cavite in a successful campaign. Aguinaldo continued to resist in the mountains until December 1897, when the Spaniards conceded some reforms. With Pedro Alejandro Paterno as mediator, the Pact of Biacnabato was concluded, whereby the Filipinos laid down their arms and Aguinaldo withdrew to Hong Kong.

Relations between Spain and the United States had continued to deteriorate. The Spanish government regarded President Cleveland's recommendation of autonomy for Cuba as a veiled threat, and some of the more chauvinistic Spaniards wanted to break relations with the United States. Cánovas had, in the meantime, proceeded to reform the

Cuban administration by opening the municipal councils, the assembly, and the Council of Administration to election by popular suffrage. Cubans were admitted to public office, even to judicial positions, and were authorized to propose budgets and customs duties. For a time the aspirations for Cuban autonomy appeared to be satisfied.

In reality, the reforms had been too long delayed and Weyler's military activities made them insignificant. Nor was American intervention impeded. Although at first moderate, McKinley followed public opinion, aroused by the clamor of the press and of the citizens whose interests in Cuba had been prejudiced. At this critical time, in August 1897, Cánovas was assassinated by an anarchist, and Sagasta, a man of great prestige and known to be pacific in policy, was restored as premier. He made Moret, regarded as an autonomist, colonial minister, and General Weyler was replaced by General Blanco, who erred in being too benevolent. The Spanish government announced its decision to concede autonomy to Cuba, and in November the new constitution for Cuba and Puerto Rico, providing self-government for the islands except in international affairs, was published. The new era in government began on January 1, 1898.

Two groups in Cuba opposed the autonomy conceded by Sagasta. Spanish residents feared they would be placed in a disadvantageous position, and the Cuban rebels were unwilling to accept anything less than complete independence. Those who hoped for the intervention of the United States did not want the problem resolved, for the American press continued to arouse sympathy for the long-suffering Cubans. Two incidents further inflamed public opinion in the United States. In February 1898 William Randolph Hearst's New York *Journal* published a private letter of Enrique Dupuy de Lôme, Spanish minister to the United States, stolen from the Habana post office by a Cuban rebel. In the letter the Spanish minister criticized McKinley as a weak man who curried favor. The American press magnified the insult, and Dupuy de Lôme was forced to resign, but the damage had already been accomplished. Then, on February 15, 1898, the USS "Maine," which had been sent to Habana, was sunk in the harbor by an explosion, killing 262 men. American technicians attributed the explosion to a submarine mine, but Spanish technicians maintained that it was internal, and the jingoist press in the United States accused Spain of responsibility for it. Later, the ship was raised to the surface for examination, to determine whether the explosion was internal or external, but no clear conclusion was ever reached.

Nevertheless, although American public opinion was violently stirred, the weary negotiations continued. In March, Woodford, American minister in Madrid, was directed to ascertain whether Spain would agree to extend an armistice to the Cuban rebels until October 1 and would immediately empty the concentration camps. Although the note was not an ultimatum, it did establish the minimum concessions which the American government regarded as necessary to halt the trend toward war. The Spanish government could not accede to any demand which implied a recognition of the belligerency of the rebels. Spanish public opinion was too sensitive to approve an armistice, but the concentration order was suspended. However, in April Spain even capitulated to the demand for an armistice, and the Spanish government ordered General Blanco to suspend hostilities. After Sagasta had directed a note requesting the advice and friendly offices of the European powers in the crisis and they urged that negotiations be continued, he recognized that Spain was without support in Europe. Only Pope Leo XIII proposed to use his good offices to gain acceptance of the armistice proposal.

President McKinley's message to Congress was already prepared when news of the Spanish order to suspend hostilities arrived in Washington. He recommended that he be authorized to use the armed forces of the United States if necessary to enforce the pacification of Cuba, and Congress extended him the required authority. On April 19, in a joint resolution, Congress declared Cuba independent, demanded that Spain withdraw from the island, and empowered the President to enforce the resolution. At the same time the Teller Amendment, which disclaimed any intention of exercising American sovereignty over Cuba after its pacification, was adopted without a dissenting vote. It was a war of popular sentiment.

War was inevitable and Sagasta was given a vote of confidence. Neither antagonist was prepared for the conflict which began on April 25, 1898. The American volunteers were without modern rifles, and their equipment was obsolete. Heavy uniforms were prescribed for a tropical climate because there was insufficient khaki cloth to provide lighter uniforms. The commissary was disorganized, and sanitation was so neglected that many died of disease. In available manpower Spain had the immediate advantage, with 200,000 soldiers in Cuba, whereas the regular army of the United States totaled only 28,000 men. The Spanish fleet consisted of cruisers and torpedo craft, but it had been neglected and was ill-armed and largely untrained. Although the American navy was composed of battleships, the North Atlantic Fleet was divided so as to protect the American seaboard from Spanish attack.

The war was short and decisive. The United States won every battle, and Spain was forced to ask for terms in three months. Admiral George Dewey was directed to undertake offensive operations in the Philippine Islands. He entered Manila Bay with four armored cruisers and three gunboats. The Spanish fleet consisted of two armored cruisers, four steel cruisers, and one wooden cruiser, which Admiral Montejo led to Cavite to await the attack. Three of the Spanish cruisers were set afire and the others were sunk. The American ships were undamaged, and only eight American sailors were wounded. Cavite was forced to surrender, and by August the Americans had taken the Philippines.

As soon as war was declared, the American fleet blockaded Cuba. Admiral Cervera was ordered to proceed to Cuba with four cruisers and six torpedo boats. Even though he recognized that it would be disastrous to face the superior American fleet, Spanish pride could not be denied, and he was blockaded in the harbor of Santiago de Cuba. On June 24 the American army landed sixteen thousand men at Daiquirí. The Spaniards, also confronted by the insurgents, never concentrated their numerical superiority. The Americans advanced on Santiago, winning the battles of El Caney and San Juan Hill. When the Spanish government ordered Admiral Cervera to sail out of Santiago harbor to oppose the American fleet, he valiantly obeyed the suicidal order and five hours later had lost all of his ships. Santiago was forced to capitulate on July 16. Ten days later an American force landed on Puerto Rico and soon captured that island.

Spain sued for peace on July 26, through Jules Cambon, French ambassador in Washington. The Treaty of Paris, signed December 10, 1898, marked a low ebb in Spanish history and the end of the Spanish empire in the New World. Spain renounced her sovereignty in Cuba and ceded Puerto Rico, Guam, and the Philippine Islands to the United States. In return, the United States agreed to pay Spain twenty million dollars for the Philippines, to transport the Spanish prisoners from Manila, and to admit Spanish trade to the Philippines on an equal basis with American trade. Spanish residents in the ceded territories were permitted to choose their nationality.

Despite the national catastrophe the Sagasta ministry remained in power until March 1899, when Silvela assumed power. The new ministry was confronted by financial insolvency, a defiant Catalonia, and the determined opposition of the National Union, a new political party led by Joaquín Costa and Santiago Alba. Eduardo Dato, minister of the Interior, succeeded in securing some social reforms, and the economic crisis was resolved with the partial reestablishment of Spanish credit.

Sagasta formed a new Liberal ministry in March 1901. He was faced with three important problems: the clerical, the social, and the regional. Anticlerical feeling, an inheritance from the French Revolution, had been accentuated by the allusions contained in *Electra,* a drama of Benito Pérez Galdós. To satisfy the opposition, taxes were imposed on the products made in the convents, and restrictions were placed on members of the religious orders who were involved in secondary education. The Catalan problem was more serious. Alejandro Lerroux, a Republican leader, was patronized by the government in his effort to divert the regional movement in Catalonia. He soon won great popularity in Barcelona, where the separatists were victorious in 1901. Their agitation contributed to the social unrest, and martial law had to be declared in Barcelona to restore order in the general strike of 1902.

A Law of Associations was adopted in the cortes in September 1901, with the object of subjecting all religious orders to a common law. The existing law of 1887 had excepted three religious orders, and all of them were now given six months in which to register. The legislation was somewhat vague, being designed principally as a threat to please the anticlerical forces, and varying interpretations made its application difficult. José Canalejas tried to enforce the Law of Associations, but his measures were regarded as too radical by the majority of the Liberals, who feared a reaction to the Right.

In May 1902 Alfonso XIII attained his majority and the regency of Maria Cristina was concluded. On the whole, it was a sorry period for Spain. There was really no one to whom the nation could look for leadership. Cánovas and Sagasta hoped to supply the deficiency, but Cánovas was an egoistic politician who looked blindly to the past for guidance and Sagasta was simply an opportunist who tried to cope with problems as they arose—unless they could be evaded. They both made use of corrupt practices and manipulated elections to maintain their majorities and the regular rotation of the two parties in office. It was an artificial system which bankrupted the political leadership of the nation. The deputies lost sight of the national welfare in their concentration on private banalities and partisan advantage. The ideals of national progress were forgotten.

The results were disastrous for Spain. In their blind faith in centralism both parties postponed autonomy for Cuba and the Philippines, thus contributing to the development of a situation which led to the Spanish-American War. Within the peninsula politicians ignored the explosive problems which confronted them. The same high regard for centralism contributed to the rise of the regional spirit in the perimeter of the peninsula, especially in Catalonia and the Basque provinces. Although Spain was growing ever poorer, little was accomplished in the solution of the continuous economic crisis. Labor organizations had newly risen to project unfamiliar complications of the social problem and to give voice to the proletariat.

Tenuous rays of hope still counteracted the intractable clouds of despair which darkened Spain. A young king, who might provide the necessary rallying point if he devoted his energy to the welfare of his people, had attained his majority. A new group of able, younger leaders —Dato, Maura, and Canalejas—had also appeared, who might yet restore the national prestige. The Spanish-American War had illumined the weakness of Spain, and the prospect had quickened the desire to formulate new policies for the regeneration of the nation. The people of the rising century might still cooperate with the popular young monarch to transform Spain.

CHAPTER XXX

The Reign of Alfonso XIII

When Alfonso XIII assumed his full prerogatives as sovereign of Spain he inherited many problems. There was general satisfaction at his accession, but he had yet to demonstrate that he was capable of providing the necessary leadership and of being a king in fact as well as in name. The social malaise and economic stagnation demanded to be dealt with by purposeful statesmanship, but the politicians surrounding the young king were primarily interested in their own careers. Alfonso XIII was so restricted by the Constitution of 1876 that the financial future of Spain, the dominance of Castile over the other regions, the orientation of Spanish policy toward Africa, and the resolution of other problems were in large measure taken out of his hands. He was personally popular, but the Spanish people had to be guided toward a realistic solution of their difficulties.

Upon the accession of the new king, Sagasta offered his resignation, but it was refused, and he was continued in office. Alfonso, after taking the customary oath, proposed a meeting of the ministers; after reading an article from the constitution he declared: "As you have just heard, the constitution confers on me the concession of honors, titles, and grandees; therefore, I warn you that I reserve the exercise of this right completely to myself." The ministers were astounded. It seemed that he betrayed either arrogance or adolescent rashness. The duke of Veragua, an outspoken liberal, pointed out another article to the king which read: "No mandate of the king can be effective unless signed by a minister." An issue had been raised between Alfonso and the ministers, and it remained to be seen whether he would try to enlarge his authority.

The enforcement of the Law of Associations was delayed, pending negotiations with the Vatican. Canalejas, minister of Agriculture, was restless, ambitious, strongly democratic, and anticlerical. He did not wish to wait and demanded that the cortes be assembled at once, and when this proposal was rejected, resigned to attack the government. The whole clerical problem was raised by the Republicans. Meanwhile, negotiations with the Vatican proceeded slowly. Moret, who was ambitious to succeed Sagasta, defended the religious orders. But Pablo Iglesias, the Socialist leader, vigorously attacked the Church as an ally of the bourgeoisie, and the Republican Salmerón declared: "I do not want either the death or the expulsion of friars; but it is necessary to deprive them of their means of livelihood. The state must prohibit institutions opposed to human nature."

Problems of education and labor were also of urgent importance. The count of Romanones, minister of Public Instruction, had adopted a progressive policy in requiring teachers in religious institutions to hold degrees. Both Catholics and Conservatives reacted immediately in defense of the old order. Moret, meanwhile, tried to establish norms for labor contracts and fixed the maximum working hours for women at sixty-six a week. He also established the legal right of workers to strike.

In Catalonia and the Basque provinces regional feeling was strongly cherished. When the count of Romanones tried to make Castilian the exclusive language of instruction this provoked an outbreak in Barcelona. For these and other reasons the attacks on Sagasta increased. Canalejas was so intransigent on the anticlerical issue that Sagasta finally expelled him from the party. Nevertheless, Sagasta was forced to resign in December 1902.

Alfonso then called Francisco Silvela to form a new cabinet. After studying law at the University of Madrid, Silvela had become a bureaucrat in the Council of State. Winning distinction as an orator at the Ateneo of Madrid and in the cortes as a representative of Ávila, he was rewarded with a position in the Ministry of the Interior under Cánovas. He continued to enjoy the confidence of the Conservative leader and succeeded him as chief of the party. As a typical Spanish gentleman, he was proud and bitter-tongued, but he was also an idealist who abhorred political corruption. Little understood by his contemporaries, he lost both faith and hope when he saw that the Spanish people were failing to accept their democratic responsibilities.

The most remarkable figure in the new cabinet was Antonio Maura, who became minister of the Interior. He was a strong advocate of local governmental reform, in which he had the support of Silvela in attempting to eliminate the influence of the local bosses in judicial affairs and elections. Except for this partnership, the Conservatives soon divided into two groups following the two leaders. The effort at local reform also raised a storm of protest in the press, which had profited from its alliance with the local bosses. Socialists, Republicans, and Liberals all joined in the attack on Maura.

The Liberals and Republicans were also divided. At the death of Sagasta in January 1903 Moret and Montero Ríos sought the leadership of the Liberal party, which in the debate over its program soon split into two factions, the Monteristas and the Moretistas. Despite the conversion of Joaquín Costa to republicanism, a division likewise soon developed in Republican ranks. In Valencia two leaders, Blasco-Ibáñez and Rodrigo Soriano, hurled insults at each other in the press, and their partisans exchanged shots in the streets. Soriano was finally expelled from the party.

When Silvela was forced to resign as a result of a debate over the message from the throne, and Raimundo Fernández Villaverde formed a ministry including a number of Galicians, Silvela retired to private life, and both major parties were left leaderless when the court moved to San Sebastián for the summer of 1903. When Antonio Maura made a brilliant oration in reply to an interrogation on the electoral procedures of the government, he was wildly applauded by the Conservative deputies; Silvela approached him, seized his arm, and pushed him toward those who acclaimed him, crying, "Take him, he is your chief!" This action evoked another ovation, prompting the Liberal marquis of La Vega de Armijo to remark, "Thus chiefs are proclaimed."

Antonio Maura duly succeeded Villaverde as premier. A Mallorcan by birth, he had studied law in Madrid, where he became a close friend and brother-in-law of German Gamazo, an influential politician. In 1881 he was elected a deputy from Palma and represented that city for the rest of his life. Maura, who soon attained a reputation as being one of the best lawyers in Spain, in 1886 withdrew from the Liberal party. He was later reconciled with Sagasta, but definitely resigned from the party in 1898 and succeeded his brother-in-law as leader of the Gamazistas in 1901.

During his career of more than twenty years as a political leader, Maura was warmly denounced and praised. An able orator, distinguished for his analytical grasp of political problems and his mastery of detail, he usually dominated the chamber when he spoke. He held such liberal views when he entered the Conservative party that Conservative extremists repudiated him. He was a man of strong convictions on municipal autonomy, regionalism, civic responsibility, and purity in politics. He firmly believed that Spain could be aroused from the apathy and pessimism into which it had fallen. Maura was especially interested in encouraging popular participation in politics and in reducing the influence of the local bosses. He was extremely religious, inflexible in his opinions, and always loath to compromise. In his later years he succumbed to the influence of friends and was charged with favoritism. Because of his legal training, he was also doctrinaire in his approach to many problems.

In April 1904 Maura accompanied the king on a visit to Barcelona, where an anarchist attempted to stab him. While the terrorists continued a campaign of violence in Barcelona, clashes also took place in Valencia between the Republicans and the Carlists. Yet the government appeared to have weathered all attacks successfully until an unexpected incident led to its fall. When General Linares, minister of War, named a chief of the newly created General Staff of the Army, Alfonso XIII rejected him. Maura rallied loyally to the support of his minister and the entire cabinet resigned in December 1904.

Alfonso XIII visited Paris in May 1905, and as he left the opera with President Loubet of France, two bombs were exploded beside their coach. Several people were wounded, and the attack was immediately blamed on the anarchists.

Villaverde had succeeded Maura as premier, but was followed by Eugenio Montero Ríos in June. The new prime minister had had a long political career. He had taught canon law in the Central University of Madrid, been a distinguished member of the constituent cortes in 1868, and named minister of Justice by Prim in 1870. Later, he was a minister in the regency. When he became premier, he was seventy-three years of age, with a well-won reputation as a jurist, a prudent and cautious politician, and an able orator.

During the elections of 1905 the Catalan separatists conducted an intensive propaganda in Barcelona, with cries of "Long Live Catalonia" and "Death to Spain." When the army was ridiculed in the journal *Cu-Cut,* a group of officers attacked its editorial offices. A heated debate in the lower chamber followed, and in November Montero Ríos suspended constitutional guarantees and resigned. He had demanded that General Weyler, minister of War, punish the military personnel who had attacked the newspaper. Weyler refused, and the Madrid garrison rallied excitedly to the support of the Barcelona contingent.

Sigismundo Moret y Prendergast then formed a Liberal ministry in December. Like Montero Ríos, he came to the premiership in his declining years. A deputy from Almadén, he supported free trade and advanced social reform and built his reputation as an orator in the Ateneo of Madrid. He served as colonial minister under Prim. At first he did not affiliate with any party when he returned to Spain after the restoration, but he finally joined Sagasta as his loyal lieutenant and friend.

Moret was an eloquent orator, but in politics he was a doctrinaire theorist, neither astute nor practical. He became an oracle to his followers, but could not restrain them. As premier he followed Sagasta, and believed firmly in the supremacy of the civil power and in a strong government.

His immediate problem was a much debated Law of Jurisdictions, which empowered military courts to consider crimes against the nation and the army. Although he proclaimed civil supremacy, his substitute proposal was as odious to the Liberals as the Law of Jurisdictions. Although the Catalans resolutely opposed it the law was approved in March 1906, and opponents at once claimed it was imposed by the army and the crown. As a result, Catalan Regionalists, Republicans, Carlists, Liberals, and Conservatives joined to form Solidaridad Catalana, a new party which indicated the increasing strength of the regional sentiment in Catalonia. Its leaders, Cambó and Prat de la Riba, were especially anxious to destroy the influence of Alejandro Lerroux in Barcelona, where he had built an effective political machine sustained even by Moret.

Late in November 1905 Alfonso XIII returned from his European travels, having selected as a bride, his cousin Victoria Eugenia Ena of Battenberg, granddaughter of Queen Victoria. Despite the warning of Moret that the Battenbergs suffered from hemophilia, the king persisted, and the wedding was celebrated in May 1906.

After several unsuccessful attempts to form ministries Antonio Maura assumed power in January 1907 and retained the premiership for two years, the longest tenure of any ministry under Alfonso XIII and one of the most prolific in legislation. The Liberals had become ineffective because of internal dissension, whereas Maura was the leader of a united and well-disciplined party. In the electoral campaign of 1907 the Basques and Solidaridad Catalana drastically increased their propaganda, and the Catalan separatists obtained forty-one of the forty-four seats, although the elections were shamelessly manipulated for the benefit of the government. The Catalans then introduced their program in the new cortes. Their spokesmen declared that they were seeking regional recognition rather than trying to undermine Spanish unity. The terrorists were not intimidated by the proclamation of martial law and the trial of two of their leaders, but continued their campaign of violence. The count of Romanones, now minister of Justice, proposed a law against terrorism, which would punish the perpetrators of crimes involving explosives, suppress anarchist newspapers, and expel anarchist propagandists. The act was attacked by the radicals and the press and its discussion was postponed.

The Liberals, Republicans, and Democrats, led by Moret, Melquíades Alvarez, and Canalejas, meanwhile attacked Maura's personal integrity and hesitated at no calumny. In the summer of 1909 the war in Morocco further complicated the political situation. Rivalry among the European powers was growing tense because of the strategic and economic importance of Morocco, and Spanish interest in that country was challenged, especially by the French. In 1880, in a conference at Madrid, the principal powers had agreed to maintain the territorial integrity of Morocco and permit all nations to trade there freely, but political and commercial rivalry soon nullified the agreement. The French sought Spanish and British support, but the Germans opposed French expansion. In 1904 Spain and France agreed to partition Morocco in a secret treaty, and in the same year the British agreed not to oppose French expansion in Morocco provided the British were given a free hand in Egypt.

When the French demanded the recognition of their protectorate over Morocco in 1905, William II of Germany landed at Tangiers from his yacht and declared that Germany would defend an independent Morocco. In the following year, the Algeciras Conference was called to provide a solution. The Spanish foreign minister presided over the representatives of Germany, France, Great Britain, Italy, and Spain. The conference agreed that German investments in Morocco would be protected, but Spanish and French interests were given special recognition. Morocco would be policed by French and Spanish forces. Under the pretext of pacifying Morocco, the French began to annex it, and in 1908 when there was friction at Casablanca the French army occupied it.

Although Abdul-Hafid, who overthrew Abdul-Aziz IV, had difficulty in maintaining order, he was desirous of cordial relations with Spain. In 1909 Antonio Maura sent Merry del Val to Morocco to undertake negotiations, but his intransigent attitude disrupted the meeting, and Maura, fearing war, began to reorganize the garrison at Melilla. The Spanish people did not want war, and Moret, Pablo Iglesias, and the Socialists opposed intervention. But when the Moors killed four laborers of the North African Company, who were working on the railway to the Spanish mines, the Spanish military governor of Melilla attacked and defeated them. Instead of acceding to Abdul-Hafid's request that he withdraw his troops, Maura decided to reinforce the garrison at Melilla and ordered the mobilization of the active reserve. The Moroccans retaliated by besieging advanced Spanish positions and harrying their supply lines. The press attacked Spanish mining interests in the Rif, and the war was patently unpopular in Spain. When the minister of War ordered troops from Madrid and Barcelona to join the expeditionary force, resentment increased. Cries of "Down with war!" were raised in Madrid, Barcelona, and Saragossa. The war in Morocco rapidly became more costly. The Rifs attacked various outposts and in July 1909 routed the inexperienced troops of General Marina. Four days later the Spaniards lost more than twelve hundred men in the disastrous battle of Barranco del Lobo. But the determined Spanish government increased the number of Spanish soldiers in Morocco to forty thousand, and General Marina, with twenty-five thousand men, undertook a successful offensive. Although the Rifs resisted furiously in a succession of bloody engagements they were forced to surrender.

Meanwhile, beginning late in July, events plunged Barcelona into violence. A general strike, called to protest against the order of mobilization, soon assumed the proportions of a rebellion. Churches and convents were burned, and other acts of vandalism were committed. The civil governor, Angel Ossorio y Gallardo, proclaimed martial law, but the outbreak spread to neighboring communities. In some cities the Republicans and Socialists encouraged the protests, attacked the government, and urged the working class to resist the war, which, they charged, was waged in the interest of the prosperous mining companies.

"Tragic Week" continued through some days of bloody fighting, and order was not completely restored in Barcelona until August 1, when the military courts began to function. The leaders of the outbreak were executed, including Francisco Ferrer Guardia, founder of a widely held school of radical thought. He was arrested, subjected to a summary trial, and shot. The execution of so prominent a political leader shocked public opinion throughout Spain, and Socialists, anarchists, and liberals in all of the capitals of Europe protested. Ferrer, an avowed anarchist and a man who had trained his followers in deeds of violence, was glorified as a martyr. While he was doubtless partly responsible for the rioting of the "Tragic Week," the summary action of the military court was a grave error and produced immediate political repercussions.

The Liberals were furious and at once withdrew their support of the government. Maura was forced to resign by his radical opponents, who included Republicans not received at court. He was succeeded by Moret, and at the end of 1909 the Republican-Socialist alliance was created.

The Socialists, who had formerly abstained from political action, now entered into an alliance which committed them to revolution. The Republicans had finally overcome the resistance of Pablo Iglesias, who had insisted on remaining aloof from politics. To solve the problems resulting from the execution of Ferrer, Moret sought to mollify the rebellious temper of eastern Spain by promising an amnesty, but he was unable to gain the necessary legislative support to consolidate his position and was forced to resign. In February 1910 Canalejas was named premier.

José Canalejas y Mendez had abandoned a teaching career for one in the railway company of which his father was a director. His earliest political sympathies were Republican, but he joined the Liberal party and became a deputy from Soria in 1880. Politically, Canalejas was radical and anticlerical. His skill as a parliamentarian drew the Liberals to him, and he became their undisputed leader. His relations with the king were always amicable, for Alfonso XIII was impressed by his intelligence and even partly converted to more liberal ideas by him. He had a prodigious memory and was an exceptional orator. Despite his liberal ideas he staunchly defended legally constituted authority, respected law and order, and defended the rights of all men.

As premier Canalejas moved farther to the left, but he was no extremist and did not draft the radical measures that some demanded. His proposed law of June 1910, prohibiting the establishment of new religious orders until a new Law of Associations was passed, produced an episcopal protest and a rupture in relations with the Vatican. The minister of Public Instruction, the count of Romanones, was also anticlerical and defended lay control of education. The radicals were not satisfied with the reforms introduced by Canalejas, and they organized a great anticlerical meeting in Madrid in July, disturbing public order with strikes and terrorism. At this time Antonio Maura was wounded by a would-be assassin in Barcelona. The Republicans and Socialists made the most of a stormy debate on the execution of Ferrer and the "Tragic Week" in the cortes. Alfonso XIII visited Melilla in January 1911, even entering the territory of the Rifs, and General García Aldave adopted a policy of conciliation toward them. But the persistent accusations of administrative corruption in Morocco in the end demoralized the army.

The Germans were provoked by French expansion in Morocco to seek their own share of African territory. In May 1911 the French occupied Fez. The Spaniards were also stirred to occupy strategic sites in their zone, Canalejas ordering the occupation of Larache and Alcázarquivir. A second Moroccan crisis occurred when the German gunboat "Panther" arrived at Agadir on July 1. Although the Germans and French soon came to an understanding, the French later became irritated by an expedition which Spain sent to occupy Ifni.

When a Spanish unit was attacked by Moroccans in August, the authorities refused to surrender those responsible for the attack. Spain then undertook a police action and forced the Moroccans to withdraw from the areas around Melilla and beyond the Kert River. Spanish expeditions were organized to pacify the area. A Moorish offensive was finally repelled, after the Spaniards lost heavily in successive engagements.

Spanish public opinion continued to oppose the war in Morocco and strikes were organized to publicize these sentiments. Rodrigo Soriano instigated a rebellion at Numantia, while the Republicans were blamed for another outbreak at Cullera. The government nevertheless persisted in its military preparations and established obligatory military service early in 1912. Conscripts were no longer permitted to purchase their exemption, and although they were required to serve only on garrison duty in times of peace, Spain now had a crippling war on hand in Morocco. Fighting continued in a desultory fashion, draining Spanish resources in an imperialist venture.

A general railway strike, which originated in Catalonia, paralyzed the Spanish economy. Canalejas at once ordered the mobilization of the railway workers, and they were forced to reestablish service under military authority. Although the Catalans were somewhat appeased by the partial satisfaction of their regional aspirations in a law authorizing greater governmental autonomy, the energetic measures of Canalejas in the railway strike alienated the workers. Manuel Pardiña, an anarchist from Bordeaux, came to Madrid to assassinate him, and on November 12 as Canalejas stopped at a bookstore in the Puerta del Sol Pardiña shot him twice and then committed suicide.

The death of Canalejas was an irreparable blow to Spain, for he was a leader of proved ability and greater promise. He was eventually succeeded as the leader of the Liberals by the wealthy count of Romanones, an energetic and ambitious politician, who enjoyed a privileged social position, but who pursued a course in imitation of Sagasta, the leader of his youth.

In November 1912 the French and Spanish negotiated a new convention in regard to Morocco, which divided the country into three zones of influence. A narrow coastal strip, including her African strongholds, was assigned to Spain. A more extensive zone was given to

France, while a small zone was internationalized and placed under the authority of the powers which had signed the Act of Algeciras.

By this time the tacit rotation of the parties in power appears to have broken down. Antonio Maura was annoyed at the royal confidence in the count of Romanones, which he regarded as proof either of the increasing liberalism of the king or of his belief in the declining popularity of the Conservative party. The Liberals had also allied themselves with the Republicans to form a solid opposition to a possible Conservative reaction. Maura therefore withdrew from political affairs, both as chief of the Conservative party and as deputy. He believed that continuation of the rotation of the monarchist parties in office was the only defense for the monarchy against the Republicans. In January 1913, when the Conservatives requested that he resume the leadership of the party, he acquiesced.

Alfonso XIII was content to bask in the praise of the Socialists and Republicans for his resistance to Maura. His reliance on the Liberals had also won approval across the Pyrenees and evoked the applause of intellectuals who had previously had little contact with the royal palace. Alfonso, in short, appeared to be a model constitutional monarch. In April 1913 an anarchist fired two shots at him, but he was not injured.

Although Maura attacked the government in the cortes for collaborating with enemies of the monarchy, Romanones continued to enjoy the confidence of the king. Gradually, the Liberals began to disintegrate, while the Republicans expelled Melquíades Alvarez for cooperating with the monarchy. Then the Liberal cabinet was defeated in the Senate, and Romanones was forced to resign. He wanted the Conservatives to assume control while he reorganized his party, but Maura declared that those who had undertaken the Moroccan war should retain power to continue it. Eduardo Dato Iradier, an intimate friend of Silvela, finally accepted the responsibility of premier. The Moroccan war dragged on, largely because of the desire of the military men to vindicate the reputations they had lost in 1898. The government tried to retain its strongholds in Morocco, win the confidence of the natives, and consolidate the protectorate. Military promotions were more rapid in time of war, and the opportunities of acquiring wealth in the administration of the army were greatly increased. The Socialists and Republicans wanted to abandon Morocco, for the war cost a million pesetas a day. But the monarchists hoped the protectorate could be peacefully maintained, and it was rumored that the king might intervene personally in partnership with the military leaders to keep it intact.

When World War I began in 1914, Dato correctly interpreted the sentiment of the people, and the Spanish government hastened to proclaim its neutrality. It had lost its enthusiasm for war on a grand scale. In general, the Conservatives sympathized with the Germans, and the intellectuals with France and Great Britain, but the discussions remained purely detached. Spain became a center of espionage and journalistic recriminations.

Committees were created to grapple with the economic problems produced by the war and contradictory policies were adopted. Prices rose, many commodities disappeared from the market, and the government tried to prevent profiteering. It prohibited the private importation of wheat and flour, arranging to import and distribute them itself. Despite these precautions many individuals pocketed large gains from a scandalous exploitation of shortages or by engaging in clandestine trade. The radicals in Catalonia accused Dato of dictatorial policies when he refused to grant them licenses for export.

The count of Romanones succeeded Dato, but the Liberals were confronted with the same problems of unemployment, rising prices, and a dissatisfied working class. The tension between sympathizers with the Germans or the Allies became more heated as the measures adopted by the belligerents affected the neutrals. Even the royal family appeared to be divided. Maria Cristina was an Austrian, Queen Victoria was English, and it was difficult to ascertain where the sympathies of Alfonso lay. He tried to be neutral, forbade discussions of the war at his dinner table, and won the appreciation of the French press because of his efforts to assist prisoners of war.

The Romanones government was attacked in the cortes in September 1916 because the merchant fleet had lost eighty thousand tons of shipping. It was charged that the owners engaged in a lucrative contraband trade and earned fabulous profits. Undeterred by fines and suspension, the press attacked the government until its position became difficult. The pro-German press attacked Romanones on the ground that he was threatening neutrality and profiting from the war. The German government demanded the termination of the contraband trade across the Pyrenees. In 1917 Germany demanded that Spain suspend all maritime commerce with her enemies. The government won a vote of confidence, but in April the torpedoing of a Spanish ship carrying coal from England to Barcelona produced a crisis. Although the government was irresolute, the partisans of the Allies and of neutrality became more bitter. Romanones, forced to resign, was succeeded by García Prieto.

Militarism had become a problem for the civil authorities of Spain early in the nineteenth century, but its existence proved only one aspect of Spanish deterioration and demoralization. Civil servants failed to discharge their duties, the professors lost their enthusiasm for teaching, the clergy intrigued for benefices, sailors abandoned their ships to waste time in the capital, the aristocrats indulged themselves frivolously, and their overseers exploited the underpaid tenants. The arrogant position to which the military aspired was not the only sign of Spanish weakness.

Politically, Spain had no real leadership on vital issues. Little distinction existed between Liberals and Conservatives except in the personal policies of the leaders. Antonio Maura continued to denounce the evils of the time and to predict dire calamities for the future, but he did not propose any solution for the omnipresent problems. He opposed one government after another without presenting a constructive program. The radicals had become generally unpopular because of their sympathies for the Allies. Only one party offered a definite program and inspired its adherents to constructive attitudes. The ability and energy of the Socialist leaders, Pablo Iglesias, Julián Besteiro, and Francisco Largo Caballero—combined with rigid party discipline—offered a formidable threat to the regime.

García Prieto's cabinet continued the policies of Romanones until a problem of internal order diverted Spanish attention from the world conflict. The existence of clandestine and illegal military organizations had already been discovered, for juntas had existed in the Artillery and Engineers for some time. They now appeared in the Infantry, with complaints of favoritism in promotion and compensation. Romanones ordered the captain general of Barcelona to dissolve the juntas and was advised that it had been accomplished. Thereupon the government issued a decree establishing seniority as the basis for promotion.

When General Aguilera became minister of War under García Prieto, he was confronted by a fresh propagandist onslaught from the juntas. He acted decisively, ordering the retirement of the captain general of Barcelona and the arrest of the disobedient officers. However, the juntas were immediately reconstituted with new members. General Marina assumed command in Barcelona and was presented with a seditious manifesto by the officers in June 1917. When he was unwilling to submit to an ultimatum but too weak to continue in office, the radicals seized the opportunity to subordinate civil authority to military pressure as a basis on which to overthrow the government.

Dato then formed a ministry and approved of measures for the regulation of the juntas, thereby giving them legal recognition. The government was impotent to control them, for many persons applauded the efforts of the juntas to eliminate current abuses, without considering the inevitable results of a revival of military intervention in civil affairs. As a counter measure, civil juntas of defense were soon organized by public employees. Many politicians used them to their own advantage: Cambó wanted to gain a victory for the Catalan separatists, Iglesias and Lerroux wanted to overthrow the monarchy. The Liberals were too absorbed in the struggle between Romanones and García Prieto for the leadership of the party to take advantage of the situation.

After their victory over the government, the military juntas continued their subversive activities. In June 1917 the Junta of Defense of the Infantry issued a public manifesto and forced Dato to suspend constitutional guarantees. The influence of the juntas was felt even in the military organization of the Palace, where tenure was restricted to four years.

When the Liberal cortes was dissolved, the town council of Barcelona demanded their convocation as an unofficial constituent assembly in Barcelona. Amid charges of collaboration between the juntas and the Catalans, the unofficial assembly—a rump cortes—met in the palace of the governor of Barcelona as scheduled, and the members reiterated the demand for a constituent cortes to resolve the problem of municipal autonomy. The gathering was ultimately forcibly dissolved by the Civil Guard. In retaliation a general strike was called by the Socialists and Republicans. Railway transportation was paralyzed and nation-wide violence resulted in eighty deaths. The leaders were arrested, and when it appeared that the strike would fail, Macía, the Catalan leader, and Lerroux fled to France. But although the government suppressed the strike with decision, it could not withstand the threat of military rebellion and, in order to satisfy the juntas, appropriated seventy-eight million pesetas for the purchase of new war material. They also forced the resignation of General Francisco Primo de Rivera as minister of War and brought about the downfall of the Dato government in October.

In the elections of February 1918, which were very corrupt, the party system further disintegrated into personal factions. García Prieto formed a weak government, but could find little support in the divided chamber. La Cierva, minister of War, forced the resignation of two Catalan ministers, made himself arbiter of the government, and proceeded with military reform by royal decree. The civil juntas tried to imitate the example of their military models, but La Cierva was firm. When the mail and telegraph services were disrupted by a strike, he militarized communications and abolished the civil service in the postal and telegraph offices. This drastic action produced a national crisis, during which

Alfonso even considered leaving Spain. Order was not restored until Antonio Maura formed a national ministry.

Maura at once undertook some fundamental reforms, placated public opinion with a decree of amnesty, and released the members of the strike committee, who had been condemned to life imprisonment for rebellion. Yet his idealism and energy failed to command the confidence of the politicians, and Romanones was returned to power. He was confronted by an even more complex situation. The Republicans demanded integral autonomy for the Catalans in November, in the conviction that free and autonomous regions were compatible with the unity of Spain. Cambó demanded complete Catalan sovereignty. In the wake of this agitation, Barcelona became the scene of increased disorder.

Aroused to action by the crisis, the Castilians and groups in Andalusia and Aragon protested against the disintegration of Spain. When the situation was debated in the cortes, Antonio Maura received an ovation for his speech in defense of national unity, whereupon the Catalans and the Republicans withdrew from the chamber.

The government adopted a conciliatory attitude toward the Catalan demands and proposed the creation of an extraparliamentary commission to establish the regional powers and submit them to the cortes for approval. When the government of Barcelona rejected the ministerial proposal and proceeded to adopt a statute of autonomy, the situation sharply deteriorated there, for the Junta of Defense opposed Catalan aspirations. Although Cambó demanded full sovereignty for Catalonia, the Catalans rejected the proposal of the commission, and Romanones announced that the government would make no further concessions. Syndicalist outrages also increased in Barcelona, and the workers in many cities became incensed over the shortage of foodstuffs, which bore with especial severity on the lower classes. As open warfare between employers and workers increased, the government declared martial law in Barcelona, but found itself powerless to restore order.

Again for a short time Maura tried to establish civil authority, but the major political parties no longer held any significance for Spaniards and disintegrated into personal factions. Joaquín Sánchez Toca, who succeeded Maura, was forced to resign by the juntas. The succeeding premier, Manuel Allendesalazar, had neither the ability nor the authority to deal with the many problems which confronted him. His tenure was made precarious by the division of the cortes into factions. It was particularly difficult to restore order in Barcelona. Employers resorted to the lockout to discipline the workers, and employees used strikes and sabotage as their weapons. The irreconcilable enmity between the two groups also produced an increasing number of crimes.

In May 1920 Dato was again named premier. He created the Ministry of Labor, but terrorism became more widespread in Barcelona, and strikes occurred throughout the nation. General Severiano Anido was named civil governor of Barcelona. Resorting to drastic action, he deported thirty-six laborers, imprisoned sixty-four syndicalists, shot prisoners under the pretext that they were trying to escape (*Ley de Fugas*), and organized the *Sindicato Libre* to combat the *Sindicato Único* of the workers. In March 1921 he was killed by an assassin, as the Syndicalists had threatened.

Meanwhile, the war had proceeded in Morocco without attracting great attention in the peninsula. General Damaso Berenguer, high commissioner of Morocco, enjoyed the full confidence of the government, but a severe famine had increased the discontent among the Moroccans. Then, General Manuel Fernández Silvestre, commander at Melilla, began to occupy more territory, and Abd-el-Krim appeared as a formidable leader of the Rifs. He was partly Hispanicized, having served as secretary in the Department of Native Affairs, professor of Arabic in a Moorish school, and judge. In April 1921 he was working under Silvestre in Melilla, when a quarrel occurred between the two. The general was unnecessarily harsh, and Abd-el-Krim left headquarters swearing that he would lead his tribesmen in a decisive blow against the Spaniards.

The Spanish army did indeed suffer a series of reverses. General Silvestre, trying to relieve an advanced outpost, was forced to withdraw to Annual and, before reinforcements could arrive, was overwhelmed by the Rifs. In the retreat—July 23–24—which was converted into a demoralized rout, the Spaniards lost fourteen thousand men and a great quantity of material.

Spanish public opinion demanded a scapegoat for the catastrophe, and found two. General Silvestre had been impetuous and had not advised the high commissioner or the government of his advance, while General Berenguer was involved because he had sent only 1500 men to the relief of Silvestre. Although Melilla was saved from falling into the hands of Abd-el-Krim, thousands of Spaniards were besieged in various outposts. The disaster produced a ministerial crisis and Antonio Maura again became premier. He at once confirmed his confidence in Berenguer as high commissioner and concentrated forty thousand men in Melilla to recover the lost territory.

Spain was overwhelmed by the disaster. The war was thoroughly debated. Miguel Primo de Rivera, captain general of Madrid, who urged that Morocco be abandoned, was relieved of his post, and General Berenguer was coldly received when he returned to the capital. Everyone desired to fix the responsibility for the debacle, punish the guilty, and recover the Spanish prisoners. One aspect of the problem remained obscure: the king's role in these events, as a friend of both Berenguer and Silvestre—perhaps even his adviser. Among the many rumors, it remained clear that Alfonso had passed the summer pleasantly at Deauville while his soldiers were being sacrificed in the African heat; accordingly his popularity began to decline from this time. The Moroccan war was more unpopular than ever, but the government still had to find some dignified way to terminate it. Maura was succeeded by José Sánchez Guerra, who became head of the Conservative party in 1922.

The new premier restored constitutional guarantees and made some concessions to the radicals in an effort to soothe the public alarm. The conclusion of General Picasso's investigation of responsibilities listed Berenguer and Silvestre among the guilty, although Alfonso tried to protect Berenguer. The report was warmly debated in the cortes, where the Liberals censured the government. Both parties continued to defend the civil authority, whose weakness was in reality responsible for the disaster.

In this sad hour García Prieto formed the last constitutional ministry under Alfonso XIII, which consisted of the ablest men in the Liberal party. Hoping to improve the situation with celerity, it divided Morocco into two zones, centering around Ceuta and Melilla, and ransomed the prisoners remaining in the hands of Abd-el-Krim.

But terrorism was continuous in Barcelona, as rival syndicates carried on open warfare in the city streets. Angel Pestaña, the Syndicalist leader, was wounded and Salvador Seguí, another anarchist leader, was killed. The government was powerless to maintain order, and a transport strike paralyzed the city. The captain general, Miguel Primo de Rivera, became more popular as the representative of order and authority. An angry exchange in the Senate between General Aguilera and José Sánchez Guerra very nearly precipitated a duel. The general threatened military action if the government did not support the armed forces. While the army continued to lose heavily in scattered engagements, the government was unable to agree on strategy to recover its lost prestige and pacify Morocco. Spain passively waited for someone to assume the leadership.

CHAPTER XXXI

The Directory of Primo de Rivera

It was now apparent that with the existing political orientation Spain's problems were intractable. The two great parties had disintegrated, and individual leadership of ambitious politicians replaced party discipline and loyalty. Ministries were unable to sustain a parliamentary majority and appeared and disappeared without constructive accomplishment.

The country lay prostrate, the treasury drained by the unwieldy bureaucracy and the Moroccan war. Stricken with poverty, Spain lost needed capital through an adverse balance of trade, while strikes paralyzed her industry and high prices made it impossible for the lower classes to live decently. Terrorism between rival syndicates stalked tragically through the streets of the principal industrial center—Barcelona. As a unified state, Spain appeared to be disintegrating. The Catalans, dissatisfied with a limited form of autonomy, demanded the recognition of their sovereignty. The Basques, proud of their distinctive culture and of the memory of their local *fueros,* also sought an approach to regional independence.

In Morocco the military campaign had been crippled by administrative corruption and political interference. A dual policy had been attempted and proved ineffective. On the one hand, the high commissioner had tried to bring the natives to a peaceful understanding with the Spanish. On the other hand, Spain had tried to maintain order in the territory. Thus, without giving the military a free hand to consolidate the Spanish position and to wipe out the memory of their defeat in 1898 with a new victory, and without pacifying the natives with a just and generous policy, the politicians had been unable to cope with the Moroccan problem. The disaster at Annual had not only been a heavy blow to Spanish pride, but had raised the question whether the abandonment of Spanish commitments in Morocco would not be preferable to the continued prosecution of an unpopular war.

The Juntas of Defense had already defied the civil authority. Undoubtedly patriotic as well as selfish in seeking to reform doubtful procedures, they set a precedent for the resumption of military interference in civil affairs. The coup d'état of 1923 had been generous and patriotic in its inception, but it violently changed the direction of the nation. Passive and indifferent citizens, confused by the impact of multiple problems, had to be aroused to action.

Miguel Primo de Rivera y Orbaneja was the heir of an ancient military tradition. He entered the General Military Academy in Toledo in 1884. Serving first in Africa in 1893 as a first lieutenant, he was promoted for heroism and awarded the coveted Cross of San Fernando. Two years later he went to Cuba as an aide to General Arsenio Martínez de Campos and remained there until 1897. When his uncle, General Fernando Primo de Rivera, was named captain general of the Philippines, he took Major Primo de Rivera along as his aide. The rising young officer participated again in the African war as a brigadier general in 1911. In 1915 he was named military governor of Cádiz, but his blunt recommendation of the abandonment of Morocco and his criticism of the government soon cost him his position. He was sent to the Allied front as an observer during World War I. In 1919, a lieutenant general, he was named captain general of Valencia, again restored to official favor, and within a few months was transferred to Madrid. His attitude on the Moroccan problem had not changed, and when he was chosen as senator from his native province of Cádiz, he again urged that Spain be relieved of the Moroccan burden. This view so offended his superiors that he was again relieved of his command.

In 1921, on the death of his uncle, who had adopted him, he became marquis of Estella, and in the next year was named captain general of Barcelona. He had long been interested in Spain's political problems, and when he witnessed the confusion produced in Barcelona by terrorism, he was not long in acquiring a reputation as a firm supporter of public order. Simple and often naive, and an opportunist rather than an artful politician, Miguel Primo de Rivera yet had an attractive personality. He has been described as a "glorified cafe politician" who aspired "to save his country by making himself its ruler." He had had little preparation for government, but as a Spaniard he had ideas on how to rule, though his garrulous decrees and fussiness over trivial details sometimes made him ridiculous in the eyes of his countrymen.

The influences which produced the coup d'état of September 1923, when Primo de Rivera was still captain general of Barcelona, are somewhat mysterious. General Aguilera had predicted a dictatorship, and it was said that he had been selected as the principal figure of the new regime. His loss of prestige in the incident with José Sánchez Guerra made him a liability rather than an asset and Miguel Primo de Rivera was selected as leader. Although the implication of the king in the coup d'état is also uncertain, in any event he acquiesced in if he did not help to plan the revolution, which effectively silenced the investigation of the disaster at Annual. It is probable that the coup d'état was inspired to permit the military to restore order in a nation which, in the opinion of the leaders, was on the verge of anarchy.

The manifesto of September 12 was directed to the nation. A few generals led by Miguel Primo de Rivera resorted to rebellion to restrain anarchy. They declared their loyalty to Alfonso XIII and Spain and asked for the confidence of the Spanish people. They could rely on the support of the garrison of Barcelona and some of the Catalans who expected to attain their regional aspirations as a result of the coup.

The rebels assumed control of all means of communication, proclaimed martial law in Barcelona, and established an interim directory on September 13. On the following day Alfonso, who was in France, returned to Madrid, accepted the resignation of the cabinet of the marquis of Alhucemas, and invited General Primo de Rivera to Madrid. The general arrived triumphantly on September 15. With the support of the army and the king, he was named chief of the government, and a definitive directory was appointed, consisting of eight generals and an admiral. Most of these were unknown, but the country as a whole at least appeared to accept them gratefully. The politicians were not so enthusiastic.

The first necessity was to restore law and order throughout the nation. Primo de Rivera was a soldier and believed in discipline. He suspended the constitutional guarantees, dissolved the cortes, restricted freedom of speech, censored the press, and abolished trial by jury. The Catalans who had aided in his elevation to power were soon undeceived. Their centers were closed. General Martinez Anido was named subsecretary of the Interior, with the responsibility of maintaining public order.

The Socialists, in a manifesto drafted by Indalecio Prieto, had immediately condemned the coup d'état, but they were afraid to challenge the military authority directly. Primo de Rivera did not wish to engage in a conflict with so powerful an organization, and fearing each other, they agreed to cooperate. As it was necessary to protect his popularity by maintaining the old political organizations, he dissolved the ayuntamientos and replaced them with juntas in which the military authority might play a part. The legislative commissions were suspended and military representatives were appointed in the judicial districts. With the king and queen Primo de Rivera paid a state visit to Italy, arriving in Rome on November 19. Although he may have gained some inspiration from the rise of the Fascist party in Italy, his dictatorship was more like that of Mustafa Kemal, which had begun about the same time in Turkey. The visit was cordial, and a favorable treaty of commerce was concluded with Italy.

In Catalonia the Lliga Regionalista had refused to support the dictator. In January 1924 provincial deputations, except in the Basque provinces and Navarre, were dissolved. A very able young Maurista, José Calvo Sotelo, who was ambitious for high office, was entrusted by the dictator with the general direction of administration. He was reputed to be well acquainted with Antonio Maura's plans for local administration.

Until January 1924 the repressive measures adopted by the Directory had been used to strengthen the popular approval of the new regime and consolidate its position. Thereafter, these measures were used against those who opposed the new policies, and any acts of protest or nonconformity were sternly punished. Rodrigo Soriano and Miguel de Unamuno —one of Spain's most distinguished writers and teachers—were exiled to Fuenterrabia for criticizing the dictator. Gradually, a little colony of émigrés and exiles assembled in Paris, although, at the same time, Primo was lenient with his friends and military colleagues. The coup d'état had been partly inspired, no doubt, by the desire to free the army from any stigma of responsibility for the Annual disaster. General Berenguer received a very light sentence for his part in the catastrophe, which produced a public reaction against the regime.

Primo was obsessed with the past. The political futility of the situation into which the party system had degenerated weighed heavily on his mind. He hoped to create from his position of a military dictator—whose authority rested on the army—a powerful national party which would restore the ancient traditions. He was unable to follow the example of Mussolini, who rode into power at the head of a national party which he had slowly built to strength. Instead, he tried to create the Patriotic Union as a mere creature of government, which would support and applaud his measures. The result was that the Patriotic Union was neither real nor effective. Many Conservatives joined the new party in good faith. Some Radicals supported the movement because of their confidence in an authoritarian doctrine. The majority of the members, however, were merely ambitious sycophants who sought an opportunity to profit from any support they might offer the dictator.

Although Moroccan negotiations had ended in Spanish recognition of the sovereignty of the sultan at Tangier, and Spain supplied officers for the local police, the muddle in Spanish Morocco was not easily straightened out. Abd-el-Krim, after careful preparation, steadily harassed the Spanish outposts. Many of the encounters were bloody. Primo went to Africa, reviewed the troops, and remarked on the lack of discipline in the Foreign Legion. After his return to Madrid, the French commander General Lyautey suggested that Spain and France cooperate in their Moroccan operations. An energetic campaign was necessary, and Primo determined to concentrate his forces in order to regain the lost territory. He went to Morocco and in October 1924 assumed personal command of the war. The first step was to abandon the advanced posts which the Spaniards had occupied. Troops were withdrawn to Tetuán, and a total of 180 positions were evacuated. During Primo's absence the marquis of Magaz presided over the Directory.

Indications had already appeared that the regime would be extremely conservative, despite the addition of Largo Caballero, the Socialist leader, to the Council of State, and the opposition began to show signs of life. A banquet in the palace in October was broken up when the police intervened to repress a demonstration of discontent. When conspiracies against the new regime were discovered, four of the guilty leaders were executed and a fifth committed suicide.

When Blasco-Ibáñez severely attacked Alfonso XIII, monarchists demonstrated their loyalty to the throne, and the Patriotic Union defended the king. Although Antonio Maura warned Alfonso of the dangers of prolonging the extra-legal constitutional situation, the only alternative that seemed open to him was an absolute monarchy, which José Sánchez Guerra, one of his staunchest defenders, declared he could never support. Both the intellectuals and politicians of Catalonia, including the Lliga Regionalista and Acció Catalana, became more hostile to the Directory.

In Morocco, Abd-el-Krim captured El Raisuni and then turned on the French and threatened Fez and Taza. General Sanjurjo successfully relieved the pressure on Melilla, but the attack on the French made possible an effective alliance, which until then had been dormant. The negotiations between the French and Spanish were conducted in Madrid, and a plan of joint operations was formulated. Troops were concentrated in Larache. Then General Sanjurjo was placed in command of a landing of 8000 men at Alhucemas in September 1925. The surprised Rifs defended themselves valiantly, but, with the aid of the combined air forces and navies, the operation was a complete success. Successive victories were won against the Moors, and the incipient republic of the Rif was overthrown.

Two enemies of the Directory became active in the absence of Primo de Rivera, who missed his great opportunity to retire and reestablish constitutional normality when he returned from Morocco. His failure to do this led inevitably to increasing opposition. In March 1925 the students of the University of Madrid began their agitation in honor of the writer Angel Ganivet, to the annoyance of Primo, who imprisoned a Mallorcan student and suspended lectures by visiting professors. The dictator had become suspicious of Damaso Berenguer, Weyler, and Cavalcanti, three of his generals, and in November, when a military conspiracy was discovered, a number of officers were imprisoned.

With the successful conquest of Alhucemas, the efforts of the Directory in settling the Moroccan question appeared to have reached success. As an initial step in the relegation of the army to its ordinary role and the restoration of normality, Primo selected a cabinet which included some civilians. The dictatorship, however, was extended, for Primo, as "protector of the nation," continued to preside over the new ministry. Alfonso acquiesced, although all of these steps were extra-legal.

Among the new members of the cabinet instituted in December 1925 were the duke of Tetuán, a man of no special distinction, and Eduardo Aunós, a Catalan member of the Lliga Regionalista. Although many on the extreme left continued to collaborate with the dictator, the civil directory was in reality conservative. The Constitution of 1876 remained suspended. The new government was challenged neither by parliamentary assessment of its measures nor public discussion in the press. Two of the ablest defenders of constitutional procedures, Pablo Iglesias and Antonio Mauro, died in December.

Rigorous measures were still taken against those who opposed the regime. *La Epoca* was fined, and Professor Jiménez Asúa was arrested for defending Miguel de Unamuno. The enemies of the Directory, on the other hand, increased daily, but their activities, under the threat of dictatorial retaliation, were necessarily clandestine. The Republicans under Alejandro Lerroux formed the Republican Alliance, and Manuel Azaña, the former editor of *España* and for many years secretary of the Ateneo of Madrid, became leader of an organization called Republican Action.

Heedless of opposition and undeterred by attacks, General Primo de Rivera continued on his arbitrary course. Hostilities were renewed in Morocco, when the French and Spanish agreed to break off negotiations with Abd-el-Krim, and the Spanish forces gained control of the plain between Nekor and the Guis. Abd-el-Krim then surrendered to the French, to evade the question of his responsibility for Spanish prisoners. His property was confiscated, and he was confined in the Island of Réunion.

In June 1926, a military revolt, led by General Aguilera and the aged General Weyler, was suppressed in the strategic city of Valencia, where there was lively animosity toward the dictatorship. As a result, many political leaders, including Marcelino Domingo, Dr. Gregorio Marañon, and Angel Pestaña were arrested and punished with heavy fines. Then the dictator dismissed the directing committee of the Ateneo of Madrid, replaced it with a group favorable to him, and lost what sympathy there remained for him in that important forum. Primo de Rivera also lost the support of the Corps of Artillery when he attempted to introduce modernizing reforms. In a decree of June 9 he broke a sacred tradition by ordering promotions to be based on merit. The corps was a very aristocratic body, in which promotion had been based on seniority. The king protested, but the general was uncompromising. The artillerymen and the cadets in the Academy of Segovia adopted a rebellious attitude, and the corps was virtually dissolved.

In foreign affairs Primo also made a decision which aroused the country. He withdrew Spain from the League of Nations in September 1926. Calvo Sotelo's financial measures had annoyed the wealthy businessmen, but Primo de Rivera's government still remained optimistic about its capability of initiating a new order. The dictator dreamed of establishing a supreme national assembly, representative of all classes and interests, which would study the important problems of government and Europeanize Spain. In a plebiscite, held in the middle of September, 6,697,164 votes were favorable to the Directory. The votes were obtained by official pressure and the propaganda of the Patriotic Union.

José Sánchez Guerra was deeply moved by the proposal to convoke an assembly, which, for him, was an attempt against the constitution. The Catalan separatists, led by Francisco Macía, conspired to organize an autonomous state, but the rebellion was easily suppressed, and Macía was exiled to Belgium.

Thus, large groups directly affected by the dictatorial measures became more embittered. The magistrates were antagonized by the role of the military, the Artillery Corps grew more hostile, the students were restrained from riots only by a display of force, and the wealthy classes were being slowly ruined by the measures of Calvo Sotelo. In Catalonia, however, where revolt against Castilian domination had long been endemic, irritation with the new regime was most powerful. The old politicians met and conspired in private houses. The Republicans plotted to overthrow the dynasty. Spain was seething with hostility toward the official regime. Even in palace circles strong criticism of Primo de Rivera was heard.

In 1927 the Federation of University Scholars became active, and the students organized. Establishment of a petroleum monopoly increased the discontent. Then Primo de Rivera resorted to fines and persecution. Ramón del Valle Inclán, the novelist and intellectual leader, defied the general. Only in Morocco, where under the leadership of General Sanjurjo steady progress had been made in the subjugation of the Spanish zone, was the new outlook hopeful. In the middle of July 1927 the victory of El-Sellitan completed the pacification of the country.

The National Assembly met in September 1927, a body handpicked by the dictator. Indalecio Prieto, the Socialist representative on the Council of State, opposed participation, but Julián Besteiro, on the other hand, held that it was logical that the Socialists should attend. José Sánchez Guerra manifested his opposition by seeking voluntary exile in Paris. The general soon revealed through his admonitions and threats that he was master of the National Assembly, which became a tame deliberative body completely under his control. While speakers who opposed him were not allowed to express themselves, those whom he favored had full latitude to praise the regime. Primo sincerely believed that he could rejuvenate the nation.

This situation continued throughout 1928, but the calm was only superficial, for there were many clandestine conspirators. Primo had suggested to one of his friends that he might retire, saying that he was tired and ill. He also planned to marry, but after announcing the wedding the couple disagreed, and he then changed his mind about retiring. He construed his successes in Morocco and with labor to mean that he could reconstruct the nation. In March 1928 there were student outbreaks. Eduardo Callejo, minister of Public Instruction, had introduced reforms, and although the dictator defended them, like other of his attempts to initiate a modernization of Spain, they were not favorably received. The National Assembly continued to meet, but no longer commanded public interest.

In 1928 a revolt of the cadets at the Academy of Segovia, in collusion with other officers, was suppressed, but the spirit of rebellion persisted, especially since civilian politicians hoped to profit from the antagonism of the military toward Primo. In January 1929 another revolt flared at Valencia, which José Sánchez Guerra, the Conservative leader, appeared from exile to direct, and which depended upon the captain general of Valencia, who, at the decisive moment, hesitated, causing the rebellion to fail. In Ciudad Real, some disgruntled artillerymen made themselves masters of the town in support of the movement at Valencia, but surrendered when that revolt collapsed. The government was victorious, but military morale and discipline appeared to be disintegrating. However, the students were more spirited in their defiance of the regime, while Republican professors and those opposed to the regime took advantage of the student disturbances for their own political purposes.

Eduardo Callejo had proposed a University Statute in 1928, conceding certain privileges to free centers under the control of clerical orders, which irritated the professors and students, who demanded the repeal of the unpopular article. Luis Bermejo, the rector of the University of Madrid, intervened, but Callejo was determined. Student demonstrations began. When the government took steps to discipline the students, they rioted and stoned the house of the dictator, whereupon the University of Madrid was closed.

In an effort to divert public feeling a great demonstration in favor of Primo de Rivera was held on April 1. But the success of the expositions held at Seville and Barcelona in May, which were expensive though brilliant spectacles, was more effective in diverting public opinion. Nevertheless, the students remained discontented and waited for the conclusion of the summer vacations to renew their agitation. The Republicans mobilized and formed the Radical Socialist party, and their leaders refused to cooperate in the expansion of the National Assembly. Although the law which had incensed the students was annulled, once their political interest was aroused, it was not easily suppressed.

The University of Valladolid sent Miguel de Unamuno as a representative to the National Assembly, while the College of Lawyers of Madrid chose Sánchez Guerra, Alba, and José Ortega y Gasset. The dictator, who sought new means to divert the public as his optimism faded, issued a bitter note in December 1929 enumerating his enemies. He yet hoped to redeem his regime, but gradually his calm and his health gave way. Some of his civilian ministers, including José Calvo Sotelo, deserted him when the peseta began to fall in value as the world economic depression was felt in Spain.

When the enemies of the regime—including students and such politicians as Maura and Martínez Barrios and General Manuel Goded—prepared a rebellion in Andalusia, the dictator resorted to an ingenious solution. Placed in authority by the army, which alone could save him at this moment, he directed a note to the army without consulting Alfonso XIII. This was an error, and the answers did not meet his expectations: generals commanding several regions spoke of their fidelity to the throne and ignored the dictator. Primo de Rivera presented his resignation and retired to Paris to die on March 17, 1930. General Damaso Berenguer, chief of the military household of the king, was then entrusted with the formation of a government. Primo had given Spain six years of peace and public order, but he had failed in his attempts to modernize Spain through a military dictatorship.

General Berenguer was confronted with the problem of the liquidation of the dictatorial regime, the restoration of constitutional guarantees, and the resumption of civil control of the government. This would have been a difficult task for any statesman, and quite impossible for a cautious general with little political experience. Moreover, he was held responsible for the disaster at Annual, which was enough for the antimonarchists. Criticism was immediately directed against the new government. Three of the ministers were conservatives, and two—the minister of War and the minister of Interior—were military men. Military interference in civil affairs and domination of the government appeared unshaken. The Ministry of State, however, was reestablished and entrusted to the duke of Alba.

An effort was made to restore normal conditions. The ministers took an oath of loyalty to the constitution, the imprisoned students were released, and professors were restored to their chairs. Unamuno was enthusiastically received in Irún and Salamanca. The ayuntamientos and provincial deputations were reconstituted in February 1930, and an amnesty was extended to the artillerymen.

Opposition to the Directory was now transformed into opposition to the monarchy; Alfonso XIII had let Primo hold power too long. Miguel Maura declared himself a Republican at San Sebastián, while Sánchez Guerra remained a monarchist, but critical of the king, and Sánchez Román denounced the infractions of the constitution. Other politicians moved from conspiracy to open political activity. The former Liberal minister Niceto Alcalá Zamora declared himself a Republican at Valencia. In view of the revolutionary activity, General Mola was named director of Security to guard against possible subversion. In May Angel Ossorio y Gallardo demanded Alfonso XIII's abdication, and in the same turbulent month the communists became active. Yet the monarchists appeared oblivious to the danger, for they had grown accustomed to revolution and to threats of revolution. Alfonso XIII visited Barcelona, and after a visit in England held an interview in Paris with Santiago Alba and Francisco Cambó, neither of whom any longer had sufficient influence to delay the progress of events.

Meanwhile, in the world economic depression the peseta declined steadily in value. In August at a meeting of special importance held at San Sebastián, the Catalan Republicans agreed to collaborate with the revolutionaries in return for recognition of the right of Catalonia to establish its own government. Republican leaders held a meeting in Madrid in September and vehemently attacked the monarchy before a large and enthusiastic audience. The signers of the Pact of San Sebastián were moving toward revolution, but they needed resources. Juan March, a wealthy smuggler who refused to supply them, was never forgiven. The military committee finally reached an understanding with the Confederación Nacional de Trabajo (CNT), the syndicalist labor union at Barcelona, and a revolution, led by General Queipo de Llano and Major Ramón Franco, was prepared for October. It was discovered by the police, and Major Franco was arrested, but he escaped from prison six weeks later.

Although Spain was now moving toward a republic, many were more against Alfonso XIII than against the monarchy, for he was held responsible for the evils of the Directory. In December 1930 the garrison at Jaca, led by Captain Fermín Galán, an African veteran, rebelled and advanced on Huesca, but the government took steps to meet the threat, and General Mola overwhelmed them with a superior force; Galán surrendered and, with Angel García Hernandez, was condemned to death and shot. The Republican movement had its martyrs.

The revolution had begun. Major Franco dropped revolutionary pamphlets over Madrid, but the outbreak at Cuatro Vientos failed when a majority of the aviators failed to support the movement. As a result, Queipo de Llano and Major Franco fled to Portugal; some members of the revolutionary committee were arrested, including Casares Quiroga, Miguel Maura, Alcalá Zamora, and Albornoz, although the police failed to capture the others—Marcelino Domingo, Alejandro Lerroux, Manuel Azaña, Nicolau d'Olwer, Martinez Barrios, and Indalecio Prieto. The Socialists' strike was ineffective, and Largo Caballero and Fernando de los Ríos surrendered. The government mistakenly believed that it had suppressed the opposition, but the opponents of the monarchy were undismayed. The revolutionary committee directed its adherents from the jail. Clandestine journals kept up the Republican propaganda. The Spanish intellectuals assumed a revolutionary attitude in organizing *Al Servicio de la República.*

General Berenguer announced general elections in February 1931, and to avoid disturbances the University of Madrid was closed. Although some monarchists announced their abstention, the Socialists agreed to participate. However, when the government could no longer find support, it resigned in February, resulting in a grave crisis for the king. Sánchez Guerra was unable to form a government, even after seeking adherents in the jail, for the revolutionaries who controlled public opinion refused to compromise. Finally, the Aznar cabinet was formed. All of its members were monarchists.

It was now decided to hold municipal elections, regarded as less dangerous than general elections, since the election of the ayuntamientos would test the revolutionary strength. The elections were held on April 12 and were the least corrupt that had ever been conducted in Spain. The Republican-Socialist coalition was triumphant in Madrid and the other large cities, and in Barcelona the Lliga Regionalista was defeated by the Esquerra. The opposition to Alfonso had found full expression—even servants of the king voting Republican.

The Monarchists were surprised, for they had not expected the elections to produce such a verdict, and they waited for loyal troops to rally to the support of the king. When the votes were counted it was seen that the rural areas voted for the regime, but the overwhelming opposition to the monarchy in the large cities was the decisive factor: the revolution continued to run its course.

Alfonso was averse to bloodshed, and at a palace meeting a majority of his ministers opposed the use of violence. Even though a provisional government had already been constituted in the house of Alcalá Zamora, the king hoped to obtain a truce until a constituent cortes could decide the fate of the monarchy. The minister of State, Romanones, held an interview with Alcalá Zamora, who would not compromise and who demanded the departure of Alfonso before sunset.

Meanwhile, in Barcelona, Maciá had proclaimed the Catalan Republic and in Madrid the banner of the republic had been hoisted amid wild rejoicing in the streets. The king bade his ministers farewell, and on April 14 left Madrid for Cartagena, where he embarked on the cruiser "Principe Alfonso." The reign of Alfonso XIII had ended, and the Second Spanish Republic was a reality.

CHAPTER XXXII

The Democratic Trend and the Cultural Scene

A reflection of the political struggle between the liberals and the conservatives may be found in the constitutional evolution of Spain from 1837 to 1876. The Constitution of 1837 restored sovereignty to the people, but the Constitution of 1845 was more in the nature of a compact. Another document formulated in 1856 never became effective. An idealistic and essentially democratic constitution was drawn up in 1869. It separated the governmental powers and provided a larger degree of religious freedom, although it maintained the Catholic Church in a favored position. A federal constitution proposed in 1873 was never approved. With the restoration of the Bourbons, Cánovas del Castillo brought about an elastic compromise between liberalism and reaction. The monarchy was established on a dynastic and hereditary basis, and Catholicism was restored as the state religion.

The Constitution of 1876 served Spain until the advent of the Second Republic in 1931, except for the seven-year period under Primo de Rivera when it was suspended. The liberal provisions of the constitution were expanded toward democracy by legislation enacted during the Regency of Alfonso XIII's mother. The Law of Associations was approved in 1887, trial by jury was provided in 1888, and universal manhood suffrage was established in 1890. The commercial, civil, and penal codes were also modified, but while the standardization of legal procedures made some headway, the ancient *fueros* persisted as the basic law of Catalonia, Navarre, and Vizcaya.

New administrative departments were created which not only added to the bureaucracy but also increased the number of persons dependent on the government. The Ministry of Industry, instituted in 1847, was given its name in 1851. In 1863 the Colonial Ministry was established, but it disappeared with the colonial empire in 1898. In 1900 the Ministry of Industry was divided into two departments, one comprehending Education and Agriculture, the other Industry and Commerce. The Council of State remained the supreme consultative body.

Provincial administration was in the hands of three agencies: the governor, the provincial deputation, and the provincial council. The governors represented the central authority and were supervised by the minister of Interior. The deputation was elective, and the council was a consultative body. A tendency to permit the expansion of local autonomy was apparent until 1876, when a counter-trend set in toward intensive centralization. By 1888 some degree of local administrative independence was again permitted.

By the end of the nineteenth century the hereditary aristocracy had lost much of its ancient political prestige, but its political influence persisted because it continued to serve the crown in diplomacy, in administrative positions, and in the militia. With the increase in democratic tendencies, on the other hand, a majority of the politicians were no longer of noble blood, even though they were sometimes given titles as a reward for services. The aristocrats retained their social dominion since they formed a closed class, united by ties of blood and marriage, by their pride, and by their ancestry. They also retained their wealth, and even increased it during the dissolution of the properties of the Church and the municipalities.

As a result of the industrial expansion of Spain, especially in Catalonia, the Basque country, and Andalusia during World War I, a class of wealthy merchants, industrialists, landlords, and shipowners emerged in Spain. Seeking to fortify their social positions with titles, honors, and even political careers, they moved to the larger cities, left their estates and businesses to the direction of overseers and managers, and enjoyed their income.

The professional groups provided most of the real rulers of Spain—the men responsible for both the progress and the decadence of the nation. Many outstanding politicians came from the universities and the Ateneo of Madrid—journalists or lawyers who acquired local reputations and followers. This fluid class, from which came most of the civil employees in public administration, lacked the solidarity of the old aristocracy, and it held diverse political ideologies. As a more stable civil service was established the positions were no longer considered legitimate booty for the triumphant party to distribute in patronage. While many administrative abuses disappeared with the colonial empire, the increase in the number of bureaucrats made them masters of the administration, though their security did not consistently increase their zeal in the performance of their duties.

The mass of the Spanish people, both in the cities and in the rural areas, led a proud but miserable existence, simply because there was not enough wealth to go around. The average wage varied from one to two pesetas, and in some villages was only a few cents. A natural resentment was felt toward those who exploited them. The gypsies, who had existed in Spain for centuries, formed a class of vagrants with a very low standard of living. They occupied prescribed districts in Madrid and Granada, served as dancers, bullfighters, beggars, or fortune-tellers, and wandered to the various fairs or markets.

As a result of poverty and the prevailing social misery among the lower classes, European revolutionary philosophies gradually penetrated the nation. Whereas the liberalism of the early nineteenth century was based on political rights, that of the later part of the century demanded the protection of economic and social rights. Under the influence of the Socialists and Anarchists, whose ideas gradually spread in Spain, the old restraints were defied, and strikes were increasingly used as weapons to win political and economic concessions.

The new theories first penetrated the coastal areas. Joaquín Abreu introduced the cooperative doctrines of the Utopian Charles Fourier into Cádiz and thence throughout Andalusia, while Fernando Garrido founded a Socialist review, *La Atracción,* in Madrid. The communistic ideas of Etienne Cabet, meanwhile, found champions in Barcelona and spread through Catalonia. Spanish misery also offered a fertile field for the revolutionary doctrines and writings of Louis Blanc, Pierre Joseph Proudhon, and Ferdinand Lassalle. The propagandists appealed especially to impecunious middle-class politicians, and by 1868 the concepts of the tyranny of capital, the rights of labor, antimilitarism, hatred of the wealthy, and atheism were widespread in Spain.

An indigenous form of socialism appeared in Andalusia, where by 1861 the peasants demanded the distribution of the land. This movement originated when the lands of the Church and the towns were divided up and the division was such that a privileged few were enriched and the masses were as miserable and landless as before.

Karl Marx's call to the workingmen of all countries to unite gave the Socialist movement some international unity, and did much to array the workers against the middle class. The International Association of Workers, founded in 1864, by 1870 had split into two irreconcilable groups which disputed the domination of the masses. The followers of

Marx expected to gain control of the forces of production, either through political action or revolution, whereas the followers of Bakunin, inspired by a mystic confidence in the goodness of man and stout individualism, hoped to abolish the state, religion, and capitalism.

Anarchism appealed especially to the individualistic Spaniard, and its greatest propagandist was an Italian, José Fanelli. After working with little success in Barcelona, he moved to Madrid in 1868, found the International Association of Workers already organized there, and spread his doctrines in impassioned discussions. His success was evident in the publication of the journal *Solidaridad* in 1870. Sagasta began to attack the anarchists and in 1872 ordered the dissolution of the International as a hotbed of crime. Instead of obeying the decree, the members defied it and held an influential Congress at Saragossa.

Meanwhile, the leader who gained the greatest prestige among Spanish workers appeared—Pablo Iglesias, who exerted a profound influence on politics for half a century. He learned the printing trade in order to assist his family, and in 1870 he joined the International Association of Workers to devote himself to the improvement of working conditions.

In 1870 Pierre Lafargue, a nephew of Karl Marx, fled from the debacle of the Paris Commune to Madrid. Pablo Iglesias cooperated with him and the orthodox Marxists. The Anarchists also grew stronger and sent delegates to the International Conference at The Hague in 1872. They were in fact strong enough to constitute an association at the Congress of Córdoba, and by 1873 had three hundred thousand members. Although its intellectual centers were in Madrid and Barcelona, anarchism made its principal appeal to the working classes of Andalusia.

Pablo Iglesias founded the Association of the Art of Printing in 1871 and became its president three years later. The Socialists failed to effect a reconciliation with the Anarchists at the Congress of Ghent, formulated their own political policy, and began to extend their influence. Iglesias, who was an effective incisive speaker, became a secretary of the central committee of the party in 1881, president four years later, and in 1886 editor of the weekly *El Socialista*. The General Union of Workers (UGT) was organized in 1888.

After 1876 the direct actions of the Anarchists led to their systematic persecution, and many migrated to Spanish America. The movement endured only in Catalonia and Andalusia. In 1878 the Anarchists initiated a campaign of arson and terrorist reprisals and extended their operations to attacks against those who revealed their secrets. One of them made an attempt on the life of Alfonso XIII and another assassinated Cánovas del Castillo.

Although defeated in their first attempts to gain political office, by 1897 the Socialists were represented in the municipal council of Bilbao. The Socialist program opposed military service, the government policy in the Cuban revolt, and the Spanish-American War. In 1899, when Iglesias became president of the Central Committee of the UGT, he steadfastly opposed collaboration with the Republicans. A few years later he had attained such prestige that Antonio Maura offered him the post of secretary of the Institute of Social Reforms. In 1905 the Socialists gained three seats in the municipal elections in Madrid, and in 1908 established the *Casa del Pueblo* in Madrid. An important force in politics, they were represented by seventy-one municipal councilors in thirty different cities and had nearly forty thousand party members.

The Socialists were responsible for the revolutionary strike of 1909 in Barcelona, called in protest against the Moroccan war. They also joined in the attack on Antonio Maura for the execution of Francisco Ferrer. This led to an alliance with the Republicans to overthrow the monarchy. In 1910 Iglesias became a deputy in the cortes. New members had joined the party and eighty-five thousand were enrolled in the UGT.

After the outbreak at Jérez and the repressive measures which followed in 1892, the Anarchists lost ground in Andalusia. Although some secret societies were dedicated to direct action, anarchist sentiment was not reawakened until the Bolshevik party appeared in Russia. A new movement was initiated in Spain about 1900. Using political tactics, the Revolutionary Syndicalists undertook methodically to organize the workers. The general strike and sabotage were the weapons to be used to establish the syndicate as the basis of production, distribution, and social organization. The Anarchists continued to agitate, strike, and propagandize, but these weapons proved futile, and they returned to terrorism. When syndicalism was imported from France it found many recruits among the Anarchists.

At a congress of workers held in Barcelona in 1910, the General Confederation of Labor (CNT) was created. When it engaged in a general strike, Canalejas acted decisively, suspending the union and breaking the strike. By 1915 the CNT had been reorganized and was publishing *Solidaridad Obrera*. In 1917, during the general strike, the Socialists began to cooperate with the Syndicalists through their labor organizations to work for a minimum standard of living, but the government arrested the leaders of the movement. By this time, however, many people had drawn closer to revolutionary ideas, and several Socialists had been elected to the cortes.

Spain also felt some strong repercussions of the Bolshevik success in Russia. In 1921 a majority of the Spanish Socialists refused to recognize the Third International, and under the leadership of Pablo Iglesias and Fernando de los Ríos followed an independent course. Their relations with the Communists were usually hostile. The Spanish Syndicalists, on the other hand, were elated at the success of the Bolsheviks, a syndicalist federation was created at Seville, and sindicatos únicos—substantially, industrial unions—were established at Barcelona. At their third congress at Madrid the Syndicalists provisionally adhered to the Third International and exerted pressure on workers to join the CNT. The intellectual leaders of the workers, both Socialist and Syndicalist, opposed cooperation with the Bolsheviks.

The government undertook an energetic repression of the syndicalist movement, and a period of ruthless terrorism ensued. Despite the efforts of the authorities to restrain them, the Syndicalists attacked their Catalan employers. The latter in response also resorted to violence and organized the Sindicato Libre. Although Barcelona was the principal scene of violence, it also extended to Madrid—where Dato was assassinated—and to other centers. Some veteran Anarchists recoiled from the crimes committed and opposed the Syndicalists. Primo de Rivera acted decisively to suppress terrorism in Barcelona, but the Syndicalists waited patiently for the opportunity to renew their activity.

The Catholics also founded clubs in the last quarter of the nineteenth century to counteract revolutionary socialism. The government, in the meantime, had taken steps to improve working conditions and provide cheap and sanitary housing for the workers. Its measures were carried out slowly and seldom equaled its good intentions. The work of women and children was regulated (1873), a Commission of Social Reform was established (1883), hospitals were established, and a workers' compensation law was placed on the statute books (1900).

Throughout the nineteenth century the Spanish army constantly intervened in civil affairs. Attempts to overthrow the government by pronunciamiento—military revolution—were common, and both extremes recognized that they could always find a military leader to support their political aspirations. The era of military interference was partly ended by the determined action of Cánovas del Castillo, but the military juntas after World War I inaugurated a period of agitation which demoralized the army and undermined the government. The problem of fixing the responsibility for the disaster at Annual again led to the threat of military intervention. Meanwhile, the respect for the Spanish armed forces declined following the disastrous results of the colonial wars. Military corruption and inefficiency caused a further loss of faith in the Spanish troops.

The Spanish military leaders had admired the successful Prussians in the Franco-Prussian War and begun to imitate them in tactics and organization. The basis of the reform proposed in 1887 was universal military service. Spain was divided into eight military districts, and a territorial reserve was established. But as a majority of the generals opposed the reforms, they were not approved. Obligatory military service was finally introduced under the leadership of Canalejas. The Spanish navy, which had played a secondary role in the colonial and civil wars, was annihilated in the Spanish-American War. Although a navy was vital to Spanish coastal defense, it was not until ten years after the war that Antonio Maura began to rebuild the fleet. Spain had, however, been a pioneer in experimentation with a submarine. In 1859 Narciso Monturial had tried out an underwater craft at Barcelona, but the Spanish government never became interested in the project. Another mariner, Isaac Peral, also made successful tests in 1889–90, but the government never approved of them.

Spanish economy was seriously disturbed by the internal disorder which preceded the restoration. Agriculture was particularly retarded. The government had hoped to remedy the situation by breaking up the landed properties of the Church and the municipalities, and although it succeeded in redistributing some of the land concentrated in latifundios, or great landed estates, it did not provide sufficient indemnity for the old owners or little real benefit to the actual cultivator—much of this land being acquired by wealthy proprietors. Feudal rights were abolished, but the serfs were transformed into tenants and merely the absentee owners of the land were changed. The towns, despoiled of their lands, were forced to levy heavier taxes to meet their obligations, and the new taxes fell most heavily on the working class. While latifundios developed in central and southern Spain, the *minifundios*—properties divided by inheritance into excessively small plots—evolved in the north and made cultivation uneconomical.

Mining, stimulated by intelligent government action and the influx of foreign capital, continued to be an important industry. In the latter half of the nineteenth century mining concessions were granted to enterprising individuals for the development of mineral resources. Despite restrictions, a great deal of foreign capital had already entered Spain.

The government had to lease the mercury mines of Almadén and the lead mines of Linares to the Rothschilds, and in 1873 the copper mines of Minas de Ríotinto were sold to an English company. A Belgian syndicate participated in the exploitation of the potassium discovered in Catalonia in 1914. The quest for iron led to the expansion of the occupied area in Morocco, which was found to be rich in minerals. Spain was really deficient in only one mineral—coal of good quality—the production of which did not meet domestic needs.

The chief Spanish industries were in chemicals and textiles, but machinery had to be imported to improve them, and Spain was slow to follow the industrialized countries. In certain respects the Spaniards imitated them, such as by the introduction of the steam engine in 1840, and the first steamship in 1852, but Spain remained largely an agricultural country. Some traditional industries were continued, and the state reserved to itself the monopoly of tobacco and matches, leasing manufacturing rights to companies. The role of Spain as an exporter of food to Europe improved during World War I, and flour mills were erected, preserved foods processed, and sugar production increased. Wine and olive oil continued to be two of the most important exports.

Normal commercial activities were also impaired by World War I, but at its close Spanish trade began to recover. Meanwhile, the unfavorable balance of trade had drained the country of capital. Spain began to export more raw materials, but she still had to import others to compensate for her deficiencies. Internal commerce was facilitated by the building of highways and railways. A railway was not built in Spain until 1848. The government wished to leave railway construction to private initiative, but in 1855 the lines were legally divided into those of general and private service, subsidies being granted to some of them. José Salamanca became the principal financier of Spanish railways. In northern and central Spain most lines were constructed by French companies, although Spanish capital and English engineers built the railroad from Tudela to Bilbao. Government regulation was strengthened by law. Rates were specified, concessions were restricted, and it was determined that the lines would eventually revert to the state.

During the reign of Isabel II more than eight thousand miles of highway were built, and after the restoration a general plan of highway construction was formulated. By 1910 Spain had more than twenty-seven thousand miles of improved highway. Primo de Rivera greatly improved Spanish highways so as to meet the needs of automobiles. Under Isabel II great interest was also displayed in canal construction, both for irrigation and transportation. The Canal of Castile and the Canal of Isabel

II were completed, and in 1859 a plan for the improvement of the Guadalquivir was adopted which again made Seville an important port. Communications had meanwhile been improved by the extension of the postal system and, in 1844, by the introduction of the telegraph. The telephone was not really introduced until Primo de Rivera granted a concession to the American International Telephone and Telegraph Company.

Although there was some agitation for free trade in Spain, the Catalans and the agricultural interests demanded that Spanish economy be protected. After the restoration, both commercial treaties and the tariffs were inspired by the principles of protection. The most alarming aspect of Spanish finances was the continuous deficit and the annual increase in the national debt. Spain had neither the industrial production nor the imperial resources to maintain her solvency. Despite efforts to reorganize Spanish finances, increase taxes, and invent new excises, expenditures continued to exceed income, because of growing bureaucracy and the demands for national defense and public works. Under Primo de Rivera, José Calvo Sotelo succeeded in accumulating a surplus, but the fall of the peseta in 1929 destroyed Spanish credit.

Relations with the Vatican fluctuated with political vicissitudes, but improved under Pope Pius IX. The Concordat of 1851 made Catholicism the exclusive religion of Spain, prelates were given increased authority over education, and the Church was authorized to acquire property in Spain. The article relating to religious orders produced much controversy, but the government agreed to the establishment of new orders approved by the pope. In 1855 the Concordat was violated when the landed property of the Church was again offered for sale. After a flurry of negotiations the Liberal Union amended the concordat so that the Pope authorized the sale of ecclesiastical property, although the Church was still permitted to acquire it. Another break with the Vatican occurred in 1864, when Pius IX condemned modern religious errors and the encyclicals were published without governmental sanction.

A wave of anticlericalism was released by the revolution of 1868, which persisted into the reign of Amadeo I. Cánovas del Castillo had restored the monarchy, but he could not restore the religious atmosphere of the later days of Isabel II. Neither extreme was satisfied with the limited religious toleration conceded by the Constitution of 1876. One of the first acts of Cánovas was to renew relations with the Vatican, but the religious unity expressed by the Concordat of 1851 was never restored. Pius X feared the anticlerical movement in Spain might disrupt her harmony with the Church, but relations with the government and the royal family remained cordial until the triumph of anticlericalism in 1931.

With the twentieth century, renewed efforts were made to improve Spanish education. The Junta for the Broadening of Studies aided students and professors in foreign studies, while the Free Institute of Education, an independently organized institution of higher education founded in 1876 by Francisco Giner de los Ríos and Manuel Bartolomé Cossio, also contributed to a zealous interest in scientific disciplines and scholarship. Journalism became very popular, for it offered not only a means of personal expression, but also opened a political career for some. The newspapers all gave vent to political opinions and publicized issues under debate, thereby increasing the trend toward democratic action. Higher education underwent many vicissitudes. The first reforms aimed at the centralization of the ten universities and the establishment of state supervision in teaching, with serious restraints on academic freedom. After a period of freedom during the revolutionary era, the state resumed its direction of education in 1875, and the reforms made after the restoration established a maze of contradictions. Nevertheless, by 1900 the universities were greatly improved. They became quasi-autonomous, alumni began to participate in their activities, and women were admitted.

While secondary education suffered vicissitudes similar to those of the universities, public opinion was deeply concerned over the improvement of literacy by better elementary education. Political battles were waged to obtain an increase in the number of schools and teachers. The reforms demanded called for better salaries for teachers, the provision of adequate buildings, an improvement in the qualifications of teachers, and the inspection of schools. While politicians were debating these matters, some individuals were acting. The Free Institute of Education provided secondary and university teaching and was responsible for the establishment of summer sessions and the creation of the Ministry of Education. Nevertheless, it was attacked because of the radical ideas of its founders, its methods of teaching, and the political activities of those connected with it. Gradually, the reforms in primary education became evident. In 1849 there were 12,357 schools, in 1908, 22,572, yet illiteracy remained a great obstacle to Spanish progress.

Philosophical studies attracted less attention in the latter part of the nineteenth century, although new trends and developments were imported. Of these, Krausism had the greatest number of disciples, and enemies; Julián Sanz del Río, whose teaching and writing had enormous influence, studied philosophy in Germany and founded the Spanish school during his academic career at the University of Madrid. Many of the revolutionaries were nourished on the principles of Krause, and many university professors subscribed to his philosophy. Among his pupils were Francisco de Paula Canalejas, Nicolas Salmerón, and Francisco Giner de los Ríos.

In the writing of history, the historians abandoned the rhetorical style of the first half of the century and became more critical and objective. Many documents were collected and published. The romantic period had not been a good one for history. Spaniards fell under the influence of French historians, especially the magniloquent Jules Michelet. Victor Balaguer (1823–1901) was a moderate representative of this school, but Emilio Castelar (1832–99) was its outstanding figure. If his historical data were inexact, at least his rhetoric and his imagination were superb. Prospero Bofarull y Mascaró (1777–1859), director of the Archive of the Crown of Aragon, composed works of solid erudition. Although Modesto Lafuente y Zamalloa (1806–66) was primarily a journalist, his *General History of Spain* was highly regarded and passed through many editions.

The entrance of Cánovas del Castillo into the Academy of History gave a decided stimulus to historical writing because of his political prestige. Probably the outstanding historian of the period was Rafael Altamira y Crevea, a professor at the Central University of Madrid, whose *History of Spain and of Spanish Civilization* marked a new era in historical analysis. The Center of Historical Studies also had great influence, partly through its director, Ramón Menéndez Pidal, another distinguished historian. Most of the Spanish historians of the modern epoch have devoted themselves to the past glories of Spain, including pre-history, the Moors, regional studies, and the Spanish American empire. The leading literary critic and historian of the nineteenth century was the erudite Marcelino Menéndez y Pelayo (1856–1912).

A number of young writers of the end of the nineteenth century sought to assist Spain after the Spanish-American War by reassessing her role in the contemporary world. One of the leaders of this so-called "Generation of '98" was Angel Ganivet (1862–98), whose *Idearium español* set the tone for a renaissance of Spanish life and thought. Manuel Bartolomé Cossio (1852–1932) also had great influence in revitalizing the Spanish spirit. Miguel Unamuno (1864–1937), rector of the University of Salamanca, wrote widely read philosophical essays as well as fiction and took an active interest in politics, although he remained independent of party affiliation. José Ortega y Gasset (1883–1955), critic and essayist, exercised a wide influence. His *The Revolt of the Masses,* a famous work, has been translated into many languages. A brilliant stylist and an illuminating commentator, he stimulated many liberal movements. Joaquín Costa y Martínez (1846–1911) was an outstanding intellectual of great influence, who wrote principally on social reform. Another important writer on social problems was a woman, Concepción Arenal (1820–93). Ramiro de Maeztu dealt with economic subjects and had a great influence on the imperial resurgence of Spain.

A principal characteristic of the literary production of the later nineteenth century was its originality. Romanticism placed less emphasis on technique and a greater emphasis on inspiration. Its influence persisted in the lyric, the drama, and the novel until the end of the century. The reign of Isabel II was rich in lyric poetry. Later, other influences such as impressionism appeared. The modern lyric poetry of Spain may be divided into two periods, the one before the impact of Rubén Darío, the Nicaraguan poet, and the succeeding one. Then, after a period of modernism, poetry came under the influence of a new generation dominated by Juan Ramón Jiménez.

Some of the earlier poets, such as Gabriel García Tassara (1817–85), were preoccupied with political problems, while others, such as Carolina Coronado (1823–1911), composed personal and erotic poetry. One of the greatest lyricists of the nineteenth century, José Zorrilla y Moral (1817–1893), migrated for a time to Mexico, where he was patronized by the Emperor Maximilian. Gustavo Adolfo Becquer (1836–70), who enjoyed a vagrant existence, wrote moving lyrics and haunting romantic prose tales. Ramón de Campoamor y Composorio (1817–1901) enjoyed an extensive popularity for his philosophizing verse. Gaspar Nuñez de Arce (1834–1903), a journalist and politician, was a poet of disillusion. Juan Ramón Jiménez (1881–1958), who was awarded the Nobel Prize, was a master of the new austere lyric and one of Spain's most distinguished poets. He also had important followers among the foremost younger poets—Federico García Lorca, Rafael Alberti, Pedro Salinas, and Jorge Guillén. The other poet of Jiménez's stature in the early twentieth century was Antonio Machado (1875–1939).

The Spanish novel both profited and suffered from the influence of foreign writers. Spaniards imitated romanticists and realists, but only in regional novels did they develop originality. Cecilia Bohl de Faber (1796–1877), who wrote under the pseudonym Fernán Caballero, had great influence on her contemporaries and is considered to have founded the modern novel. Her first novel, *La Gaviota,* won her a considerable public. In addition to her novels of local color she was an important collector of Spanish folk tales. Of the many writers of historical novels perhaps the best was Enrique Gil, author of *El Señor de Bembibre*. The master of exuberant and romantic prose was Pedro Antonio de Alarcón (1833–91), who attained popular fame with his stories of rustic life. Among his best-known novels are *El Final de Norma, El Sombrero de tres picos,* and *El Capitán Veneno*. Another important writer, Juan Valera (1827–1905), followed a diplomatic career. A versatile critic, poet, and dramatist, he excelled in the novel. His masterpiece was *Pepita Jiménez*.

Benito Pérez Galdós (1843–1920), the most famous modern Spanish novelist, was a liberal in ideology. He wrote more than seventy historical and social novels and was also successful as a dramatist. His novels include *Doña Perfecta* and *Angel Guerra*. His dramas, such as *La Loca de la casa* and *Mariucha,* were enthusiastically acclaimed, but his greatest stage success, *Electra,* has been attributed to political circumstances rather than merit. Vicente Blasco-Ibáñez (1867–1928) was a regional novelist, a revolutionary politician, and an aggressive Republican. Reared in Valencia, the majority of his novels deal with that region. Two of his best works are *La Barraca* and *Cañas y barro,* but his most popular novel is the melodramatic *Los Cuatro jinetes del apocalipsis* (*The Four Horsemen of the Apocalypse*).

An aristocrat, Emilia Pardo Bazán (1852–1921), who became one of the leading realistic novelists of Spain, owed her success to her energetic, masculine style. Her most famous novels are *Un Viaje de novios, Los Pozos de Ulloa, La Madre natureleza,* and *La Serena negra*. Armando Palacio Valdés (1853–1938) was a realistic novelist preoccupied with cultural problems. His works include *Marta y María* and *La Hermana de San Sulpicio*. Pío Baroja (1872–1956) wrote many novels on Basque life; Ramón del Valle Inclán (1869–1936) gained attention as an exotic stylist; Gabriel Miró (1879–1929) wrote elegantly for a select group; and Ramón Pérez de Ayala (b. 1880), who was in the Spanish diplomatic service, wrote masterly and satirical delineations of character in such novels as *Tiger Juan*.

The modern Spanish theater was marked by two trends, one toward historic and romantic drama and the other toward the comedy of manners. Later, a third trend appeared in the theater of ideas, but the public was only partly prepared for these subtleties of style and thought and in general continued to prefer gay comedy. The prolonged romantic period was best represented by Antonio García Gutiérrez (1813–84), who had a brilliant career. Of his plays the most popular was *El Travador*. Juan Eugenio Hartzenbusch (1806–1880), whose *Los Amantes de*

Teruel achieved contemporary popularity, was prominent in the romantic movement. A new era was inaugurated by José Echegaray y Eizaguirre (1832–1916), who produced play after play with intricate themes and psychological problems. The most popular dramatist of the new school, Jacinto Benavente, who, like Echegaray, won the Nobel Prize, was well known for his satiric comedies. Gregorio Martínez Sierra, whose psychological perceptivity was remarkable, obtained an immediate success with his *Canción de cuna,* and a pair of brothers, Serafín Quintero (1871–1938) and Joaquín Alvarez Quintero (1873–1944), captured the popular fancy with their lively and graceful plays.

The period was marked by a revival of the regional languages, which had partly succumbed to the influence of Castilian. The renaissance was essentially political, but its leaders appealed to regional pride by an emphasis on regional literature and traditions. The principal centers of separatism were Galicia and Catalonia, although there was some activity in the even more particularistic Basque country. Rosalia de Castro (1837–85), a sensitive Galician poet, reflected the life and restlessness of the people in that area. The best-known Galician poet, Manuel Curros Enríquez (1851–1900), worked in Madrid as a Republican journalist, but wrote in the Galician dialect.

The principal Catalan poet was Mosén Jacinto Verdaguer (1845–1900). His masterpiece, *La Atlántida,* is one of the great modern epics. Juan Maragall y Gorina (1860–1911), one of the foremost poets of the day, was a fervent Catalan, who won his first literary triumph in the Floral Games of Barcelona in 1881. Catalonia also produced some excellent playwrights. Federico Soler y Hubert (1838–95) was regarded by his contemporaries as the founder of the Catalan theater. He wrote under the pseudonym of Serafi Pitaira and won the Queen Regent's prize for his play *Batalla de reines* in 1888. Angel Guimerá y Jorge (1847–1924), both a poet and dramatist, produced romantic masterpieces. Other well-known Catalan dramatists were Ignacio Iglesias y Peyades (1871–1928) and Santiago Rusiñol y Prats (1861–1931). The Catalan theater declined after 1900, but a number of able Catalan novelists appeared, such as Narciso Oller y Moragas (1846–1930), Catarina Albert y Paradis, and Eugenio d'Ors.

In architecture the two most renowned figures were Luis Domènech y Muntaner (d. 1923) and Antonio Gaudí (1852–1926), both Catalans, whose best work is in Barcelona. Gaudí, the most widely discussed architect of Spain, demonstrated such great originality in his church of the Holy Family in Barcelona that his innovations have been called revolutionary. He adapted historic styles to modern materials and embellished his works by an extraordinary command of the auxiliary arts.

During the second half of the century, after the romantic vogue entered Spain from France and Germany, Spanish painting developed remarkably. Federico Madrazo (1815–94) and Carlos Luis de Ribera introduced the new influence into Spain. The realistic school originated by Goya persisted into the later nineteenth century with Eugenio Lucas (1824–70), who adopted his style so completely that his pictures are often confused with those of Goya. One of the greatest Spanish artists of the nineteenth century was Mariano Fortuny (1838–74). He studied in Rome and took part in the Moroccan war. His African pictures contributed especially to his fame. A Belgian, Carlos de Ilaes (1829–98), who became a naturalized Spaniard, revived interest in landscape painting. Spanish art was brilliantly represented at the Paris Exposition in 1878, and Madrid, Seville, Barcelona, and Valencia became the principal artistic centers.

A new style flourished in interpreting atmosphere and light. Its leading exponent, Joaquín Sorolla y Bastida (1863–1923), was the great Spanish impressionist. Julio Romero y Torres (1880–1930) was a highly individual artist of Córdoba, specializing in portraits. Ignacio Zuloaga, a Basque, attained considerable acclaim for his vigorous and vivid pictures, and the brothers Ramón and Valentín de Zabiaurre combined primitiveness with audacious decoration. The great Pablo Picasso and Salvador Dali left Spain early in their careers and lived and achieved fame abroad.

New styles and new tastes developed in music. While critics and many musicians defended the Italian opera and official patronage was extended to foreign music, some attempts were made to create a Spanish opera based on popular music. Although its devotees applauded the resultant light operas, many critics regarded them as unworthy of the efforts of Spanish musicians. Eventually, the consolidation of the zarzuela as a true musical type was accomplished by Rafael Hernandos y Palomar (1822–88) and Cristobal Oudrid (1825–77). Francisco Ascensio Barbieri (1823–94) wrote operas and zarzuelas and was very popular in the middle of the century. In Catalonia, Antonio Nicolau (1858–1933) was the composer of many operas. Felipe Pedrell (1841–1923) also wrote operas and collected the folk music of Spain. He dedicated himself to the revival of the Spanish musical idiom. Isaac Albéniz (1860–1909), who gave his first concert at the age of four, became one of the leading inspirations of Spanish music with such works as *Iberia*. Basque music was maintained as a national tradition by José María Usandisaga (1887–1915) and Jesus Guridi. Enrique Granados will long be remembered for his *Goyescas*. But the Spanish composer who attained the greatest fame, however, was Manuel de Falla (1876–1946) of Cádiz. He achieved recognition and success with his opera *La Vida breve*. It is said that some of his music is Andalusia transmuted. And perhaps the greatest virtuoso of modern times is Pablo Casals.

Despite the continuous internal conflict and the loss of Spain's colonial empire, the century preceding the establishment of the Second Republic was one of increasing democracy, economic progress, and expanding cultural interest. Inspired by the removal of restrictions on political and economic activity, Spaniards entered with enthusiasm into the development of their culture. Yet beneath the surface of this intellectual and artistic ferment the seeds of decentralization and anarchy lay dormant. The country was impoverished, drained of capital by war and an adverse trade balance. Reforms were contemplated and even put into statutes, but usually their effectiveness was left in the realm of good intentions.

The Spanish people were beginning to take matters into their own hands. Some continued to expect to gain social reform through political agencies, others relied on direct action through terrorism. The nation was exposed to the threat of regional decentralization as the hegemony of Castile was weakened and aspirations for regional autonomy were revived. Meanwhile, Spanish politicians continued to seek private advantage with little regard for the common good. The tension increased, awaiting only the arrival of some political crisis to expend its force in a tremendous upheaval.

CHAPTER XXXIII

The Second Republic

The Revolutionary Committee of the Republican-Socialist coalition had constituted itself as the Provisional Government (April 14, 1931) when Alfonso XIII became a voluntary exile, although he did not abdicate his authority. The Provisional Government which assumed control of the destinies of Spain included: president, Niceto Alcalá Zamora y Torres; minister of State, Alejandro Lerroux y García; minister of Justice, Fernando de los Ríos Urruiti; minister of War, Manuel Azaña Díaz; minister of Interior, Miguel Maura y Gamazo; minister of Finance, Indalecio Prieto Tuero; and minister of Labor, Francisco Largo Caballero.

Most members of the government were experienced politicians. Niceto Alcalá Zamora, a former Liberal deputy and minister, was a skillful orator whose declaration of Republican principles in Valencia a year earlier had produced a sensation in political circles. Alejandro Lerroux was the master of the Radical party. An opportunist in his methods, he had built up a strong political machine in Barcelona and had opposed the resurgence of Catalan regionalism. He was the oldest man in the new government. Francisco Largo Caballero, Indalecio Prieto, and Fernando de los Ríos were leading Socialists. The others were Republicans. Miguel Maura, the son of Antonio Maura, had not become a Republican until 1925, but his sharp criticism of the dictator had given him stature in his adopted party.

The group included some of the ablest propagandists in Spain. Two of them, Los Ríos and Maura, had attained reputations as lawyers. Others were men of letters or journalists. Manuel Azaña had won the National Prize for Literature in 1926 and was an incisive speaker, both moving and satiric. On the whole their political attitudes were more intellectual and idealistic than practical. They had become the leaders of the government because they represented the liberal reaction to the dictatorial methods of Primo de Rivera. They had had long political experience and were determined to make Spain a modern state.

For the moment the conservative opposition was disorganized as a result of the failure of the Directory and the impact of the election, but it was deeply rooted in tradition. The radical opposition, while abstaining from political action, was impatient to secure reforms through direct action. It consisted of the Anarchists and Syndicalists, who had to be restrained in the interest of public order. The new government had the task of combating both extremes while it consolidated its position and undertook the modernization of Spain. To establish a republican regime, its members were determined to be liberal and democratic.

Nevertheless, the Provisional Government had only de facto authority. This rendered it more vulnerable to attacks and made a legalization of its position imperative. In mid-April the ministers issued a Juridical Statute, justifying their authority and promising to submit their collective and individual work to the approval of a constituent cortes. They assumed the authority to govern Spain for three months and proceeded to reorganize the branches of government. The permanent membership of the Senate, as provided by the Constitution of 1876, was dissolved and the senators were deprived of their special rights. The Council of State was abolished, and the security police were reorganized in an effort to protect the nascent republic against subversion and to maintain order. Then the legislative work of the Directory was revised.

The government sought to establish a new social order in keeping with the modern responsibilities of the state. All contracts, services, and monopolies were reexamined to ascertain whether they were contrary to the national interest. The penal laws of the Directory were annulled, and the Penal Code of 1870 was revised. Jury trial was reestablished, while the final decision in most matters was reserved to the constituent cortes. The new government was impatient to renovate Spain, restore individual rights, and introduce social legislation.

The assessment of responsibility for the Annual disaster and for the arbitrary measures of the dictatorship provided another important task. An attempt was made to obliterate every vestige of the monarchy which had been overthrown—names of warships were changed, and it was proposed to rename many of the streets of Madrid. The property of the crown was confiscated and the income reserved to the public treasury. The tricolor of red, yellow, and dark violet was adopted as the National banner, and the "Hymn of Riego" was substituted for the "Royal March." Sweeping measures were enacted in an effort to abolish or modify the principal supports of the old regime. The army was subjected to drastic reorganization and its power was restricted. The old Law of Jurisdictions was abrogated. Likewise, the military orders of Santiago, Calatrava, Alcántara, and Montesa, rich in ancient tradition and landed wealth, were suppressed. More than twenty thousand officers were given the opportunity to retire on full pay, and the admission of new students to the military academies was suspended. The rank and file of the army was drastically reduced. Thirty-four divisional commands were reduced to nine, and the number of field officers was decreased by a ratio of ten to one. The Ministry of War was thoroughly reorganized. By the middle of June the power of the army to intervene in civil affairs had been theoretically diminished.

An attempt was also made to resolve the religious issue. Miguel Maura declared that the primary objective of the new regime was the separation of Church and state. Complete religious liberty was authorized in Spain, and when the Catholics protested, the final decision in the matter was left to the cortes. The Church had been an ally of the monarchy, and it was essential to restrict its political influence in the approaching elections for the constituent cortes. Yet Miguel Maura, for one, recognized that caution had to be exercised lest the Catholics be aroused to united action by a direct assault on the Church. Cardinal Segura y Saenz, archbishop of Toledo, had already urged Catholics to elect deputies who would defend the Church. As a result he was expelled from the country. Aroused by this act, the Catholics began to mobilize in defense of their interests. The body called Catholic Action was organized to defend clerical interests.

Educational reform was the next item on the Republican program. The Council of Public Instruction was reorganized and obligatory religious education was abolished. Local and provincial councils of primary instruction were established. Seven thousand new places for teachers, each endowed with five thousand pesetas, were created. The dictatorial decree prohibiting the use of Catalan in the primary schools of Catalonia was abrogated, and the regional language was ordered taught in the normal schools there. Thus, the regional identity of Catalonia was recognized, and relations between the Catalans and the Provisional Government became cordial. The Catalans had already undertaken the formulation of a regional statute to submit to the people and to the cortes.

Perhaps the greatest achievement of the Second Republic lay in the peaceful revolution by which it was inaugurated. Alcalá Zamora wrote that the indomitable will of the people had overthrown a monarchy that had existed for fifteen centuries in forty-eight hours in a bloodless revolution. The boast of the president of the Provisional Government was somewhat premature. The new regime was not a month old before serious disorders occurred as a result of the rivalry of the Socialist and Syndicalist unions, and the intransigent attitude of Cardinal Segura y Saenz aroused the anticlerical passion of the radicals and extremists.

A riot took place in Madrid on May 10. The following day several churches and convents in Madrid were burned while the Provisional Government deliberated and blamed the reactionary Monarchists. Finally, the Monarchist newspaper *A B C* and the Catholic daily *El Debate* were suspended. The incendiarism in Madrid was a signal for similar attacks in other parts of the nation, where the anticlerical sentiment was unrestrained. While there were no disturbances north of Madrid, convents and churches blazed in Valencia, Alicante, Murcia, Granada, Seville, Córdoba, Cádiz, and Málaga, and martial law had to be proclaimed. Then, after five days of turmoil, the disorder subsided and the country became completely quiet.

The anarchy in the southern part of Spain, where the situation of the rural laborers was painful, had emphasized the need for agrarian legislation. The exodus of the rural laborers to the cities was alarming. The new cabinet believed that land should be distributed among those who tilled it, and agrarian legislation to this effect was immediately enacted. Moreover, employers of agricultural labor were required to give preference to the day laborers in their neighborhoods, and the municipal police were ordered to investigate uncultivated lands and to dictate the norms for their use. Accident indemnification was also extended to agricultural workers. A commission on agrarian reform was appointed to formulate bases for the solution of the land problem and for presentation to the constituent cortes. Labor problems were likewise considered. The eight-hour day was adopted, regulations for the maintenance of labor standards were issued, a board was established to encourage employment, and mixed tribunals were created to arbitrate disputes between employers and laborers.

Indalecio Prieto was confronted with a more nearly insoluble task than any of his colleagues. As minister of Finance, he had to stabilize Spanish currency. This old problem, inherited from the monarchy, was made more difficult by the world-wide economic depression of the time. The peseta had dropped in value long before the advent of the Second Republic. By the end of April 1931 it had fallen to a value lower than at any time since 1898, as the efforts at stabilization failed and the anxiety produced by the bloodless revolution caused a sharp decline. Various members of the Spanish aristocracy tried to emigrate with their fortunes and increased the financial strain. Funds withdrawn for export were ordered redeposited, but the peseta continued to drop—from twenty-five pesetas to the pound sterling in 1926 to fifty-eight in 1931.

It was under these circumstances that the elections for the constituent cortes were held. The principal aim of the Provisional Government was the restoration of a normal governmental existence. The suspension of constitutional guarantees and the clamor for constitutional reform had been important factors in the fall of the monarchy. The minimum age for the franchise was reduced from twenty-five to twenty-three as a reward to the young men who had helped establish the republic. Eligibility for membership in the cortes was extended to women and priests. The electoral divisions were revised so that each province could choose one deputy for every fifty thousand inhabitants. The elections were to be held in June, and the cortes was convoked for July 14. It was to consist of a single chamber, elected by direct popular suffrage, and was invested with wide legislative powers.

The primary issue of the electoral campaign was the confirmation of the republic and the reconstruction of Spain on liberal and socialist lines. The parties were divided into three main groups. The conservatives desired to protect traditional institutions and vested interests of the Church and the landlords. They had been disorganized as a result of the municipal elections and now sought to awaken their adherents and the indifferent masses to the threat to Spanish traditions. They hoped to profit by the reaction against the reforms already undertaken by the Provisional Government and the violence of the impatient radicals. The new Spanish Action party was more thoroughly organized, under the leadership of the marquis of Luna and Angel Herrera, editor of *El Debate*. The clergy also rallied to the defense of their interests. Cardinal Segura y Saenz, who had returned to Spain, issued a pastoral letter urging Spanish Catholics to participate in the elections and to support candidates who would defend the rights of the Church and the social order. Alfonso XIII issued similar instructions to the Monarchists, but they showed less energy.

The Republican-Socialist coalition, which had been held intact until the convocation of the cortes, was the strongest group in the electoral contest. It included parties of varying political opinions, and the alliance was difficult to maintain in view of the individualism of the Spaniards and the differences which threatened to disrupt it. The Provisional Government, however, maintained its cohesion and threw all of its energies into the campaign.

The third group consisted of the extremists who wished to reconstruct Spain by revolution rather than evolution. They created disorder and violence in the campaign, which was accentuated by the rivalry between the Socialist and Syndicalist labor organizations for the support of the laborers. The small Communist party was also active in the campaign, conducting meetings and distributing masses of propaganda, but it was not as effective as the Syndicalists, whose anarchist tendencies held a greater appeal to Spanish individualism. Their object in boycotting the elections was to paralyze the country by strikes and violence, and thus by direct action to force the acceptance of their program. Angel Pestaña was their effective leader in Barcelona, but they also conducted an intensive campaign in Andalusia. They opposed domination from the Communists at Moscow.

In the elections the Republican-Socialist alliance won a resounding victory. The disorder had discredited the extremists, and the Monarchists had not yet recovered from their surprise. The Socialists won 130 seats, the Radical Republicans 100, the Right Republicans 75, the Catalans 40, and the Catholics, Carlists, and Monarchists 90. The remaining seats were scattered among the extremists. Significantly enough, not a single Communist was elected.

The newly elected cortes debated the republican constitution throughout the summer. A preliminary draft had already been formulated, and the parliamentary commission proceeded to revise it in leisurely fashion. The last article of the constitution was finally approved in November, and the final draft was approved by a vote of 368–0 on December 9.

The Constitution of 1931 was a liberal document—too liberal for all sections of the country for which it was designed. It declared Spain to be "a democratic republic of workers of every class, organized in a regime of liberty and justice." Its authority sprang from the people, all of whom were equal before the law. Spain surrendered her proud isolation by engaging to respect "the universal rules of international law" and by renouncing "war as an instrument of national policy." The existing municipal and provincial organization was retained under the new constitution, but it was provided that groups of provinces might organize and apply for a Statute of Autonomy.

In the important section on guarantees of political and individual rights, equality and freedom were emphasized. Titles of nobility were abolished. Neither birth, social class, wealth, political ideas, nor religious beliefs would provide a basis for privilege in Spain. The equality of women before the law was established. Freedom of thought, the right of petition, freedom of assembly, and a free press were guaranteed. Protection was given against arbitrary arrest and imprisonment. After a heated debate between Victoria Kent and Clara Campoamor—the two women members of the constituent cortes—the suffrage was extended to women. The government could suspend any part of the constitution when the security of the state so required, subject to the subsequent approval of the cortes. The suspension would be valid, however, for only thirty days.

A crisis arose over the treatment to be given private property. In the end a compromise was effected by providing for nationalization or expropriation with adequate compensation, but forbidding confiscation.

No crisis, however, so racked the cortes and the country as did that produced by the attack on the Church. The new constitution provided for the separation of Church and state. Every individual was guaranteed freedom of conscience, but the problem also involved the religious orders, divorce, and education. There is little doubt that the idealists in their anticlerical enthusiasm made a fundamental error. They attacked the Church in abolishing it as the official religion, in providing for the dissolution of the Jesuit order, in nationalizing the property of the religious orders, and in prohibiting them from engaging in industry, commerce, or education.

To the Catholics this was persecution, and it aroused Catholic sentiment throughout the country. Its immediate consequence was the resignation of Alcalá Zamora and Miguel Maura from the Provisional Government. They undertook a campaign to revise the constitution before it was promulgated. The Catholic deputies also withdrew from the constituent cortes. Manuel Azaña was named president of the Provisional Government.

Another group of articles regulated marriage, divorce, and the education of children. Marriage was based on the equality of the sexes and could be dissolved on the petition of either party. Parents were obligated to educate their children, whether they were legitimate or illegitimate. Primary education was to be free and compulsory. All education, however, would be subject to lay control.

As for governmental organization, the Constitution of 1931 provided that the president of the Republic, elected for six years, would personify the nation. He nominated the prime minister and could direct foreign affairs, subject to the approval of the cortes. His power was strictly subordinated to that of the cortes, which represented the sovereign will of the Spanish people. Even in convoking and dissolving the cortes he was subjected to restrictions and to possible censure and deposition.

The cortes or congress of deputies was converted into a unicameral body, "composed of representatives elected by universal, equal, direct, and secret suffrage." The deputies, who had to be twenty-three years of age, were elected for four years. The cortes was to meet annually on October 2 for a period of four months. Both the government and the deputies could initiate legislation. The cortes might authorize the government to legislate by decree upon matters reserved to it, but the power was restricted to specific matters.

The debates in the constituent cortes had been accompanied by sporadic strikes and disturbances throughout the country. Nevertheless, the deputies had persisted in their labors, and the constitution was approved. The disorder, however, had forced the deputies to add the Law for the Defense of the Republic to the constitution, to be effective for the duration of the constituent cortes unless expressly repealed. It had been proposed by President Azaña in an effort to restrain the extremists of both Right and Left. The conservatives attacked it as a continuation of dictatorial procedures, for they also hoped to profit from dissatisfaction with the disorder and to prevent the consolidation of the republic.

After the approval of the constitution it was necessary to choose the first president of the Second Republic. Although the Socialists constituted the largest single party in the chamber, they were divided. Some wished to remain in the opposition and await developments before assuming the responsibility for governing Spain. Others were inclined to accept the task with all of its consequences, hoping to form a government of the Left.

The election of the president was held in the cortes in December. Although Alcalá Zamora had been practically ostracized for a time after his resignation as president of the Provisional Government, he had not withdrawn from the chamber and soon recovered his popularity. It appeared that he would be the unanimous choice for the new chief executive, and when the ballots were counted, he had received 362 of the 410 votes cast. A new government was immediately constituted, following the resignation of the Provisional Government. Manuel Azaña was named premier, and Alejandro Lerroux became the leader of the opposition. The Second Republic was thus constitutionally consolidated but it had yet to consolidate Spain.

Meanwhile, the constituent cortes had also considered other matters. Trying Alfonso XIII *in absentia,* it condemned him to perpetual exile. He was charged with neglect of his duties as a constitutional sovereign, acceptance of the coup d'état of Primo de Rivera, treason against the sovereign people, and complicity in administrative immorality. In vain was he defended by the veteran count of Romanones, the only confessed

Monarchist in the cortes. Manuel Azaña remained as premier of Spain for nearly two years.

At the close of 1931 an incident occurred in Castelblanco, a little village of nine hundred inhabitants in Estremadura. When the authorities refused permission for a political meeting, four civil guards were killed by a mob. A general strike was called in neighboring Badajoz. Such outbreaks were due to the extremists—the Syndicalists, Anarchists, and Communists—who hoped to profit from disorder to discredit any duly authorized government. They were impatient for a complete revolution, attained by direct action, which would overthrow all vestiges of the old order. They were rivals of the Socialists and also sought to discredit them. Unrest, rioting, and arson appeared in Bilbao and Valencia, where the civil guards were a target for the fury of the mobs. But the most serious disturbance occurred in Catalonia. The Catalans had won the cooperation of the Syndicalists for their regional aspirations, but the Communists, who had been returning from exile, sought to undermine the Statute of Autonomy. This was the first organized attempt to establish a Communist state in Spain. Although sympathetic outbreaks took place in Bilbao, Lérida, and Seville, the revolt was localized and quickly suppressed by Azaña's firm and prompt action.

The next move of the government was to expel the Jesuits by a decree ordering the confiscation of their property in February 1932. While the measure was enacted to enforce the constitution against religious orders which took an oath of allegiance to the pope, and was in accord with the prevailing anticlerical sentiment in the government, it was unwise. It was unpopular with many segments of the population and produced a reaction even among Catholics who were in general sympathetic toward the republic. The Jesuits had a great educational influence in the nation through their seventy residences and thirty colleges. The Republic could provide neither teachers nor schools to replace them. Nevertheless, their residences and schools were abandoned as they went into exile.

Azaña, however, continued to act with decision. He deported a hundred Communist rebels to Spanish Guinea without trial. As a result some twenty general strikes were called, but most of them lasted only a day or two and the country quickly regained normality. Despite a few riots, Spain was tranquil until August.

During February new divorce laws were also approved. This further alienated the Catholics, because, although the Church held marriage to be indissoluble, the law conceded divorce after five years of agreed separation for various causes. The lack of social discipline which accompanied the greater freedom provided by the Republic unhappily multiplied the number of beggars in the streets of Madrid and the provincial capitals. An increased migration from the rural communities to the cities was already making itself manifest.

An agrarian law was passed during the summer of 1932. Reformers had long agreed that the only remedy for the low wages and agrarian misery and discontent lay in the expropriation and redistribution of the large estates. The new law tried not only to meet the demands of the Syndicalists, but to provide compensation for the landlords. All land above a certain limit was made liable to expropriation, with compensation allowed on the basis of the assessed value for taxation. Usually, this was below real value, but payment was made in government bonds. The law was applied to the area of the great latifundios in central and southern Spain and to all other estates of feudal origin. While royal holdings and lands belonging to those who conspired against the Republic were confiscated, aristocrats were indemnified for recent improvements. The expropriated land became national property and was ordered cultivated by peasant tenants. A central Institute of Agrarian Reform was created, with a general board representing the various interests involved. It had the task of working through regional committees to take censuses and proceed with the redistribution, which would take a number of years. The law was welcomed by the mass of Spaniards, but for the extremists of the Left it was inadequate and too impartial and for the conservatives it was too drastic.

In August 1931 the Catalans voted on their Statute of Autonomy, which had already been submitted to the municipal councils and approved by them. The verdict was overwhelmingly in favor of the statute —592,961 to 3,276. Two-thirds of the negative votes were polled in Barcelona, while 99 percent of the remainder of the Catalans favored the statute. When the document was presented to the cortes there was a violent reaction against it. The conservatives, who had not questioned the principle of regional autonomy in the constitution, opposed the statute as a part of the government program. They protested the dismemberment of the nation in an effort to defeat and weaken the government.

Debate on the Catalan statute occupied the cortes from May to September 1932. Many of the fundamental clauses of the original document were sadly mutilated, but the Catalans showed admirable restraint. They held their regional language in great sentimental regard. The Catalan statute provided two official languages, Catalan in Catalonia, and Castilian in relations with the government of the republic. This clause was modified, finally declaring that "the Catalan language, like the Castilian language, is the official language in Catalonia." Although the compromise was meaningless, it produced an adverse effect on the sensitive Catalans.

Castile had always controlled Catalan education. Professors and school teachers from Catalonia had been unable to obtain posts in other parts of the nation, while their institutions were filled with natives of other parts of Spain, unfamiliar with Catalan. The University of Barcelona was administered from Madrid. The statute was modified to give the Generalitat control of the Catalan educational and cultural institutions. The University of Barcelona was to be granted autonomy under a board of control. This caused some Catalans to threaten to abstain from voting on the article. Azaña exerted great influence in favor of the bill, but although he succeeded in soothing public opinion in Barcelona, he failed to reconcile the Catalan deputies.

Finally, in September the statute was approved by 314 votes to 24. The Catalans were jubilant despite the amendments to their original statute. The statute and the decree promulgating it were appropriately signed at San Sebastián, and the document was formally presented to the assembled Generalitat on September 25. The Catalans had won an equal partnership in the Spanish union of states and had reasserted their individuality.

The Basque provinces—Guipúzcoa, Álava, Vizcaya, and Navarre—also had definite regional characteristics, a proud cultural heritage, and a unique language. Three days after the proclamation of the Catalan state in Madrid, an attempt to establish a Basque state at Guernica, under the famous national oak, was prevented by the police. While the movement for autonomy was based largely on a synthetic revival of the Basque language, it was distinguished by the religious attitude of the Basques. They were devout Catholics who protested against the anticlerical provisions of the constitution. The Navarrese, who were the most rural of the four provinces, were less enthusiastic about the Statute of Autonomy in the discussion at Pamplona than the other three provinces. The action of the municipal councils in approving the statute in Guipúzcoa, Álava, and Vizcaya was confirmed by plebiscites. In the cortes, however, parliamentary delays kept the document in committee until the government resigned and its postponement was inevitable.

Many Galicians also desired autonomy for economic reasons, chiefly through a desire to improve their own economic condition. They had formed an autonomist movement and, with the advent of the republic, prepared a draft statute. The proposal was approved by the municipal councils, but the government was forced to resign before it could be approved by the cortes.

The cortes was still in session when two pronunciamientos, long familiar to Spaniards, were made simultaneously in Madrid and Seville. In Madrid the military revolt in August marked a violent resurgence of the Monarchists. It was organized by aristocrats and retired army officers, but the citizens resisted stubbornly, and the rebels were opposed by many police and loyal soldiers. The outbreak was quickly suppressed.

General Sanjurjo, marquis of the Rif, director general of the civil guard, led a more serious revolt in Seville, aimed at the government in power rather than at the republic itself. There was fighting throughout the city between the rebel troops and the forces loyal to the republic and between radicals of both extremes. Most of the civil guard remained loyal to the republic and reinforcements, rushed to Seville, soon suppressed the insurrection. Repercussions were felt throughout Andalusia, however, as Socialists and Syndicalists declared strikes. Azaña's prompt action in suppressing the revolt strengthened the government. General Sanjurjo and his fellow conspirators, who had been captured, were leniently treated. He was sentenced to death, but popular opinion forced the president to commute the sentence to life imprisonment.

The government made a serious error, however, in suspending eight Madrid newspapers, including *A B C* and *El Debate,* and a number of provincial periodicals. Although they eventually resumed publication, the crisis did not merit the severe action, which increased the discontent of the moderates and conservatives. During the autumn the civil service was purged, creating uneasiness and a feeling of insecurity in areas which would otherwise have remained loyal to the republic.

To enforce the constitutional provision and satisfy the anticlericals, the Law of Confessions and Congregations was presented in October 1932 and promulgated seven months later. While this confirmed guarantees in the constitution and tried to provide religious equality, it was aimed largely at restricting the freedom of the religious orders. This punitive intent increased the opposition of the Catholics without really satisfying the anticlericals. The restrictions on the educational activity of the orders were drastic. They had provided facilities for primary education which when terminated—by the end of 1933—would seriously handicap the efforts to reduce illiteracy. Many educators who realized that there were insufficient lay schools believed the change should have been effected more gradually.

Marcelino Domingo had already authorized the creation of twenty-seven thousand schools, of which three thousand had been completed and seven thousand were to be ready within a year. However, it was difficult to train sufficient teachers to staff the schools. In 1932 twenty-five hundred more schools were opened, and the salaries of the school teachers were raised to a minimum of three thousand pesetas. Traveling schools were established for remote areas, and the municipalities were obliged by law to contribute to the cost of constructing new schools. Fernando de los Ríos became minister of Education at the end of 1932. He built new secondary schools or used those confiscated from the Jesuits. The number of students receiving secondary training was increased to seventy thousand, as compared with the twenty thousand three years earlier.

Little was done in higher education. The University City in Madrid, which had been begun by Primo de Rivera, was under construction, but professorial abuses and student strikes continued. Only in Barcelona was there university autonomy. Nevertheless, the republic had accomplished a great deal in education. Schools of Arabic studies were created, a summer session was inaugurated at Santander, and the budget for higher educational activities was increased to forty-five million pesetas in 1932.

By the early part of 1933, however, the government of Azaña had failed to maintain its popularity. Anarchist revolts in Madrid, Barcelona, Lérida, Valencia, and Seville were easily suppressed, but the escape of twenty-nine of the prisoners from Africa again raised the charges of tyranny against the government. The event which led directly to its fall, however, was a revolt in Casas Viejas. This little village lay on the borders of a forty-thousand-acre estate owned by the duke of Medinaceli, which was to be confiscated and distributed among the peasants. On January 11 a group of rebels proclaimed a Communist regime there and demanded the surrender of the civil guard. They had accumulated firearms and ammunition and opened fire on the civil guards. Reinforcements drove the rebels from the village, but resistance continued in one house. After the defenders suffered heavy losses the house was bombed and set on fire, and eight persons were killed. The rebels finally surrendered the following morning, after the death of more than twenty persons.

The government was charged with issuing orders which were barbarous and inhuman, and the indignation found expression in the cortes. Lerroux and his radical followers were insistent in their attack, and the coalition supporting the government was split. Azaña was sustained by a small majority of only forty-three. An official investigation was undertaken, and the report of the commission censured the director general of Security for having ordered the application of the *ley de fugas* —the shooting of a person under the pretext that he was trying to escape. The government was sustained, but its prestige had disappeared because of its severity.

The government was fearful of popular opinion and postponed the municipal elections. Partial elections in twenty-five hundred rural districts, which had been deprived of their representation because they had returned Monarchists in 1931, were announced, and in these the government was defeated, winning only some five thousand of the sixteen thousand offices to be filled. Battle was immediately joined when the cortes met. The parties in opposition demanded that the government resign. Azaña staunchly refused, and the Radicals went into parliamentary revolt, forming a bloc to obstruct legislative activity and force the government to resign. The Syndicalists initiated disturbances throughout Spain. A traffic strike in Barcelona was followed by general strikes throughout the country, and the university students organized demonstrations in Madrid. The unrest was not hostile to the republic, because a vast majority of the people opposed both communism and the monarchy. They were fearful only of a prolongation of conflict.

The Law of Religious Confessions and Congregations was approved by the cortes in May 1933 by a vote of 278 to 50. The conservative press and the bishops condemned it sharply, but Alcalá Zamora finally decided to sign it. A more liberal Law of Public Order replaced the Law for the Defense of the Republic late in July. Even after all the legislation necessary to implement the constitution had been passed, Azaña was unwilling to relinquish office. But the Radicals continued to demand the dissolution of the chamber because the country now desired a more conservative government, and finally he resigned. Lerroux then tried to form a short-lived government supported by the Radicals and Radical-Socialists. The only course which remained was to hold new elections. Alcalá Zamora dissolved the constituent cortes, and general elections were fixed for the first ordinary cortes in November 1933.

While the Azaña government was desperately trying to consolidate the republic and maintain order, the threat of Spanish Fascism had already appeared. Interest in Italian Fascism had been aroused in the intellectual circles of Madrid by Ernesto Giménez Caballero. He went to Italy in 1928, where he absorbed the doctrines of Fascism, and on his return to Spain he became a propagandist for it. He regarded Rome as the seat of Catholic tradition in Europe and the symbol of Latin Europe against northern Europe, which had assumed Continental leadership as the prestige of the Mediterranean nations declined. He regarded Russia, which had also been a victim of the greed of the northern powers, as a comrade and ally of the aggrieved nations of Latin Europe.

Another Spaniard looked to Berlin for leadership. Ramiro Ledesma Ramos, the impoverished son of a village school teacher, was enrolled at the University of Madrid, where he soon acquired a following and became an open admirer of Hitler. Intolerant and harsh in temperament, he felt a passion for proletarian justice. In the end he contributed more to the development of the ideas of Spanish Fascism than did any other Spaniard. He appealed directly to the urban proletariat and provincial peasantry, regarding Karl Marx as an apostle in the battle for proletarian justice. He condemned the Spanish Church and Catholicism as reactionary influences, and as enemies of social justice as dangerous as the industrialists, bankers, and landlords of Spain.

Ledesma founded an organization which he named Juntas de Ofensiva Nacional-Sindicalista (JONS). Anticlericalism remained a powerful ally of the new movement, both for its value in enlisting the anticlerical Anarchists and in maintaining its solidarity against the Popular Action party led by Gil Robles. JONS, like its syndicalist adherents, was extremely revolutionary. It, too, believed in direct action through street fighting, attacks on opposition clubs, and heckling political orators until rioting began. JONS appealed to tough, intolerant, and fanatical young men.

The Spanish Fascist movement had no leader until the emergence of José Antonio Primo de Rivera, the handsome, widely respected, and popular son of Miguel Primo de Rivera. He had received an excellent education and although a devout Catholic, deplored the political influence of the Spanish clergy. He was admired not only by his followers but by the Socialist Indalecio Prieto, and the Anarchist Angel Pestaña. Yet Ledesma Ramos regarded José Antonio as a "political dilettante" and an "immature aristocrat," who dreamed only of vindicating the name of his father. Ledesma feared he would betray the Fascists into reaction.

After unsuccessfully attempting to launch a new publication, *El Fascio,* José Antonio Primo de Rivera organized the Falange Española at a rally attended by several thousand persons in October 1933. His principal associates were Julio Ruiz de Alda, who had accompanied Ramón Franco on his famous flight to Buenos Aires, and Alfonso Garcia Valdecasas, a Republican deputy who deserted his colleagues for the Monarchist party.

In the elections of November 1933 Spain swung definitely to the Right. When the election returns were finally reported the conservatives held 207 of the 473 seats in the cortes, the moderates 167, and the parties of the Left only 99. Among the conservatives were forty-three Traditionalists or Monarchists and sixty-two members of the Popular Action party. The moderates included one hundred Radicals and twenty-five members of the Catalan Lliga. The Left was also divided between Socialists and members of the Catalan Esquerra.

As the conservatives had no clear majority and had to depend on the cooperation of the moderates, who exercised decisive control, the most practicable course was to let the moderates govern. Lerroux, leader of the Radical party, had the largest following in the cortes and was a subtle and experienced politician. The people were optimistic concerning the future. They hoped for less precipitate progress and fewer revolutionary strikes, but they were doomed to wait in political inaction while the radicals of both extremes gathered their strength.

Finally, Alejandro Lerroux assumed the prime ministership. Eight of his cabinet of thirteen men were Radicals, and four of the remainder were moderates. José María Gil Robles, however, remained the principal force in the cortes. He was the leader of the Confederación Española de Derechos Autónomos (CEDA), the strongest party coalition in the country. Completely inexperienced in governmental affairs, he had been the hope of the Catholics as a protégé of the Jesuits, who expected him to undo much that Azaña had accomplished during the preceding two years. Gil Robles was willing to cooperate with Lerroux, although he was prepared to take office if the Radicals lost the confidence of the chamber. Alcalá Zamora, despite his own Catholic leanings, distrusted Gil Robles as a statesman and never called on him to form a government. He remained without portfolio, and this fact contributed to the unpopularity of Alcalá Zamora with the conservatives, who regarded his attitude as an affront to their leader.

One of the first objects of the Radical government was to relieve the Catholic Church from the measures passed under Azaña. The substitution of lay schools for religious schools was indefinitely postponed—many Jesuits were still teaching openly in Madrid—and salaries were voted for the parish priests. Negotiations were undertaken with the Vatican. Despite the tranquility of the country and the reduction in the number of strikes, it soon became evident that the new government could accomplish little. Unstable for lack of policy, it was forced to resign in March, because the Spaniards were unwilling to cooperate. Salvador de Madariaga became minister of Education in the new government of Ricardo Samper. A distinguished author and professor and an able ambassador in Washington and Paris for the republic, he aroused great expectations for educational reform, but he remained in office only six weeks. Samper was a provincial politician of little ability.

Francisco Macía, first president of the Generalitat and a leader in the struggle for Catalan autonomy, died in December 1933. Thereafter, the Catalan political path began to diverge from that of the republic. Political opinion in Catalonia had not changed, while the rest of Spain had become more conservative. The reaction elsewhere simply solidified radical opinion in Catalonia. Luis Companys, who succeeded Macía as president of the Generalitat, was able to hold the confidence of the Catalan Esquerra.

Underneath the surface Spain was still republican. The attempt to reestablish capital punishment was exceedingly unpopular, and the minister of Justice, Alvarez Valdez, was forced to resign, even though there was a continuous succession of crimes in the larger towns. The Amnesty bill, which proposed to extend a pardon to political offenders for crimes committed before December 3, 1933, also aroused a heated debate, but was passed. General Sanjurjo emerged from prison and removed to Lisbon, where he again began to participate in conspiracies against the republic. Juan March, who had been expelled from the constituent cortes, also resumed his former activities. Calvo Sotelo returned to the cortes, where he attacked the financial policies of the republic in fiery speeches.

During the summer portents of future troubles appeared. The Basque provinces held the right to assess their own taxes and pay a fixed annual sum to the national treasury. New taxes threatened this privilege, and the Basque ayuntamientos resolved to elect representatives to defend their privileged position. The government declared the elections illegal, but the Basques stubbornly held them without disturbance, despite the protest of civil governors and the presence of police and armed guards. Many of the mayors of these municipalities were arrested, but the matter was held in abeyance until the cortes could discuss it.

In Catalonia the Generalitat had passed a law designed to settle an old dispute between tenants and proprietors. Many of the former had been dispossessed because the depression had prevented them from fulfilling their contracts. Disputes were to be settled by arbitration tribunals, but the proprietors protested the reinstatement of the tenants and their payment of reduced rentals. The Spanish Court of Constitutional Guarantees, as the final court of appeal, declared the law illegal because the Catalan parliament had exceeded its authority in legislating on the matter. In Barcelona the Lliga Catalana supported the court but the Esquerra remained intransigent. The deputies and the Basque nationalists walked out of the cortes, but Luis Companys publicly ratified the law. As a result the Catalans attacked the government for following a centralist policy and threatened revolution.

Meanwhile, instead of resuming the role of an opposition party, the Socialists, led by Indalecio Prieto and Francisco Largo Caballero, also veered toward revolt. Although Manuel Azaña was disappointed at the trend of events, he sought to prevent the outbreak. In Madrid the Socialists, Syndicalists, and Communists protested against a meeting of the Catalan landowners through a general strike, and concern increased when the Socialists bought arms for the labor unions from the government and delivered them in Asturias and the Basque country under the personal supervision of Prieto. Samper had been forced to resign, and Lerroux was entrusted with the formation of a government. Gil Robles demanded a portfolio for the CEDA. It was rumored that if his adherents entered the ministry, there would be a revolutionary strike. Three CEDA men were included in the new cabinet. The hour for revolution had struck.

On the morning of October 5 a general strike was declared throughout the country. Asturias was the critical area. Martial law was proclaimed there, and the police and civil guard were reinforced by the army. Barcelona was tranquil until October 6, when Companys announced the Catalan state as part of the "Federal Spanish Republic" and invited the anti-Fascist leaders in the nation to establish a provisional government at Barcelona. The issue had been joined between the reactionary conservatives who wanted to impede reform and the parties of the Left who were impatient to proceed rapidly with the reconstruction of the nation. Companys demanded that General Batet transfer his allegiance to the new federal regime. Batet, whose troops were in possession of the central Plaça de Catalunya, refused. Fighting began by midnight, and early the following morning Companys and his followers were forced to surrender.

In Asturias the rebellion produced a short and bloody civil war, accompanied by barbaric atrocities on both sides. The rebels massed in the hills and mines of Asturias. The government rushed reinforcements, but they were too late to prevent a determined attack on Oviedo. The people supported the rebels and fired on the soldiers from their houses. Some six thousand rebels under arms, equipped with tanks, machine guns, armored cars, and dynamite, carried on continuous fighting in Oviedo for three days. General López Ochoa, who commanded the government troops, fought a fierce engagement with four hundred men near Aviles. He routed them, but had difficulty in returning to Oviedo because the bridges had been destroyed and trees blocked the road. By mid-October the city was under government control. Moors and members of the Foreign Legion had been rushed from Africa to suppress the miners. During the fighting more than thirteen hundred persons were killed and three thousand wounded, of whom more than two-thirds were civilians.

Madrid had also experienced the terror of civil strife. Soldiers entered the crowded Puerta del Sol and fired without provocation at imaginary foes on roofs and into the apartments of inoffensive people. Lerroux had declared the entire nation under martial law for two months. Azaña, who had opposed the rebellion and sought to persuade Largo Caballero that it would play into the hands of the conservatives, was arrested in Madrid. Throughout Spain the enemies of the government were arrested. Largo Caballero was sent to the Model Prison. Only Prieto remained at large, and from his refuge he denied the extravagant charges which were leveled against him.

The net result of the revolt was to increase the prestige of the conservatives and momentarily to accelerate the reaction. Catalonia lost her autonomous position and local administration was again centralized. In the cortes the Monarchists demanded that the Catalan statute be annulled, but the Radicals supported Cambó, the leader of the Lliga Catalana, who blamed the revolt on the Esquerra. As the CEDA deputies resisted the efforts of the Monarchists to enlist their support and agreed with the Radicals, a compromise was arranged. The Catalan statute would only be suspended until the cortes determined the details of its gradual restoration. The functions of the president of the Generalitat were delegated to a governor general.

Although Azaña had been acquitted of complicity in the revolt, a number of prominent persons had been condemned to death by the military courts, and the government was confronted with the difficult question of ordering their execution or granting a reprieve. Either decision would be attacked by some sectors of public opinion. The fate of the government hung on the issue. The Radicals favored the commutation of the sentences, while the CEDA and agrarian leaders voted for execution. No agreement could be reached and the ministry resigned. When Gil Robles demanded six portfolios, Lerroux formed a minority cabinet, but it was shortlived. Gil Robles believed that his opportunity had arrived and that he would be called to form a government. His adherents demanded either his appointment or elections, which, according to them, would signify chaos. Instead, Alcalá Zamora entrusted the government to Lerroux again. Gil Robles became minister of War with four followers in the coalition cabinet.

Two trials meanwhile excited the public mind. In Catalonia, Companys and six fellow conspirators were sentenced to prison for thirty years, while the cortes debated the guilt of Azaña. Although the final vote was 189 to 68 in a chamber half-filled, an absolute majority was not attained and the charges collapsed. The debate was full of personalities and marked the lowest point of Azaña's prestige and popularity. Thereafter, they rose steadily.

An effort was also made to revise the Constitution of 1931. It provided for its own revision four years after promulgation. In 1935 the cabinet published a summary of its proposals including the modification of regional autonomy, the ending of expropriations of private property, a redefinition of educational policy, and the restoration of the Senate. Indications appeared that the religious articles would be modified.

The government adopted an energetic program of public economy. The minister of Finance, Chapaprieta, hoped to balance the budget by 1936–37. No budgets had been presented since 1932, and the deficit had increased. Chapaprieta's economy legislation became effective in October. It was aimed at the reform of the bureaucratic civil service, many posts being abolished and salaries cut. All civil servants were required to work as well as draw their salaries. This reform, however, was detrimental to education. The teachers were miserably compensated, some forty-three thousand in elementary schools earning less than $250 a year; although the republic had created thirty thousand new schools, it was also necessary to pay the teachers a living wage.

In the autumn of 1935 a series of crises disrupted the coalition between the conservatives and the Radicals. When Lerroux was forced to resign, Chapaprieta formed a cabinet of nine ministers, including three Radicals, Gil Robles and two followers, an Agrarian, and a member of the Lliga Catalana. When it broke up in disorder after lasting only eleven weeks, no one wanted to assume the premiership. A general election appeared to be the only hope. Manuel Portela Valladares, ex-civil governor of Barcelona and ex-governor general of Catalonia, finally became premier, but despite his experience, he was unable to stabilize the shifting sands of national politics. The president of the Republic, who had the responsibility for signing the decree of dissolution of the Cortes, adjourned that body, and general elections were fixed for mid-

February 1936. In preparation for them Valladares raised the States of Alarm and Prevention in the districts in which they were in force and abolished the censorship of the press.

The Communists had never gained the foothold in Spain that the Socialists and Anarcho-Syndicalists had obtained. They acquired their first influence in the government when the technique of the Popular Front was adopted by the Seventh Congress of the Communist International in 1935. By seeking electoral alliances with other left-wing parties and bourgeois groups they obtained some share in governmental authority. They hoped to fuse the Socialists with the Communists, and to make Francisco Largo Caballero the future leader of the Spanish proletarian parties. Only the Spanish Communist party, which had a branch in Catalonia, was directly linked with the Comintern. The Partido Obrero de Unificación Marxista (POUM)—the Workers' Marxist Unity party led by Andres Nin and Joaquín Maurín—also limited to Catalonia, represented a Trotskyite influence. Prior to the emergence of the Popular Front there were not more than twenty thousand members of the Spanish Communist party, which had not even been registered until the advent of the Republic. In June 1931 it became a legally constituted party, but nine months later it had no more than eleven thousand members.

The Falange Española had adopted a policy of frank terrorism in its revolutionary tactics of direct action. It not only initiated a campaign of agitation, but also undertook reprisals against the Marxist enemies of the Falangists. In its syndical organization, it was essential that it obtain workers in its membership. The workers were more numerous than their enemies and had a practical organization, powerful resources, and had worked in the shadow of the weak reactionary government of Lerroux. The leaders of the two opposed factions were merciless in their nearly open warfare, which kept Madrid in a state of disorder and led to assassinations and retaliations. The Falange had a man charged with the murder of its rivals. José Antonio Primo de Rivera would telephone him that another Falangist had been killed and order him to avenge the murder at once, and, in the words of the "hatchetman," "It was done."

It was in this atmosphere that Spaniards prepared for the elections. The radical parties—the Republican Left, the Republican Union, the Socialists, the Syndicalists, the Anarchists, the Marxists, and the Communists—formed the Popular Front. They hoped to maintain their unity long enough to restore the Republican regime and bring progress and increasing prosperity to the workers after two years of apathetic reaction. The conservatives united under the banner of law and order, with Gil Robles as their principal leader. They called all of their opponents Marxists or Anarchists, despite the variety of their real political creeds.

The electoral returns revealed a remarkable victory for the groups of the Left. They won a total of 256 seats against 52 for the moderate or center group, and 165 for the Right or conservative group. The moderates had lost at the expense of the radicals. The largest single party in the cortes remained CEDA, with one hundred members, followed by the Socialists with 87, and Azaña's Republican Left, with 81. In addition, the conservative parties were solidly united, while there was a possibility that the Popular Front coalition might divide on subsequent issues.

As soon as it became clear that the Popular Front had gained a majority, its supporters became impatient. They wanted the amnesties promised for their friends and relatives. Dispossessed civil servants demanded reinstatement. Demonstrations were staged in Madrid, and the political excitement increased. Portela, the retiring premier, proclaimed a State of Alarm for a week throughout the country, reinstated some employees, and resigned.

A strong man was necessary to restrain the gross lawlessness of the mobs, who believed in direct action, and to maintain order. Manuel Azaña, who was entrusted with the formation of a government, immediately reinstated the former ayuntamientos, appointed new civil governors, and signed a decree of amnesty, to be approved later by the cortes. Thousands of vengeful prisoners were released throughout the country. Companys returned to Barcelona and soon resumed his office. In Catalonia the restored Generalitat began to enforce its Agrarian Law. The high court was no longer willing to enforce its decision.

The primary targets of the popular violence were the churches. The anticlericals, encouraged by the inactivity of the police, burned churches and convents, while the government remained patient in an effort to restrain mob feeling. Although the press was rigidly censored, rumors spread panic in Madrid, and many persons emigrated or remained fearfully in their houses. There was a growing suspicion that Fascists were responsible for the epidemic of murders. Leading citizens were shot down in cold blood or escaped by good fortune. There was street fighting and many of the Fascists, including José Antonio, were imprisoned.

In the central and southern agricultural districts the impatient peasants began to seize the land. The Lerroux government had postponed the application of the Agrarian Law of 1932, but bad weather and unemployment had increased the distress. Although the work of the Institute of Agrarian Reform was accelerated, the peasants frequently took action themselves, normally without disorder or violence. They simply marked out the strips they proposed to occupy and cultivate under the new system. Then they held a demonstration in front of the local government offices and sought formal approval for their action. In some cases their *fait accompli* was approved, in others they were driven from the land. There was confusion but little disorder.

Then the cortes, when passions were already tense, deposed the president of the republic and changed the administration. Alcalá Zamora had become increasingly unpopular. He had another year to complete his term of office, but he was attacked under the constitutional right of the new cortes to examine his second dissolution of the parliament. An unfavorable vote by an absolute majority would automatically involve his deposition. Although Azaña remained inactive, Indalecio Prieto led the attack on the president. The debate lasted for five hours, but the result could be foreseen. CEDA had no more regard for Alcalá Zamora than had the Popular Front and abstained from voting. He had never recognized the political statesmanship of Gil Robles. The result was 238 of 417 votes for the deposition of the president. Alcalá Zamora refused to receive the committee sent to advise him of his deposition, and it made its report to his principal secretary.

Martínez Barrios, the speaker, assumed the presidency until the new election, held on May 10. It was already evident that the president would be a member of the Popular Front, and the name of Manuel Azaña was most often mentioned. At the same time his strength was desirable in the position of prime minister. He was the leader of the Popular Front and alone could save it from possible dissolution. By the day of the election, he was the sole candidate. Of the 911 electors—deputies of the cortes and an equal number of delegates—874 cast their votes. The deputies of the Right abstained, and thus 115 votes were blank. Alejandro Lerroux, Francisco Largo Caballero, and José Antonio Primo de Rivera each received one vote. Ramón González Peña, who had shouted "Viva Asturias!" at the deposition of Alcalá Zamora, was given two votes. Manuel Azaña Díaz received 754 votes. After taking his oath of office he made his permanent residence in the National Palace. The electors had shown their confidence in him.

Casares Quiroga became the next premier. The government once again tried to enforce the Agrarian Law and the Law of Confessions and Congregations. Throughout the country, however, there was serious social unrest—strikes, demonstrations, assassinations, riots, and arson, with the complications of gang warfare and street fighting. Spain was rapidly moving toward chaos. The conservatives attacked the government for its inability to maintain order. Gil Robles and Calvo Sotelo, the most vocal of the opposition, held that Spain was in a state of anarchy which could not be allowed to persist.

The government could not control the extremists of the Left, but it tried to restrain those of the Right. By June the Fascists had become intensely active and violent. The advent of the Popular Front had stimulated them to redoubled activity. While they were disappointed, even depressed, by the victory of the Left, they were encouraged by Nazi progress in Germany and Fascist victories in Abyssinia. They were also conspiring for the overthrow of the Republic with the leading military officers and with their Fascist allies in Italy.

CHAPTER XXXIV

The Civil War

The assassination of José Calvo Sotelo was the signal for armed rebellion in Spain against the Republican government. The gang warfare between the radicals of the Left and the Falangists, both inspired by theories of direct action that would lead to revolution, had gradually driven the neutral masses into two extreme camps. The neutral center, the bulwark maintaining the equilibrium in any democracy, had been eliminated. Civil war gradually became inevitable and needed only a spark to ignite it.

While the CEDA adherents under Gil Robles had hoped to gain control of the government by political action, the Falange Español had been created with the primary purpose of overthrowing the Second Republic by violence. For a while it had been led in the cortes by José Antonio Primo de Rivera, but after the elections of 1936 it was no longer represented. The Falange had resorted to violence with impunity because of the laxity of the forces expected to maintain order, but it had gradually alienated many of the Monarchists who had joined it. José Antonio wanted especially to vindicate his father, since Alfonso XIII had failed to support the dictator in his hour of crisis. For that reason and because of his revolutionary social ideology, the head of the Falange was no Monarchist. Many of the Monarchists, therefore, turned to another leader prepared to challenge the republic.

After his return from exile José Calvo Sotelo had enjoyed increasing prestige in the cortes as an ardent adversary of the government. He was never sympathetic with José Antonio, who refused to accept him as an equal, but he was no less a revolutionary. As a result he became the leader of a new organization of Monarchists of all kinds, the National Bloc, which aimed at the overthrow of the republic, by force if necessary. Its manifesto, issued early in 1935, was signed by a hundred representatives of varied economic interests and high social and professional standing. The executive committee included José Calvo Sotelo and Juan Antonio Ansaldo. Like other conservative movements which opposed the republic, it organized a militia, initially a thousand strong, which was carefully drilled and armed.

The government tried rather ineffectually to proceed with its daily duties, but the impunity with which assassinations were committed led to the arrest of thousands of Fascists. Still the murders continued. Seven Socialists were killed and a dozen wounded as they left a meeting of the Casa del Pueblo. When an Assault Guard lieutenant, José Castillo, was murdered on July 12, one of his companions swore vengeance, and two days later the lifeless body of José Calvo Sotelo was found. An experienced politician, he had frequently been indicated as the future dictator. His murder unleashed three years of civil strife.

The Falange showed signs of disintegration, as the Monarchists continued to abandon it. Arredondo, the first leader of the Falange militia, became active in the creation of the Unión Militar Española (UME) and was later active in the revolution. Another militia leader of the Falange, Rada, became national commander of the Requetes, an organization founded by the Carlists in the nineteenth century and reborn under the Second Republic. The Requetas wore red berets, scapularies, medals, and crucifixes and played a decisive part in the civil war.

Preparations for the overthrow of the republic had been carefully made. Ansaldo had visited Rome in 1931 to confer with Marshal Balbo and secure Italian aid in the attack on the liberal regime. Two years later Calvo Sotelo, accompanied by Ansaldo, had made another trip to Rome while he was still an exile in Paris. He had a cordial interview with the Italian air marshal, and they prepared for future cooperation against the Second Republic. Cardinal Segura was in Rome at that time and the eloquent Jesuit, Father Torres, also consulted with the conspirators. Although General Sanjurjo had failed in the revolt of 1932 in Seville, after his release from prison he again became the central figure in the plans for revolution. He remained in Portugal, but the plans of the conspirators were laid around him.

During the Asturian revolt in 1934, plans were made to bring General Sanjurjo from Portugal to Asturias, where in alliance with Lieutenant Colonel Yagüe he might have established a basis for the assumption of authority. Such a movement might have succeeded, for Sanjurjo had great prestige with the armed forces and the Spanish people. It might then have remained purely Spanish, without foreign commitments, secret alliances, and subsequent debts to pay. General Franco, who was also a military conspirator, had been brought to the Ministry of War and charged with the suppression of the revolt in Oviedo. He had ordered Yaguë to Asturias. But just when the rebellion was about to be launched, Franco changed the plans because he did not believe the moment propitious.

Another opportunity occurred in 1936, when Alcalá Zamora dissolved the cortes. The conservatives were enraged at what they considered a political coup d'état. Gil Robles was minister of War and General Franco was chief of staff. Many members of the armed forces who had been implicated in the 1932 revolt had disconsolately returned to active duty after the amnesty, not reconciled to the republic. The chief of staff and others, however, concluded that the moment was not yet opportune and that the armed forces might fail to rally to the revolt.

With José Calvo Sotelo assassinated, the situation was different. His murder not only had to be avenged, but the time was ripe for military action to prevent anarchy. Moreover, the morale of the army was on the point of disintegration as a result of the desire of the Republican authorities to relegate it to a secondary role in Spanish affairs. The National movement, then, was initiated as a pronunciamiento, not only to protect the role of the military but to restore order in the country. It was more carefully planned, however, and had greater civilian participation than was characteristic of the coups d'état of the nineteenth century. Thus, the movement launched on July 18, 1936, "was both improvised and premeditated." Perhaps the national temper had been misinterpreted and the military, traditionally blind to public opinion, had failed to recognize the strength of Republican opinion. The Nationalists had nevertheless arranged for such a contingency by securing a pledge of Italian cooperation.

The Communist party had taken advantage of its alliance with the Popular Front to elect seventeen deputies to the cortes. Only a few of these, however, assumed roles of importance. José Díaz Ramos, general secretary of the party, was an ex-Anarchist who had the greatest prestige. Dolores Ibarruri, *"La Passionaria,"* was a deputy from Oviedo, with a long and significant career as an agitator in Vizcaya. As editor of *Mundo Obrero* she was one of the most effective Communist propagandists. While the numbers of the Communists were not impressive, they had succeeded in infiltrating the provincial governments and gaining control of municipal administration. They thus held strategic positions from which they could control public opinion and encourage subversion and disorder. The Communists believed in direct action and tried to link their parliamentary activity with the struggle in the street. Their principal aim was the mobilization of the masses.

The Socialists had come to collaborate more fully with the Communists, recognizing the importance of the unity of the proletariat while ignoring the danger of infiltration. The Communists hoped ultimately to fuse with the Socialists and, by their greater cohesion and discipline, to dominate them. The Communists also hoped to coordinate the various trade unions: The Communist union was the Confederación General de Trabajo Unitaria, the Unión General de Trabajadores (UGT) was controlled by the Socialists, and the Confederación Nacional del Trabajo (CNT) was Anarcho-Syndicalist in ideology.

Internally, the Socialists were divided. The conservative or reformist branch was led by Julián Besteiro and Indalecio Prieto, while the more radical or revolutionary wing was under the leadership of Francisco Largo Caballero. This branch was the more popular, and the doctrine of revolution was especially strong in the Socialist youth organizations. It was evident that Largo Caballero might be the leader to guide Spain toward a Communist regime under the direction of the Communist International. The Communist press praised him as the accepted chieftain of a sovietized Spain.

By the summer of 1936 the Communist trade unions had made progress in their union with the UGT, but it was more difficult to secure the cooperation of the Anarcho-Syndicalists. They opposed the authoritarianism of the Communists and did not accept active participation in the normal political activities of the state as a method of action. They also hoped to gain the cooperation of the Socialists in a revolutionary movement which would refuse to collaborate in the government.

The most powerful weapon of the Communists, however, was their youth organizations. They hoped to unite them with the Socialist Youth and had discussed unified action as early as 1934. In March 1936 a joint youth delegation went to Moscow to discuss the plans for a union and a month later created a joint committee. In a short time their separate publications had been fused and an appropriate uniform of a blue shirt and a red tie had been adopted.

In their Spanish campaign the Communists created many "front" organizations, designed to catch the unwary through ambiguous titles and the use of democratic terms to cover their intrigue and subversion. In the same way, the term "Red" was applied by the opposition to all supporters of the government, who by no means were all Communists. The adherents of the government ranged from liberals to extreme

Anarchists, and their reasons for supporting the government varied widely.

Like the Anarchists and the Falangists, the Communists were responsible for many of the incidents and disturbances that racked Spain during the Second Republic. They sought to profit from all social movements which attracted workers, and condemned those which by their faults or their independence impeded the Communist activities. They believed in a strong, well-disciplined organization. By the advent of the Popular Front each extremist group had developed its own special objects and methods of attack. The Anarchists engaged in bombings and armed holdups, while the Communists attacked the political centers of opposing parties and burned churches.

The Communists also engaged in a vigorous pro-Soviet propaganda, which increased after the victory of the Popular Front. They flooded Spain with cheap pamphlets and books and organized motion-picture clubs which exhibited revolutionary films at low prices. Attempts were also made to develop a revolutionary theater in Spain, but the motion picture was the most effective weapon of propaganda. Efforts were made to popularize broadcasts from Radio Moscow and to form sports clubs along Communist lines. The Communists prepared to use armed militia on the day of the uprising. It has been estimated that one hundred thousand members belonged to the youth organizations dominated by the Communists. The government, however, paid little attention to the drills and target practice of the extremists of both sides and let them proceed with impunity. The schools were one of the most effective channels of Communist activity. They enlisted six thousand of the fifty thousand teachers in the country in their controlled union and sought to indoctrinate the students.

There was little danger that the Communists would suddenly seize power in 1936. They had rivals more powerful than themselves in the Anarchists, and they had not completely won the cooperation of the Socialists. Nevertheless, they were contributing to the demoralization of Spain by undermining morality, encouraging attacks on the social order, and trying to weaken the government so as eventually to obtain control.

Thus the stage was set. The military leaders intervened to save Spain from the threat of communism and anarchy by seizing control of numerous cities. Then, with these as bases, they hoped to overthrow the government. The Republican authorities sought to thwart such a move by weakening the army and exiling its more outspoken leaders. They also permitted the arming of the militia, the trade unions, and the syndicates, perhaps with the hope that the arms distributed would be used in the defense of the Second Republic.

Neither side realized that the midsummer fighting in 1936 marked the beginning of a long and bloody war. Neither side recognized the possibility that the extremes were so widely separated that no amount of compromise or good will could eradicate their animosity. The Republicans regarded the revolt as little more threatening than uprisings they had suppressed in the past. They were unprepared for war. The army was somewhat demoralized, but it had vigorous and audacious leaders. They had had little opportunity, however, to appeal to the mass of the people. In the beginning both sides had to resort to improvisation.

Yet the Nationalists had already begun to organize their militia. Thousands of Navarrese, moved by love of tradition, flocked to join the Requetes. The Nationalists also controlled the well-disciplined and tough Foreign Legion, the Moorish troops—who were imported to redress the balance of Spanish political power—and most of the regular army. The Republicans had most of the navy, a small air force, and the well-organized trade unions, which were partly armed. And the government was in Republican hands. They also held the principal urban centers of Madrid, Barcelona, and Valencia, and the industrial centers of the nation.

The civil war opened with the successful rising of the garrisons in various parts of Spain—in Asturias, León, Álava, Navarre, Castile, Aragon, Cádiz, and Algeciras. The garrisons were small and the areas controlled by the Nationalists were widely separated. Hostilities began on July 18, 1936, when the Spanish army in Morocco rebelled against the government. The rebels occupied Melilla, Ceuta, and Tetuán and took control of Spanish Morocco. On the following day General Francisco Franco, who had been relegated to oblivion in the Canary Islands by the Popular Front, flew to Morocco in a plane rented from the English.

First reports from Spain were confused. In Seville, General Queipo de Llano had succeeded in dominating the city with a small force. He successfully resisted attack and undertook radio propaganda. This initial triumph gave the Nationalists a secure base for the invasion of Spain from Morocco. The rebellion had also been successful in Saragossa, the capital of Aragon. From the capital the Nationalists had secured control of Jaca, Huesca, Calatayud, and Teruel. Valladolid, in the heart of Castile, had been seized by General Saliquet. Córdoba, Jérez de la Frontera, and Cádiz joined the revolt the same day.

Nationalist sentiment in the north was already strong. Zamora,

Burgos, and Pamplona were the source of recruits for the rebellious army. In Oviedo, General Aranda was opposed by the miners, who supported the republic. Colonel Moscardó, in Toledo, withdrew to the military academy in the Alcázar and prepared to sustain a siege, for most of the citizens remained loyal to the republic. Sharp fighting in Granada and La Coruña gave the Nationalists control of both. They also succeeded in dominating El Ferrol, Cáceres, Segovia, Ávila, and the Balearic and Canary Islands.

General Goded was heavily outnumbered in Barcelona. Although he tried to hold the principal thoroughfare, the revolt was soon suppressed. Catalonia as a whole remained loyal to the Second Republic, which had recognized its autonomy. The Republicans soon gained control of Madrid. The Nationalist center in the Montaña barracks was overwhelmed and the defenders massacred. From the capital the Republicans gained control of Guadalajara and Alcalá de Henares.

The Nationalist movement was suppressed in Málaga, Albacete, and Almería. By July 23 the Republicans had overpowered the Nationalists in San Sebastián, and the Basque provinces of Guipúzcoa and Vizcaya remained loyal to the government, which had only recently conceded them their autonomy. The rebellious garrison in Valencia resisted for several weeks, but was forced to submit early in August.

Thus, while the Republicans had the advantage of controlling the central nucleus and the Mediterranean coast, the Nationalists held widely separated zones. Old Castile and León, combined with Navarre and Aragon to the east, and Galicia and Estremadura to the west, were under Nationalist control, as was western Andalusia. While the Republican masses wasted their energies in badly coordinated attacks on their opponents, the Nationalists undertook to form a well-disciplined military organization.

Meanwhile, according to plans already formulated, General Sanjurjo prepared to assume supreme command of the Nationalist forces. Ansaldo, who had refused to fly Franco from the Canaries to Morocco, was ordered by General Mola in Pamplona to bring Sanjurjo from Portugal to Burgos. The flight was undertaken on July 20, but the plane crashed and Sanjurjo was killed. Thus, the Nationalist leaders at first had difficulty in pressing their operations. General Emilio Mola was left as commander in the north, while General Franco commanded the south, although technically General Queipo de Llano commanded the forces in Seville and Franco only the expeditionary forces from Africa.

The Republican fleet had blockaded the southern coast, and the Nationalists had to transport their African forces to the peninsula against the naval superiority of the Republicans. The crews of the fleet had forced their officers to declare for the Republican cause. Concentrated at Tangier, the navy bombarded Ceuta, Melilla, and Cádiz. After Franco had protested against the use of Tangier in the International Zone, the fleet retired to Cartagena and Málaga. Finally, a convoy was organized between Ceuta and Algeciras, and soldiers and war matériel were landed in the peninsula. Many of the supplies and soldiers were transported by air in Italian and German planes.

The war soon became one of fixed positions. General Mola sought to oust the Republicans from the Sierra de Guadarrama north of Madrid in order to support a possible Nationalist rising in the capital. Local operations were undertaken so as to control positions which would serve as bases for more ambitious attacks. The northern front was stabilized with the Nationalist capture of Siguenza in mid-October.

It was more difficult to consolidate the Aragonese front. The Republicans held a convenient base in Barcelona from which to attack the Nationalist positions. On the other hand, the Nationalists held Saragossa, the natural center of communications between Madrid and Catalonia. They also controlled the Balearic Islands as a base for air attacks. This gave them a defensive advantage. In Andalusia the Nationalists began to consolidate their position and establish effective communication with Granada. They raised the siege of Córdoba and invaded the province of Málaga, but it was not until February 1937 that Málaga was taken.

The revolution had not been as immediately successful as the Nationalists had hoped. It was now evident, as the masses rallied to the support of the Second Republic, that the war would be prolonged. The African army, consisting of Foreign Legionnaires and Moors, was ferried across the Straits of Gibraltar in ever-increasing numbers by air and sea. In August, General Franco transferred his headquarters to Seville, and in October the Junta established at Burgos transferred its authority to him as supreme commander of the armed forces and chief of the government. Attacking columns were to converge on Madrid, but communications, however tenuous, had to be established with the Nationalists in the north. By August 10 the Nationalists had taken Mérida to establish a link in the communications. Then, moving on Badajoz, with the Foreign Legion leading the attack, they took the fortified city by storm in a fierce battle.

The combined armies of Castile and Andalusia then moved to Cáceres and Trujillo, and General Franco set up his headquarters at Cáceres. The Nationalists took Talavera and Máqueda, vital outposts in the outer defenses of Madrid, but Franco decided to relieve the garrison of the Alcázar in Toledo instead of attacking Madrid immediately. Colonel

Moscardó, military governor of the province, had defended the military academy for sixty-seven days with some eleven hundred men who joined the Nationalist cause. Some 60 percent of the defenders were killed or wounded in the siege. The building was mined by the Republicans, and on September 18 a great explosion occurred, but few were killed. The defenders beat off the ensuing attack and reorganized their defenses. On September 26 Toledo was relieved.

Then the advance on Madrid was resumed. It took a month for the Nationalist forces to move from Toledo to Madrid. Meanwhile, other columns advanced from the north and from Sigüenza. By the latter part of October the encirclement of Madrid was complete, and thereafter the siege of the capital was one of slow attrition. The Republicans were divided over the defense of the city: Largo Caballero wanted to resist until the end, but Indalecio Prieto urged a more moderate policy. Finally, the Republican government moved over the only remaining road in Republican hands to Valencia. Reinforcements continued to reach the defenders from Valencia and Barcelona.

The siege of Madrid developed into a war of stubborn maneuvering for advantage and of minor offensives. A battle at Jarama in February was ferocious and prolonged. The following month the Italian allies of the Nationalists were routed at Guadalajara by the International Brigades, and as a result, the front was temporarily stabilized. The battle for Madrid raged principally in the University City, where the most bitter fighting occurred in 1937. This position formed the advanced defenses of the city after the Nationalist attack was repelled.

The Nationalists were particularly anxious to control the Cantabrian coast, which was important to them because Santander, Bilbao, and the surrounding area were highly industrialized, with shipyards, factories, and communication with France. The Basque provinces of Vizcaya and Guipúzcoa had remained loyal to the Second Republic. In Asturias the lingering memories of the revolt of 1934 had not been eradicated.

In 1937 an attack on Guipúzcoa was launched from Navarre, and some six thousand Requetes and Falangists overcame the urban militia in savage guerrilla warfare. By late September the Nationalists had conquered Irún and controlled the entire province of Guipúzcoa. Oviedo had remained a besieged Nationalist stronghold, for Colonel Aranda had driven out the Republican elements and made himself master of the city in July. The Republicans, however, controlled the surrounding mountains and relentlessly shelled the defenders. After two and a half months of siege, they occupied outlying sections of the city and its relief became urgent. Colonel Teijeiro led the first columns from Galicia, which on penetrating the city discovered that there were only seven hundred of the original five thousand defenders alive.

Thereupon, the Nationalists launched an offensive in Vizcaya. The modern, mechanized army under General Mola began the siege of Bilbao on March 31, 1937. After an intensive bombardment and more than two and a half months of fighting the city was forced to surrender. General Dávila was then in command, for General Mola had been killed in a plane crash. On April 26 the town of Guernica, sacred to the Basques as an ancient capital and as a national shrine, was subjected to an intense aerial bombardment by German planes, and two days later it was occupied.

Late in the summer of 1937 a campaign for the control of Santander was undertaken. The Republicans, who had lost fifteen thousand men at the fall of Bilbao, were so demoralized that many units surrendered. By late August Santander was in Nationalist hands. Asturias was next surrounded, but General Aranda was forced to resort to guerrilla tactics in the mountainous interior, for the Asturians fought desperately and destroyed their own villages to impede the Nationalist advance. Meanwhile, General Solchaga advanced along the Asturian coast, and in October occupied the ancient shrine of Covadonga. On October 21 General Franco announced that the northern part of the peninsula had been conquered.

Somewhat earlier, as a diversion to relieve the pressure of the campaign in the north and to weaken the siege of Madrid, the Republicans launched a determined offensive at Brunete in July. The first breakthrough was complete, but it was threatened by the Nationalists on both flanks and was stopped by July 11. The Nationalists launched a counteroffensive and advanced as much as a mile, but the relief of Madrid had been averted.

The Aragonese front then became the center of interest. It extended from Teruel through Belchite northward to Huesca and ended near Jaca. The Republicans undertook a series of thrusts against this front from August 24 until the middle of November 1937, using an estimated force of eighty-five thousand men. Belchite was finally taken and a temporary advance was made near Jaca, but the offensive was generally ineffective. In a new offensive launched in December on Teruel, the pressure was so heavy that General Franco was forced to discard his preparations for an offensive against Madrid and launch a counter-attack in Aragon. Teruel was captured by the Republicans and held until February 1938.

The decisive campaign of the war, lasting from July 25 to the middle of November 1938, was fought on the Ebro. The Republicans crossed the river and penetrated the Nationalist lines, but after August the battle became one of trench warfare. When the Republican offensive was stopped the issue was no longer in doubt. The recovery of Teruel paved the way for an advance by the Nationalists down the Ebro Valley to the Mediterranean. The Republican territory was now split into two sectors. From Viñaroz the Nationalists moved to Castellón, which they captured in June 1938. Between December 23, 1938, and February 10, 1939, Catalonia was conquered, the advancing Nationalists moving into the ancient principality from all directions. Tarragona fell and the siege of Barcelona began. Its resistance was less stubborn than had been anticipated. Bombarded on January 22, the city soon fell, and the remnants of the defenders fell back toward the north on Gerona near the French frontier.

Chaos now gripped Madrid, which was so hopelessly isolated that it could no longer expect relief. Despite this, there was fighting between extremist groups within the city. Although a Defense Council under General Miaja did its utmost, Madrid was occupied by the Nationalists by the end of March. Resistance also collapsed in Valencia and other cities which had remained loyal to the Second Republic until the end. General Franco announced on April 1, 1939, that the civil war was over.

One of the reasons for the conversion of the traditional pronunciamiento into a prolonged and savage civil war lay in foreign intervention. Although the democratic Western Powers tried to isolate the struggle by an elaborate façade of nonintervention, their efforts did not prevent individual volunteers from rallying to the aid of the Republicans, nor the Axis Powers from seeking in Spain the first test of their military might as a prelude to World War II.

In the attempt to isolate the Spanish civil war a diplomatic struggle developed between Germany, Italy, and Portugal on the one hand and France and Russia on the other. Great Britain was involved as a collaborator with the French, while American corporations were interested in Spanish markets, especially for gasoline. The various powers gave as much moral and material aid as was possible without expanding the civil war into a general war. Twenty-six nations sent representatives to a Non-Intervention Committee established in London in September 1936. Portugal joined the committee in October, although she held the Madrid government illegal and broke relations with it three weeks later. In November, Germany and Italy announced in similar notes that they no longer recognized the Second Republic and acknowledged Franco's headquarters as the government of Spain.

The Republican propagandists, meanwhile, used the Assembly of the League of Nations as a sounding board. Alvarez del Vayo, the foreign minister, addressed that body, arguing that the effect of nonintervention was to blockade the legitimate Spanish government. England and France removed their ambassadors to Biarritz, where they were on neutral ground and could meet the representatives of either side. Nevertheless, the resignation of the Republican diplomats had made Madrid's representation abroad insecure. Although the pope had denounced the violence in Spain and the pro-Republican ambassador was prevented from entering the embassy to the Holy See, it was not until October that Franco assumed control of that embassy.

As the sympathies of Europe became aligned on one side or the other, the Non-Intervention Committee continued to meet in London under the presidency of Lord Plymouth, parliamentary under-secretary for Foreign Affairs. It appointed a subcommittee to consider charges against countries which intervened. When Russia accused Italy, Portugal, and Germany of sending the rebels continuous aid, the Portuguese representative walked out and the Italian ambassador brought countercharges against Russia. Nazi Germany followed a similar policy, and charges were bandied back and forth without result.

The Non-Intervention Committee remained quiet and observed developments with increasing cynicism, but it did accomplish two things. In the first place it disclosed the extent to which the war was being conducted in Spain by non-Spaniards. It also did something to limit this foreign intervention. In November, England, in an effort to enforce neutrality, decided not to grant belligerent rights to either side. The Western Powers were also disturbed by the possibility of Italian aggression in Mallorca and German penetration into Morocco. Both these nations announced that they had no designs on Spanish territory. Finally, on February 15 the Continental Powers imposed a ban on volunteers to Spain and established a plan of supervision, effective in March 1937, to prevent persons from being recruited as volunteers or of going to Spain to fight. Arrangements were later made to police the French and Portuguese frontiers and to allot zones of naval control. More than 855 observers were stationed on the frontiers and along the Spanish coasts. The committee also considered the problem of withdrawing the volunteers already in Spain.

England was as neutral as her own interests would permit. She had to keep the confidence of the Left in Parliament and to protect her strategic interests in the Mediterranean from possible Italian aggression. The victory of Franco would strengthen Fascist power in the Mediterranean and might endanger British possession of Gibraltar. Germany, Italy, and Portugal, on the other hand, were inspired by a desire to help another authoritarian state and by their hatred of communism. None of the countries wanted a general war, but each of them had a special interest in the Spanish war.

One of the most serious threats to peace was the appearance of piracy in the Mediterranean. The Republicans both searched and fired on German vessels. The situation became more acute when the Board of International Control gave various nations the task of keeping their naval vessels strictly neutral. The attacks on German and Italian ships continued. When the "Deutschland" was attacked at Ibiza in the Balearic Islands in May the Germans were indignant, and severely bombarded Almería in retaliation. More German submarines were sent to the Mediterranean. After an attempt was made to torpedo the "Leipzig," the Germans withdrew from the work of enforcing neutrality. Finally, a conference was called—on French initiative—at Nyon in September 1937 to cope with piracy. The Italians refused to attend the deliberations, but adhered to the agreement which finally disposed of this kind of lawlessness.

However futile the efforts of the Non-Intervention Committee were to halt assistance to either side in the civil war, they did prevent the spread of the conflict into a general war. Although in many respects the war was already an international conflict, the general war did not occur until Spain was at peace and able to maintain a precarious neutrality.

As soon as the revolution broke out, the Republican government sought foreign aid. Agents were sent to Paris to purchase war matériel and planes. The Republicans also sought to recruit volunteers for their International Brigades. France was a member of the Non-Intervention Committee, but her government was unable to prevent the French trade unions from recruiting volunteers for the Republican cause or to stop the shipment of supplies across the frontier.

Russian intervention was slight during the early hostilities, but after Largo Caballero assumed control of the government it increased. Supplies were shipped from Odessa to Barcelona, Valencia, Alicante, and Cartagena. This aid was important, and the Russians also sent agents, including technicians, business specialists, and instructors to aid the Republicans. However, the Soviet citizens did not themselves engage in combat, since the International Brigades assumed that responsibility. In addition, the Soviets took over some administrative functions in Barcelona and Madrid. Other countries also contributed to the Republican cause, and Greece served as a base for shipments of war matériel in the eastern Mediterranean. A great deal of Czech material was sent through the Polish port of Gdynia. Even German firms sold supplies to the Republicans through Greek and Turkish agents.

By far the most effective aid to the Republican cause was rendered by the International Brigades. After the fall of Talavera de la Reina these volunteer units were formed as a result of an agreement between Maurice Thorez and Largo Caballero in September 1936. Recruiting centers were opened in France, and a complex system of enlistment, transportation, and entry into Spain through Perpignan was organized. The training and organization of the volunteers was undertaken at Albacete. The advance on Madrid made it necessary to use the volunteers before their training had been completed.

Foreign volunteers also served in the Nationalist ranks, including Portuguese, White Russians, French, and Irish. The major assistance came, however, from the Italians. Marshal Balbo had agreed to support the Fascist counter-revolution in Spain as early as 1931, and the Italians were loyal to his commitment. They immediately provided aviation aids for the Nationalists. Their first infantry assistance was supplied by volunteers in the Málaga campaign in 1937, but the men were ill-prepared and generally did not prove good soldiers. Between January 1 and the middle of February 1937 the Italians sent forty thousand fully equipped men to Spain. The attack on Guadalajara, which ended in a bitter defeat for the Nationalists and the numerous Italian units involved, seriously injured their morale. Some thirty thousand Italians took part in the fighting around Santander, and they also participated in the Aragonese and Catalan campaigns. The Nationalists were never able to use Italians as shock troops as the Republicans employed the International Brigades, for they did not stand up under fire.

Many German volunteers also fought in the Nationalist forces. They were never as numerous as the Italians, but they gave valuable service, especially as aviators in the bombing of Guernica and as technicians. Estimated as numbering six thousand they were organized in the Condor Legion, which was extremely mobile and technically perfect. The Germans were also valuable in training the Nationalists in specialized branches of warfare.

During the war, Barcelona, with the ample autonomy conceded by the Republic, was an almost independent center. It was at first subjected to different political influences from the capital, but the government in Madrid lost control of the Barcelona administration after the rising of General Goded. Thereafter, the regional government reigned supreme. The revolution progressed more rapidly there as the labor unions assumed control. The slogan of the extremists from CNT, UGT, POUM, and the FAI (Federación Anarquista Iberica) became the letters UHP, "Unite Proletarian Brothers," which decorated walls and cars. There was little police protection for the individual or his property.

Madrid was less proletarian and less anarchist in atmosphere, for the militiamen who had rallied to the defense of the capital represented all of the various sections in the Popular Front. Since Casares Quiroga had been blamed for not foreseeing the military revolt, Azaña summoned Martínez Barrios to form a government. Then the extremists, tired of compromise, took control, and Azaña was forced to give up all pretense of constitutional government. In July 1936 José Giral Pereira, an apothecary, became prime minister, but two months later Francisco Largo Caballero succeeded him. When the government was reorganized after the fall of Irún, Largo Caballero also served as minister of War, Julio Alvarez del Vayo was minister of State, and Juan Negrin was minister of Finance. Jesus Hernández, as minister of Education, represented the Communists.

A primary object of the new government was to restore military order. Volunteers were conscripted and severe measures were taken to enforce discipline. Censorship was rigidly imposed on newspapers and radio, wireless sets were seized, and Nationalist broadcasts were jammed. The cortes, reduced to one hundred members of the extreme Left, met occasionally, but had little authority. The war crisis had caused the suspension of ordinary constitutional processes.

In May 1937 Juan Negrin became prime minister and Indalecio Prieto minister of Defense. When the government had moved to Valencia in the previous November, it took the gold reserves of the Bank of Spain, amounting to some $700,000,000; some of this was shipped to Russia in exchange for goods, but it was charged that Juan Negrin shipped $50,000,000 to Mexico. As a result a controversy developed between Negrin and Prieto which split the Republican government.

After the government had moved to Valencia, a Junta of Defense ruled Madrid under the direction of General Sebastián Pozas, commander of the Civil Guard. Those in control of the Republican center vented their fury on all who could be considered hostile to the popular regime. While the appalling list of murders was in part designed to eliminate potential enemies, it also was an indication of the anarchy which became dominant in the crisis. The moderate Republicans were unable to control the extremists, for the civil war unleashed the savage fury of the lower classes. Among the victims were Ramiro de Maeztu and José Antonio Primo de Rivera, who was killed in an Alicante prison to which he had been sent before the war started.

While the mob committed savage atrocities on the Republican side, especially venting its anticlerical fury on priests and in the burning of churches, the Nationalists also retaliated with massacres of their own. On the Republican side most crimes might be attributed to the anarchy, in which rapine and violence became common, but the Nationalists theoretically had a military organization, and their massacres were often officially inspired and carried out with military precision. The propagandist agencies of both sides in the conflict hurled charges and counter-charges. Before long, humanity and judicial processes had disappeared.

One of the principal reasons for the inability of the Republican government to maintain order and control the trade unions may be attributed to the struggle for power which rent it internally. The Communists sought to take advantage of the crisis and gain complete control. They liquidated or expelled POUM, representing the Trotskyite Communists, and the CNT, representing the Anarchists, was reduced to impotence. The Socialist-Communist alliance came to dominate Republican affairs. Indalecio Prieto lost his influence in the government when he refused to become subservient to the Soviets, and in April 1938 Juan Negrin assumed the real leadership of the Republican government. Manuel Azaña, president of the Second Republic, ceased to be a force in the government, and remained at Montserrat until, with Luis Companys and José Antonio Aguirre, president of the Basque government, he went to France after the capture of Gerona.

On the Nationalist side a similar lack of harmony was evident. The members of Renovación Española believed in the traditions of a conservative monarchy, and disliked the Falangists, who were neither monarchical nor conservative, but on the contrary had a radical social program of their own. As the revolt had been launched as a negative movement, its leaders had to undertake a positive program in order to appeal to the country. The conflicting elements indicated an urgent need for unity, and as a result, in April 1937, a decree consolidated them. A National Council was established to give proportional representation to the various parties and groups. The Falange Española, however, secured the major position in the new regime.

The decree of unification was not well received by some members of the Falange. Manuel Hedilla, one of its leaders, was accused of sedition, because of a telegram he addressed to provincial leaders, and sentenced to death. Although the execution was not carried out, other leaders of the

Falange were imprisoned. The traditionalists were not convinced of the virtues of the unification and had no illusions about their own role in it, but accepted the *fait accompli* in the hope that the monarchy would ultimately be restored. The army, which controlled the Fascist militia, approved of the consolidation.

On January 30, 1938, the Nationalists transferred their capital from Salamanca to Burgos. The new government represented all parties in an attempt to unite the nation. Franco was now chief of the Spanish state as caudillo, and the count of Jordana became minister of Foreign Affairs. The Falangists were directly represented only by Pedro González Bueno in the Ministry of Trade Union Organization, and Ramón Serrano Suner, Franco's brother-in-law, as minister of the Interior. The regime remained in Burgos for two years, until it had concluded the war victoriously and restored internal stability.

When the war began the Republican government had reserves of gold, some of which was exported for supplies by orders of Juan Negrin. The Ministry of Finance also assumed control of the gold in private banks, which were operated by the employees. As business became disorganized in the general anarchy, Republican credit declined abroad. Franco's resources were originally provided by Juan March, and he had no immediate difficulties about finance. He established a rigid control of credit and exchange, encouraged the activity of small business, and granted credits to the big companies. As he took over Republican territory he established a new monetary system. Later, he accepted and endorsed the notes of the Bank of Spain and guaranteed small properties. Finally, the leading capitalists who had backed him placed credit at his disposal.

The resources of his territory also played a part in assisting in the maintenance of a favorable balance of trade. Franco held territory rich in food supplies, the wheatlands of Castile and Estremadura and the fertile valley of the Guadalquivir. He also had rich mineral resources, such as the mines of Andalusia, which were increased after he conquered the Cantabrian coast. He maintained firm control of the exchange and increased his trade with Germany and England. The Republicans, on the other hand, foolishly counted on their gold reserves to last indefinitely. They controlled three large towns, two with great resources, but Madrid was difficult to feed, the industry of Barcelona declined for lack of raw material and because trade was dislocated, and Valencia lost her principal customers for agricultural products.

In three years the Republican regime in Spain had collapsed and had been replaced by a dictatorship closely connected with the Axis Powers.

The failure of the Second Republic may in large measure be attributed to its own weakness. It was inspired originally by the highest democratic ideals and strove to renovate Spain as a modern state, to leap the abyss between the medievalism of a reactionary monarchy and the modern concept of a socially responsive nation.

Like all liberal, democratic regimes, to achieve its purposes the Second Republic had to attempt to represent all segments of popular opinion. It could not maintain its policy with a firm hand. When it did it was accused of tyranny. It was caught between two forces which sought its destruction. The reactionary elements of the Right were divided between those who sought to restore the monarchy and those who wished to renovate Spain by a revival of dictatorial procedures. Both groups were uncompromising in their hostility to the government. Some depended on ballots, others resorted to bullets. On the other hand, the extremists of the Left were intent on the destruction of the regime from its inception, either by violent direct action or by infiltration. The neutral mass of public opinion was sharply split and began to take sides in the controversy as a means of maintaining a political equilibrium.

When the war began, the true liberals were left without allies. Those whose real interest lay in preserving public order were in revolt against it. Those who sought impatiently to make it subservient to Communist ideology that had no real strength in the nation became its only allies. Instead of protecting the Republican ideals they subverted them by infiltration, and in the end came to dominate the tottering Second Republic. Chaos and anarchy were inevitable. Under the circumstances only a strong government could have survived. The least that can be said for the Nationalist victory is that it rescued Spain from a worse fate, and although a fearful price of six hundred thousand lives had to be paid, it restored peace and order with a strong hand.

CHAPTER XXXV

The Franco Regime

In March 1939 Francisco Franco, the caudillo of the triumphant Nationalists, held his victory parade in Madrid. Born in Galicia in 1892, he had originally intended to follow a naval career. When he found he could not be admitted to the Naval Academy, he entered the Military Academy of Toledo at fifteen. Two years after his graduation in 1910 he was assigned to a regiment in Africa as an officer and participated in a series of operations against the Moroccans. By 1915 he was a captain. Wounded a year later, he was awarded the Cross of Maria Cristina for bravery in action and promoted to major.

In 1920 he returned to Africa, where he assisted in the organization of the Spanish Foreign Legion. In 1923, at the suggestion of Alfonso XIII, he was given command of the Foreign Legion. During a brief interlude in his military activities in 1923 he married Carmen Polo y Martínez Valdés, daughter of a noble and well-known Asturian family.

The Moroccan rebellion had again endangered the position of the Spaniards. Franco participated in the withdrawal from Xauen and the evacuation of Alhucemas in 1925. Before the campaign was concluded he was a brigadier general, one of the youngest men of that rank in Europe. After his return to Spain he was named director of the newly created General Military Academy of Saragossa, remaining there until it was closed by Azaña as minister of War in 1931.

During his military career Franco had built a reputation as leader and strategist. In 1932 he was entrusted with the command of an infantry brigade in La Coruña. Although his brother Ramón had dropped revolutionary pamphlets over Madrid in 1931 and had been involved in the rebellion at Cuatro Vientos, Francisco Franco was not sympathetic toward the Second Republic. He was named military commander of the Balearic Islands in 1933 in order to remove him from the temptation of armed rebellion in the peninsula. Diego Hidalgo, minister of War, became acquainted with him in 1934 and was so impressed with him that when the Asturian revolt occurred he brought him to the Ministry of War. Franco, who was familiar with the Asturian terrain, was placed in charge of the suppression of the revolt with orders to use his old Foreign Legion and the Moors against the Asturian miners. He was in command of the Army of Morocco in 1935, when Gil Robles, becoming minister of War, appointed him chief of staff.

On two occasions Franco's refusal to proceed with the revolutionary conspiracy of the Nationalists in which he was involved, because the time was not propitious, forced the postponement of the date set for the rising. It is also interesting to note that fortune as well as reputation played a part in his ascent to the leadership of the Nationalists. General Sanjurjo, the designated leader of the conspirators, was killed in an attempt to leave Portugal in an overloaded plane, and his other principal rival, General Emilio Mola, was likewise killed in an airplane accident. Franco, a man from the Celtic northwest and a striking embodiment of the character of that area, had developed a stubborn and shrewd caution which prevented him from overplaying his hand. Tenacious in pursuing his objectives and adroit in attaining them, he resolutely clung to the position he had won, and his sinuous nature enabled him to reconcile its contradictions and to rationalize its inconsistencies.

After leading the Nationalists to victory, he was confronted with the problems of internal reconstruction. Although Galicia and Andalusia were little damaged, the remainder of Spain had been devastated. The civil war had divided families and one segment of the nation had defeated the other. A pronunciamiento could easily have been forgotten, but the memory of members of a family lost by execution or massacre was not so easily obliterated. The principal task of Franco was that of reconciling those who had won with those who had lost. He has given Spaniards peace by maintaining order with a strong hand. He had always been a military man, but his savage reprisals on those responsible for anarchy under the Popular Front, his attempt to Castilianize Spain despite its regional diversity, and his devotion to the establishment of myths glorifying the Nationalist cause drove the injustices of military rule more deeply into the consciousness of the Spanish people instead of reconciling them.

Perhaps it is futile to believe that anything but ruthless repression might have restored faith in a common destiny among the individualists who compose the Spanish nation. The Spaniards are delighted with the peace that has been maintained, but, except for his immediate supporters and those who profit from the regime, they have not been happy with

Franco. After the victory, Spanish jails were crowded with the defeated. Throughout the peninsula those who had collaborated with the republic and those who had been guilty of violence were arrested as a measure of security, sometimes also in a spirit of vengefulness. Republican officials surrendered in order to ensure their survival. All available places of confinement were jammed. Thousands of soldiers of the Republican army were detained until they could be restored to a civil status. More than three hundred thousand political prisoners were awaiting trial or examination.

As chief of the Spanish state, and, later, as caudillo of the only recognized political party, Franco had already indicated that the government of Spain was founded on totalitarian concepts, "with full respect for the traditions, and with consideration for the historical nationality, unity, and continuity of Spain." During the war years, policies had to be improvised and the leadership of a military insurrection had to be authoritarian. The government created was designed largely to conduct the war. A National Defense Council was established on a provisional basis in July 1936. Its purpose was to concentrate all power in the hands of one supreme military chief who would also serve as head of the government. A provisional government was set up October 1, 1936, and on December 29, 1936, Franco assumed full powers as chief of the Spanish state. Various ministries were created in 1938, and in August 1939 the full mechanism of the state was restored. After the *fait accompli* of the Nationalist victory, a majority of the nations recognized the new regime as the government of Spain.

It was not until July 1945 that the *Fuero de los españoles,* which is basic to an understanding of the activities of the present Spanish state, was issued. As a bill of rights, defining the privileges and duties of the citizens of Spain, it was drawn up and debated in a cortes and was promulgated by General Franco as the fundamental law of the land. It is obviously a body of glittering generalities with only a distant relationship to political and economic realities, but as a statement of ideal principles, it deserves some attention.

The Spanish state proclaimed in the *fuero* that its guiding principle is respect for the dignity, integrity, and liberty of the human being, but declared at the same time that all Spaniards are bound to render faithful service to the country, remain loyal to the chief of the state, and obey the laws. They are guaranteed equality before the law and full respect of their personal and family honor. They not only have the right to be educated, but they also have the duty of acquiring an education, either informally or formally. The state pledges that no talent will be neglected for lack of funds. The Catholic Church was restored as the state religion, but a limited toleration was provided in a pledge to respect the religious beliefs of individuals and to permit non-Catholics to worship privately.

As might be expected in a state born of military revolt and dedicated to authoritarian principles in an era of international suspicion, all Spaniards were obliged by the *fuero* to render military service. They were also required to pay taxes. All had a right to participate in public affairs, and freedom of speech and correspondence was guaranteed, but one might not express ideas hostile to the fundamental laws of the state. Spaniards were permitted to assemble and associate for licit ends, and the state reserved the right to create and maintain organizations necessary for the fulfillment of its obligations. Spaniards were guaranteed juridical security. They could not be arbitrarily arrested or condemned nor deprived of their nationality except for treason or service to a foreign state.

The family was recognized by the *fuero* as the fundamental social institution, and marriage was regarded as indissoluble. Large families were encouraged, with the prospect of state protection. While parents were obliged to maintain and educate their children, those who failed to do this properly might have their authority transferred by the state.

As in the Second Republic, all Spaniards had the right under the *fuero* to work and the duty to engage in some socially useful activity. The state recognized a community of interest in work, shared equally by the technicians, the laborers, and the capitalists—all three elements in industry having a right to share in its benefits. The state was to regulate carefully the relations among them, maintaining strict justice and the principle that economic gain—profit—is subordinate to human values, the interests of the nation, and the common welfare.

All workers were to be protected by the state in their right to a just wage, sufficient to maintain a decent and dignified standard of living. They were to be guaranteed a wide range of social protections, covering old age, illness, maternity, and unemployment. To this end the state was not only to provide necessary institutions of its own but also to foster those created by the Church, corporations, and private philanthropy. The state undertook to recognize and protect private property in all its forms as essential to a healthy social system.

Such is theoretically the present constitution of Spain, but theory and fact have rarely coincided. Elaborate laws may be passed, but remain ineffective because no one takes the trouble to enforce them. Custom and tradition are too strong to permit ideals to be converted into realities. The Spaniard is too rugged an individualist to subordinate his freedom of action to the general welfare. Nevertheless, some progress is evident in this *fuero*. Indeed, it perhaps gained something from the fact that it was formulated and promulgated under a dictatorial regime. One proposed by the representatives of all the people would have been much more liberal, but it might not have included enough safeguards to prevent a relapse into anarchy. The charter represents an effort to clothe the hand of the dictator in a velvet glove.

The cortes of the Franco regime remains the legislative branch of the Spanish state. It was established by a law of July 17, 1942, which marked a distinct innovation in Spanish political life. The old term "deputy" has been replaced by the still older *procurador*—used when the kings were absolute and conceded *fueros* to their subjects. Since partisan politics was abolished in Spain with the unification of various groups into the single party, the Falange, the old free play of party politics, which involved political compromises between groups, disappeared. Already in 1923, when political leadership had so decayed that Primo de Rivera established a Directory, the statesmen had become politicians, following the people instead of leading them, as they concentrated primarily on their own careers. It is highly doubtful if more able statesmen will appear in a regime in which politicians become sycophants to gain and retain an official status and a single authoritarian party denies admission to many persons with political aspirations because of the system in which it is conceived.

The present cortes has functional representation. It consists of permanent ex officio members, including the ministers; the national councilors of the Falange; the president of the Council of State and the Supreme Courts of Justice and Military Justice; the representatives of the national syndicates, who may not exceed one-third of the total number of *procuradores;* the mayors of the fifty provincial capitals and an elected representative of the other municipalities of each province; the rectors of the universities; the president of the Institute of Spain; two representatives of the royal academies; the president and two representatives of the Superior Council of Scientific Investigation; one or two representatives of each of the various professional organizations, including lawyers, engineers, physicians, pharmacists, veterinarians, and architects; and outstanding persons who, by their rank or service to Spain, may be designated by the chief of state to a number not to exceed fifty.

The cortes is the supreme organ for the participation of the Spanish people in the tasks of the state. Its principal mission is the preparation of laws for the sanction of the chief of state. The professional representation was based on the theories of José Antonio Primo de Rivera, who believed that "the most authentic representation of the mass of the people is through the family, the municipality, and the trade union." *Procuradores* must be Spaniards in the full exercise of their civil rights. They are either elected or permanent. The designated members either serve ex officio, because of the position they hold, or may be named by Franco. The usual term of office is three years, although short-term elections may be held to fill vacancies.

Extensive powers are assigned to the cortes, subject, of course, to the approval of the chief of state. It formulates all budgets, economic and financial legislation, and the basic laws affecting the duties and rights of Spaniards. It regulates the institutions of the state, local government, the legal codes, judicial organization, and public administration. It establishes the bases for agrarian, mercantile, industrial, and educational legislation. In case of war or national emergency, however, the government may intervene in these matters and issue decrees having the force of law. Legislative commissions and individuals may also submit proposals to the cortes, and the chief of the state may return any law to the cortes for further study.

Under these provisions the cortes is not a sovereign legislative body representing the popular will. Spain has abandoned the idea of legislative supremacy in favor of the concept of the strong executive. It may be the beginning of a parliament in the older sense, but its members offer more of a sounding board for the support and flattery of the chief of the state than a medium for expressing the will of the people. The national sovereignty has been subverted. Many Spaniards recall with nostalgia the national crises produced by partisan political intrigue and the freedom of individual expression thus offered.

It is natural that Spanish administration should now be highly centralized. Regional personality and political aspirations are ignored. The emblem of the new regime is that of the Catholic Kings, the yoke and the arrows of the Personal Union. The yoke signifies the union, the arrows the several kingdoms which composed that union, now bound together under the domination of Castile. It was the emblem of the Falange; it has become the emblem of Franco. Madrid has indeed become the administrative and regulating economic center of the kingdom.

The fifty Spanish provinces—purely artificial political districts and in no sense related to regional aspirations—are administered by governors named in Madrid. The provincial deputations, representing the strictly provincial interests, consist of local representatives chosen on both a territorial and corporate basis. The provincial authorities have considerable latitude in many local matters. The alcaldes of the municipal governments are also designated in Madrid. The municipal councils are indirectly elected.

A supreme court stands at the head of the judicial system. It is divided into several chambers, according to the nature of the case—civil, criminal, administrative, and social. The intermediate district courts are the old territorial audiencias, and below them are the local courts. The ecclesiastical courts, independent under the Rota, were established in Spain by an agreement between the government and the Holy See in 1947. Other special courts are the military courts, fiscal tribunals, and the *Tribunal de las Aguas* in Valencia, which is the vestige of an ancient court which without appeal distributes and assigns water for irrigation. Other local usages and customs have survived in the laws of the several regions.

On July 26, 1947 the next important step in the restoration of a more normal regime was taken in the promulgation of the Law of the Chieftainship of the State and of the Succession. It was submitted to the people after being approved by two-thirds of the cortes in June 1947 and received 82 percent of the votes of the electoral body in a referendum in July. It declared that Spain, "as a political unity a Catholic, social and representative State," was "constituted as a kingdom," with Generalissimo Franco as the chief of the state. In the event that this position becomes vacant a Council of Regency is to assume its powers. This council will consist of the president of the cortes, the prelate of highest rank, and the captain general or the senior lieutenant general of the armed forces. The president of the cortes will assume the presidency of the council, the decisions of which will be valid on his approval and that of at least one other member.

The new law also created a Council of the Kingdom to collaborate with the chief of the state. This consisted of the president of the cortes, the senior prelate, the head of the armed forces, the chief of the General Staff, the president of the Council of State, the president of the Supreme Court, the president of the Institute of Spain, and seven councilors. Four of these were to be elected, one by each of the groups represented in the cortes: the Syndicalists, local administration, and the rectors of the universities and professional colleges. The other three were to be designated by the chief of the state, one from the ex officio members of the cortes, one from those he appointed, and one at large.

This body is consultative on matters relating to the return of a law to the cortes, the declaration of war or conclusion of peace, the proposal to the cortes of the successor to the chief of the state, and affairs of similar import. At any time the chief of the state may propose to the cortes the person whom he considers should be called to succeed him as king or regent.

The Council of Regency will assume the designated ruler's powers and convoke the cortes and the Council of the Kingdom will witness his oath and proclaim him king. If no successor has been named in the event of the death or incapacity of the chief of the state, the government and the Council of the Kingdom will choose him within three days and propose him to the cortes either as king or as regent. To be eligible for the chieftainship of the state, the king or regent must be a male, a Spaniard, thirty years of age, a Catholic, possess the qualities necessary for the discharge of his mission, and have taken an oath of loyalty to the fundamental laws and the National Movement.

Once the crown is given to a king the regular order of succession is by primogeniture. The nearest male heir will succeed. A female may not reign, but can transmit the right to her male heirs. Every cession of rights, renunciation of rights, or royal marriage must be approved by the cortes. With the advice of the Council of State, the chief of the state may propose the exclusion of those who are notoriously incapacitated or who by their acts lose their rights for the succession. Thus, Spain is a monarchy without a king. Franco does not aspire to that position because the succession is guaranteed to one of royal blood.

Naturally, the army is one of the principal supports of the Franco regime. It was the basis for his accession to power and remains loyal to him as the chief of the state. The army has been the bulwark of many regimes in modern Spain, intervening in political affairs time and again. It is important to understand the Spanish military psychology in this role. Since every Spaniard is a unique political party in his own right and the military men are not immune to this individualism, they intervene in civil affairs not as soldiers but as Spaniards for what they consider the general welfare. They have led the nation out of many difficult situations, just as their subservience to tradition has produced others. They are loyal to their chiefs as long as they are interested in the welfare of the nation.

Yet the Spanish army has been traditionally as monarchist as it has been conservative. The only explanation for its stubborn fidelity to a regime which has thus far denied the restoration of the Bourbons is its loyalty to the profession. To its members the national welfare is well served if the interest of the army is served. Vehemently anticommunist, somewhat cynical of public opinion, it has a strong reverence for private property and the maintenance of social order.

For fifteen years it has been pampered by the chief of the state. It has been given new barracks, which occupy a strategic site in every town. Its needs are carefully provided in a budget that devotes more to military expenditure than to the other agencies of government. The army has received not only the authority but also the equipment, the training schools, special rations as a privileged economic caste, and political influence for the senior officers for their role in the national defense. The younger officers, trained in admiration for dictatorial institutions, have no concept of constitutional government or attachment to the monarchy. Consequently, the allegiance of the officers and their control over their units are directed to the genuine, unquestioning, and determined support of the regime.

Some of the older officers have proved exceptions to this rule, but they have been quickly removed. Generals Kindelán and Varela lost their influence and careers because they were more loyal to the ideal of a restored monarchy than to the caudillo. General Franco has obviated any inclination of the army to engage in conspiracy against him with great dexterity. His loyal divisions are scattered throughout Spain, and he has the military strength to suppress the least symptom of rebellion.

There is a single political party, the Falange, which constitutes not only one of Franco's principal supports and contributes much of his political, economic, and social program, but also often provides his political appointees. Originally, inspired by Fascist principles and organized like a Fascist party, its members wore a Fascist uniform. It has been intensely nationalistic, and it has no political competition. It enrolled thousands of young men in its ranks during the civil war and, in the end, emerged as the sole party when the various groups were unified in 1937.

General Franco was not originally a Falangist, but was the leader of the military group in the civil war. He became the caudillo of the National Movement and consequently the leader of the Falange when it became the sole party. In that capacity he changed its original purpose by adopting its program and making it a bulwark of his regime. After 1939 when it received state support until the end of World War II, when Fascism became less stylish in Spain, it enjoyed great influence and prestige. Many Spaniards in high position as well as many Communists and Anarchists found in it a key to influence and political office and a haven from political persecution.

As caudillo of the *Falange Española Tradicionalista y de las J.O.N.S.*, Franco is an absolute chief without responsibility to any member of its National Council of elected members—who are drawn from Spanish public life—or to the smaller group of ex officio members. The Falange is actually administered, however, by a political Junta, the permanent Committee of the National Council, of which Franco is president. A secretary general in Madrid directs the practical operation of the movement, which is extended into every province and among the women and the youth of the nation. While it has lost, in recent years, a great deal of its political influence, its women's section and youth's section are of continuing importance. The women's organization was established in 1939. Its program includes both political education and civic training. It supervises the social service system through Auxilio Social, which extends into every Spanish community. By a decree of May 1940 Spanish women who are single or childless widows are obliged to devote some time to social service under the Falange. They take part in educational affairs, are active in sports, health, and sanitation, and foster such cultural activities as the traditional local dances.

The principal aim of the youth organizations is to capture the imagination and loyalty of the young people of Spain. In creating the Frente de Juventudes in 1940, the Falange had two purposes. One was to prepare good party members, and the other was to propagandize the doctrines of the Falange among the youth of the nation. It has both a masculine and a feminine section, divided into age groups. Through the Frente, the Falange intervened in the political education of many who are not affiliated with it. The Frente has directed trade schools and has been active in higher education through the Sindicato Español Universitario (SEU), a trade union for the institutions of higher learning.

The Falange has also controlled censorship in the national office of the press and has devoted a great deal of time to propaganda through the radio, the theater, and the motion pictures. It has its own chain of newspapers. In Madrid *Arriba* and *Pueblo* are its principal organs, and it controls a number of newspapers in the provinces.

As a reaction to the Republican persecution of the Church in Spain, clerical interests and Catholics rallied to the defense of their institutions. Catholic Action was organized with Popular or National Action as its political party. Later, the defense of Catholic interests was undertaken by CEDA, the bloc led by Gil Robles. Catholics who sought to defend Christian society against the extremists of the Left played an important part in supporting the Nationalist cause. Naturally, therefore, the Franco regime has remained favorable to the Church and not only supports it generously but recognizes it as a collaborator in the reconstruction of Spain.

Thus, the Church has been one of the principal supports of the regime in an effort to restore the religious unity of the past. The savage attacks of the extremists on priests and clerical property under the Second Republic left it no alternative. As a means of defending itself against a repetition of the past, the Church has again intervened in politics, from which the Republicans tried to disassociate it. Traditionally, the bishops have always supported the political power which guaranteed their privileges and the prerogatives of the Church. They believed that a Nationalist victory would secure public order and relax the Republican legislation in matters relating to religion and education.

The Spanish bishops in 1939 would probably have preferred a monarchist restoration for traditional reasons. The monarchy in the past had always supported their interests. There were, perhaps, some doubts as to the objectives of some of the groups supporting Franco. The army was an ancient ally, but the Falange, with its totalitarian program, might prove dangerous. Consequently, after the victory, full of hope for the restoration of its privileges the Church adopted a dual policy. It was anxious to perpetuate a regime which promised security, but it also wished to maintain a favorable balance of power with the other rival political groups. To this the well-organized Catholic Action party dedicated its political activity.

Franco had recognized the power of Catholic Action by 1944, when he named its secular head, Alberto Martin Artajo, as foreign minister. While it professes to be apolitical and aims only at the mobilization of the Catholic laymen, the Junta Suprema, a conference of all of the Spanish bishops under the presidency of the archbishop of Toledo, is the highest authority in Catholic Action. Its power is delegated to a permanent body of six members, five bishops, and one layman. The latter is the director of the Junta Técnica Nacional, which implements the policies formulated by the bishops. It is predominantly secular with only one ecclesiastic among its thirty-one members.

The party is active in provincial and municipal life. Its alleged purpose is to rechristianize Spain, a program with many implications. It appeals to intellectuals and businessmen and is most active in the field of social welfare and philanthropy. It is closely connected with Editorial Católica, which controls six of Spain's best newspapers, including *Ya,* published in Madrid.

Gradually, as its suspicions of the Falange increased, the members of Catholic Action decided to intervene more actively in the struggle for the control of power. It began to develop a powerful organization among the intellectual elite known as Opus Dei, founded originally in 1928 by José Maria Escriva de Balaguer, a Catalan. After the conclusion of the civil war it began to attract attention and was approved by the Vatican in June 1950. It also received the aid of Franco as he sought to de-emphasize its chief rival, the Falange, after the victory of the Western democracies. The Jesuits have opposed Opus Dei as a strong threat to their own position.

Opus Dei numbers among its members both men and women, subordinated to the rule of chastity but permitted marriage. All Catholics do not support the Opus Dei, for it often seems to emphasize politics more strongly than it does religion. It appears to emulate the Masons in their intimate cooperation and mutual aid to each other. Its control of the teaching profession aids it in recruiting new members.

The Falange and Catholic Action are rivals in the field of social welfare, and both desire to become the predominant influence among the forces allied with Franco. The Church, however, won its most decisive victory in the field of education in 1943. Archbishop Plá y Deniel proposed a new national law of education to the minister of Education, Ibañez Martin, but the Falangist ministers in the Council of Ministers, led by José Luis Arrese, opposed the draft which reaffirmed clerical control of the schools of the nation. When the council agreed on terms which left the authority of the clergy in doubt, the archbishop brought pressure to bear on Franco, and the Law of Primary Education of July 1945 was passed. It invested the clergy with more educational authority than they had enjoyed before the Second Republic.

In the spring of 1945, when the German allies of the Falange finally succumbed, the Church consolidated its position. The prestige of the Falange was at a low ebb. A pastoral letter defended the legitimacy of the Franco regime and praised its religious policy, while the Spanish episcopate denounced the Potsdam condemnation of Spain and foreign intervention.

In 1952 the schism between the Falange and some Catholics was indicated by the pastoral letters issued by Cardinal Archbishop Pedro Segura y Saenz of Seville. He attacked *Arriba,* the Falangist periodical, because of an editorial opposing the Catholic demands for a curb on the twenty thousand Protestants in Spain. He halted the circulation of the letter only when he learned that Franco had written the editorial, but he later declared that Spanish Catholics must preserve Catholic unity "even if it means shedding our blood." In August he again challenged the legal status of non-Catholic sects in Spain on the ground that the Vatican had not approved the article in the Charter of Rights of 1945 allowing them the private exercise of their faith. In August 1953, however, a concordat was negotiated with the Vatican, and while confirming Catholicism as "the only religion of the Spanish people" and guaranteeing the teaching of Catholicism in all schools, it recognized the validity of the prohibition against molesting persons because of the private exercise of their worship. The concordat had been in process of negotiation for nineteen months. The cortes approved it on October 26.

In November 1952 the archbishop of Seville attacked the Falange as neopagan. He issued a warning to youths studying for the priesthood against spending vacations in the youth camps of the Falange, which he considered detrimental to Catholic interests. While the Falange had obtained great influence in national education, the National Board of Catholic Bishops complained in 1952 that the government had extended the Church only minimum influence in secondary education. After the conclusion of the alliance with the United States, the Spanish primate, Cardinal Enrique Plá y Deniel endorsed the pact, but warned the government that the Church would condemn "external manifestations" of worship by non-Catholic Americans in Spain.

Many Spanish Monarchists were exiled or have become hostile to the Franco regime because of their loyalty to Don Juan, son of Alfonso XIII. A large number of Spanish people would probably favor a restoration of a constitutional monarchy. Certainly the majority is opposed to Franco. Although the Monarchists suffered a defeat when the Act of Unification merged the entire Traditionalist or Carlist movement with the Falange, their ranks were already divided. Esteban Bilbao led the conciliatory Monarchist faction, while the more uncompromising Monarchists have followed Dr. Gregorio Marañon and José Ortega y Gasset. Between these two extremes the mass of the Monarchists have wavered as speculations on General Franco's intentions have varied. Many Falangists as well as Monarchists have defected to Franco to become apostles of his order.

Don Juan de Borbón y Battenberg, count of Barcelona, is the most prominent Spanish political refugee. He has waited since 1931 for the moment to ascend the Spanish throne. Most of his exile was spent in Switzerland, but in January 1946, he moved to Estoril, Portugal. After unsuccessfully attempting to bring the issue of restoration to a head in 1943, Don Juan a year later denounced the Franco regime. By 1945 it was evident that General Franco did not intend to sponsor a restoration, considering it unlikely that the victorious Western Powers would apply political pressure on his regime. It was also apparent that no nation could recover the "normalcy" of prewar years.

When Juan again appealed to General Franco in 1945 to reconcile all Spaniards by a restoration of the traditional monarchy, he promised an eventual restoration. Juan flew to Lisbon, with the tacit approval of Franco, who thereby had him near at hand for a dramatic countermove to meet, if necessary, the threat of the United Nations' condemnation of the Fascist regime in Spain. In reality Franco has remained indifferent to Juan's pretensions. Inspired by hope kindled by the inclusion of nine Monarchists in the first reorganization of the Franco cabinet since 1946, Juan again demanded the throne in 1951 and urged that all restrictions on personal liberty be removed. This demand was unheeded, but reports from Madrid claimed that Juan had become more conciliatory and had concluded that the restoration of the monarchy was feasible only with Franco.

A division of opinion has existed among the Monarchists as to who should be the next king of Spain. Although the majority favor Don Juan, there are other aspirants to the throne. Nevertheless, all Monarchists fervently anticipate the eventual restoration of a member of the Bourbon family. This expectation has been postponed daily since the conclusion of the civil war, but from Portugal and France the aspirants continue to look to the fulfillment of their hopes.

Opposition to Franco is also alive in those who hope to restore the Republic. Some of these are in exile in France and others migrated to Mexico or South America. If they remained in Spain they are reduced to underground activity. It has been estimated that five hundred thousand political refugees crossed the frontier into France at the termination of the civil war.

In March 1939 the Permanent Deputation of the last Republican cortes met in Paris and declared that it was the only permanent representation of the Spanish Republicans and the only legitimate organ of the Second Republic. Martinez Barrios, as president of the last Republican cortes, assumed the duties of the presidency indefinitely, since, under the circumstances, no new election could be held. Despite the efforts of Juan Negrin to contend that he retained his authority as premier, the Permanent Deputation established a junta, the Auxilio a los Republicanos Españoles (JARE) and named Luis Nicolau d'Olwer its president.

Nevertheless, personal ambition divided the exiles until they were reunited in 1944 in the Alianza Nacional de Fuerzas Democráticas ("National Alliance of Democratic Forces"), composed of representatives of the Socialist, Republican, and Anarchist underground movements. They accepted the necessity of a regime of transition which would gradually restore personal freedom and firmly maintain public order. The exiles, however, possessed no means of overthrowing a government protected by an army and secret police, and the National Alliance remained a political forum rather than a political force.

Within Spain, despite security precautions, the Communists, Socialists, and Anarchists have maintained the most active underground organizations. The principal activity of these groups is the distribution of clandestine propaganda. The Communists have had the advantage of international assistance in the supply of arms, money, propaganda, and men. Their Junta Suprema de Unión Nacional, formed in 1943 and for a year the only underground organization, is dedicated to the overthrow of the Franco regime, and to that end it has appealed to all groups opposing Franco and has avoided divisive issues. Nevertheless, other underground movements were wary of the Communists and suspicious of their objectives.

As a party of direct action, the Anarchist underground has hoped to aid the Spanish workers, but it has had more courage and energy than a concrete program for an attack on the Falangist state. The Socialists, more representative of the middle class, have looked to the Western democracies, especially to England, for assistance, but their prestige has declined and rifts have appeared in their ranks as a result of the English demand that they consider a Monarchist restoration as the best means of transition to a democratic regime.

The whole Spanish underground might aptly be termed Republican, because the restoration of a republic is the object of all the clandestine activity. This effort also has the passive support of many who have no role in the underground. The Republican underground specifically is a middle-class party without any Marxist doctrines. Some members are moderate, others are violently anticlerical. Their program is similar to that of the Socialists.

It is impossible to organize this opposition to Franco effectively, since he is supported by the armed might of a police state. Many have been enlisted in secret units of resistance, but these cannot emerge as political parties, and the participants are also anxious to avoid violence. If they attained political freedom, however, they would undertake social and economic reform on a sweeping scale. As the power of the clergy has increased in Spain, those who harbor anticlerical prejudices have also increased in number and hostility to the Church.

After more than twenty-five years of stability, the Franco regime is fairly secure against conspiracy and armed rebellion within the state. Secret agents are numerous and subversive activity is ultimately denounced. Nevertheless, a strong government is necessary to maintain order. All Spaniards are looking to the future with some degree of concern. It is possible that the death of Franco would bring chaos. There might be rivalry among the military leaders for control, despite the appointment of Captain General Augustin Muñoz Grandes as vice-premier, in July 1962. The animosity between the army, the Falange, and the Church might develop and further handicap even a strong successor. In any event, after the years of restraint the majority of the people, led by underground conspirators, might so react as to bring anarchy again to Spain. Discipline imposed from without does not inculcate self-discipline—that can only be cultivated in the Spanish people with time and patience through education and experience in governing.

Spain is still a poor country economically. Approximately two-thirds the size of Texas, with about five times the population and probably less than half the resources, it can hardly be expected to maintain its people on an equivalent standard of living. For economic progress, it has long been in especial need of two commodities—water and capital. Nature does not usually supply the water, and it takes capital to establish a system of irrigation to make up for the deficiency.

Spain has endeavored to balance the budget, but unsuccessfully. The rise in government expenditure has been attributable to the inflationary trend in prices and to the increase in the budget for the armed services. Taxation, also increased, amounts to about 15 percent of a national income of approximately sixty billion dollars. The national debt has grown steadily.

Despite the efforts to repress inflation by controls over prices, wages, and profits in all branches of economy, Spanish prices have consistently increased. The controls have been disregarded and the efforts to enforce them have been ineffectual. As a result of meager food rations the public has resorted to the black market to secure even a low diet. In addition, production in both industry and agriculture tends to concentrate on less strictly controlled nonessential goods.

The whole population of Spain is organized economically into a vertical system of twenty-six branches of production called syndicates. These were made compulsory by the Labor Charter of March 1938. The syndicates control production, wages, prices, distribution, and the erection of new industries. The objective of this organization of society is to eliminate the parasite and the class struggle. The syndicates elect a national committee of three members who are all ex officio members of the cortes. They also nominate some sixty members of the cortes. The syndical committeemen and delegates serve as an advisory body to the government. They recommend wages, hours of work, and prices for controlled goods. They also advise the government on import and export matters and administer parts of the social insurance program. Syndical courts of industrial arbitration, composed of employers and employees, have also been established.

Although Spain is primarily an agricultural country, nature has not been generous to its farmers. The high central meseta has been extensively cultivated, but much of the land is constantly threatened by drought. While irrigation was practiced in the Middle Ages by the Moslems, constant warfare and lack of capital, engineering personnel, and equipment have prevented its development. Less than a third of the cultivable land is irrigated. Even though three-fourths of the farming area in Spain is devoted to cereals, wheat especially, since the civil war an increasing amount of foodstuffs has had to be imported. Olives form an important crop with a varying yield, subject to freezes from time to time, and potatoes and oranges are also raised in quantity.

The future of Spanish economy is uncertain. Under Franco, attempts are being made to industrialize Madrid, but Spain can never compete as an industrial nation with other powers as long as she has to import raw materials and machine tools. Manpower is abundant in Spain, and it seems more economical—and easier to maintain a degree of content—to employ it in a way that appears primitive to American eyes. Oxen are used in the fields instead of tractors, grain is harvested with a scythe or a sickle, and roads are laboriously built by hand instead of with bulldozers. The methods of modern agriculture would put many out of work. Poverty is a natural result of the Spanish predicament.

The wealth of Spain is still unequally distributed and the balance is not being corrected. Even to a casual observer it is evident that Spain is undergoing a social revolution. The political influence of the aristocracy as a class is being restricted, and a new middle class is rapidly extending its influence and wealth, although charges of graft and corruption are leveled against it. The lower classes are no better off than they were under the republic. Prices are high. Wages are low. Housing cannot keep pace with the growing population. To attract the support of the lower classes the government tries to improve their condition by extensive public housing developments and by the apportioning of the great latifundios of Andalusia, initiated by the Second Republic. Modern villages have been erected, the farmers have been encouraged to purchase land on a twenty-year basis, sanatoria have been built in the Guadarramas, and technical institutes have been opened to train laborers in more specialized skills.

It will require time, however, before these projects have an effect on the national economy. Reform by political action, when confronted by both tradition and inertia, is a slow process. One of the vital questions in Spain is whether the lower classes can be restrained from a violent reaction to their condition until the reforms become effective. In large measure the answer depends on the continuation of a strong national government, capable of maintaining order.

The Spaniard has always had an intense devotion to individual liberties, and the restriction of these has always provided a demand for their restoration. Contemporary Spaniards feel keenly the heavy hand of dictatorial procedures. In a sense they have surrendered their freedom in order to save themselves from communism. Perhaps it is the only way to resist that threat, but it is a great price to pay when by reform the state might be made so strong that no citizen would be attracted to the Communist ideology.

CHAPTER XXXVI

Spain and the World

Spain emerged from the civil war to find herself confronted with World War II. The paramount aim of the Franco regime was to maintain neutrality in that struggle so that it might heal the wounds of civil strife and undertake the economic and social reconstruction of the nation. Franco's position was not an enviable one. His country was exhausted and poor, his people were weary of bloodshed, and his own position, established after three years of fighting, remained to be consolidated.

Ideologically, as a dictator, he was inclined to favor the Axis Powers. They had contributed substantially to his triumph in Spain, and their methods were similar to his. The democracies, on the other hand, had maintained an attitude of marked hostility or indifference toward him. But Spain was forced both by her internal condition and her desire for peace to remain neutral throughout the war. Her strategic position on both the Altantic and the Mediterranean, and the importance of Gibraltar, placed her under pressure from both belligerent alliances.

Franco's policy, therefore, had to be devious and deceptive. It was based on the defense of Spanish interests and his avowed opposition to communism. He could not risk an adventure which might result in the loss of his own hard-won power. He had to walk the tight rope of neutrality and accept even the Nazi alliance with the Soviets in an effort to protect himself. He had to be prepared both to participate in the victory of his fellow dictators and to avoid the consequences of their defeat.

Consequently, Madrid resounded with pro-Axis speeches and Ramón Serrano Suner, his brother-in-law and the Falangist foreign minister, followed a definite pro-Axis policy from 1940 to 1942. As long as the Spanish government believed in the possibility of an Axis victory it definitely cooperated with the Nazi and Fascist governments. Its representatives received instructions to favor them. It harbored German and

Italian spies and agents and was a sounding board for Axis propaganda. It joined in denouncing the degenerate democracies and sent the Blue Division to fight its traditional enemies, the Communists, when Hitler attacked the Soviet Union.

Yet the threat of German invasion was very real for Spain, from the collapse of France in 1940 and the advance of the Nazi forces to the Pyrenees until the tide began to turn against the Axis in 1943. The government had to take that menace into consideration in formulating its own policies and in its official utterances. And despite his adherence to the Anti-Comintern Pact of March 1939, despite his pro-Axis speeches and protection of German espionage, Franco never followed up his words with deeds. However great his sympathy for the Axis cause, he maintained his armed neutrality even when the Allied invasion of Africa and the ensuing Mediterranean operations might have been crippled by Spanish entry into the war as an Axis ally.

Throughout the conflict Spain had never lost sight of two important rewards for such assistance as she might give the Axis. She was not willing to fight for them, but she hoped to obtain them as a reward for her cooperation. The most urgent of these aims was the long cherished design of recovering Gibraltar from the British. The other was an expansion of Spanish authority into French Morocco, long regarded as properly a Spanish sphere of influence. In short, in recalling the days of the Catholic Kings, the Franco government hoped to re-create an empire. Despite the hopes of obtaining these crumbs of victory from a triumphant Axis, Spain remained officially neutral. While she threatened Gibraltar and continued to intrigue among the Moroccan nationalists she took no active advantage of British or French preoccupation to seize them.

Nevertheless, Franco took one step to protect his African interests for which he was later accused of perfidy. In November 1940, General Yuste occupied Tangier, which had been under international control since 1923. The other signatories to the international agreement, except Portugal, were at war, and Spain was the only power capable of maintaining the neutrality of Tangier. By February 1941 an agreement had been concluded with the principal powers concerned.

The first perceptible change in the attitude of the Franco government occurred when, in August 1942, General Jordana replaced Serrano Suner as foreign minister. The landing of the Allies in North Africa three months later provided a severe test of Spanish neutrality. The Allied forces would have been in a grave situation had Franco altered his policy. Franco, however, had already begun to believe that an Axis victory was not as certain as it had formerly appeared. His utterances lost much of their pro-Axis flavor during the next year. In May 1943, in a speech at Almería, he urged that peace negotiations be undertaken. The fall of Mussolini increased the pro-Allied sentiment in Spain. As the tide of Spanish opinion had begun to favor the Allies more strongly by October 1943, the United States assumed the responsibility of outbidding Germany for Spanish exports, thereby dealing the Nazis a severe blow in economic warfare.

During the latter part of World War II, Franco tried more and more to ingratiate himself with the Allies, who he now assumed would be the ultimate victors. He gave permission to French combatants to cross Spain to join the Free French forces in North Africa, even over German protests. Spain offered other facilities to refugees. American fliers who crashed or made forced landings in the country were released. Permission was given the United States to use Spanish air fields. Finally, for his own interests as well as the Allied cause, Franco developed more intimate commercial relations with the democracies than with the Axis.

Thus, Spain, as a result of the devious policy of Franco, remained neutral. An ideological ally of the Axis, she was the only member of the Anti-Comintern Pact to survive the defeat. To the victorious democratic powers, and especially to the Soviet Union, the Franco regime remained a reactionary and Fascist force. Many people in both Great Britain and the United States expected that the Franco government would be overthrown by the Spanish people.

They counted on this eventuality without considering the fact that Franco had remained neutral and consolidated his strong rule during World War II. The exiled extremists—Republicans and Monarchists—and the underground were impotent when confronted by a dictator in a police state, supported by a loyal army. No power was willing to intervene to restore either a monarchy or a republic and even the Soviet Union was unwilling and unable to risk helping in the "democratization" of Spain.

Nevertheless, in the hope that the last stronghold of Fascism might be eliminated in Spain, the victorious powers exerted pressure to accelerate the disintegration of the Franco regime. The Spanish question became an issue which met nearly unanimous agreement at the Conference of the United Nations in San Francisco in 1945. It appeared possible to oust Franco by concerted international pressure. Exiled Spanish Republicans gathered in San Francisco to present their case.

In June 1945 the Mexican delegate to the United Nations and a former ambassador to Moscow, Luis Quintanilla, presented a resolution to exclude Spain from membership in the United Nations. While the name of Spain was not mentioned there was little doubt that this was the nation whose regime had "been established with the aid of the armed forces of countries that had fought against the United Nations."

The next denunciation of Franco occurred at Potsdam. The Spanish exiles placed considerable faith in the new Labour prime minister of England, Clement Attlee. It was well known that Stalin would denounce the Franco regime. It was therefore agreed that the nature, history, and associations of the Franco regime precluded its consideration as a member of the United Nations. It was Fascist in character and had collaborated with the Axis before and during World War II. When the United Nations Assembly met in London in February 1946, it reiterated the Potsdam condemnation, recommending that the United Nations base their future relations with Spain on the spirit and letter of that statement.

The French even proposed a joint plan of action against Spain to Great Britain and the United States. When this failed the French government in March 1946 closed the frontier between Spain and France, thereby interrupting Spanish land communication with the rest of Europe. The three powers thereupon condemned the regime in a joint declaration that while they had "no intention of interfering in the internal affairs of Spain," they hoped the Spanish people might "work out their own destiny" by obtaining the "peaceful withdrawal" of Franco, the abolition of the Falange and the establishment of an interim government which would offer political amnesty, freedom of assembly and political association, and provide for free elections. Spain would then receive the recognition and support of all freedom-loving nations.

The campaign against Franco culminated in the Security Council in April 1946, when the Polish delegate, Oscar Lange, proposed that action be taken against the generalissimo. Arguing that the regime threatened world peace and security, Lange urged the United Nations to break diplomatic relations with it. Only the Soviet Union, France, and Mexico supported the proposal, but a subcommittee was created to study the matter, ascertain the validity of the charges, and recommend appropriate political measures. In its report the subcommittee concluded that the regime was a "potential danger to peace and security," although it was not an immediate threat. It recommended that this potential menace be considered and that the members of the United Nations individually terminate diplomatic relations with Spain.

Determined to prosecute the attack on the Franco regime, the Soviet Union in June 1946 vetoed the measure as too moderate. Australia proposed as a compromise that the Security Council maintain constant surveillance of the Spanish situation and be ready to take appropriate steps at any time. The issue was then raised again in the General Assembly. It not only recommended that the Franco government be "debarred from membership in international agencies" under the United Nations, but that the members of the United Nations individually "refuse to maintain diplomatic relations" with it. It also recommended in a draft resolution that members terminate imports from Spain until they were assured these products were not essential for the food requirements of the Spanish people.

Meanwhile, the exiled Republican government in France, led by José Geral y Pereira, had inspired angry newspaper protests over the execution of some French resistance leaders for underground activity in Spain. They were supported by the French Communists and even by distinguished Frenchmen who demanded a rupture of relations with Spain. Their protests were echoed by the Communist press throughout the world. Coincidental with the formal indictment of Spain by the United Nations, Soviet Russia also conducted a violent campaign against Franco as a threat to peace.

By 1950, however, the United States was becoming aroused by the threat of international communism, and American military planners recognized the strategic position of the Iberian peninsula and the necessity of including it in the defense plans of the Western Powers as a site for air and naval bases. The Spaniards, even under the dictatorship of Franco, had gradually reemerged as a nation with which relations could be reestablished.

Latin American nations had taken the lead in the restoration of Spanish diplomatic relations. In August 1950 Peru and Bolivia asked the General Assembly of the United Nations to revoke the ban on the admission of Spain as a member of the specialized agencies of the United Nations and the decision made in 1946 that the members of the United Nations should not maintain full diplomatic relations with Spain. The United States supported the resolution in the Special Political Committee of the General Assembly, where it was adopted by a vote of thirty-seven to ten and sent to the General Assembly for final action. It was already evident that the diplomatic boycott had failed, for seventeen members of the United Nations still maintained diplomatic relations with Spain. On November 4, 1950, the General Assembly voted thirty-eight to ten, with twelve abstentions, to remove Spain from the blacklist and admit her to participation in the specialized agencies. Although the United States voted for the resolution, President

Truman declared that it would be a long time before the United States would send an ambassador to Spain. Later in November Spain was admitted to the Food and Agricultural Organization Conference in Washington, despite the protests of the Spanish Republican government-in-exile.

As a result of her position of isolation, Spain had been forced to undertake and partly complete her reconstruction in the years after World War II without external aid. As late as June 1950 Franco had complained that the major powers were deliberately hindering Spanish industrial development for their own benefit. In August 1950, however, Senator Pat McCarran proposed that the United States lend Spain one hundred million dollars through the Export-Import Bank for economic aid. The reasons advanced in support of the loan were Spain's strategic position and her anti-Communist attitude. Administration Democrats rallied to the support of President Truman, who proposed to place any assistance under the Economic Cooperation Administration. The Senate approved the loan sixty-five to fifteen, but in the appropriation bill which passed both houses, it was reduced to $62,500,000. President Truman signed the bill in September.

Finally, on December 27, 1950, the United States appointed an ambassador to Spain—the first since Norman Armour had been withdrawn in accordance with the United Nations boycott. Stanton Griffis was chosen by President Truman for the post, and Franco named José Lequerica, a former Axis sympathizer and Spanish representative to Vichy, France, as his ambassador in the United States. Great Britain had already appointed Sir John Balfour as her ambassador to Spain. Despite an announced reluctance to resume diplomatic relations with Spain, France agreed to exchange ambassadors early in 1951.

With diplomatic relations thus restored, Franco was anxious to obtain further economic aid and modern weapons to replace the obsolete equipment of his army. He was reportedly interested in a military alliance. General Omar Bradley, chairman of the Joint Chiefs of Staff of the United States, indicated in June 1951 that the Atlantic defensive bloc would be stronger with the admission of Spain. Portugal had been admitted to the North Atlantic Treaty Organization in 1949. The inclusion of Spain would not only make the Western bloc complete, but would enable the Western Powers to extend their defensive bases. Great Britain, already possessed of Gibraltar as a Spanish base, was reluctant to admit Spain to the Atlantic bloc because of the political opposition of the Labour party. France had no need of bases south of the Pyrenees, which she feared might be established as a line of defense in Europe, leaving her undefended in the event of Soviet aggression and diverting aid from the NATO states.

The United States, however, needed naval bases in the Mediterranean for the Sixth Fleet, and the establishment of air bases in Spain behind the protective barrier of the Pyrenees was considered highly desirable. In July 1951 Admiral Forrest P. Sherman conferred with Franco on the possibility of concluding an Hispano-American defense arrangement. It was agreed in principle that the United States might be permitted to use Spanish air and naval bases, whereupon Secretary of State Acheson declared that Spain was "of strategic importance to the general defense of Western Europe." President Truman then announced that American policy toward Spain had been reoriented on the advice of the Department of Defense. By the middle of November an American military mission had published a report on the Spanish bases that might be of potential use.

Thus, negotiations were inaugurated for a military alliance between Spain and the United States. In an effort to adopt a policy more acceptable to the West, Franco had reorganized his cabinet for the first time since 1946. Nine Monarchists were included in it, and some observers anticipated a restoration of the Monarchy. Nevertheless, the Spaniards were justly proud of the progress toward reconstruction which they had already made without external aid. In August 1951 Spain had received only a little more than half of the loan administered by the Economic Cooperation Administration. This was used for agricultural supplies and the development of hydro-electric power. In January 1952 Franco announced to his Council: "Thanks both to God and the tenacity of Spaniards, the sun of our hopes begins to shine in the world." At the end of the year he declared that Spain was then "sought after by those who in years past scorned our offer to cooperate against communism." Spain had won "triumphs both at home and abroad unknown in our history since the sixteenth century."

Negotiations for the American use of Spanish bases were progressing slowly. Confident that they would be independent partners in any alliance, the Spanish agents were careful to make no concessions that would offend Spanish pride. It was to Franco's advantage to use the negotiations to obtain every possible form of assistance that would bulwark his own position in Spain. The United States had promised an additional one hundred million dollars for economic aid, but the Spanish price for the bases was the same kind of assistance in military equipment which had been extended to other European countries. In

December 1952 General J. Lawton Collins, chief of staff of the United States Army, went to Spain to hasten the negotiations.

Meanwhile, Spain had placed an embargo on the shipment of strategic materials to the Soviet Union and her satellites. She was admitted to the World Health Organization and the Economic and Social Council of the United Nations in 1951 and to the United Nations Educational, Scientific, and Cultural Organization in 1952. Three members of UNESCO, including Pablo Casals, the Spanish cellist, resigned in protest. In July 1952, Great Britain changed her policy toward Franco for the first time since the war by lifting the embargo on the export of military equipment to Spain. Although the Labourites objected to this policy it gave Great Britain certain commercial advantages of economic value and enabled her to export obsolescent equipment.

By September 1953 the negotiations between the United States and Spain were completed. The United States was authorized to "develop, maintain and use" military bases in Spain in return for at least $226,-000,000 in economic and military aid. The three pacts, signed after two years of continuous negotiation, provided for the joint use of air and naval bases to strengthen the defense of the West. Spain retained sovereignty over the bases. It was agreed that she would receive the installations erected on the bases by the United States intact when the United States stopped using them. Although either government might terminate the alliance, it was effective for ten years and would continue automatically for two successive five-year periods. Although the treaties did not specify the location of the air bases, which were left to be designated by competent authorities, the United States received the right to use four air fields and to develop naval facilities in the harbors of Cartagena on the Mediterranean, Cádiz on the southeast coast, and El Ferrol and La Coruña on the northwest tip of the peninsula.

The Congress of the United States had already appropriated $226,-000,000 to support the base agreement, and, of this sum, $85,000,000 was designated for economic aid and $141,000,000 for military assistance. It was estimated that the improvement of the Spanish bases would cost $200,000,000. Spain had been included in the Western defense orbit without involving either of the Atlantic allies of the United States opposed to Franco. Although Great Britain and France accepted the *fait accompli* as an affair between Spain and the United States, Franco was opposed also to direct Spanish military ties with Great Britain, France, or NATO. He held that the pact with the United States completely assured the West of Spanish assistance against the Soviet Union. It is significant, however, that in December 1953 the British Foreign

Office lifted its ban on the export of modern military equipment to Spain. This change in policy, probably inspired by commercial rivalry with the United States, enabled the Spaniards to buy older models of British jet fighter planes. The cortes unanimously ratified the alliance with the United States on November 30, 1953.

Thus, the Communist threat to the Western world brought the United States in alliance with the only undefeated member of the Anti-Comintern Pact of 1939. It was an alliance which had mutual advantages and in which the Spaniards considered themselves as equal partners. The alliance with Franco, however, required a delicate diplomacy on the part of the United States. While the Franco faction is at present the dominant one in Spain, supported by the army, the Church, and the Falange, there is no assurance that it will forever remain dominant, especially if chaos should follow the death of Franco. The United States has had to exercise caution, lest in buttressing the rule of Franco with economic and military aid, and with the prestige of American assistance, the other factions are not completely alienated. Already, the Monarchists claim that Franco would have reestablished the monarchy had it not been for the timely American support. Thus, American assistance must be carefully administered for the welfare of all Spaniards.

The economic and military reconstruction of Spain also presents the danger that once the country is restored as a modern military state, Spanish pride, feeding on memories of past glories, may again become imperialistic. For economic reasons also she may attempt to extend her influence to the detriment of her neighbors. The Portuguese, despite the apparent understanding which exists between Salazar and Franco, are already concerned lest a powerful Spain attempt to reunite the entire peninsula. Some Spaniards, recalling the unity of the peninsula under Philip II, speak casually of Portugal as a province of Spain. The attempt to develop such a policy would not only constitute an aggressive step against a member of NATO, but would surely be opposed by the ancient ally of Portugal, Great Britain. While the Portuguese colonies in Africa undoubtedly constitute a tempting lure to imperialism, the attempt to reunite the peninsula would split the Western democracies into hostile groups.

One of the fundamental objectives of the Falange has been the restoration of Spanish sovereignty over Gibraltar. In December 1950 Franco declared that Great Britain must return Gibraltar to Spain. The Spaniards maintain that the British occupied Gibraltar in 1704 on behalf of their Spanish allies and should return it. They appear to forget that Philip V and not Charles, archduke of Austria, the British candidate, ascended the Spanish throne and that Spain approved, however reluctantly, the cession of Gibraltar by Louis XIV.

The Spaniards are sentimentally and officially united in their desire to recover Gibraltar. The student demonstrations and the restrictive measures against the British in Gibraltar have undoubtedly been officially inspired. Gibraltar is a convenient rallying point for Spanish sentiment behind Franco, and the inspired agitation may continue. As Franco has declared, however, it is not worth fighting for. After two and a half centuries it has also become a sentimental symbol to the British, however much its strategic value has decreased. The British will probably not surrender their sovereignty of Gibraltar without defending it, while Franco would not dare risk an open break with such a valuable customer for agricultural exports. Nevertheless, Spanish policy is once again a continuing source of friction.

In the civil war the Nationalists recalled the Moslems of Morocco to redress the balance of power in Spain. Since his victory Franco has followed a policy of friendship toward the Arab League and the Moslems of North Africa, both as a means of extending Spanish influence and in an effort to attract the Moslem populations in the French colonies in North Africa. Foreign Minister Alberto Martin Artajo undertook a friendly mission in the Middle East in 1952. He signed pacts of friendship with Syria, Transjordan, Egypt, and Iran. Spain was pledged to resist communism and indicated a desire to join a Mediterranean defensive alliance. In March 1952 Spain authorized the formation of political parties in Spanish Morocco to win Moslem support there. Immediately, nationalist leaders in Spanish Morocco began a campaign for the independence of Spanish and French Morocco as a united state. Finally, in August 1961, Spain evacuated its remaining Moroccan bases, although an independent Morocco still demanded the liberation of Ifni, Villa Sanjurjo, Ceuta, and Melilla.

The close tie between the Germans and the Spaniards has persisted. Since the emergence of West Germany as an ally of the West in the struggle against communism, friendly feeling between Germans and Spaniards has increased. Germans travel in Spain in ever increasing numbers as tourists and businessmen. With their industrial efficiency, they are increasing their commercial ties with Spain. The Spaniards recall with something akin to nostalgia their imperial greatness, when in Charles V they had a common ruler with the Germans. While this attachment, based both on economics and sympathy, strengthens the Western alliance, it also poses a problem for the other nations of Western Europe. Spain has not been admitted to NATO, but she has been included in the Organization for European Economic Cooperation (OEEC) and its successor, the Organization for Economic Cooperation and Development (OECD).

While the tendency of the Spaniards—like all people who recall their ancient glories—is to live in the past, there is little doubt that by carefully planning their destiny and adopting wise policies, Spain may once again become an influential European power. She has linguistic and sentimental ties with half of the New World. Her people are industrious, virile, and energetic. They have the qualities which may enable them once again to play a role in world affairs.

It is to be hoped that in their revival they will take wise internal measures to retain the unity of their diverse regions and that they will not succumb externally to the dangerous threat of imperialism. Franco, as chief of the state, is the successor to two dynasties of foreign rulers, who were interested more in family affairs than in Spain. He is the first Spaniard to guide the destinies of Spain since the era of Ferdinand and Isabel. His symbol is the same as that of the Catholic Kings, the yoke and the arrows of the Personal Union. If he demonstrates their wisdom in internal policy, if he does not divert Spanish energy into foreign adventures, and if chaos does not follow his exit from the scene, Spain may well have a future as well as the past in which to glory.

SUGGESTED READINGS

I. GENERAL

Adams, Nicholson B. *The Heritage of Spain. An Introduction to Spanish Civilization.* New York, 1943.

Aguado Bleye, Pedro. *Manual de historia de España.* 2 vols. Bilbao, 1927–28.

Altamira, Rafael. *Historia de España y de la civilización española.* 4 vols. Barcelona, 1900–11.

———. *A History of Spain.* Translated by Muna Lee. New York, 1949.

Atkinson, William C. *A History of Spain and Portugal.* Baltimore, 1960.

Ballasteros y Beretta, Antonio. *Historia de España y su influencia en la historia universal.* 10 vols. Barcelona, 1918–41.

Bertrand, Louis, and Sir Charles Petrie. *The History of Spain.* Translated by W. B. Wells. New York, 1934.

Blánquez Fraile, Agustin. *Historia de España.* Barcelona, 1931.

Chapman, Charles E. *A History of Spain.* New York, 1927.

Diccionario de historia de España. 2 vols. Madrid, 1952.

Hume, Martin. *The Spanish People: Their Origin, Growth and Influence.* London, 1901.

Livermore, Harold. *A History of Spain.* New York, 1958.

Madariaga, Salvador de. *The Rise and Fall of the Spanish American Empire.* 2 vols. London, 1947.

Menéndez Pidal, Ramón, ed. *Historia de España.* Madrid, 1940.

Moran, Catherine. *Spain: Its Story Briefly Told.* London, 1931.

Sedgwick, H. D. *A Short History of Spain.* New York, 1925.

Vicens Vives, J., ed. *Historia social y económica de España y America.* 4 vols. Barcelona, 1957–58.

II. SPECIALIZED TOPICS

Almirante, José. *Bosquejo de la historia militar de España, hasta fines del siglo XVIII.* 3 vols. Madrid, 1923.

Arranz Velarde, Fernando. *Compendia de historia maritima de España.* Barcelona, 1940.

Ballesteros, Manuel. *España en los mares.* Madrid, 1943.

Chaytor, H. J. *A History of Aragon and Catalonia.* London, 1933.

Hume, Martin. *Queens of Old Spain.* Edinburgh, 1906.

———. *Spain: Its Greatness and Decay, 1479–1788.* Cambridge, 1905.

Klein, Julius. *The Mesta. A Study in Spanish Economic History (1273–1836).* Cambridge, Mass., 1920.

Lea, Henry Charles. *A History of the Inquisition of Spain.* 4 vols. New York, 1906–8.

———. *The Inquisition of the Spanish Dependencies: Sicily, Naples,*

Sardinia, Milan, the Canarias, Mexico, Peru, New-Granada. New York, 1908.

Llorente, Juan Antonio. *Historia crítica de la Inquisición de España.* 2 vols. Barcelona, 1870–80.

Mayer, August L. *La pintura española.* Translated by Manuel Sánchez Sarto. Barcelona, 1937.

Menéndez Pelayo, Marcelino. *Historia de los heterodoxos españoles.* 8 vols. Madrid, 1946–48.

Merriman, Roger Bigelow. *The Rise of the Spanish Empire in the Old World and in the New.* 4 vols. New York, 1918–34.

Miller, Townsend. *The Castles and the Crown. Spain, 1451–1555.* New York, 1963.

Neumann, Abraham A. *The Jews in Spain: Their Social, Political and Cultural Life During the Middle Ages.* 2 vols. Philadelphia, 1942.

Ramos Oliveira, A. *Politics, Economics and Men of Modern Spain, 1808–1946.* Translated by Teener Hall. London, 1946.

Ríos, Jose Amador de los. *Historia social, política, y religiosa de los Judíos en España y Portugal.* 3 vols. Madrid, 1875–76.

Roviri i Virgili, A. *Historia nacional de Catalunya.* 6 vols. Barcelona, 1922–31.

Smith, R. S. *The Spanish Guild Merchant. A History of the Consulado, 1250–1700.* Durham, 1940.

Soldevila, Ferrán. *Historia de Catalunya.* 3 vols. Barcelona, 1934–35.

Washburn, Oliver D. *Castles in Spain.* Mexico, 1957.

III. ANCIENT SPAIN

Bosch Gimpera, Pedro. *Etnologia de la peninsula Ibérica.* Barcelona, 1932.

———. *El poblamiento antiqua y la formación de los pueblos de España.* Mexico, 1944.

Bouchier, E. S. *Spain Under the Roman Empire.* Oxford, 1914.

Carpenter, Rhys. *The Greeks in Spain.* Bryn Mawr, 1925.

Dixon, P. *The Iberians of Spain.* New York, 1940.

García y Bellido, Antonio. *Fenicios y Carthagineses en occidente.* Madrid, 1942.

———. *Hispania Graeca.* 2 vols. Barcelona, 1948.

Melida, José R. *Arquelogia española.* Barcelona, 1929.

Obermaier, Hugo. *El hombre prehistórica y los origines de la humanidad.* Translated by Antonio García Bellido. Madrid, 1932.

———. *Fossil Man in Spain.* New Haven, 1924.

Sutherland, C. H. V. *The Romans in Spain, 217 B.C.–A.D. 117.* London, 1939.

IV. THE BARBARIANS IN SPAIN

Bradley, Henry. *The Goths, from the Earliest Times to the End of the Gothic Domination in Spain.* London, 1888.

Ortega Rubio, Juan. *Los Visgodos en España.* Madrid, 1903.

Pérez Pujol, Eduardo. *Historia de las instituciones sociales de la España Goda.* 4 vols. Valencia, 1896.

Vicetto, Benito. *Los reyes suevos de Galicia.* 3 vols. Coruña, 1860.

V. THE MOORS IN SPAIN

Bourke, Thomas. *A Concise History of the Moors in Spain.* London, 1811.

Condé, José Antonio. *Historia de la dominación de los Arabes en España.* 3 vols. Madrid, 1820–21.

González Palencia, Angel. *Historia de la España Musulmana.* Barcelona, 1935.

———. *Los Mozárabes de Toledo en los siglos XII y XIII.* 4 vols. Madrid, 1926–30.

Herrera Oria, Enrique. *Historia de la Reconquista de España.* Madrid, 1943.

Lane-Poole, Stanley. *The Moors in Spain.* London, 1893.

Watts, Henry Edwards. *Spain . . . History from the Moorish Conquest to the Fall of Granada (711–1492).* London, 1893.

VI. THE MEDIEVAL CHRISTIAN STATES: LEON AND CASTILE

Clarke, H. Butler. *The Cid Campeador and the Waning of the Crescent in the West.* New York, 1897.

Cotarelo Valledor, Armando. *Historia crítica y documentada de la vida y acciones de Alfonso III el Magno, ultimo rey de Asturias.* Madrid, 1933.

Llampayas, José. *Alfonso X. El hombre, el rey y el sabio.* Madrid, 1947.

Menéndez Pidal, R. *La España del Cid.* 2 vols. Madrid, 1929.

Pérez de Urbel, Justo. *Historia del Condado de Castilla.* 3 vols. Madrid, 1945.

———. *Fernán González.* Madrid, 1943.

Prado, Manuel. *Covadonga.* Madrid, 1915.

Ríos Sarmiento, J. *La vida y los libros de Alfonso el Sabio.* Barcelona, 1943.

Storer, Edward. *Peter the Cruel. The Life of the Notorious Don Pedro of Castile; Together With an Account of His Relations With the Famous Maria de Padilla.* Baltimore, 1910.

VII. THE MEDIEVAL CHRISTIAN STATES: ARAGON

Calmette, Joseph. *La question des Pyrenees et la marche d'Espagne au Moyen Age.* Paris, 1947.

Jiménez Soler, Andrés. *La Edad Media en la Corona de Aragon.* Barcelona, 1930.

Llampayas, José. *Jaime I el Conquistador.* Madrid, 1942.

Lluch Arnal, Emili. *Historia de l'antic regne de Valencia.* Valencia, 1926.

Miron, E. L. *The Queens of Aragon; Their Lives and Times.* London, 1913.

Nicolau d'Olwer, L. *L'expansió de Catalunya en la Mediterrania oriental.* Barcelona, 1926.

Ríos Sarmiento, Juan. *Jaime I de Aragon, el Conquistador.* Barcelona, 1941.

VIII. HOUSE OF TRASTAMARA

Bermejo de la Rica, Antonio. *El triste destino de Enrique IV y la Beltraneja.* Madrid, n.d.

Calmette, Joseph. *Louis XI et la revolution catalane (1461–1473).* Toulouse, 1902.

García Mercadal, José. *Don Carlos de Aragon, Principe de Viana.* Barcelona, 1944.

Gutiérrez Gili, J. *Alvaro de Luna (Condestable de Castile).* Barcelona, 1929.

Iribarren, Manuel. *El Principe de Viana (un destino frustrado).* Barcelona, 1948.

Marañon, Gregorio. *Ensayo biológico sobre Enrique IV de Castilla y su tiempo.* Madrid, 1930.

Silió, César. *Don Alvaro de Luna y su tiempo.* Madrid, 1934.

Sitges, Juan B. *Enrique IV y la Excelente Señora llamada vulgarmente la Beltraneja, 1425–1530.* Madrid, 1912.

Vicens Vives, J. *Juan II de Aragon (1398–1479).* Barcelona, 1953.

IX. THE UNION OF SPAIN

Cedillo, Conde de. *El Cardenal Cisneros, Gobernador del Reino. Estudio histórico.* 3 vols. Madrid, 1921–28.

Clemencin, Diego. *Elogio de la Reina Católica Doña Isabel.* Madrid, 1820.

Doussinague, José M. *La Political internacional de Fernando el Católico.* Madrid, 1944.

Giménez Soler, Andrés. *Fernando el Católico.* Barcelona, 1941.

Hare, Christopher. *A Queen of Queens and the Making of Spain.* London, 1906.

Lacadena y Brualla, Ramón. *El gran Cardenal de España, don Pedro Gonzalez de Mendoza.* Saragossa, 1939.

Llampayas, José. *La España imperial. Fernando el Católico.* Madrid, 1941.

Mattingly, Garrett. *Catherine of Aragon.* Boston, 1941.

Merino, Abelardo. *El Cardenal Mendoza.* Barcelona, 1942.

Merton, R. *Cardinal Ximénes and the Making of Spain.* London, 1934.

Plunket, Irene L. *Isabel of Castile and the Making of the Spanish Nation, 1451–1504.* New York, 1915.

Prescott, William Hickling. *History of the Reign of Ferdinand and Isabella the Catholic.* 2 vols. New York, 1838.

Silió Cortés, César. *Isabel la Católica, fundadora de España. Su vida. Su tiempo. Su reinado (1451–1504).* Valladolid, 1938.

Starkie, Walter. *Grand Inquisitor. Being an Account of Cardinal Ximénes de Cisneros and His Times.* London, 1940.

Walsh, William Thomas. *Isabella of Spain, the Last Crusader.* New York, 1930.

Williamson, James A. *Maritime Enterprise, 1485–1558.* Oxford, 1913.

X. THE HOUSE OF AUSTRIA

Arbó, Juan Sebastián. *Cervantes, The Man and His Time.* Translated by Ilsa Barea. New York, 1955.

Armstrong, Edward. *The Emperor Charles V.* 2 vols. London, 1902.

Babelon, Jean. *Charles-Quint, 1500–1558.* Paris, 1947.

Carande, Ramón. *Charles V y sus banqueros. La vida económica de España en una fase de su hegemony, 1516–1556. Vol. II. La Hacienda Real de Castilla.* 2 vols. Madrid, 1943–49.

Davies, R. Trevor. *The Golden Century of Spain, 1501–1621.* London, 1937.

Hume, Martin. *Court of Philip IV. Spain in Decadence.* New York, 1907.

———. *Two English Queens and Philip.* London, 1908.

Ibarra y Rodrigues, Eduardo. *España bajo los Austrias.* Barcelona, 1935.

Lewis, D. B. Wyndham. *Charles of Europe.* New York, 1931.

Loth, David. *The Master of the Armada, Philip II of Spain.* New York, 1932.

MacElwee, W. L. *The Reign of Charles V, 1516–1558.* London, 1936.

Marañon, Gregorio. *El Conde-Duque de Olivares.* Madrid, 1936.

———. *Antonio Pérez.* 2 vols. Madrid, 1947.

Mattingly, Garrett. *The Armada.* New York, 1959.

Motley, John Lothrop. *The Rise of the Dutch Republic. A History.* 3 vols. London, 1855.

Parr, Charles McKew. *So Noble a Captain. The Life and Times of Ferdinand Magellan.* New York, 1953.

Prescott, William Hickling. *History of the Reign of Philip the Second.* 3 vols. Philadelphia, 1916.

Rea, L. *The Armada.* London, 1933.

Seaver, Latimer H. *The Great Revolt in Castile. A Study of the Comunero Movement, 1520–1521.* Boston, 1928.

Serrano, L. *España en Lepanto.* Madrid, 1935.

Tomas, Mariano. *Felipe II, rey de España y monarca del universo.* Saragossa, 1939.

Walsh, William Thomas. *Philip II.* London, 1937.

Yeo, Margaret. *Don John of Austria.* London, 1934.

XI. THE BOURBONS

Addison, Joseph. *Charles the Third of Spain.* Oxford, 1900.

Armstrong, Edward. *Elizabeth Farnese, "the Termagant of Spain."* London, 1892.

Auvergne, Edmund B. d'. *Queen at Bay: the Story of Maria Cristina and Don Carlos.* Baltimore, 1910.

Benton, Elbert Jay. *International Law and Diplomacy of the Spanish-American War.* Baltimore, 1908.

Bermejo, Ildefonso Antonio. *Historia de la interinidad y guerra civil de España desde 1868.* 3 vols. Madrid, 1875–77.

Chadwick, French Ensor. *Relations of the United States and Spain: The Spanish-American War.* 2 vols. New York, 1911.

Challice, Rachel. *The Secret History of the Court of Spain During the Last Century*. London, 1909.

Ciges Aparicio, M. *España bajo la dinastia de los Borbones* (*1701–1931*). Madrid, 1932.

Clarke, Henry Butler. *Modern Spain, 1815–1898*. Cambridge, 1906.

Cortés Cavanillas, Julián. *Alfonso XIII, el Rey romántico*. Madrid, 1943.

———. *María Cristina de Austria, madre de Alfonso XIII*. Madrid, 1944.

Cotte, S. de. *Madame des Ursins, roi d'Espagne*. Paris, 1946.

Custine, Marquis de. *L'Espagne sous Ferdinand VII*. 4 vols. Paris, 1838.

Danvila y Collado, Manuel. *Reinado de Carlos III*. 6 vols. Madrid, 1891.

Desdevises du Dezert, G. *L'Espagne de l'ancien regime*. 3 vols. Paris, 1893–94.

Diaz-Plaja, Fernando. *La vida española en el siglo XVIII*. Barcelona, 1946.

Erskine, S. *Twenty-Nine Years: the Reign of King Alfonso XIII of Spain*. London, 1931.

Fernandez Almagro, M. *Historia del reinado de Alfonso XIII*. Barcelona, 1933.

———. *Historia política de la España contemporánea*. 2 vols. Barcelona, 1956–59.

Gambra, Rafael. *La primera guerra civil en España* (*1820–1823*). Madrid, 1949.

García Escudero, José Maria. *De Cánovas a la Republica*. Madrid, 1953.

Gomez del Campillo, Miguel. *Relaciones diplomáticas entre España y los Estados Unidos según los documentos del Archive Histórico Nacional*. 2 vols. Madrid, 1944.

Hannay, David. *Don Emilio Castelar*. London, 1896.

Harcourt-Smith, Simon. *Cardinal of Spain. The Life and Strange Career of Alberoni*. New York, 1941.

Hill, Constance. *Story of the Princess des Ursins in Spain*. Boston, 1913.

Hume, Martin. *Modern Spain, 1788–1898*. New York, 1900.

Kany, Charles E. *Life and Manners in Madrid, 1750–1800*. Berkeley, 1932.

Latimer, Elizabeth (Wormeley). *Spain in the Nineteenth Century*. Chicago, 1897.

Luz, Pierre de. *Isabelle II, reine d'Espagne*. Paris, 1935.

Marañon, Gregorio. *El Empecinado*. Madrid, 1932.

Maura Gamazo, G. *Historia crítica del reinado de D. Alfonso XIII durante su minoridad*. Barcelona, 1919.

Millis, Walter. *The Martial Spirit, a Study of Our War With Spain*. Boston, 1931.

Oman, Charles William Chadwick. *Wellington's Army, 1809–1814.* London, 1912.

———. *A History of the Peninsular War.* 5 vols. Oxford. 1902–14.

Parnell, Arthur. *The War of the Succession in Spain During the Reign of Queen Anne, 1702–1711.* London, 1888.

Romanones, Conde de. *Doña María Cristina de Habsburgo y Lorena, la discreta Regente de España.* Madrid, 1933.

———. *Notas de una vida (1868–1901).* Madrid, 1934.

———. *Notas de una vida (1868–1912).* Madrid, n.d.

———. *Notas de una vida (1912–1931).* Madrid, 1947.

Rousseau, François. *Regne de Charles III d'Espagne (1759–1788).* 2 vols. Paris, 1907.

Sencourt, Robert. *King Alfonso. A Biography.* London, 1942.

Strobel, Edward Hunt. *Spanish Revolution, (1868–1875).* Boston, 1898.

Trend, J. B. *The Origins of Modern Spain.* New York, 1934.

Wallaton, Henry. *Alfonso XIII.* Geneva, 1943.

Wells, W. B. *The Last King Don Alfonso XIII of Spain.* London, 1934.

Wheeler, Harold F. B. *The Story of Wellington.* London, 1912.

White, George F. *A Century of Spain and Portugal (1788–1898).* London, 1909.

Zabala y Lera, Pio. *España bajo los Borbones.* Barcelona, 1936.

———. *Historia de España y de la civilización española. Edad contemporánea.* 2 vols. Barcelona, 1930.

XII. CONTEMPORARY SPAIN SINCE 1931

Alba, Victor. *Histoire des republiques espagnoles.* Translated by Louis Parrot. Paris, 1948.

Ansaldo, Juan Antonio. *Memoires d'un monarchiste espagnol.* Monaco, 1953.

———. *¿Para Que? De Alfonso XIII a Juan III.* Buenos Aires, 1951.

Arraras, Joaquín. *France.* San Sebastián, 1937.

Barea, Arturo. *The Forging of a Rebel.* Translated by Ilsa Barea. New York, 1946.

Basaldua, Pedro de. *En España sale el sol.* Buenos Aires, n.d.

Bowers, Claude G. *My Mission to Spain. Watching the Rehearsal for World War II.* New York, 1954.

Brenan, Gerald. *South from Granada.* New York, 1957.

———. *The Spanish Labyrinth. An Account of the Social and Political Background of the Civil War.* New York, 1943.

Cattell, David T. *Communism and the Spanish Civil War.* Berkeley, 1956.

———. *Soviet Diplomacy and the Spanish Civil War.* Berkeley, 1957.

Cleugh, James. *Spain in the Modern World.* New York, 1953.

Feis, Herbert. *The Spanish Story. Franco and the Nations at War.* New York, 1948.

Foltz, Charles, Jr. *The Masquerade in Spain.* Boston, 1948.

Hamilton, Thomas J. *Appeasement's Child. The Franco Regime in Spain*. New York, 1943.
Hayes, Carlton J. H. *Wartime Mission in Spain*. New York, 1946.
Hoare, Sir Samuel. *Complacent Dictator*. New York, 1947.
Hughes, Emmet John. *Report from Spain*. New York, 1947.
Knickerbocker, H. R. *The Siege of the Alcazar*. Philadelphia, 1936.
Loveday, Arthur F. *Spain, 1923–1948. Civil War and World War*. Ipswich, n.d.
Madariaga, Salvador de. *España. Ensayo de historia contemporánea*. Buenos Aires, 1942.
Manuel, Frank E. *The Politics of Modern Spain*. New York, 1938.
Matthews, Herbert L. *The Yoke and the Arrows*. New York, 1957.
Merin, Peter. *Spain Between Death and Birth*. Translated by Charles Fullman. London, 1938.
Mirandet, François. *L'Espagne de France*. Paris, 1948.
Palencia, Isabel. *Smouldering Freedom. The Story of the Spanish Republicans in Exile*. New York, 1945.
Pattee, Richard. *This Is Spain*. Milwaukee, 1951.
Payne, Stanley G. *Falange, a History of Spanish Fascism*. Stanford, 1961.
Peers, E. Allison. *The Spanish Tragedy, 1930–1936. Dictatorship, Republic, Chaos*. New York, 1936.
Pla, José. *Historia de la Segunda República Española. Barcelona*. 1940–41.
Plenn, Abel. *Wind in the Olive Trees. Spain from the Inside*. New York, 1946.
Reid, John T. *Modern Spain and Liberalism*. Stanford, 1937.
Sieberer, A. *Espagne contre Espagne*. Translated by Berthe Medici-Cavin. Geneva, n.d.
Smith, Rhea Marsh. *The Day of the Liberals in Spain*. Philadelphia, 1938.
Taylor, F. Jay. *The United States and the Spanish Civil War, 1936–1939*. New York, 1956.
Thomas, Hugh. *The Spanish Civil War*. New York, 1961.

RULERS OF SPAIN

Kings of the Visigoths, Moorish caliphs and kings, and kings of León, Asturias, Castile, Aragon, and Navarre

Ferdinand II of Aragon and Isabel of Castile	1479–1504
Philip I and Juana	1504–1506
Ferdinand V (II of Aragon)	1506–1516
Charles I (Emperor Charles V)	1516–1556
Philip II	1556–1598
Philip III	1598–1621
Philip IV	1621–1665
Charles II	1665–1700
Philip V	1700–1724
Luis I	1724
Philip V	1724–1746
Ferdinand VI	1746–1759
Charles III	1759–1788
Charles IV	1788–1808
Ferdinand VII	1808
Joseph Bonaparte	1808–1813
Ferdinand VII (restored)	1814–1833
Isabel II	1833–1868
Amadeus	1870–1873

REPUBLIC

Emilio Castelar y Ripoll, head	1873–1874
Alfonso XII	1874–1885
Alfonso XIII	1886–1931

PRESIDENTS

Niceto Alcalá Zamora y Torres	1931–1936
Manuel Azaña	1936–1939

CHIEF OF STATE

Francisco Franco	1939–

INDEX

DATE DUE

NOV 21 '66			
NOV 22 '66			
MAR 7 '67			
MAR 18 '67			
APR 7 '67			
APR 19 '67			
JUL 5 '67			
MAR 12 '68			
APR 9 '68			
APR 24 '68			
OCT 19 '68			
NOV 21 '68			
DEC 2 '68			
MAR 26 '73			
DEC 6 '73			
OC 25 '77			
NO 22 '78			
DE 5 '78			